PowerShell Deep Dives

PowerShell Deep Dives

Edited by Jeffery Hicks ▪ Richard Siddaway
Oisín Grehan ▪ Aleksandar Nikolić

MANNING
SHELTER ISLAND

For online information and ordering of this and other Manning books, please visit www.manning.com. The publisher offers discounts on this book when ordered in quantity. For more information, please contact

Special Sales Department
Manning Publications Co.
20 Baldwin Road
PO Box 261
Shelter Island, NY 11964
Email: orders@manning.com

Manning Publications Co.
20 Baldwin Road
PO Box 261
Shelter Island, NY 11964

Development editor: Cynthia Kane
Copyeditor: Gwen Burda, Tiffany Taylor, and Lianna Wlasiuk
Proofreader: Melody Dolab
Typesetter: Dennis Dalinnik
Cover designer: Marija Tudor

ISBN 9781617291319
Printed in the United States of America

1 2 3 4 5 6 7 8 9 10 – MAL – 18 17 16 15 14 13

To the memory and indomitable spirit of Will Steele
@pen_test

authors and their chapters

brief contents

contents

preface

While I was finishing another book project for Manning, a discussion developed about a PowerShell Deep Dives book. In the past Manning published two volumes of a SQL Server Deep Dives book written by a number of SQL Server MVPs and members of the SQL community. The chapters were intended as in-depth content on specific aspects of SQL Server. At the time, many of us involved in this book were also part of the developing PowerShell Deep Dives conference.

That event brought Microsoft MVPs and community members together for a few days of intense PowerShell togetherness. Think of it as a geeky Woodstock festival for PowerShell. The intent was to share PowerShell experiences and ideas on specific—or even niche—topics that would be hard to cover in a larger conference like Microsoft TechEd. The PowerShell Deep Dives conference eventually became the PowerShell Summit that we enjoy today.

The idea behind this book was to take that conference concept and put it into book format. The chapters would be short explorations of specific PowerShell ideas—things that might be presented at the PowerShell Summit. Some of the content in this book has actually been presented at these conferences.

I was "volunteered" to serve as lead editor and began my new career as cat wrangler. A call went out and many people offered to contribute chapters to the book as well as act as section editors. Eventually, we had a tentative table of contents and our volunteer authors started writing.

Volunteer is the key word here as nobody associated with this project is receiving any royalties or advances. Instead, all royalties will be donated to charity, which was also a part of the SQL Server Deep Dives project. In purchasing this book in any format, you are supporting the outstanding work of Save the Children.

On behalf of the authors and my coeditors, we are grateful for your support and interest in our collective work. Are you ready to dive in deeply and uncover some PowerShell treasures?

JEFFERY HICKS

acknowledgments

First, I must thank all of the contributors to this book, including their families and employers. Writing a book is a major undertaking, regardless of whether you are writing 30 chapters or one. For many of my coauthors this book is their first publication, so not only do I want to thank them, I also want to congratulate them. This book would never have happened without the contributions of these members of the PowerShell community.

Next, I couldn't have shepherded this book to completion without the assistance and advice of section editors Oisín Grehan, Richard Siddaway, and Aleksandar Nikolić. I think the project was more involved than they anticipated and I appreciate their willingness to stick it out with me—especially Richard who volunteered for section editor duty in addition to contributing three chapters of his own!

All of us would like to thank the terrific people at Manning: Cynthia Kane, Michael Stephens, Mary Piergies, Barbara Mirecki, Kevin Sullivan, Melody Dolab, Lianna Wlasiuk, Tiffany Taylor, Gwen Burda, and Maureen Spencer. These few are just the tip of a fantastic iceberg of enthusiastic people who kept us on track, supported this project, and, in the end, made it all possible.

Special thanks to our peer reviewers, who read the chapters during development and provided invaluable feedback: Adam Rodgers, Allan Miller, Dave Pawson, Don Westerfield, Douglas Duncan, James Berkenbile, Jeff Dykstra, Klaus Schulte, Mike Shepard, Subhasis Ghosh, and Thomas Lee.

Finally, a sincere thank-you to the PowerShell community. It is no overstatement to say that this community is extremely active, supportive, and welcoming. I'm amazed not only at how members of the community absorb and welcome contributions like this book, but also at how they give and share so much of what they've learned with others. This is an incredible group of people. Without their interest and support, this project would not have come to fruition. Your enthusiasm enriches us all, and especially the lives touched by Save the Children.

about this book

This book is for anyone with an interest in PowerShell. Perhaps you want to learn what you can accomplish or perhaps you're trying to solve a problem and you see a chapter that will help. While the majority of the chapters in the book are written for IT pros, there is plenty of content for developers and others whose PowerShell experience may be more peripheral.

We're assuming you have some fundamental PowerShell knowledge. If you're an absolute beginner, much of the content will be lost on you. This book isn't intended as a tutorial for learning PowerShell, but it should teach you how to accomplish certain tasks or take advantage of a PowerShell feature that goes beyond the core documentation.

In any event, this is PowerShell content you likely won't find any place else, written by PowerShell experts and MVPs.

What version of PowerShell do I need?

This book isn't targeted at any particular version of PowerShell. There are some chapters that are PowerShell 3.0-specific and that should be evident from reading the chapter. The safest assumption is that you're using at least PowerShell 2.0.

Where's coverage of Microsoft Exchange?

As we were assembling content for this book, we had to use what contributors wanted to write about, but we also wanted to keep the book broad in scope. Yes, there are a few chapters that are SQL Server-related, but many of the concepts and techniques can apply to other PowerShell situations.

Frankly, products like Microsoft Exchange, which rely heavily on PowerShell, deserve their own Deep Dives book, and we hope someone from the Exchange community will step up and lead the effort for a similar book, hopefully with some good PowerShell content. The same is true of other Microsoft products such as SharePoint and Active Directory.

How the book is organized

This book is divided into 4 parts, each centered on a PowerShell theme:

- Part 1—PowerShell administration
- Part 2—PowerShell scripting
- Part 3—PowerShell for developers
- Part 4—PowerShell platforms

This isn't necessarily a hard and fast division. Some chapters could easily have been assigned to multiple parts. Since the book isn't intended as a tutorial, you can jump from chapter to chapter as you see fit. An effort was made within each section to order content in such a way as to facilitate learning.

Code conventions and downloads

All source code in listings or in text is in a `fixed-width font like this` to separate it from ordinary text. We've tried to make any code that's shown as a listing available as a download. You should test and review all code samples in a non-production environment. None of the code listings should be considered production-ready.

Throughout the book you will see shorter code examples. Many of these are one-line expressions. Due to printing limitations we have had to take a few liberties with how code is presented. You might see a command presented like this:

```
PS C:\> Get-service | where {$_.status -eq 'running'} | select
  ➥ status,displayname
```

or like this

```
Get-service |
where {$_.status -eq 'running'} |
select status,displayname
```

It is the same one-line command. We are trusting that you have enough fundamental PowerShell knowledge to understand what a basic command looks like and how to use it either in the shell or a script.

The source code for the examples in this book is available online from the publisher's website at www.manning.com/PowerShellDeepDives.

Author Online

The purchase of *PowerShell Deep Dives* includes free access to a private web forum run by Manning Publications, where you can make comments about the book, ask technical questions, and receive help from the authors and from other users. To access the forum and subscribe to it, point your web browser to www.manning.com/PowerShellDeepDives. The Author Online forum and the archives of previous discussions will be accessible from the publisher's website as long as the book is in print.

This is the place to go to report errors in the book or to receive help with title-specific content. If you're looking for more general help with PowerShell, please visit the forum at http://PowerShell.org. Registration is free and many authors of this book are active on the site.

About the editors

Jeffery Hicks is the lead editor for *PowerShell Deep Dives*. The bios and photographs of the section editors can be found at the end of the introductions for their respective sections.

- Part 1—PowerShell administration, edited by Richard Siddaway
- Part 2—PowerShell scripting, edited by Jeff Hicks
- Part 3—PowerShell for developers, edited by Oisín Grehan
- Part 4—PowerShell platforms, edited by Aleksandar Nikolić

Jeffery Hicks is a Microsoft MVP in Windows PowerShell, a Microsoft Certified Trainer, and an IT veteran with over 20 years of experience, much of it spent as an IT consultant specializing in Microsoft server technologies with an emphasis in automation and efficiency. He works today as an independent author, trainer, and consultant. Jeff writes the popular Prof. PowerShell column for MPCMag.com, and is a regular contributor to the Petri IT Knowledgebase, 4SysOps and the Altaro Hyper-V blog, as well as a frequent speaker at technology conferences and user groups.

Jeff's latest books are Manning's *Learn PowerShell 3 in a Month of Lunches, Second Edition* and *Learn PowerShell Toolmaking in a Month of Lunches,* both with Don Jones, and *PowerShell in Depth: An Administrator's Guide,* coauthored with Don Jones and Richard Siddaway.

about Save the Children

Save the Children is the leading independent organization creating lasting change in the lives of children in need in the United States and around the world. Recognized for their commitment to accountability, innovation, and collaboration, Save the Children goes into the hearts of communities, where they help children and families help themselves. The charity works with other organizations, governments, non-profits, and a variety of local partners while maintaining their own independence without political agenda or religious orientation.

When disaster strikes around the world, Save the Children is there to save lives with food, medical care, and education, and remains to help communities rebuild through long-term recovery programs. As quickly and as effectively as Save the Children responds to tsunamis and civil conflict, it also works to resolve the ongoing struggles children face every day—poverty, hunger, illiteracy, and disease—and replaces them with hope for the future.

Save the Children serves impoverished, marginalized, and vulnerable children and families in nearly 120 countries. Their programs reach both children and those working to save and improve their lives, including parents, caregivers, community members, and members of our partner organizations. They help save children's lives, protect them from exploitation, and assist them in accessing education and health care.

Through disaster risk-reduction, emergency preparedness, rapid humanitarian relief, and long-term recovery programs, Save the Children also assists millions of girls and boys at risk of or affected by natural disasters, conflicts, and ethnic violence.

The editors and contributors of *PowerShell Deep Dives* are proud to donate the royalties from this book to this worthy cause. Learn more at www.savethechildren.org.

PART 1

PowerShell administration

Edited by Richard Siddaway

PowerShell is a tool for administrators enabling the automation of administrative processes. This first part of the book gives you an overview of the range of administrative tasks you can tackle and some superb examples of administering systems with PowerShell.

PowerShell remoting is fantastic for administering tens, hundreds, or thousands of remote machines. But sometimes, things go wrong. Chapter 1 will show you how to diagnose and correct problems with PowerShell remoting.

In PowerShell 1.0 we only had WMI for working with remote machines. PowerShell 3.0 introduces a new way to work with WMI on local and remote machines—the CIM cmdlets and CIM sessions, which are analogous to PowerShell remoting sessions but only for WMI access, and which are discussed in chapter 2.

How many times have you heard the phrase, "Users say that server X is running slowly"? You now need to investigate the server—chapter 3 shows you how to use PowerShell to collect and analyze the data from performance counters.

Your network is fundamental to your environment. Chapter 4 presents a set of PowerShell-based tools that enable you to investigate networking issues, such as which ports are available, and how to test connectivity by sending data to and from specific ports.

The ability to administer servers remotely is key to managing a large environment. Chapter 5 shows how this concept can be extended to remote management from almost any device using PowerShell Web Access (a Windows Server 2012 feature). It provides true role-based access for your remote administration.

Do you know who is logging onto to your machines, what they're doing, and when they're doing it? The techniques presented in chapter 6 will enable you to audit your user logons so you know, and can prove, who is doing what and when. You could extend these techniques to investigate other events recorded in your event logs.

Security is one aspect of an administrator's work that never goes away. Certificates are used in a number of situations including authentication and encryption. Managing certificates can be a time-consuming activity, but chapter 7 comes to the rescue by showing you how to use PowerShell to administer your certificate authority database.

Part 1 closes with chapter 8 which shows you how to manage the size of the Active Directory token used for authorization. If this token gets too large, users will experience difficulties logging on and accessing their resources.

The chapters in this part of the book have one thing in common—the techniques presented are designed to make your job easier. Automate the mundane and repetitive, and you'll find the time to proactively make your job, and therefore your environment, better.

Enjoy!

About the editor

Richard Siddaway has worked with Microsoft technologies for 25 years and is currently automating for Kelway (UK) Ltd. PowerShell caught his interest during the early beta releases for version 1.0 back in 2005. Richard blogs extensively about PowerShell and founded the UK PowerShell User Group in 2007. A PowerShell MVP for the last six years, Richard gives numerous talks on PowerShell at various events in the UK, Europe, and the US. He has published a number of articles on PowerShell.

After writing two PowerShell books—*PowerShell in Practice* (Manning 2010) and *PowerShell and WMI* (Manning 2012)—Richard then collaborated with Don Jones and Jeff Hicks to write *PowerShell in Depth* (Manning 2013). Richard is currently writing an introductory book for Active Directory administrators that features PowerShell. He can be contacted through his blog at http://msmvps.com/blogs/RichardSiddaway/Default.aspx.

1 Diagnosing and troubleshooting PowerShell remoting

Don Jones

Troubleshooting and diagnosing remoting can be one of the most difficult tasks for an administrator. When remoting works, it works; when it doesn't, it's often hard to tell why. Fortunately, PowerShell v3 and its accompanying implementation of remoting offer much clearer and more prescriptive error messages than prior versions. But even v2 included an undocumented and little-appreciated module named `PSDiagnostics`, which was designed specifically to facilitate remoting troubleshooting. The module lets you turn on detailed trace log information before you attempt to initiate a remoting connection. You can then use that detailed log information to get a better idea of where remoting is failing.

In this chapter I'll walk you through several troubleshooting examples. The idea is to help you recognize specific failure situations so that you'll know what to do in each case to get things working. Each example focuses on a single scenario, such as a failed or blocked connection.

Diagnostics examples

For the following scenarios I started by importing the `PSDiagnostics` module (note that this is implemented as a script module and requires an execution policy that permits it to run, such as `RemoteSigned` or `Unrestricted`). Figure 1 also shows that I ran the `Enable-PSWSManCombinedTrace` command, which starts the extended diagnostics logging.

For each scenario I then ran one or more commands that involved remoting, as demonstrated in figure 2. Afterward, I disabled the trace by running `Disable-PSWSManCombinedTrace`, so that the log would only contain the details from that

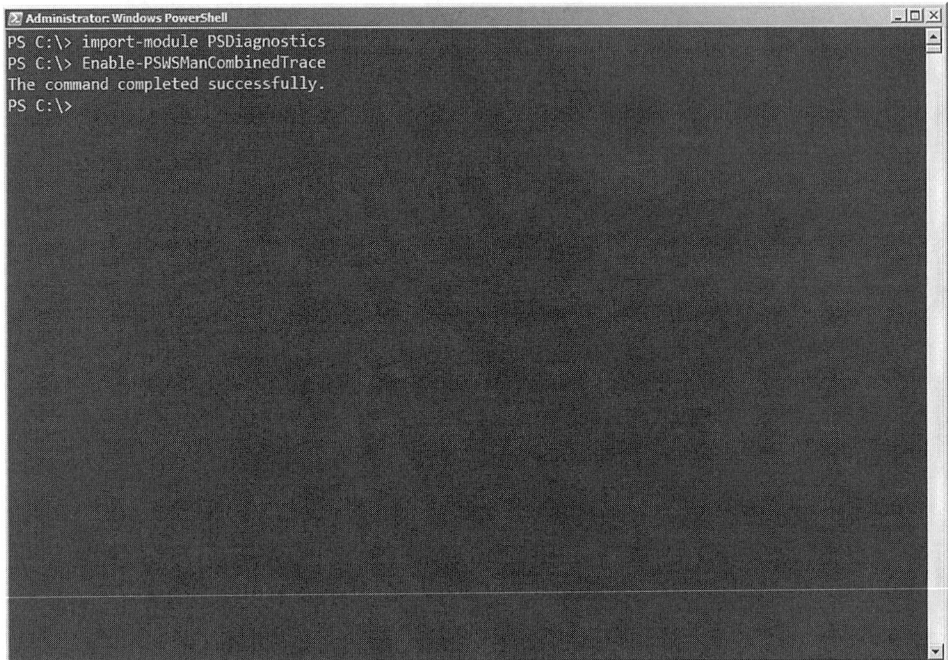
Administrator: Windows PowerShell
PS C:\> import-module PSDiagnostics
PS C:\> Enable-PSWSManCombinedTrace
The command completed successfully.
PS C:\>

Figure 1 Loading the diagnostics module and starting a trace

```
Administrator: Windows PowerShell
PS C:\> Enable-PSWSManCombinedTrace
The command completed successfully.
PS C:\> Enter-PSSession dc01
[dc01]: PS C:\Users\Administrator\Documents> dir
[dc01]: PS C:\Users\Administrator\Documents> cd ..
[dc01]: PS C:\Users\Administrator> dir

    Directory: C:\Users\Administrator

Mode                LastWriteTime     Length Name
----                -------------     ------ ----
d-r--         3/19/2012   5:24 PM            Contacts
d-r--         3/19/2012   5:24 PM            Desktop
d-r--         3/19/2012   5:24 PM            Documents
d-r--         3/19/2012   5:24 PM            Downloads
d-r--         3/19/2012   5:24 PM            Favorites
d-r--         3/19/2012   5:24 PM            Links
d-r--         3/19/2012   5:24 PM            Music
d-r--         3/19/2012   5:24 PM            Pictures
d-r--         3/19/2012   5:24 PM            Saved Games
d-r--         3/19/2012   5:24 PM            Searches
d-r--         3/19/2012   5:24 PM            Videos

[dc01]: PS C:\Users\Administrator> exit
PS C:\> Disable-PSWSManCombinedTrace
The command completed successfully.
The command completed successfully.
```

Figure 2 Entering a session and running a command

```
Administrator: Windows PowerShell

PS C:\> get-winevent microsoft-windows-winrm/operational

   ProviderName: Microsoft-Windows-WinRM

TimeCreated                     Id LevelDisplayName Message
-----------                     -- ---------------- -------
4/13/2012 7:19:04 PM           142 Error            WSMan operation SignalShell failed, error co...
4/13/2012 7:19:04 PM           254 Information      Activity Transfer
4/13/2012 7:19:04 PM            16 Information      Closing WSMan shell
4/13/2012 7:19:04 PM            15 Information      Closing WSMan command
4/13/2012 7:19:04 PM            13 Information      Running WSMan command with CommandId: 3836B8...
4/13/2012 7:19:01 PM            15 Information      Closing WSMan command
4/13/2012 7:19:01 PM            13 Information      Running WSMan command with CommandId: BA8242...
4/13/2012 7:19:01 PM            15 Information      Closing WSMan command
4/13/2012 7:19:01 PM            13 Information      Running WSMan command with CommandId: 64BB35...
4/13/2012 7:19:00 PM            15 Information      Closing WSMan command
4/13/2012 7:19:00 PM            13 Information      Running WSMan command with CommandId: 8013C6...
4/13/2012 7:19:00 PM            15 Information      Closing WSMan command
4/13/2012 7:19:00 PM            13 Information      Running WSMan command with CommandId: F34270...
4/13/2012 7:18:57 PM            15 Information      Closing WSMan command
4/13/2012 7:18:57 PM            13 Information      Running WSMan command with CommandId: 61FC69...
4/13/2012 7:18:57 PM            15 Information      Closing WSMan command
4/13/2012 7:18:57 PM            13 Information      Running WSMan command with CommandId: AA7365...
4/13/2012 7:18:52 PM            15 Information      Closing WSMan command
4/13/2012 7:18:52 PM            13 Information      Running WSMan command with CommandId: 0A29F2...
4/13/2012 7:18:52 PM            15 Information      Closing WSMan command
4/13/2012 7:18:52 PM            13 Information      Running WSMan command with CommandId: 297D4F...
```

Figure 3 Examining the logged diagnostic information

particular attempt (I cleared the log between attempts, so that each scenario provided a fresh diagnostics log).

Finally, as shown in figure 3, I retrieved the messages from the log. In the scenarios I'll provide an annotated version of these.

NOTE In the examples I'll typically truncate much of this output so that you can focus on the most meaningful pieces. Also note the difference between reading the information from the event log architecture, as in figure 3, and reading the .EVT trace file directly, as you'll do in some of the scenarios. The latter will provide combined information from different logs, which can sometimes be more useful.

I'll also make use of the Microsoft Windows Remote Management (WinRM)/Analytic log, which doesn't normally contain human-readable information. In order to use the log's contents I'll use an internal Microsoft utility to translate the log's contents into something you can read. (I've been given permission to distribute the utility, which you can find at http://files.concentratedtech.com/psdiagnostics.zip.)

Trace information is stored in PowerShell's installation folder (run `cd $pshome` to get there, then change to the Traces folder). The filename extension is .ETL, and you can use `Get-WinEvent -path filename.etl` to read a particular file. The `Construct-PSRemoteDataObject` command, included in the zip file I referenced, can translate

Figure 4 Dot-sourcing the Construct-PSRemoteDataObject.ps1 script

portions of the Analytic log's `Message` property into human-readable text. A demo script included in the zip file shows how to use it. As shown in figure 4, I dot-sourced the Construct-PSRemoteDataObject.ps1 file into my shell in order to gain access to the commands it contains.

I also deleted the contents of C:\Windows\System32\WindowsPowerShell\v1.0\Traces prior to starting each of the following examples. That way, I start each one with a fresh trace.

A perfect remoting connection

Time for the first scenario: a perfect remoting connection. In this example you go from a Windows 7 client computer in a domain named AD2008R2 to the domain's DC01 domain controller. On the DC, change to the C:\ folder, run a directory, and then end the session. Figure 5 shows the entire scenario.

Now read the log in chronological order. You need to be careful; running `Enable-PSWSManCombinedTrace` and `Disable-PSWSManCombinedTrace` creates log events for those commands. You might want to run the `Enable` command and then wait a few minutes before doing anything with remoting. That way, you can tell by the timestamp in the log when the "real" traffic begins. Wait a few more minutes before running the `Disable` command, again so that you can easily tell when the "real" log traffic ends. Also note that you'll get information from two logs, WinRM

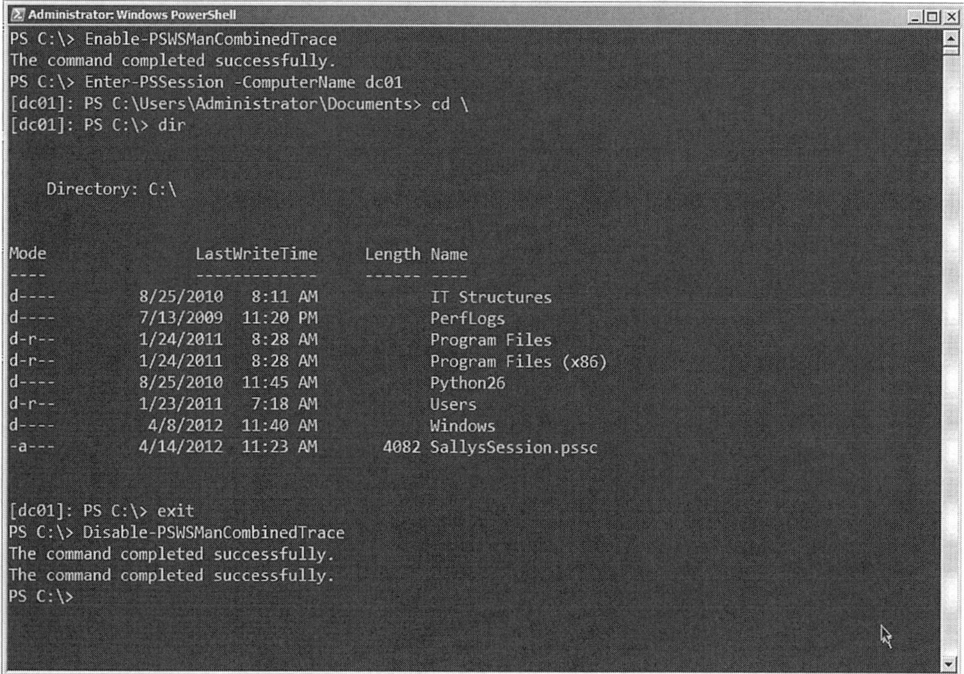
```
PS C:\> Enable-PSWSManCombinedTrace
The command completed successfully.
PS C:\> Enter-PSSession -ComputerName dc01
[dc01]: PS C:\Users\Administrator\Documents> cd \
[dc01]: PS C:\> dir


    Directory: C:\


Mode                LastWriteTime     Length Name
----                -------------     ------ ----
d----         8/25/2010   8:11 AM            IT Structures
d----         7/13/2009  11:20 PM            PerfLogs
d-r--         1/24/2011   8:28 AM            Program Files
d-r--         1/24/2011   8:28 AM            Program Files (x86)
d----         8/25/2010  11:45 AM            Python26
d-r--         1/23/2011   7:18 AM            Users
d----          4/8/2012  11:40 AM            Windows
-a---         4/14/2012  11:23 AM       4082 SallysSession.pssc


[dc01]: PS C:\> exit
PS C:\> Disable-PSWSManCombinedTrace
The command completed successfully.
The command completed successfully.
PS C:\>
```

Figure 5 The example for this scenario: a perfect remoting connection

and PowerShell, although reading the .EVT file with `Get-WinEvent` will grab everything in sequence.

The connection begins with (in this example) `Enter-PSSession` and name resolution, as shown in figure 6.

WinRM has to spin up a runspace (a PowerShell process) on the remote computer. That includes setting several options for locale, timing, and so on, as shown in figure 7.

This will go on for a while. Eventually you'll see WinRM beginning to send "chunks," which are packetized communications. These are sent via the Simple Object Access Protocol, so expect to see SOAP referenced a lot. (Web Services Management [WS-MAN] is a Web service, remember, and SOAP is the communications language of Web services.) Figure 8 shows a couple of these 1500-byte chunks. Notice that the payload is pretty much gibberish.

This gibberish is what the `Construct-PSRemoteDataObject` command can translate. For example, those "sending" messages have an event ID of 32868; by looking for only those events you can see what's being sent, as shown in figure 9.

In this case, the client was asking the server (which is listed as the destination) about its capabilities, and for some metadata on the `Exit-PSSession` command (that's the second message). This is how the client figures out what kind of server it's talking to and other important, preliminary information. Now the client knows what

```
4/14/2012 3:03:39 PM Command Enter-PSSession is Started.


                     Context:
                             Severity = Informational
                             Host Name = ConsoleHost
                             Host Version = 3.0
                             Host ID = 5daaddbe-8c9d-4ee4-ab44-fac774eedc6f
                             Engine Version = 3.0
                             Runspace ID = f47408cf-bd95-4ced-ace8-e799421d646b
                             Pipeline ID = 294
                             Command Name = Enter-PSSession
                             Command Type = Cmdlet
                             Script Name =
                             Command Path =
                             Sequence Number = 89
                             User = AD2008R2\Administrator
                             Shell ID = Microsoft.PowerShell


                     User Data:


4/14/2012 3:03:39 PM ComputerName resolved to localhost
4/14/2012 3:03:39 PM ComputerName resolved to dc01
4/14/2012 3:03:39 PM ComputerName resolved to dc01
4/14/2012 3:03:39 PM ComputerName resolved to dc01
```

Figure 6 Starting the remoting connection

version of the serialization protocol will be used to send data back and forth, what time zone the server is in, and other details.

NOTE Event ID 32868 is client-to-server traffic; ID 32867 represents server-to-client traffic. Using those two IDs along with `Construct-PSRemoteDataObject` can reveal the majority of the session transcript once the connection is established.

```
4/14/2012 3:03:39 PM Creating Runspace object
                           Instance Id: cd32125b-0290-4887-89a9-910ca224b3f7
4/14/2012 3:03:39 PM Creating RunspacePool object
                           InstanceId 4358d585-0eab-47ef-a0e6-4b98e71f34ab
                           MinRunspaces 1
                           MaxRunspaces 1
4/14/2012 3:03:39 PM Creating WSMan Session. The connection string is: dc01/wsman?PSVersion=3.0
4/14/2012 3:03:39 PM WSMan Create Session operation completed successfuly
4/14/2012 3:03:39 PM Getting WSMan Session Option (29) - INVALID_SESSION_OPTION.
4/14/2012 3:03:39 PM Getting WSMan Session Option (11) - WSMAN_OPTION_MAX_RETRY_TIME.
4/14/2012 3:03:39 PM Setting WSMan Session Option (26) - WSMAN_OPTION_UI_LANGUAGE with value
                     (en-US) completed successfully.
4/14/2012 3:03:39 PM Setting WSMan Session Option (25) - WSMAN_OPTION_LOCALE with value (en-US)
                     completed successfully.
4/14/2012 3:03:39 PM Setting WSMan Session Option (1) - WSMAN_OPTION_DEFAULT_OPERATION_TIMEOUTMS
                     with value (180000) completed successfully.
4/14/2012 3:03:39 PM Setting WSMan Session Option (12) - WSMAN_OPTION_TIMEOUTMS_CREATE_SHELL with
                     value (180000) completed successfully.
4/14/2012 3:03:39 PM Setting WSMan Session Option (17) - WSMAN_OPTION_TIMEOUTMS_CLOSE_SHELL with
                     value (60000) completed successfully.
4/14/2012 3:03:39 PM Setting WSMan Session Option (16) - WSMAN_OPTION_TIMEOUTMS_SIGNAL_SHELL with
                     value (60000) completed successfully.
4/14/2012 3:03:39 PM Opening RunspacePool
4/14/2012 3:03:39 PM Runspace state changed to Opening
```

Figure 7 Starting the remote runspace

```
4/14/2012 3:03:39 PM SOAP [client sending index 1 of 6 total chunks (1500 bytes)] <s:Envelope
                     xmlns:s="http://www.w3.org/2003/05/soap-envelope"
                     xmlns:a="http://schemas.xmlsoap.org/ws/2004/08/addressing"
                     xmlns:w="http://schemas.dmtf.org/wbem/wsman/1/wsman.xsd" xmlns:p="http://schem
                     as.microsoft.com/wbem/wsman/1/wsman.xsd"><s:Header><a:To>http://dc01:5985/wsma
                     n?PSVersion=3.0</a:To><w:ResourceURI s:mustUnderstand="true">http://schemas.mi
                     crosoft.com/powershell/Microsoft.PowerShell</w:ResourceURI><a:ReplyTo><a:Addre
                     ss s:mustUnderstand="true">http://schemas.xmlsoap.org/ws/2004/08/addressing/ro
                     le/anonymous</a:Address></a:ReplyTo><a:Action s:mustUnderstand="true">http://s
                     chemas.xmlsoap.org/ws/2004/09/transfer/Create</a:Action><w:MaxEnvelopeSize s:m
                     ustUnderstand="true">512000</w:MaxEnvelopeSize><a:MessageID>uuid:86AACA6B-4F66
                     -42A9-A267-8C287AA011E1</a:MessageID><w:Locale xml:lang="en-US"
                     s:mustUnderstand="false" /><p:DataLocale xml:lang="en-US"
                     s:mustUnderstand="false" /><p:ActivityId s:mustUnderstand="false">01911C40-F80
                     0-0000-66BA-A1FC9D15CD01</p:ActivityId><p:SessionId s:mustUnderstand="false">u
                     uid:5EB0B40D-C79B-4114-908E-8AAC76B78C42</p:SessionId><p:OperationID s:mustUnd
                     erstand="false">uuid:8076355C-7892-4C0A-9F7C-2198B60CDAF2</p:OperationID><p:Se
                     quenceId s:mustUnderstand="false">1</p:SequenceId><w:OptionSet
                     xmlns:xsi="http://www.w3.org/2001/XMLSchema-instance"
                     s:mustUnderstand="true"><w:Option Name="protocolversion" MustComply="true">2.2
                     </w:Option></w:OptionSet><w:OperationTimeout>PT180.000S</w:OperationTimeout><r
                     sp:CompressionType s:mustUnderstand="true" xmlns
4/14/2012 3:03:39 PM SOAP [client sending index 2 of 6 total chunks (1500 bytes)] :rsp="http://sche
                     mas.microsoft.com/wbem/wsman/1/windows/shell">xpress</rsp:CompressionType></s:
                     Header><s:Body><rsp:Shell
                     xmlns:rsp="http://schemas.microsoft.com/wbem/wsman/1/windows/shell"
                     Name="Session10"
                     ShellId="4358D585-0EAB-47EF-A0E6-4B98E71F34AB"><rsp:InputStreams>stdin pr</rsp
                     :InputStreams><rsp:OutputStreams>stdout</rsp:OutputStreams><creationXml xmlns=
                     "http://schemas.microsoft.com/powershell">AAAAAAAAACgAAAAAAAAAAAMAAALwAgAAAAIA
                     AQCF1VhDqw7vR6DmS5jnHzSrAAAAAAAAAAAAAAAAAAAAAO+7vzxPYmogUmVmSWQ9IjAiPjxNUz48Vm
                     Vyc2lvbiBOPSJwcm90b2NvbHZlcnNpb24iPjIuMjwvVmVyc2lvbj48VmVyc2lvbiBOPSJQU1ZlcnNp
                     b24iPjIuMDwvVmVyc2lvbj48VmVyc2lvbiBOPSJTZXJpYWxpemF0aW9uVmVyc2lvbiI+MS4xLjAuMT
                     wvVmVyc2lvbj48QkEgTj0iVGltZVpvbmUiPkFBRUFBQUQvLy8vL0FRQUFBQUFBQUFBRUFRQUFBQnhU
                     ZVhOMFpXMHVRM1Z5Y21WdWRGTjVjM1JsYlZScGJXVmFiMjVsQkFBQUFCZHRYME5oWTJobFpFUmhlV3
                     hwWjJoMFEyaGhibWRsY3cxdFgzUnBZMnR6VDJabWMyVjBEbTFmYzNSaGJtUmhjbVJPWVcxbERtMWZa
                     R0Y1YkdsbmFIUk9ZVzFsQXdBQkFSeFRlWE4wWlcwdVEyOXNiR1ZqZEdsdmJuTXVTR0Z6YUhSaFlteG
                     xDUWtDQUFBQUFQZ3BGOWIvLy84S0NnUUNBQUFBSEZ0NWMzUmxiUzVEYjJ4c1pXTjBhVzl1Y3k1SVlY
                     Tm9kR0ZpYkdVSEFBQUFDa3h2WVdSR1lXTjBiM0lIVm1WeWMybHZiZ2hEYjIxd1lYSmxjaEJJWVhOb1
                     EyOWtaVkJ5YjNacFpHVnlDRWhoYzJoVGFYcGxCRXRsZVhNR1ZtRnNkV1Z6QUFBREF3QUZCUXNJSEZ0
                     NWMzUmxiUzVEYjJ4c1pXTjBhVzl1Y3k1SlEyOXRjR0Z5WlhJa1UzbHpkR1Z0TGtOdmJHeGxZM1JwYj
                     I1ekxrbElZWE5vUTI5a1pWQnliM1pwWkdWeUNPeFJPRDhBQUFBQUNnb0RBQUFBQ1FNQUFBQUpCQUFB
                     QUJBREFBQUFBQUFBQUJBRUFBQUFBQUFBQUFzPTwvQkE+PC9NUz48L09iaj4AAAAAAAAAAKQAAAAAAAA
                     AAAwAADfkCAAAABAABAIXVWEOrDu9HoOZLmOcfNKsAAAAA
```


Figure 8 Data begins to transfer over the connection

Moving on. As shown in figure 10, you'll see some authentication back-and-forth, during which some errors can be expected. The system will eventually get over it and, as shown, start receiving chunks of data from the server.

A rather surprising amount of back-and-forth can ensue as the two computers exchange pleasantries, share information about each other and how they work, and so on. Change your event log output to include event ID numbers, because those can be useful when trying to grab specific pieces of data. At this point the log will consist mainly of the client sending commands and the server sending back the results. This is more readable when you use `Construct-PSRemoteDataObject`, so here's the complete back-and-forth from that perspective. First up is the client's statement of its session capabilities:

```
destination : Server
messageType : SessionCapability
pipelineId  : 00000000-0000-0000-0000-000000000000
```

```
runspaceId   : 4358d585-0eab-47ef-a0e6-4b98e71f34ab
data         : <Obj RefId="0"><MS><Version
               N="protocolversion">2.2</Version><Version
               N="PSVersion">2.0</Version><Version
               N="SerializationVersion">1.1.0.1</Version><BA N="TimeZon
               e">AAEAAAD/////AQAAAAAAAAAEAQAAABxTeXN0ZW0uQ3VycmVudFN5c
               3RlbVRpbWVab25lBAAAABdtX0NhY2hlZERheWxpZ2h0Q2hhbmdlcw1tX
               3RpY2tzT2Zmc2V0Dm1fc3RhbmRhcmROYW1lDm1fZGF5bGlnaHROYW1lA
               wABARxTeXN0ZW0uQ29sbGVjdGlvbnMuSGFzaHRhYmxlCQkCAAAAAPgpF
               9b///8KCgQCAAAAHFN5c3RlbS5Db2xsZWN0aW9ucy5IYXNodGFibGUHA
               AAACkxvYWRGYWN0b3IHVmVyc2lvbghDb21wYXJlchBIYXNoQ29kZVByb
               3ZpZGVyCEhhc2hTaXplBEtleXMGVmFsdWVzAAADAwAFBQsIHFN5c3Rlb
               S5Db2xsZWN0aW9ucy5JQ29tcGFyZXIkU3lzdGVtLkNvbGxlY3Rpb25zL
               klIYXNoQ29kZVByb3ZpZGVyCOxROD8AAAAACgoDAAAACQMAAAAJBAAAA
               BADAAAAAAAAAABAEAAAAAAAAAAAs=</BA></MS></Obj>
```

Then the server's:

```
destination : Client
messageType : SessionCapability
pipelineId  : 00000000-0000-0000-0000-000000000000
runspaceId  : 00000000-0000-0000-0000-000000000000
data        : <Obj RefId="0"><MS><Version
              N="protocolversion">2.2</Version><Version
              N="PSVersion">2.0</Version><Version
              N="SerializationVersion">1.1.0.1</Version></MS></Obj>
```

```
Administrator: Windows PowerShell
PS C:\> get-winevent -path $pshome\traces\pstrace.etl -oldest  | ? { $_.id -eq '32868' } | % { $idx
= $_.message.indexof("Payload Data: 0x"); $str = $_.message.substring($idx + ("Payload Data: 0x".len
gth));Construct-PSRemoteDataObject $str }


destination : Server
messageType : SessionCapability
pipelineId  : 00000000-0000-0000-0000-000000000000
runspaceId  : 4358d585-0eab-47ef-a0e6-4b98e71f34ab
data        : <Obj RefId="0"><MS><Version N="protocolversion">2.2</Version><Version
              N="PSVersion">2.0</Version><Version N="SerializationVersion">1.1.0.1</Version><BA N="
              TimeZone">AAEAAAD/////AQAAAAAAAAAEAQAAABxTeXN0ZW0uQ3VycmVudFN5c3RlbVRpbWVab25lBAAAABd
              tX0NhY2hlZERheWxpZ2h0Q2hhbmdlcw1tX3RpY2tzT2Zmc2V0Dm1fc3RhbmRhcmROYW1lDm1fZGF5bGlnaHRO
              YW1lAwABARxTeXN0ZW0uQ29sbGVjdGlvbnMuSGFzaHRhYmxlCQkCAAAAAPgpF9b///8KCgQCAAAAHFN5c3Rlb
              S5Db2xsZWN0aW9ucy5IYXNodGFibGUHAAAACkxvYWRGYWN0b3IHVmVyc2lvbghDb21wYXJlchBIYXNoQ29kZV
              Byb3ZpZGVyCEhhc2hTaXplBEtleXMGVmFsdWVzAAADAwAFBQsIHFN5c3RlbS5Db2xsZWN0aW9ucy5JQ29tcGF
              yZXIkU3lzdGVtLkNvbGxlY3Rpb25zLklIYXNoQ29kZVByb3ZpZGVyCOxROD8AAAAACgoDAAAACQMAAAAJBAAA
              ABADAAAAAAAAAABAEAAAAAAAAAAAs=</BA></MS></Obj>

destination : Server
messageType : GetCommandMetadata
pipelineId  : 03460806-3011-42a6-9843-c54f39ee6fb8
runspaceId  : 4358d585-0eab-47ef-a0e6-4b98e71f34ab
data        : <Obj RefId="0"><MS><Obj N="Name" RefId="1"><TN RefId="0"><T>System.String[]</T><T>Sys
              tem.Array</T><T>System.Object</T></TN><LST><S>Out-Default</S><S>Exit-PSSession</S></L
              ST></Obj><Obj N="CommandType" RefId="2"><TN RefId="1"><T>System.Management.Automation
              .CommandTypes</T><T>System.Enum</T><T>System.ValueType</T><T>System.Object</T></TN><T
              oString>Alias, Function, Filter, Cmdlet</ToString><I32>15</I32></Obj><Nil
              N="Namespace" /><Nil N="ArgumentList" /></MS></Obj>
```

Figure 9 Translating the data that was sent

```
4/14/2012 3:03:39 PM An error was encountered while processing an operation.
                     Error Code: 11001
4/14/2012 3:03:39 PM The chosen authentication mechanism is Kerberos
4/14/2012 3:03:39 PM Sending the request for operation CreateShell to destination machine and port
                     dc01:5985
4/14/2012 3:03:39 PM An error was encountered while processing an operation.
                     Error Code: 11001
4/14/2012 3:03:39 PM The chosen authentication mechanism is Kerberos
4/14/2012 3:03:39 PM Received the response from Network layer; status: 200 (HTTP_STATUS_OK)
4/14/2012 3:03:39 PM Received the response from Network layer; status: 200 (HTTP_STATUS_OK)
4/14/2012 3:03:39 PM Activity Transfer
4/14/2012 3:03:39 PM Activity Transfer
4/14/2012 3:03:39 PM SOAP [client receiving index 1 of 2 total chunks (3000 bytes)] <s:Envelope
                     xml:lang="en-US" xmlns:s="http://www.w3.org/2003/05/soap-envelope"
                     xmlns:a="http://schemas.xmlsoap.org/ws/2004/08/addressing"
                     xmlns:x="http://schemas.xmlsoap.org/ws/2004/09/transfer"
                     xmlns:w="http://schemas.dmtf.org/wbem/wsman/1/wsman.xsd"
                     xmlns:rsp="http://schemas.microsoft.com/wbem/wsman/1/windows/shell" xmlns:p="h
                     ttp://schemas.microsoft.com/wbem/wsman/1/wsman.xsd"><s:Header><a:Action>http:/
                     /schemas.xmlsoap.org/ws/2004/09/transfer/CreateResponse</a:Action><a:MessageID
                     >uuid:67E26C83-FCD7-41EA-9B26-636BBE961791</a:MessageID><p:OperationID s:mustU
                     nderstand="false">uuid:8076355C-7892-4C0A-9F7C-2198B60CDAF2</p:OperationID><p:
```

Figure 10 Taking care of authentication

Next is the server's `$PSVersionTable` object, which lists versioning information:

```
destination  : Client
messageType  : ApplicationPrivateData
pipelineId   : 00000000-0000-0000-0000-000000000000
runspaceId   : 4358d585-0eab-47ef-a0e6-4b98e71f34ab
data         : <Obj RefId="0"><MS><Obj N="ApplicationPrivateData"
               RefId="1"><TN RefId="0"><T>System.Management.Automation.
               PSPrimitiveDictionary</T><T>System.Collections.Hashtable
               </T><T>System.Object</T></TN><DCT><En><S
               N="Key">PSVersionTable</S><Obj N="Value"
               RefId="2"><TNRef RefId="0" /><DCT><En><S
               N="Key">PSVersion</S><Version
               N="Value">2.0</Version></En><En><S
               N="Key">PSCompatibleVersions</S><Obj N="Value"
               RefId="3"><TN RefId="1"><T>System.Version[]</T><T>System
               .Array</T><T>System.Object</T></TN><LST><Version>1.0</Ve
               rsion><Version>2.0</Version><Version>3.0</Version></LST>
               </Obj></En><En><S N="Key">BuildVersion</S><Version
               N="Value">6.2.8314.0</Version></En><En><S
               N="Key">PSRemotingProtocolVersion</S><Version
               N="Value">2.2</Version></En><En><S
               N="Key">WSManStackVersion</S><Version
               N="Value">3.0</Version></En><En><S
               N="Key">CLRVersion</S><Version
               N="Value">4.0.30319.261</Version></En><En><S
               N="Key">SerializationVersion</S><Version N="Value">1.1.0
               .1</Version></En></DCT></Obj></En></DCT></Obj></MS></Obj
               >
```

Next the server sends information about the runspace that will be used:

```
destination : Client
messageType : RunspacePoolStateInfo
```

```
pipelineId   : 00000000-0000-0000-0000-000000000000
runspaceId   : 4358d585-0eab-47ef-a0e6-4b98e71f34ab
data         : <Obj RefId="0"><MS><I32
               N="RunspaceState">2</I32></MS></Obj>
```

The client sends information about its `Exit-PSSession` command:

```
destination : Server
messageType : GetCommandMetadata
pipelineId  : 03460806-3011-42a6-9843-c54f39ee6fb8
runspaceId  : 4358d585-0eab-47ef-a0e6-4b98e71f34ab
data        : <Obj RefId="0"><MS><Obj N="Name" RefId="1"><TN RefId="0"
              ><T>System.String[]</T><T>System.Array</T><T>System.Obje
              ct</T></TN><LST><S>Out-Default</S><S>Exit-PSSession</S><
              /LST></Obj><Obj N="CommandType" RefId="2"><TN RefId="1">
              <T>System.Management.Automation.CommandTypes</T><T>Syste
              m.Enum</T><T>System.ValueType</T><T>System.Object</T></T
              N><ToString>Alias, Function, Filter,
              Cmdlet</ToString><I32>15</I32></Obj><Nil N="Namespace"
              /><Nil N="ArgumentList" /></MS></Obj>
```

Later you'll see the result of the `CD C:\` command, which is the new PowerShell prompt reflecting the new folder location:

```
destination : Client
messageType : PowerShellOutput
pipelineId  : c913b8ae-2802-4454-9d9b-926ca6032018
runspaceId  : 4358d585-0eab-47ef-a0e6-4b98e71f34ab
data        : <S>PS C:\&gt; </S>
```

Next, let's look at the output of the `Dir` command. The first bit is writing the column headers for Mode, LastWriteTime, Length, Name, and so forth. This is all being sent to the client. I've included the first few lines for you, each of which comes across in its own block:

```
destination : Client
messageType : RemoteHostCallUsingPowerShellHost
pipelineId  : c259c891-516a-46a7-b287-27c96ff86d5b
runspaceId  : 4358d585-0eab-47ef-a0e6-4b98e71f34ab
data        : <Obj RefId="0"><MS><I64 N="ci">-100</I64><Obj N="mi"
              RefId="1"><TN RefId="0"><T>System.Management.Automation.
              Remoting.RemoteHostMethodId</T><T>System.Enum</T><T>Syst
              em.ValueType</T><T>System.Object</T></TN><ToString>Write
              Line2</ToString><I32>16</I32></Obj><Obj N="mp"
              RefId="2"><TN RefId="1"><T>System.Collections.ArrayList<
              /T><T>System.Object</T></TN><LST><S>Mode
              LastWriteTime     Length Name
                                        </S></LST></Obj></MS></Obj>

destination : Client
messageType : RemoteHostCallUsingPowerShellHost
pipelineId  : c259c891-516a-46a7-b287-27c96ff86d5b
runspaceId  : 4358d585-0eab-47ef-a0e6-4b98e71f34ab
data        : <Obj RefId="0"><MS><I64 N="ci">-100</I64><Obj N="mi"
              RefId="1"><TN RefId="0"><T>System.Management.Automation.
```

```
              Remoting.RemoteHostMethodId</T><T>System.Enum</T><T>Syst
              em.ValueType</T><T>System.Object</T></TN><ToString>Write
              Line2</ToString><I32>16</I32></Obj><Obj N="mp"
              RefId="2"><TN RefId="1"><T>System.Collections.ArrayList<
              /T><T>System.Object</T></TN><LST><S>----
              -------------     ------ ----
                                       </S></LST></Obj></MS></Obj>

destination : Client
messageType : RemoteHostCallUsingPowerShellHost
pipelineId  : c259c891-516a-46a7-b287-27c96ff86d5b
runspaceId  : 4358d585-0eab-47ef-a0e6-4b98e71f34ab
data        : <Obj RefId="0"><MS><I64 N="ci">-100</I64><Obj N="mi"
              RefId="1"><TN RefId="0"><T>System.Management.Automation.
              Remoting.RemoteHostMethodId</T><T>System.Enum</T><T>Syst
              em.ValueType</T><T>System.Object</T></TN><ToString>Write
              Line2</ToString><I32>16</I32></Obj><Obj N="mp"
              RefId="2"><TN RefId="1"><T>System.Collections.ArrayList<
              /T><T>System.Object</T></TN><LST><S>d----
              8/25/2010   8:11 AM            IT Structures
                                             </S></LST></Obj></MS></Obj>

destination : Client
messageType : RemoteHostCallUsingPowerShellHost
pipelineId  : c259c891-516a-46a7-b287-27c96ff86d5b
runspaceId  : 4358d585-0eab-47ef-a0e6-4b98e71f34ab
data        : <Obj RefId="0"><MS><I64 N="ci">-100</I64><Obj N="mi"
              RefId="1"><TN RefId="0"><T>System.Management.Automation.
              Remoting.RemoteHostMethodId</T><T>System.Enum</T><T>Syst
              em.ValueType</T><T>System.Object</T></TN><ToString>Write
              Line2</ToString><I32>16</I32></Obj><Obj N="mp"
              RefId="2"><TN RefId="1"><T>System.Collections.ArrayList<
              /T><T>System.Object</T></TN><LST><S>d----
              7/13/2009  11:20 PM            PerfLogs
                                             </S></LST></Obj></MS></Obj>
```

Eventually the command finishes and you get the prompt again:

```
destination : Client
messageType : PowerShellOutput
pipelineId  : f5c8bc7a-ec54-4180-b2d4-86479f9ea4b9
runspaceId  : 4358d585-0eab-47ef-a0e6-4b98e71f34ab
data        : <S>PS C:\&gt; </S>
```

You'll also see periodic exchanges about the state of the pipeline. The following indicates that the command is done:

```
destination : Client
messageType : PowerShellStateInfo
pipelineId  : f5c8bc7a-ec54-4180-b2d4-86479f9ea4b9
runspaceId  : 4358d585-0eab-47ef-a0e6-4b98e71f34ab
data        : <Obj RefId="0"><MS><I32
              N="PipelineState">4</I32></MS></Obj>
```

A lot of data passes back and forth, but it's possible to make sense of it using these tools. Frankly, most remoting problems take place during the connection phase, meaning once that's completed successfully you'll have no further problems. The next scenarios focus on specific connection errors.

NOTE To clear the log and prepare for a new trace, try deleting the .EVT files and going into Event Viewer to clear the Applications and Services Logs > Microsoft > Windows > Windows Remote Management log. If you're getting errors when running `Enable-PSWSManCombinedTrace`, one of those two tasks probably hasn't been completed.

Connection problem: Blocked port

Figure 11 shows what happens when you try to connect to a computer and the necessary port—5985 by default—isn't open all the way through. Let's look at how this appears in the log.

NOTE I'm assuming you've already checked the computer name, made sure it resolves to the proper IP address, and so forth; what you're looking at is *definitely* a blocked port (because I set it up that way) in this example.

Figure 12 shows that you successfully resolved the computer name. You'll find that testing with `Enter-PSSession` is easiest, because it's easy to spot that command in the log and see when the "real" log data begins.

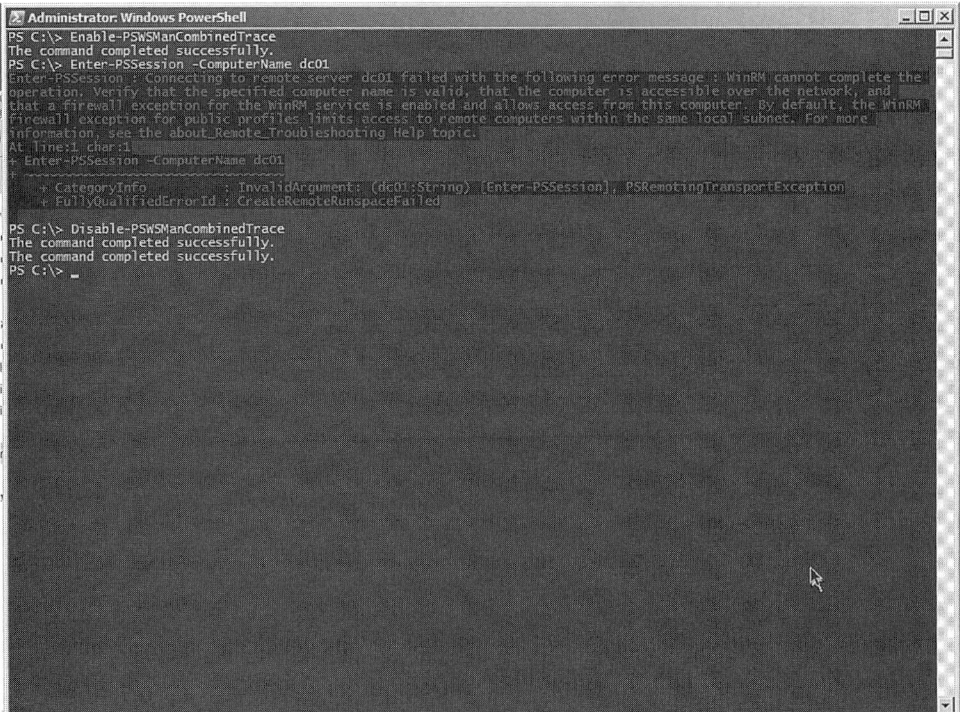

Figure 11 Connection failure due to a firewall or other port-blocking problem

```
7937 4/14/2012 4:01:11 PM Command Enter-PSSession is Started.


                          Context:
                                  Severity = Informational
                                  Host Name = ConsoleHost
                                  Host Version = 3.0
                                  Host ID =
                          8fd53e17-bd16-456a-8c6e-174acb89ce8c
                                  Engine Version = 3.0
                                  Runspace ID =
                          f42d6bb0-43d6-4f7d-81e9-376113a63428
                                  Pipeline ID = 66
                                  Command Name = Enter-PSSession
                                  Command Type = Cmdlet
                                  Script Name =
                                  Command Path =
                                  Sequence Number = 255
                                  User = AD2008R2\Administrator
                                  Shell ID = Microsoft.PowerShell


                          User Data:


12035 4/14/2012 4:01:11 PM ComputerName resolved to localhost
12035 4/14/2012 4:01:11 PM ComputerName resolved to dc01
12035 4/14/2012 4:01:11 PM ComputerName resolved to dc01
12035 4/14/2012 4:01:11 PM ComputerName resolved to dc01
```

Figure 12 Starting the connection attempt

A lot of the initial log traffic is still WinRM talking to itself, getting set up for the connection attempt. Keep scrolling through that until you start to see problem indications. Figure 13 shows a timeout—never a good sign—and the error message generated by WinRM. As you can see, this is exactly what's on-screen, so PowerShell isn't hiding anything.

This is one of the trickiest bits of remoting: WinRM can't tell why the server didn't respond. It doesn't realize that the port isn't open. For all WinRM knows, you could have specified a computer name that doesn't exist. All it sees is that it sent a message out to the network and nobody replied. In the end, nearly all of the possible "low-level" problems—bad IP address, bad computer name, blocked port, and so forth—all look the same to WinRM. You're on your own to troubleshoot these problems.

One useful technique is to use the old command-line Telnet client. Keep in mind that WS-MAN is HTTP, and HTTP, like many Internet protocols, sends text back and forth, more or less exactly like Telnet. HTTP has specific text it sends and looks for, but the transmission is old-school Telnet. Run something like `telnet dc01 5985` to see if you can connect. A blank screen is normal: press Ctrl-C to break out, and you'll see an HTTP "Bad Request" error. That's fine. It means you got through. That confirms the computer name, IP address, port, and everything else "low-level."

```
 138 4/14/2012 4:01:34 PM The client got a timeout from the network layer
                          (ERROR_WINHTTP_TIMEOUT)
1840 4/14/2012 4:01:34 PM An error was encountered while processing an
                          operation.
                          Error Code: 2150859046
                          Error String:<f:WSManFault xmlns:f="http://schemas.mi
                          crosoft.com/wbem/wsman/1/wsmanfault"
                          Code="2150859046"
                          Machine="C3096161287.AD2008R2.loc"><f:Message>WinRM
                          cannot complete the operation. Verify that the
                          specified computer name is valid, that the computer
                          is accessible over the network, and that a firewall
                          exception for the WinRM service is enabled and
                          allows access from this computer. By default, the
                          WinRM firewall exception for public profiles limits
                          access to remote computers within the same local
                          subnet. </f:Message></f:WSManFault>
1840 4/14/2012 4:01:34 PM An error was encountered while processing an
                          operation.
                          Error Code: 2150859046
                          Error String:<f:WSManFault xmlns:f="http://schemas.mi
                          crosoft.com/wbem/wsman/1/wsmanfault"
                          Code="2150859046"
                          Machine="C3096161287.AD2008R2.loc"><f:Message>WinRM
                          cannot complete the operation. Verify that the
                          specified computer name is valid, that the computer
                          is accessible over the network, and that a firewall
                          exception for the WinRM service is enabled and
                          allows access from this computer. By default, the
                          WinRM firewall exception for public profiles limits
                          access to remote computers within the same local
                          subnet. </f:Message></f:WSManFault>
```

Figure 13 The timeout error in the diagnostics log

Connection problem: No permissions

This problem can be tricky, because you need to be an Administrator to enable a diagnostics trace. On the other hand, WinRM is usually quite clear when you can't connect because your account doesn't have permission to the endpoint: "Access Denied" is the error message, and that's pretty straightforward.

But you can also log on as an Administrator (or open a shell under Administrator credentials), enable a trace, and then have another user (or your other user account) make the attempt. Go back in as Administrator, disable the trace, and then examine the log. Figure 14 shows what you're looking for.

The log data after that shows you the user account that tried to create the connection (AD2008R2\SallyS, in our example, which is why the command failed—she's not an Administrator). A quick check with `Get-PSSessionConfiguration` on the remote machine will confirm the permissions on whatever remoting endpoint you're attempting to connect to. Also, as shown in figure 15, running `Set-PSSessionConfiguration` can be useful. Provide the `-Name` of the endpoint you're checking, and add `-ShowSecurityDescriptorUI`. That will let you confirm the endpoint's permissions in a friendlier GUI form, and you can modify it right there if need be.

```
 1840 4/14/2012 4:18:53 PM An error was encountered while processing an
                           operation.
                           Error Code: 5
                           Error String:<f:WSManFault xmlns:f="http://schemas.mi
                           crosoft.com/wbem/wsman/1/wsmanfault" Code="5"
                           Machine="dc01"><f:Message>Access is denied.
                           </f:Message></f:WSManFault>
  254 4/14/2012 4:18:53 PM Activity Transfer
  142 4/14/2012 4:18:53 PM WSMan operation CreateShell failed, error code 5
32786 4/14/2012 4:18:53 PM Runspace Id 0d91c610-3c82-4b15-8858-76d833a013a3.
                           Callback received for WSMan Create Shell
 1840 4/14/2012 4:18:53 PM An error was encountered while processing an
                           operation.
                           Error Code: 122
                           Error String:<f:WSManFault xmlns:f="http://schemas.mi
                           crosoft.com/wbem/wsman/1/wsmanfault" Code="122"
                           Machine="C3096161287.AD2008R2.loc"><f:Message>The
                           data area passed to a system call is too small.
                           </f:Message></f:WSManFault>
  319 4/14/2012 4:18:53 PM Getting message for error code 5 completed
                           successfully. The languageCode parameter was: en-US
 8196 4/14/2012 4:18:53 PM Modifying activity Id and correlating
12039 4/14/2012 4:18:53 PM Modifying activity Id and correlating
32784 4/14/2012 4:18:53 PM Runspace Id: 0d91c610-3c82-4b15-8858-76d833a013a3
                           Pipeline Id: 00000000-0000-0000-0000-000000000000.
                           WSMan reported an error with error code: 5.
                            Error message: Connecting to remote server dc01
                           failed with the following error message : Access is
                           denied. For more information, see the
                           about_Remote_Troubleshooting Help topic.
                            StackTrace:
32776 4/14/2012 4:18:53 PM Runspace Id: 0d91c610-3c82-4b15-8858-76d833a013a3
                           Pipeline Id: 00000000-0000-0000-0000-000000000000.
                           WSMan reported an error with error code: 5.
                            Error message: Connecting to remote server dc01
                           failed with the following error message : Access is
                           denied. For more information, see the
                           about_Remote_Troubleshooting Help topic.
```

Figure 14 "Access Denied" in the diagnostics log

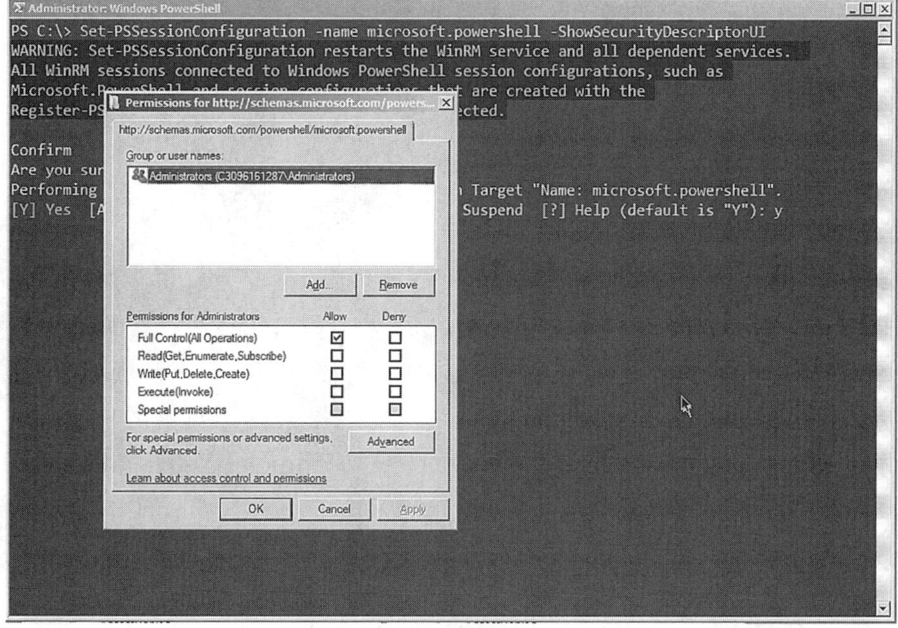

Figure 15 Checking an endpoint's permissions using `Set-PSSessionConfiguration`

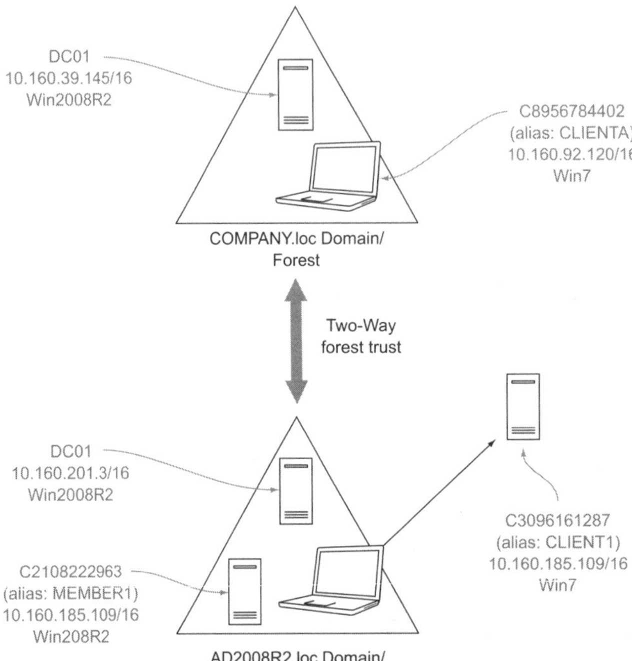
DC01
10.160.39.145/16
Win2008R2
C8956784402
(alias: CLIENTA)
10.160.92.120/16
Win7
COMPANY.loc Domain/
Forest
Two-Way
forest trust
DC01
10.160.201.3/16
Win2008R2
C2108222963
(alias: MEMBER1)
10.160.185.109/16
Win208R2
AD2008R2.loc Domain/
Forest
C3096161287
(alias: CLIENT1)
10.160.185.109/16
Win7

Figure 16 Attempted connection for this scenario: untrusted host

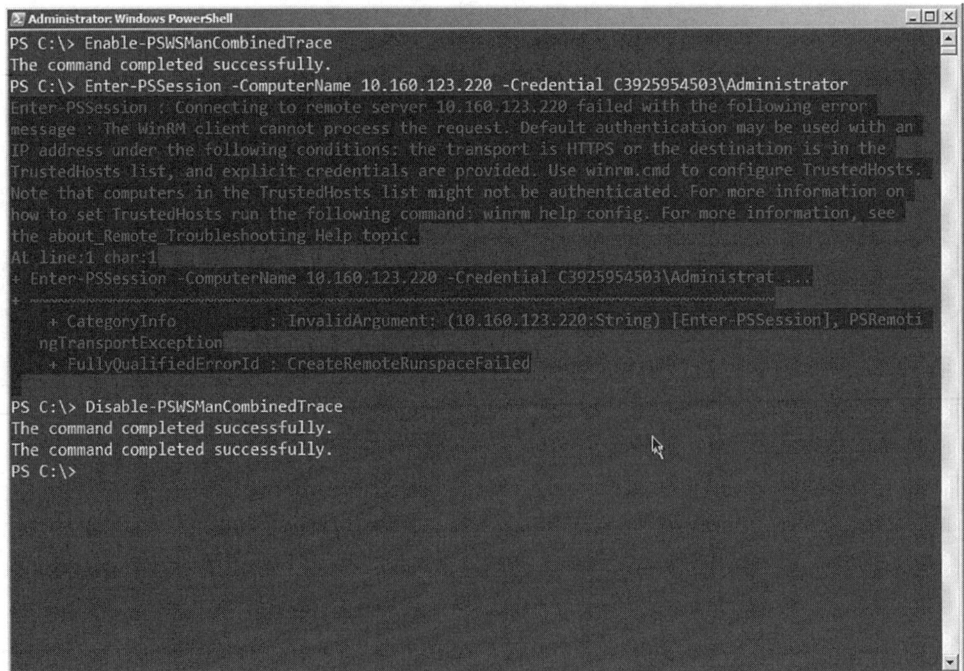
Administrator: Windows PowerShell
PS C:\> Enable-PSWSManCombinedTrace
The command completed successfully.
PS C:\> Enter-PSSession -ComputerName 10.160.123.220 -Credential C3925954503\Administrator
Enter-PSSession : Connecting to remote server 10.160.123.220 failed with the following error message : The WinRM client cannot process the request. Default authentication may be used with an IP address under the following conditions: the transport is HTTPS or the destination is in the TrustedHosts list, and explicit credentials are provided. Use winrm.cmd to configure TrustedHosts. Note that computers in the TrustedHosts list might not be authenticated. For more information on how to set TrustedHosts run the following command: winrm help config. For more information, see the about_Remote_Troubleshooting Help topic.
At line:1 char:1
+ Enter-PSSession -ComputerName 10.160.123.220 -Credential C3925954503\Administrat ...
+ CategoryInfo : InvalidArgument: (10.160.123.220:String) [Enter-PSSession], PSRemotingTransportException
+ FullyQualifiedErrorId : CreateRemoteRunspaceFailed
PS C:\> Disable-PSWSManCombinedTrace
The command completed successfully.
The command completed successfully.
PS C:\>

Figure 17 The error message when attempting to connect to an untrusted host. The message gives good clues as to how to solve this problem.

Connection problem: Untrusted host

In this scenario you try to connect from the client in the AD2008R2 domain to a standalone computer that isn't part of a domain, as shown in figure 16.

As shown in figure 17, the error comes quickly, even though you provided a valid credential. You're in a situation where WinRM can't get the mutual authentication it wants, and that requires additional setup, which I won't cover here (grab my free *Secrets of PowerShell Remoting* from http://PowerShellBooks.com for a walkthrough on fixing this problem). But what does the problem look like in the diagnostics log?

Figure 18 shows that WinRM still sends its initial salvo of traffic to the server. The error is generated when the reply comes back that the client can't authenticate this server. What you see in the log is pretty much what shows up in the shell, verbatim.

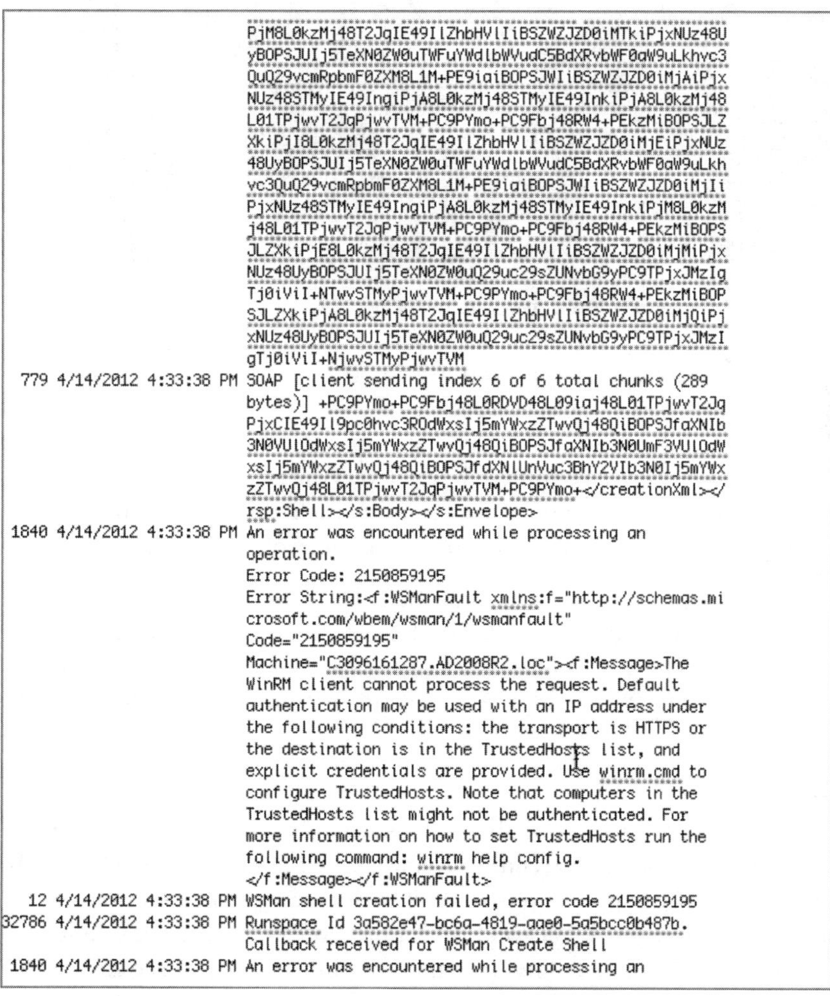

```
                               PjM8L0kzMj48T2JqIE49IlZhbHVlIiBSZWZJZD0iMTkiPjxNUz48U
                               yBOPSJUIj5TeXN0ZW0uTWFuYWdlbWVudC5BdXRvbWF0aW9uLkhvc3
                               QuQ29vcmRpbmF0ZXM8L1M+PE9iaiBOPSJWIiBSZWZJZD0iMjAiPjx
                               NUz48STMyIE49IngiPjA8L0kzMj48STMyIE49InkiPjA8L0kzMj48
                               L01TPjwvT2JqPjwvTVM+PC9PYmo+PC9Fbj48RW4+PEkzMiBOPSJLZ
                               XkiPjI8L0kzMj48T2JqIE49IlZhbHVlIiBSZWZJZD0iMjEiPjxNUz
                               48UyBOPSJUIj5TeXN0ZW0uTWFuYWdlbWVudC5BdXRvbWF0aW9uLkh
                               vc3QuQ29vcmRpbmF0ZXM8L1M+PE9iaiBOPSJWIiBSZWZJZD0iMjIi
                               PjxNUz48STMyIE49IngiPjA8L0kzMj48STMyIE49InkiPjM8L0kzM
                               j48L01TPjwvT2JqPjwvTVM+PC9PYmo+PC9Fbj48RW4+PEkzMiBOPS
                               JLZXkiPjE8L0kzMj48T2JqIE49IlZhbHVlIiBSZWZJZD0iMjMiPjx
                               NUz48UyBOPSJUIj5TeXN0ZW0uQ29uc29sZUNvbG9yPC9TPjxJMzIg
                               Tj0iViI+NTwvSTMyPjwvTVM+PC9PYmo+PC9Fbj48RW4+PEkzMiBOP
                               SJLZXkiPjA8L0kzMj48T2JqIE49IlZhbHVlIiBSZWZJZD0iMjQiPj
                               xNUz48UyBOPSJUIj5TeXN0ZW0uQ29uc29sZUNvbG9yPC9TPjxJMzI
                               gTj0iViI+NjwvSTMyPjwvTVM
  779 4/14/2012 4:33:38 PM SOAP [client sending index 6 of 6 total chunks (289
                               bytes)] +PC9PYmo+PC9Fbj48L0RDVD48L09iaj48L01TPjwvT2Jq
                               PjxCIE49Il9pc0hvc3ROdWxsIj5mYWxzZTwvQj48QiBOPSJfaXNIb
                               3N0VUlOdWxsIj5mYWxzZTwvQj48QiBOPSJfaXNIb3N0UmF3VUlOdW
                               xsIj5mYWxzZTwvQj48QiBOPSJfdXNlUnVuc3BhY2VIb3N0Ij5mYWx
                               zZTwvQj48L01TPjwvT2JqPjwvTVM+PC9PYmo+</creationXml></
                               rsp:Shell></s:Body></s:Envelope>
 1840 4/14/2012 4:33:38 PM An error was encountered while processing an
                               operation.
                               Error Code: 2150859195
                               Error String:<f:WSManFault xmlns:f="http://schemas.mi
                               crosoft.com/wbem/wsman/1/wsmanfault"
                               Code="2150859195"
                               Machine="C3096161287.AD2008R2.loc"><f:Message>The
                               WinRM client cannot process the request. Default
                               authentication may be used with an IP address under
                               the following conditions: the transport is HTTPS or
                               the destination is in the TrustedHosts list, and
                               explicit credentials are provided. Use winrm.cmd to
                               configure TrustedHosts. Note that computers in the
                               TrustedHosts list might not be authenticated. For
                               more information on how to set TrustedHosts run the
                               following command: winrm help config.
                               </f:Message></f:WSManFault>
   12 4/14/2012 4:33:38 PM WSMan shell creation failed, error code 2150859195
32786 4/14/2012 4:33:38 PM Runspace Id 3a582e47-bc6a-4819-aae0-5a5bcc0b487b.
                               Callback received for WSMan Create Shell
 1840 4/14/2012 4:33:38 PM An error was encountered while processing an
```

Figure 18 The diagnostic log content when attempting to connect to an untrusted host

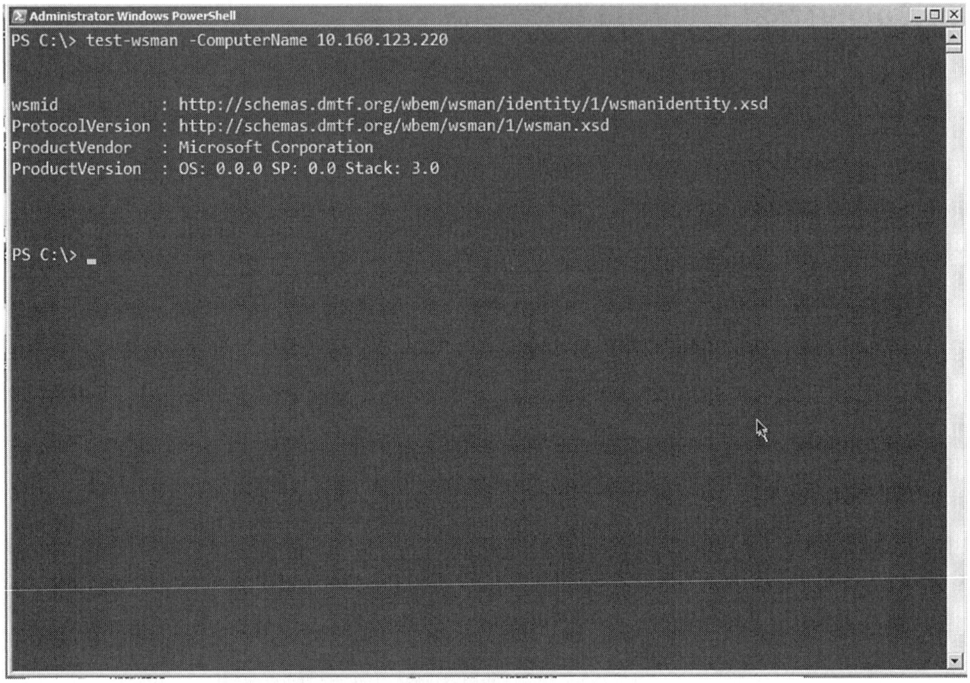

```
Administrator: Windows PowerShell
PS C:\> test-wsman -ComputerName 10.160.123.220


wsmid           : http://schemas.dmtf.org/wbem/wsman/identity/1/wsmanidentity.xsd
ProtocolVersion : http://schemas.dmtf.org/wbem/wsman/1/wsman.xsd
ProductVendor   : Microsoft Corporation
ProductVersion  : OS: 0.0.0 SP: 0.0 Stack: 3.0



PS C:\> _
```

Figure 19 **`Test-WSMan` is like a "ping" for remoting**

Figure 19 shows a good second step to take: run `Test-WSMan`. Provide the same computer name or IP address, but leave off the `-Credential` parameter. The cmdlet can at least tell you that WS-MAN and WinRM are up and running on the remote computer, and what version they're running. That narrows the problem down to one of authentication, involving either your permissions (which would have resulted in "Access Denied") or the mutual authentication component of remoting.

NOTE You see substantially the same behavior when you attempt to connect using HTTPS (the `-UseSSL` switch on the various remoting commands) and the remote machine's SSL certificate name doesn't match the name you used in your command. The error message is unambiguous both onscreen and in the log.

Summary

Why did I bother going through the logs when, in most of the examples, the logs echoed what was on the screen? It's simple: as PowerShell becomes embedded in more and more GUI applications you might not always have a console to rely on, with its nice error messages. What you can do, however, is use the console to start a trace, run whatever GUI app is failing, and then dig into the log to see if you find some of the signs I've shown you.

As for solving these problems, in many cases you'll have to perform some additional remoting setup. That can be complex in anything but a "we all live in the same domain" environment. I've put together a step-by-step guide to every configuration scenario I could think of, complete with screen shots, in a free PDF called *Secrets of PowerShell Remoting*, available from http://PowerShellBooks.com. (That site will at least get you to the guide's current location.)

About the author

Don Jones is a senior partner and principal technologist for Concentrated Tech (ConcentratedTech.com). He's authored and co-authored six books on Windows PowerShell, including *Learn Windows PowerShell 3 in a Month of Lunches*, *Learn PowerShell Toolmaking in a Month of Lunches*, and *PowerShell in Depth*. Don is a Microsoft MVP Award recipient and writes the monthly Windows PowerShell column for Microsoft's *TechNet Magazine* (TechNetMagazine.com). Don is also the co-founder and CEO for PowerShell.org, where you'll find him answering questions in the "General Q&A" and "Remoting" discussion forums.

2 CIM sessions

Richard Siddaway

PowerShell v3 introduces a great deal of new functionality. The biggest changes are associated with Windows Management Instrumentation (WMI).

NOTE WMI is Microsoft's implementation of the industry standard Common Information Model (CIM). With the Windows 8/2012 wave of products, Microsoft started moving to a more standards-based approach for WMI, and new terminology has emerged based on these changes.

With WMI in PowerShell v3, you get

- A new API
- New objects and .NET classes
- A new set of cmdlets
- CIM sessions
- The ability to create cmdlets from WMI classes

One chapter can't cover all of these topics, so I'm going to concentrate on CIM sessions with a side trip through the CIM cmdlets. For the other topics, see my book *PowerShell and WMI* (Manning 2012).

I start the chapter with a look at how WMI has been used in the past and some of the problems associated with it, followed by a quick look at the new CIM cmdlets, including comparisons to the existing WMI cmdlets where applicable.

Then I discuss CIM sessions, and I close the chapter by showing you how to configure CIM sessions to work with systems that still use legacy versions of PowerShell.

WMI

The WMI cmdlets in PowerShell v2 are great—if you've ever tried working with WMI through VBScript, you'll appreciate how great they are! But WMI cmdlets do come with a few problems.

WMI is a terrific tool for working with remote systems (in PowerShell v1 it was the *only* remote tool). The problem is that the WMI cmdlets work over Distributed

Component Object Model (DCOM) for access to remote systems. DCOM isn't a firewall-friendly protocol; it needs to be explicitly allowed. The remote machine also has to allow DCOM access. You can access a remote system by using the -ComputerName parameter:

```
PS> Get-WmiObject -Class Win32_ComputerSystem -ComputerName DC02
```

If DCOM isn't configured, you get an error like this:

```
Get-WmiObject : The RPC server is unavailable. (Exception from HRESULT:
     0x800706BA)
At line:1 char:1
+ Get-WmiObject -Class Win32_ComputerSystem -ComputerName DC02
+ ~~~~~~~~~~~~~~~~~~~~~~~~~~~~~~~~~~~~~~~~~~~~~~~~~~~~~~~~~~~
    + CategoryInfo          : InvalidOperation: (:) [Get-WmiObject],
     COMException
    + FullyQualifiedErrorId :
     GetWMICOMException,Microsoft.PowerShell.Commands.GetWmiObjectCommand
```

The other place where DCOM bites you is on the -Authentication parameter of Get-WmiObject. This causes confusion because you aren't authorizing yourself; you're determining the level of encryption on the DCOM connection to the remote machine. The most common scenario is when the WMI provider needs PacketPrivacy—full encryption on the connection—and won't allow remote access without it. This issue occurs with the Internet Information Services (IIS) and cluster WMI providers, for example.

NOTE Local access ignores the need for PacketPrivacy.

You can use PowerShell remoting to overcome the DCOM problems. You're effectively running the commands locally and bypassing DCOM. In PowerShell v3 you get another way to access WMI classes—the CIM cmdlets.

CIM cmdlets

CIM is an industry standard, owned and maintained by the Distributed Management Task Force (DMTF), which is also responsible for the WS-MAN protocols. WMI is Microsoft's implementation of CIM.

Try this:

```
Get-WmiObject -List *_ComputerSystem
```

You'll get two classes returned:

- CIM_ComputerSystem
- Win32_ComputerSystem

The CIM_ComputerSystem class is the original DMTF standard. The Win32_ComputerSystem class is Microsoft's version. In the root\cimv2 namespace, many of the classes have a CIM_ and a Win32_ version. They may be identical, or the Win32_ may be a modified version of the CIM_ class, usually with extra properties. I use the Win32_ class if there's a choice.

The new CIM API and cmdlets are part of an effort to further the use of CIM/WMI by a closer adoption of standards, and to link in with the Open Management Infrastructure initiative.

The new CIM cmdlets are listed in table 1 with their corresponding WMI cmdlets.

Table 1 Comparison of CIM cmdlets and WMI cmdlets

CIM cmdlet	WMI cmdlet
`New-CimInstance`	n/a
`Get-CimInstance`	`Get-WmiObject`
`Set-CimInstance`	`Set-WmiInstance`
`Invoke-CimMethod`	`Invoke-WmiMethod`
`Remove-CimInstance`	`Remove-WmiObject`
`Get-CimAssociatedInstance`	n/a
`Get-CimClass`	n/a
`Register-CimIndicationEvent`	`Register-WmiEvent`

The functioning of the CIM cmdlets is obvious—they do the same job as their WMI equivalents. But some cmdlets don't have a WMI equivalent:

- `New-CimInstance`—Creates a new instance of a CIM class. In practice, it has limited applicability. I usually use the `Create` method of a class through `Invoke-CimMethod`.
- `Get-CimAssociatedInstance`—Works through WMI associations. Easier to use than the `ASSOCIATORS OF` queries in WMI.
- `Get-CimClass`—Investigates a CIM class. You can discover properties and methods (including arguments). Arguably the most useful CIM cmdlet.

Using the CIM cmdlets is similar to using the WMI cmdlets, but note these two differences:

- You get a different type of object returned.
- You get an inert object—no WMI methods. Use `Invoke-CimMethod` to use the methods of a class.

You can see the differences by comparing the output of the WMI and CIM cmdlets. Try this code:

```
Get-WmiObject -Class Win32_ComputerSystem | Get-Member
Get-CimInstance -Class Win32_ComputerSystem | Get-Member
```

Compare the results to see the changes. You may also see a difference in the default output from a class because the CIM cmdlets produce a different object; therefore, the formatting can be different.

The WMI cmdlets had a `-ComputerName` parameter for accessing remote systems. The CIM cmdlets give you a choice: the `-CimSession` parameter for working with CIM sessions, or the `-ComputerName` parameter, which works with one or more computer names.

Using CIM sessions

Let's take a look at the syntax of `Get-CimInstance`:

```
Get-Command Get-CimInstance -Syntax

Get-CimInstance [-ClassName] <string> [-ComputerName <string[]>]
[-KeyOnly] [-Namespace <string>] [-OperationTimeoutSec <uint32>]
[-QueryDialect <string>] [-Shallow] [-Filter <string>]
[-Property <string[]>] [<CommonParameters>]

Get-CimInstance [-ClassName] <string> -CimSession <CimSession[]>
[-KeyOnly] [-Namespace <string>] [-OperationTimeoutSec <uint32>]
[-QueryDialect <string>] [-Shallow] [-Filter <string>]
[-Property <string[]>] [<CommonParameters>]
```

This is an abbreviated version of the output. The important point is that there is a `-ComputerName` parameter and a `-CimSession` parameter. Which should you use? The following rules control the usage of these parameters:

- *No* `-ComputerName` *or* `-CimSession`—Access the local machine using Component Object Model (COM).
- `-ComputerName`—Access the named machine(s) over WS-MAN. Create the connection, retrieve the data, and break the connection.
- `-CimSession`—Access the machine(s) contained in the open session by WS-MAN by default. DCOM is available as an option.

Those descriptions are reminiscent of PowerShell remoting. Use `-ComputerName` to access once or create a session for multiple round trips. The comparison is quite apt. Table 2 compares the CIM session cmdlets with the PowerShell remoting session cmdlets.

Table 2 Comparison of CIM session cmdlets and PowerShell remoting cmdlets

CIM session	Remoting session
Get-CimSession	Get-PSSession
New-CimSessionOption	New-PSSessionOption
New-CimSession	New-PSSession
Remove-CimSession	Remove-PSSession

Start by using the `-ComputerName` parameter:

```
PS> Get-CimInstance -ClassName Win32_OperatingSystem `
-ComputerName W12Standard | Format-List
```

```
SystemDirectory : C:\Windows\system32
Organization    :
BuildNumber     : 9200
RegisteredUser  : Windows User
SerialNumber    : 00183-80000-02976-AA135
Version         : 6.2.9200
PSComputerName  : W12Standard
```

That looks similar to what you would get from `Get-WmiObject`, so you can assume it's working. The system W12Standard is a Windows Server 2012 machine running PowerShell v3.

Now try the same thing against another system, WebR201 running PowerShell v2:

```
PS> Get-CimInstance -ClassName Win32_OperatingSystem `
-ComputerName webr201 | Format-List

Get-CimInstance : The WS-Management service cannot process the request. A
     DMTF resource URI was used to access a non-DMTF class. Try again using a
     non-DMTF resource URI.
At line:1 char:1
+ Get-CimInstance -ClassName Win32_OperatingSystem -ComputerName webr201 |
     Format- ...
+ ~~~~~~~~~~~~~~~~~~~~~~~~~~~~~~~~~~~~~~~~~~~~~~~~~~~~~~~~~~~~~~~~~~~~~~
    + CategoryInfo          : NotSpecified:
    (root\cimv2:Win32_OperatingSystem:String) [Get-CimInstance],
    CimException
    + FullyQualifiedErrorId : HRESULT
    0x80338139,Microsoft.Management.Infrastructure.CimCmdlets.GetCimInstance
    Command
    + PSComputerName        : webr201
```

Oops. You have a problem. The problem is that PowerShell isn't installed in isolation. The WS-MAN protocol is also installed with it as part of the WinRM service, which is used for remoting. Comparing the WS-MAN versions on the two machines, you can see the difference:

```
PS> Test-WSMan -ComputerName W12Standard -Authentication Default

wsmid           : http://schemas.dmtf.org/wbem/wsman/identity/1/
     wsmanidentity.xsd
ProtocolVersion : http://schemas.dmtf.org/wbem/wsman/1/wsman.xsd
ProductVendor   : Microsoft Corporation
ProductVersion  : OS: 6.2.9200 SP: 0.0 Stack: 3.0

PS> Test-WSMan -ComputerName WebR201 -Authentication Default

wsmid           : http://schemas.dmtf.org/wbem/wsman/identity/1/
     wsmanidentity.xsd
ProtocolVersion : http://schemas.dmtf.org/wbem/wsman/1/wsman.xsd
ProductVendor   : Microsoft Corporation
ProductVersion  : OS: 6.1.7601 SP: 1.0 Stack: 2.0
```

You can see that W12Standard (running PowerShell v3) uses WS-MAN 3.0, but WebR201 (running PowerShell v2) uses WS-MAN 2.0.

NOTE You must use PowerShell v3 and WS-MAN 3.0 on the remote system for the `-ComputerName` parameter on CIM cmdlets to work, including `New-CimSession`. You also need the WinRM service running, but you don't need to have enabled PowerShell remoting.

The WS-MAN version appears to be a problem. It has a solution, which I'll get to in a bit. But first, how do you use a CIM session?

```
PS> $s = New-CimSession -ComputerName W12Standard
PS> Get-CimInstance -ClassName Win32_OperatingSystem -CimSession $s |
➥ Format-List

SystemDirectory : C:\Windows\system32
Organization    :
BuildNumber     : 9200
RegisteredUser  : Windows User
SerialNumber    : 00183-80000-02976-AA135
Version         : 6.2.9200
PSComputerName  : W12Standard
```

Create a new CIM session using the `New-CimSession` cmdlet. Supply one or more computer names to be part of the session. Then use the session variable with the `-CimSession` parameter. When you create a CIM session you can give it a name, but you can't use the name as input to the `-CimSession` parameter!

When you create a CIM session involving multiple machines, use a variable like this:

```
PS> $s = New-CimSession -ComputerName W12Standard, DC02
PS> Get-CimSession

Id           : 3
Name         : CimSession3
InstanceId   : 18d79ba0-9cbc-4462-8c35-063222e5ec6c
ComputerName : W12Standard
Protocol     : WSMAN

Id           : 4
Name         : CimSession4
InstanceId   : 28c91894-2384-4416-861c-09c80dddd8f5
ComputerName : DC02
Protocol     : WSMAN
```

You can then access all machines in the session:

```
Get-CimInstance -ClassName Win32_OperatingSystem -CimSession $s
```

Alternatively, you can access individual machines within the session:

```
Get-CimInstance -ClassName Win32_OperatingSystem `
-CimSession (Get-CimSession -ComputerName DC02)

Get-CimInstance -ClassName Win32_OperatingSystem `
-CimSession (Get-CimSession -Id 4)

Get-CimInstance -ClassName Win32_OperatingSystem `
-CimSession (Get-CimSession -Name CimSession4)
```

```
Get-CimInstance -ClassName Win32_OperatingSystem `
-CimSession (Get-CimSession `
-InstanceId 28c91894-2384-4416-861c-09c80dddd8f5)
```

You can use any of these methods, though the computer name is probably the easiest to work with.

So far, you have worked with remote machines running PowerShell v3 and WS-MAN 3.0. How do you deal with machines running older versions of WS-MAN?

CIM session options

You saw earlier that when you use the `-ComputerName` parameter with the CIM cmdlets, the connections are made over the WS-MAN protocol. This connection mechanism fails for versions of WS-MAN earlier than 3.0; that is, for PowerShell v2.

When you create a CIM session you can use the `-SessionOption` parameter to define one or more options to configure the session. These options are created using the `New-CimSessionOption` cmdlet:

```
PS> Get-Command New-CimSessionOption -Syntax

New-CimSessionOption [-Protocol] <ProtocolType>
  ➥ [-UICulture <cultureinfo>]
  ➥ [-Culture <cultureinfo>] [<CommonParameters>]

New-CimSessionOption [-NoEncryption] [-SkipCACheck] [-SkipCNCheck]
[-SkipRevocationCheck] [-EncodePortInServicePrincipalName]
[-Encoding <PacketEncoding>] [-HttpPrefix <uri>]
[-MaxEnvelopeSizeKB <uint32>]
[-ProxyAuthentication <PasswordAuthenticationMechanism>]
[-ProxyCertificateThumbprint <string>]
[-ProxyCredential<pscredential>]
[-ProxyType <ProxyType>] [-UseSsl] [-UICulture <cultureinfo>]
[-Culture <cultureinfo>] [<CommonParameters>]

New-CimSessionOption [-Impersonation <ImpersonationType>]
[-PacketIntegrity] [-PacketPrivacy]
[-UICulture <cultureinfo>]
[-Culture <cultureinfo>] [<CommonParameters>]
```

The important parameter for connecting to legacy versions of WS-MAN is the `-Protocol` parameter. This enables you to create a session using DCOM as your transport mechanism:

```
PS> $o = New-CimSessionOption -Protocol DCOM
PS> $sd = New-CimSession -ComputerName webr201 -SessionOption $o
PS> Get-CimInstance -ClassName Win32_OperatingSystem
  ➥ -CimSession $sd | Format-List

SystemDirectory : C:\Windows\system32
Organization    :
BuildNumber     : 7601
RegisteredUser  : Windows User
SerialNumber    : 55041-437-0002014-84878
Version         : 6.1.7601
PSComputerName  : webr201
```

If you create a session using WS-MAN as well, like this

```
PS> $sw = New-CimSession -ComputerName w12standard
```

you can use them together, like this:

```
Get-CimInstance -ClassName Win32_OperatingSystem -CimSession $sd,$sw
```

NOTE If your connection to a remote machine is broken and restored within about four minutes, for instance due to a reboot of the remote machine, then the CIM session over WS-MAN will automatically reconnect. A CIM session over DCOM won't reconnect.

CIM sessions over DCOM also solve another problem. A number of WMI namespaces require `PacketPrivacy` authentication for remote access. IIS is an example. This fails:

```
PS> Get-WmiObject -Namespace 'root\webadministration' -Class Server
  ➥ -ComputerName webr201

Get-WmiObject : Access denied
At line:1 char:1
+ Get-WmiObject -Namespace 'root\webadministration'
-Class Server -ComputerName we ...
+ ~~~~~~~~~~~~~~~~~~~~~~~~~~~~~~~~~~~~~~~~~~~~~~~~~~~~~~~~~
  ➥ ~~~~~~~~~~~~~~~~~~~~~~~~~
    + CategoryInfo          : InvalidOperation: (:) [Get-WmiObject],
     ManagementException
    + FullyQualifiedErrorId : GetWMIManagementException,Microsoft.PowerShell.
      ➥ Commands.GetWmiObjectCommand
```

You need to use `PacketPrivacy`, which is specified using the `-Authentication` parameter:

```
PS> Get-WmiObject -Namespace 'root\webadministration'
  ➥ -Class Server -ComputerName webr201 -Authentication 6

__GENUS                   : 2
__CLASS                   : Server
__SUPERCLASS              : Object
__DYNASTY                 : Object
__RELPATH                 : Server=@
__PROPERTY_COUNT          : 4
__DERIVATION              : {Object}
__SERVER                  : WEBR201
__NAMESPACE               : root\webadministration
__PATH                    : \\WEBR201\root\webadministration:Server=@
ApplicationDefaults       : System.Management.ManagementBaseObject
ApplicationPoolDefaults   : System.Management.ManagementBaseObject
SiteDefaults              : System.Management.ManagementBaseObject
VirtualDirectoryDefaults  : System.Management.ManagementBaseObject
PSComputerName            : WEBR201
```

When you create a CIM session and set the protocol to DCOM, you get `PacketPrivacy` automatically set for you. Unfortunately, the information returned by `Get-CimSession` doesn't show this, but it does work:

```
PS> Get-CimInstance -Namespace 'root\webadministration' `
-Class Server -CimSession $sd

ApplicationDefaults        : ApplicationElementDefaults
ApplicationPoolDefaults    : ApplicationPoolElementDefaults
SiteDefaults               : SiteElementDefaults
VirtualDirectoryDefaults   : VirtualDirectoryElementDefaults
PSComputerName             : webr201
```

The other nice thing about CIM cmdlets is that you don't get the system properties, so you have a cleaner output.

Other options available through the `New-CimSessionOption` cmdlet include

- *The option to set the culture*—By default, `New-CimSessionOption` uses the culture of the client machine, but you can set the culture to match the server.
- *WS-MAN options* (such as skipping certificate checks, using proxies, and maximum envelope size)—These are analogous to configuring a remoting session and are used in the same scenarios.
- *WMI impersonation*—This is usually not required, as the default is to impersonate.

Summary

CIM sessions provide a more robust, firewall-friendly way to access WMI on remote machines than using DCOM in the WMI cmdlets. Get to know them; they will save you work, time, and effort.

About the author

Richard Siddaway has worked with Microsoft technologies for 25 years and has spent time in most IT roles. He currently works for Kelway (UK) Ltd as an automation consultant. He has a long-standing interest in automation techniques, and PowerShell has been his primary automation tool since the early beta versions. Richard founded the UK PowerShell User Group in 2007 and is a PowerShell MVP. He frequently speaks at PowerShell user groups in the UK, Europe, the US, and elsewhere around the world, and judges the Microsoft Scripting Games. In addition to writing his blog (http://msmvps.com/blogs/RichardSiddaway/), Richard has authored two PowerShell books: *PowerShell in Practice* (Manning 2010) and *PowerShell and WMI* (Manning 2012), and co-authored *PowerShell in Depth* (Manning 2013) with Don Jones and Jeffery Hicks. Currently he is writing an introductory book for Active Directory administrators that features PowerShell.

3 Collecting and analyzing performance counter data

Arnaud Petitjean

Most of the time, performance management is a topic that interests IT pros who have to troubleshoot performance issues. But assessing performance can be important in a number of other scenarios, such as before you upgrade a machine to new hardware, before updating an application to a newer version, when defining performance baselines, or, worse, when users are complaining because their desktop PC or their business application is performing badly.

The good news is that Windows embeds all the technologies that allow you to collect bunches of valuable data, from the global CPU, memory, network, and disk I/O usage data to detailed information like the resource consumption of a specific process.

In this chapter, I'll cover how to collect, store, and analyze performance counter data using a dedicated set of PowerShell cmdlets. But first I'll talk a bit about the API that PowerShell relies on and what this API can do.

Windows Performance Logs and Alerts

The technology called Performance Logs and Alerts (PLA) is both a protocol and a software component for logging diagnostic data on remote computers or on local computers as well. The software component is a set of DCOM interfaces. To summarize, PLA allows you to

- *Collect performance data.* That data can be pulled from hardware (a CPU, network, or disk, for example) or software (an application, a process, or a thread, for example). The logged performance counter data is often useful for the analysis of performance trends and bottlenecks. The PLA protocol also supports logging performance counter data in a SQL database format, a text comma-separated values (CSV) file, or a binary performance log (BLG) file.

- *Collect event tracing data (Event Tracing for Windows, or ETW).* The event provider is software that can create event notifications and generate events when certain activities, such as a disk I/O operation or a page fault, occur. ETW provides a tracing mechanism for events raised by both user-mode applications and kernel-mode device drivers.
- *Collect API tracing data.* PLA lets you gather API call activity of an executable in order to diagnose various issues (for example, detecting unnecessary API calls).
- *Collect configuration information.* PLA collects computer settings at the time of collection. You can use the configuration information to verify the system state or track changes.
- *Generate alerts.* PLA allows you to create alerts based on performance counters. An alert can trigger running a program, logging the alert as an event, or starting another data collection.
- *Start, stop, or schedule data collection.* Gathering the data can consist of grouping sets of counters into collections. PLA lets you start, stop, and schedule the collections in a precise manner.

In this chapter, I'll focus on PLA's abilities to gather performance data, create collections, and manage them. I won't talk about the other functionalities of PLA.

PLA relies on DCOM, which uses Remote Procedure Call (RPC) as its transport. That means if you want to use PLA on remote computers using the built-in mechanism, you have to be careful about the firewall configuration. But that isn't an issue if you use Windows PowerShell remoting (based on WinRM) to manage your systems remotely. PowerShell remoting uses an HTTP/HTTPS-based protocol for the transport that is much more firewall-friendly than RPC.

Enumerating the counter groups

Before collecting data from the performance counters, you need to identify which ones are the most relevant for your needs and identify their names.

To do this, use the PowerShell cmdlet `Get-Counter` and its `-ListSet` parameter. If you ask for help for this cmdlet you'll see two different parameter sets. For now, focus on the second help syntax:

```
Get-Counter [-ListSet] <String[]> [-ComputerName <String[]>]
      [<CommonParameters>]
```

Counters are grouped into list sets that are a convenient way to identify all the relevant counters for a particular field. For example, all the counters related to the memory diagnostics are located under the `Memory` list set. Similarly, all the counters related to branch cache management data, network, or PowerShell are put in the following list sets, respectively: `BrancheCache`, `Network Interface`, and `PowerShell Workflow`.

Here's how to get them all:

```
PS > Get-Counter -ListSet *
```

Although this command line works, the output isn't user-friendly; there's too much information on the screen. For better readability, use a command line that returns a small number of properties:

```
PS > Get-Counter -ListSet * | Sort-Object -Property CounterSetName |
  ➥ Format-Table CounterSetName, Description -AutoSize

CounterSetName         Description
--------------         -----------
...
.NET CLR Data          .Net CLR Data
.NET CLR Memory        Counters for CLR Garbage Collected heap.
ASP.NET                ASP.NET global performance counters
BITS Net Utilization   BITS Per Job Network Utilization
BranchCache            Counters for measuring bandwidth and latency for Br...
Database               Database provides performance statistics for each p...
HTTP Service           Set of HTTP service counters...
LogicalDisk            The Logical Disk performance object consists of cou...
Memory                 The Memory performance object  consists of counters...
Network Interface      The Network Interface performance object consists of..
PowerShell Workflow    Displays performance counters for PowerShell Workfl...
Processor              The Processor performance object consists of counte...
Telephony              The Telephony System
Terminal Services      Terminal Services Summary Information
...
```

Or better yet, try the `Out-GridView` cmdlet:

```
PS > Get-Counter -ListSet * | Out-GridView
```

This returns a screen like that shown in figure 1. Then you can sort on the `CounterSetName` property by clicking the column's name.

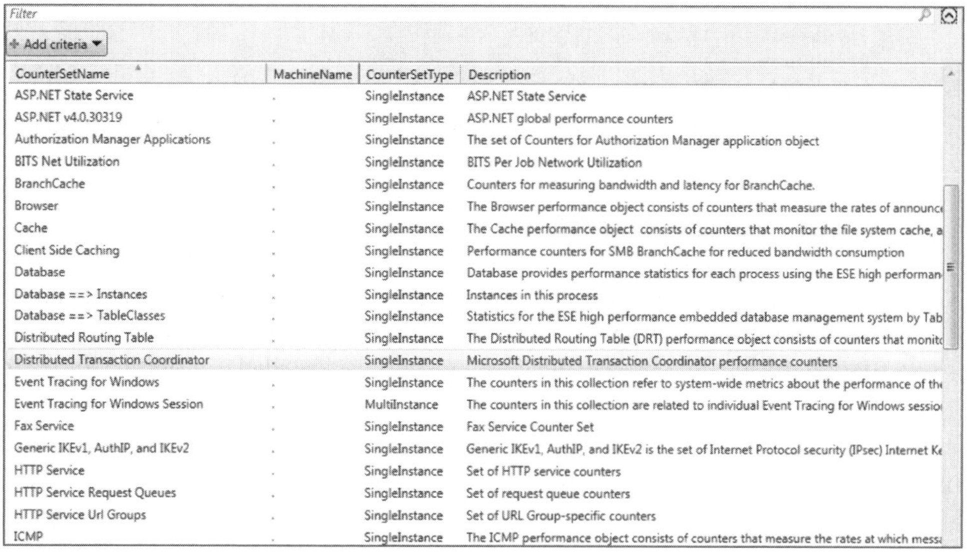

Filter

Add criteria ▾

CounterSetName	MachineName	CounterSetType	Description
ASP.NET State Service	.	SingleInstance	ASP.NET State Service
ASP.NET v4.0.30319	.	SingleInstance	ASP.NET global performance counters
Authorization Manager Applications	.	SingleInstance	The set of Counters for Authorization Manager application object
BITS Net Utilization	.	SingleInstance	BITS Per Job Network Utilization
BranchCache	.	SingleInstance	Counters for measuring bandwidth and latency for BranchCache.
Browser	.	SingleInstance	The Browser performance object consists of counters that measure the rates of announc
Cache	.	SingleInstance	The Cache performance object consists of counters that monitor the file system cache, a
Client Side Caching	.	SingleInstance	Performance counters for SMB BranchCache for reduced bandwidth consumption
Database	.	SingleInstance	Database provides performance statistics for each process using the ESE high performan
Database ==> Instances	.	SingleInstance	Instances in this process
Database ==> TableClasses	.	SingleInstance	Statistics for the ESE high performance embedded database management system by Tab
Distributed Routing Table	.	SingleInstance	The Distributed Routing Table (DRT) performance object consists of counters that monit
Distributed Transaction Coordinator	.	SingleInstance	Microsoft Distributed Transaction Coordinator performance counters
Event Tracing for Windows	.	SingleInstance	The counters in this collection refer to system-wide metrics about the performance of th
Event Tracing for Windows Session	.	MultiInstance	The counters in this collection are related to individual Event Tracing for Windows sessio
Fax Service	.	SingleInstance	Fax Service Counter Set
Generic IKEv1, AuthIP, and IKEv2	.	SingleInstance	Generic IKEv1, AuthIP, and IKEv2 is the set of Internet Protocol security (IPsec) Internet Ke
HTTP Service	.	SingleInstance	Set of HTTP service counters
HTTP Service Request Queues	.	SingleInstance	Set of request queue counters
HTTP Service Url Groups	.	SingleInstance	Set of URL Group-specific counters
ICMP	.	SingleInstance	The ICMP performance object consists of counters that measure the rates at which mess

Figure 1 List sets in `Out-GridView`

If you're curious and want to count how many list sets you have at your disposal, it's easy:

```
PS > Get-Counter -ListSet * | Measure-Object |
➥ Select-Object -ExpandProperty Count

115
```

You have 115 list sets on your freshly installed Windows Server 2012 machine. Now enter a command to get the total number of counters available:

```
PS > Get-Counter -ListSet * | Select-Object -ExpandProperty Counter |
➥ Measure-Object | Select-Object -ExpandProperty Count

1773
```

Wow! That's an amazing number of counters, isn't it? Is it possible to determine how many counters you have per list set? Sure:

```
PS > Get-Counter -ListSet * | Select-Object -Property CounterSetName,
➥ @{n='#Counters';e={$_.counter.count}} |
➥ Sort-Object -Property CounterSetName | Format-Table -AutoSize

CounterSetName                                              #Counters
--------------                                              ---------
...
.NET CLR Data                                                       6
.NET CLR Memory                                                    23
ASP.NET                                                            19
BITS Net Utilization                                                8
BranchCache                                                        21
Database                                                           35
HTTP Service                                                        6
...
LogicalDisk                                                        23
Memory                                                             35
Network Interface                                                  18
PowerShell Workflow                                                29
Processor                                                          15
...
```

Windows Server 2012 owns more than 1700 performance counters that belong to more than 110 categories (called the list set).

Finding the right counters

Given the huge number of counters available in Windows, finding the right ones may not be an easy task. You could browse the web and read numerous documents about how to assess performance in order to find the appropriate counters, or you could be more efficient and browse the existing counters installed on your machine. To do this, you have two options:

- *Option 1*—Launch the graphical Performance Monitor console (shown in figure 2), click the Add Counters icon (the plus sign), and browse the list. Note that if you check the Show Description box you gain access to detailed information about the purpose of every counter.
- *Option 2*—Use PowerShell to browse and search the internal repository.

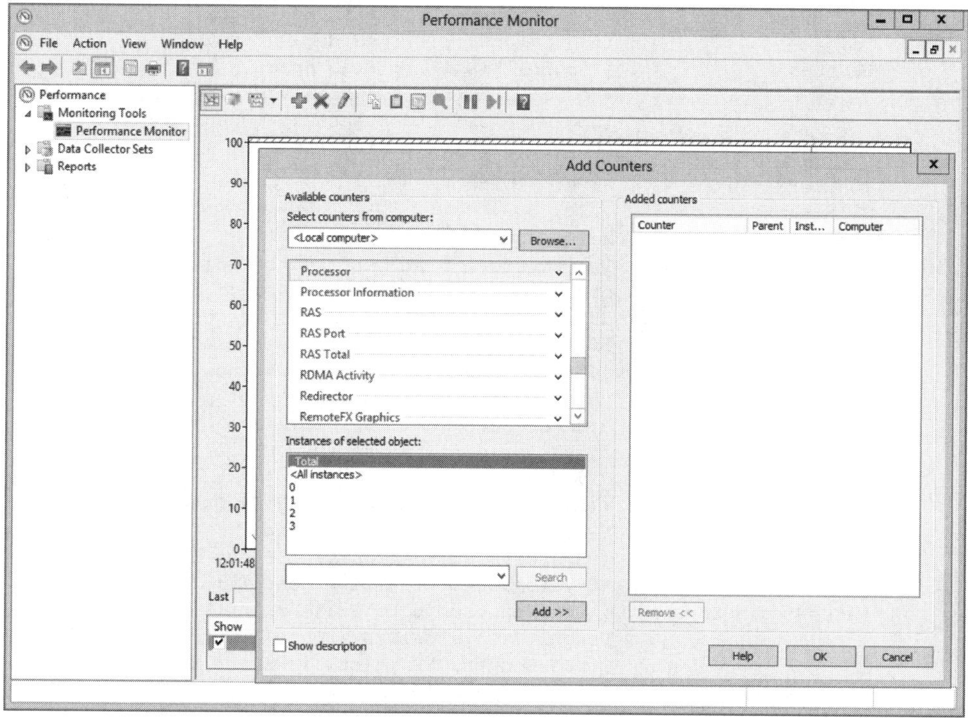

Figure 2 Performance Monitor console—browsing the counters

Although option 1 is a valid approach, it doesn't allow you to copy and paste the counters' paths, and you'll need that information later in order to get the data. This is why I'll focus on option 2, the PowerShell option.

You've seen that to view the counters' sets (the list sets) you need to use the `Get-Counter` cmdlet with the `-ListSet` parameter.

Suppose you want to find all the counters related to disks. Try this:

```
PS > Get-Counter -ListSet *disk*

CounterSetName     : LogicalDisk
MachineName        : .
CounterSetType     : MultiInstance
Description        : The Logical Disk performance object consists of
                     counters that monitor logical partitions of a
                     hard or fixed disk drives.  Performance Monitor
                     identifies logical disks by their a drive
                     letter, such as C.
Paths              : {\LogicalDisk(*)\% Free Space,
                     \LogicalDisk(*)\Free Megabytes,
                     \LogicalDisk(*)\Current Disk Queue Length,
                     \LogicalDisk(*)\% Disk Time...}
PathsWithInstances : {\LogicalDisk(E:)\% Free Space,
                     \LogicalDisk(C:)\% Free Space,
```

```
                      \LogicalDisk(_Total)\% Free Space,
                      \LogicalDisk(E:)\Free Megabytes...}
Counter             : {\LogicalDisk(*)\% Free Space,
                      \LogicalDisk(*)\Free Megabytes,
                      \LogicalDisk(*)\Current Disk Queue Length,
                      \LogicalDisk(*)\% Disk Time...}

CounterSetName      : PhysicalDisk
MachineName         : .
CounterSetType      : MultiInstance
Description         : The Physical Disk performance object consists
                      of counters that monitor hard or fixed disk
                      drive on a computer.  Disks are used to store
                      file, program, and paging data and are read to
                      retrieve these items, and written to record
                      changes to them.  The values of physical disk
                      counters are sums of the values of the logical
                      disks (or partitions) into which they are
                      divided.
Paths               : {\PhysicalDisk(*)\Current Disk Queue Length,
                      \PhysicalDisk(*)\% Disk Time,
                      \PhysicalDisk(*)\Avg. Disk Queue Length,
                      \PhysicalDisk(*)\% Disk Read Time...}
PathsWithInstances  : {\PhysicalDisk(0 E: C:)\Current Disk Queue
                      Length, \PhysicalDisk(_Total)\Current Disk
                      Queue Length, \PhysicalDisk(0 E: C:)\% Disk
                      Time, \PhysicalDisk(_Total)\% Disk Time...}
Counter             : {\PhysicalDisk(*)\Current Disk Queue Length,
                      \PhysicalDisk(*)\% Disk Time,
                      \PhysicalDisk(*)\Avg. Disk Queue Length,
                      \PhysicalDisk(*)\% Disk Read Time...}
```

The counters are located under the `Paths` and `Counter` properties. These two properties are referencing the same thing because the `Counter` property is an alias of the `Paths` property. In order to extract the counters' names (or `Counter` paths in the terminology), use the extremely useful `-ExpandProperty` parameter of the `Select-Object` cmdlet:

```
PS > Get-Counter -ListSet *disk* | Select-Object -ExpandProperty Paths

\LogicalDisk(*)\% Free Space
\LogicalDisk(*)\Free Megabytes
\LogicalDisk(*)\Disk Transfers/sec
\LogicalDisk(*)\Disk Reads/sec
\LogicalDisk(*)\Disk Writes/sec
\LogicalDisk(*)\Disk Bytes/sec
\LogicalDisk(*)\Disk Read Bytes/sec
\LogicalDisk(*)\Disk Write Bytes/sec
...
\PhysicalDisk(*)\Current Disk Queue Length
\PhysicalDisk(*)\% Disk Time
\PhysicalDisk(*)\% Idle Time
\PhysicalDisk(*)\Split IO/Sec
```

Now all you have to do is to pick up the right counter, but that's another story, and will depend on your needs at the time. But to help prepare for that task, try using option 1 first to browse the available counters and read their descriptions, and then use PowerShell (option 2) to get their data once you've identified them.

Accessing the counters' data

Once you determine the counters you want to query, getting the information is straightforward. Have a look at the first help syntax:

```
Get-Counter [[-Counter] <String[]>] [-ComputerName <String[]>] [-Continuous
 [<SwitchParameter>]] [-MaxSamples <Int64>] [-SampleInterval <Int32>]
[<CommonParameters>]
```

The `-Counter` parameter allows you to specify the names of multiple counters. The same goes for the second parameter, `-ComputerName`, which allows a string array of computer names.

The `-Continuous` switch parameter allows you to indicate whether you want to get the counters' data continuously, that is, whether the collection should continue while the PowerShell process is running. The `-MaxSamples` parameter indicates the number of samples of data you want to collect. `-SampleInterval` determines the frequency of the data collection in seconds. If, for example, you use a value of 10 for `-MaxSamples` and 2 for `-SampleInterval`, you'll get a total of 10 samples, and each sample will be collected every 2 seconds.

Now, try it!

Suppose you've identified an interesting counter, one that returns the current CPU load of the physical processors. Enter this:

```
PS > Get-Counter -Counter '\Processor(*)\% Processor Time'

Timestamp                 CounterSamples
---------                 --------------
08/10/2012 10:50:32 PM    \\ws2012us-0\processor(0)\% processor time :
                          32.9234067811321

                          \\ws2012us-0\processor(1)\% processor time :
                          0.165070557964087

                          \\ws2012us-0\processor(2)\% processor time :
                          39.1630898712594

                          \\ws2012us-0\processor(3)\% processor time :
                          0.165070557964087

                          \\ws2012us-0\processor(_total)\% processor time :
                          18.1041644417939
```

As you can see, this shows not only the general CPU load of the computer, but also the details for all the cores. This example is for a machine with a quad-core CPU, so you see four instances, one for each core. If you had more physical CPUs you'd see more instances. For example, a two-socket system with four cores in each CPU would show eight instances. The `_total` instance is the average load of all the cores (the sum of the load of all the cores divided by the number of cores).

If you only want one instance, instead of using an asterisk in the parentheses, specify the instance name:

```
PS > Get-Counter -Counter '\Processor(_total)\% Processor Time'

Timestamp                 CounterSamples
---------                 --------------
15/10/2012 11:04:16 PM    \\ws2012us-0\processor(_total)\% processor time :
                          5.7687964656473
```

Controlling the sampling and the collection interval

If you don't ask `Get-Counter` for a particular number of samples, you only get one. Although this information can be useful as an instantaneous value, it's generally best to be able to get more data.

The `-MaxSample` parameter specifies the number of samples to get from each counter. (To get samples continuously you have to use the `-Continuous` switch.) In the following command line you ask for five samples of the selected counter:

```
PS > Get-Counter -Counter '\Processor(_total)\% Processor Time'
➥ -MaxSample 5

Timestamp                 CounterSamples
---------                 --------------
16/10/2012 12:26:38 AM    \\ws2012us-0\processor(_total)\% processor time :
                          9.62628218427481

16/10/2012 12:26:39 AM    \\ws2012us-0\processor(_total)\% processor time :
                          11.0301526757573

16/10/2012 12:26:40 AM    \\ws2012us-0\processor(_total)\% processor time :
                          18.8230172314685

16/10/2012 12:26:41 AM    \\ws2012us-0\processor(_total)\% processor time :
                          14.6256781806885

16/10/2012 12:26:43 AM    \\ws2012us-0\processor(_total)\% processor time :
                          14.0962802715194
```

If you don't specify an interval, you get the data every second. You can adjust this by setting the interval with the `-SampleInterval` parameter. Suppose you want to collect three samples of data at five-second intervals:

```
PS > Get-Counter -Counter '\Processor(_total)\% Processor Time'
➥ -MaxSample 3 -SampleInterval 5

Timestamp                 CounterSamples
---------                 --------------
16/10/2012 12:32:24 AM    \\ws2012us-0\processor(_total)\% processor time :
                          10.388804621813

16/10/2012 12:32:29 AM    \\ws2012us-0\processor(_total)\% processor time :
                          15.1723817764828

16/10/2012 12:32:34 AM    \\ws2012us-0\processor(_total)\% processor time :
                          17.2179883236179
```

Getting the data from remote computers

With the -ComputerName parameter you have the ability to query the counters of remote computers this way:

```
PS > Get-Counter -Counter '\Processor(_total)\% Processor Time'
  ➥ -Computer ws2012us-0, ws2012us-1
```

Or:

```
PS > Get-Counter -Counter
  ➥ '\\ws2012us-0\Processor(_total)\% Processor Time',
  ➥ '\\ws2012us-1\Processor(_total)\% Processor Time'
```

Although that sounds interesting, it may not be the best option because

- The servers (the remote machines) and the client have to be in the same domain.
- You have to be logged in as a domain administrator because Get-Counter doesn't have any -Credential parameter that could give you the ability to use an alternate account.
- The firewalls on the remote computers have to accept DCOM/RPC protocol because Get-Counter relies on it.

Because of these drawbacks, and if the requirements aren't fulfilled, the best option is to use the PowerShell remoting mechanism; therefore, you could write something like this:

```
PS > $scriptblock = {
Get-Counter -Counter '\Processor(_total)\% Processor Time'}
PS > Invoke-Command -ComputerName ws2012us-0,ws2012us-1 `
  ➥ -Credential $cred -ScriptBlock $scriptblock
```

That being said, you have to be careful because there's a little trick. When you use the remoting mechanisms with cmdlets like Invoke-Command, PowerShell uses serialization. That means the data you receive from a remote computer is serialized into XML to cross the network and then deserialized on your local machine. Hence the object you get isn't a live object anymore but a "rehydrated" object that has lost all the methods from the original object and only has static properties. Furthermore, only one level of depth is serialized by default, which means that if the original object contains nested objects you can't reach them.

To get around this, you have two options: either dig into the object on the remote side in order to return the data you're interested in, or change the default settings to return more than one level of depth for your data. For the second option, setting a value of two levels of depth would be sufficient.

To illustrate, try this snippet:

```
PS > $scriptblock = {
     Get-Counter -Counter '\Processor(_total)\% Processor Time'}
PS > $r = Invoke-Command -ComputerName ws2012us-0 -ScriptBlock $scriptblock
PS > $r.CounterSamples

Microsoft.PowerShell.Commands.GetCounter.PerformanceCounterSample
```

Because of the serialization mechanism, you get a string containing the type name of the CounterSamples property instead of getting the expected result.

Now extract the expected property on the remote computer side:

```
PS >  $scriptblock = {
   Get-Counter -Counter '\Processor(_total)\% Processor Time' |
   foreach { $_.CounterSamples }
}

PS > Invoke-Command -ComputerName ws2012us-0 -ScriptBlock $scriptblock

Path                    InstanceName     CookedValue        PSComputerName
----                    ------------     -----------        --------------
\\ws2012us-0\proce...   _total           1.43665925470344   ws2012us-0
```

The other technique consists of modifying the PowerShell type data by using the new functionality available with PowerShell v3's Update-TypeData, which allows you to update a type dynamically without using a ps1xml file.

Although that's nicer than the previous technique (even if it seems more complicated), the advantage is that you can specify the level of serialization depth you want. Hence, you get more data. Be careful with the depth level you choose because you could get too much data and consume unnecessary extra bandwidth:

```
PS > $scriptblock = {
     Update-TypeData -TypeName `
     Microsoft.PowerShell.Commands.GetCounter.PerformanceCounterSampleSet `
                  -SerializationDepth 2 -force
     Get-Counter -Counter '\Processor(_total)\% Processor Time'
  }

PS > $r = Invoke-Command -ComputerName ws2012us-0 -ScriptBlock $scriptblock
PS > $r | Select-Object -ExpandProperty CounterSamples

Path               : \\ws2012us-0\processor(_total)\% processor time
InstanceName       : _total
CookedValue        : 4,36866636762234
RawValue           : 120415781250
SecondValue        : 129989286481071543
MultipleCount      : 1
CounterType        : Timer100NsInverse
Timestamp          : 02/12/2012 14:30:48
Timestamp100NSec   : 129989322481070000
Status             : 0
DefaultScale       : 0
TimeBase           : 10000000
```

Using jobs for long-running tasks

Because data collection is often a long-running process, it presents a good opportunity to use jobs to get the work done in the background and avoid blocking the PowerShell console.

To create jobs, add the -AsJob parameter to Invoke-Command, and that's it:

```
PS > $scriptblock = {
   Update-TypeData -TypeName
```

```
    ➥ Microsoft.PowerShell.Commands.GetCounter.PerformanceCounterSampleSet
    ➥ -SerializationDepth 2 -force
   Get-Counter -Counter '\Processor(_total)\% Processor Time' -MaxSample 5
}

PS > $r = Invoke-Command -Computer ws2012us-0
  ➥ -ScriptBlock $scriptblock -AsJob

PS > $r | Receive-Job | Select-Object -ExpandProperty CounterSamples
```

NOTE In order to make this work you need PowerShell 3 because we update a type with the new functionality exposed by `Update-TypeData`.

Saving the performance data to a file

Saving performance data to a file is an efficient way to diagnose performance issues afterward. Also, if you choose to export your data into a binary file format you have the chance to view the counter values into the Windows Performance Monitor.

Even though you can collect performance data using the PowerShell cmdlets exclusively, it may not always be the best option. PLA offers the ability to create Data Collectors (via COM objects) and to schedule them. I won't cover setting up Data Collectors in this chapter because it's not PowerShell-related, but keep in mind that it exists and may be the option of choice for large deployments.

The key cmdlet here is `Export-Counter`. Have a look at its parameter set:

```
Export-Counter [-Path] <String> [-Circular [<SwitchParameter>]]
[-FileFormat <String>] [-Force [<SwitchParameter>]] [-MaxSize <UInt32>]
-InputObject <PerformanceCounterSampleSet[]> [<CommonParameters>]
```

The first parameter to set up is `-Path`, which you use to indicate a location for storing the data. Then you specify the file type you want to get. Three file types are available: CSV, TSV (tab separated values), and BLG. Whereas CSV and TSV are text files that use, respectively, the comma and the tab character as delimiters, BLG is a binary file format.

The two other parameters, `-Circular` and `-MaxSize`, work hand in hand in the sense that you can use `-MaxSize` to define a maximum file size. When you do so, and if you use the `-Circular` switch, the oldest data is overwritten by the newest data when the maximum size is reached. If you omit `-Circular` while specifying a maximum size, when the limit is reached PowerShell stops gathering the data and returns a nonterminating error.

Saving the data to a binary file (BLG)

Let's see how it works. In this example you'll collect a bunch of counters for 120 seconds. I want you to take a snapshot every second and send the data into a binary file named capture1.blg. Here's how:

```
PS > $counters = '\Processor(*)\% Processor Time',
                 '\Memory\Committed Bytes',
                 '\Memory\Available Bytes', '\Memory\Pages/sec',
```

```
                '\Process(*)\Working Set - Private',
                '\PhysicalDisk(_Total)\Disk Reads/sec',
                '\PhysicalDisk(_Total)\Disk Writes/sec'

PS > Get-Counter -Counter $counters -MaxSamples 120 -SampleInterval 1 |
➥ Export-Counter -Path C:\PerfLogs\capture1.blg -FileFormat blg
```

When the collection is over, to see the data, double-click the resulting BLG file in Windows Explorer; the data automatically displays in the Windows Performance Monitor GUI, as shown in figure 3.

The Windows Performance Monitor GUI is extremely useful in determining, at first glance, how a system behaved. You can also display the performance counters that belong to every process. By default, in Windows Server 2012 they aren't shown in order to lighten the view.

Triggering a data collection on remote computers using PowerShell remoting is easy. All you have to do is to enclose the `Get-Counter` cmdlet and its parameters into a script block and invoke that script block with `Invoke-Command`, as shown in the following listing.

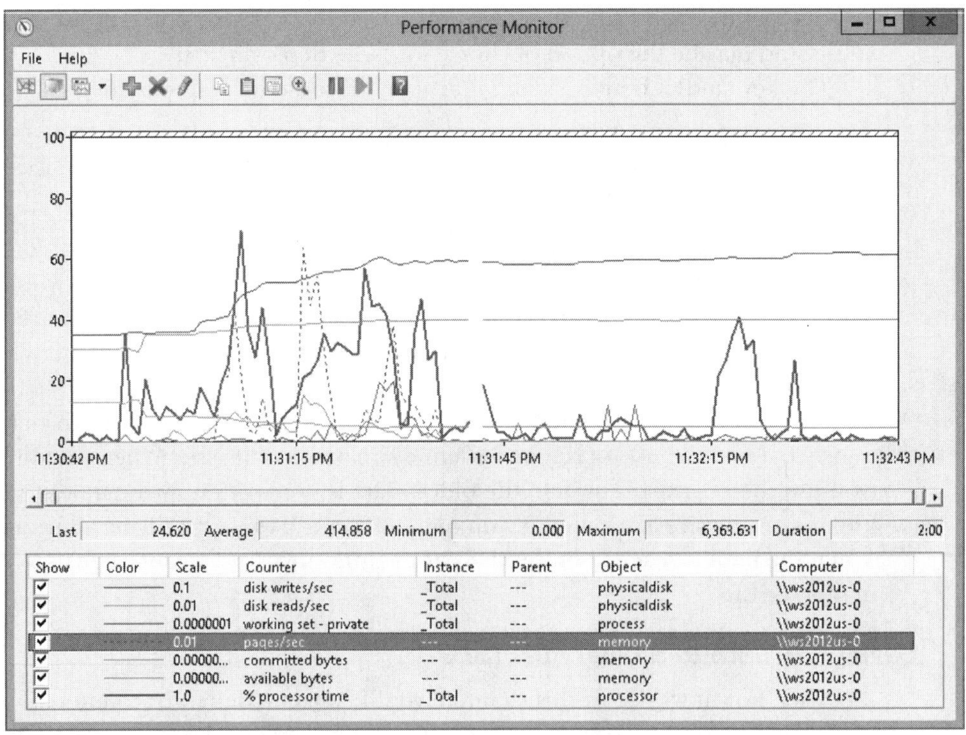

Figure 3 Performance Monitor showing a BLG file

Listing 1 Collecting and saving remote performance data to disk in a BLG file

```
#requires -version 3.0

$counters = '\Processor(*)\% Processor Time',
            '\Memory\Committed Bytes',
            '\Memory\Available Bytes', '\Memory\Pages/sec',
            '\Process(*)\Working Set - Private',
            '\PhysicalDisk(_Total)\Disk Reads/sec',
            '\PhysicalDisk(_Total)\Disk Writes/sec'

Invoke-Command -ScriptBlock {
  Get-Counter -Counter $using:counters -MaxSamples 120 -SampleInterval 1 |
 Export-Counter -Path C:\PerfLogs\capture1.blg -FileFormat blg } `
 -AsJob -ComputerName ws2012us-0, ws2012us-1
```

This script creates a file named capture1.blg on each remote machine in the C:\PerfLogs directory.

TIP Notice the use of `$using` here. This is a new scope in PowerShell v3 that references a variable declared in the current session's scope. You can only use `$using` inside `Invoke-Command`, `Start-Job`, or workflows. It's useful for passing arguments to a command that will be executed remotely.

Saving the data to an Excel file (CSV)

`Export-Counter` lets you save performance data to CSV files. This format is convenient for viewing, sorting, and organizing the data with Microsoft Excel.

To do this, set the `-FileFormat` parameter to the CSV value, like this:

```
Get-Counter -Counter $counters -MaxSamples 120 -SampleInterval 1 |
➥ Export-Counter -Path C:\PerfLogs\capture1.csv -FileFormat csv
```

The data is saved in a CSV file named capture1.csv, which can be viewed in Excel, as shown in figure 4.

The other value the `-FileFormat` parameter accepts is TSV, which uses the tab character as a delimiter instead of a comma.

NOTE In my experience, whether you choose to export data to a CSV file or a binary file, the first line of data (not the header) is always incomplete or erroneous; hence, I strongly recommend ignoring it.

Manipulating stored performance data from a file

Now that you've acquired some data, it's time to make the data talk. Although you could double-click any BLG file and see the graphical representation of the data, it could be interesting to get access to the raw data programmatically. This way, you can process, slice, and dice the data, and automate production of statistics or reports.

You could, for instance, easily find out if a machine is correctly sized "CPU-wise" or "memory-wise" and find the responsible processes in cases of CPU pegging, memory

	A	B	C	D	E	F	G	H	I	J
1	(PDH-CSV 4.0) (Romance Daylight Time)(-120)	\\ws2012us - 0\processor (0)\%	\\ws2012us - 0\processor (1)\%	\\ws2012us - 0\processor (2)\%	\\ws2012us - 0\processor (3)\%	\\ws2012us - 0\processor (_total)\%	\\ws2012us - 0\memory\ committed	\\ws2012us - 0\memory\ available	\\ws2012us - 0\memory\ pages/sec	\\ws2012us - 0\process(i dle)\workin
2	10/25/2012 00:32:14.323						3512725504	933130240		20480
3	10/25/2012 00:32:15.353	2.99539629	0	1.47969936	0	0.72185575	3512733696	932745216	9.71582881	20480
4	10/25/2012 00:32:16.367	6.17938296	4.64134006	6.17938296	4.64134006	5.41035658	3516923904	923275264	0	20480
5	10/25/2012 00:32:17.378	13.5927368	22.8506578	8.96377624	4.33481571	12.4354942	3520765952	917909504	0	20480
6	10/25/2012 00:32:18.392	4.61586436	1.53895675	7.69277196	1.53895675	3.84664239	3520638976	918769664	42.4061963	20480
7	10/25/2012 00:32:19.412	2.1261545	0.59687566	3.65543334	0.59687566	1.74383724	3521314816	919171072	0	20480
8	10/25/2012 00:32:20.419	2.41413258	2.41413258	8.61006067	2.41413258	3.96311461	3522011136	917491712	36.7400491	20480
9	10/25/2012 00:32:21.431	0	2.88777573	0	0	0.57557497	3521257472	918126592	0	20480
10	10/25/2012 00:32:22.447	15.5583193	3.27589302	4.8111963	1.74058973	6.34649959	3528818688	908967936	8.85760944	20480
11	10/25/2012 00:32:23.461	7.69487474	6.15645599	9.2332935	1.54119972	6.15645599	3528003584	912089088	7.88919561	20480
12	10/25/2012 00:32:24.475	3.07704734	1.53858777	1.53858777	1.53858777	1.9232002	3528749056	911503360	0	20480
13	10/25/2012 00:32:25.489	3.07724806	3.07724806	0.0003353	1.53879168	1.92341317	3527471104	912322560	23.6673814	20480
14	10/25/2012 00:32:26.503	30.7694561	26.1540865	30.7694561	27.692543	28.846378	3103002624	1450422272	86.721656	20480
15	10/25/2012 00:32:27.561	11.485982	7.06028106	4.1098138	7.06028106	7.42909657	3093667840	1336094720	23.6403627	20480
16	10/25/2012 00:32:28.778	3.84644622	7.69258838	12.8207779	3.84644622	7.05156057	3093098496	1337540608	61.6784388	20480
17	10/25/2012 00:32:29.814	0.6080574	0.6080574	5.12587297	0.6080574	1.7375137	3092914176	1336885248	0	20480
18	10/25/2012 00:32:30.850	0.63520296	2.14073019	3.64625741	2.14073019	2.14073019	3092918272	1337020416	0	20480
19	10/25/2012 00:32:31.868	21.8890726	20.3574858	29.5470067	28.0154198	24.9522462	3118432256	1325551616	28.453194	20480
20	10/25/2012 00:32:32.882	81.5385271	10.7695476	9.23109149	15.3849158	29.2310205	3025309696	1431879680	0	20480

Figure 4 CSV file opened in Excel

shortage, I/O overconsumption, and so on. In a previous job I was in charge of collecting performance data on 15,000 virtual desktops. The goal was to understand why some computers were pegging for several hours in a row, and thanks to PowerShell I found some interesting results.

The key cmdlet here is `Import-Counter`. This command takes input from any file containing performance data (CSV, TSV, BLG) that has been generated by either `Export-Counter` or the PLA COM object. This is expected because, as I said earlier, the `*-Counter` family relies on the PLA interface.

Have a look at the help file to figure out how to use this command:

```
Import-Counter [-Path] <String[]> [-Counter <String[]>]
[-EndTime <DateTime>] [-MaxSamples <Int64>] [-StartTime <DateTime>]

Import-Counter [-Path] <String[]> -ListSet <String[]>

Import-Counter [-Path] <String[]> [-Summary [<SwitchParameter>]]
```

The last two syntaxes give access to metadata such as the counters' names contained in the file, the number of samples, and information about the collection's start and end times.

Let's look at some examples to help you better understand:

```
PS > Import-Counter -Path C:\Temp\DataCollector01.blg -Summary

OldestRecord                NewestRecord                SampleCount
------------                ------------                -----------
06/11/2012 10:59:28 PM      06/11/2012 11:55:28 PM      57
```

If you use the asterisk as the value of the `-ListSet` parameter, `Import-Counter` enumerates all the counter names embedded in the file and displays them grouped by list set:

```
PS > Import-Counter -Path C:\Temp\DataCollector01.blg -Listset *

CounterSetName     : Processor
MachineName        : \\WS2012US-1
CounterSetType     : SingleInstance
Description        :
Paths              : {\\WS2012US-1\Processor(*)\% Processor Time}
PathsWithInstances : {\\WS2012US-1\Processor(_Total)\% Processor Time}
Counter            : {\\WS2012US-1\Processor(*)\% Processor Time}

CounterSetName     : PhysicalDisk
MachineName        : \\WS2012US-1
CounterSetType     : SingleInstance
Description        :
Paths              : {\\WS2012US-1\PhysicalDisk(*)\Disk Transfers/sec}
PathsWithInstances : {\\WS2012US-1\PhysicalDisk(_Total)\Disk Transfers/sec}
Counter            : {\\WS2012US-1\PhysicalDisk(*)\Disk Transfers/sec}

...

CounterSetName     : Memory
MachineName        : \\WS2012US-1
CounterSetType     : SingleInstance
Description        :
Paths              : {\\WS2012US-1\Memory\Available Bytes,
                      \\WS2012US-1\Memory\Pages/sec}
PathsWithInstances : {}
Counter            : {\\WS2012US-1\Memory\Available Bytes,
                      \\WS2012US-1\Memory\Pages/sec}
```

Only the first syntax of the command gives access to the raw data. If you don't specify any counter's name, `Import-Counter` imports all the data from all the counters. Now try importing all the data into the variable `$data` and see what happens:

```
PS > $data = Import-Counter -Path C:\Temp\DataCollector01.blg

import-counter : The data in one of the performance counter samples is not
valid. View the Status property for each PerformanceCounterSample object to
 make sure it contains valid data.
At line:1 char:6
+ $data = import-counter -path C:\Temp\DataCollector01.blg
+         ~~~~~~~~~~~~~~~~~~~~~~~~~~~~~~~~~~~~~~~~~~~~~~~~
    + CategoryInfo          : InvalidResult: (:) [Import-Counter], Exception
      + FullyQualifiedErrorId :
      CounterApiError,Microsoft.PowerShell.Commands.ImportCounterCommand
```

The first thing to note is the error saying that at least one counter sample isn't valid. As usual, reading PowerShell's error messages is important and valuable.

Here, PowerShell is cautioning you to check the Status property of each `PerformanceCounterSample` object before using it. Don't worry, data collection isn't an exact science, and this happens often.

Next, you'll import data, and in order to avoid flooding the console with errors like you just saw, you can hide them using the well-known common parameter `-ErrorAction` by setting it to the value `SilentlyContinue` (or to the value 0, which is exactly the same):

```
PS > $data = Import-Counter -Path C:\Temp\DataCollector01.blg
➥ -ErrorAction 'SilentlyContinue'
```

Now, your `$data` variable is populated with `PerformanceCounterSampleSet` objects. To be more precise, `$data` is an array of `PerformanceCounterSampleSet` objects. You can dig into the array and examine what's in there:

```
PS > $data[1]

Timestamp                 CounterSamples
---------                 --------------
06/11/2012 11:00:29 PM    \\ws2012us-1\processor(_total)\% processor time :
                          59.7149893297773

                          \\ws2012us-1\process(system)\% processor time :
                          3.08500400793026

...

                          \\ws2012us-1\physicaldisk(_total)\disk
                          transfers/sec:
                          208.797799242242

                          \\ws2012us-1\network adapter(microsoft hyper-v
                          network adapter)\bytes total/sec :
                          2773.05258695793

                          \\ws2012us-1\memory\available bytes :
                          37879808

                          \\ws2012us-1\memory\pages/sec :
                          1807.12422401212
```

I couldn't show all the data here—it would be too much for a book page—but understand that you've collected a certain number of counters at a given time interval. You have your data from `$Data[0]` to `$Data[TotalNumberOfSamples-1]`.

While we're talking about intervals, let's determine the interval of your collection:

```
PS > $data[1].Timestamp - $data[0].Timestamp | Select-Object TotalSeconds

 TotalSeconds
 ------------
       60.559
```

That's correct; you set up your Data Collector Set to gather data every minute.

Now you're going to calculate the average of total percentage of processor time consumed during the period of the data collection in order to see if your system was performing well or poorly.

First, because you're only interested in one particular counter, and because the performance data files can be big, you can reduce the memory footprint (and also simplify your script a little bit) by importing only the counters you want. You could also specify a time interval by using the `-StartTime` and `-EndTime` parameters, but considering that your collection lasted less than an hour you don't need to do that; instead, import all the data:

```
PS > $data = Import-Counter -Path C:\Temp\DataCollector01.blg
  ➥ -Counter '\\WS2012US-1\Processor(_Total)\% Processor Time'
# Overall average calculation
PS > $d = $data | Select-Object -Expand countersamples | where status -eq 0
PS > $d[1..($d.Count-1)] | Measure-Object -Property cookedvalue -Average

Count    : 56
Average  : 74.9717228805766
Sum      :
Maximum  :
Minimum  :
Property : CookedValue
```

Note that you took the precaution of avoiding erroneous data by filtering out the status. Indeed, a zero value means the data is valid, so you take into account only the data that has a zero value assigned to its status property.

In this code snippet, you averaged the data for the duration of the whole collection (about one hour) and determined that the CPU usage was high—around 75 percent. In this case, the machine probably had a performance issue, but it's not completely obvious. You could have had the CPU pegged for 20 minutes, then no load at all. If that were the case, the average would have lowered to 30 percent and could have looked almost like a normal load.

In order to get a more precise overview, try creating a script that offers the ability to slice the data and compute the average at the interval you want, like in the next listing.

Listing 2 Get-AvgCPULoad.ps1

```
#requires -version 3.0

Param (
    [parameter(Mandatory=$true)]
    [string]$File,
    [parameter(Mandatory=$false)]
    [int]$interval = 5    # default value
)

$counter = '\\*\Processor(_Total)\% Processor Time'
$data = Import-Counter -path $file -Counter $counter

$d = $data | Select-Object -Expand countersamples |
             Where status -eq 0

for ($i=1; $i -lt $d.count ; $i+=$interval)
{
```

Counter's path to collect

Filters out the erroneous counter values

Loop starts at index I to avoid bad data at index 0

```
    New-Object -TypeName PSObject -Property @{
         Timestamp = $d[$i].Timestamp;
         CPUAvg    = $d[$i..($i+($interval - 1))] |
            Measure-Object -Prop cookedvalue -Average |
            Select-Object -ExpandProperty Average
    }
}
```

Average calculation

Custom object creation with two properties (`timestamp` and `CPUAvg`)

Now all you have to do is call the script and provide a BLG file path and an interval:

```
PS > ./Get-AvgCPULoad.ps1 -File C:\temp\DataCollector01.blg -interval 10

Timestamp                              CPUAvg
---------                              ------
06/11/2012 11:00:29 PM      89.7425991823448
06/11/2012 11:10:28 PM      99.9192712443985
06/11/2012 11:20:28 PM      99.2941515599998
06/11/2012 11:30:28 PM      96.1755994404801
06/11/2012 11:40:28 PM      18.2450261493011
06/11/2012 11:50:28 PM      27.4416675911747
```

TIP Instead of specifying the machine name inside the counter's name you can use an asterisk, which stands for any machine name. The counter name could have been represented like this: `'\\*\Processor(_Total)\% Processor Time'`

The interval in listing 2 is the same as the number of minutes. This is because the data in the binary file was collected this way. Keep in mind that an interval can represent any time interval.

You could improve this script a little in order to extract more information and gain a better understanding of the data. In the improved version, shown in the following listing, you also process the physical memory available (in bytes) and the page file usage (expressed in number of pages per second).

Listing 3 Get-AvgGlobalLoad.ps1

```
Param (
    [parameter(Mandatory=$true)]
    [string]$File,
    [parameter(Mandatory=$false)]
    [int]$interval = 5
)
$counter = '\\*\Processor(_Total)\% Processor Time',
           '\\*\Memory\Available Bytes',
           '\\*\Memory\Pages/sec'

$data = Import-Counter -path $file -Counter $counter
$d = $data | where {$_.countersamples.status -eq 0}

for ($i=1; $i -lt $d.count ; $i+=$interval)
{
  $UBound = $i+($interval-1)
  New-Object -TypeName PSObject -Property ([Ordered]@{
    Timestamp = $d[$i].Timestamp;
```

Counter's path to collect

Filters out the erroneous counter values

Loop starts at index l to avoid bad data at index 0

Custom object creation containing ordered hash table

```
    CPUAvg    = [int]($d[$i..$UBound] |
      where {$_.CounterSamples.Path -like $counter[0]} |
      foreach {$_.countersamples[0].cookedvalue} |
      Measure-Object -Average |
      Select-Object -ExpandProperty Average );
    MemoryAvailableByteAvg = [int](($d[$i..$UBound] |
      where {$_.CounterSamples.Path -like $counter[1]} |
      foreach {$_.countersamples[1].cookedvalue} |
      Measure-Object -Average |
      Select-Object -ExpandProperty Average) / 1MB);
    MemoryPageAvg = [int]($d[$i..$UBound] |
      where {$_.CounterSamples.Path -like $counter[2]} |
      foreach {$_.countersamples[2].cookedvalue} |
      Measure-Object  -Average |
      Select-Object -ExpandProperty Average)
  })
}
```

Average calculation

Here's what you get:

```
PS> ./Get-AvgGlobalLoad.ps1 -File C:\temp\DataCollector01.blg -interval 10

Timestamp              CPUAvg MemoryAvailableByteAvg MemoryPageAvg
---------              ------ ---------------------- -------------
06/11/2012 11:00:29 PM     90                     48           313
06/11/2012 11:10:28 PM    100                     36           314
06/11/2012 11:20:28 PM     99                     24           701
06/11/2012 11:30:28 PM     96                    108           498
06/11/2012 11:40:28 PM     18                     70           393
06/11/2012 11:50:28 PM     27                     58           945
```

This presents a pretty clear picture. Your monitored system, in addition to the CPU performance issue, is also running out of physical memory and is using the swap file a lot. It would be worth digging deeper in order to find the responsible process or processes. As long as the data is available you could write such a script to find the source of the problem.

Summary

In this chapter I not only showed you how to collect, save, and analyze performance data with PowerShell, but I also covered the methodology for finding the appropriate counters to help you diagnose a machine's performance issues.

The hardest part of the troubleshooting process isn't the data acquisition—as you've seen, that's pretty straightforward with PowerShell—but understanding the counter values. To do this, if the performance file is a binary file you have two options: open the file into the GUI, or use the `Import-Counter` cmdlet and dig into the raw data. This second option is best when it comes to automating the analysis. I covered this topic through a few examples in the last part of the chapter, where you calculated the average of several counters. Calculating the average of small samples of data helps avoid spikes and gives you a better understanding of how a machine is behaving.

A topic I didn't cover, because it's not completely PowerShell-related, is the use of Data Collectors. If you need to collect data from lots of machines on a regular basis, using Data Collectors is the way to go. To create them you need to use COM objects or wrap the logman.exe utility.

About the author

Arnaud Petitjean is a passionate and experienced IT professional with more than 15 years in the field. He started his career as a Microsoft Exchange administrator and progressively moved to system administration and virtualization, a field in which he developed scripts in various languages. In 2006 he literally fell in love with the beta version of PowerShell and has been writing scripts ever since. He's the founder of the French-speaking PowerShell community (http://powershell-scripting.com) and the author of *Windows PowerShell: Reference Guide for Windows Administration* (ENI Editions, in French only; first edition, 2008; second edition, 2010; third edition, 2013). He's been a PowerShell MVP since 2007.

4 TCP port communications with PowerShell

Boe Prox

PowerShell can be a powerful network troubleshooting tool thanks to its reach back into the .NET framework. In this chapter I'll take you through some of the more useful .NET classes that you can harness to help with your network troubleshooting and with building some fun scripts. By the end of the chapter you'll know how to create a port scanner to check for open ports on your network, send and receive data between ports, create formatted packets to send a Lightweight Directory Access Protocol (LDAP) request to a domain controller, and process the return packets to emulate the same type of output from another command-line interface (CLI) tool, portqry.exe. You'll also learn about creating a TCP listener object that will serve as an open port on your system to allow clients to connect to your system, and lastly, you'll put everything together to create an Echo server that can repeat back to you every key that you've typed! By using these techniques and scripts you'll be able to troubleshoot applications communicating on your network by checking to see if the ports required are available on the system or if they're being blocked, either by software on the server or by something else, such as a hardware firewall or an access control list (ACL) on a switch.

Before I begin, let's review some terminology.

A *port* identifies different applications, services, or processes running on a single system and enables them to share a single physical connection in a network. Think of it as a door to the application instance on a server. If the door is open you can communicate with the application on the other side, but you can't make a connection if the door shut or blocked.

An *endpoint* is the end of the network link between a client and server that allows the use of network streams to communicate between one another. The endpoint also provides utilities to see if the connection is active and if the streams are readable or writable, and to configure the size of the buffers for the streams.

A *socket* is an endpoint instance of two-way communication between two applications on the same network by pairing an IP address with a port.

Testing for an open port

When troubleshooting server communications you sometimes have to test a port on the server to see if it's accepting any sort of communication. To do that, a TCP (or a User Datagram Protocol [UDP]) socket is opened up from a client that attempts to make a connection to the remote server port. Let's assume that you're trying to troubleshoot a possible issue with clients that are authenticating in an Active Directory domain and you need to see if LDAP (port 389) is being blocked, either by a software firewall on the domain controller or a hardware firewall.

To do this you must first create the client TCP object using the `System.Net.Sockets.TCPClient` class. Table 1 shows the available constructors for creating the `TCPClient` object. You use a constructor (also known as a ctor) to create an object and to supply initial values as parameters to give the object a default value to prepare it for use.

Table 1 Potential `TCPClient` constructors

Name	Description
`TcpClient()`	Creates a new instance of the `TcpClient` class
`TcpClient(AddressFamily)`	Creates a new instance of the `TcpClient` class with the specified family (scheme of IP address, such as Internetwork Packet Exchange, InterNetwork, AppleTalk, and so on)
`TcpClient(IPEndPoint)`	Creates a new instance of the `TcpClient` class and binds it to the specified local endpoint
`TcpClient(String, Int32)`	Creates a new instance of the `TcpClient` class and connects to the specified port on the specified host

For this example you'll select the fourth option, creating a `TCPClient` object by supplying a hostname or an IP address and a port. Using the `New-Object` cmdlet, you can create the object with the supplied arguments. I'm recommending this option because it can help you to quickly determine if the port specified on the system is open. You'll work through this example as if you're running commands from my client system, Boe-Pc, which will make the port connection to the remote domain controller, DC1:

```
PS C:\> New-Object System.Net.Sockets.TCPClient -Argument "DC1","389"

Client              : System.Net.Sockets.Socket
Available           : 0
Connected           : True
ExclusiveAddressUse : False
ReceiveBufferSize   : 65536
SendBufferSize      : 65536
ReceiveTimeout      : 0
```

```
SendTimeout          : 0
LingerState          : System.Net.Sockets.LingerOption
NoDelay              : False
```

From this you can see by the `Connected` property that you've connected to the port, meaning it's open! This is a pretty simple one-liner for checking whether or not a port is open. What happens if the port isn't open or is being blocked? For instance, you can check if FTP (port 21) is enabled and running on the domain controller like this:

```
PS C:\> New-Object System.Net.Sockets.TCPClient -Argument "DC1","21"
New-Object : Exception calling ".ctor" with "2" argument(s): "No connection
could be made because the target machine
actively refused it 192.168.1.18:21"
At line:1 char:1
+ New-Object System.Net.Sockets.TCPClient -Argument "DC1","21"
+ ~~~~~~~~~~~~~~~~~~~~~~~~~~~~~~~~~~~~~~~~~~~~~~~~~~~~~~~~~~~~
    + CategoryInfo          : InvalidOperation: (:) [New-Object],
     MethodInvocationException
    + FullyQualifiedErrorId :
     ConstructorInvokedThrowException,Microsoft.PowerShell.Commands.NewObject
     Command
```

As you can see, the port was "actively refused" by the server, as shown by the bolded text in the message. You could wrap this up in a `Try/Catch` to better handle the error message, but this example is more about what happens when an attempt to connect to a port is done against a closed or blocked port. Another possibility is that the connection attempt may time out. To better handle the situation I'll show you how to wrap this up into a simple function that can scan multiple ports and hosts.

Building a more robust port checker

Checking a single port on a single system is fine for a quick check with only a simple line of code, but you can do much more with an advanced function. You'll be able to handle errors more gracefully and also provide timeout mechanisms to handle areas where the query seems to hang for an extended period of time because the client connection is attempting to connect to a port that isn't open but isn't actively blocking the port. Finally, you'll also be able to specify parameter attributes such as allowing values from the pipeline, meaning that you can pipe specific data into the new function and it will know exactly how to handle it.

The function you're going to create (shown in the following listing) is called `Test-TCPPort`, and it meets all of these requirements, making it a robust port checker.

NOTE Use caution whenever you're running a port scanner of any kind on a corporate network. This could be mistaken for an adversary attempting to get information about the infrastructure.

Listing 1 `Test-TCPPort`

```
Function Test-TCPPort {
  [cmdletbinding()]
```

```
  Param (
    [parameter(ValueFromPipeline=$True,
    ValueFromPipelineByPropertyName=$True)]
    [Alias("CN","Server","__Server","IPAddress")]
    [string[]]$Computername = $env:COMPUTERNAME,
    [parameter()]
    [Int32[]]$Port = 23,
    [parameter()]
    [Int32]$TimeOut = 5000
  )
  Process {
    ForEach ($Computer in $Computername) {
      ForEach ($p in $port) {
        Write-Verbose ("Checking port {0} on {1}" -f $p, $computer)
        $tcpClient = `
New-Object System.Net.Sockets.TCPClient
        $async = $tcpClient.BeginConnect($Computer,
$p,$null,$null)
        $wait = $async.AsyncWaitHandle.WaitOne(`
$TimeOut,$false)
        If (-Not $Wait) {
          [pscustomobject]@{
            Computername = $Computername
            Port = $P
            State = 'Closed'
            Notes = 'Connection timed out'
          }
        } Else {
          Try {
            $tcpClient.EndConnect($async)
            [pscustomobject]@{
              Computername = $Computer
              Port = $P
              State = 'Open'
              Notes = $Null
            }
          } Catch {
            [pscustomobject]@{
              Computername = $Computer
              Port = $P
              State = 'Closed'
              Notes = ("{0}" -f $_.Exception.Message)
            }
          }
        }
      }
    }
  }
}
```

Set up parameters for the advanced function

Create `TCPClient` object

Begin connection to remote system on specified port

Set timeout for attempted port connection

If connection times out, create appropriate object

If port connection is good, create appropriate object

Handle connection errors with appropriate output object

Here is a demonstration against the domain controller to check for ports 389, 636, 21, and 23:

```
Test-TCPPort -Computername DC1 -Port 389,636,21,23
```

```
PS C:\> Test-TCPPort -Computername DC1 -Port 389,636,21,23

Computername                                   Port State                   Notes
------------                                   ---- -----                   -----
DC1                                             389 Open
DC1                                             636 Open
DC1                                              21 Closed                  Exception calling "EndConn...
DC1                                              23 Closed                  Exception calling "EndConn...
```

Figure 1 `Test-TCPPort` **run against DC1**

The output is shown in figure 1.

What you have now is a nice reusable function that you can use to troubleshoot either your server or your network. You can even pipe out the output to a CSV file using `Export-CSV` to provide a report on the port scan. Keep in mind that if you plan to do this across the network against multiple systems and multiple ports, your network security team might interpret it as malicious activity. Be sure to communicate with others when you do this!

Sending and receiving data

Knowing how to check if a port is open is one thing, but being able to send data across the network to that port and being able to handle the response from the remote server requires a little more work. Although sending data from your local port to a remote port is simple, the trick is to understand what the port on the other end is expecting. Merely sending a stream of text from one port to another won't work. Transmissions are sent and received as bytes, and all text must be converted to bytes before being sent to a port as a packet. Some ports are expecting a byte to be in a specific format, whereas others only require some sort of data (a single byte, for instance) before responding back. I'll show you an example of this later in this section.

Sending data

As mentioned, sending the data isn't the most complicated part, but it's vital. In order to send anything between ports the data must be converted into bytes, which is required for the data transmission process. To do this follow these steps:

1. Create the `TCPClient` object.
2. Create a network stream that will be used to transmit the data.
3. Take the input data to be transmitted and convert it into bytes.
4. Transmit the bytes to the remote port using the network stream.

As you did earlier, connect to the remote server port. This time, connect to port 7:

```
$tcpClient = New-Object System.Net.Sockets.TCPClient
$tcpClient.Connect("DC1",7)
```

Port 7 is the Echo port. Fortunately, each installation of Windows has a list of common ports available to reference. You can find this list at C:\Windows\System32\Drivers\etc\services. Open the file with Notepad or another text editor to see all the ports. The

Echo port can be a useful network troubleshooting tool; it repeats back everything sent to it, making it a nice example. For more information about the Echo port and how to configure it see http://mng.bz/FRj1.

NOTE Some of the ports mentioned in this chapter may be blocked by firewalls. Make sure the ports are open before trying these examples.

Next, take some text that you wish to send across the network and convert it into a collection of bytes using the `Text.Encoding` class along with the `GetBytes()` method (this can also be referred to as a buffer):

```
$Text = "This is a test message"
[byte[]]$bytes  = [text.Encoding]::Ascii.GetBytes($Text)
```

The resulting `$bytes` collection will look like figure 2.

Now that you have your data converted into bytes, create a network stream object that you can use to transmit the bytes over to the remote port. For this, use the `GetStream()` method on the `TCPClient` object:

```
$clientStream = $tcpClient.GetStream()
```

With the network stream established you can begin transmitting the bytes to the remote client using the `Write()` method of the network stream object. The `Write()` method takes three parameters to successfully transmit the data. The first parameter should contain the buffer of bytes being sent across the network, and the second parameter should be the location within the buffer that the stream should begin writing the data to on the remote port. The final parameter is the total size (or length) of data that will be transmitted through the stream. Once the data has been transmitted,

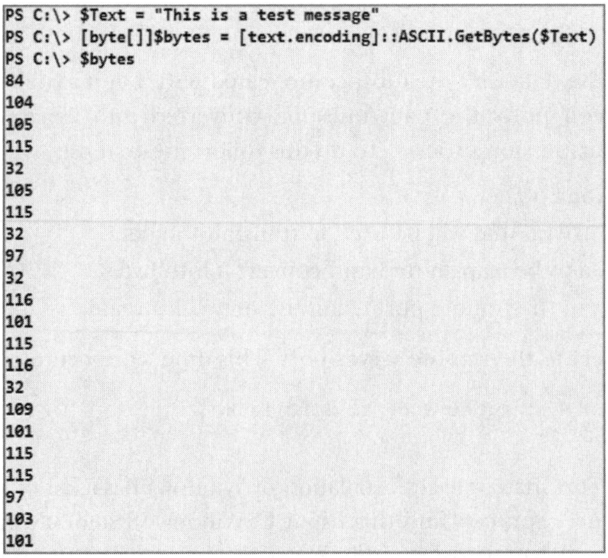

```
PS C:\> $Text = "This is a test message"
PS C:\> [byte[]]$bytes = [text.encoding]::ASCII.GetBytes($Text)
PS C:\> $bytes
84
104
105
115
32
105
115
32
97
32
116
101
115
116
32
109
101
115
115
97
103
101
```

Figure 2 Output from `$bytes` showing the collection of bytes

the network stream will flush the contents by using the `Flush()` method of the network stream object, like this:

```
$clientStream.Write($bytes,0,$bytes.length)
$clientStream.Flush()
```

That's all there is to sending data across a TCP port to another TCP port. As long as the port is open and you know exactly what type of packet can be sent to it, the remote port should accept the packet and respond with its own packet.

Receiving data

Now that you've sent some data to your destination port, how do you receive the data that has been sent back? First you have to know if data has, in fact, been sent back to your port. To do that, look at the network stream object created earlier and check its `DataAvailable` property. If the property is set to `True` you know data is available:

```
PS C:\> $clientStream.DataAvailable
True
```

Next, configure a buffer to store the data. You can find out exactly how much data is available by checking the `Available` property of the `$tcpClient` object:

```
PS C:\> $tcpClient.Available
22
```

Now you can create the proper buffer to get the data. If you attempt to guess how large a buffer you need to get the return data stream, there's a chance you'll guess too small and only get a chunk of the total data rather than all of it:

```
[byte[]]$inStream = New-Object byte[] 22
```

Using the `Read()` method of your network stream object, you use the same skills learned from the `Write()` method to add the correct parameters to read the bytes from the remote port:

```
$response = $clientStream.Read($inStream, 0, $inStream.count)
```

Notice that you're saving the output of the `Read()` method to `$response`. This is the number of bytes received from the remote port in the stream, not the bytes themselves. The bytes are saved in the buffer you created, `$inStream`. In this case, the number of bytes returned from the remote port is 22 (which matches what was seen earlier with the `Available` property):

```
PS C:\> $response
22
```

This is important to know for when you begin to translate the bytes into human-friendly text. Because you created a 1 MB buffer it becomes unnecessary to translate anything larger than what was already received, and doing so would cause extra spaces in the translated text. If the amount of data is greater than what your buffer can support, then you have to implement a loop to handle the extra data that needs translating

(I'll show you how to do this later in the chapter). For this example, you only get the first 22 bytes of the buffer (starting at the 0 index and going to the 21st index of the array). This way, you have only the text you need:

```
[Int]$response = $clientStream.Read($inStream, 0, $inStream.count)
[System.Text.Encoding]::ASCII.GetString($inStream[0..($response - 1)])
This is a test message
```

Now you can perform some cleanup of the objects to free up all of the resources, such as memory that has been allocated to your examples:

```
PS C:\> $tcpClient.Dispose()
PS C:\> $clientStream.Dispose()
```

And just like that, you have your data sent back to you from the remote server. And if you notice, it's exactly the same thing you sent to the port—the Echo port is living up to its name.

LDAP port communications

In this section, I'll show you how to send and receive formatted packets using PowerShell to communicate with a domain controller in the same way you'd use another command-line utility: portqry.exe.

Testing port 389 and receiving data with portqry.exe

You may have used portqry.exe (http://support.microsoft.com/kb/310099) in the past to query various ports. If so, you may be aware that if portqry.exe knows the type of formatted packet to send to a port, it will attempt to send the packet and return the response from that port to your console. Let's see exactly what happens when running portqry.exe against your domain controller, like this:

```
.\PortQry.exe -n DC1.rivendell.com -e 389
```

The result is shown in figure 3.

The complete flow from beginning the `Bind` request to the final `Unbind` request is illustrated in figure 4. You can use this same concept to generate and run a script for communicating with a domain controller using PowerShell.

The output from this shows you a number of things, such as the `supportedLDAPVersion`, whether the domain controller is a global catalog, its `servername`, and several other things. Wouldn't it be nice if you could do this type of query with PowerShell? You could query for the same information and put the results into a nice object that you could work with.

Testing port 389 and receiving data with PowerShell

PowerShell is more than capable of emulating portqry.exe by not only finding that port 389 is open, but also by sending and receiving the formatted packets required to successfully query LDAP. To get to that point you have to determine the kind of

```
Attempting to resolve name to IP address...

Name resolved to 192.168.1.18

querying...

TCP port 389 (ldap service): LISTENING

Using ephemeral source port
Sending LDAP query to TCP port 389...

LDAP query response:

currentdate: 01/21/2013 21:48:50 (unadjusted GMT)
subschemaSubentry: CN=Aggregate,CN=Schema,CN=Configuration,DC=rivendell,DC=com
dsServiceName: CN=NTDS Settings,CN=DC1,CN=Servers,CN=Default-First-Site-Name,CN=Sites,CN=Configuration,DC=rivendell,DC=c
om
namingContexts: DC=rivendell,DC=com
defaultNamingContext: DC=rivendell,DC=com
schemaNamingContext: CN=Schema,CN=Configuration,DC=rivendell,DC=com
configurationNamingContext: CN=Configuration,DC=rivendell,DC=com
rootDomainNamingContext: DC=rivendell,DC=com
supportedControl: 1.2.840.113556.1.4.319
supportedLDAPVersion: 3
supportedLDAPPolicies: MaxPoolThreads
highestCommittedUSN: 123048
supportedSASLMechanisms: GSSAPI
dnsHostName: dc1.rivendell.com
ldapServiceName: rivendell.com:dc1$@RIVENDELL.COM
serverName: CN=DC1,CN=Servers,CN=Default-First-Site-Name,CN=Sites,CN=Configuration,DC=rivendell,DC=com
supportedCapabilities: 1.2.840.113556.1.4.800
isSynchronized: TRUE
isGlobalCatalogReady: TRUE
domainFunctionality: 0
forestFunctionality: 0
domainControllerFunctionality: 2

======== End of LDAP query response ========
```

Figure 3 Output from running `portqry.exe` against a domain controller

formatted packets you need to send to the port. If you don't know how to format the packets you'll never get past the initial query attempt.

For this example you're going to use Network Monitor (NetMon) to capture packets during your query with portqry.exe in order to determine what kind of packets you need to send to the LDAP port. You can obviously use another sniffer, such as

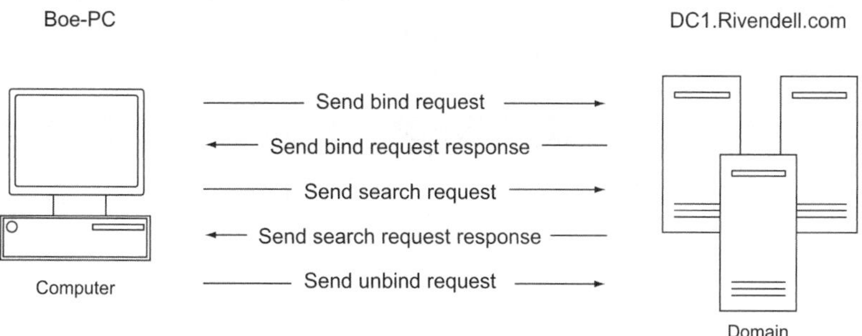

Figure 4 Flow of LDAP communication between Boe-PC and DC1.Rivendell.com

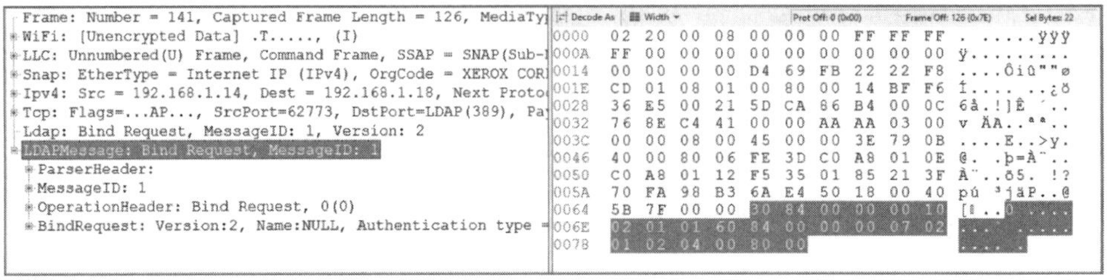

Figure 5 **`BindRequest` packet to the domain controller**

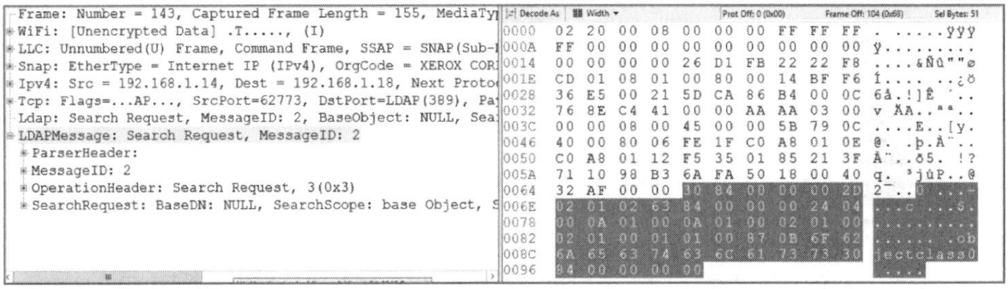

Figure 6 **`searchRequest` packet to the domain controller**

Wireshark, if you have access to it. Figure 5 shows the packet and the highlighted data that you'll need to send as the initial `Bind` request to the domain controller.

If the `Bind` is successful the server will respond with a `Bind` response packet back to you. If the packet is 22 bytes you know it's safe to proceed with a `searchRequest` packet back to the domain controller. Once again, use NetMon to figure out what packet you should create in order to get the response you want. In figure 6 you can see that more data will have to be sent to the domain controller; this is necessary in order to successfully complete the search request.

The packet sent after your search request is the search response from the domain controller, which contains all the information you need. With this information you can put together a script that will not only send the proper packets to the domain controller, but also take the `searchResponse` packet and properly format it as an object. The script is shown in the following listing.

Listing 2 Test-LDAP.ps1

```
[cmdletbinding()]
Param (
  [string]$Computername = "DC1.rivendell.com",
  [Int]$Port = 389
)

Try {

  $tcpClient = New-Object System.Net.Sockets.TCPClient
  $tcpClient.Connect($Computername,
```

```
                    $Port
                   )

If ($tcpClient.Connected) {

  [byte[]]$bindRequest = 0x30,0x84,0x00,0x00,
  0x00,0x10,0x02,0x01,
   #10x01,0x60,0x84,0x00,0x00,0x00,
  0x07,0x02,0x01,0x02,0x04,0x00,0x80,0x00

  [byte[]]$searchRequest = 0x30,0x84,0x00,
  0x00,0x00,0x2d,0x02,0x01,
   #10x02,0x63,0x84,0x00,0x00,
  0x00,0x24,0x04,0x00,0x0a,0x01,0x00,0x0a,
   #10x01,0x00,
  0x02,0x01,0x00,0x02,0x01,0x00,0x01,0x01,0x00,0x87,
  0x0b,0x6f,
   #10x62,0x6a,0x65,0x63,0x74,0x63,0x6c,0x61,
  0x73,0x73,0x30,0x84,0x00,0x00,
   #10x00,0x00

  [byte[]]$unbindRequest = 0x30,0x84,0x00,
  0x00,0x00,0x05,0x02,0x01,
   #10x03,0x42,0x00

  $bindResponseBuffer = New-Object Byte[] -ArgumentList 22

  $stream = $TcpClient.GetStream()

  $stream.Write($bindRequest,
                0,
                $bindRequest.length
                )
  $stream.Flush()

  Start-Sleep -Milliseconds 1000

  If ($tcpClient.Available -eq 22) {
    Try {
      [Int]$response = $stream.Read($bindResponseBuffer,
                                     0,
                                     $bindResponseBuffer.count
                                     )

      $stream.Write($searchRequest,0,$searchRequest.length)
      $stream.Flush()

      Start-Sleep -Milliseconds 1000
      $availableBytes = $tcpClient.Available
      $searchResponse = $Null
      [int]$response = 0
      Do {
        $searchResponseBuffer = New-Object Byte[] -ArgumentList 1024
        [Int]$response = $response + $stream.Read($searchResponseBuffer,
                                                   0,
                                               $searchResponseBuffer.count
                                                  )
        [byte[]]$searchResponse += $searchResponseBuffer
```

❶ Define the packets to be used for requests

Create the network stream to send and receive packets

Send and receive data from the DC

```
  Write-Progress `
-Activity ("Downloading LDAP Response from {0}" -f $Computername) `
-Status ("Bytes Received: {0}" -f ($response)) `
-PercentComplete (($response / $availableBytes)*100) -Id 0
} While ($stream.DataAvailable)


Try {
  $stream.Write($unbindRequest,0,$unbindRequest.length)
  $stream.Flush()
} Catch {
  Write-Warning ("Line: {0} -> {1}" -f `
  $_.invocationInfo.ScriptLineNumber,$_.Exception.Message)
}

$MemoryStream = new-object System.IO.MemoryStream `
-ArgumentList $searchResponse[0..$availableBytes],0,$availableBytes
$binaryReader = new-object System.IO.BinaryReader `
-ArgumentList $MemoryStream

$binaryReader.ReadBytes(6) | Out-Null
$binaryReader.ReadBytes(3) | Out-Null
$binaryReader.ReadBytes(6) | Out-Null
   $binaryReader.ReadBytes(2) | Out-Null
   $binaryReader.ReadBytes(6) | Out-Null

[byte[]]$bytes = $Null

$isHeader = $True
$isPropertyHeader = $True

$Object = New-Object PSObject

Do {
  Write-Verbose ("Begin of Do: {0}" -f `
  ($binaryReader.BaseStream.Position -eq `
$binaryReader.BaseStream.Length))
  If ($isHeader) {
    Write-Verbose ("Removing Header information")
    $binaryReader.ReadBytes(6) | Out-Null
    $isHeader = $False
  } Else {
    If ($binaryReader.ReadByte() -eq 0x04) {
      $expectedBytes = $binaryReader.ReadByte()
      [byte[]]$bytes += $binaryReader.ReadBytes($expectedBytes)
    }
    If ($isPropertyHeader) {
      Try {
        Write-Verbose ("Reached the end of the Property Header")
        $propertyHeader = `
        [System.Text.Encoding]::ASCII.GetString($bytes)
      } Catch {}
      $isPropertyHeader = $False
      $isHeader = $True
      $bytes = $Null
    } Else {
    If ($binaryReader.PeekChar() -eq 0x30) {
      Try {
```

Annotations:
- ❷ Display a progress bar and message
- ❸ Strip out headers that serve no purpose
- ❹ Begin formatting the `searchResponse` packet
- Determine next available bytes

```
                Switch ($propertyHeader) {              <-- Add multiple
                  "currentTime" {                           items to collection
                    $time = `
                    ([System.Text.Encoding]::ASCII.GetString($bytes) `
                    -split "\.")[0]
                    $property = `
                    [datetime]::ParseExact($time,
                                          'yyyyMMddHHmmss',
                                          $Null
                                         )
                  }
                  Default {
                    $property = `
                    [System.Text.Encoding]::ASCII.GetString($bytes)
                    If ($Property -match "\t") {
                      $property = $property -split "\t"
                    }
                  }
                }
                Write-Verbose ("Reached the end of the Property")
                $Object = Add-Member -InputObject $Object `
                -MemberType NoteProperty -Name $propertyHeader `
                -Value $property -PassThru
              } Catch {}
              $isPropertyHeader = $True
              $isHeader = $True
              $bytes = $Null
            } Else {
            [byte[]]$bytes += 0x09
          }
        }
      }                                                    5 Use a progress
      Write-Verbose ("Reached end of Do Statement")          bar to show
                                                             formatting
      Write-Progress -Activity "Formatting LDAP Response" `  <-- status
                     -Status ("Bytes Remaining: {0}" -f `
($binaryReader.BaseStream.Length - $binaryReader.BaseStream.Position)) `
                     -PercentComplete `
(($binaryReader.BaseStream.Position / binaryReader.BaseStream.Length)*100)`
-Id 1
      Write-Verbose ("End of Stream: {0}" -f `
      ($binaryReader.BaseStream.Position -eq `
      $binaryReader.BaseStream.Length))
    } Until ($binaryReader.BaseStream.Position -eq `
      $binaryReader.BaseStream.Length)
                                                            Insert new
    $object.pstypenames.insert(0,'Net.TCP.LDAPMessage')  <-- typename
    Write-Output $Object
  } Catch {
    Write-Warning ("Line: {0} -> {1}" -f `
    $_.invocationInfo.ScriptLineNumber,$_.Exception.Message)
  }
} Else {
  Write-Warning ("Bind was unsuccessful with {0} on port {1}!" -f `
                $Computername, $port)
}
```

```
$stream.Close(1)
$TcpClient.Close()
} Else {
  Write-Warning ("{0}: LDAP Connection Failed!" -f $Computername)
}
} Catch {
Write-Warning ("{0}: {1}" -f $Computername, $_.Exception.Message)
}
```

The LDAP packet payloads ❶ are bytes that aren't in a human-readable format but are used to communicate with the domain controller. Use `Write-Progress` to help track the progress of downloading the response from the domain controller ❷.

Because a lot of the data isn't needed and will only make formatting the returned data more complicated, ignore the unneeded data by removing it from the buffer using the `ReadBytes()` method ❸. Once you have all the data from the domain controller you can begin translating the data into a human-readable format that will be displayed as an object ❹. As you did earlier, use `Write-Progress` to track the activity of converting the data into a human-readable format ❺.

The output of the script is shown in figure 7.

The finished product is a script that's able to query the LDAP port and not only send formatted packets found using NetMon, but also receive the formatted packets sent back from the domain controller. Taking the `searchRequest` packets and formatting them into usable objects provided the finishing touch. You were able to strip out all of the headers and get down into the data. Reviewing the NetMon captures helped you to figure out how to handle the response packets and write the code that handled the formatting.

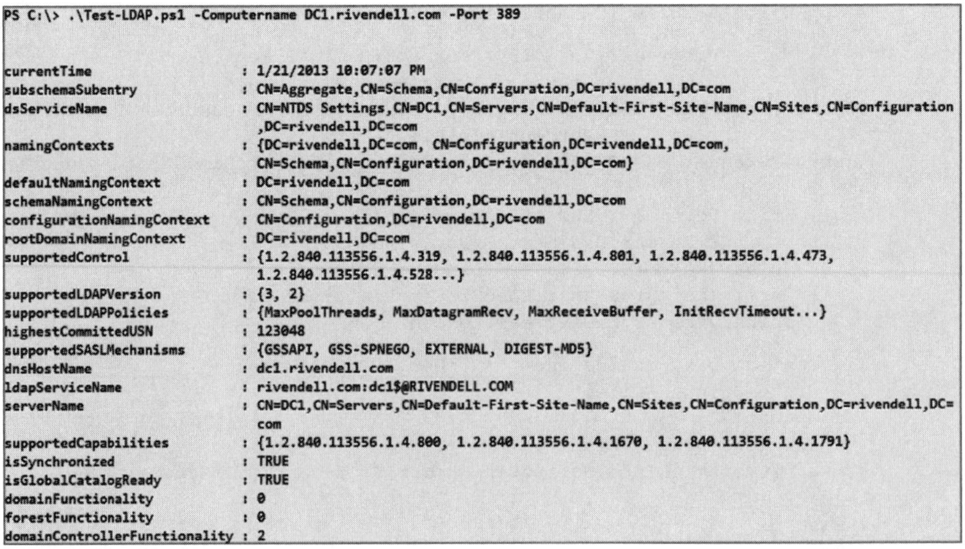

```
PS C:\> .\Test-LDAP.ps1 -Computername DC1.rivendell.com -Port 389


currentTime                   : 1/21/2013 10:07:07 PM
subschemaSubentry             : CN=Aggregate,CN=Schema,CN=Configuration,DC=rivendell,DC=com
dsServiceName                 : CN=NTDS Settings,CN=DC1,CN=Servers,CN=Default-First-Site-Name,CN=Sites,CN=Configuration
                                ,DC=rivendell,DC=com
namingContexts                : {DC=rivendell,DC=com, CN=Configuration,DC=rivendell,DC=com,
                                CN=Schema,CN=Configuration,DC=rivendell,DC=com}
defaultNamingContext          : DC=rivendell,DC=com
schemaNamingContext           : CN=Schema,CN=Configuration,DC=rivendell,DC=com
configurationNamingContext    : CN=Configuration,DC=rivendell,DC=com
rootDomainNamingContext       : DC=rivendell,DC=com
supportedControl              : {1.2.840.113556.1.4.319, 1.2.840.113556.1.4.801, 1.2.840.113556.1.4.473,
                                1.2.840.113556.1.4.528...}
supportedLDAPVersion          : {3, 2}
supportedLDAPPolicies         : {MaxPoolThreads, MaxDatagramRecv, MaxReceiveBuffer, InitRecvTimeout...}
highestCommittedUSN           : 123048
supportedSASLMechanisms       : {GSSAPI, GSS-SPNEGO, EXTERNAL, DIGEST-MD5}
dnsHostName                   : dc1.rivendell.com
ldapServiceName               : rivendell.com:dc1$@RIVENDELL.COM
serverName                    : CN=DC1,CN=Servers,CN=Default-First-Site-Name,CN=Sites,CN=Configuration,DC=rivendell,DC=
                                com
supportedCapabilities         : {1.2.840.113556.1.4.800, 1.2.840.113556.1.4.1670, 1.2.840.113556.1.4.1791}
isSynchronized                : TRUE
isGlobalCatalogReady          : TRUE
domainFunctionality           : 0
forestFunctionality           : 0
domainControllerFunctionality : 2
```

Figure 7 Output of the Test-LDAP.ps1 script

Although this was only used for LDAP, you can easily take the same concepts from this script and apply them to check for RPC and other ports like portqry.exe does. You can even send web requests to a web server, as long as you know the proper syntax to use in the request. Be sure you review the sniffer captures to know exactly what you need to send and to view the expected return packets.

Creating an Echo server

At this point, you've been doing mostly client-based work that involved testing ports, sending and receiving data, and working with formatted packets to send and receive data. You haven't yet worked on the server side of the house. This final section will cover setting up a server that echoes back the text sent to it.

Creating a TPC port listener

The first step in creating an Echo server is setting up a listener to make it available on the network. Using the `System.Net.Sockets.TcpListener` class you can easily configure and run a server that can listen for requests and respond to them.

To start, create the listener object on a port of your choosing; in this example you'll use port 7:

```
$Listener = New-Object System.Net.Sockets.TcpListener -ArgumentList 7
$Listener

Server                     LocalEndpoint ExclusiveAddressUse
------                     ------------- -------------------
System.Net.Sockets.Socket 0.0.0.0:7                    False
```

This doesn't do anything yet. If you try to run `Get-NetTCPConnection` (which requires PowerShell v3 under the NetTCP module) to look for port 7 and you don't already have the Simple TCP Services component installed, you'll receive an error stating the port isn't available:

```
Get-NetTCPConnection -LocalPort 7
```

To start up the listener, use the `Start()` method. If a software firewall asks for permission to open this port, go ahead and give it permission to do so:

```
$Listener.Start()
```

Now check for listening ports again to see if anything has shown up:

```
Get-NetTCPConnection | Where LocalPort -eq 7

LocalAddress LocalPort RemoteAddress RemotePort State  AppliedSetting
------------ --------- ------------- ---------- -----  --------------
0.0.0.0      7         0.0.0.0       0          Listen
```

You now have a listening port that's available to any system with network access to this system. If a system attempts to connect to the port very little will happen, as nothing has been coded to handle incoming connections and data requests.

Handling connections and data

With the TCP port listener open you can now tell it to listen for and accept client connections. To enable the object to accept new connections, use the `AcceptTCPConnection()` method. Once you call this method you'll be unable to do anything else in the console, as this is a "blocking" method. You can get around this by using a PowerShell job or creating a new background PowerShell runspace, but that's beyond the scope of this chapter. Only after a connection has occurred will the listener allow execution of the script to continue, or in this case, allow access to the console again:

```
$incomingClient = $Listener.AcceptTcpClient()
```

Notice the `$incomingClient` variable assigned to this method. You do this because once a connection has been made, the `AcceptTcpClient()` method will output a `System.Net.Sockets.TcpClient` object that you'll need to manipulate in order to complete the connection and handle incoming data:

```
$incomingClient

Client              : System.Net.Sockets.Socket
Available           : 0
Connected           : True
ExclusiveAddressUse : False
ReceiveBufferSize   : 65536
SendBufferSize      : 65536
ReceiveTimeout      : 0
SendTimeout         : 0
LingerState         : System.Net.Sockets.LingerOption
NoDelay             : False
```

You can find out the IP address of the incoming connection by digging into the `Client` property of the `System.Net.Sockets.TcpClient` object:

```
$incomingClient.Client
Available           : 0
LocalEndPoint       : 192.168.1.13:7
RemoteEndPoint      : 192.168.1.18:1093
Handle              : 1332
Blocking            : True
UseOnlyOverlappedIO : False
Connected           : True
AddressFamily       : InterNetwork
SocketType          : Stream
ProtocolType        : Tcp
IsBound             : True
ExclusiveAddressUse : False
ReceiveBufferSize   : 65536
SendBufferSize      : 65536
ReceiveTimeout      : 0
SendTimeout         : 0
LingerState         : System.Net.Sockets.LingerOption
NoDelay             : False
Ttl                 : 128
DontFragment        : True
```

```
MulticastLoopback    :
EnableBroadcast      :
DualMode             :
```

You can see both the server IP address and port (192.168.1.13:7), as well as the client that's connecting to the port (192.168.1.18:1093).

The next step is to create the network stream object from the `System.Net.Sockets.TcpClient` object returned from the client connection:

```
$stream = $incomingClient.GetStream()
```

If all of this seems familiar, it should, because you're at the same point you were earlier in the chapter when receiving and sending data. Using what you learned earlier you can now start sending and receiving data using the same methods. As a refresher, the code you used earlier is listed here:

```
$tcpClient = New-Object System.Net.Sockets.TCPClient
$tcpClient.Connect("DC1",7)
$Text = "This is a test message"
[byte[]]$bytes  = [text.Encoding]::Ascii.GetBytes($Text)
$clientStream = $tcpClient.GetStream()
$clientStream.Write($bytes,0,$bytes.length)
$clientStream.Flush()
$clientStream.DataAvailable
[byte[]]$inStream = New-Object byte[] 22
$response = $clientStream.Read($inStream, 0, $inStream.count)
[Int]$response = $clientStream.Read($inStream, 0, $inStream.count)
[System.Text.Encoding]::ASCII.GetString($inStream[0..($response - 1)])

$tcpClient.Dispose()
$clientStream.Dispose()
```

This method is generally used for a single client connection, as each blocking connection method makes it hard to handle more than one client at a time if used in a loop. If you want to set up a more robust server I suggest getting familiar with creating your own PowerShell runspaces and learning more about sharing variables, which makes the handling of multiple remote connections and the sending and receiving of data much easier.

Creating the Echo server

I've gone over sending data, receiving data, and working with TCP listeners to set up your own server to listen on a port of your choosing and then handle data that's transmitted both ways. The last step in this process is to put all of this together by creating your own Echo server. This doesn't have much practical use other than testing network communication between a client and server, but it does bring together all of the techniques in this chapter.

Earlier I mentioned how you can install the Simple TCP Services feature that includes the Echo server via port 7. Using Telnet on a client, connect to the remote server running the Echo port:

```
telnet dc1.rivendell.com 7
```

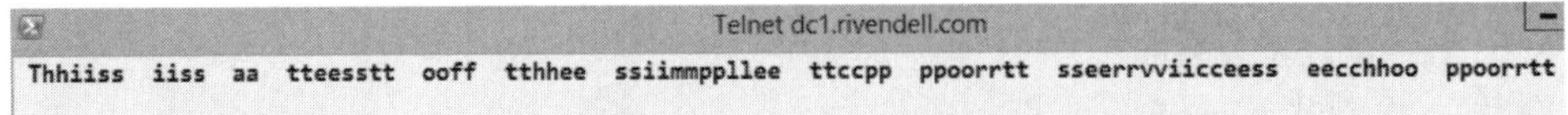

Figure 8 Sample input to the Echo port on the remote system

Now type a simple sentence and watch as each letter typed is repeated back, as shown in figure 8.

This is simple to emulate with PowerShell and doesn't require setting up multiple runspaces to handle incoming connections, although if you're expecting more than one client you'll need multiple runspaces to effectively handle multiple connections. Again, building runspaces is beyond the scope of this chapter.

The script shown in the following listing opens up port 7 as the Echo server port that will receive and resend the data sent from the client.

Listing 3 Start-EchoServer.ps1

```
[cmdletbinding()]
Param()
[console]::Title = "Echo Server"
$Listener = New-Object System.Net.Sockets.TcpListener `
 -ArgumentList 7

$Listener.Start()
Write-Verbose "Server started"

While ($True) {
    $incomingClient = $Listener.AcceptTcpClient()
    $remoteClient =
     $incomingClient.client.RemoteEndPoint.Address.IPAddressToString
    Write-Verbose ("New connection from {0}" -f $remoteClient)

    Start-Sleep -Milliseconds 1000

    $stream = $incomingClient.GetStream()
    $activeConnection = $True

    While ($incomingClient.Connected) {
        If ($Stream.DataAvailable) {
            Do {
                [byte[]]$byte = New-Object byte[] 1024
                Write-Verbose ("{0} Bytes Left from {1}" -f
                  $return.Available,$remoteClient)
                $bytesReceived = $stream.Read($byte, 0, $byte.Length)
                If ($bytesReceived -gt 0) {
                    Write-Verbose ("{0} Bytes received from {1}" -f
                    $bytesReceived,$remoteClient)
                    $String +=
     [text.Encoding]::Ascii.GetString($byte[0..($bytesReceived - 1)])
                } Else {
                    $activeConnection = $False
                    Break
                }
            } While ($Stream.DataAvailable)
```

Create TCP listener object; wait for incoming connections

Ensure always in a listening state

Continue processing client messages and echoing them back

Check if data is still available to process

```
            If ($String) {
                Write-Host -Foreground Green -background Black `
                ("Message received from {0}:`n {1}" -f
                  $remoteClient,$string) -Verbose

                $bytes  = [text.Encoding]::Ascii.GetBytes($string)
                $string = $Null
                Write-Verbose ("Echoing {0} bytes to {1}" -f
                               $bytes.count, $remoteClient)
                $Stream.Write($bytes,0,$bytes.length)
                $stream.Flush()
            }
        }
    }
}
```

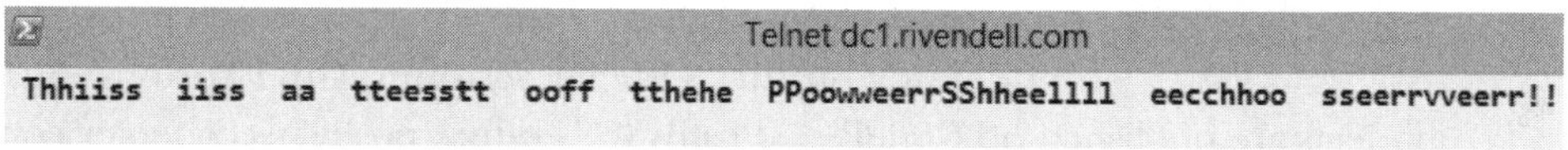

```
Telnet dc1.rivendell.com
Thhiiss  iiss  aa  tteesstt  ooff  tthehe  PPoowweerrSShheellll  eecchhoo  sseerrvveerr!!
```

Figure 9 Sample input to the PowerShell Echo server

```
PS D:\SharedStorage> .\Start-EchoServer.ps1
VERBOSE: Server started
VERBOSE: New connection from 192.168.1.14
VERBOSE:  Bytes Left from 192.168.1.14
VERBOSE: 1 Bytes received from 192.168.1.14
Message received from 192.168.1.14:
 t
VERBOSE: Echoing 1 bytes to 192.168.1.14
VERBOSE:  Bytes Left from 192.168.1.14
VERBOSE: 1 Bytes received from 192.168.1.14
Message received from 192.168.1.14:
 h
VERBOSE: Echoing 1 bytes to 192.168.1.14
VERBOSE:  Bytes Left from 192.168.1.14
VERBOSE: 1 Bytes received from 192.168.1.14
Message received from 192.168.1.14:
 i
```

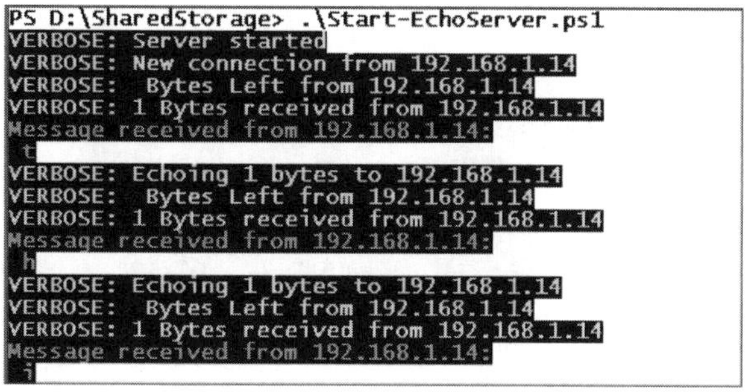

Figure 10 The PowerShell Echo server handling the responses from a client and "echoing" back the data

Figure 9 shows a message being typed into the console from Telnet, with the data being sent back. You'll notice that the first letter only appears once. The first letter you type doesn't get displayed on the console; instead, the single "T" is the reply from the Echo server.

Figure 10 shows the PowerShell Echo server responding to each and every sent character.

Summary

As you've seen, you can do many things with PowerShell to take advantage of TCP port communications. The possibilities with these techniques are limited only by your imagination and what you can build. Be sure to use tools such as sniffers to help you in your exploration of TCP communications.

Whether you're creating a simple port scanner to emulate an Echo port or building your own PowerShell chat room and client (which I happened to do, and it's available for download and use at http://poshchat.codeplex.com), PowerShell is more than capable of meeting your needs. Whatever you do, have fun with it and be sure to share it with the rest of the PowerShell community!

About the author

Boe Prox is a Senior Windows Systems Administrator. He has been in the IT industry since 2003 and has worked with Windows PowerShell since 2009. He is also the recipient of the Microsoft Community Contributor award for 2011 and 2012. Boe holds several IT certifications, including MCITP:Enterprise Administrator, VCP 4, and Microsoft Certified Solutions Associate. You can find him on Twitter (@proxb) and at his blog (http://learn-powershell.net). He is also a moderator on the "Official Scripting Guys Forum!" His current projects are published on CodePlex: PoshWSUS (http://poshwsus.codeplex.com), PoshPAIG (http://poshpaig.codeplex.com), and PoshChat (http://poshchat.codeplex.com).

5 Managing systems through a keyhole

Bartosz Bielawski

Imagine you're sitting on the beach with your smartphone. You'd love to ignore calls from work, but you just got a text saying that an important client's account is locked. It's the middle of vacation season, and for whatever reason nobody in the office is able to solve the problem. You roll your eyes and take a deep breath. Then you open the appropriate web page on your phone, log on, and run a single command. You send a text to your colleagues that the problem is solved. Is it possible? With PowerShell v3 and Windows Server 2012, the answer is yes.

Windows Server 2012 comes with PowerShell Web Access (PSWA). A question that concerns many administrators is this: do I really want to be able to do everything I can normally do from my workstation when I'm connected to my systems from my phone or tablet? Maybe I want to be able to perform only those tasks that are safe but may be seen as crucial by some (important if "some" includes your manager), like unlocking a client's active directory account.

PSWA can't restrict the list of commands available, but because it uses PowerShell remoting at the backend you can configure it to only use a dedicated-session configuration. And you can set up this session configuration in a way that meets your goals—in a way that will let you do what you must but hide anything that could potentially cause harm to the managed system.

PowerShell remoting

PowerShell remoting is functionality that Windows administrators can use to connect to remote computers if they're running PowerShell v2 (at least) and have this option enabled. To control who can connect to the computer and what operations can be performed on it you'll use session configurations (endpoints). Let's take a look at the different types of endpoints.

Endpoints

When you use PowerShell remoting you usually connect to the default endpoint, `Microsoft.PowerShell`. You can change this either by using the parameter `ConfigurationName` on `*-PSSession` cmdlets or by changing the preference variable `$PSSessionConfigurationName`. To work with remoting endpoints on your computer you use cmdlets with the common noun `PSSessionConfiguration`:

```
PS C:\> Get-Command -Noun PSSessionConfiguration | select Name

Name
----
Disable-PSSessionConfiguration
Enable-PSSessionConfiguration
Get-PSSessionConfiguration
Register-PSSessionConfiguration
Set-PSSessionConfiguration
Unregister-PSSessionConfiguration
```

For example, if you want to see all the endpoints available on your computer, run the `Get-PSSessionConfiguration` cmdlet:

```
PS C:\> Get-PSSessionConfiguration

Name          : microsoft.powershell
PSVersion     : 3.0
StartupScript :
RunAsUser     :
Permission    : BUILTIN\Administrators AccessAllowed, BUILTIN\Remote
     Management Users AccessAllowed

Name          : microsoft.powershell.workflow
PSVersion     : 3.0
StartupScript :
RunAsUser     :
Permission    : BUILTIN\Administrators AccessAllowed, BUILTIN\Remote
     Management Users AccessAllowed

Name          : microsoft.powershell32
PSVersion     : 3.0
StartupScript :
RunAsUser     :
Permission    : BUILTIN\Administrators AccessAllowed, BUILTIN\Remote
     Management Users AccessAllowed

Name          : microsoft.windows.servermanagerworkflows
PSVersion     : 3.0
StartupScript :
RunAsUser     :
Permission    : NT AUTHORITY\INTERACTIVE AccessAllowed,
     BUILTIN\Administrators AccessAllowed
```

Your default remoting endpoint (`Microsoft.PowerShell`) is configured to only allow members of the local Administrators group, and it doesn't restrict them at all. In v3 a new group was added with the same access to this endpoint: Remote Management

Users. Almost everything can be done using this default configuration. Although this is a good thing, you may want to have different, custom endpoints available on your computer. You may want to have an endpoint that would have some elements configured specifically for you—such as variables, aliases, and loaded modules—configured in the same way you would your local environment using profile scripts.

Another option is to create an endpoint that would expose only a limited set of commands—a constrained endpoint. Both operations require creating a custom endpoint (`Register-PSSessionConfiguration`) or modifying one that already exists (`Set-PSSessionConfiguration`).

You'll use these cmdlets to create and configure your remoting endpoint.

Constrained endpoints, take one

You customize remoting endpoints in PowerShell v2 with startup scripts. When you want to build a constrained endpoint in v2 you have to know exactly what is required. No cmdlet can help you with that. You create a startup script and take a few actions to limit the users in it:

- Hide all variables and cmdlets (change them to private).
- Remove all scripts and applications.
- Change the language mode to `NoLanguage`.
- Define the proxies necessary for the remoting endpoint to work.
- Define any public commands that you want to expose.

Next, register or set the custom endpoint and pass the path to the configuration script you've created to the `StartupScript` parameter. But there's no built-in way to delegate such an endpoint. You could change the security descriptor and allow a nonadministrative account to connect to the endpoint, but you can't change the context in which commands run to the context of another user with higher privileges.

Constrained endpoints, take two

A nice addition to remoting in PowerShell v3 is the option to use configuration files. When you register or configure an endpoint you can specify the path to the `PSSessionConfiguration` file that covers the same elements that v2's `StartupScript` did, but in a more structured way that's easier to follow and change. The cmdlet for creating configuration files for remoting endpoints is `New-PSSessionConfigurationFile`. With this cmdlet you can focus on the things you want to achieve rather than on how to achieve them.

CREATING A SAMPLE ENDPOINT

The sample endpoint you're going to create has only one purpose: finding locked Active Directory accounts and unlocking selected accounts. That's it. You want to be as restrictive as possible and have only the cmdlets you need. When using the `New-PSSessionConfiguration` cmdlet to create your configuration file, for the most part PowerShell will support you with parameters (that you can complete with the tab key) and help you with arguments (ones that have a closed list of possible values). Run this command to create your configuration file:

```
New-PSSessionConfigurationFile -Path v3config.pssc `
    -SessionType RestrictedRemoteServer `
    -LanguageMode NoLanguage `
    -ModulesToImport ActiveDirectory `
    -VisibleCmdlets Unlock-ADAccount, Search-ADAccount
```

This creates a file containing all the fields that are supported in the session configuration file. All optional fields that you haven't specified are marked as comments, making it easy to edit the file later and enable additional fields by "uncommenting" them. Use the `RestrictedRemoteServer` configuration type to make sure your endpoint contains all the commands necessary for basic operations (connecting to the endpoint, disconnecting from it, listing available commands). Set `LanguageMode` to `NoLanguage` to disable any language elements (such as script blocks, variables, or operators). By specifying `ModulesToImport` and `VisibleCmdlets` you enable the performance of both actions you need: searching for locked accounts and unlocking accounts in Active Directory.

The configuration file (with comments removed) can be seen in the following listing.

Listing 1 Configuration file (v3config.pssc) for the sample endpoint

```
@{
SchemaVersion = '1.0.0.0'
GUID = '607136de-2811-42f3-b526-ea2b1d5b59a2'
Author = 'BielawB'
CompanyName = 'PAREXEL'
Copyright = '(c) 2012 BielawB. All rights reserved.'

ExecutionPolicy = 'Restricted'
LanguageMode = 'NoLanguage'
SessionType = 'RestrictedRemoteServer'

ModulesToImport = 'ActiveDirectory'
VisibleCmdlets = 'Unlock-ADAccount','Search-ADAccount'
}
```

Setting endpoint properties

Configuring elements important for constrained endpoint

Selecting visible module and cmdlets

The file generated is easy to update—open it in your PowerShell editor of choice and modify the keys you want to change. It's always possible you'll make a mistake, and this is where the `Test-PSSessionConfigurationFile` cmdlet comes in handy (particularly when used with the `Verbose` parameter). For example, suppose you decide to define an alias in your configuration. As shown in figure 1, the `Test-PSSessionConfigurationFile` cmdlet tells you exactly what mistakes you've made.

When you're sure the configuration file is error-free you can register the new endpoint:

```
Register-PSSessionConfiguration -Name Unlock -Path v3config.pssc
```

You have two options here: run it on the domain controller (which will make it easier to test) or run it on any member server (but the `ActiveDirectory` module won't work

```
Administrator: Windows PowerShell
PS v3 > Test-PSSessionConfigurationFile -Verbose -Path .\v3config.pssc
VERBOSE: The member 'AliasDefinitions' must contain the required key 'Name'.
Add the require key to the file D:\Tests\v3config.pssc.
False
PS v3 > # Adding 'Name' key to our alias definition...
PS v3 > Test-PSSessionConfigurationFile -Verbose -Path .\v3config.pssc
VERBOSE: The member 'AliasDefinitions' must contain the required key 'Value'.
Add the require key to the file D:\Tests\v3config.pssc.
False
PS v3 > # Adding 'Value' and 'Opt'...
PS v3 > Test-PSSessionConfigurationFile -Verbose -Path .\v3config.pssc
VERBOSE: The key 'Opt' in the member 'AliasDefinitions' is not valid. Change
the key in the file D:\Tests\v3config.pssc.
False
PS v3 > # Changing 'Opt' to 'Options' - optional key.
PS v3 > Test-PSSessionConfigurationFile -Verbose -Path .\v3config.pssc
True
```

Figure 1 The `Test-PSSessionConigurationFile` cmdlet will help you avoid errors in your configuration file.

until you configure `RunAs` credentials and bypass the double-hop issue). Your first remoting endpoint has been created. Now you need to learn how to delegate it. As you'll see, delegating is not only supported in v3, it's also pretty easy to do.

> **The double-hop issue**
>
> PowerShell remoting, by default, uses Kerberos for authentication. Unless the computer you connect to is configured as "trusted for delegation" it won't be able to delegate a Kerberos token on the user's behalf to other network resources. As a result, anything that requires delegation will fail. This issue is known as the double-hop issue, and you can work around it in a few ways, including using `RunAs` credentials. You can also use Credential Security Support Provider (CredSSP) or configure the remote computer as "trusted for delegation."

DELEGATION

Constrained endpoints are perfect candidates for delegation. With them you can hand over authorizations to less privileged users in a controlled manner. Delegating an already configured endpoint is a matter of running a single command (usually `Set-PSSessionConfiguration`) with two parameters that will define whose credentials will be delegated (`RunAsCredential`) and who will be allowed to use the endpoint. For the latter, you can use either `ShowSecurityDescriptorUI`, if you prefer using a GUI to set up access rights, or `SecurityDescriptorSddl`, if you know security descriptor definition language (SDDL) syntax. You can do it during registration or modify the endpoint already registered. In my opinion it's better to test constraints first and enable delegation later. (When you invite guests to your home, you want to clean up the house first, rather than run around with a mop once they're already there!) Your endpoint has been tested, so now you can delegate it:

```
Set-PSSessionConfiguration -Name Unlock `
    -RunAsCredential MONAD\Administrator -ShowSecurityDescriptorUI -Force
```

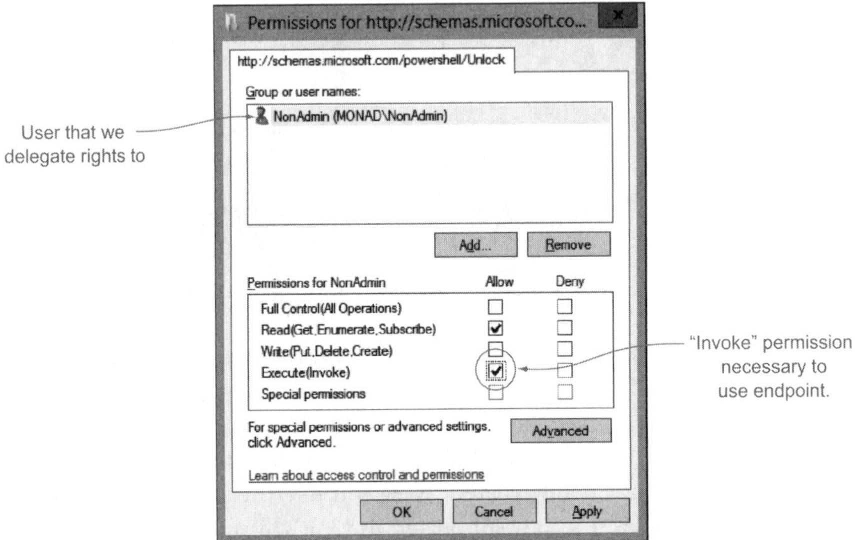

Figure 2 Giving the `NonAdmin` user access to the endpoint by assigning read and execute rights

Using `ShowSecurityDescriptorUI` gives you a user-friendly GUI to configure permissions to your endpoint. You want to be sure only designated users can access it, so remove the default groups and add only the `NonAdmin` user, as shown in figure 2.

Now that your endpoint is up and running you can invite your "guests."

PowerShell Web Access

You've got remoting set up, and now it's time to configure a feature added in Windows Server 2012: PowerShell Web Access. PSWA allows you to use PowerShell on almost any device. It's a gateway between your web browser and the remoting endpoint you want to connect to. Security concerns are involved, but you can mitigate those risks by carefully designing your infrastructure. I'll walk you through how to configure PSWA.

To get PSWA up and running you need an IIS server that's running Windows Server 2012 and is accessible from outside and able to connect to your internal network. It has to support HTTPS binding, preferably with a proper certificate (to avoid an "untrusted certificate" warning). You have to install the PSWA feature first:

```
Install-WindowsFeature -Name WindowsPowerShellWebAccess `
    -IncludeAllSubFeature -IncludeManagementTools
```

Next, run a script to install the PSWA application, in this case giving it a custom name:

```
Install-PswaWebApplication -WebApplicationName MyPosh
```

It's important to have a limited user on your IIS server who can log in to the PSWA gateway but do nothing more. Let's name this user `WebRestricted`. The IIS server that will run the PSWA gateway is appropriately named `PSWA`.

Once you've created your limited user (keep in mind that it can be a nondomain user, depending on the demilitarized-zone configuration you use), you need to add the appropriate authorization rule:

```
Add-PswaAuthorizationRule -ComputerName dc.monad.ps1 `
    -UserName PSWA\WebRestricted -ConfigurationName Unlock
```

You've given access to one user, one computer, and one specific configuration on this computer. `ComputerName` matches the name of the computer running the constrained endpoint, and `ConfigurationName` matches the name you specified when you registered the constrained endpoint. If your IIS server is outside the domain you need to make sure it will be able to connect to the host that the authorization rule points to. Do this by entering

```
Set-Item -Path WSMan:\localhost\Client\TrustedHosts `
    -Value dc.monad.ps1 -Concatenate
```

NOTE Be aware that the PSWA gateway can have PowerShell remoting disabled: this technology doesn't require it on the gateway host. It uses an HTTPS connection from your browser to the gateway, and a WinRM connection from the gateway to final host.

Once the configuration is complete you can open a connection to the PSWA gateway using a web browser. The address depends on the initial configuration, in this case https://PSWA/MyPosh, as shown in figure 3.

The disadvantage in setting PSWA to work with only one endpoint, other than the default, is that you have to specify almost all the parameters available during the connection, as shown in figure 4.

Figure 3 Structure of the PowerShell Web Access URI

Windows PowerShell Web Access

Enter your credentials and connection settings

User name: PSWA\WebRestricted

Password: ••••••••

Connection type: Computer Name

Computer name: dc.monad.ps1

Optional connection settings

Destination computer credentials (if different from gateway)

User name: MONAD\NonAdmin

Password: ••••••••

Configuration name: Unlock

Figure 4 Logging on to PowerShell Web Access with a specific authorization rule configured

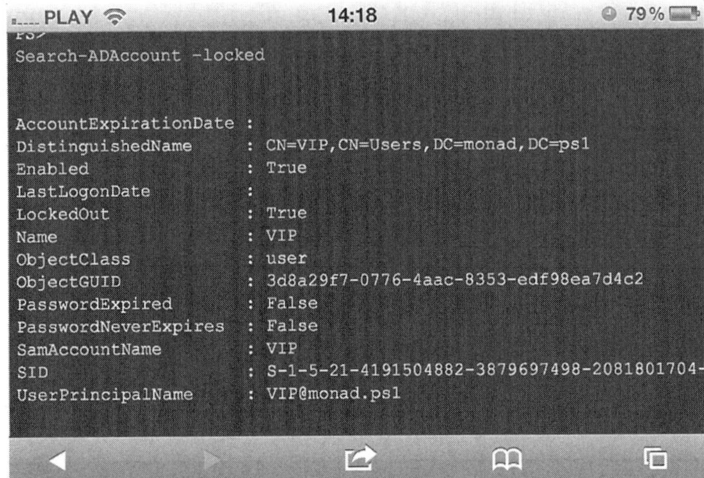

Figure 5 Searching for locked accounts from a smartphone is almost the same as searching from a workstation.

Once you connect you have your two cmdlets available, plus a few proxy functions needed for the remoting endpoint to work. You can now check for locked accounts in the same way you would if you were running PowerShell on a normal workstation, as shown in figure 5.

If you try to connect to a different host with a different user it won't work—either the gateway or the endpoint will stop you. With all the settings configured correctly you can connect to the endpoint from any device, including a smartphone, tablet, or netbook. All you need is a web browser and the ability to type letters and other characters (a pipeline can be tricky).

The only commands available in this session are the ones you decide to expose, so there's no way to remove an account, for example, or disable it. If you decide you need more commands you can add them by modifying your configuration file and resetting the endpoint. If you need another endpoint you can configure one and add a new authorization rule on the PSWA gateway to allow the connection. With PSWA, you have granular control over who can perform certain tasks, where, and how, all without leaving the door to your system wide open. If all you need is a small keyhole, a keyhole is what you'll get.

Summary

Your initial problem was solved with two elements: a constrained endpoint and PSWA. The constrained endpoint is your back-end and limits the actions you can perform. PSWA is the front-end that allows access from any device with a web browser. But this is only the beginning. You can create your own tools that would use your back-end to perform actions, group several constrained endpoints, and create a single application (with a GUI) for the help-desk staff to perform their tasks. You can define as many authorization rules for your PSWA application as you need to manage your organization. Everything can be done in a secure fashion, without fully opening the doors to your system.

Is it safe? There's always risk, but the safeguards I've shown you can minimize it. PSWA makes it possible to connect to a PowerShell remoting endpoint even if direct connection isn't possible. You connect using a regular account to both a web application and a remoting endpoint, using authorization rules in the first case and delegation in the second. It's all about careful design. You have full control. It's not an all-or-nothing decision: you control what is exposed, where, and how.

You face two situations. In one, whenever something requires your attention, you need a good and stable Internet connection to use a virtual private network, and a trusted and well-protected laptop to perform operations. The second is slightly different: when you're away from your desk, you need a gateway to connect to and an underprivileged account so you can perform important tasks in a way that doesn't put your system at risk. In this chapter you gave yourself the option to perform them from any device with an Internet connection, web browser, and keyboard (even if the keys were only a few pixels on a touchscreen). To move between the two you needed only to constrain the remoting endpoints and PSWA. In my opinion, this transition was worth the price.

About the author

Bartosz (Bartek) Bielawski is a busy IT Administrator with an international company, PAREXEL. He loves PowerShell and automation. That love earned him the honor of Microsoft MVP. He shares his knowledge mainly on his blogs and through articles published in the Polish *IT Professional* magazine.

6 Using PowerShell to audit user logon events

Mike F. Robbins

Event logs are special files on Windows-based workstations and servers that record system activity. Do you want to know if there's a problem with your Windows-based servers? Almost anything you'd want to know about what has occurred on your servers, whether an informational event, a warning, an error, or a security event, is contained in the event logs. When's the last time you took a look at all of the event logs on each of your servers?

Beginning with Windows Vista and Windows Server 2008 the event logs were redesigned in an XML-based log format, and newer operating systems such as Windows Server 2012 can contain over 200 different event logs, depending on what roles have been enabled. Each of these event logs is an individual file located in the %SystemRoot%\System32\Winevt\Logs folder by default. Event Viewer is the graphical user interface tool that most administrators are familiar with when it comes to event logs, but with an overwhelming amount of data being contained in so many individual logs on each of their servers, administrators have to learn more efficient ways to retrieve the specific information they're looking for.

This chapter focuses on using PowerShell to retrieve auditing information for user logon events from the security event log of your Windows-based servers. Although you can use many different tools to perform this task, PowerShell is one of the most efficient and versatile options—it allows you to control the specific details of how you query for the information, where most of the processing takes place, and where the data filtering occurs. It can also translate cryptic numeric codes contained in specific events into meaningful information.

Event log basics

You can search event logs in a number of ways, depending on the piece of information you have and the type of data you're looking for. Because you'll be focusing on a few different security-related user-logon events in this chapter you'll search by event ID.

An event ID is a numeric code that uniquely identifies a specific type of event. How do you determine what the event IDs are for successful logons, logon failures, and user account lockouts? The event IDs and their descriptions can be found in the article "Description of security events in Windows 7 and in Windows Server 2008 R2" at http://support.microsoft.com/kb/977519. Similar information is also available as an Excel spreadsheet at www.microsoft.com/en-us/download/details.aspx?id=21561. I've listed them here for you in table 1. These event IDs were changed from three- to four-digit numeric codes with Windows Vista and Windows Server 2008, so you won't find them in the event logs of older operating systems. The event IDs in table 1 are valid for Windows Vista, Windows Server 2008, and higher.

Table 1 Event IDs

Event ID	Description
4624	An account was successfully logged on.
4625	An account failed to log on.
4740	A user account was locked out.

Querying the event logs with PowerShell

The two PowerShell cmdlets specifically designed for querying information in the event logs are `Get-EventLog` and `Get-WinEvent`.

The `Get-EventLog` cmdlet has been around since PowerShell v1, but the initial version of this cmdlet didn't include a `ComputerName` parameter for support to query the event logs of remote computers. That functionality was added to `Get-EventLog` with the release of PowerShell v2. This means you'll need at least PowerShell v2 on your machine in order to run this cmdlet and query the event logs of remote machines.

The `Get-WinEvent` cmdlet, added in PowerShell v2, is much more powerful and efficient in certain scenarios for querying the event logs. One issue with the `Get-WinEvent` cmdlet is that it doesn't natively support running against multiple remote computers, as the `Get-EventLog` cmdlet does. Looking at the help for the `ComputerName` parameter of the `Get-WinEvent` cmdlet confirms that it only supports a string and not an array of strings:

```
PS C:\> help Get-WinEvent -Parameter ComputerName
-ComputerName <string>
```

Viewing the help for the `ComputerName` parameter of the `Get-EventLog` cmdlet shows that it supports an array of strings, which means it can accept multiple computer names:

```
PS C:\> help Get-EventLog -Parameter ComputerName
-ComputerName <string[]>
```

You'd have to use a Foreach or ForEach-Object loop or PowerShell remoting in order to use the Get-WinEvent cmdlet with multiple computer names in a single command. Foreach iterates through a collection of objects, and ForEach-Object obtains its collection of objects through the pipeline. For a small number of items in a collection the performance difference of these two is negligible, but when you have a large number of items and they're already known, Foreach is faster than ForEach-Object, as it doesn't have to collect the objects before the loop starts.

The following PowerShell script shows an example of using the Get-WinEvent cmdlet in a Foreach loop:

```
$ComputerName = 'server1', 'server2'
foreach ($Computer in $ComputerName)
{
 Get-WinEvent -ComputerName $Computer -Logname 'security' -MaxEvents 10
   ➥ -FilterXPath '*[System[EventID=4624]]'
}
```

This script is an example of using the Get-WinEvent cmdlet in a ForEach-Object loop:

```
'server1', 'server2' |
ForEach-Object {
 Get-WinEvent -ComputerName $_ -Logname 'security' -MaxEvents 10
   ➥ -FilterXPath '*[System[EventID=4624]]'
}
```

I've chosen to use the FilterXPath parameter set with the Get-WinEvent cmdlet in the examples in this chapter because the FilterHashTable parameter set isn't supported when run from Windows Vista or Windows Server 2008, although remote queries against either of those operating systems using the FilterHashTable parameter set work without issue when the client performing the query is running Windows 7, Windows Server 2008 R2, or higher.

What if your servers are running Windows Server 2008 and your security team won't allow PowerShell to be enabled or a newer version of PowerShell to be installed? That's certainly not the optimum environment for remotely managing your Windows-based servers with PowerShell, but it's possible to remotely query the event logs of your servers that don't have PowerShell installed or enabled using the Get-EventLog and Get-WinEvent cmdlets.

To do this you need at least one machine running Windows Vista, Windows Server 2008, or higher that has PowerShell v2 or higher installed on it from which to perform the remote querying. One issue you're likely to run into is the "RPC Server is unavailable" error, which is probably due to the firewall on the remote server blocking the request. The simplest way to resolve this is to allow the Remote Event Log Management exception in the firewall of the remote servers whose event logs you're trying to query. It's also possible that the security team won't allow a generic firewall exception to be made on the servers, but in most cases at least a single specific IP address exception is allowed for a management workstation that's used for this type of remote administration.

Both the Get-EventLog and Get-WinEvent cmdlets run asynchronously, or against one computer (specified using the ComputerName parameter) at a time. You can place either cmdlet inside the script block {} of the Invoke-Command cmdlet to take advantage of PowerShell remoting, which runs synchronously, or against multiple computers in parallel at the same time.

To use Invoke-Command you must have at least PowerShell v2 installed and PowerShell remoting enabled on the remote machines you're targeting. PowerShell remoting is enabled by default on Windows Server 2012. By taking advantage of PowerShell remoting you'll eliminate many of the issues I've discussed, such as the issue with the FilterHashTable parameter set of Get-WinEvent and most of the firewall-related issues.

The following PowerShell script shows the Get-WinEvent example you previously used, now modified for use with Invoke-Command. It places the script inside the script block and moves the computer names you're targeting to the ComputerName parameter of Invoke-Command. It also eliminates the Foreach or ForEach-Object loop because the ComputerName parameter of the Invoke-Command cmdlet supports multiple computer names:

```
Invoke-Command -ComputerName 'server1', 'server2' {
 Get-WinEvent -Logname 'security' -MaxEvents 10
   ➥ -FilterXPath '*[System[EventID=4624]]'
}
```

Now that we've covered the basics of event logs and how to query them with PowerShell, let's take a look at a real-world scenario for each of the querying methods covered in this section.

Auditing logon failures

Suppose you have external users who access a private section of your website that runs on IIS and uses Windows Authentication. These users frequently experience difficulties when trying to log in to the website. Your goal is to provide your help desk staff with a quick and efficient method for gaining insight into the login issues so they can determine the problem. To enable the help desk staff to read the event logs of the servers where the website resides, but for which they don't have administrative privileges, they've been added to a global group in Active Directory, and that global group has been made a member of the local Event Log Readers group on the servers. Also, the local Event Log Readers group has been granted read access to the HKLM\SYSTEM\CurrentControlSet\services\eventlog\Security hive in the registry on those servers; otherwise, the help desk staff still wouldn't be able to read the security event log.

Earlier you learned that the event ID for "An account failed to log on" is 4625. Viewing one of the 4625 events on the web server through Event Viewer, shown in figure 1, you'll see status and sub-status codes that may provide additional information that could help determine why a user can't log on.

Figure 1 Event 4625—example of sub-status code for Account Does Not Exist

You can see that the status and sub-status codes are part of the message property by using the `Get-WinEvent` cmdlet to retrieve one of the logon failure events and then piping it to `Select-Object` using the `-ExpandProperty` parameter to view its contents:

```
PS C:\> Get-WinEvent -ComputerName 'www' -MaxEvents 1 -Logname 'security'
  ➥ -FilterXPath '*[System[EventID=4625]]' | select -expand message
An account failed to log on.

Account For Which Logon Failed:
     Security ID:           S-1-0-0
     Account Name:          laurac
     Account Domain:        MIKEFROBBINS

Failure Information:
     Failure Reason:        Unknown user name or bad password.
     Status:                0xc000006d
     Sub Status:            0xc0000064
```

Unfortunately, there's no easy way to pull a single piece of information out of the message property. Usually these individual items are accessible via the properties collection of `Get-WinEvent`, but that isn't the case in this particular scenario.

The `Get-EventLog` cmdlet has a `ReplacementStrings` collection similar to the properties collection of `Get-WinEvent`. Both the status and sub-status codes are accessible as individual elements in the `ReplacementStrings` collection, so you'll use the `Get-EventLog` cmdlet instead of `Get-WinEvent`. In the following results I've added bracketed numbers that correspond to the position in the collection where each of these items is located. You'll need that information to access the specific elements individually when creating your script:

```
PS C:\> Get-EventLog -ComputerName 'www' -LogName 'security'
  ➥ -InstanceId 4625 -Newest 1 | select -expand replacementstrings
[0]  S-1-0-0
[1]  -
[2]  -
[3]  0x0
[4]  S-1-0-0
[5]  laurac
[6]  mikefrobbins
[7]  0xc000006d
[8]  %%2313
[9]  0xc0000064
[10] 3
```

```
[11] NtLmSsp
[12] NTLM
[13] PC2
[14] -
[15] -
[16] 0
[17] 0x0
[18] -
[19] 192.168.1.99
```

A little research on the Microsoft Developer Network (MSDN) turns up something called "NTSTATUS values," which contains the descriptions for the status and sub-status codes at http://mng.bz/z88n. The most common ones are shown in table 2.

Table 2 Common logon failure status codes

Code	Description
0xC0000064	Account does not exist
0xC000006A	Incorrect password
0xC000006D	Incorrect username or password
0xC000006E	Account restriction
0xC000006F	Invalid logon hours
0xC000015B	Logon type not granted
0xC0000070	Invalid Workstation
0xC0000071	Password expired
0xC0000072	Account disabled
0xC0000133	Time difference at DC
0xC0000193	Account expired
0xC0000224	Password must change
0xC0000234	Account locked out

Now you're ready to create your PowerShell script, to which you'll add these status and sub-status codes. You want the script to be parameterized for the computer name and the number of records to retrieve. You'll pipe the results to `Select-Object` and use a hash table to display custom column names, along with adding a function named `Get-FailureReason` to automatically translate the status and sub-status codes into their meaningful descriptions from table 2. The script is shown in the following listing.

Listing 1 Auditing logon failures

```
param (
  $ComputerName = $Env:ComputerName,
  $Records = 10
)
```

```
function Get-FailureReason {
  Param($FailureReason)
    switch ($FailureReason) {
      '0xC0000064' {"Account does not exist"; break;}
      '0xC000006A' {"Incorrect password"; break;}
      '0xC000006D' {"Incorrect username or password"; break;}
      '0xC000006E' {"Account restriction"; break;}
      '0xC000006F' {"Invalid logon hours"; break;}
      '0xC000015B' {"Logon type not granted"; break;}
      '0xc0000070' {"Invalid Workstation"; break;}
      '0xC0000071' {"Password expired"; break;}
      '0xC0000072' {"Account disabled"; break;}
      '0xC0000133' {"Time difference at DC"; break;}
      '0xC0000193' {"Account expired"; break;}
      '0xC0000224' {"Password must change"; break;}
      '0xC0000234' {"Account locked out"; break;}
      '0x0' {"0x0"; break;}
      default {"Other"; break;}
  }
}
Get-EventLog -ComputerName $ComputerName -LogName 'security'
  ➥ -InstanceId 4625 -Newest $Records |
  select @{Label='Time';Expression={$_.TimeGenerated.ToString('g')}},
    @{Label='User Name';Expression={$_.replacementstrings[5]}},
    @{Label='Client Name';Expression={$_.replacementstrings[13]}},
    @{Label='Client Address';Expression={$_.replacementstrings[19]}},
    @{Label='Server Name';Expression={$_.MachineName}},
    @{Label='Failure Status';Expression={Get-FailureReason
      ➥ ($_.replacementstrings[7])}},
    @{Label='Failure Sub Status';Expression={Get-FailureReason
      ➥ ($_.replacementstrings[9])}}
```

A subset of the columns returned by this script is shown in figure 2. Based on these results, it appears that the user is attempting to log in with the username of laurac. The correct username is lcallahan.

As shown in figure 3, had the password been incorrect instead of the username, the generic reason for failure and status code would have been the same, but the substatus code would have been different.

In this section you've used PowerShell to determine why a user is unable to log on by translating cryptic status codes retrieved from the security event log of an IIS web server into meaningful information. Finding and translating these same codes with

```
PS C:\> .\Get-LogonFailures.ps1 -ComputerName www -Records 7 | Format-Table

User Name       Failure Status                 Failure Sub-Status
---------       --------------                 ------------------
adodsworth      Account restriction            Account disabled
afuller         Password must change           0x0
jleverling      Account restriction            Invalid logon hours
laurac          Incorrect username or password Account does not exist
mpeacock        Account expired                0x0
msuyama         Account restriction            Invalid Workstation
ndavolio        Incorrect username or password Incorrect password
```

Figure 2 Results of the `Get-LogonFailures.ps1` PowerShell script from listing 1

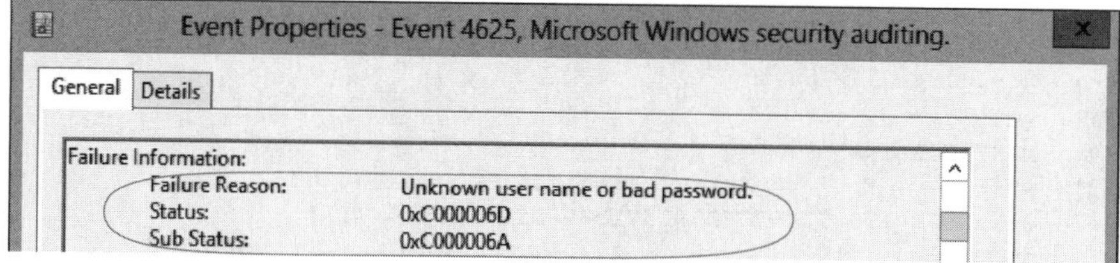

Figure 3 Event 4625—example of sub-status code for Incorrect Password

the Event Viewer graphical interface tool into something meaningful would be a manual and time-consuming process, so it's easy to see how much more efficient PowerShell is in this situation than Event Viewer or another tool that's unable to automatically translate the codes.

In the next section you'll use PowerShell to determine the logon type and authentication protocol for individual user logon requests to specific servers based on information in the security event log of the server where the logon event took place. This can help you locate incorrectly configured servers, which can cause security vulnerabilities because the systems are using weak logon authentication protocols.

Auditing logon type and authentication protocol

Suppose a new SharePoint farm has been built and you want to verify that Kerberos is the authentication protocol being used between the web frontends and their dedicated backend SQL Server. As previously determined, successful logons are identified by event ID 4624 in the security event log. The numeric values for Logon Type and Authentication Package are the two key pieces of information you're looking for. As with the example in the previous section, they can both be seen in the message property of `Get-WinEvent`:

```
PS C:\> Get-WinEvent -ComputerName 'sql' -MaxEvents 1 -Logname 'security'
  ➥ -FilterXPath '*[System[EventID=4624]]' | select -expand message
An account was successfully logged on.
Subject:
     Security ID:            S-1-5-18
     Account Name:           PC3$
     Account Domain:         MIKEFROBBINS
     Logon ID:               0x3e7

Logon Type:             10

Detailed Authentication Information:
     Logon Process:          User32
     Authentication Package:       Negotiate
```

The difference this time is that they're available in the properties collection of `Get-WinEvent` as individual elements. The logon-type code is in position 9, which is number [8], and the logon authentication protocol is in position 11, which is number [10] of the properties collection, as shown in the following results:

```
PS C:\> Get-WinEvent -ComputerName 'sql' -MaxEvents 1 -Logname 'security'
➥ -FilterXPath '*[System[EventID=4624]]' | select -expand properties
[0]  S-1-5-18
[1]  PC3$
[2]  MIKEFROBBINS
[3]  999
[4]  S-1-5-21-1998522977-2393571580-1109924844-1113
[5]  mpeacock
[6]  MIKEFROBBINS
[7]  273615
[8]  10
[9]  User32
[10] Negotiate
[11] PC3
[12] 00000000-0000-0000-0000-000000000000
[13] -
[14] -
[15] 0
[16] 2208
[17] C:\Windows\System32\winlogon.exe
[18] 192.168.1.86
```

Articles about logon-type numeric codes and their values are available on TechNet at http://mng.bz/VD00 and on MSDN at http://mng.bz/adZz. These codes and values are shown in table 3.

Table 3 Logon-type codes and values

Numeric Code	Value
0	System
2	Interactive
3	Network
4	Batch
5	Service
6	Proxy
7	Unlock
8	NetworkCleartext
9	NewCredentials
10	RemoteInteractive
11	CachedInteractive
12	CachedRemoteInteractive
13	CachedUnlock

For the SharePoint-to-SQL-Server authentication test you want to run the PowerShell script shown in listing 2, which has the logon-type codes and values incorporated, against the SQL Server and look for the Active Directory service accounts that are used by SharePoint on the web frontends. As with the previous script, this script is parameterized for the computer name and the number of records to return. This script uses a `Switch` statement in a hash table to return a meaningful name for the logon-type code, which indicates the type of logon session that took place when a user logged onto the server. It then customizes the column header names in a hash table, and finally sorts by server name in ascending order and then by time in descending order.

Listing 2 Auditing logon type and authentication protocol

```
param (
  $ComputerName = $Env:ComputerName,
  $Records = 10
)
Foreach ($Computer in $ComputerName) {
  Get-WinEvent -Computer $Computer -LogName 'security' -MaxEvents
    ➥ $Records -FilterXPath '*[System[EventID=4624]]' |
  select @{Label='Time';Expression={$_.TimeCreated.ToString('g')}},
    @{Label="Logon Type";Expression={switch
      ➥ (foreach {$_.properties[8].value}) {
      0 {"System"; break;}
      2 {"Interactive"; break;}
      3 {"Network"; break;}
      4 {"Batch"; break;}
      5 {"Service"; break;}
      6 {"Proxy"; break;}
      7 {"Unlock"; break;}
      8 {"NetworkCleartext"; break;}
      9 {"NewCredentials"; break;}
      10 {"RemoteInteractive"; break;}
      11 {"CachedInteractive"; break;}
      12 {"CachedRemoteInteractive"; break;}
      13 {"CachedUnlock"; break;}
      default {"Other"; break;}}}},
    @{Label='Authentication';Expression={
     $_.Properties[10].Value}},
    @{Label='User Name';Expression={$_.Properties[5].Value}},
    @{Label='Client Name';Expression={$_.Properties[11].Value}},
    @{Label='Client Address';Expression={$_.Properties[18].Value}},
    @{Label='Server Name';Expression={$_.MachineName}} |
sort @{Expression="Server Name";Descending=$false},
     @{Expression="Time";Descending=$true}}
```

Parameterize for computer name and number of records to return

`Switch` statement to return meaningful name for authentication type

Customize column header names

Sort by server name in ascending order, time in descending order

A subset of the columns returned by this script is shown in the following results. You can see that the two SharePoint service accounts are using the network logon type and the Kerberos authentication protocol:

```
PS C:\> .\Get-AuthType.ps1 -ComputerName 'sql' | Format-Table

Logon Type           Authentication User Name  Client Name Client Address
----------           -------------- ---------  ----------- --------------
RemoteInteractive    Negotiate      mpeacock   PC3         192.168.1.65
Network              Kerberos       spExtFarm              -
Network              Kerberos       spExtApp               -
RemoteInteractive    Negotiate      mpeacock   PC3         192.168.1.65
```

You can run this script against other servers, such as an Exchange server that's running Outlook Web Access (OWA), to see how users are authenticating to it. You may be surprised to find that some users are being authenticated using the Network Cleartext logon type in that particular scenario, but at least those logon events are protected by the SSL encryption on the OWA website, assuming you're using SSL encryption on your OWA website.

In this section you used PowerShell to query the event logs of a SQL Server to retrieve successful user logon events containing numeric logon type codes. You translated those codes into meaningful descriptions from information to determine how users are logging onto the system and what authentication protocol is being used for their logon sessions.

Next you're going to use PowerShell to query the event logs of all the Active Directory domain controllers in a specific domain to determine what computer or device is causing a specific user account to be constantly locked out.

Auditing Active Directory user-account lockout events

Scenario: A help desk ticket has been escalated to the engineering team. It states that a user has called the help desk three times in the past 10 minutes because their Active Directory user account is constantly being locked out. Each time the help desk staff unlocks the account, within a few minutes the account is locked out again, and the user is not attempting to log in when this happens.

In this scenario you'll use a PowerShell script to identify the computer or device that's locking out the user. The event ID for account lockouts is 4740. These events only occur on domain controllers for Active Directory user-account lockouts, but they could happen on any domain controller in the entire domain, so you'll need to query each one. The script needs to complete as quickly as possible while keeping the network bandwidth it uses to a minimum, and the majority of the work should be performed on the domain controllers where the lockouts occurred. This is a perfect situation for the `Invoke-Command` cmdlet, as PowerShell remoting is enabled on all of the domain controllers in this environment. By default, to use PowerShell remoting you must be an administrator on the remote machines you're targeting.

The script shown in listing 3 will retrieve only the Active Directory user lockout events that have occurred in the past two hours and for which the username is AFuller. PowerShell v2 and the remote server administration tools must be installed on the computer running the script. PowerShell v2 or higher must be installed and PowerShell remoting must be enabled on each of the domain controllers that the script is running against.

Listing 3 Auditing Active Directory user-account lockouts

```
Import-Module ActiveDirectory
Invoke-Command -ComputerName (
    Get-ADDomainController -Filter * |
     select -expand name
    ){
     Get-WinEvent -Logname security -FilterXPath "*[System[EventID=4740
       ➥ and TimeCreated[timediff(@SystemTime) <= 7200000]]
       ➥ and EventData[Data[@Name='TargetUserName']='afuller']]" |
      select TimeCreated,
             @{Label='User Name';Expression={$_.Properties[0].Value}},
             @{Label='Client Name';Expression={$_.Properties[1].Value}}
     }
```

A subset of the columns returned by this script is shown in the following results. `Invoke-Command` returns an additional property named `PSComputerName` that tells you what server each of the results are from:

```
TimeCreated             User Name     Client Name  PSComputerName
-----------             ---------     -----------  --------------
9/22/2012 9:57:51 PM    afuller       PC1          dc02
9/22/2012 9:57:51 PM    afuller       PC1          dc01
9/22/2012 9:49:07 PM    afuller       PC1          dc03
9/22/2012 9:49:07 PM    afuller       PC1          dc01
```

What if you have hundreds of domain controllers in your environment? Isn't there a more efficient way of finding the user-account lockout events without having to query every domain controller in the entire domain? If replication is working properly in your domain, all of the user-account lockout events for the entire domain will be replicated to the security event log of the domain controller that holds the Primary Domain Controller (PDC) emulator Flexible Single Master Operations (FSMO) role. You can make a slight modification to the script, replacing the `Get-ADDomainController` cmdlet with the `Get-ADDomain` cmdlet to determine which domain controller holds this role. This results in the script only querying that individual domain controller for the user-account lockout events. The modified script is shown in the following listing.

Listing 4 Auditing Active Directory user-account lockouts via the PDC emulator

```
Import-Module ActiveDirectory
Invoke-Command -ComputerName (
    Get-ADDomain |
     select -expand PDCEmulator
    ){
     Get-WinEvent -Logname security -FilterXPath "*[System[EventID=4740
       ➥ and TimeCreated[timediff(@SystemTime) <= 7200000]]
       ➥ and EventData[Data[@Name='TargetUserName']='afuller']]" |
      select TimeCreated,
             @{Label='User Name';Expression={$_.Properties[0].Value}},
             @{Label='Client Name';Expression={$_.Properties[1].Value}}
     }
```

As shown in the following results, this script has the same server name in the PSComputerName column for each of the results because you only queried the domain controller that holds the PDC emulator FSMO role:

```
TimeCreated            User Name    Client Name  PSComputerName
-----------            ---------    -----------  --------------
9/22/2012 9:57:51 PM   afuller      PC1          dc01
9/22/2012 9:49:07 PM   afuller      PC1          dc01
```

The name of the computer that's causing the user account to be locked out will be returned by either of these scripts in the Client Name column of the results. In this example the user account was being locked out by a computer named PC1. PC1 had stale credentials saved on it in the credential manager for AFuller's user account. Once those credentials are removed and the account is unlocked again, the problem will be resolved.

Summary

Several options are available to administrators when using PowerShell to query the event logs of their remote Windows-based servers. In this chapter you learned how to use the PowerShell cmdlets designed for querying the information contained in these logs, eliminating the tedious task of manually sifting through them for specific data. You also used PowerShell to automate the translation of cryptic numeric codes contained in the properties of specific events from the security event log into meaningful information, eliminating the time-consuming process of translating each code manually.

The concepts covered in this chapter can be applied to any of the event logs, not just the security event log. The PowerShell scripts I showed you are customizable for many different scenarios; you can schedule them to run automatically at predefined intervals, and the results can be logged to a file or a web page, or sent to an email address without any user intervention.

About the author

Mike F. Robbins is a senior systems engineer with almost 20 years of experience as an IT professional. He currently works for a healthcare company in Meridian, Mississippi. A PowerShell enthusiast, Mike uses PowerShell on a daily basis to administer Windows Server, Hyper-V, SQL Server, Exchange, SharePoint, Active Directory, Terminal Services, EqualLogic Storage Area Networks, and Backup Exec. He has written PowerShell guest blog articles for the *Hey, Scripting Guy!* blog and *PowerShell Magazine*. He's a Microsoft Certified IT Professional and three-time Microsoft Certified Systems Engineer (Windows NT 4.0, Windows 2000, and Windows Server 2003). Mike blogs at http://mikefrobbins.com and can be found on Twitter: @mikefrobbins.

7 Managing and administering a certification authority database with PowerShell

Vadims Podans

Since the introduction of Windows 2000 Server, the Windows operating system has provided a built-in component that allows companies to use public key infrastructure (PKI) features in their private networks—either Certificate Services or, starting with Windows Server 2008, Active Directory Certificate Services (AD CS).

Unlike with commercial certificate providers (like VeriSign/Symantec, DigiCert, and others), private AD CS allows unlimited certificate issuance at minimal cost. The high level of security provided by digital certificates, coupled with a low price and automatic certificate distribution (through automatic enrollment), has allowed network administrators to use certificates to secure many internal (and, in some cases, external) services and applications.

Although Windows provides some command-line tools, they aren't ready for PKI task automation. Only Windows PowerShell allows systems administrators to automate almost all PKI-related management tasks. In this chapter you'll learn about using PowerShell to automate the PKI tasks related to your certification authority database.

For convenience, I'll use the abbreviation AD CS to denote Active Directory Certificate Services as a technology, and the abbreviation CA to denote an instance of the certificate services—a certification authority.

Existing tools

Windows provides two built-in tools for accessing your CA database:

- The Certification Authority Microsoft Management Console (MMC) snap-in (certsrv.msc)
- The certutil.exe command-line tool

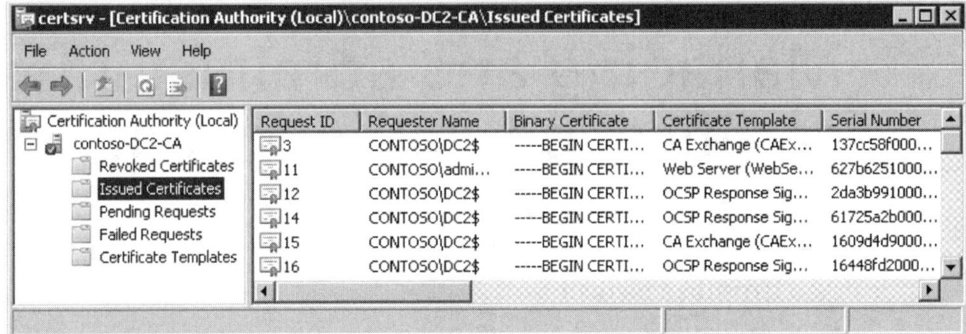

Figure 1 Certification Authority MMC snap-in

Figure 1 illustrates the Certification Authority MMC snap-in.

In figure 1 you see several folders in the left pane, and CA database contents—certificate-request rows and columns—in the right. The folders represent logical groups of certificate requests in the CA database by their statuses. Each column in the right pane contains detailed information about each request row. For example, you can see information about who requested the certificate and which certificate template was used.

Although this is a useful tool, you can't automate or script actions in the MMC. To provide automation features the certutil.exe tool was developed. Although certutil.exe can be scripted, the output is text-based, so it's difficult to do anything with it, and the output depends on various input factors, because the certutil.exe tool composes the output based on returned data and may not follow any text pattern for a certain command.

Windows Server 2012 and Windows 8 provide a set of cmdlets that you can use to automate a few PKI management tasks but don't provide built-in cmdlets for CA database management.

Querying the CA database

Fortunately, both of the aforementioned tools use publically available COM interfaces. Although COM interfaces are quite complex in managed programming languages (such as C# or VB.NET), a great COM provider in PowerShell makes life much easier.

NOTE If you plan to automate CA management tasks with PowerShell, be ready to dive into a COM world. There are no built-in .NET classes to manage CA servers. But don't worry, CryptoAPI COM interfaces are smart and powerful.

For the most part, you'll explicitly use two COM interfaces:

- `ICertView`—Intended to access and query the CA database. The `ProgId` for this interface is `CertificateAuthority.View`, and online documentation can be found at http://msdn.microsoft.com/library/aa385417.aspx.

- `ICertAdmin`—Intended to perform advanced CA database administration tasks. The `ProgId` for this interface is `CertificateAuthority.Admin`, and online documentation can be found at http://msdn.microsoft.com/library/aa383234.aspx.

WARNING These interfaces are not installed by default. In order to install them you have to install AD CS management tools. Use Server Manager (Windows Server 2008 and newer) or install AD CS Management components of the Remote Server Administration Tools (RSAT) on Windows Vista and newer client operating systems.

Before getting started I'd like to outline the basic steps required for accessing a CA database schema:

1. Open the connection to the CA database.
2. Specify the desired database table.
3. Open the schema view and iterate over each schema column in a loop.
4. Put some logic in the loop to fetch schema details.

Accessing the database

Now you're ready to establish a connection to your CA database. First, instantiate an `ICertView` object and review the exposed members:

```
PS C:\> $CaView = New-Object -ComObject CertificateAuthority.View
PS C:\> $CaView | Get-Member

   TypeName: System.__ComObject#{d594b282-8851-4b61-9c66-3edadf848863}

Name                  MemberType Definition
----                  ---------- ----------
EnumCertViewColumn    Method     IEnumCERTVIEWCOLUMN EnumCertViewColumn (...
GetColumnCount        Method     int GetColumnCount (int)
GetColumnIndex        Method     int GetColumnIndex (int, string)
OpenConnection        Method     void OpenConnection (string)
OpenView              Method     IEnumCERTVIEWROW OpenView ()
SetRestriction        Method     void SetRestriction (int, int, int, Vari...
SetResultColumn       Method     void SetResultColumn (int)
SetResultColumnCount  Method     void SetResultColumnCount (int)
SetTable              Method     void SetTable (int)
```

Next, open a connection. `ICertView` supports remote CA access, and you have to specify a CA configuration string in the `OpenConnection` method call.

What is a CA configuration string? It's a string that uniquely identifies the CA host name and CA certificate name, separated by a slash. For example, suppose you have a default AD CS installation on a computer called dc2.contoso.com, and the CA name is Contoso-dc2-CA. The resulting configuration string will be dc2.contoso.com\contoso-dc2-ca. For the CA host name you can use either a short (NetBIOS) name or a fully qualified domain name:

```
PS C:\> $CaView.OpenConnection("dc2\contoso-dc2-ca")
```

If the method succeeds, it doesn't return anything; if it fails, an error is thrown.

Getting the database schema

What's next? What can you query? At this point, nothing. You don't even know the CA database schema. The `ICertView` interface has the `SetTable` method, which tells you that there are multiple tables. All modern Windows CA versions define these four tables, shown here with their numerical values in parentheses:

- *Request* (0x0)—Stores all issued and revoked certificates, and failed and pending certificate requests. Usually you'll deal only with the Request table, as other tables aren't of interest to administrators.
- *Extension* (0x3000)—Stores extensions for each certificate.
- *Attribute* (0x4000)—Stores attributes passed along with the certificate request.
- *CRL* (0x5000)—Stores the certificate revocation list (CRL) information (along with CRLs themselves) for each CRL ever issued by the CA server.

Call the `SetTable` method to select the desired table:

```
PS C:\> $CaView.SetTable(0x0)
```

Now tell the CA server that you want to query the table schema. You can do this with the `EnumCertViewColumn` method call:

```
PS C:\> $Columns = $CaView.EnumCertViewColumn(0)
```

The `$Columns` variable will contain a column iterator. Now create a simple `While..Do` loop to iterate over the columns. In the loop you can extract the column information, such as column name, display name, max length for stored data, and data type for the column:

```
PS C:\> while ($Columns.Next() -ne -1) {
>>     New-Object psobject -Property @{
>>         Name = $Columns.GetName()
>>         DisplayName = $Columns.GetDisplayName()
>>         Type = switch ($Columns.GetType()) {
>>             1 {"Long"}
>>             2 {"DateTime"}
>>             3 {"Binary"}
>>             4 {"String"}
>>         }
>>         MaxLength = $Columns.GetMaxLength()
>>     }
>> }
>>

Name                        DisplayName                 Type     MaxLength
----                        -----------                 ----     ---------
Request.RequestID           Request ID                  Long             4
Request.RawRequest          Binary Request              Binary       65536
Request.RawArchivedKey      Archived Key                Binary       65536
Request.KeyRecoveryHashes   Key Recovery Agent Hashes   String        8192
Request.RawOldCertificate   Old Certificate             Binary       16384
Request.RequestAttributes   Request Attributes          String       32768
Request.RequestType         Request Type                Long             4
```

```
Request.RequestFlags         Request Flags                 Long          4
Request.StatusCode           Request Status Code           Long          4
Request.Disposition          Request Disposition           Long          4
Request.DispositionMessage Request Disposition Message String        8192
Request.SubmittedWhen        Request Submission Date       DateTime      8
Request.ResolvedWhen         Request Resolution Date       DateTime      8
Request.RevokedWhen          Revocation Date               DateTime      8
<...>
```

Call the `Next` method for each column and call the appropriate methods to get the relevant column properties.

NOTE Regarding the `Binary` data type, in unmanaged languages like C++ this means a pure byte array, but the interface doesn't support the classic byte array (also known as `safearray`); therefore, the best way to store binary data is to return the data as a base64 string and convert the string to a managed byte array.

The database schema differs slightly between versions, so it may be reasonable to query the database schema for your CA version to determine whether the particular column exists. To practice with the code you can manually query schema for other tables. The following listing contains our example wrapped to a simple function.

Listing 1 Get-CADataBaseSchema.ps1

```
function Get-CADataBaseSchema {
[CmdletBinding()]
  param(
    [Parameter(Mandatory = $true)]
    [string]$ConfigString,
    [ValidateSet('Request','Extension','Attribute','CRL')]
    [string]$Table = "Request"
 )
  $CaView = New-Object -ComObject CertificateAuthority.View
  $CaView.OpenConnection($ConfigString)
  switch ($Table) {
    "Request" {$CaView.SetTable(0x0)}
    "Extension" {$CaView.SetTable(0x3000)}
    "Attribute" {$CaView.SetTable(0x4000)}
    "CRL" {$CaView.SetTable(0x5000)}
  }
  $Columns = $CaView.EnumCertViewColumn(0)
  while ($Columns.Next() -ne -1) {
    New-Object psobject -Property @{
      Name = $Columns.GetName()
      DisplayName = $Columns.GetDisplayName()
      Type = switch ($Columns.GetType()) {
        1 {"Long"}
        2 {"DateTime"}
        3 {"Binary"}
        4 {"String"}
      }
```

```
            MaxLength = $Columns.GetMaxLength()
        }
    }
}
```

You must set the target table to query before you call the `EnumCertViewColumn` method. Otherwise you'll get an error message after iterating over the last column.

Querying the database

Once you get the CA database schema you can query the database for request rows and their details. To perform any query follow these steps:

1. Open a connection to the CA database.
2. Specify the desired database table to query.
3. Specify the query filters (if necessary).
4. Set the result column count.
5. Set the desired columns you want to return.
6. Open the database view and iterate over each returned row and column in a loop.

QUERY FILTERS

When you access the CA database it's impractical to dump the entire database for performance reasons, particularly when the data is transmitted over a network. Instead, I recommend filtering out unnecessary rows on the server side. PowerShell's built-in filtering cmdlet `Where-Object` performs filtering on the client side. The `ICertView` interface has built-in filtering capabilities via the `SetRestriction` method, and you should use them whenever possible. Let's recall the Certification Authority MMC snap-in, as shown in figure 2.

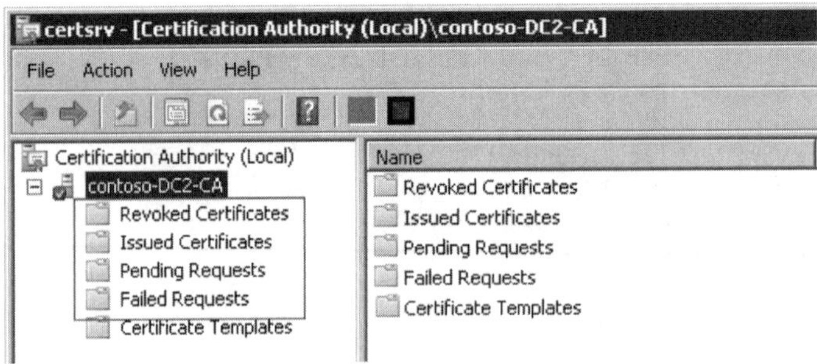

Figure 2 Database contents logically grouped in Certification Authority MMC snap-in

The Certification Authority MMC snap-in groups all request rows by their statuses in four logical groups: revoked, issued, pending, and failed. Most likely you'll want to do the same thing in PowerShell. First, let's look at the `SetRestriction` method description, which can be found on MSDN at http://msdn.microsoft.com/library/aa385439.aspx. Here's a brief summary of the method parameters:

- `ColumnIndex`—Specifies the column index. Alternatively you can use predefined tables. In real situations you'll most likely use filters based on a specific column or entire table with failed or pending requests.
- `SeekOperator`—Specifies the logical operator. The operators are almost identical to standard PowerShell logical operators, like `-eq`, `-le`, `-lt`, `-ge`, and `-gt`. The following numerical values are defined:
  - `CVR_SEEK_EQ` (0x1)—Can be used for all data types; the only operator supported for `String` and `Binary` data types.
  - `CVR_SEEK_LE` (0x2)—Can be used for `DateTime` and `Long` (or `integer`) data types.
  - `CVR_SEEK_LT` (0x4)—Can be used for `DateTime` and `Long` (or `integer`) data types.
  - `CVR_SEEK_GE` (0x8)—Can be used for `DateTime` and `Long` (or `integer`) data types.
  - `CVR_SEEK_GT` (0x10)—Can be used for `DateTime` and `Long` (or `integer`) data types.
- `SortOrder`—Specifies how to sort results. I can't think of any real situation in which you would need to sort the output in a special manner, so you can pass zero to this parameter.
- `pvarValue`—Specifies the data query qualifier.

The following snippet retrieves the column index for the RequestID column by using the `GetColumnIndex` method:

```
$ColumnIndex = $CaView.GetColumnIndex(0,"RequestID")
```

As the first parameter, specify the table you want to query and the column name (non-localized name). Now set the filter to restrict the output to a specific RequestID value:

```
$operator = @{"eq" = 1;"le" = 2; "lt" = 4; "ge" = 8; "gt" = 16}
$CaView.SetRestriction($ColumnIndex,$operator["eq"],0,100)
```

In this case the CA server returns only one row with RequestID = 100. Another example uses date/time filters:

```
$ColumnIndex = $CaView.GetColumnIndex(0,"NotAfter")
$CaView.SetRestriction($ColumnIndex,$operator["lt"],0,[datetime]::Now)
```

This example sets the filter to return request rows for expired certificates, where the NotAfter column value is less than the current date/time.

You can specify multiple filters, and the CA will restrict the output to rows that match the filters. One of the most popular ways to filter is by certificate-request status: revoked, issued, pending, or failed (as shown in figure 2). You can use the following predefined table to restrict output to pending requests:

```
$CaView.SetRestriction(-1,0,0,0)
```

And you can use the following predefined table to restrict output to failed requests:

```
$CaView.SetRestriction(-3,0,0,0)
```

No predefined tables exist for filtering rows to issued and revoked certificates. Instead you have to set a filter based on the Disposition column. Table 1 lists useful disposition codes.

Table 1 Request-row disposition codes

Disposition code	Disposition meaning
9	The request is pending for approval
15	CA certificate
16	CA certificate chain
20	Issued certificate
21	Revoked certificate
30	Request is failed
31	Request is denied

For a complete list of disposition values please refer to the CertSrv.h header file in the Windows Software Development Kit.

If you want to look only for revoked certificates set a restriction as follows:

```
$ColumnIndex = $CaView.GetColumnIndex(0,"Disposition")
$operator = @{"eq" = 1;"le" = 2; "lt" = 4; "ge" = 8; "gt" = 16}
$CaView.SetRestriction($ColumnIndex,$operator["eq"],0,21)
```

Here's another filter example for finding all issued certificates that will expire in one month:

```
$ColumnIndex = $CaView.GetColumnIndex(0,"Disposition")
$operator = @{"eq" = 1;"le" = 2; "lt" = 4; "ge" = 8; "gt" = 16}
$CaView.SetRestriction($ColumnIndex,$operator["eq"],0,20)
$ColumnIndex = $CaView.GetColumnIndex(0,"NotBefore")
$CaView.SetRestriction($ColumnIndex,$operator["gt"],0,[datetime]::Now)
$ColumnIndex = $CaView.GetColumnIndex(0,"NotAfter")
$CaView.SetRestriction($ColumnIndex,
➥ $operator["lt"],0,[datetime]::Now.AddMonths(1))
```

As shown, you can create various filters to make the query quicker and return only the data you need without having to filter the output by using external means.

SELECTING THE OUTPUT COLUMNS

The next step is to identify the output columns. `ICertView` has a predefined output-column view depending on the certificate-request status. You can use the following default column-view sets, shown here with their numerical values in parentheses:

- `CV_COLUMN_QUEUE_DEFAULT` (-1)—Contains the default column view for pending requests
- `CV_COLUMN_LOG_DEFAULT` (-2)—Contains the default column view for issued, failed, and revoked requests
- `CV_COLUMN_LOG_FAILED_DEFAULT` (-3)—Contains the default column view for failed or denied requests
- `CV_COLUMN_LOG_REVOKED_DEFAULT` (-7)—Contains the default column view for revoked certificates

Alternatively you can define your own column-view sets based on internal requirements. A custom output column assignment is performed in two steps:

1. Set the output column count by using the `SetResultColumnCount` method.
2. Specify the output columns by using the `SetResultColumn` method.

Suppose you want to display only basic information about all issued certificates. You're interested in the following columns: RequestID, Request.RequesterName, CommonName, NotBefore, NotAfter, and SerialNumber. You could use the following command sequence:

```
$OutColumns = "RequestID", "Request.RequesterName", "CommonName",
➥ "NotBefore", "NotAfter", "SerialNumber"
$CaView.SetResultColumnCount($OutColumns.Length)
$OutColumns | ForEach-Object {$CaView.SetResultColumn($_)}
```

The first line contains an array of columns to add, the second line sets the result column count, and the last line sets specific columns to add.

TIP Columns used to set query filters aren't required to appear in the output.

In certain cases you may want to get all columns for each output row (but use this option carefully, as it may consume a lot of local and network resources). Instead of specifying all columns explicitly you can simplify the code with the following trick. Get the overall column count by invoking the `GetColumnCount` method and set the columns as follows:

```
$ColumnCount = $CaView.GetColumnCount(0)
$CaView.SetResultColumnCount($ColumnCount)
0..($ColumnCount - 1) | ForEach-Object {$CaView.SetResultColumn($_)}
```

Get column count for default Request table (line 1)
Set column count to return (line 2)
Use `ForEach-Object` loop to add all columns (line 3)

Although you're free to select any columns you want to return I recommend always including the RequestID column in the output. This column's value is frequently used for other method calls.

PROCESSING THE OUTPUT

Once you've configured the filters and the output view you're ready to process the database results. First, call the `OpenView` method to inform the CA database that you're ready to receive data:

```
$Row = $CaView.OpenView()
```

The `$Row` variable holds the row iterator. The row iterator must be set in a `While..Do` loop as follows:

```
While ($Row.Next() -ne -1) {#loop body}
```

Once the method returns -1 you've reached the last row and must exit the loop. The following code fragment displays the row and column iteration loops:

```
while ($Row.Next() -ne -1) {                                  ❶ Start row iterator
  $cert = New-Object psobject -Property @{
    ConfigString = $ConfigString;                             Create custom psobject
  }                                                           to store current row
  $Column = $Row.EnumCertViewColumn()
  while ($Column.Next() -ne -1) {                             ❷ Start column iterator
    $current = $Column.GetName()
    $Cert | Add-Member -MemberType NoteProperty $($Column.GetName()) `
      -Value $($Column.GetValue(1)) -Force
    if ($Cert.CertificateTemplate -match "^(\d\.){3}") {     ❸ Add special handling for the CertificateTemplate column
      $cert.CertificateTemplate =
        ([Security.Cryptography.Oid]$Column.GetValue(1)).FriendlyName
    }
  }
  $Cert
}
```

The code represents a simple database iterator. By starting the first loop ❶ you create the row iterator. Inside this loop you create the row object and the inner column iterator. In the second loop ❷ you iterate over columns and fill the row object with column values. But the column called CertificateTemplate may return a template name (for version 1 templates) or a template-associated object identifier. As you are interested in only the template name, you add a special converter for the CertificateTemplate column ❸.

REUSING THE CODE

At first glance the code looks complex, but don't worry—you can write the code once and reuse it at any time without having to make modifications. You do this by creating a universal function called, say, `Get-RequestRow` with several parameters to perform various queries. Let's try to determine which parameters you can use.

As you already know, you have to specify the CA server you want to query. The CA server is identified by a CA configuration string; therefore, the first parameter would be something like `-ConfigString`. Because the CA configuration string is more than a computer name I recommend not using the common `-ComputerName` for this parameter to avoid parameter misuse.

Based on my experience and that of other PKI administrators, most likely you'll query certificate rows based on a particular certificate status or certificate-request status—issued, revoked, pending, or failed (to match the Certification Authority MMC snap-in view); therefore you should add a second parameter called `-Status`.

FILTERS

You'll use filters extensively to get output that's more relevant. Obviously, the parameter should be called `-Filter`. As the `ICertView.SetRestriction` method allows you to specify multiple filters per query, the parameter should accept an array of filters.

As you've learned, you can specify columns (properties) to return, and you specify the last parameter, `-Property`, which accepts an array of properties (column names) to return. The following code snippet displays parameter definitions:

```
param(
  [string]$ConfigString,
  [ValidateSet('Revoked','Issued','Pending','Failed')]
  [string]$Table,
  [String[]]$Filter,
  [String[]]$Property
)
```

The next step is to open a connection to a database:

```
$CaView = New-Object -ComObject CertificateAuthority.View
$CaView.OpenConnection($ConfigString)
```

Process the `-Status` parameter to set the initial filter:

```
$RColumn = $CaView.GetColumnIndex(0, "Disposition")
switch ($Status) {
  "Revoked" {$CaView.SetRestriction($RColumn,1,0,21)}
  "Issued" {$CaView.SetRestriction($RColumn,1,0,20)}
  "Pending" {$CaView.SetRestriction(-1,0,0,0)}
  "Failed" {$CaView.SetRestriction(-3,0,0,0)}
}
```

Retrieve Disposition column index for use in filters

Revoked certificates are identified by Disposition = 21

Issued certificates are identified by Disposition = 20

Default restriction tables for pending and failed requests

Now you have to process other user-defined filters. Most likely you've already noticed that the `ICertView` filter semantics are similar to the default PowerShell comparison-operator semantics. It would be convenient to use the following filter semantic: "ColumnName <operator> value". You'll use the default PowerShell operator names that match the filter operators: `-eq`, `-le`, `-lt`, `-ge`, and `-gt`. Although it looks trivial, a lot of work is involved in writing a proper and smart parameter handler. To write a good handler follow these steps:

1. Split each filter line into three tokens: column name, operator, and column value.
2. Because filters are passed in strings, convert string values to integers and date/time. Column values must be the exact type as identified in the database schema. For example, if you filter requests by the RequestID column the value must be converted to integers. If you filter requests by the NotAfter or NotBefore column the value must be converted to a `DateTime` object.

3 Perform additional transformations if necessary. For example, certificate templates internally aren't strings but object identifiers (OIDs), and OID values are stored in the CertificateTemplate column. It's tough to remember template OID values, so you should use the `Oid` class to convert template display names to `Oid` class and retrieve the OID value.

The following code snippet displays the `-Filter` parameter processor:

```
if ($Filter -ne $null) {
  foreach ($line in $Filter) {
    if ($line -match "^(.+)\s(-eq|-lt|-le|-ge|-gt)\s(.+)$") {
      try {$Rcolumn = $CaView.GetColumnIndex($false, $matches[1])}
      catch {Write-Warning "Specified column '$($matches[1])' does not
        ➥ exist."; return}
      $Seek = switch ($matches[2])
        "-eq" {1}
        "-lt" {2}
        "-le" {4}
        "-ge" {8}
        "-gt" {16}
      }
      $Value = $matches[3]
      if (($Value -as [int]) -is [int]) {$Value = $Value -as [int]}
      else {
        try {
          $dt = [DateTime]::ParseExact(
            $Value,
            "MM/dd/yyyy HH:mm:ss",
            [Globalization.CultureInfo]::InvariantCulture
          )
          if ($dt -ne $null) {$Value = $dt}
        } catch {}
      }
      if ($matches[1] -eq "CertificateTemplate") {
        if (([Security.Cryptography.Oid]$Value).FriendlyName) {
          $Value = ([Security.Cryptography.Oid]$Value).Value
        }
      }
      try {$CaView.SetRestriction($RColumn,$Seek,0,$Value)}
      catch {Write-Warning "Specified pattern '$line' is not valid!";
        ➥ return}
    } else {Write-Warning "Malformed pattern: '$line'.!"; return}
  }
}
```

Split each line to three tokens: column name, operator, column value

Retrieve Disposition column index

Convert textual operator to an `integer` value

❶ Try to cast value to integer

❷ Try to cast value to `DateTime`

❸ Try to cast value to object identifier

This code snippet shows all the steps defined earlier. You split the filter expression to tokens by using the `match` operator. Then you attempt to cast the filter qualifier value to `integer` ❶ and `DateTime` ❷. If the casting still fails the qualifier value is a simple string. You add an additional value converter ❸, as the CertificateTemplate column requires a template-associated object identifier, rather than a template common or display name.

Let me point out a trick used in the code:

```
$dt = [DateTime]::ParseExact(
  $Value,
  "MM/dd/yyyy HH:mm:ss",
  [Globalization.CultureInfo]::InvariantCulture
)
if ($dt -ne $null) {$Value = $dt}
```

Why use the `TryParse` static method in `DateTime` class to convert a date/time string to a `DateTime` object? Why not explicitly cast the string to a `DateTime` class? A while ago I faced an issue with such castings, because explicit casting doesn't always work, depending on regional settings. The answer came to me after I ran the following commands:

```
PS C:\> (Get-Date).ToString()
2012.08.25. 16:54:35
PS C:\> "$(Get-Date)"
08/25/2012 16:54:50
PS C:\>
```

You see that the `ToString` method on the `DateTime` object respects the regional settings, and after calling this method you can still explicitly cast a returned string to a `DateTime` object. But when you enclose a `DateTime` object in double quotes a returned string contains a culture-invariant date/time representation. This is what happens in our example when a `DateTime` object is enclosed in double quotes. Depending on the culture settings, a backward conversion (explicit casting) may not work. Because a culture-invariant date/time string has the same format on all systems regardless of culture settings it's best to use the `TryParse` method to convert a date/time string to a `DateTime` object.

Now process the `-Property` parameter in the manner described:

```
if ($Property -contains "*") {
  $ColumnCount = $CaView.GetColumnCount(0)
  $CaView.SetResultColumnCount($ColumnCount)
  0..($ColumnCount - 1) | ForEach-Object {$CaView.SetResultColumn($_)}
} else {
  $properties = switch ($Status) {
    "Revoked" {"RequestID", "Request.RevokedWhen", "Request.RevokedReason",
      ➥ "CommonName", "SerialNumber"}
    "Issued" {"RequestID", "Request.RequesterName","CommonName",
      ➥ "NotBefore", "NotAfter", "SerialNumber"}
    "Pending" {"RequestID", "Request.RequesterName",
      ➥ "Request.SubmittedWhen", "Request.CommonName", "CertificateTemplate"}
    "Failed" {"RequestID", "Request.StatusCode",
      ➥ "Request.DispositionMessage", "Request.SubmittedWhen",
      ➥ "Request.CommonName", "CertificateTemplate"}
  }
  $properties = $properties + $Property | Select-Object -Unique | Where-
    ➥ Object {$_}
  $CaView.SetResultColumnCount($properties.Count)
  $properties | ForEach-Object {$CaView.SetResultColumn(
    $CaView.GetColumnIndex(0, $_))
  }
}
```

The column views used in this code are based on my experience. If you feel you need a different default column view you can change it in the `switch` statement.

The last step is to open the view and enumerate the rows and columns, as already discussed in the "Processing the output" section:

```
$Row = $CaView.OpenView()
while ($Row.Next() -ne -1) {
  $cert = New-Object psobject -Property @{
    ConfigString = $ConfigString;
  }
  $Column = $Row.EnumCertViewColumn()
  while ($Column.Next() -ne -1) {
    $current = $Column.GetName()
    $Cert | Add-Member -MemberType NoteProperty $($Column.GetName()) -Value
      ➥ $($Column.GetValue(1)) -Force
    if ($Cert.CertificateTemplate -match "^(\d\.){3}") {
      $cert.CertificateTemplate =
        ➥ ([Security.Cryptography.Oid]$Column.GetValue(1)).FriendlyName
    }
  }
  $Cert
}
Remove-Variable Row, Column, CaView -ErrorAction SilentlyContinue
[GC]::Collect()
```

The complete function code can be found in the code download available with this book.

FUNCTION USAGE

Let's look at a few examples of how to use your function. Suppose you want to get certificates based on a specified certificate template that will expire in the next two months:

```
PS C:\> Get-RequestRow -ConfigString "dc2\contoso-dc2-ca" -Status "Issued"
  ➥ -Filter "CertificateTemplate -eq WebServer", "NotAfter -gt $(Get-
  ➥ Date)", "NotAfter -lt $((Get-Date).AddMonths(2))"

ConfigString          : dc2\contoso-dc2-ca
RequestID             : 1460
Request.RequesterName : CONTOSO\WEB$
CommonName            : www.contoso.com
NotBefore             : 2011.08.28. 16:05:26
NotAfter              : 2012.08.27. 16:05:26
SerialNumber          : 659bb31735250f080002000005b4

ConfigString          : dc2\contoso-dc2-ca
RequestID             : 1465
Request.RequesterName : CONTOSO\WEB$
CommonName            : ev2.contoso.com
NotBefore             : 2011.09.03. 17:57:44
NotAfter              : 2012.09.02. 17:57:44
SerialNumber          : 659bb31735250f080002000005b9
```

The function returned two objects, meaning that two Secure Sockets Layer (SSL) certificates are about to expire. You can use this information to notify the web server administrators about these certificates so they can take appropriate steps to renew them in a timely fashion.

As a second example, suppose a user named Mike Smith leaves the company and you need to determine which certificates were issued to him and revoke them to prevent certificate usage. The best way is to filter by the UPN (user principal name) column:

```
Get-RequestRow -ConfigString "dc2\contoso-dc2-ca" -Status "Issued" -Filter
➥ "UPN -eq msmith@contoso.com", "NotAfter -gt $(Get-Date)"
```

This sets two filters: one by UPN value, and one that instructs the CA to return rows only for nonexpired certificates (where the NotAfter column value is set to a future time). You can use the returned information to identify which certificates should be revoked.

You can export returned objects to a CSV, XML, or other type of file for analytical, accounting, and other purposes. As this code doesn't change in the database you can spend time constructing various filters based on your needs.

Advanced administration of the CA database

With PowerShell you can do even more with a CA database. You've learned how to query a CA database and now you can dramatically extend your experience by using PowerShell to do certain CA administrative tasks. I'll cover the following administrative tasks in this section:

- Certificate revocation
- Certificate request approval or denial
- Request row deletion (database cleanup)

Before getting started let's look at what APIs are required.

Required APIs

In the examples to come you'll use the `Get-RequestRow` function (wherever possible) and the `ICertAdmin` COM interface. The following shows how to instantiate the `ICertAdmin` interface and displays the exposed members:

```
PS C:\> $CertAdmin = New-Object -ComObject CertificateAuthority.Admin
PS C:\> $CertAdmin | Get-Member

   TypeName: System.__ComObject#{f7c3ac41-b8ce-4fb4-aa58-3d1dc0e36b39}

Name                     MemberType Definition
----                     ---------- ----------
DeleteRow                Method     int DeleteRow (string, int, Date, in...
DenyRequest              Method     void DenyRequest (string, int)
GetArchivedKey           Method     string GetArchivedKey (string, int, ...
GetCAProperty            Method     Variant GetCAProperty (string, int, ...
GetCAPropertyDisplayName Method     string GetCAPropertyDisplayName (str...
GetCAPropertyFlags       Method     int GetCAPropertyFlags (string, int)
GetConfigEntry           Method     Variant GetConfigEntry (string, stri...
GetCRL                   Method     string GetCRL (string, int)
GetMyRoles               Method     int GetMyRoles (string)
GetRevocationReason      Method     int GetRevocationReason ()
```

```
ImportCertificate         Method     int ImportCertificate (string, strin...
ImportKey                 Method     void ImportKey (string, int, string,...
IsValidCertificate        Method     int IsValidCertificate (string, string)
PublishCRL                Method     void PublishCRL (string, Date)
PublishCRLs               Method     void PublishCRLs (string, Date, int)
ResubmitRequest           Method     int ResubmitRequest (string, int)
RevokeCertificate         Method     void RevokeCertificate (string, stri...
SetCAProperty             Method     void SetCAProperty (string, int, int...
SetCertificateExtension   Method     void SetCertificateExtension (string...
SetConfigEntry            Method     void SetConfigEntry (string, string,...
SetRequestAttributes      Method     void SetRequestAttributes (string, i...

PS C:\>
```

In this console output you see that the `ICertAdmin` interface implements many powerful methods that allow you to manage various aspects in CA management. In the next sections I'll discuss several useful scenarios and PowerShell techniques.

Certificate revocation

Frequently an issued certificate must be explicitly revoked before it expires, such as when a user leaves the company, changes positions, and so forth. In addition, special cases arise, as when a notebook is stolen or a smart card is lost. Certificate revocation rules must be written in a certificate practice statement (CPS) or in the company's security policy.

To revoke a certificate use the `RevokeCertificate` method in the `ICertAdmin` interface. The method description can be found at http://msdn.microsoft.com/library/aa383251.aspx. As per this documentation the method accepts four arguments:

- The CA configuration string
- The certificate serial number to revoke
- The revocation reason (enumerated)
- The effective revocation date and time (optional)

Two special notes: first, the certificate serial number must be an even-length hex string. How do you determine whether the string contains an even number of characters? Divide the string length by two with remainder, and if the division operation returns 1 you must prepend the serial number with an extra zero character:

```
if ($string.Length % 2) {$string = "0" + $string}
```

If the string contains an even number of characters the expression in the `IF` statement returns zero, zero is evaluated as False, and the `THEN` clause won't be executed.

Second, the `Date` argument expects Coordinated Universal Time (UTC), also known as Greenwich Mean Time (GMT). It's a common mistake for a caller to pass a `DateTime` object with desired date/time. Instead, invoke the `ToUniversalTime` method on the `DateTime` object and pass the resulting value.

Now let's create a sample function for revoking a certificate. The function will accept three parameters:

- `Request`—Specifies the request object. This object can be retrieved by running the `Get-RequestRow` function. You can directly pipe objects from the `Get-RequestRow` function.
- `Reason`—An enumeration that contains the possible revocation reasons. `Unspecified` is used by default.
- `RevocationDate`—Specifies the date and time at which the certificate is supposed to be revoked. The current date and time is used by default.

The function is shown in the following listing.

Listing 2 Revoke-Certificate.ps1

```
function Revoke-Certificate {
[CmdletBinding()]
  param(
    [Parameter(
      Mandatory = $true,
      ValueFromPipeline = $true,
      ValueFromPipelineByPropertyName = $true
    )]
    [Object]$Request,
    [ValidateSet(
      "Unspecified","KeyCompromise","CACompromise","AffiliationChanged",
      "Superseded","CeaseOfOperation","Hold","Unrevoke"
    )]
    [string]$Reason = "Unspecified",
    [datetime]$RevocationDate = [datetime]::Now
  )
  process {
    $CertAdmin = New-Object -ComObject CertificateAuthority.Admin
    $Reasons = @{
      "Unspecified" = 0;
      "KeyCompromise" = 1;
      "CACompromise" = 2;
      "AffiliationChanged" = 3;
      "Superseded" = 4;
      "CeaseOfOperation" = 5;
      "Hold" = 6;
      "ReleaseFromCRL" = 8;
      "Unrevoke" = [int]::MaxValue
    }
    if ($Request.SerialNumber.Length % 2) {
      $Request.Serialnumber = "0" + $Request.Serialnumber
    }
    try {
      $CertAdmin.RevokeCertificate(
        $Request.ConfigString,
        $Request.SerialNumber,
        $Reasons[$Reason],
        $RevocationDate.ToUniversalTime()
      )
      Write-Host "SerialNumber = $($Request.SerialNumber) is revoked
        ➥ ($Reason)."
```

❶ `ICertAdmin` instantiation must be placed in a `Process` clause

Revocation reason enumeration

Serial number must be an even-length string

Passed date/time is converted to UTC time

```
      # throw error if fails
      } catch {Write-Error $_}
    }
  }
```

Take note of two important points: first, the ICertAdmin object instantiation must be placed in a Process block ❶ (instead of a Begin block). This is because the ICert-Admin methods cache the ConfigString argument parameter and don't clear it when the configuration string is changed. Therefore, if you change the configuration string without instantiating a new interface object the method will contact the previous CA server. Second, look at the RevokeCertificate method call and the last parameter (highlighted in bold):

```
$CertAdmin.RevokeCertificate(
    $Request.ConfigString,
    $Request.SerialNumber,
    $Reasons[$Reason],
    $RevocationDate.ToUniversalTime()
)
```

The method expects UTC, not local time. You have to call the ToUniversalTime method on the DateTime object to convert local time to UTC.

The usage is simple. Suppose you want to decommission a website (in this example, www2.contoso.com) that used SSL to secure data transmission. The following one-liner could be used:

```
Get-RequestRow -ConfigString "dc2\contoso-dc2-ca" -Status "Issued" -Filter
  ➥ "NotAfter -gt $(Get-Date)","CommonName -eq www2.contoso.com" | Revoke-
  ➥ Certificate -Reason "CeaseOfOperation"
```

The command retrieves all active (nonexpired) certificates issued to www2.contoso.com and passes the returned objects to the Revoke-Certificate function.

You already saw an example of retrieving all active certificates issued to a user (Mike Smith) who left his company. Now pipe the results to the Revoke-Certificate function and specify the suitable revocation reason (say, CeaseOfOperation):

```
Get-RequestRow -ConfigString "dc2\contoso-dc2-ca" -Status "Issued" -Filter
  ➥ "UPN -eq msmith@contoso.com", "NotAfter -gt $(Get-Date)" | Revoke-
  ➥ Certificate -Reason "CeaseOfOperation"
```

Be careful with this method, because once a certificate is revoked this operation can't be undone.

Certificate request approval and denial

By default Enterprise CA automatically issues certificates once they're requested. This behavior allows for the automatic distribution of certificates to a large number of clients. But sometimes approval from the previous CA manager (or CA administrator) is required. For example, smart-card and code-signing certificates shouldn't be automatically issued. An enrollment agent or CA manager must process them manually. Another example is when a certificate template constructs a certificate subject from an incoming request. The CA manager must verify whether the requester has permission to enroll certificates for a specified name or verify other certificate-request properties and manually issue or deny the request.

If the certificate template is configured to pend all requests, then all requests are placed in the Pending Requests folder (see figure 1). A certificate request review is an out-of-band process and you don't need to be concerned with it here. In order to issue a pending request you can use the `ResubmitRequest` method. (Information on this method can be found in the MSDN library at http://msdn.microsoft.com/library/aa383250.aspx.) The method accepts two arguments: the CA configuration string and the request ID, which is stored in the RequestID column. The function in the following listing approves (issues) a specified pending request and accepts only a single argument, `-Request`, which identifies the request to approve.

Listing 3 Approve-CertificateRequest.ps1

```
function Approve-CertificateRequest {
[CmdletBinding()]
  param(
    [Parameter(
      Mandatory = $true,
      ValueFromPipeline = $true,
      ValueFromPipelineByPropertyName = $true
    )]
    [Object]$Request
  )
  process {
    $CertAdmin = New-Object -ComObject CertificateAuthority.Admin
    try {
      $DM = $CertAdmin.ResubmitRequest(
        $Request.ConfigString,$Request.RequestID
      )
      switch ($DM) {
        0 {Write-Warning "The request '$($Request.RequestID)' was not
          ➥ completed."}
        1 {Write-Warning "The request '$($Request.RequestID)' failed.'"}
        2 {Write-Warning "The request '$($Request.RequestID)' was denied."}
        3 {Write-Host "The certificate '$($Request.RequestID)' was
          ➥ issued.'" -ForegroundColor Green}
        4 {Write-Warning "The certificate '$($Request.RequestID)' was
          ➥ issued separately."}
        5 {Write-Warning "The request '$($Request.RequestID)' was taken
          ➥ under submission."}
        default {
          $hresult = "0x" + $("{0:X2}" -f $DM)
          Write-Warning "The request with ID = '$($Request.RequestID)' was
            ➥ failed due to the error: $hresult"
        }
      }
    } catch {Write-Warning "Unable to issue request with ID =
      ➥ '$($Request.RequestID)'"; $_}
  }
}
```

And the following example approves the certificate request with ID = 100, which is in a pending state:

```
Get-RequestRow -ConfigString "dc2\contoso-dc2-ca" -Status "Pending" -Filter
  ➥ "RequestID -eq 100" | Approve-CertificateRequest
```

NOTE You can't approve a request that's already been issued.

What if a CA manager decides to reject (deny) a certificate request? The function in the following listing denies a specified pending request and accepts only a single argument, `-Request`, which identifies the request to deny.

Listing 4 Deny-CertificateRequest.ps1

```
function Deny-CertificateRequest {
[CmdletBinding()]
  param(
    [Parameter(
      Mandatory = $true,
      ValueFromPipeline = $true,
      ValueFromPipelineByPropertyName = $true
    )]
    [Object]$Request
  )
  process {
    $CertAdmin = New-Object -ComObject CertificateAuthority.Admin
    try {
      $hresult = $CertAdmin.DenyRequest(
        $Request.ConfigString,$Request.RequestID
      )
    } catch {throw $_}
    if ($hresult -eq 0) {
      Write-Host "Successfully denied request with ID =
        ➥ $($Request.RequestID)"
    } else {
      Write-Warning "The request's with ID = $($Request.RequestID) current
        ➥ status does not allow this operation."
    }
  }
}
```

A similar syntax to that for the `Approve-CertificateRequest` function could be used:

```
Get-RequestRow -ConfigString "dc2\contoso-dc2-ca" -Status "Pending" `
  ➥ -Filter "RequestID -eq 100" | Deny-CertificateRequest
```

NOTE You can't deny a request that has already been issued or denied.

CA database cleanup

Normally CAs last many years and the CA database stores all the requests that were submitted from the time the CA server was installed. Over time the CA database can grow to be quite large. Large databases cause big delays when the CA service (certsvc) starts. If you think your CA database is too large you can delete request rows that are no longer needed. This is an important process and you must plan your database cleanup carefully. In short, you can remove all failed and pending requests and remove issued requests that have expired. For more information I recommend the following article written by the Ask the Directory Services Team: http://mng.bz/JB7j.

Once you have a plan to clean up your CA database you can take a look at the `DeleteRow` method. (Information on this method can be found in the MSDN library at http://msdn.microsoft.com/library/aa383235.aspx). Although the method accepts five parameters you can use it in a more granular way, using only the following two arguments to provide better support for your `Get-RequestRow` function:

- `Request`—Specifies the request-row object to delete. This object can be retrieved by running the `Get-RequestRow` function. You can directly pipe objects from the `Get-RequestRow` function.
- `Force`—Suppresses all removal-confirmation prompts.

The following listing removes a specified request row from the CA database.

Listing 5 `Remove-RequestRow.ps1`

```
function Remove-RequestRow {
[CmdletBinding(
  ConfirmImpact = 'High',
  SupportsShouldProcess = $true
)]
  param(
    [Parameter(
      Mandatory = $true,
      ValueFromPipeline = $true,
      ValueFromPipelineByPropertyName = $true
    )]
    [Object]$Request,
    [switch]$Force
  )
  process {
        $CertAdmin = New-Object -ComObject CertificateAuthority.Admin
        if ($Force -or $PSCmdlet.ShouldProcess(
        $Request.ConfigString,
        "Remove request row with ID = '$($Request.RequestID)'"
      )
    ) {$Return = $CertAdmin.DeleteRow(
         $Request.ConfigString,0,0,0,$Request.RequestID
       )}
    if ($Return -eq 1) {
      Write-Host "Deleted request row with ID = $($Request.RequestID)."
    } else {
      Write-Warning "Request row with ID = $($Request.RequestID) does not
      ➥ exist."
    }
  }
}
```

A destructive method; you must confirm your action.

Here's how you use the function to remove all failed requests:

```
Get-RequestRow -ConfigString "dc2\contoso-dc2-ca" -Status "Failed" |
➥ Remove-CertificateRequest
```

This function uses advanced parameters in the `CmdletBinding` attribute. This means that the function will prompt users to confirm their actions. You can suppress confirmation prompts by adding the `-Force` switch parameter. Everything is quite straightforward and self-explanatory. In the method call you specify only the CA configuration string and ID of the row you want to remove. All other parameters will be set to zero.

Summary

In this chapter you learned several great lessons about CA database management in PowerShell. Even though you can now do more now than you could before, you learned only a little of the functionality exposed by CryptoAPI COM interfaces. With COM you can automate almost all aspects of CA management. You can find a PowerShell PKI module on CodePlex (http://pspki.codeplex.com) that uses the described techniques to access and automate your CA database management tasks. With your new knowledge you can extend the code and/or modify it to fit your administration requirements. By adding the powerful PowerShell engine you can dramatically increase your productivity and save time and money on administrative-task automation. Stay connected with Windows PowerShell!

About the author

Vadims Podans is an independent security and automation consultant with four years of experience in PKI and administrative-task automation with Windows PowerShell. He has a blog where he writes about advanced topics in PowerShell and cryptography, located at http://en-us.sysadmins.lv.

8 Using PowerShell to reduce Active Directory token bloat

Ashley McGlone

As a Microsoft Premier Field Engineer I work with companies of all sizes to get their Active Directory environment healthy. One of the most common issues I find is called *token bloat.* When users become members of too many groups, their access token grows so large that it no longer fits inside some of the default OS settings. Users can experience issues logging in, applying group policies, and authenticating to web servers.

Token size issues are usually due to a combination of three scenarios:

- Leftover security identifier (SID) history from Active Directory migrations
- Heavy group nesting
- Stale group memberships

This chapter will address the SID history scenario, because in my field experience it seems to be the most common. Many scripts are available online to help with group cleanup, but little has been published on automating SID history removal.

The scripts provided in this chapter will do the following:

- Document the extent of SID history in the environment
- Create a SID mapping file for use with the Active Directory Migration Tool (ADMT)

Armed with these two key pieces of information you can move forward with SID history remediation. Once remediation is complete end-user support should notice a decline in the aforementioned troubleshooting mysteries associated with token bloat.

SIDs 101

Here are the key facts about SIDs and how they're used:

- Every domain has a SID that originates from the Security Accounts Manager (SAM) database of the first domain controller (DC) promoted in that domain.

- Every *security principal* in the domain has its own SID (users, computers, groups, and others). The SID of each security principal is composed of the domain SID and a *relative identifier* (RID).
- RIDs are handed out by the domain's *RID Master Flexible Single Master Operations* (FSMO). Domain controllers have a pool of RIDs that they pull from any time they create a security principal. By default, domain controllers keep a pool of 500 RIDs, refreshed by requests to the RID Master.
- *Access control lists* (ACLs) store SIDs in *access control entries* (ACEs) to identify the user, computer, or group receiving permissions to a resource.
- During domain migrations the new domain account gets a SID in the new domain. Then the old domain account SID can be appended as an alias that gives this new account identical access to the old domain. This is called *SID history*. Domain migrations can be implemented without SID history, but most people choose this option.
- SID history is intended as a temporary bridge for access during a domain migration project, but too often the project wraps up without removing it. The accumulation of SID history in the forest can lead to *token bloat*. For companies that do frequent mergers and acquisitions this piles up quickly.

NOTE For more information on the SID data structure see the Windows Data Type open specifications at http://msdn.microsoft.com/en-us/library/gg465313.aspx.

NOTE For more information on calculating token size, see KB 327825 at http://support.microsoft.com/kb/327825.

Where does the SID history come from?

Consider this scenario. You're doing an Active Directory migration with the ADMT or a similar product. You migrate the users and groups with the SID history option. The project schedule falls behind. You take a shortcut with the member servers. Instead of using the ADMT security translation process you rejoin the servers to the new domain, leaving all of the old ACLs and SIDs untouched. You leave the SID history in place and move on to the next big project and deadline. Everything seems to work fine.

Management is happy that you met the deadline, but little do they know that you created a hidden issue with the potential for generating many help desk calls.

This scenario is common and presents the following risks:

- Down the road you're likely to encounter token bloat because now most users and groups have at least two SIDs. This effectively doubles a user's group memberships.
- If you decide to clean up the SID history in the future you have the potential of orphaning users from their data because the old SIDs were still giving them access.
- When the ADMT server is decommissioned you'll lose all of the SID migration data needed to clean the ACL SID history on your migrated resource servers.

Many companies that I work with find themselves in this place. Users are calling the help desk with mysterious symptoms when trying to log on or access secure web servers (like SharePoint). They aren't sure what's causing the problem. Often it's token bloat and the SID history is a significant component. At this point you might purge the SID history, but then you could lose access to all of the migrated data with old SIDs in the ACLs. The best way forward is to go back and finish the Active Directory migration by doing security translation on all of the migrated servers.

NOTE To better understand the domain migration process, SID history, and SID mapping files, download the ADMT guide at www.microsoft.com/en-us/download/details.aspx?id=19188.

The solution

In order to right these wrongs from previous migrations you need a combination of PowerShell scripting and the ADMT. The following steps will rid your environment of SID history:

1. Identify all servers in the environment that were involved in the Active Directory migration(s). Hopefully you have a share with the project documentation or you can interview staff who participated in the original project. Otherwise, you can scan servers for SID history using the `Convert-SIDHistoryNTFS` function provided in the `SIDHistory` module referenced in the "Summary" section at the end of this chapter.
2. Install the latest version of the ADMT on a member server in your domain (not a DC).
3. Run the PowerShell script from this chapter (listing 1) to create a SID mapping file.
4. Run the ADMT security translation wizard against each of the old servers and use the SID mapping file when prompted to retrieve objects for security translation. View the ADMT log files to see where changes were made. The wizard will translate SIDs in the following locations:
   - Files and Folders
   - Local Groups
   - Printers
   - Registry
   - Shares
   - User Profiles
   - User Rights
5. In phases, purge SID history from users and groups, starting with a small test population and then going by department until it's entirely removed from the environment. Rerun the script provided later in this chapter (listing 1) to see where SID history remains.

WARNING *Do not purge all SID history at once.* That could be a resume-generating event if you missed some resources in the re-migration. Do it in smaller batches to be safe.

NOTE To remove SID history easily with PowerShell use the `Remove-SIDHistory` function provided in the `SIDHistory` module referenced in the "Summary" section at the end of this chapter.

NOTE Be aware that there are other places where the ADMT process doesn't translate SID history, including DCOM permissions, scheduled tasks, IIS, Exchange, and SharePoint. The PowerShell module referenced in the "Summary" section includes a function called `Convert-SIDHistoryNTFS` that will assist with translating NTFS permissions on network-attached storage (NAS) file resources.

Because the ADMT database is long gone you have to rebuild the SID mapping between old and new SIDs. Luckily for you this data is all present in Active Directory because you told the ADMT to store it in the `sidHistory` attribute. You need to put it into a file that the ADMT wants, called the SID mapping file. This file format is a CSV file where the first column contains the old SID and the second column contains either the new SID or the new user name in DOMAIN\USERNAME format. The script in this chapter (listing 1) will do this for you. This script is entirely safe for your environment because it makes no changes and only reads data.

In addition to the mapping file the script will also generate a CSV report of all SID history in your domain. It includes the following columns: `samAccountName`, `DisplayName`, `objectClass`, `OldSID`, `NewSID`, and `DistinguishedName`. Use this report before the cleanup to assess the scope of the issue. Run it again after the cleanup to make sure you got it all.

TIP Another handy way to view SID history for a specific user is with the NTDSUTIL command-line tool. You can use the command `group membership evaluation` to view all of a user's groups and it will tell you which ones come from SID history. This is another process to spot-check SID history before and after the cleanup.

The script

Now let's look at the code to inventory SID history and create the ADMT mapping file. The heart of this script is five lines that are wrapped in the following listing.

Listing 1 SID history reports

```
Import-Module ActiveDirectory

$ADQuery = Get-ADObject -LDAPFilter "(sIDHistory=*)" `
    -Property objectClass, samAccountName, DisplayName, `
    objectSid, sIDHistory, distinguishedname |
    Select-Object * -ExpandProperty sIDHistory
```

1 Import Active Directory module

2 Query all objects with SID history

```
$ADQuery |
    Select-Object objectClass, `
    @{name="OldSID";expression={$_.Value}}, `
    @{name="NewSID";expression={$_.objectSID}}, `
    samAccountName, DisplayName, DistinguishedName, `
    @{name="DateTimeStamp";expression={Get-Date -Format g}} |
    Export-CSV SIDReport.csv -NoTypeInformation
```

❸ Export results as CSV report

```
$ADQuery |
    Select-Object @{name="OldSID";expression={$_.Value}}, `
    @{name="NewSID";expression={$_.objectSID}} |
    Export-CSV SIDMap0.csv -NoTypeInformation
```

❹ Export results as ADMT mapping file

```
Get-Content .\SIDMap0.csv |
    ForEach-Object {$_.Replace("`"","")} |
    Set-Content .\SIDMap.csv
```

❺ Clean quotes out of mapping file

```
Remove-Item .\SIDMap0.csv

"Output complete:"
"SIDReport.csv  - full SID History report for reference in Excel"
"SIDMap.csv     - file for use with ADMT to do security translation"
```

The Active Directory module for PowerShell is automatically available on any DC that's Windows Server 2008 R2 or above. You can also install it from the Remote Server Administration Tools (RSAT) for Windows 7 or above. After importing the module ❶ you're able to use a number of handy cmdlets, many of which begin with `Get-AD*`.

Because you're going to format the output into two separate files you'll do the Active Directory query ❷ only once and capture it into the variable `$ADQuery`. This is obviously more efficient than doing the query twice and piping it out twice. Using the LDAP filter `"(sidHistory=*)"` will return all Active Directory objects that have a value for SID history.

The trick to the query is that SID history is a *multivalue* attribute. It's possible that a security principal has been migrated more than once creating multiple SID history values. The following syntax will *not* work:

```
Get-ADObject -LDAPFilter "(sidHistory=*)" -Property sidHistory |
  ➥ Export-CSV SIDHistory.csv
```

This will get you a list of the objects, but the SID history column on every row will say "Microsoft.ActiveDirectory.Management.ADPropertyValueCollection". To see the data you must use the `ExpandProperty` switch on the `Select-Object` cmdlet. When you display a list of object properties at the PowerShell console sometimes one of those properties may be what we call *multivalued*. That means the property contains multiple entries in an array or object collection. In Active Directory several user attributes are multivalues (including `postalAddress`, `sIDHistory`, `description`, and `userCertificate`). By expanding these properties in your query you can get one row for each SID history value that's present, making the result set friendlier for exporting and reporting. This report treats the multivalue attributes as separate rows so that you get a one-to-one list of `OldSID`/`NewSID` entries. The working syntax looks similar to this:

```
Get-ADObject -LDAPFilter "(sidHistory=*)" -Property sidHistory |
➥ Select-Object * -ExpandProperty sidHistory |
➥ Export-CSV SIDHistory.csv
```

Finally, the script exports the SID mapping data into two separate CSV files for convenience: ❸ a detailed report for viewing in Excel and ❹ an ADMT SID mapping file. For the ADMT mapping file you have to remove the quotes ❺ from the CSV file, because the ADMT doesn't like those in the input file.

This code appears in the `SIDHistory` module as the function `Export-SIDMapping` and creates two CSV files: SIDMap.csv and SIDReport.csv.

Listing domain SIDs and trusts

When you view the SID history output the SIDs look like a bunch of random numbers, but they're not random at all. Remember how earlier you learned that the first portion of a SID identifies the domain where the object was created? In order to make sense of this SID history data you need to label the accounts with the name of the source domain from whence they came.

First you need a legend that maps SID history domains to their names. The domain SID is stored on the root of the domain partition. You can get this easily enough for the present domains in the forest, and you'll look at that code in a minute. But what about the old domains? If your environment is like many of those I encounter in my line of work you may have stale trusts scattered across the forest, remnants of past migrations never cleaned up afterward. These trusts are the clues you need to understand the past.

Luckily for you each trust is stored in the domain partition of the Active Directory database as a `trustedDomain` object. One of the attributes on this object is the domain SID of the trusted domain. Now you can see that all you need is a well-crafted Active Directory query to retrieve these domain SIDs and build your list.

On the flip side it's possible that the trusts are long gone, and you won't be able to identify every domain in your past. I've met a couple of administrators who maintain a list of all former trusted domain SIDs for such occasions. It's a good idea; otherwise you won't know the names of some old domains.

The challenge

Exactly how many domain SIDs do you need to find? Consider each of these scenarios:

- You need to identify every domain in the forest.
- Each one of these forest domains could have external trusts. You need to enumerate those external, nontransitive trusts for each of the forest domains.
- The forest root domain could have a transitive forest trust. In this case you need to enumerate not only the remote member of the trust, but also any child domains that may exist in the remote trusted forest. This is one of the most challenging situations and requires adequate permissions in the remote forest domains.

- Those remote transitively trusted domains in other forests may have external trusts as well, but "a trust of a trust of a trust" is too many hops for you to make. Permissions and the lack of transitivity prevent you from getting there. In this case you can rerun the PowerShell code again in the remote trusted domains and manually merge the output into a single list.

PowerShell options

PowerShell has a number of ways to get domain SIDs and trusted domain SIDs. Each of these has their own strengths and weaknesses. I have listed them in order of my personal preference:

1. The Active Directory module cmdlets
2. Windows Management Instrumentation (WMI)
3. The NLTEST command-line tool
4. Active Directory Service Interfaces (ADSI)
5. .NET code in PowerShell

Active Directory cmdlets

This method is appropriate for environments where you have at least one DC that's Windows Server 2008 R2 or newer in each forest domain (or you have the Active Directory Web Service running on a legacy DC; see http://aka.ms/ADPS2003). Here are the steps to collect the data using these cmdlets:

1. Get a list of domains in the forest:

   ```
   (Get-ADForest).Domains
   ```

2. Get the SID of the domain:

   ```
   (Get-ADDomain).DomainSID
   ```

3. List the name and SID of all trusted domains that aren't forest members (filtering on `trustAttributes` where the bit `TRUST_ATTRIBUTE_WITHIN_FOREST` is not set):

   ```
   Get-ADObject -SearchBase "CN=System,DC=Contoso,DC=com" `
     -SearchScope OneLevel `
     -LDAPFilter "(&(objectClass=trustedDomain)(!trustAttributes=32))" `
     -Property name, securityIdentifier
   ```

The downside here is that Active Directory queries across domains usually complain about permissions. You could prompt for credentials but that could require unique credentials for every domain. You'll use the WMI method to avoid this scenario.

NOTE This PowerShell solution was developed using the cmdlets available in PowerShell v2 and the Windows Server 2008 R2 Active Directory module. Since then the Windows Server 2012 Active Directory module has been upgraded to include the new cmdlet `Get-ADTrust`, which would satisfy the needs of this script. But in order to maintain compatibility in legacy environments that new functionality hasn't been used.

WMI

This method is handy when you have older domains where the Active Directory cmdlets can't reach. Put differently, there may be Windows Server 2003 domains where the Active Directory Web Service isn't installed but WMI is available. The WMI method is also easier when trying to connect to trusted domains. Each of these WMI queries will list the SID of the domains involved:

```
Get-WmiObject -Namespace root\MicrosoftActiveDirectory `
   -Class Microsoft_LocalDomainInfo

Get-WmiObject -Namespace root\MicrosoftActiveDirectory `
   -Class Microsoft_DomainTrustStatus
```

If you don't run these commands from a DC, you'll need to add the `ComputerName` switch and pass the name of a DC. These WMI classes only exist on DCs.

The downside here is that there's no quick way to enumerate all of the domains in the forest. You would have to crawl all of the trusts to discover every domain and its trusts.

NOTE WMI support for Active Directory has been deprecated in Windows Server 2012, meaning that it still works but may not be available in future releases.

NLTEST

NLTEST does some stunning trust enumeration, complete with domain SIDs. This is exactly what you want—almost. What you *don't* want is to parse a bunch of command-line output. (NLTEST is a little-known utility that's been in the resource kit for a long time. It has a load of handy switches. Check it out.)

```
NLTEST /server:dc1 /domain_trusts /all_trusts /v
```

NOTE Refer to *PowerShell in Depth* (Manning 2013), chapter 18, for examples of parsing output from legacy utilities.

ADSI

ADSI, as painful as it is for IT pros, can query `trustedDomain` objects as well, but it will have the same permissions limitations you ran into earlier with the Active Directory cmdlets when reaching across domain and forest boundaries:

```
$ADSI = [ADSISEARCHER][ADSI]""
$ADSI.SearchRoot = [ADSI]"LDAP://CN=System,DC=Contoso,DC=com"
$ADSI.SearchScope = "onelevel"
$ADSI.Filter = "(&(objectClass=trustedDomain)(!trustAttributes=32))"
$ADSI.PropertiesToLoad.Add("name")
$ADSI.PropertiesToLoad.Add("securityIdentifier")
$ADSI.FindAll()
```

My preference is to use the simpler syntax of the Active Directory module cmdlets, but in this case neither the cmdlets nor ADSI fits our needs exactly.

.NET

To meet all the requirements you have to use .NET. I came to this realization after many hours of blood, sweat, and tears at the PowerShell console in my lab. Once I saw the impressive results from `NLTEST` I suspected there had to be a way to call the same APIs in PowerShell. From .NET you get a forest object and then call the `GetAllTrustRelationships` method. Then you peel down into the `TrustRelationshipInformation`, which holds the `TrustedDomainInformation`, where you find the domain SID of the trust partners. The code for this is provided in the next section.

The script solution

You're going to use a combination of WMI and .NET for the solution. The following listing contains the code that will build the domain SID list.

Listing 2 Domain SID report

```
$DomainSIDList = @{}

$MyDomainSID = Get-WmiObject `
    -Namespace root\MicrosoftActiveDirectory `
    -Class Microsoft_LocalDomainInfo |
    Select-Object DNSname, SID

$DomainSIDList.Add($MyDomainSID.DNSname, $MyDomainSID.SID)

$forest = `
    [System.DirectoryServices.ActiveDirectory.Forest]::`
    GetCurrentForest()

$forest.Domains | ForEach-Object {
     Get-WmiObject `
     -Namespace root\MicrosoftActiveDirectory `
     -Class Microsoft_DomainTrustStatus `
     -ComputerName $_.Name |
     ForEach-Object {
       $DomainSIDList.Add($_.TrustedDomain, $_.SID)
      }
}

$trusts = $forest.GetAllTrustRelationships()

ForEach ($trust in $trusts) {

  $trust.TrustedDomainInformation |
    ForEach-Object {

        $DomainSIDList.Add($_.DnsName, $_.DomainSid)

        $context = New-Object `
            System.DirectoryServices.ActiveDirectory.DirectoryContext`
            ("Forest",$_.DnsName)

        $remoteforest = `
            [System.DirectoryServices.ActiveDirectory.Forest]::`
            GetForest($context)
```

1. Empty hash table to hold the list
2. Get current domain SID with WMI
3. Store domain name and SID
4. Connect to forest with .NET
5. Enumerate trusts for each domain using WMI
6. .NET equivalent to NLTEST /DOMAIN_TRUSTS /ALL_TRUSTS
7. `TrustedDomainInformation` property holds name and SID for each trust

```
        $remotetrusts =
          ➥ $remoteforest.GetAllTrustRelationships()      ❽ Repeat trust enumeration
                                                              for trusted domains
        ForEach ($remotetrust in $remotetrusts) {
          $remotetrust.TrustedDomainInformation |
            ForEach-Object { $DomainSIDList.Add($_.DnsName, $_.DomainSid) }
        }

    }
}                                            ❾ Display the
                                                results
$DomainSIDList
```

This code may look somewhat busy but it boils down to two WMI calls and a couple of .NET calls. First you create an empty hash table ❶ to hold all of the domain name/SID results. The first WMI call ❷ gets the local domain name and SID, which you add to the hash table ❸. You repeat this hash table insertion for each domain name/SID pair found throughout the script.

The first .NET call ❹ establishes a connection with the current forest. (Behind the scenes the cmdlet `Get-ADForest` does the same thing.) The forest object then has a list of domains ❺ that you'll pipe to WMI to gather all SIDs from the trusts of each of those domains. This effectively gets the SID of every domain in the forest and any external trusts.

That gets all of the domain-level external trusts scattered throughout the forest, but now you need to get any external forest trusts ❻ in the root. Looping through ❼ that trust information you'll repeat the same trust enumeration steps ❽ to find trusts in the remote forests as well. In the end you'll have a pretty thorough report of trusts. But due to permissions issues and the number of trust hops there may be more trusts to be discovered (for example, a series of trusts chaining three or more forests together, albeit unlikely in most environments). In such cases rerun the script directly in those remote forests and then manually merge the output into a single CSV file. Finally, you'll print the results ❾.

This code appears in the `SIDHistory` module as the function `Export-DomainSIDs`, and it will give you a CSV file containing all of the domain names and domain SIDs. Use `Get-Help Export-DomainSIDs -Full` to see the syntax and notes. As a bonus there's also a function called `Update-SIDMapping`. This function will take the SID report file generated by `Export-SIDMapping` and insert a new column showing the source domain name for each SID history entry based on the output of `Export-DomainSIDs`.

The following is a list of the functions you'll find in the module:

```
PS C:\> Import-Module SIDHistory
PS C:\> Get-Command -Module SIDHistory

CommandType   Name                      ModuleName
-----------   ----                      ----------
Function      Convert-SIDHistoryNTFS    SIDHistory
Function      Export-DomainSIDs         SIDHistory
Function      Export-SIDHistoryShare    SIDHistory
Function      Export-SIDMapping         SIDHistory
```

```
Function      Get-SIDHistory          SIDHistory
Function      Merge-CSV               SIDHistory
Function      Remove-SIDHistory       SIDHistory
Function      Update-SIDMapping       SIDHistory
```

For more information on modules see `Help about_Modules`.

Summary

I began this chapter lamenting the mysterious troubleshooting issues associated with Active Directory token bloat, and you learned that often SID history can be the culprit. Now you have the tools in PowerShell to generate a list of all objects that have SID history in the forest and then match that data to the old domain name where available. Using this information you can plan your SID history cleanup project with precision. With the ADMT and the SID mapping file you created you're now empowered to translate the SID history on your resource servers. Once the translation is complete you can safely remove the SID history from your Active Directory objects, reducing token bloat across the forest and winning the praise of users everywhere.

For more information check out my blog series online, where you can find the full PowerShell module download, additional functions to help with ACL cleanup, and links to more resources for the topic, at http://aka.ms/SIDHistory.

About the author

Ashley McGlone is a Microsoft Premier Field Engineer (PFE). He started writing code on a Commodore VIC20 back in 1983, and he's been hooked ever since. As a former Microsoft Certified Trainer Ashley used to teach Microsoft Certified Systems Engineer (MCSE) classes on NT 4.0 and Windows 2000. Ashley spent eight years of his IT career administering a large enterprise where he scripted for Active Directory and thousands of workstations. Today he specializes in Active Directory and PowerShell, helping Microsoft Premier customers reach their full potential through risk assessments and workshops. Ashley's TechNet blog (http://aka.ms/GoateePFE) focuses on real-world solutions for Active Directory using Windows PowerShell. He can be found on Twitter at @GoateePFE.

PART 2

PowerShell scripting

Edited by Jeffery Hicks

When PowerShell first appeared, many people thought, "Great. Another scripting language from Microsoft like VBScript that I have to learn." Actually, that's only half the story. IT pros have since discovered that PowerShell is an effective interactive management engine that just happens to have a scripting interface. PowerShell pros know that anything they can do in the shell they can put into a script. Scripts save time and offer flexibility and reusability. The fact that PowerShell can also incorporate native .NET code means that you can create some pretty awesome PowerShell-based tools.

Whether you're writing a basic PowerShell script, beginning to dabble in advanced functions, or creating full-blown modules, there's something for everyone in this section. Everyone should at least read chapter 9 from James O'Neill on the ten commandments of PowerShell scripting. Even if you don't agree with all of them, his suggestions will certainly get you thinking about how you're approaching PowerShell script writing.

This section has a number of chapters that center on tips, from Will Steele, Jeff Wouters, and Jonathan Medd, that will help you write more effective scripts. And because there's really no difference between running a script and typing a command, some of their tips might carry over into your shell.

PowerShell MVPs Bartosz Bielawksi and Adam Driscoll have contributed chapters on scripting-related topics that I think many PowerShell scripters don't think about or haven't used much. These chapters go beyond the PowerShell help files, and while aimed at more experienced users, even beginners should learn what they can do in PowerShell.

The final chapters in the section are what I refer to as "tool building." In chapter 15, Matthew Reynolds offers some advice on improving performance when your script needs to work with big data. PowerShell MVP and author Richard Siddaway introduces us to the very cool world of CDXML in chapter 16. With PowerShell 3 we can now create new tools leveraging CIM, in much the same way Microsoft did for Windows 8 and Windows Server 2012. Finally, my contribution in chapter 17 guides you into creating PowerShell tools from command line tools. I bet there are still a number of legacy command line tools you use. Wouldn't it be nice to make them more PowerShell-like so they can be integrated into your PowerShell commands? That's what the chapter is all about.

The authors and I can't guarantee you'll be a world-class PowerShell scripter, but this section should add some new tools to your scripting toolkit.

About the editor

Jeffery Hicks is a longtime PowerShell MVP. He writes and speaks wherever he can about PowerShell, efficiency, and Microsoft technologies, in between training engagements. Jeff is also known as Prof. PowerShell from his long-running column on MCPMag.com. His latest book is *PowerShell in Depth: An Administrator's Guide*, co-written with Don Jones and Richard Siddaway (Manning 2013). You can follow Jeff on his blog, http://jdhitsolutions.com/blog or on Twitter as @JeffHicks.

9 The 10 PowerShell scripting commandments

James O'Neill

In my view, PowerShell succeeds because it provides a kit of small, general-purpose commands to be linked together to make larger, specific commands. Extending the toolkit is a good thing, and my approach to extending the toolkit can be summarized as "10 commandments" (which I jokingly call cmdments):

1. Create functions for reuse, scripts for a single task.
2. Choose names for commands and parameters wisely.
3. One task, one function: the "DoStuffWith" verb doesn't exist for a reason.
4. Build flexibility into parameters.
5. Ask whether constants are better as defaults for parameters.
6. Ask "What could I receive?" and "What could I pass on?"
7. Use `Write-` and `Out-` cmdlets properly.
8. Use comment-based help, and include examples.
9. Learn to use the `Try{} Catch{}` scriptblocks; don't rely on `$ErrorActionPreference`.
10. Choose either to support `-WhatIf` or to restore data.

This chapter will give you more insight into each commandment.

Constructing a sound function

Scripts do a complete job—you can have "Download new pictures from my RSS feed.ps1" as a script that runs as a scheduled job and doesn't rely on taking user input. Whereas scripts are specific and self-contained, functions do small jobs, like the built-in commands, and add tasks to the shell making them building blocks for scripts. Functions aim to be part of one or more bigger commands.

Select your function name carefully

From a syntax point of view almost any name that you use is valid, but whether it's a good name is another issue. The convention in PowerShell is for commands to be in the form `Verb-Noun`. Nouns are always in the singular (which saves nonnative speakers of English from having to learn irregular plurals). I've heard arguments for prefixing nouns so that two sets of functions don't clash, but in practice I've never found it necessary; the noun need only convey the meaning of what the function does.

I recommend following the naming conventions and sticking to PowerShell's list of standard verbs for two reasons: (1) users expect it and (2) if you put your code into a PowerShell module, the `Import-Module` command gives warnings if the module contains nonstandard names. `Get-Verb` gives a list of approved verbs, which includes the following:

- *GET*—Returns something that already exists
- *NEW*—Creates something new and independent
- *ADD*—Creates something "attached" to something that exists

The name also indicates the scope of the function's work. An example I've used is creating functions `Get-Sine`, `Get-Cosine`, and `Get-Tangent`. These names mean I don't use `Get-Tangent -inverse`; I use a separate function, `Get-ArcTangent`. Defining separate functions keeps your aliases simple (`Sin`, `Cos`, `Tan`, and `ArcSin`, `ArcCos`, `ArcTan`) and you avoid "Ipconfig syndrome." Ipconfig is the classic example of anything loosely related to the original purpose being lashed onto a command: in Ipconfig it's not the command name that determines the work to be carried out, but switches (such as `/release`). In PowerShell the command name determines what will be done, and the parameters determine the details of how it should be done and to which target(s) it should be done.

Start help early

Traditionally programmers write their code and then hand it over to someone else to write help. Command-line tools often support a `-?` parameter, which gets a programmer's explanation of how the command works. PowerShell always returns help derived from a function's structure, and suitably formatted comments allow PowerShell to create substantive help. Specifying a one-line synopsis as part of the help reinforces the scope of work you set when you selected the function name, and providing a set of examples illustrates what the function should do. Help is useful not only when you return to a function you wrote some months before but also helps to give you a specification to work to. You don't need to fill in all of the descriptive parts of the help at the outset, but it's useful to document how you expect your function to be used at the start and then implement to that documentation.

In PowerShell v3 the Integrated Scripting Environment (ISE) comes with built-in script snippets for cmdlets (see figure 1). From the ISE, right-click in the editor and

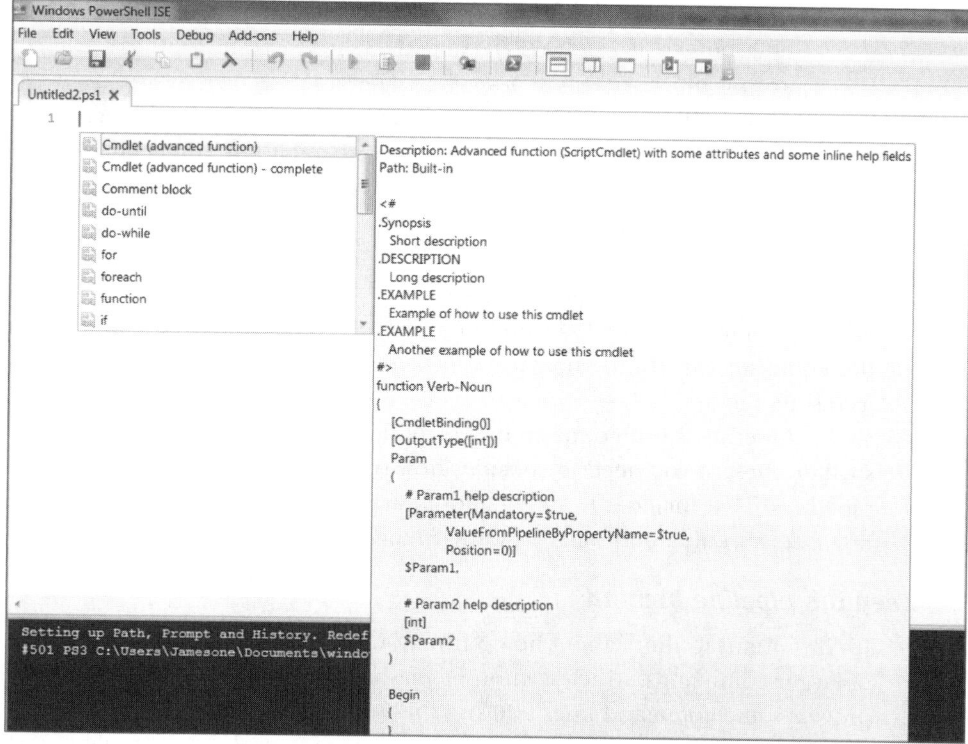

Figure 1 Inserting the Cmdlet (advanced function) snippet jump-starts the entry of help code.

then choose Start Snippets or press CTRL-J. Snippets provide good practice templates for which you fill in the blanks.

This snippet includes the following items:

- *Comment-based Help*—Help can appear before, after, or inside the function. The snippet puts it at the top of the file.
- `Verb-Noun` *name*—Name of the function.
- `[CmdletBinding()]` *header*—Enables common parameters, such as `WarningAction` and `ErrorAction`, among other things.
- `[OutputType()]` *header*—Allows the output type to be returned by help and helps PowerShell v3 IntelliSense to suggest the right properties and methods in an expression that contains the output of the function.

  There's no enforcement of this, unlike declaring a function in a compiled language such as C#. If you don't know what type your function returns you can put `Object` here.
- `Param()` *block*—Provides example parameters (and a reminder to insert comment-based help for the parameter).

Note that it's valid to write `Function name (Param1, Param2) {body}` in PowerShell, but *not* if `[CmdletBinding()]` is specified; in that case you must use a `param()` block.

One of the example parameters accepts input from the pipeline.

- *`Begin{}`, `Process{}` and `End{}` blocks*—Used when input comes from the pipeline. `Begin` runs before the first item, `Process` repeats for each item, and `End` runs after the last item.

Output

With the function named, an outline of what it does, and a barebones structure for the code, we can think about the input parameters it receives and how it returns its results.

In PowerShell you compose big, complicated commands by forming pipelines of smaller ones, so you need to consider how the functions you create fit into a world of pipelines. That includes thinking about parameters that come from the pipeline and how to ensure that output is "pipeline-friendly."

Keep the pipeline in mind

It's important to think about how a function can act as a small command and be part of larger commands, which is another reason to sketch out early in the development process some command lines that use the function. As a general guideline, functions should be able to pass rich objects to the next command. An example I use is finding an MD5 hash for a file. The hash allows me to identify files uniquely even when they've been renamed. I've saved over 50,000 picture files on my laptop, and if I want to find duplicates I can run the following command:

```
Get-FilesWithHash | Group -Property hash | where {$_.Count -gt 1}
```

This gives me a group object containing a set of files for each hash that occurs more than once.

But how should `Get-FilesWithHash` work? I contend that it's more useful to return a file object with the hash as a property than to return the hash, and that a function that accepts files as input and adds a hash to them is more flexible (and easier to write) than one that tries to do all the selection itself. A more efficient implementation of `Get-FilesWithHash` is

```
Get-Some-Files | Add-MD5Hash
```

When I write the help I can then include examples like these:

- `Dir | Add-MD5Hash`

  Returns a set of files with an MD5 hash added. PowerShell's default formatting won't show the hash.
- `DIR | Add-MD5Hash | Format-Table -property Name,MD5`

  Shows file names and their hash.

- `$duplicates = dir | add-MD5hash | group-object Length,md5 |`
  `➥ where { $_.Count -gt 1 }`

  Saves groups with duplicate files to `$duplicates`.

Although the assumption is that `Add-MD5Hash` will have files piped into it, it would be an oversight if the function didn't allow the user to specify files as a parameter.

Some objects (such as WMI ones) are ugly; or more accurately, PowerShell doesn't include formatting XML for them by default. If you're going to do in-depth work with such objects it may make sense to create your own formatting XML file. Tools that make this easier include James Brundage's EZOut (http://ezout.start-automating.com), but this can be overkill. Often the most practical thing to do is to use `Format-List` or `format-table` inside the function. After the data is formatted it's useless to anything later in the pipeline, so give your function either a `-Formatted` switch to turn formatting on or a `-Raw` switch to turn it off.

Handle and provide a path property

Many PowerShell commands that accept files as input don't care what kind of object they're passed, provided the object has a `.Path` property. If your function returns objects that are (or can refer to) files, setting a `.Path` property ensures that your objects can be piped straight into commands that work with files.

For example, PowerShell's `Select-String` cmdlet outputs `MatchInfo` objects that return what was found, where, and so on. `MatchInfo` also contains a path, which means you can put together a command like this:

```
Select-String -list -Pattern "while" -path *.ps1 |
  ➥ Copy-Item -Destination e:\WhileFiles
```

Use Write- commands properly

One of the telltale signs of people who are new to PowerShell is the way they use (or misuse) `Write-Host` and `Write-Output`. Heavy use of `Write-Host` is usually a mistake because it's for outputting only information that isn't to be passed into a pipeline. For example, I use a `Get-SQL` command to fetch data using ODBC. I want to know how many rows of data it returned, but I don't want "4000 rows returned" to go into the next command in the pipeline; this is the proper use for `Write-Host`. I also have a `-quiet` switch to turn this off.

New users also learn that PowerShell has an `echo` command like the batch file command, but `echo` is an alias for `Write-Output`, so they use `Write-Output` everywhere they'd have used `echo`. Writing `$x` does the same as `Write-Output $x`. The only reason to use this cmdlet is if you need to make clear where a result is being returned.

Everyone has experienced commands that take a long time to run. `Write-Progress` is *the* way to tell the user what's happening in long-running tasks.

`Write-Verbose` provides the user with extra information if they want it, but also puts pseudo comments in the code. For example,

```
Write-Verbose "About to fetch data from $URL"
```

reports progress to the user, but there's no need to write a comment saying you're about to fetch data from that URL. Write-Debug allows the user to break into the execution, and Write-Warning tells the user when things don't go according to plan. If you specify [CmdletBinding()] it enables the common parameters, which control what the script does when it gets to a verbose, debug, or warning message. By default only warnings are displayed, but you can hide or stop warnings or show more information by adding a switch, with no extra coding effort. Before PowerShell, users had to modify a script to output information when debugging and then reverse the changes out when they got it working. When you use Write- commands properly the debugging lines turn themselves off when not needed.

People who work with batch files know that output including errors can be suppressed by redirecting to NUL. PowerShell allows output to be sent to Out-Null (or cast to the [Void] type), but it treats errors differently. One of my pet peeves is when users set $ErrorActionPreference to hide a possible error. PowerShell allows commands to be wrapped in a try{} block and errors to be handled in a catch{} block, but this is usually overkill: cmdlets (and functions that specify [CmdletBinding()]) allow error messages to be managed with a parameter, just like verbose, debug and warning messages.

For example, if a function calls something that might produce a nonterminating error (for instance, searching recursively through directories might result in access denied for some), you can suppress errors with -ErrorAction SilentlyContinue or you can force them to be terminating errors with -ErrorAction Stop.

Parameters

When you write a specification for a function you include its name, its output and its inputs, and a description of what it does. The code that you write to produce the output from the inputs *implements* that specification.

The use of the term *function* in PowerShell is a source of confusion for people who have some programming background in systems programming languages. At one time the term script cmdlet began to be used, but it never replaced function. A function is one of the five kinds of PowerShell commands—the others being aliases, cmdlets, workflows and external programs. Ultimately users don't care whether a command is implemented as a function or a cmdlet; they want to know what to put in and what comes out.

Systems programmers who work in C#, VB, or some other compiled language use the term function to refer to a pedantic section of code. C# programmers don't bat an eye over a "function" that processes files but doesn't accept a string that contains a path to a file—they write an extra line to get the file from the path first. That's not acceptable in PowerShell; commands shouldn't say, "You gave that to me in a way I don't like." For example, you could write

```
[System.Management.Automation.PathInfo]$x = Resolve-Path profile.ps1
Copy-Item $x ..
```

or

```
[system.io.fileinfo]$x = Get-Item profile.ps1
Copy-Item $x ..
```

or

```
[System.String]$x = "profile.ps1"
Copy-Item $x ..
```

Each of these examples forces `$X` to hold a different data type, and yet they all work with `Copy-Item`. Anything you write that extends the set of commands users can type in PowerShell should behave like the built-in cmdlets. You, therefore, need to anticipate what users will want to use as parameters and cater to that.

Use standard parameter names and aliases

Existing PowerShell commands use `-Path`, not `-File`; `-Recurse`, not `-Subdirectories`; and so on. Your function's parameters will be more easily understood if you follow conventions, but you don't need to be slavish about it. For example, PowerShell uses `ComputerName`, but when I wrote a library to manage Hyper-V virtual machines on Windows Server 2008 I thought that using `Computer` risked confusion between `Virtual Machine` and `Host`, so I used `Server` for the host and `VM` for the guests. The library was widely used and I didn't receive a single complaint that it confused people or was "nonstandard," so it seems to have been a good decision.

A parameter doesn't have to have a single name; aliases can be helpful. Long names can be shortened to give de facto aliases; for example, `-HeartBeatTimeOut` could be `-HeartBeat` or more likely `-h`. You might prefer an alias of `-TimeOut`. Consider a function that takes a `-Describe` parameter; `-d` is ambiguous and so is `-de` (it could be `-debug`), but that's no reason not to define an alias `-d` for this parameter.

Avoid restoring data: make full use of the common parameters

As well as enabling the `-Debug` and `-Verbose` switches and the `-ErrorAction` and `-WarningAction` parameters, `[cmdlet binding()]` enables `-WhatIf` and `-Confirm`.

If the function makes big changes you can specify an impact level of low, medium, or high:

```
[CmdletBinding(SupportsShouldProcess=$true, ConfirmImpact='High' )]
```

If `ConfirmImpact` isn't specified it defaults to medium. If the impact level is higher than the value of `$ConfirmPreference` confirmation will be requested. Specifying `-Confirm` sets `$ConfirmPreference` for the function to low. An if statement determines whether the impacting action should proceed. For example:

```
if ($pscmdlet.shouldProcess($file.name,"Delete file") {Del $file}
```

Here's how the `.ShouldProcess` method works with the following switches:

- *`-Confirm`*—Prints the message and returns true or false depending on the user's input

- `-WhatIf`—Prints the message and returns false
- `-Verbose`—Prints the message and returns true

Assign default values (so constants can be parameters)

Writing a parameter in the form

```
ComputerName = "."
```

assigns it a default value—in this case `"."`, which means the local computer—if no value is provided for the parameter when the function is called. It's not necessary to require users to supply a computer name if you can assume the current machine. In the same way, it's not necessary to make "Local computer" a hardcoded default: any constant like that can be written in the parameters section, and then the user can override it.

For example, a function that calls `Get-WMIobject` shouldn't be limited to working only on the local machine. You can use a `-ComputerName` parameter that defaults to the current computer. If there's a business rule embedded in your function it might even make sense for that part of your function to be the default value of a `scriptblock` parameter. The script block gets run in the appropriate place, but to change the rule you can specify a new one in the command line.

For functions that return information about files it makes sense to assume `*.*` (all files in the current directory), but for functions that change files it's safer to make no assumptions.

Be mindful of your users

Don't expect other people to know the syntax for things inside your function. For example, WMI uses the percent sign (`%`) for wildcards (SQL style) instead of the more typical asterisk (`*`). In this case you either expect users to learn the SQL syntax or you keep them in mind and include something like this in your functions:

```
-Replace "*","%"
```

Is it bad form to expect users to learn the SQL syntax? I'd argue it's the programmer's job to take on work to save the user time (not vice versa). I'll return to this theme later.

Provide parameters to switch off parts of a complex function (or script)

I use a script that updates remote systems and can be run as

```
Update-System -noBackup
```

Just as moving business rules into script blocks allows a script to do a second job without rewriting, so providing switches that examine a large `If {}` block allows a single script to do `Update-SystemWithBackup` and `Update-SystemWithoutBackup`.

Accept input from the pipeline

Piping in is key to the *Shell* part of PowerShell. The telltale construction that says, "This should accept pipeline input" generically looks like this:

```
Get-thing | ForEach-Object {Verb-Thing -thing $_}
```

For example, if I implemented my `Add-MD5Hash` and found I was using it as

```
Dir | ForEach {Add-MD5Hash -path $_.name}
```

I'd know that path needs to take input. It's easy for a parameter to accept its value from a piped object; you prefix the parameter like this:

```
[parameter(ValueFromPipeLine= $true)]
```

In PowerShell v3 it's only necessary to write

```
[Parameter(ValueFromPipeline)]
```

The `=$true` is optional, but if your work might be used with v2 it's worth including it.

To support multiple items being passed via the pipe a function needs the following blocks:

- *`Begin {}`*—runs before the first item
- *`Process {}`*—runs once for each set of parameters (so in case of piped input, once for each item)
- *`End {}`*—runs after the last item

These blocks are optional; if the function doesn't have any of them the entire function body is treated as an end block.

Another way to tag parameters that work with the pipeline is to use `ValueFromPipeLineByPropertyName`:

```
[parameter(ValueFromPipelineByPropertyName =
     $true)][Alias('Fullname','Path')]
             $Include=@("*.ps1","*.js","*.sql"),
```

This says to PowerShell, "If the piped object has a property with the same name as this parameter or any of its aliases, then use the value of that property as the parameter value." This function supports `-include`, which defaults to an array of values. If it receives piped input that has an `.Include`, `.FullName`, or `.Path` property, then the value of that property is used.

All PowerShell commands that work with files deal with piped objects in this manner. For example,

- a `PathInfo` object from `Resolve Path`,
- a `FileInfo` object from `Get Item` or `Get ChildItem` (a.k.a. `Dir` or `ls`),
- a `directorySecurity` object from `Get ACL`, or
- a `matchinfo` object from `Select String`.

Be flexible about what is acceptable in parameters

You've seen that PowerShell can be flexible about the data type of parameters and that well-written scripts don't require the user to express parameters in an unnatural way. Another aspect of flexibility is what you treat as "valid" input. In PowerShell you can often do validation on parameters, but beware of validation that shifts the effort from the writer of the script to its user.

Flexibility also includes the number of items you accept in a parameter. The built-in PowerShell commands accept multiple values, as shown here:

```
PS> stop-process 4472,5200,5224
```

Users will, therefore, expect this feature in your functions, too. One of your parameters is usually the target of the command. If the name of the command indicates *what* the command does, you can think about parameters like this:

- The "target" parameter indicates *which* object or objects it acts on.
- The remaining parameters define *how* it goes about it.

The "which" parameters require more flexibility than the "how" parameters.

The target of a command could be an object or it could be an ID or a name from which the desired object can be obtained. A name could be a wild card that expands to more than one object, so a single-value target parameter resolves an array of target objects.

It's best to expand names first and then either loop through the values or call the function recursively for each item. Recursion copes with nested arrays or arrays of names that need to be resolved. The script shown in listing 1 is a function called `test-file`, which handles exactly this scenario.

The function starts with online help that explains that the function gets the first line of a file; it works with file-related objects via the pipeline or as a variable or strings, and if given something it can't handle as a file, it returns null. Some people may prefer to see a warning if the item isn't a file, but when something like `Get-ChildItem -Recurse` (or `dir -r`) is used it includes directories in the stream of objects sent down the pipeline, and my own preference is to avoid printing a warning for each.

Listing 1 The `test-file` function

```
<#
.Synopsis
   Gets the first line of a file for demo purposes
.EXAMPLE
   get-acl *.* | where {$_.Owner -match "james"} | test-file
   It works with file-related objects
.EXAMPLE
   test-file p*.*
   It works with strings
.EXAMPLE
   $f = Get-Item '.\100 Meter Event.txt' ; test-file $f
   It works with stored objects
```

```
.EXAMPLE
   Get-Date | test-file
   Input that cannot be converted to a file returns Null
#>
function test-file
{    [CmdletBinding()]
     [OutputType([String])]
     Param
     (    # The File to test
          [parameter(ValueFromPipeline=$true)]
          $Path = "*.*"
     )
     Process
     {    if ($path -isnot [array] -and $path -isnot [system.io.fileinfo])
              {$path = $path | Get-Item -ErrorAction SilentlyContinue}
          if ($path -is [array])
              {foreach ($p in $path) {Test-File $p} }
          if ($path -is [System.IO.FileInfo])
              {
                Get-Content -TotalCount 1 $path
              }
     }
}
```

The first two `if` statements in the `Process{}` block deal with the two cases the function handles when the parameter isn't a single file. If it isn't an array or a file then the function uses `Get-Item` to try to get the correct file or files. If what is passed works with `Get-Item` it works with the function, so the function delegates the responsibility of checking validity to `Get-Item`. If the parameter is an array or if `Get-Item` returns an array the function is called recursively for each item in the array.

The third `if` is the main part of the function, which runs for the real object(s), not for a name or the array object. If no input, or input of an impossible type, is provided the function quietly returns nothing. In most cases "null in/null out" is a valid rule, but on occasion when the function cannot assume a default a *mandatory* parameter makes more sense.

Using parameter types and validation properly

Specifying parameter types in PowerShell isn't *validation* but *casting*. For example, in compiled languages like C#,

```
string MD5(string fileName) {}
```

declares `MD5` as a function that returns a string and takes a string parameter, so

```
S = MD5(7)
```

causes a compiler error because 7 isn't a string.

In PowerShell,

```
Function Get-MD5{ Param([string]$FileName)     }
```

also declares a string parameter, but

```
Get-MD5 7
```

converts 7 to a string.

This behavior is helpful, for example, if a variable `F` holds a `fileInfo` object—the type that PowerShell's `Get-Item` and `Get-ChildItem` (alias `dir` and `ls`) commands return. In C#,

```
S = MD5(F)
```

returns a compiler error because, as in the previous C# example, `F` is the wrong type.

PowerShell converts the object to a string, and fortunately the `.toString()` method of a `fileInfo` object returns a string containing the path to the file.

But casting doesn't always do the conversion you expect. For example,

```
[System.IO.FileInfo]$file
```

won't reject a string such as

```
'.\100 Meter Event.txt'
```

but converts it to an object representing a file in \windows\system32. The file doesn't exist and is read-only!

A better approach is to leave parameters untyped and then resolve types and perform other validation in code, as shown in listing 1. The function works whether the user passes a name of something or an object that represents it. At a minimum, a command should allow a `-name` or `-path` parameter as well as an `-InputObject` parameter. For example, the following all do the same thing:

```
PS> stop-process 4472,5200,5224
PS> Get-Process -Name "calc" | Stop-Process
PS> $p = get-process calc; Stop-Process -InputObject $p
PS> stop-process -name calc
```

It's better to support this kind of behavior without the parameter. For example, the `Rename-Item` command (alias `ren`) doesn't care if it's passed a file object or a path:

```
PS> ren '.\100 Meter Event.txt' "100 Metre Event.txt"
PS> $f = get-item '.\100 Metre Event.txt' ; ren $f '100 Meter Event.txt'
```

You're probably doing something wrong if your function forces the user to use the equivalent of

```
PS> Stop-Process (get-process Calc)
```

or

```
PS> Ren (get-item '.\100 Metre Event.txt') "100 M Event.txt"
```

PowerShell provides a battery of validation that can be performed on parameters, the most common of which is to say a parameter is mandatory. Mandatory parameters were introduced in PowerShell v2, so you still see code that sets the default of a parameter to "throw." This was the only way to make a parameter mandatory in PowerShell v1.

The advantage of the mandatory parameter attribute is that it prompts users for input and even offers limited help about what the input should be. The disadvantage is that

```
$x = pipeline ; test-Stuff $x ;
```

isn't the same as

```
pipeline | test-stuff
```

In the former, if the pipeline outputs nothing, `$x` is null, and if a mandatory parameter contains null or an empty array, a runtime error occurs. In the latter version, when there is nothing to pass down the pipeline no error occurs. The parameter validation options available let you specify that null and/or empty are allowed.

If a parameter fails validation a runtime error is generated. Where functions are units of a larger program—as in the systems programming world—this can provide extra validation as values pass between different parts of a script. But when a function is a command run by a real user it can be a user interface disaster. Consider this function, which takes a possible ID, uses a regular expression to validate it, and if it's valid, outputs it:

```
Function Test-ID {
    Param
         (
            [parameter(Mandatory=$true)]
            [ValidatePattern("^\d{3}-\d{2}-\d{4}$")]
            [String[]]
           $ID
         )
         process {$ID}
}
```

Let's see what happens when the user enters the ID using an incorrect format:

```
C:\ps > Test-ID 123456789
Test-ID : Cannot validate argument on parameter 'ID'.
The argument "123456789" does not match the "^\d{3}-\d{2}-\d{4}$" pattern.
Supply an argument that matches "^\d{3}-\d{2}-\d{4}$" and try the command
     again.
```

Users are told to make their input match `"^\d{3}-\d{2}-\d{4}$"` and try again. Really? Even experienced PowerShell users need a few moments to decode a regular expression. An alternative way to write the function is to provide users with informative feedback:

```
Function Test-ID {
        Param
          (
            [parameter(Mandatory=$true)]
            [String[]]
```

```
            $ID
        )
        process {
          If ($id -notmatch"^\d{3}-\d{2}-\d{4}$")
               {Write-Warning "ID Needs to be a US Social Security"+
                              "Number in the form 123-45-6789"
                return }
          else { $ID}
        }
}
```

This second version isn't ideal, though. The function should attempt to convert digits with missing or incorrect separators into a correctly formatted string. Forcing users to change their input to save you work isn't a good use of validation. In this case I'd test for any number of nonalphanumeric characters, including 0, inserted between the digits:

```
If ($id -notmatch"^\d{3}\W*\d{2}\W*\d{4}\W*$")
```

This identifies bad input where digits are grouped with the separators in the wrong places, sequences that include letters, or sequences with too many or too few digits. But if users enter a space or no separator at all it doesn't make their input invalid.

This next regular expression then converts the ID to the desired format:

```
$id = $id -replace "^(\d{3})\W*(\d{2})\W*(\d{4})\W*$" ,'$1-$2-$3'
```

This is a variation on the theme that users shouldn't need to know what's inside your function to use it, and you should go out of your way to save users from learning any new syntax to use your work. Replacing "`*`" with "`%`" to get expected wildcard behavior was an example of this, but there are plenty of other cases in which user interface design should go the extra mile to help the user.

Example: finding duplicate files

Listing 2 comes from an Internet posting. The code looks at music files and checks for duplicate files based on finding the MD5 hash for the files and grouping them. Although the code works—otherwise it wouldn't have made it to the Internet—the initial version, shown here, includes none of the best practices I've advocated in this chapter.

Listing 2 The initial code for finding duplicates

```
function Get-MD5(
      [System.IO.FileInfo]$file = $(Throw 'Usage: Get-MD5
     [System.IO.FileInfo]')
)
{
  $stream = $null;
  $cryptoServiceProvider =
     [System.Security.Cryptography.MD5CryptoServiceProvider];
  $hashAlgorithm = new-object $cryptoServiceProvider
```

```
  $stream = $file.OpenRead();
  $hashByteArray = $hashAlgorithm.ComputeHash($stream);
  $stream.Close();
  return [string]$hashByteArray;
}

filter AttachMD5
{
  $md5hash = Get-MD5 $_;
  return ($_ | AddNote MD5 $md5Hash);
}
filter AddNote([string] $name, $value)
{
$mshObj = [System.Management.Automation.psObject] $_;
$note = new-object System.Management.AUtomation.psNoteProperty $name, $value
$mshObj.psObject.Members.Add($note);
return $mshObj
}

Get-ChildItem i:\music\*.* |
  where { $_ -is [System.IO.FileInfo] } |
  AttachMD5 |
  group-object Length,MD5
```

I'll mention several nitpicks at the outset: the C/C#/Java style of using semicolons at the end of lines, the use of `return`, and the absence of `param` blocks and `[CmdletBinding()]`. Also the filter doesn't have a standard name, and it could be a function instead.

Thinking back to my design rules, ask yourself, "What is the script trying to do?" It's trying to add an MD5 hash to an item. Therefore, it should be one function named `Add-MD5`, not a filter that uses one function to get the hash, and a second function to add the hash as a note property. The hash is currently in the form of an array of bytes, but a single hex-formatted string is a better choice. Let's pare down `Get-MD5`, `AttachMD5`, and `AddNote` to one `Add-MD5` function:

```
Function Add-MD5(
[System.IO.FileInfo] $file = $(Throw 'Usage: Add-MD5 [System.IO.FileInfo]')
)
{
  $hashAlgorithm = new-object
    ➥ System.Security.Cryptography.MD5CryptoServiceProvider
  $stream        = $file.OpenRead()
  $hashalgorithm.ComputeHash($stream)|
        foreach -begin {$h=""} -process {$h+=$_.tostring("x2")}
  $stream.Close()
  $file | add-member -Force -PassThru -MemberType noteproperty `
                     -Name "MD5"      -Value $h
}
```

This version doesn't support piping, but changing the body to a `process{}` block and changing the parameter declaration solves this. Also, because the variable `$hashAlgorithm` is reused, let's put it in a `begin{}` block:

```
Function Add-MD5 {
Param    ([parameter(ValueFromPipeLine= $true, mandatory=$true)]
          [System.IO.FileInfo]$file
         )
Begin    { $hashAlgorithm = `
             new-object System.Security.Cryptography.MD5CryptoServiceProvider
     }
Process { $stream  = $file.OpenRead()
...
```

This is a good step forward, but the `$file` parameter should be `$path` to be consistent with PowerShell naming conventions. Also the specification of the type requires the user to get file objects; if anything else is passed strange results may be returned.

Let's improve the function in listing 3 so that it can accept a string and convert it to one or more files. It can handle an array (either passed as a parameter or resulting from converting a string) by calling itself recursively, and it can process a single file object. If it receives anything else—for example, a directory object—it can ignore it.

Listing 3 The refactored code for getting duplicates

```
Function Add-MD5 {
Param    ([parameter(ValueFromPipeLine= $true)]$Path)
Begin    {$hashAlgorithm = new-object
  ➥ System.Security.Cryptography.MD5CryptoServiceProvider }
Process { If (($Path -is [string]) -and (test-path $file))
                {$Path = get-item -path $file}
          If (($Path -is [array])
                {$Path | Add-MD5  }
          If ( $Path -is [System.IO.FileInfo])
                {
                  $stream = $Path.OpenRead()
                  $hashalgorithm.ComputeHash($stream) |
                     foreach -begin {$h=""} -process {$h+=$_.tostring("x2")}
                     $stream.Close()
                     $Path |
                     add-member -Force -PassThru -MemberType noteproperty `
                     -Name "MD5" -Value $h
                }
.         }
}
```

Now the function works if it's called with

```
PS> Dir -recurse | Add-MD5
PS> Add-MD5 *.PS1
```

and so on. Filtering out the directories with a recursive `dir` or `Get-ChildItem` isn't necessary.

Extra tricks for file parameters

As is, the `Add-MD5` function works well for passing `object` or `name-of-object` for most objects. But when the objects in question are expected to be files you can optimize the code even more.

Convert to paths

If you convert `fileInfo` or `pathinfo` objects to strings the results contain the path of the object. Although this doesn't work for all objects (`fileSecurity` objects, for example), declaring `$path` as a string array and converting objects gives one or more strings, which can then be converted to file objects:

```
Param    (
           [String[]]
           $Path = "*"
         )
Begin    {
    $hashAlgorithm =
      ➥ new-object System.Security.Cryptography.MD5CryptoServiceProvider
         }
Process {  $files = (Get-Item $path -ErrorAction SilentlyContinue |
           Where-Object {$_ -is [System.IO.FileInfo] }  )
            if ($files)  {
                  foreach ($f in $files) {
                        $stream = $f.OpenRead()
                        .
                        .
                        .    etc
                  }
            }
            else{ Write-Warning "$path didn't yield any valid files"}
         }
```

As a result, `$files` contains the specified file(s), whether what was passed is a string containing a file name or a wildcard, a single file object, an array of file objects, or nothing at all (in which case it contains all files in the current directory). Anything that comes back that isn't a file (a directory, or a path pointing to somewhere that isn't in the file system) is filtered out. If the result is no files a warning is printed; otherwise the function gets the result for each file.

We could extend the function by using `Get-ChildItem` instead of `Get-Item` and by adding support parameters such as `-recurse` and `-include`.

Use a path property if it exists

File-related .NET objects have a `.Path` property (and PowerShell adds a `.PSPath` property to some). By specifying the parameter as

```
[parameter(ValueFromPipeLineByPropertyName = $true,
           ValueFromPipeLine               = $true   )]
[String[]]
$Path
```

the `$Path` parameter is the piped object's path (if it has one) or the object as a string (if it doesn't have a path property). This can be extended by using known aliases for the path:

```
[parameter(ValueFromPipeLineByPropertyName = $true,
           ValueFromPipeLine               = $true   )]
```

```
[Alias('Fullname','Filename','PSPath')]
[String[]]
$Path = "*"
```

If the object has properties with any of these names (or if the function is written with `-FileName` instead of `-Path`), `$Path` will contain the path to the item.

Pipe the same item into multiple parameters

There's no reason for a piped object to provide the value for only one parameter. Defining a second parameter to go with the one already defined ensures that the object is captured:

```
[parameter(valueFromPipeLine = $true  )]
$InputObject
```

In the body of the function it's possible to write the following:

```
if (-not $inputObject.path) {$inputObject = $f}
Add-Member -PassThru -Force -InputObject $InputObject -MemberType
➥ NoteProperty -Name "MD5" -Value $h
```

If the pipeline supplies an input object and the object has a path (it isn't a string, for example), that object is returned with the hash added; otherwise the file object is returned with the hash.

The entire optimized function is shown in the next listing.

Listing 4 The finished code for getting duplicates

```
Function Add-MD5 {
Param     ( [Parameter(ValueFromPipeLineByPropertyName = $true,
                       ValueFromPipeLine = $true  )]
            [Alias('Fullname','Filename','PSPath')]
            [String[]]
            $Path = "*" ,
            [parameter(valueFromPipeLine = $true  )]
            $InputObject
          )
Begin     { $hashAlgorithm = `New-Object
  ➥ System.Security.Cryptography.MD5CryptoServiceProvider}
Process   { $files = (Get-Item $path -ErrorAction SilentlyContinue |
                        Where-Object {$_ -is [System.IO.FileInfo] }  )
            if ($files)  {
               foreach ($f in $files) {
                   $stream = $f.OpenRead()
                   $hashalgorithm.ComputeHash($stream)|
                       foreach -begin {$h=""} -process
                           ➥ {$h+=$_.tostring("x2")}
                   if (-not $inputObject.path) {$inputObject = $f}
                   Add-Member -InputObject $InputObject -Name "MD5" `
                              -MemberType NoteProperty  -PassThru `
                              -Value $h
               }
            }
```

```
            Else    { Write-Warning "$path didn't yield any valid files"}
         }
}
```

The improved function now supports being called with the following:

- A single, unique file name

  ```
  Add-MD5 '.\100 Meter Event.txt'
  ```

- Multiple file names and/or names that use wild cards

  ```
  Add-MD5 '*.txt',*.ps1
  ```

- File objects as a parameter

  ```
  $psfiles = get-item *.ps1 ; Add-MD5 $psfiles
  ```

- File objects via the pipeline

  ```
  DIR  -Recurse -Include *.TXT | Add-MD5
  ```

- Other objects with a file property via the pipeline

  ```
  Select-String -Pattern  "hash" -Path *.ps1 -List | Add-MD5
  ```

- File names via the pipeline

  ```
  Type FileList.txt | Add-MD5
  ```

Write code for another person to read

Don't try to imagine what everyone else in the world might want. Instead, imagine yourself a few months from now, working late, up against a deadline, trying to use the function you're writing now. What will your future self thank you for doing, or curse you for not doing?

If you already use comment-based help to describe what the function does and to list all the different ways it can be called the next step is to use `Write-Verbose` for progress messages. These messages are a useful hybrid of debugging information, which can be turned on at will but also serve as comments when you read the code. As for other comments, unless the code is difficult to read don't bother to explain what it's doing, but do explain why.

In scripts I try to avoid PowerShell "golf" in which the smallest number of [key]strokes wins. Generally if it's easier to see what the script is doing with a name or parameter written out in full, it goes in, but I find that some additions don't add clarity. For example, which version of the following code is clearer?

```
get-item -Path  "*.txt" | where-object -FilterScript {$_.length -gt 1024} |
  ➥ foreach-object -Process {$_.name}
```

or

```
get-item "*.txt" | where {$_.length -gt 1024} | foreach {$_.name}
```

I think the second is easier to read, but it's at odds with a general guideline of avoiding the use of aliases in scripts. Whether to allow yourself any aliases at all is a valid question to ask. Generally if the alias is either the verb or noun part of the full name (Where, Sort, ForEach), I think it's OK. The following is too terse:

```
ls "*.txt" | ? {$_.length -gt 1024} | % {$_.name}
```

But at least `ls`, `?`,and `%` are things I use at the command line. If I encounter `SLS` in a script I need to check what it's an alias for (`Select-String`), which cancels out the savings in typing time.

How you choose to lay out and indent code is a personal choice. The style preferences that worked well for poring over printed listings on 80-column wide fanfold paper don't work as well for today's wide-but-not-tall monitors. There's a compromise to be made between excessively long lines that extend off the side of the screen (the eye doesn't like reading long lines, which is why newspapers uses multicolumn layouts) and splitting lines so many times that the reader must scroll up and down. Personally, I vary my formatting style to make code easier to read. For example, if the condition, collection, and action are all short I might write the following:

```
If (Condition) {ForEach ($item in $Collection) {act-on $f}}
```

If they're long I might write this instead:

```
If ($conditionA -or $conditionB -and $conditionC -or $conditionD)
    {
        foreach ($f in (Something -long -complicated $files))
            {
                action1
                action2
                action3 $f | action4
            }
    }
```

Trying to write rules that dictate when to combine as one line and when to break as two is difficult. Tasks that involve a single pipeline with many steps can be easier to follow if written in shorter pieces that use variables to hold intermediate values. At the other extreme are people who feel they can use variables only as parameters, never literal values, so they'd never write the following:

```
"A circle, radius 2 has a circumference of 12.566"
```

Instead, they'd write this:

```
[double]$pi       = 3.1415
[double]$radius   = 2
[double]$diameter = $radius * 2
[double]$circ     = $pi * $diameter
$Template = "A circle radius {0} has circumference of {1:f3}"
$OutText  = $Template -f $radius, $circ
Write-output -inputObject $outText
```

The easy-to-follow code lies somewhere in the middle.

Summary

This chapter opened with 10 statements about what you should and should not do. Perhaps the golden rule is to remember that PowerShell functions don't exist in a vacuum. When you write functions they should resemble cmdlets and functions that other people have implemented. Use established naming conventions. Provide help, debugging, and feedback that you can implement without excessive overhead. Most importantly, PowerShell commands are flexible enough with their inputs and outputs that you can and should chain them together in pipelines. If your function works in the middle of a long pipeline then you're getting it right.

About the author

James O'Neill was born in 1965 and insists that he is still alive. He used his first Microsoft product at the age of 13 and has scarcely stopped since. From the year 2000, he served 10 years at Microsoft where he became evangelical about PowerShell and was best known for adding PowerShell support to the first releases of Hyper-V. He lives near Oxford, England with his wife and two children and occasionally manages to find time for photography and teaching people to scuba dive. He has a worrying tendency to write about himself in the third person.

10 Avoiding the pipeline

Jeff Wouters

Whether you're new to PowerShell or you're at a more advanced level, I encourage you to always consider performance and execution time when you write a script.

One of the most powerful features of PowerShell is its ability to use the pipeline. Finding objects, filtering them to return the ones you want, and performing an action on those objects is easy to do with *pipelined expressions*, which I refer to as the pipeline. Every step is one pipe in the pipeline. In general, the fewer pipes you use, the shorter the execution time and the fewer resources that are used.

Although creating one-liners is easy to learn and understand, following best practices yields the best performance. If you don't implement best practices your script may still work, but you'll experience negative performance and/or long execution times.

When writing scripts I always keep this goal in mind: to complete the task at hand in the most efficient way.

In this chapter I'll show you how to combine parameters so that you won't have long commands in which objects are piped from one cmdlet to another. This approach improves performance, decreases the execution times of your scripts, and generally reduces the amount of code you write.

Requirements

The only requirement for this chapter is the ability to execute PowerShell code. You have a few ways to accomplish this:

- On a PowerShell prompt.
- Through a scripting editor. (Ensure that it supports PowerShell, allows for code execution to test your code, and includes the ability to view the output of your code.)
- Execute scripts manually.

To measure the execution time for each command I provide in this chapter I use the `Measure-Command` cmdlet, like this:

```
PS D:\> Measure-Command {
➥ Get-WmiObject -Class win32_bios -Property manufacturer |
➥ Where-Object {$_.Manufacturer -eq "Hewlett-Packard"}}

Days              : 0
Hours             : 0
Minutes           : 0
Seconds           : 0
Milliseconds      : 131
Ticks             : 1315776
TotalDays         : 1,52288888888889E-06
TotalHours        : 3,65493333333333E-05
TotalMinutes      : 0,00219296
TotalSeconds      : 0,1315776
TotalMilliseconds : 131,5776
```

Execution times are based on my environment. These numbers are indicative and not definitive. Their purpose is to illustrate the benefits of the alternative scripting techniques I'll show you. Results may vary based on your system.

To make these numbers more reliable measure the execution time multiple times and then calculate the average. The numbers won't change much, though.

Rules of engagement

When I started to use PowerShell I was introduced to the pipeline first. When I saw how easy it was I began to pipe everything together, never noticing execution times or performance impact. Over the last few years the best practices I've learned have enabled me to run scripts in a fraction of the execution time of my previous scripts.

For example, consider a script I wrote that provisions 1,500 user objects in Active Directory. The script uses a CSV file, in which 25 or more properties are defined per user, to assign users to the appropriate groups. Previously, this script took about 12 minutes to execute, and now it takes somewhere between 55 and 60 seconds. Times vary depending on your Active Directory server(s), but you get the idea.

Before I introduce the pipeline best practices let's take a look at the pipeline itself. A pipeline uses a technique called *piping* to pass objects from one command to the next. One way of piping is as follows (in order): get all processes, filter based on the process name, and then stop the process. For example,

```
Get-Process | Where-Object {$_.Name -eq "notepad"} | Stop-Process

Execution time: 61 milliseconds
```

All objects (in this case processes) are received by the `Get-Process` cmdlet. Those objects are piped to the `Where-Object` cmdlet where the objects are filtered based on their name. Only processes with the name "notepad" are piped to the `Stop-Process`, which in turn stops the processes. Let's look at what can happen when your script returns large amounts of data and how you can address the consequences.

Filtering objects sooner

You may encounter situations in which your code must handle large numbers of objects. In these cases filtering that list of objects is imperative to gain the best performance.

Let's revise the notepad example so that it filters the objects sooner. The `Get-Process` cmdlet has a `-Name` parameter that allows you to filter based on the `name` property and eliminates the need to use the `Where-Object` cmdlet:

```
Get-Process -Name notepad | Stop-Process

Execution time: 49 milliseconds
```

The `Get-Process` cmdlet now receives and filters all processes. Only then are they piped to the `Stop-Process` cmdlet. Filtering on object properties instead of using the `Where-Object` cmdlet significantly reduces the number of objects (processes) passed from the first to the second pipe. It also shortens the pipeline. This allows for shorter execution times and less resource utilization.

Let's take a deeper look at this technique.

Filtering by property

Suppose you need to get all files with the .docx or .txt extension and with "PowerShell" in their names. You could use the `Where-Object` cmdlet in the pipeline:

```
PS D:\> Get-ChildItem -Recurse | Where-Object {
➥ (($_.Extension -eq ".docx") -or ($_.Extension -eq ".txt")) -and
➥ ($_.Name -like "*PowerShell*")}

    Directory: D:\

Mode           LastWriteTime   Length  Name
----           -------------   ------  ----
-a---     12-9-2012    10:36   510229  PowerShell ft Hyper-V.docx
-a---     12-9-2012    10:36   8233    PowerShell ft Hyper-V Notes.txt
-a---     2-9-2012     16:24   433672  PowerShell Deep Dives.docx
-a---     2-9-2012     16:24   1285    PowerShell Deep Dives Notes.txt
-a---     21-6-2012    00:52   306913  Practical PowerShell.docx
-a---     21-6-2012    00:52   9835    Practical PowerShell Notes.txt

Execution time: 162 milliseconds
```

This script uses a pipelined expression, but if you use the `Get-ChildItem` cmdlet's parameters instead the script will run more efficiently.

The `Get-ChildItem` cmdlet provides `-Include` and `-Filter` parameters. Let's use those instead of the pipeline:

```
PS D:\> Get-ChildItem -Recurse -Include *.docx, *.txt -Filter *PowerShell*

    Directory: D:\

Mode           LastWriteTime   Length  Name
----           -------------   ------  ----
-a---     12-9-2012    10:36   510229  PowerShell ft Hyper-V.docx
-a---     12-9-2012    10:36   8233    PowerShell ft Hyper-V Notes.txt
-a---     2-9-2012     16:24   433672  PowerShell ft Windows.docx
```

```
-a---        2-9-2012     16:24    1285     PowerShell ft Windows Notes.txt
-a---        21-6-2012    00:52    306913   Practical PowerShell.docx
-a---        21-6-2012    00:52    9835     Practical PowerShell Notes.txt

Execution time: 82 milliseconds
```

As you can see, it's possible to get the same output without using the pipeline.

In PowerShell v3 the `Get-ChildItem` cmdlet also provides `-File` and `-Directory` parameters which allow you to filter for only files or directories. If you're looking for files only, using the `-File` parameter decreases the execution time of the command because directories are skipped entirely.

This is why I always find it useful to know what parameters are offered, and if I don't know, the `Get-Help` cmdlet saves the day.

Filtering by condition

Cmdlets that have parameters that can do the object filtering for you avoid the pipeline altogether. Let's look at an example of how you could filter a list of objects based on a condition. We'll use the pipeline first and then I'll show you an alternative. The following script filters objects based on the value of the `Manufacturer` property:

```
PS D:\> Get-WmiObject -Class win32_bios -Property manufacturer |
  ➥ Where-Object {$_.Manufacturer -eq "Hewlett-Packard"}

__GENUS          : 2
__CLASS          : Win32_BIOS
__SUPERCLASS     :
__DYNASTY        :
__RELPATH        :
__PROPERTY_COUNT : 1
__DERIVATION     : {}
__SERVER         :
__NAMESPACE      :
__PATH           :
Manufacturer     : Hewlett-Packard
PSComputerName   :

Execution time: 82 milliseconds
```

The more efficient way of doing this is to use the `-Query` parameter of the `Get-WmiObject` cmdlet. You can use this parameter to search for the object and show it based on a condition set on the value of the `Manufacturer` property:

```
PS D:\> Get-WMIObject -Query "SELECT Manufacturer FROM Win32_BIOS WHERE
  ➥ Manufacturer='Hewlett-Packard'"

__GENUS          : 2
__CLASS          : Win32_BIOS
__SUPERCLASS     :
__DYNASTY        :
__RELPATH        :
__PROPERTY_COUNT : 1
```

```
__DERIVATION      : {}
__SERVER          :
__NAMESPACE       :
__PATH            :
Manufacturer      : Hewlett-Packard
PSComputerName    :

Execution time: 27 milliseconds
```

Filtering this way is faster and uses fewer resources. To round out this section let's look at how you can conserve resources when filtering many objects.

Returning only the properties that you need

When you're done filtering objects you still have all of the properties attached to them. This information consumes resources that you may not even need and can slow your script and/or system down. To clean this up the `Select-Object` cmdlet and the pipeline come into play:

```
PS D:\> Get-ChildItem -Recurse -Include *.docx, *.txt -Filter *PowerShell*|
➥ Select-Object LastWriteTime, Name

    Directory: D:\

     LastWriteTime  Name
     -------------  ----
12-9-2012    10:36  PowerShell ft Hyper-V.docx
12-9-2012    10:36  PowerShell ft Hyper-V Notes.txt
2-9-2012     16:24  PowerShell ft Windows.docx
2-9-2012     16:24  PowerShell ft Windows Notes.txt
21-6-2012    00:52  Practical PowerShell.docx
21-6-2012    00:52  Practical PowerShell Notes.txt
...
```

There isn't another way to filter the objects and return only the ones you want. `Select-Object` is the way to go here.

NOTE The only reason I'm piping to `Select-Object` here is to make the output appropriate for a book format (due to its width).

Providers and filtering parameters

Filtering with parameters instead of piping to `Where-Object` can have an impact, as I've shown. Let's go one step further and look at a type of parameter that's more powerful than others. *Filtering* parameters, as they're called, work with PowerShell system providers. To understand how filtering parameters work you need to know something about the providers.

PowerShell providers are part of the `Microsoft.PowerShell.Core` module, and filtering parameters let these providers do the work for them. Providers let you access a variety of data stores as though they were file system drives, and they show you these stores the same way a drive is shown. These providers offer power, short execution times, and low overhead on your system. To find out which providers offer filtering capabilities use the `Get-PSProvider` cmdlet:

```
PS D:\> Get-PSProvider | Select-Object -Property *

ImplementingType : Microsoft.PowerShell.Commands.FileSystemProvider
HelpFile         : System.Management.Automation.dll-Help.xml
Name             : FileSystem
PSSnapIn         : Microsoft.PowerShell.Core
ModuleName       : Microsoft.PowerShell.Core
Module           :
Description      :
Capabilities     : Filter, ShouldProcess, Credentials
Home             : C:\Users\Administrator
Drives           : {C, D, F}
...
```

The `Capabilities` property indicates that the file system provider offers filtering capabilities.

Cmdlets that are designed to work with providers have one of the following nouns:

- `ChildItem`
- `Content`
- `Item`
- `ItemProperty`
- `Location`
- `Path`
- `PSDrive`
- `PSProvider`

When you use the `Get-ChildItem` cmdlet PowerShell asks the file system for all of the objects, receives them from the file system, and does the filtering itself. This is when a filtering parameter comes in handy.

The `Get-ChildItem` cmdlet has an `-Include` parameter which tells PowerShell to ask the file system for the objects that comply with the given filter. The file system therefore does the filtering before giving the requested objects to PowerShell. PowerShell doesn't do any filtering and the number of objects/data transferred between PowerShell and the provider (and by extension the system) is kept to a minimum.

Also, the file system provider is more low-level in the system architecture than PowerShell. Because the filtering is accomplished on a level "closer" to the actual data it causes less overhead.

What's in a name?

Here we get to a nice gotcha. You may presume that every cmdlet that offers, for example, a `-Query` parameter automatically uses a provider, but this isn't the case. For example, the `Get-WMIObject` and `Get-ChildItem` cmdlets both have a `-Filter` parameter, but only one uses a provider.

The `Get-ChildItem` cmdlet has a noun from the list you saw previously, which indicates that this cmdlet uses a provider, specifically the file system provider. The `Get-WMIObject` cmdlet doesn't have a noun from the list. When you think about it, is there any provider for WMI? No, there isn't. To check, run the `Get-PSProvider` command.

Where-Object isn't bad

I used the `Where-Object` cmdlet to show you a few examples of how you can avoid the pipeline. But don't get me wrong; the point is that when you don't need to use the pipeline, don't. When you do need to use the pipeline, `Where-Object` has its place.

This powerful cmdlet allows you to filter based on several statements at once. Suppose you need to find all files with "PowerShell" in the name, that are between 1 and 4 MB, and that have the .docx extension. You also want to find all files with "Hyper-V" in the name that are between 1 and 4 MB and have either the .doc or .docx extension. Use the pipeline and the `Where-Object` cmdlet to do this:

```
PS D:\> Get-ChildItem -Recurse -File |
➥ Where-Object {(($_.Name -like "*PowerShell*") -and ($_.Extension -eq
➥ ".docx")) -or (($_.Name -like "*Hyper-V*") -and (($_.Extension -eq
➥ ".doc") -or ($_.Extension -eq ".docx"))) -and (($_.Length -gt 1MB) -and
➥ ($_.Length -lt 4MB))}

    Directory: D:\

     LastWriteTime  Name
     -------------  ----
21-6-2012     00:52  Practical PowerShell.docx
12-7-2012     18:32  PowerShell ft Hyper-V.docx
16-7-2012     12:16  Hyper-V Beyond.doc
2-9-2012      16:24  Hyper-V Design - Standard.docx

Execution time: 180 milliseconds
```

In this example you need to use `Where-Object` and the pipeline because parameters alone don't meet the requirements.

Using regular expressions

You can use regular expressions (regex) in multiple ways. In this section I'll show you one example to give you an idea of the impact regex can have.

Let's say that you need to get all files with "PowerShell" or "Hyper-V" in the name and that have the .docx or .txt extension. You can use pattern matching to find the files:

```
PS D:\> Get-ChildItem -Recurse -File |
➥ Where-Object {(($_.Name -match '.*PowerShell.*\.(docx|DOCX)\b') -or
➥ ($_.Name -match '.*Hyper-V.*\.(doc|DOC|docx|DOCX)\b')) -and (($_.Length
➥ -gt 1MB) -and ($_.Length -lt 4MB))}

    Directory: D:\

     LastWriteTime  Name
     -------------  ----
21-6-2012     00:52  Practical PowerShell.docx
```

```
12-7-2012     18:32  PowerShell ft Hyper-V.docx
16-7-2012     12:16  Hyper-V Beyond.doc
2-9-2012      16:24  Hyper-V Design - Standard.docx

Execution time: 298 milliseconds
```

The execution time is longer, but it's easier to use pattern matching (in this case by using regex) because you can apply this pattern to objects. Matching a pattern offers much more flexibility than a "hard-coded" compare.

I'm using regex for pattern matching only, but you can do much more with it. For example, you could replace text that fits a pattern, split strings, and so on. To give you an idea of all the possibilities, think of regex as wildcards on steroids.

Using member enumeration

In previous versions of PowerShell the only way to perform a task on multiple objects with a one-liner was to use the `ForEach-Object` cmdlet in the pipeline.

For example, in PowerShell v2 if you wanted to get a single property for a group of objects, say the `name` of the objects, some code such as this was needed:

```
PS C:\> Get-Process | Select-Object -Property Name

Name
----
armsvc
conhost
csrss
csrss
dasHost
dwm
explorer
...
```

You needed to use the pipeline to give the group of objects to the next pipe, in this case, a pipe in which the `Select-Object` cmdlet is used to filter the properties to a single one: the name of the objects.

Now let me introduce you to the ultimate avoid-the-pipeline feature brought to you by PowerShell v3: member enumeration. To use this feature you place in parentheses anything that would've previously come in the pipeline before the `Foreach-Object` and/or `Select-Object` pipe. This syntax isn't new to PowerShell v3. What's new here is how it handles the fact that it doesn't know if it's a single object or an entire array of objects.

Before member enumeration you had to do some fancy tricks to handle this. PowerShell now does it for you under the hood. Member enumeration also enumerates, among other things, all possible properties and methods for these objects, which you can use.

Member enumeration and properties

You can use member enumeration to get all the values of a single property on one or a bunch of objects, like so:

```
PS C:\> (Get-Process).Name

Name
----
armsvc
conhost
csrss
csrss
dasHost
dwm
explorer
...
```

Note that member enumeration works only with a single property. To select multiple properties use the `Select-Object` cmdlet in the pipeline.

I didn't provide the execution time of this script because it can be misleading. In this example I'm getting the names of the processes, and using member enumeration takes more time than using the pipeline.

The gotcha with member enumeration is that the more objects you handle, the faster it gets relative to using the pipeline. For example, on a disk with many files and directories, time the execution of the following two commands:

```
Get-ChildItem -Recurse | Select-Object -Property Name
(Get-ChildItem).Name
```

You'll find that member enumeration yields the shorter time.

Let's look at another example of member enumeration. This time we'll use it with a method instead of a property.

Member enumeration and methods

Suppose you need to close all applications named "App1" on all devices in your environment. You could use the `CloseMainWindow()` method attached to the process objects in a one-liner:

```
PS C:\> Get-Process -Name App1 | ForEach-Object { $_.CloseMainWindow() }
True
```

Just as you can use member enumeration with properties, the same syntax works with methods, and that's how you avoid the pipeline:

```
PS C:\> (Get-Process -Name App1).CloseMainWindow()
True
```

Counting objects

All methods that are available on variables that hold objects are also available with member enumeration. Again, let's take a practical example.

To count objects in previous versions of PowerShell you have to use the `Measure-Object` cmdlet:

```
PS C:\> Get-Process | Measure-Object

Count    : 52
Average  :
Sum      :
Maximum  :
Minimum  :
Property :
```

If you only need to know the number of objects, not the name of objects and such, this script gives you more than you need, so you have to select only what you want:

```
PS C:\> Get-Process | Measure-Object | Select-Object -ExpandProperty Count
52
```

This is complex code relative to the information it returns. With member enumeration you can count in a far easier way:

```
PS C:\> (Get-Process).Count
52
```

Instead of `Count` you can also use `Length`; if the object(s) doesn't have such a property it returns `1` (or `0` for `$Null`).

It doesn't matter if you handle one or a thousand objects; under the hood, PowerShell does the filtering and replaces what the `Foreach-Object` cmdlet was doing. In fact, the `ForEach-Object` cmdlet isn't used at all—it's all native PowerShell!

NOTE In PowerShell v2 this syntax to get the count of objects works only when you have multiple objects. In the case of a single object it gives no value back. In PowerShell v3 using member enumeration returns the correct value for both single and multiple objects.

Summary

You've seen how easy it is to avoid the pipeline—when you don't need it. The *when-you-don't-need-it* part is important here. Piping itself is one of the best and most powerful features of PowerShell.

Although this chapter's title suggests avoiding the pipeline, my goal was to show you how to use the commands, parameters, and pipeline in the most efficient way. In some of the examples efficiency removed the need to use the pipeline. So, in fact, does following the PowerShell best practices and filtering on the left.

I've shown you how to combine parameters instead of piping, but there are use cases in which it's prudent to use the pipeline because parameters may not offer the desired functionality. But I've also shown that filtering parameters offer better performance. So when you filter on the left, use the most efficient parameter.

Learning how to best-use the power of the shell results in performance and execution-time improvements. Remember the goal when writing your scripts: to complete the task at hand in the most efficient way.

About the author

Jeff Wouters is a freelance technical consultant with a focus on high availability, delivery, and deployment of applications/desktops/servers using Microsoft and Citrix products. He designs and implements solutions based on technologies such as virtualization, redundancy, clustering, replication, and automation. He also has a great passion for PowerShell and uses it to automate tasks and reports on the job.

Jeff is a PowerShell MVP and has been a speaker at IT events, such as E2E Virtualization Conference, BriForum Chicago, and Microsoft TechDays. He is also the founding member of the Dutch PowerShell User Group. You can find Jeff on social media by searching for his name; he blogs at http://www.jeffwouters.nl (mainly about PowerShell but also about anything that piques his interest).

11 A template for handling and reporting errors

Will Steele

> *Writing programs that work when everything goes as expected is a good start. Making your programs behave properly when encountering unexpected conditions is where it really gets challenging.*
>
> —Marijn Haverbeke
>
> *Eloquent JavaScript: A Modern Introduction to Programming*

Efficient, predictable error handling has been at the core of PowerShell's design since its earliest days and has allowed scripters to design robust automation solutions with minimal effort. In small scripts a balanced combination of common parameters, the use of `Write-Error`, or perhaps `Write-Warning`, and some well-placed `if/then` statements generally prove to be enough for most scripter's daily automation problems. As the size and complexity of my scripts have grown, though, so, too, has my need for a hands-off integration of error handling. With these larger scripts my focus on problem management has dwindled relative to how much the amount of time and energy spent on properly automating the task has increased. In this chapter we'll explore an approach I developed to automatically and precisely report errors using a reusable script template.

Many of the concepts I used to develop this template rely on PowerShell variables and language structures. What's unique is how these items are combined so that anyone with a PowerShell script or Integrated Scripting Environment (ISE) can wrap their commands in my template and end up with an error-aware script designed not only to highlight that a problem has occurred but also exactly what, where, and why the error happened.

To help you understand my approach I'll cover the following PowerShell concepts:

1. The `$ErrorActionPreference` variable
2. The `try/catch/finally` error-handling structure

3. The `$Error` object
4. `InvocationInfo` property bag

After examining these items I'll consolidate them into a single script template to illustrate their practical application.

Using preference variables: $ErrorActionPreference

Preference variables are a set of built-in PowerShell variables that allow you to customize the shell's behavior. You use the `$ErrorActionPreference` variable to control how PowerShell responds to a nonterminating error at the command line or in a script, cmdlet, or provider. Nonterminating errors, such as those generated by the `Write-Error` cmdlet, don't stop the cmdlet processing.

The `$ErrorActionPreference` variable has four possible values:

- `Stop`
- `Inquire`
- `Continue` (the default)
- `SilentlyContinue`

Setting `$ErrorActionPreference` at the script level makes that action the default for all commands inside that script. Usually, though, you want to control error actions at the command level. In that case, use the `-ErrorAction` (or `-EA`) common parameter, which is available for all commands and enables you to set an error action for an individual command.

Because only `Stop` errors can be trapped it's important to set the error action to `Stop` for any command that might generate an error that you can anticipate and that you want to trap and deal with.

NOTE Setting `$ErrorActionPreference` to `SilentlyContinue` at the top of a script is considered a poor practice. Doing so suppresses all errors except for commands that specify a different `-ErrorAction`. Either handle errors (`-ErrorAction Stop`) or allow them to display, but avoid suppressing them.

For the remainder of this chapter I assume that you've identified the commands in your script that might cause an error that you want to handle, and you've either set `$ErrorActionPreference="Stop"` in your script (which would be unusual because that requires you to trap every error for every command in the script), or you've set `-ErrorAction Stop` for those commands.

Also keep in mind that `-ErrorAction` and `$ErrorActionPreference` deal only with nonterminating errors—errors that a command encounters that don't cause it to discontinue. If a command runs into something beyond which it can't continue, it always behaves as if `-ErrorAction Stop` were specified.

Using structured error handling: try/catch/finally

PowerShell is built on top of the .NET Framework. As a result, many of the underlying PowerShell features are adaptations and/or extensions of .NET objects and ideas. The error-handling structures are no different. In fact, .NET offers a variety of language constructs for dealing with errors, including `trap`, `throw`, and `try/catch/finally`. The `-ErrorAction` common parameter deals with cmdlet-level, nonterminating errors. When you need to deal with heavier exceptions use one of these three structures.

In working with each construct the `try/catch/finally` structure has proven to be the most robust. It places the code you want to run in the `try` block. When the code executes the shell monitors for exceptions. If an exception is encountered in the `try` block it's first saved to the `$Error` automatic variable, and PowerShell then attempts to match it to a `trap` or `catch` block. If none is found it passes control to the `finally` block. If it can't be handled at all it's written to the error stream.

One of the powerful features of .NET, and, inherently, the PowerShell `catch` block, is its ability to track both general and specific types of errors. This ability gives you two different approaches to error handling. The first approach is to let any and all errors bubble up to the `catch` block. For large scripts I tend to use this approach because I'm looking for anything that has failed along the way. The second approach is to specify one or more exceptions that you may want to handle in the `catch` block. This can come in handy if the conditions for which you want to handle errors are precise, but in other situations you may not want to provide handling at all. In this chapter we'll focus on the catchall approach because you want as broad a set of exception notifications raised as possible.

To begin building the error-handling template let's combine what we've covered so far into this pattern:

```
$ErrorActionPreference = 'Stop'

try
{
   # Do work
}
catch
{
   $Error
}
finally
{
   # Finalize work
}
```

If we place commands in this pattern and cause a failure on purpose—a divide-by-zero exception, for example—let's see what it does:

```
$ErrorActionPreference = 'Stop'

try
{
    1/0
```

```
}
catch
{
    $_
}
finally
{
    "Completed."
}
```

Running this script returns the following results:

```
Attempted to divide by zero.
At line:5 char:5
+     1/0
+     ~~~
    + CategoryInfo          : NotSpecified: (:) [], RuntimeException
    + FullyQualifiedErrorId : RuntimeException
Completed.
```

As you can see from this output, several important pieces of data are returned: the error message, the error location (both the line and offset), the exception information, and confirmation that it reached the last block with the "Completed" remark.

With a few lines of boilerplate code you have a structured approach to try running code, catching errors, and running clean-up code (in the `finally` block), if necessary. This is the type of information you want from an organized, hands-off exception-handling template.

Now we can move to the final pieces of the puzzle: the `$Error` object and its `InvocationInfo` properties.

Using $Error and InvocationInfo objects

As you work with PowerShell you'll find that many processes hide the mechanics behind how they handle things. For instance, when we ran the command `1/0` PowerShell returned a .NET error and placed it in the `$Error` object. To get a glimpse of what the `$Error` object is, run the following two commands:

```
PS > 1/0
PS > $Error | Get-Member | Format-Table -AutoSize -Wrap
```

Running this pair of commands returns the following results:

```
   TypeName: System.Management.Automation.ErrorRecord

Name                  MemberType     Definition
----                  ----------     ----------
Equals                Method         bool Equals(System.Object obj)
GetHashCode           Method         int GetHashCode()
GetObjectData         Method         System.Void
     GetObjectData(System.Runtime.Serialization.SerializationInfo
     info,System...
GetType               Method         type GetType()
ToString              Method         string ToString()
CategoryInfo          Property       System.Management.Automation.ErrorC...
```

```
ErrorDetails            Property       System.Management.Automation.ErrorD...
Exception               Property       System.Exception Exception {get;}
FullyQualifiedErrorId Property       string FullyQualifiedErrorId {get;}
InvocationInfo          Property       System.Management.Automation.Invoca...
PipelineIterationInfo Property       System.Collections.ObjectModel.Read...
ScriptStackTrace        Property       string ScriptStackTrace {get;}
TargetObject            Property       System.Object TargetObject {get;}
PSMessageDetails        ScriptProperty System.Object PSMessageDetails {get...
```

The MSDN documentation for the ErrorRecord object (http://msdn.microsoft.com/en-us/library/system.management.automation.errorrecord(v=vs.85)) includes a few members worth checking out. Let's revise the divide-by-zero script so that you can examine the properties and see what sort of useful details you can dredge out of this object. The following command gives you some items to look at:

```
$ErrorActionPreference = 'Stop'

try
{
    1/0
}
catch
{
    "CategoryInfo: $($_.CategoryInfo)"
    "ErrorDetails: $($_.ErrorDetails)"
    "Exception: $($_.Exception)"
    "FullyQualifiedErrorID: $($_.FullyQualifiedErrorID)"
    "InvocationInfo: $($_.InvocationInfo)"
    "PipelineIterationInfo: $($_.PipelineIterationInfo)"
    "ScriptStackTrace: $($_.ScriptStackTrack)"
    "TargetObject: $($_.TargetObject)"
    "PSMessageDetails: $($_.PSMessageDetails)"
}
finally
{
    "Completed."
}
```

Running this command returns the following results:

```
CategoryInfo: NotSpecified: (:) [], RuntimeException
ErrorDetails:
Exception: System.Management.Automation.RuntimeException: Attempted to
divide by zero. ---> System.DivideByZeroException: Attempted to divide by
zero.
   --- End of inner exception stack trace ---
   at
     System.Management.Automation.ExceptionHandlingOps.CheckActionPreference(
     Fun
ctionContext funcContext, Exception exception)at
  System.Management.Automation.Interpreter.ActionCallInstruction`2.
  Run(InterpretedFrame frame)
   at
  System.Management.Automation.Interpreter.Interpreter.HandleException
  (InterpretedFrame frame, Exception exception)
```

```
  FullyQualifiedErrorID: RuntimeException
  InvocationInfo: System.Management.Automation.InvocationInfo
PipelineIterationInfo:
ScriptStackTrace:
TargetObject:
PSMessageDetails:
Completed.
```

Most of these details don't tell you much, but the `InvocationInfo` object still has some unpacking to do. As noted in the MSDN documentation, the `InvocationInfo` object (http://msdn.microsoft.com/en-us/library/system.management.automation.invocationinfo_members(v=vs.85).aspx) has a lengthy list of properties that you can tap into to get explicit details about the invoked commands. In this case, the invoked commands are passed to the pipeline object via the `$Error` collection. With some experimentation you can take advantage of a variety of properties accessible through the `InvocationInfo` object.

Listing 1 is a revised version of the divide-by-zero script with a new helper function called `Get-TimeStamp` and a cleared `$Error` object to prevent cross-contamination of stale and new error records. It also includes details about the error's exact nature. Keep in mind that this listing is one example of how you could display error information; it isn't the only way.

Listing 1 Enhanced template that gets error details

```
function Get-TimeStamp                                  <-- Captures formatted time stamps
{
    Get-Date -Format 'yyyy-MM-dd HH:mm:ss'
}

$ErrorActionPreference = 'Stop'                         <-- 1 Sets preference variable

try
{
    1/0                                                 <-- 2 Throws intentional error
}
catch
{
Write-Warning @"                                        <-- 3 Outputs error notification
   $(Get-TimeStamp):
   $(Get-TimeStamp): $('-' * 50)
   $(Get-TimeStamp): -- SCRIPT PROCESSING CANCELLED
   $(Get-TimeStamp): $('-' * 50)
   $(Get-TimeStamp):
   $(Get-TimeStamp): Error in $($_.InvocationInfo.ScriptName).
   $(Get-TimeStamp):
   $(Get-TimeStamp): $('-' * 50)
   $(Get-TimeStamp): -- Error information
   $(Get-TimeStamp): $('-' * 50)
   $(Get-TimeStamp):
   $(Get-TimeStamp): Line Number: $($_.InvocationInfo.ScriptLineNumber)
   $(Get-TimeStamp): Offset: $($_.InvocationInfo.OffsetInLine)
   $(Get-TimeStamp): Command: $($_.InvocationInfo.MyCommand)
```

```
    $(Get-TimeStamp): Line: $($_.InvocationInfo.Line.Trim())
    $(Get-TimeStamp): Error Details: $($_)
    $(Get-TimeStamp):
"@
}
finally
{
    "$(Get-TimeStamp): Completed."
}
```

I set `$ErrorActionPreference = Stop` ❶ because I'm generating an error by attempting to divide by zero ❷. You can't specify an `-ErrorAction` for that division operation, so setting the preference variable is my only recourse. At ❸, I use `Write-Warning` to output the error notification. I could've written it to a file (perhaps by using `Set-Content` or `Out-File`), but onscreen display is sufficient for this demonstration.

When you rerun the script with these refinements you get a clear picture of what went wrong:

```
2012-09-14 21:25:47:
2012-09-14 21:25:47: --------------------------------------------------
2012-09-14 21:25:47: -- SCRIPT PROCESSING CANCELLED
2012-09-14 21:25:47: --------------------------------------------------
2012-09-14 21:25:47:
2012-09-14 21:25:47: Error in C:\Users\owner\Desktop\Powershell\
SampleErrorHandling.ps1.
2012-09-14 21:25:47:
2012-09-14 21:25:47: --------------------------------------------------
2012-09-14 21:25:47: -- Error information
2012-09-14 21:25:47: --------------------------------------------------
2012-09-14 21:25:47:
2012-09-14 21:25:47: Line Number: 10
2012-09-14 21:25:47: Offset: 5
2012-09-14 21:25:47: Command:
2012-09-14 21:25:47: Line:     1/0
2012-09-14 21:25:47: Error Details: Attempted to divide by zero.
2012-09-14 21:25:47:
2012-09-14 21:25:47: Completed.
```

In a sample script like this, where the majority of the code is designed to show proof of concept, you may not appreciate the usefulness of details like this. But when your scripts push into the 3,500-line range you want an error-handling framework that reports, with pinpoint precision and accuracy, what went wrong and where. If I run a script and it spits out an error telling me that on line 1,764, offset 24 an error occurred with a `Get-WebConfiguration` cmdlet call, it's no mystery as to where I need to look to find my problem or what I'm looking for when I get there.

Handling custom business-logic errors with throw and try

Sometimes a business-logic need, not a PowerShell terminating error, requires a script to stop running. From a purely syntactical, processing logic standpoint this is a nonissue.

Consider a unique case in which you look at a directory to see if it has more than 100 files. The business logic here is that if more than 100 files are in a directory, processing must stop and an error must be raised, thereby cancelling the script's processing. In a lower level .NET language you could write your own exceptions, but in PowerShell you don't need to go to the trouble of all that. Using `throw` gives you complete control over when you choose to raise these exceptions or not.

Let's look at two approaches to handling self-raised exceptions. The `Write-Error` cmdlet is the standard cmdlet, which breaks the flow of command and places output on the error pipeline:

```
try
{
    if((Get-ChildItem -Path "C:\windows\system32").Count -gt 100)
    {
        Write-Error "File count surpassed processing limit."
    }
}
```

Because much of the reporting remains the same I'll display only the key portion of the error reporting. When this script runs I get this output from my framework:

```
2012-09-17 13:35:19: Error Details: File count surpassed processing limit.
2012-09-17 13:35:19: Line Number: 24
2012-09-17 13:35:19: Offset: 9
2012-09-17 13:35:19: Command: ErrorHandlingTemplate_002.ps1
2012-09-17 13:35:19: Line:         Write-Error "File count surpassed
     processing limit."
```

Alternatively you can replace the `Write-Error` cmdlet with the `throw` keyword:

```
try
{
    if((Get-ChildItem -Path "C:\windows\system32").Count -gt 100)
    {
        Throw "File count surpassed processing limit."
    }
}
```

This approach yields identical output in terms of the template, yet I've found that using `Write-Error` sometimes fails to properly represent the source of the error if you're dealing with embedded modules and/or functions due to scoping issues. The most effective and consistent results I've found come from using `throw`.

Final template

The final script template (listing 2) contains a few additional features for the sake of completeness. The `transcript` cmdlets (`Start-Transcript` and `Stop-Transcript`) are excellent single-line tools to build a logged record of everything that happened from start to finish of a script. Note that these cmdlets typically work only in the PowerShell console host and not in the ISE.

Listing 2 Complete error-handling template

```
function Get-TimeStamp                                   <-- Function to capture
{                                                            formatted time stamps
    Get-Date -Format 'yyyy-MM-dd HH:mm:ss'
}
                                                             Transcribes
Start-Transcript "$loggingdirectory\$($Host.Name)_          output
➥ $($Host.Version)_$(Get-TimeStamp).txt"                <--

Set-StrictMode -Version 2.0                              <-- Configures script

$ErrorActionPreference = 'Stop'                          <-- Sets preferences
                                                             (1) Clears error
$Error.Clear();                                          <--     variable

try
{
    # Do work - Put the main body of your script here
    <#
    If specific errors are encountered, use throw to break out
    of try for non-terminating/business logic errors.

    Throw "$(Get-TimeStamp): Include custom reporting on business
     logic/non-terminating errors."
    #>
}
catch                                                        Implements
{                                                            try/catch/
@"                                                           finally
   $(Get-TimeStamp): $('-' * 50)                             pattern
   $(Get-TimeStamp): -- SCRIPT PROCESSING CANCELLED
   $(Get-TimeStamp): $('-' * 50)
   $(Get-TimeStamp):
   $(Get-TimeStamp): Error in $($_.InvocationInfo.ScriptName).
   $(Get-TimeStamp):
   $(Get-TimeStamp): $('-' * 50)
   $(Get-TimeStamp): -- Error information
   $(Get-TimeStamp): $('-' * 50)
   $(Get-TimeStamp):
   $(Get-TimeStamp): Error Details: $($_)
   $(Get-TimeStamp): Line Number: $($_.InvocationInfo.ScriptLineNumber)
   $(Get-TimeStamp): Offset: $($_.InvocationInfo.OffsetInLine)
   $(Get-TimeStamp): Command: $($_.InvocationInfo.MyCommand)
   $(Get-TimeStamp): Line: $($_.InvocationInfo.Line)
"@
}
finally
{
    Stop-Transcript
}
```

Clearing the error variable ❶ ensures that any stops encountered are legitimately raised by this `try` block and not another PSSession, script, or variable.

By incorporating the following four PowerShell concepts it's possible to build a robust, "always-on" error-handling template that nails down with 100-percent accuracy the problems in a script:

- `$ErrorActionPreference` variable
- `try/catch/finally` construct
- `$Error` object
- `InvocationInfo` property of the `ErrorRecord`

Summary

Although you can't always catch every problem that may arise while running a script, using techniques like these allows you to worry less about the problems you can't foresee and focus more on the ones you can. In light of this error-handling template, even if you don't gracefully handle 99 percent of problems you'll know about them with a high degree of exactitude.

Thinking back to the opening quote, my goal was to "(m)ak(e) programs behave properly when encountering unexpected conditions ... where it really gets challenging." With this template you now have at your disposal a practical, easy-to-use snippet, which provides an embedded error-handling/reporting mechanism with a minimal amount of code. Instead of focusing on how to handle what could go wrong, now you can focus on making sure you nail down what you need to get right.

About the author

Will Steele was an IT professional and Windows PowerShell enthusiast. He helped get PowerShell.org up and running by acting as a community liaison and building the site's initial calendar of user group meetings and other events. Will attended Christian Brothers University, worked at Fiserv, blogged at http://LearningPCs.blogspot.com, and tweeted as @pen_test. Will passed away in December 2012, shortly after making his contribution to this book. He's survived by his wife and three children and is deeply missed by the PowerShell community.

12 Tips and tricks for creating complex or advanced HTML reports with PowerShell

Jonathan Medd

One of PowerShell's most common uses is to collect data and then generate reports from that data, which makes it an excellent tool. PowerShell can export data for reporting purposes to a number of different formats, including CSV, XML, and HTML. But typically you can only export the data in a raw form, and you'll have to use other tools to make the report look pretty.

In this chapter I'll show you ways to improve the quality of an HTML-based report using PowerShell tips and tricks, without needing to depend on other tools. By means of a Systems Inventory report example you'll see what you can achieve with a small amount of extra knowledge.

To create the Systems Inventory report I'll use some standard PowerShell techniques for scripts, but the focus of the chapter will be on PowerShell tips in HTML. Throughout the chapter I'll be putting together the following sections to build up the script, and I'll include the complete code at the end of this chapter:

- Script parameters and help
- A `begin` block to include generating the HTML header and report image
- A `process` block to generate the queries that will produce the report data for each computer included in the report
- An `end` block to join together the various HTML code parts and export them to a file

Standard ConvertTo-HTML output

Since PowerShell v1, a cmdlet called `ConvertTo-HTML` has been included as standard. Most PowerShell books and learning materials typically have covered this cmdlet since early on as a means to export data, alongside others such as Export-CSV and Export-CLIXML, but these have usually only been covered as a basic tool. The tale usually follows something like "...take the following example, pipe it to ConvertTo-HTML, and you have a great report to send to your manager or display on the company intranet." But when you examine that report it's unlikely to be something that's going to get you that promotion from your manager or look great on the intranet. Look at the following listing.

Listing 1 ConvertTo-HTML example with Out-File

```
$os = Get-WmiObject win32_operatingsystem
$bios = Get-WmiObject win32_bios

$report = [pscustomobject]@{
        ComputerName        = $OS.__Server
        Description         = $OS.Caption
        BuildNumber         = $OS.BuildNumber
        BIOSSerial          = $BIOS.SerialNumber
    }
$report | ConvertTo-Html | Out-File BasicReport.html
```

This listing will produce a report, shown in figure 1, that isn't particularly pleasing to the eye as it only displays black text on a white background.

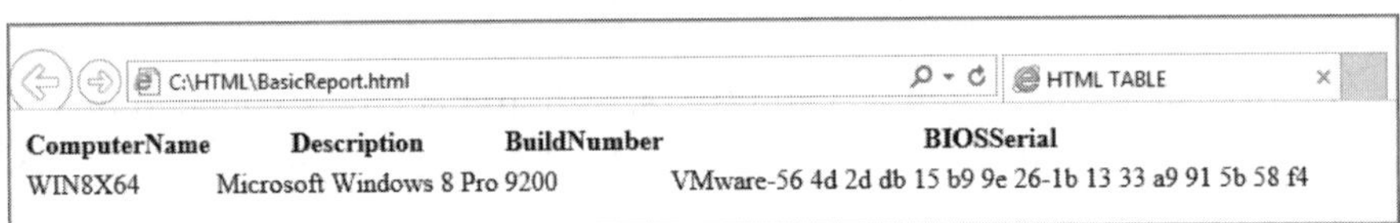

C:\HTML\BasicReport.html
HTML TABLE
ComputerName
Description
BuildNumber
BIOSSerial
WIN8X64
Microsoft Windows 8 Pro 9200
VMware-56 4d 2d db 15 b9 9e 26-1b 13 33 a9 91 5b 58 f4

Figure 1 Basic HTML report using the ConvertTo-HTML cmdlet

NOTE ConvertTo-HTML sends data to the pipeline, not directly to an HTML file; consequently the data is typically sent down the pipeline to Out-File.

With the help of the tips and tricks in this chapter you can turn the report in figure 1 into something more appealing, such as you'll see in figure 2.

Script parameters and help

The tips and tricks illustrated in this chapter will form part of an example Systems Inventory report. Some of these examples will use parameters from the script, which is why I introduce the script in the next listing. This script includes standard PowerShell help and parameters, explanations that are out of the scope of this chapter.

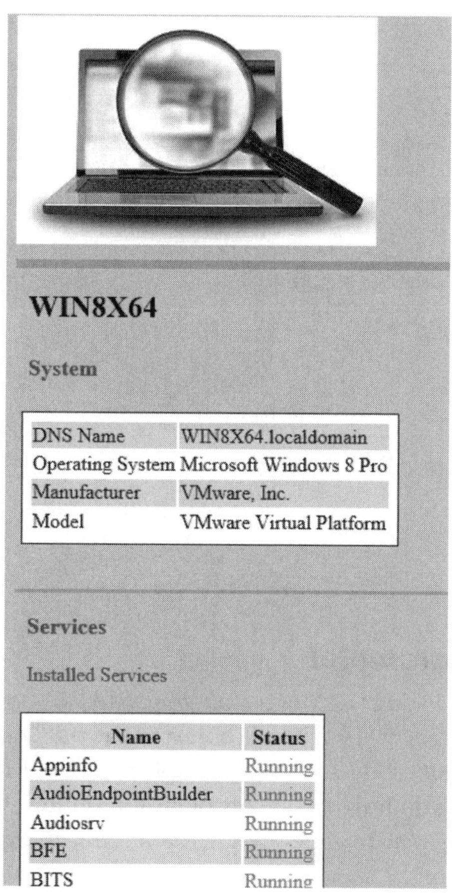

WIN8X64
System
DNS Name
WIN8X64.localdomain
Operating System
Microsoft Windows 8 Pro
Manufacturer
VMware, Inc.
Model
VMware Virtual Platform
Services
Installed Services
Name
Status
Appinfo
Running
AudioEndpointBuilder
Running
Audiosrv
Running
BFE
Running
BITS
Running

Figure 2 HTML report using tips and tricks from this chapter

Listing 2 Script parameters and help

```
<#
.SYNOPSIS
   HTML Systems Inventory Report

.DESCRIPTION
   Create an HTML Systems Inventory Report for multiple computers

.PARAMETER ComputerName
   Supply a name(s) of the computer(s) to create a report for

.PARAMETER ReportFile
   Path to export the report file to

.PARAMETER ImagePath
   Path to an image file to place at the top of the report

.EXAMPLE
   Get-HTMLSystemsInventoryReport -ComputerName Server01 -ReportFile `
     C:\Report\InventoryReport.html -ImagePath C:\Report\Image.jpg
#>
```

```
[CmdletBinding()]

Param
    (
        [Parameter(Mandatory=$true,
                   ValueFromPipeline=$true,
                   ValueFromPipelineByPropertyName=$true,
                   Position=0)]
        [ValidateNotNullOrEmpty()]
        [Alias("CN","__SERVER","IPAddress","Server")]
        [String[]]
        $ComputerName,

        [Parameter(Mandatory=$true,
                   Position=1)]
        [ValidateNotNullOrEmpty()]
        [String]
        $ReportFile,

        [Parameter(Position=2)]
        [String]
        $ImagePath
    )
...
```

ConvertTo-HTML's -Fragment parameter

If you examine the HTML code in listing 1, which was generated by `$report | ConvertTo-Html | Out-File BasicReport.html`, you'll observe that the `ConvertTo-HTML` cmdlet generates all of the HTML code for you, as displayed in the following snippet. Nice and easy, but this leaves you little in the way of customization. Wouldn't it be great if you could use `ConvertTo-HTML` to generate the report data and then handle the style of the document elsewhere?

```
PS C:\HTML> $report | ConvertTo-Html
<!DOCTYPE html PUBLIC "-//W3C//DTD XHTML 1.0 Strict//EN"  "http://www.w3.org/
     TR/xhtml1/DTD/xhtml1-strict.dtd">
<html xmlns="http://www.w3.org/1999/xhtml">
<head>
<title>HTML TABLE</title>
</head><body>
<table>
<colgroup><col/><col/><col/><col/></colgroup>
<tr><th>ComputerName</th><th>Description</th><th>BuildNumber</th><th>
 BIOSSerial</th></tr>
<tr><td>WINDOWS8X64</td><td>Microsoft Windows 8 Pro</td><td>9200</
     td><td>VMware-56 4d f3 6e 62 f3 f0 8a-24 92 69 21 a6 cc
 6b ed</td></tr>
</table>
</body></html>
```

My first tip is to use the `-Fragment` parameter of `ConvertTo-HTML` to generate your data and to separately create the formatting HTML code yourself. Notice that using the following parameter gives you only the data in HTML, but not the header:

```
PS C:\HTML> $report | ConvertTo-Html -Fragment
<table>
<colgroup><col/><col/><col/><col/></colgroup>
<tr><th>ComputerName</th><th>Description</th><th>BuildNumber</th><th>
BIOSSerial</th></tr>
<tr><td>WINDOWS8X64</td><td>Microsoft Windows 8 Pro</td>
<td>9200</td><td>VMware-56 4d f3 6e 62 f3 f0 8a-24 92 69 21 a6 cc
6b ed</td></tr>
</table>
```

I'll use this technique a number of times to generate report data. To create the header HTML code I'll use a here-string and manually store the header in a variable.

Using a PowerShell here-string to create the HTML header

It's possible for you to manually create the HTML header and store it in a variable ready for use later. Combining this method with the previously mentioned `-Fragment` parameter means that you can better control the style of the HTML document and concentrate on using PowerShell to collect the data for the report. I've set out the HTML header in the following listing—you're only limited by your imagination and level of HTML knowledge, but you'll find plenty of examples online if you need a decent starting point. A good place to check out is www.w3schools.com, as it not only has excellent free resources on CSS styles, but also HTML in general. Let's take a look at the next listing, which shows a possible example for our HTML header that will be placed in the `begin` section of our script.

Listing 3 HTML header stored in a variable

```
$HTMLHeader = @"

    <!DOCTYPE html PUBLIC "-//W3C//DTD XHTML 1.0 Strict//EN" "http://
     www.w3.org/TR/xhtml1/DTD/xhtml1-strict.dtd">

    <html xmlns="http://www.w3.org/1999/xhtml" lang="en" xml:lang="en">
    <head>
    <title>Systems Inventory</title>
    <style type="text/css">
    <!--

    body {
        background-color: #66CCFF;
    }

    table {
        background-color: white;
        margin: 5px;
        top: 10px;
        display: inline-block;
        padding: 5px;
        border: 1px solid black
    }
```

```
    h2 {
        clear: both;
        font-size: 150%;
        margin-left: 10px;
        margin-top: 15px;
    }
    h3 {
        clear: both;
        color: #FF0000;
        font-size: 115%;
        margin-left: 10px;
        margin-top: 15px;
    }
    p {

        color: #FF0000;
        margin-left: 10px;
        margin-top: 15px;
    }
    tr:nth-child(odd) {background-color: lightgray}
    -->
    </style>
    </head>
    <body>
"@
...
```

In listing 3 I've stored the HTML header in a PowerShell here-string, mostly setting style information such as colors and table formatting for upcoming sections in the Systems Inventory report. I'll include this listing in the `begin` block of the script because it's only required to be executed once, no matter how many computers are included in the report. It'd also be good to brighten up the HTML report further by adding an image. In the next section we'll look at a way to do this.

Encoding an image into the HTML report

Our HTML Systems Inventory report will begin to look a lot smarter if we include an image and make it look similar to figure 3.

It's possible to do this using base64 to encode the image using PowerShell, then creating the necessary HTML and storing the result in a variable. By encoding the image into the document you won't have a dependency on the image file any longer. Consequently it may make it easier to distribute the report, say by email, as you don't need to include the image alongside the

Figure 3 Encoded image in HTML document

report file. You'll place the code in the next listing in the begin section of the script because you only have to include it once.

Listing 4 Encode an image into an HTML document

```
Function Get-Base64Image ($Path) {
        [Convert]::ToBase64String((Get-Content $Path -Encoding Byte))
    }
if ($ImagePath) {
        if (Test-Path -Path $ImagePath) {

        $HeaderImage = Get-Base64Image -Path $ImagePath

        $ImageHTML = @"
            <img src="data:image/jpg;base64,$($HeaderImage)" style="left:
 150px" alt="System Inventory">
"@
        }
    else {
        throw "$($ImagePath) is not a valid path to the image file"
        }
...
```

In listing 4 I created a function called Get-Base64Image that I'll use to encode the image. Then I'll check that the image file exists with Test-Path and create the HTML code that's necessary to display an encoded image.

Because we've been storing the HTML code in variables we'll be able to put it all together by joining the variables to create one large block of HTML code. At this point we've created the header and an image, which means the end block of our script is populated with the HTML header and encoded image, as shown in the following listing.

Listing 5 Preparing the end block with the HTML header and encoded image

```
end {
    $HTMLHeader +$ImageHTML | Out-File $ReportFile
}
```

Now I only need to prepare the required data for each system, store the result in a variable, and add it to the end block to create the full HTML report.

Adding charts to the report

To brighten up the report further I'm going to use the Microsoft Chart Controls next. This tool will help me to generate a pie chart to illustrate the Service StartMode on the computer being reported on, such as that shown in figure 4.

NOTE You can use the Microsoft Chart Controls to create charts of any type you can think of to illustrate data in a professional format for your reports. In this particular example I'm using a pie chart, but the code required need only be adjusted slightly depending on the type of chart you wish to use for your report.

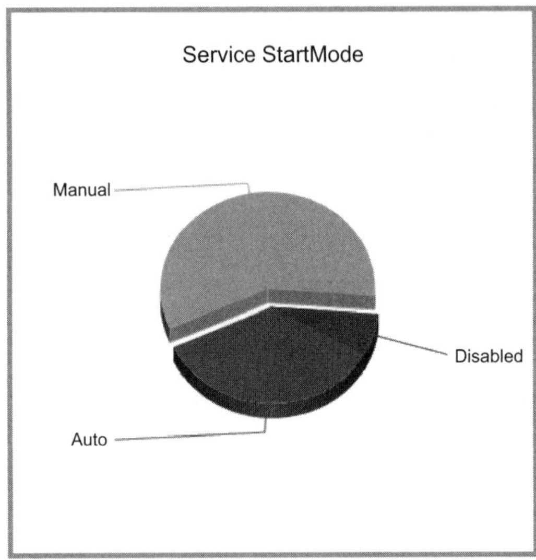

Figure 4 Service StartMode pie chart

If you've installed .NET Framework 4 you have everything you need to use the Microsoft Chart Controls. If you have .NET Framework 3.5 SP1 you'll need to run an additional download, which you can find at: www.microsoft.com/en-us/download/details.aspx?id=14422.

I've created the `New-PieChart` function and stored it in the `begin` code block (see the next listing). I've created it in order to create the pie chart I need for each system, using the reporting script.

Listing 6 Code for the `New-PieChart` function

```
function New-PieChart {
    <#
    .SYNOPSIS
       Create a new Pie Chart using .Net Chart Controls

    .DESCRIPTION
       Create a new Pie Chart using .Net Chart Controls

    .PARAMETER Title
       Title of the chart

    .PARAMETER Width
       Width of the chart

    .PARAMETER Height
       Height of the chart

    .PARAMETER Alignment
       Alignment of the chart

    .PARAMETER SeriesName
        Name of the data series

    .PARAMETER xSeries
        Property to use for x series
```

```
.PARAMETER ySeries
    Property to use for y series

.PARAMETER Data
   Data for the chart

.PARAMETER ImagePath
   Path to save a png of the chart to

.EXAMPLE
   New-PieChart -Title "Service Status" -Series "Service" -xSeries
      ➥ "Name" -ySeries "Count" -Data $Services
      ➥ -ImagePath C:\Report\Image.jpg
#>

[CmdletBinding()]

Param
    (
        [Parameter(Mandatory=$true)]
        [ValidateNotNullOrEmpty()]
        [String]$Title,

        [Parameter(Mandatory=$false)]
        [ValidateNotNullOrEmpty()]
        [Int]$Width = 400,

        [Parameter(Mandatory=$false)]
        [ValidateNotNullOrEmpty()]
        [Int]$Height = 400,

        [Parameter(Mandatory=$false)]
        [ValidateSet("TopLeft","TopCenter","TopRight",
                    "MiddleLeft","MiddleCenter","MiddleRight",
                    "BottomLeft","BottomCenter","BottomRight")]
        [String]$Alignment = "TopCenter",

        [Parameter(Mandatory=$true)]
        [ValidateNotNullOrEmpty()]
        [String]$SeriesName,

        [Parameter(Mandatory=$true)]
        [ValidateNotNullOrEmpty()]
        [String]$xSeries,

        [Parameter(Mandatory=$true)]
        [ValidateNotNullOrEmpty()]
        [String]$ySeries,

        [Parameter(Mandatory=$true)]
        [ValidateNotNullOrEmpty()]
        [PSObject]$Data,

        [Parameter(Mandatory=$true)]
        [ValidateNotNullOrEmpty()]
        [String]$ImagePath
    )

[void][Reflection.Assembly]::LoadWithPartialName `
 ("System.Windows.Forms.DataVisualization")
```

```
    $Chart = New-Object `
     System.Windows.Forms.DataVisualization.Charting.Chart
       $Chart.Width = $Width
       $Chart.Height = $Height

    [void]$Chart.Titles.Add("$Title")
       $Chart.Titles[0].Alignment = $Alignment
       $Chart.Titles[0].Font = "Calibri,20pt"

    $ChartArea = New-Object `
     System.Windows.Forms.DataVisualization.Charting.ChartArea
       $ChartArea.Area3DStyle.Enable3D = $true
       $Chart.ChartAreas.Add($ChartArea)

       [void]$Chart.Series.Add($SeriesName)
       $Chart.Series[$SeriesName].ChartType = "Pie"
       $Chart.Series[$SeriesName]["PieLabelStyle"] = "Outside"
       $Data | ForEach-Object `
{$Chart.Series[$SeriesName].Points.Addxy( $_.$xSeries , $_.$ySeries) } | Out-
     Null
       $Chart.Series[$SeriesName].Points.FindMaxByValue()["Exploded"] =`
$true

       $Chart.SaveImage("$ImagePath","png")
    }
 }
```

I'll use the New-PieChart function in the next section to process services for each computer in the report and pass that data into the function. The final step of the function exports the chart to a PNG file. I'll use the Get-Base64Image function again to encode the chart image into the report.

Preparing the data for the report

To generate data for this report I'm using a mixture of WMI queries and some standard PowerShell cmdlets to give an example of some typical data you might wish to include in an inventory report. The results of each WMI query are stored in variables for later reference and shown in the following listing. You'll place this code in the process block because it'll need to execute for every computer you want to include in the report.

Listing 7 Preparing the inventory queries, variables, and pie chart

```
$OperatingSystem = Get-WmiObject Win32_OperatingSystem -ComputerName `
     $Computer
$ComputerSystem = Get-WmiObject Win32_ComputerSystem -ComputerName `
     $Computer
$LogicalDisk = Get-WmiObject Win32_LogicalDisk -ComputerName $Computer
$NetworkAdapterConfiguration = Get-WmiObject -Query "Select * From `
     Win32_NetworkAdapterConfiguration Where IPEnabled = 1" -ComputerName `
     $Computer
$Services = Get-Service -ComputerName $Computer
$Hotfixes = Get-HotFix -ComputerName $Computer
```

```
$Hostname = $ComputerSystem.Name
$DNSName = $OperatingSystem.CSName +"." + `
     $NetworkAdapterConfiguration.DNSDomain
$OSName = $OperatingSystem.Caption
$Manufacturer = $ComputerSystem.Manufacturer
$Model = $ComputerSystem.Model

$Resources = [pscustomobject] @{
    NoOfCPUs = $ComputerSystem.NumberOfProcessors
    RAMGB = $ComputerSystem.TotalPhysicalMemory /1GB -as [int]
    NoOfDisks = ($LogicalDisk | Where-Object {$_.DriveType -eq 3} | Measure-
     Object).Count
    }

$StartMode = $Services | Group-Object StartMode
        $PieChartPath = Join-Path (Split-Path `
     $script:MyInvocation.MyCommand.Path) -ChildPath ServicesChart.png
        New-PieChart -Title "Service StartMode" -Series "Service ` StartMode
     by Type" -xSeries "Name" -ySeries "Count" -Data $StartMode `
-ImagePath $PieChartPath

        $PieImage = Get-Base64Image -Path $PieChartPath

$ServiceImageHTML = @"
<img src="data:image/jpg;base64,$($PieImage)" style="right: 150px" `
     alt="Services">
"@
...
```

Now you can construct the HTML for each data section using the `-Fragment` parameter technique I previously demonstrated. For example, in the next listing I create the HTML code for the system services information. Note the boldfaced syntax I use to sort multiple properties in different directions.

Listing 8 Building the HTML for the system services information

```
$ServicesHTML = $Services | Sort-Object `
     @{Expression="Status";Descending=$true},@{Expression="Name" `
     ;Descending=$false} | Select-Object Name,Status | ConvertTo-Html
     -Fragment
```

This process will be repeated for each section of the report and will generate HTML code for us to insert into the report later (this code is cut for brevity).

```
<table>
<colgroup><col/><col/></colgroup>
<tr><th>Name</th><th>Status</th></tr>
<tr><td>Appinfo</td><td>Running</td></tr>
<tr><td>AudioEndpointBuilder</td><td>Running</td></tr>
<tr><td>Audiosrv</td><td>Running</td></tr>
<tr><td>BFE</td><td>Running</td></tr>
<tr><td>BITS</td><td>Running</td></tr>
<tr><td>BrokerInfrastructure</td><td>Running</td></tr>
.................
</table>
...
```

Again, though, this is quite static-looking data—let's brighten it up somewhat.

Differentiating report data with color

In the previous example of system services data turned into HTML you'll typically end up with services that have a status of either 'Running' or 'Stopped.' It'd be great to differentiate these with color and make them stand out better in our report. Figure 5 illustrates an example of this using the report.

VMTools	Running
Wcmsvc	Running
WdiServiceHost	Running
WinDefend	Running
WinHttpAutoProxySvc	Running
Winmgmt	Running
wscsvc	Running
WSearch	Running
AeLookupSvc	Stopped
ALG	Stopped
AllUserInstallAgent	Stopped
AppIDSvc	Stopped
AppMgmt	Stopped
AxInstSV	Stopped
BDESVC	Stopped

Figure 5 Differentiating report data with color

I achieve this by using the -Replace operator. Any text with <td>Running</td> will be replaced with HTML code to turn the word 'Running' green:

```
$ServicesFormattedHTML =  $ServicesHTML |
     ForEach {

   $_ -replace "<td>Running</td>","<td style='color: green'>Running</td>"

}
```

I need to assign more than one color, though: green for 'Running' and red for 'Stopped.' But I can do this without much extra effort, because I can use multiple -Replace operators on the same line:

```
$ServicesFormattedHTML =  $ServicesHTML | ForEach {

   $_ -replace "<td>Running</td>","<td style='color: green'>Running</td>"
   ➥ -replace "<td>Stopped</td>","<td style='color: red'>Stopped</td>"

}
```

The report's almost ready. Now I just need to put everything together.

Final steps

I'll put the report data together for each computer (we're still inside the process block) with a mixture of manual HTML and dynamically generated HTML stored in variables. Each time I process a computer I add the result to the $HTMLSystemReport variable. Then to round off things I close out the script with the end block, putting all of the different HTML pieces together, as shown in the next listing.

Listing 9 Building the HTML code for each computer in the report

```
$ItemHTML = @"
    <hr noshade size=5 width="100%">

    <p><h2>$Hostname</p></h2>
    <h3>System</h3>
    <table>
    <tr>
```

```
    <td>DNS Name</td>
    <td>$DNSName</td>
    </tr>
    <tr>
    <td>Operating System</td>
    <td>$OSName</td>
    </tr>
    <tr>
    <td>Manufacturer</td>
    <td>$Manufacturer</td>
    </tr>
    <tr>
    <td>Model</td>
    <td>$Model</td>
    </tr>
    </table>

    <br></br>

    <hr noshade size=1 width="100%">

    <h3>Services</h3>
    <p>Installed Services</p>
    $ServicesFormattedHTML

    <hr noshade size=1 width="100%">

    <h3>Hotfixes</h3>
    <p>Installed Hotfixes</p>
    $HotfixesFormattedHTML
    <br></br>

    <hr noshade size=1 width="100%">

    <h3>Resources</h3>
    <p>Installed Resources</p>
    $ResourcesHTML
"@
$HTMLSystemReport += $ItemHTML
}
end {
    $HTMLHeader +$ImageHTML + $HTMLSystemReport | Out-File $ReportFile
}
```

The end block to finish

You can view the complete script in the next listing.

Listing 10 Completed Systems Inventory script

```
<#
.SYNOPSIS
   HTML Systems Inventory Report

.DESCRIPTION
   Create an HTML Systems Inventory Report for multiple computers

.PARAMETER ComputerName
   Supply a name(s) of the computer(s) to create a report for

.PARAMETER ReportFile
   Path to export the report file to
```

```
.PARAMETER ImagePath
   Path to an image file to place at the top of the report

.EXAMPLE
   Get-HTMLSystemsInventoryReport -ComputerName Server01 `
 -ReportFile C:\Report\InventoryReport.html -ImagePath C:\Report\Image.jpg
#>

[CmdletBinding()]

Param
    (
        [Parameter(Mandatory=$true,
                   ValueFromPipeline=$true,
                   ValueFromPipelineByPropertyName=$true,
                   Position=0)]
        [ValidateNotNullOrEmpty()]
        [Alias("CN","__SERVER","IPAddress","Server")]
        [String[]]
        $ComputerName,

        [Parameter(Mandatory=$true,
                   Position=1)]
        [ValidateNotNullOrEmpty()]
        [String]
        $ReportFile,

        [Parameter(Position=2)]
        [String]
        $ImagePath
    )

begin {

    $UsedParameter = $False
    if ($PSBoundParameters.ContainsKey('ComputerName')){
        $UsedParameter = $True
        $InputObject = $ComputerName
    }

    if (!(Test-Path (Split-Path $ReportFile))){

        throw "$(Split-Path $ReportFile) is not a valid path to the report
   file"
    }

    $HTMLHeader = @"

    <!DOCTYPE html PUBLIC "-//W3C//DTD XHTML 1.0 Strict//EN" "http://
     www.w3.org/TR/xhtml1/DTD/xhtml1-strict.dtd">

    <html xmlns="http://www.w3.org/1999/xhtml" lang="en" xml:lang="en">
    <head>
    <title>Systems Inventory</title>
    <style type="text/css">
    <!--

    body {
        background-color: #66CCFF;
    }
```

```
    table {
        background-color: white;
        margin: 5px;
        top: 10px;
        display: inline-block;
        padding: 5px;
        border: 1px solid black
    }

    h2 {
        clear: both;
        font-size: 150%;
        margin-left: 10px;
        margin-top: 15px;
    }

    h3 {
        clear: both;
        color: #FF0000;
        font-size: 115%;
        margin-left: 10px;
        margin-top: 15px;
    }

    p {

        color: #FF0000;
        margin-left: 10px;
        margin-top: 15px;
    }

    tr:nth-child(odd) {background-color: lightgray}

    -->
    </style>
    </head>
    <body>
"@

    function Get-Base64Image ($Path) {
        [Convert]::ToBase64String((Get-Content $Path -Encoding Byte))
    }

        if ($ImagePath) {
        if (Test-Path -Path $ImagePath) {

        $HeaderImage = Get-Base64Image -Path $ImagePath

        $ImageHTML = @"
            <img src="data:image/jpg;base64,$($HeaderImage)" `
 style="left: 150px" alt="System Inventory">
"@
        }
    else {
        throw "$($ImagePath) is not a valid path to the image file"
        }
    }
```

```
function New-PieChart {
<#
.SYNOPSIS
   Create a new Pie Chart using .Net Chart Controls

.DESCRIPTION
   Create a new Pie Chart using .Net Chart Controls

.PARAMETER Title
   Title of the chart

.PARAMETER Width
   Width of the chart

.PARAMETER Height
   Height of the chart

.PARAMETER Alignment
   Alignment of the chart

.PARAMETER SeriesName
    Name of the data series

.PARAMETER xSeries
    Property to use for x series

.PARAMETER ySeries
    Property to use for y series

.PARAMETER Data
   Data for the chart

.PARAMETER ImagePath
   Path to save a png of the chart to

.EXAMPLE
   New-PieChart -Title "Service Status" -Series "Service" `
-xSeries "Name" -ySeries "Count" -Data $Services -ImagePath `
  C:\Report\Image.jpg
#>

[CmdletBinding()]

Param
    (
        [Parameter(Mandatory=$true)]
        [ValidateNotNullOrEmpty()]
        [String]$Title,

        [Parameter(Mandatory=$false)]
        [ValidateNotNullOrEmpty()]
        [Int]$Width = 400,

        [Parameter(Mandatory=$false)]
        [ValidateNotNullOrEmpty()]
        [Int]$Height = 400,

        [Parameter(Mandatory=$false)]
        [ValidateSet("TopLeft","TopCenter","TopRight",
                     "MiddleLeft","MiddleCenter","MiddleRight",
                     "BottomLeft","BottomCenter","BottomRight")]
        [String]$Alignment = "TopCenter",
```

```
            [Parameter(Mandatory=$true)]
            [ValidateNotNullOrEmpty()]
            [String]$SeriesName,

            [Parameter(Mandatory=$true)]
            [ValidateNotNullOrEmpty()]
            [String]$xSeries,

            [Parameter(Mandatory=$true)]
            [ValidateNotNullOrEmpty()]
            [String]$ySeries,

            [Parameter(Mandatory=$true)]
            [ValidateNotNullOrEmpty()]
            [PSObject]$Data,

            [Parameter(Mandatory=$true)]
            [ValidateNotNullOrEmpty()]
            [String]$ImagePath
        )

    [void][Reflection.Assembly]::LoadWithPartialName `
     ("System.Windows.Forms.DataVisualization")

       $Chart = New-Object `
     System.Windows.Forms.DataVisualization.Charting.Chart
       $Chart.Width = $Width
       $Chart.Height = $Height

       [void]$Chart.Titles.Add("$Title")
       $Chart.Titles[0].Alignment = $Alignment
       $Chart.Titles[0].Font = "Calibri,20pt"

       $ChartArea = New-Object `
     System.Windows.Forms.DataVisualization.Charting.ChartArea
       $ChartArea.Area3DStyle.Enable3D = $true
       $Chart.ChartAreas.Add($ChartArea)

       [void]$Chart.Series.Add($SeriesName)
       $Chart.Series[$SeriesName].ChartType = "Pie"
       $Chart.Series[$SeriesName]["PieLabelStyle"] = "Outside"
       $Data | ForEach-Object `
{$Chart.Series[$SeriesName].Points.Addxy( $_.$xSeries , $_.$ySeries) } | Out-
     Null
       $Chart.Series[$SeriesName].Points.FindMaxByValue()["Exploded"] = $true

           $Chart.SaveImage("$ImagePath","png")
    }
}

process {

    if (!($UsedParameter)){

        $InputObject = $_
    }

    foreach ($Computer in $InputObject){

        $OperatingSystem = Get-WmiObject Win32_OperatingSystem `
-ComputerName $Computer
        $ComputerSystem = Get-WmiObject Win32_ComputerSystem `
```

```
-ComputerName $Computer
        $LogicalDisk = Get-WmiObject Win32_LogicalDisk -ComputerName
     $Computer
        $NetworkAdapterConfiguration = Get-WmiObject -Query `
"Select * From Win32_NetworkAdapterConfiguration Where IPEnabled = 1" `
-ComputerName $Computer
        $Services = Get-WmiObject Win32_Service -ComputerName $Computer
        $Hotfixes = Get-HotFix -ComputerName $Computer

        $Hostname = $ComputerSystem.Name
        $DNSName = $OperatingSystem.CSName +"." `
+ $NetworkAdapterConfiguration.DNSDomain
        $OSName = $OperatingSystem.Caption
        $Manufacturer = $ComputerSystem.Manufacturer
        $Model = $ComputerSystem.Model

        $Resources = [pscustomobject] @{
            NoOfCPUs = $ComputerSystem.NumberOfProcessors
            RAMGB = $ComputerSystem.TotalPhysicalMemory /1GB -as [int]
            NoOfDisks = ($LogicalDisk | Where-Object {$_.DriveType -eq 3} |
     Measure-Object).Count
        }

        $StartMode = $Services | Group-Object StartMode
        $PieChartPath = Join-Path (Split-Path `
     $script:MyInvocation.MyCommand.Path) -ChildPath ServicesChart.png
        New-PieChart -Title "Service StartMode" -Series `
"Service StartMode by Type" -xSeries "Name" -ySeries "Count" `
-Data $StartMode -ImagePath $PieChartPath

        $PieImage = Get-Base64Image -Path $PieChartPath

$ServiceImageHTML = @"
            <img src="data:image/jpg;base64,$($PieImage)" `
style="right: 150px" alt="Services">
"@

        $ServicesHTML = $Services | Sort-Object `
     @{Expression="State";Descending=$true}, `
     @{Expression="Name";Descending=$false} | Select-Object Name,State |
     ConvertTo-Html -Fragment
        $ServicesFormattedHTML =  $ServicesHTML | ForEach {

           $_ -replace "<td>Running</td>","<td style='color: green'>Running</
     td>" -replace "<td>Stopped</td>", `
"<td style='color: red'>Stopped</td>"

        }

        $HotfixesHTML = $Hotfixes | Sort-Object Description |
Select-Object HotfixID,Description,InstalledBy,Installedon |
ConvertTo-Html -Fragment
        $HotfixesFormattedHTML =  $HotfixesHTML | ForEach {

           $_ -replace "<td>Update</td>","<td style='color: blue'>Update</
     td>" -replace "<td>Security Update</td>", `
"<td style='color: red'>Security Update</td>"

        }

        $ResourcesHTML = $Resources | ConvertTo-Html -Fragment
```

```
$ItemHTML = @"
    <hr noshade size=5 width="100%">

    <p><h2>$Hostname</p></h2>
    <h3>System</h3>
    <table>
    <tr>
    <td>DNS Name</td>
    <td>$DNSName</td>
    </tr>
    <tr>
    <td>Operating System</td>
    <td>$OSName</td>
    </tr>
    <tr>
    <td>Manufacturer</td>
    <td>$Manufacturer</td>
    </tr>
    <tr>
    <td>Model</td>
    <td>$Model</td>
    </tr>
    </table>

    <br></br>

    <hr noshade size=1 width="100%">

    <h3>Services</h3>
    <p>Installed Services</p>
    $ServicesFormattedHTML

    $ServiceImageHTML

    <hr noshade size=1 width="100%">

    <h3>Hotfixes</h3>
    <p>Installed Hotfixes</p>
    $HotfixesFormattedHTML
    <br></br>

    <hr noshade size=1 width="100%">

    <h3>Resources</h3>
    <p>Installed Resources</p>
    $ResourcesHTML
"@
        $HTMLSystemReport += $ItemHTML
    }
}

end {
    $HTMLHeader +$ImageHTML + $HTMLSystemReport | Out-File $ReportFile
}
```

The script can be executed to generate the report, as this example shows:

```
PS C:\HTML> "WIN8X64","WIN701","WIN702" | ./SystemReport.ps1 -ReportFile `
 C:\HTML\InventoryReport.html -ImagePath C:\HTML\Header.jpg
```

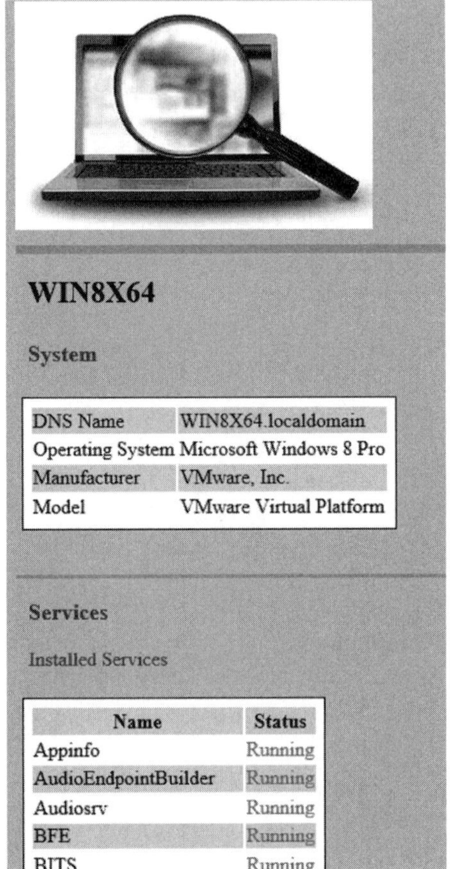

Figure 6 Sample of the finished Systems Inventory report

Figure 6 shows how the report now takes on a more colorful appearance than the report with which I first started.

Summary

I hope these PowerShell tips and tricks have helped you to see a few of the possibilities for transforming basic HTML reports with black text on white backgrounds that use only `ConvertTo-HTML`, to something more colorful that's presentable as a management type of report.

I recommend you break up the report into sections, build up the different HTML parts, and join them together at the end to turn the report into a file. If you're experienced with HTML or happy to carry out some deeper research you should be able to take these reports even further than I have in this chapter—for example, by adding charts, multiple columns and pages, and collapsing sections—and in turn produce even better-looking reports.

About the author

Jonathan Medd has been working with IT infrastructure products since 1997. A few years ago he discovered Windows PowerShell, and he now cohosts the *Get-Scripting* PowerShell podcast. Since April 2010 he's been a Microsoft MVP for Windows PowerShell, and in 2011 he was honored as a VMware vExpert. He is co-author of *VMware vSphere PowerCLI Reference.*

13 Using and "abusing" dynamic parameters

Bartosz Bielawski

In our lives we make choices all the time; some choices are obligatory, but sometimes they're optional. Imagine you're buying a bike. You need to customize it, and although some choices are "static," such as selecting the frame or the wheels, some aren't. For example, you'd consider stabilizers only if you were looking for a bike for a small child. At a bike shop a salesperson probably wouldn't start a conversation about your purchase of a new bike with the question: "Which stabilizers do you prefer: ones with Spiderman or ones with Lightning McQueen?" But if you mention that you're looking for a bike for your little son, these questions would seem natural. Dynamic parameters are additional options that only make sense in your current context and only then will you have a chance to use them.

Version 1 of the PowerShell scripting language already was powerful and flexible and with each new version it improves. PowerShell almost always uses some language elements in production scripts, such as parameter validation, comment-based help, and pipeline binding. But one rarely used feature (mainly because of complexity of application, limitations it brings to the table, and relatively small number of use cases) is the dynamic parameter. If you've ever been in a situation where you needed additional control over code, the dynamic parameter feature may be the solution for you.

What are dynamic parameters? They're a way to customize your command to the point where parameter presence and options depend on conditions, both external and internal. Unlike static parameters, they usually show up when they're needed. Input parameters in any scripting language have one main purpose: they provide flexibility to change the behavior of scripts, functions, and procedures, without having to edit the code. PowerShell supports several levels of parameter control:

- automatic `$args`
- simple named parameters

- parameters with `[Parameter()]` decoration
- parameters grouped in parameter sets
- dynamic parameters

It's the script author's decision to determine the level of complexity and control to use. To put our main topic in correct context we'll first take a look at static parameters to see what we can achieve in PowerShell, without implementing dynamic parameters.

Static parameters

As I mentioned previously, each version of PowerShell has introduced new language elements that allow script authors to control parameters. In v1 they were already robust, but the advanced functions built into v2 made them all the more powerful. Let's first take a look at v1 functionality, and then spend some time on the features that were added in v2.

INITIAL DESIGN

PowerShell v1 was built to support three ways of accepting inline input to functions and scripts: using the automatic `$args` variable, using `named` parameters, and using `positional` parameters. You'll have situations where `$args` is a sufficient way to accept external input, particularly in ad hoc scripting. But this way of passing parameters is fragile and can cause unexpected behavior. This is because you depend on order and you can't change this order or skip any of the parameters. Obviously, for some functions you won't have any negative effects, such as when you use the function that turns lists of words into string arrays:

```
function New-StringArray {
    [string[]]$args
}
```

Once you start writing more robust functions, named parameters become a natural way of accepting input and offer the added benefits of passing parameters in any order you choose, or skipping parameters you don't need (see the following listing). It's also a good idea to put parameters in the `param` block—this way you have consistent syntax between scripts, functions, and script blocks.

Listing 1 Example function with named parameters

```
function Get-ADSIComputer {
param (
    $Filter,
    $Root
)

    if (!$Filter) {
        Write-Warning "Filter is required."
        return
    }

    $Searcher = New-Object ADSISearcher -ArgumentList @(
        [ADSI]$Root,
```

```
        "(&(objectClass=computer)($Filter))"
    )
    $Searcher.FindAll()
}
```

You can call your function using the parameter's positions (as we did with `$args`). You can also take advantage of how the PowerShell parser handles parameters: you don't have to specify a full parameter name; you only need enough from its name to differentiate it from the other parameters. In our case, the first letter would be sufficient (F for *Filter* and R for *Root*). Version 1 of PowerShell also allows you to specify type for named parameters and give them a default value. Because the default value can be a subexpression it can be used to make the parameter mandatory. I've slightly improved the function so you don't have to check for the presence of the required parameter. A trick related to the default value, shown in the next listing, will help us with that.

Listing 2 Example of function that uses parameters with types and default values

```
function Get-ADSIComputer {
param (
    [string]$Filter = $(throw "Filter is required!"),
    [ADSI]$Root = ''
)

    $Searcher = New-Object ADSISearcher -ArgumentList @(
        $Root,
        "(&(objectClass=computer)($Filter))"
    )
    $Searcher.FindAll()
}
```

And that's all you can do with v1. Let's look at what v2 has to offer.

ADVANCED FUNCTIONS

When you're writing functions or scripts in PowerShell v2 you can make them so robust that it may be hard to tell the difference between your code and a compiled cmdlet. Parameters can be mandatory (with the same prompt you get for mandatory parameters in cmdlets), take value from a pipeline (both by property and value), have aliases, and have validated input. You can support different scenarios using sets of parameters. Parameters can be shared between sets and also be unique to one of them. Although improved parameter binding is just one of the advanced functions in v2, I want to focus on parameters, so I won't discuss other advantages of writing advanced function. The following listing is an example of the same function we defined previously, rewritten with everything the advanced function has to offer in the parameter definition area.

Listing 3 Sample advanced function

```
function Get-ADSIComputer {
[CmdletBinding(
    DefaultParameterSetName = 'Filter'
)]
```

```
param (
    [Parameter(
        Mandatory = $true,
        HelpMessage = "LDAP Filter",
        ParameterSetName = 'Filter'
    )]
    [ValidatePattern('^\w+=[\w*]+$')]
    [string]$Filter,
    [Parameter(
        Mandatory = $true,
        ParameterSetName = 'All'
    )]
    [switch]$All,
    [ValidateScript({
        $Pattern = '(^(?-i:LDAP)://.*?,DC=\w+$|^$)'
        if ($_.Path -match $Pattern) {
            $true
        } else {
            throw "Wrong path specified!"
        }
    })]
    [ADSI]$Root = ''
)

    if ($All) {
        $Filter = 'name=*'
    }
    $Searcher = New-Object ADSISearcher -ArgumentList @(
        [ADSI]$Root,
        "(&(objectClass=computer)($Filter))"
    )
    $Searcher.FindAll()
}
```

As you can see, all those elements can help you define functions in a production-ready fashion. You can write functions and scripts that can prevent future users from shooting themselves in the foot.

Dynamic parameters

All of the parameters I've mentioned up to this point are static. Even if we grouped them in sets, all of the parameters I've defined are available all the time. Dynamic parameters behave differently: their existence depends on conditions that the code author defines. Dynamic parameters are added at runtime, which forces a different syntax than the one reserved for static parameters: you need to explicitly use .NET types that you use implicitly in a normal parameter definition. Dynamic parameters can have the same elements as static parameters—that is, they can be mandatory, have validation, aliases, and so on. As always, this technique has both advantages and disadvantages, which we'll explore next.

ADVANTAGES AND DISADVANTAGES

Before we dig into the applications of dynamic parameters take a look at table 1, which lists the reasons why you may want to use them, and why you may want to avoid them.

Table 1 Advantages and disadvantages of dynamic parameters

Advantages	Disadvantages
You can investigate the context in which your command will run Binding after all other parameters (late binding)	Dynamic parameters are harder to discover Binding after all other parameters Complex implementation

One main advantage of dynamic parameters is that you can investigate the context in which your command will run: mainly the current state (for example, path—something that provider cmdlets do) and the values of other parameters. Then you can perform actions based on that information. This conditional nature makes your final product more user-friendly, because you don't show parameters that wouldn't work in a particular situation.

Late binding (binding after all static parameters) shows up in both columns. It's an advantage because it gives you the added benefit of defining some options (like validation attributes) depending on your situation at runtime. This means even if you always want to use a parameter you may want to adapt its behavior to the current situation, something only dynamic parameters can help with. At the same time this may cause some issues. A perfect example of that is the disambiguating of shortened parameters that we mentioned previously: if a unique static parameter matches the short version it'll be always used, even if other dynamic parameters would also match.

The biggest disadvantage is the fact that dynamic parameters are hard to discover. Because of their dynamic nature they won't show up in help for command, nor will they be present in the parameter list retrieved by `Get-Command`, unless you run the following command in the required context (if the context is the only factor used, as it is for most provider-related cmdlets):

```
PS C:\> Set-Location -Path C:
PS C:\> (Get-Command -Name Set-Item).Parameters['Type']
PS C:\> Set-Location -Path HKLM:\
PS HKLM:\> (Get-Command -Name Set-Item).Parameters['Type']

Name            : Type
ParameterType   : Microsoft.Win32.RegistryValueKind
ParameterSets   : {[__AllParameterSets,
    System.Management.Automation.ParameterSetMetadata]}
IsDynamic       : True
Aliases         : {}
Attributes      : {__AllParameterSets}
SwitchParameter : False
```

Alternatively, you can specify the optional parameter `ArgumentList`, with all of the positional parameters required by the definition of dynamic parameter:

```
PS HKLM:\> Set-Location -Path C:
PS C:\> (Get-Command -Name Set-Item -ArgumentList HKLM:).Parameters['Type']

Name            : Type
ParameterType   : Microsoft.Win32.RegistryValueKind
```

```
ParameterSets    : {[__AllParameterSets,
     System.Management.Automation.ParameterSetMetadata]}
IsDynamic        : True
Aliases          : {}
Attributes       : {__AllParameterSets}
SwitchParameter : False
```

The last disadvantage to cover from the previous table is complexity of implementation. You have to use .NET classes directly to define dynamic parameters. Rather than memorizing the syntax you'll probably have to use templates or snippets.

Why would you want to use dynamic parameters? Let's take a look first at existing implementations of dynamic parameters; then we'll cover a few scenarios where this language element may be justified, regardless of the disadvantages related to it.

EXISTING IMPLEMENTATIONS OF DYNAMIC PARAMETERS

Dynamic parameters were used in all versions of PowerShell. Most dynamic parameters can be found in provider-related cmdlets. Provider cmdlets were designed with supporting common functionality in mind. But what if the provider that you'd like to use has some unique capabilities? Should you implement this as the cmdlet parameter for all of your providers? If you do, it may cause confusion, as users would see this parameter and expect it to work against providers that aren't able to understand it. That's why provider-related cmdlets have many dynamic parameters. You can apply this same philosophy to any command you create. But you don't have to stop there—dynamic parameters can give you even more, if you can think outside the box and "abuse" them.

Practical applications

Dynamic parameters are a way to make more general cmdlets (like provider-related cmdlets) adaptable to current circumstances. Even though most providers support similar operations and try to expose objects in a similar fashion, you don't lose any provider-specific functionality thanks to dynamic parameters. With that in mind let's look at practical examples of dynamic parameter implementations. As I mentioned previously, it's not as straightforward as it is with static parameters. You have to call .NET classes directly, put pieces together, and test, test, test. It may not work at first, so testing is crucial and it usually takes some time (and/or experience) to do it right.

We'll first try to do something similar to what provider cmdlets do. Then we'll explore some other situations where dynamic parameters can also be useful.

Using dynamic parameters

We'll start slowly with a basic function that will support a dynamic parameter, depending on the current date. We'll use it to show the structure of an advanced function that supports dynamic parameters. The next listing shows what this kind of function looks like.

Listing 4 Basic advanced function with dynamic parameter defined

```
function Get-Drink {
[CmdletBinding()]                                    <-- Changing regular function into advanced function
param (
    [switch]$Soft,
    [switch]$Hot
)

DynamicParam {

if (0, 6 -contains (Get-Date).DayOfWeek) {
    $SM = 'System.Management.Automation'
    $Type = 'Collections.ObjectModel.Collection[System.Attribute]'
    $Name = 'Strong'
    $Param = @{
        TypeName = "$SM.ParameterAttribute"
        Property = @{
            ParameterSetName = "__AllParameterSets"
            Mandatory = $false
        }
    }
    $Attributes = New-Object @Param                  Creating attribute object with selected options set

    $AttributeCollection = New-Object $Type
    $AttributeCollection.Add($Attributes)            Creating attributes collection from previously created attributes

    $Param = @{
        TypeName = "$SM.RuntimeDefinedParameter"
        ArgumentList = @(
            $Name,
            [switch],
            $AttributeCollection
        )
    }
    $Parameter = New-Object @Param                   Defining dynamic parameter

    $Param = @{
        TypeName =
            "$SM.RuntimeDefinedParameterDictionary"
    }
    $Dictionary = New-Object @Param
    $Dictionary.Add($Name, $Parameter)
    $Dictionary                                      Defining and returning parameters dictionary
}
}

end {
    if ($PSBoundParameters.ContainsKey('Strong')) {
        "It's weekend, let's try something strong!"  Using dynamic parameter value
    }
    if ($Soft) {
        "Time for some soft drinks!"
    }
    if ($Hot) {
        "Tea or coffee - what will it be?"
    }
}
}
```

NOTE Once you decide to define dynamic parameters you have to use the `begin`, `process`, and `end` scriptblocks; otherwise you'll end up with errors. But adding blocks that logically divide code into things that happen before pipeline processing starts (`begin`), then happen for every item passed into the pipeline (`process`), and then things that happen after the last item in the pipeline is processed (`end`) is a good idea even if you don't plan to use dynamic parameters.

The entire process of creating dynamic parameter(s) requires several steps:

1. Create parameter attributes (this includes things like validation attributes)
2. Create collection from parameter attributes
3. Create parameter object with name, type, and previously created collection of attributes
4. Add parameters to dictionary with their names as key, and parameter object as value
5. Return parameters dictionary
6. In function body retrieve parameter value from `$PSBoundParameters` dictionary

The code shown in listing 4 may be hard to read at first (as I mentioned, it looks a lot like C# with all `New-Object` calls). It's probably a good idea to have your template handy with the code necessary to build a parameter collection. But it's also a good idea to check the MSDN documentation for classes used inside this construct to make sure you're doing it right, particularly in the case of validation attributes.

When would you want to use dynamic parameters in production? They're justified when material that your function or script should work with is dynamic as well. Another possible scenario is to add a parameter only if it can be used when the value of some other parameter meets some criteria.

For example, the `Get-WmiObject` will accept the `Credential` parameter only for remote computers. If you're writing an inventory function using this cmdlet you may want to make sure that the `ComputerName` parameter points to a remote box and only then allow users to specify alternate credentials. The following listing presents a few things: it adds a dynamic parameter based on the value of another parameter, sets a default value for the created parameter, and uses `ArgumentTransformationAttribute` in the `DynamicParam` block.

Listing 5 Using a dynamic parameter to decide if the `Credential` parameter is needed

```
function Get-Inventory {
[CmdletBinding()]
param (
    [Parameter(
        Mandatory = $true
    )]
    [string]$ComputerName
)
```

```
DynamicParam {
    $IPAddresses =  [net.dns]::GetHostAddresses($env:COMPUTERNAME) |
        select -ExpandProperty IpAddressToString

    $HostNames = $IPAddresses | ForEach-Object {
            try {
                [net.dns]::GetHostByAddress($_)
            } catch {
                # We do not care about errors here...
            }
        } | select -ExpandProperty HostName -Unique

    $LocalHost = @(
        '',
        '.',
        'localhost',
        $env:COMPUTERNAME,
        '::1',
        '127.0.0.1'
    ) + $IPAddresses + $HostNames

    if ($LocalHost -notcontains $ComputerName -and
        $ComputerName) {
        $SMA = 'System.Management.Automation'
        $Type = 'Collections.ObjectModel.Collection[System.Attribute]'
        $Name = 'Credential'
        $AttributeCollection = New-Object $Type

        $Attribute1 = New-Object "$SMA.ParameterAttribute" -Property @{
            ParameterSetName = "__AllParameterSets"
            Mandatory = $false
        }
        $AttributeCollection.Add($Attribute1)

        $Attribute2 = New-Object "$SMA.CredentialAttribute"
        $AttributeCollection.Add($Attribute2)

        $Parameter = New-Object "$SMA.RuntimeDefinedParameter"`
            -ArgumentList @(
                $Name,
                [Management.Automation.PSCredential],
                $AttributeCollection
            ) -Property @{
                Value = [Management.Automation.PSCredential]::Empty
            }

        $Dictionary = New-Object "$SMA.RuntimeDefinedParameterDictionary"
        $Dictionary.Add($Name, $Parameter)
        $Dictionary
    }
}

end {
    $Options = $PSBoundParameters + @{
        ErrorAction = 'Stop'
    }
```

Collecting local computer names in array of strings

Using collection to check if computer is local

```
    try {
        $Param = $Options + @{
            Class = 'Win32_OperatingSystem'
        }
        $OpertingSys = Get-WmiObject @Param
        $Param.Class = 'Win32_OperatingSystem'
        $ComputerSys = Get-WmiObject @Param

        New-Object PSObject -Property @{
            Name = $ComputerSys.Name
            User = $ComputerSys.UserName
            OSName = $OpertingSys.Caption
            SP = $OpertingSys.ServicePackMajorVersion
        } | select Name, User, OSName, SP
    } catch {
        "{0}: error - {1}" -f $PSBoundParameters.ComputerName, $_ |
            Write-Warning
    }
}
}
```

Using PSBoundParameters directly on cmdlet

Now whenever you try to get inventory from a remote computer you have the option to specify credentials, and if you try to connect a local computer this parameter won't show up, as figure 1 shows.

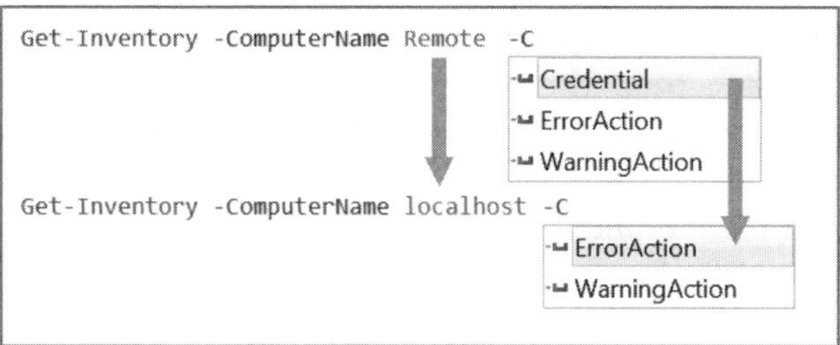

Figure 1 Different parameters available for connecting to different computers

"Abusing" dynamic parameters

In some situations you may want to use dynamic parameters not because of the conditional nature of their creation, but because of late binding and its ability to read an environment at runtime. Because `DynamicParam` runs before PowerShell will perform any operation inside a script or function you can mitigate errors, avoiding issues with missing prerequisites.

A good example of this kind of situation is defining type for parameters. An example of such a function is shown in the next listing.

Listing 6 Function that uses type defined inside the module for its parameter

```
function Test-Type {
param (
    [Parameter(
        Mandatory = $true,
        ValueFromPipeline = $true
```

```
    )]
    [Microsoft.ActiveDirectory.Management.ADUser]$User
)
begin {
    if (!(Get-Module ActiveDirectory)) {
        "You need to load ActiveDirectory module." |
            Write-Error
    }
}
process {
    Get-ADUser $User -Properties *
}
}
```

Using custom type for static parameter

Checking Active Directory module presence

If an assembly that contains a selected type isn't loaded before the function is used it will cause errors that usually make sense for the author only, as you can see in figure 2.

As the previous figure shows we've tried to use the function `Test-Type`. We haven't explicitly used any type; the function tried to do that on our behalf. Even though PowerShell v3 by default would try to load the module when the command can't be found, it won't work for the missing types. This means the autoloading feature didn't help for using our function. The friendly error message the function author included didn't make it to the user. It may be hard to understand what went wrong. The fix is to load the module first, but the function author can't check for it nor inform the user about it in a friendly error message.

You can avoid this issue by testing the presence of the module before the function runs, but you can also use dynamic parameters and try to import the module or throw a friendly error message if the module isn't available. Once you set up the dynamic parameters you will have two benefits:

- A module (or other required assembly) will be loaded before binding parameters.
- If the module isn't present on the system you'll get an error message that clearly states the nature of the problem.

You can see this friendly error message in figure 3.

As you can see, the function grew a little bit. The parameter was moved to the `DynamicParam` block without losing any attributes. The only thing you've added is code that checks if you have the necessary type available, as shown in the next listing.

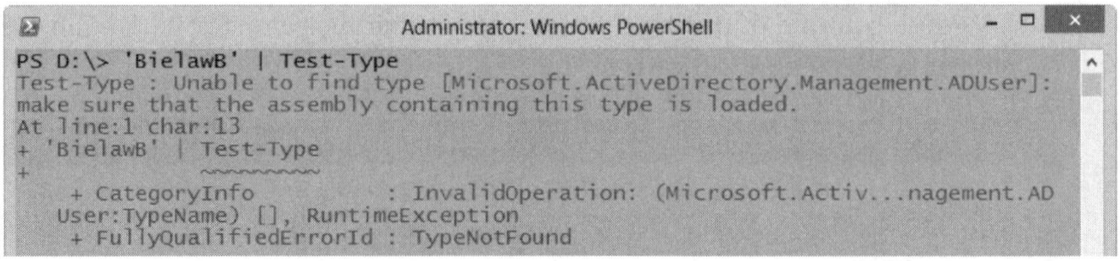

```
Administrator: Windows PowerShell
PS D:\> 'BielawB' | Test-Type
Test-Type : Unable to find type [Microsoft.ActiveDirectory.Management.ADUser]:
make sure that the assembly containing this type is loaded.
At line:1 char:13
+ 'BielawB' | Test-Type
+             ~~~~~~~~~
    + CategoryInfo          : InvalidOperation: (Microsoft.Activ...nagement.AD
   User:TypeName) [], RuntimeException
    + FullyQualifiedErrorId : TypeNotFound
```

Figure 2 Error message that user will receive, instead of a friendly warning built into the function

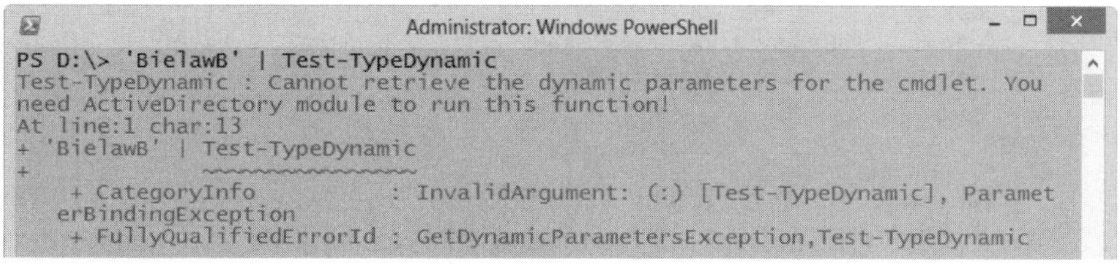

```
Administrator: Windows PowerShell
PS D:\> 'BielawB' | Test-TypeDynamic
Test-TypeDynamic : Cannot retrieve the dynamic parameters for the cmdlet. You
need ActiveDirectory module to run this function!
At line:1 char:13
+ 'BielawB' | Test-TypeDynamic
+             ~~~~~~~~~~~~~~~~
    + CategoryInfo          : InvalidArgument: (:) [Test-TypeDynamic], Paramet
   erBindingException
    + FullyQualifiedErrorId : GetDynamicParametersException,Test-TypeDynamic
```

Figure 3 The friendly error message generated by code inside a `DynamicParam` block

Listing 7 Dynamic parameter supports loading the missing module to avoid error

```
function Test-TypeDynamic {
[CmdletBinding()]
param ()
DynamicParam {
    $Message = "You need ActiveDirectory module to run this function!"
    if (!(Get-Module ActiveDirectory)) {
        try {
            $Param = @{
                Name = 'ActiveDirectory'
                ErrorAction = 'Stop'
            }
            Import-Module @Param
        } catch {
            throw $Message
        }
    }
    $SMA = 'System.Management.Automation'
    $Type = 'Collections.ObjectModel.Collection[System.Attribute]'
    $Name = 'User'

    $Attributes = New-Object "$SMA.ParameterAttribute" -Property @{
        ParameterSetName = "__AllParameterSets"
        Mandatory = $true
        ValueFromPipeline = $true
    }
    $AttributeCollection = New-Object $Type
    $AttributeCollection.Add($Attributes)

    $Param = @{
    TypeName = "$SMA.RuntimeDefinedParameter"
    ArgumentList = @(
        $Name,
        [Microsoft.ActiveDirectory.Management.ADUser],
        $AttributeCollection
    )
    }
    $Parameter = New-Object @Param

    $Dictionary = New-Object "$SMA.RuntimeDefinedParameterDictionary"
    $Dictionary.Add($Name, $Parameter)
    $Dictionary
}
```

Checking Active Directory module presence and loading it

Defining parameter using custom type from module

```
process {
    $User = $PSBoundParameters.User
    Get-ADUser $User -Properties *
}
}
```

As you can see, instead of using a condition to decide whether or not to add a parameter, you'll test the presence of the module that contains the type used for the example parameter. If it's absent we'll try to load it. If loading fails we'll provide a user-friendly error message that informs the user what went wrong. This isn't exactly what this feature was designed for, but that shouldn't stop you.

Another example situation where you may want to take advantage of late binding without making the parameter itself optional is when you want to apply a validation attribute that changes, depending on the value of the already bounded parameter. The next listing contains the function that will decide on the validation attribute for the `Suffixes` parameter once the `Prefix` is defined.

Listing 8 Function that validates second parameter based on value of first parameter

```
function Ping-Host {
[CmdletBinding()]
param (
    [ValidatePattern('^\d{1,3}(\.\d{1,3}){0,2}$')]      <-- Using ValidateSet for our static Prefix parameter
    [string]$Prefix
)

DynamicParam {
    if ($Prefix -match '^\d{1,3}(\.\d{1,3}){0,2}$') {      <-- Checking if Prefix meets requirement first
        $SMA = 'System.Management.Automation'
        $Type = 'Collections.ObjectModel.Collection[System.Attribute]'
        $Name = 'Suffixes'
        $AttributeCollection = New-Object $Type

        $Attribute1 = New-Object "$SMA.ParameterAttribute" -Property @{
            ParameterSetName = "__AllParameterSets"
            Mandatory = $true
        }
        $AttributeCollection.Add($Attribute1)

        switch -Regex ($Prefix) {                     <-- Using switch to define pattern for Suffixes parameter
            '^\d{1,3}$' {
                $Pattern = '^\d{1,3}(\.\d{1,3}){2}$'
            }
            '^\d{1,3}\.\d{1,3}$' {
                $Pattern = '^\d{1,3}\.\d{1,3}$'
            }
            '^\d{1,3}(\.\d{1,3}){2}$' {
                $Pattern = '^\d{1,3}$'
            }
        }
        $Attribute2 = New-Object "$SMA.ValidatePatternAttribute" $Pattern

        $AttributeCollection.Add($Attribute2)
```

```
        $Parameter = New-Object "$SMA.RuntimeDefinedParameter"`
            -ArgumentList @(
                $Name,
                [string[]],
                $AttributeCollection
            )
        $Dictionary = New-Object "$SMA.RuntimeDefinedParameterDictionary"
        $Dictionary.Add($Name, $Parameter)
        $Dictionary
    }
}

end {
    $Output = @{}
    $Type = 'System.Net.NetworkInformation.Ping'
    $Suffixes = $PSBoundParameters.Suffixes
    Write-Verbose ($Suffixes -join ',')
    foreach ($Suffix in $Suffixes) {
        $IP = "{0}.{1}" -f $Prefix, $Suffix
        $Output.Add($IP,
            (New-Object $Type).SendPingAsync(
                $IP
            )
        ) | Out-Null
    }
    do {
        foreach ($Key in ($Output.Keys |
                    where { $Output.$_.IsCompleted})) {
            $Output.$Key.Result | select Status, RoundTripTime, @{
                Name = 'Address'
                Expression = { $Key }
            }
            $Output.Remove($Key)
        }
    } until (!$Output.Count)
}
}
```

Using .NET 4.5 method to simplify asynchronous pinging

We know that the IPv4 address consists of four octets expressed individually in decimal numbers and separated by periods. Depending on the number of octets covered by the `Prefix` you'll define the pattern for the `Suffixes` so that joining them together will produce a valid IP address. As a result, if you specify the correct number of octets you'll get asynchronous ping results:

```
PS C:\> Ping-Host -Prefix 192.168.1 -Suffixes (1..3)

                     Status              RoundtripTime Address
                     ------              ------------- -------
                    Success                          4 192.168.1.1
                    Success                          0 192.168.1.3
DestinationHostUnreachable                           0 192.168.1.2
```

But if the number of octets is incorrect you'll get the error message:

```
PS C:\> Ping-Host -Prefix 192.168 -Suffixes (1..3)
Ping-Host : Cannot validate argument on parameter 'Suffixes'. The argument
```

```
"1" does not match the "^\d{1,3}\.\d{1,3}$" pattern. Supply an argument
that matches "^\d{1,3}\.\d{1,3}$" and try the command again.
At line:1 char:37
+ Ping-Host -Prefix 192.168 -Suffixes (1..3)
+                                     ~~~~~~
    + CategoryInfo          : InvalidData: (:) [Ping-Host], ParameterBindin
   gValidationException
    + FullyQualifiedErrorId : ParameterArgumentValidationError,Ping-Host
```

This gives us the option to make our command flexible, without losing appropriate parameter validation.

Summary

The Windows PowerShell scripting language is flexible and potentially dynamic. Commands may adapt their behavior and parameters to the circumstances at runtime and dynamic parameters are a powerful technique to implement it.

Dynamic parameters by definition are present depending on predefined conditions. But it's also possible to use this language element to implement parameters that can always be present, but which require late binding. This is because of some dependencies that have to be met, or some flexibility you'd like to implement in the validation of attributes. The requirement to run code during the parameter binding phase is enough to justify using dynamic parameters.

This flexibility, though, comes at a price that may discourage script authors from using the technique. It's complex and it harms discoverability of parameters. But I recommend that you know how to use this technique and have it handy for whenever circumstances justify using it. In my opinion it's great that this option exists, and I'm happy that most provider-related cmdlets use it to make providers more practical and easier to use.

About the author

Bartosz (Bartek) Bielawski is a busy IT Administrator with an international company, PAREXEL. He loves PowerShell and automation. That love earned him the honor of Microsoft MVP. He shares his knowledge mainly on his blogs and through articles published in the Polish *IT Professional* magazine.

14 PowerShell type formatting

Adam Driscoll

Type formatting is used to define how a .NET type will be displayed on the PowerShell command line or host. Without the use of formatting a large number of .NET types would prove difficult to read. This chapter focuses on defining a custom formatting file for the `PrintSystemJobInfo` class. This class defines the print jobs that are in progress on local and remote print servers. The following script outputs all the print jobs on the local machine:

```
Add-Type -AssemblyName "System.Printing"

foreach($pq in (New-Object -TypeName
  ➥ System.Printing.PrintServer).GetPrintQueues())
{
    $pq.Refresh()
    $pq.GetPrintJobInfoCollection()
}
```

The script creates a new `PrintServer` object, iterates over the print queues on the system, and then returns the print jobs for each of the print queues. Running the script yields output similar to what's shown here:

```
HostingPrintServer          : System.Printing.PrintServer
HostingPrintQueue           : System.Printing.PrintQueue
JobName                     : Print System Document
IsRetained                  : False
IsUserInterventionRequired  : False
IsBlocked                   : False
IsDeleted                   : False
IsPaperOut                  : False
IsOffline                   : False
IsPrinting                  : False
...
```

This particular class has 33 properties. Although most of them are useful, viewing all of them at once makes it difficult to find the most important information. This is especially true when many print jobs are running on a machine.

One example of type formatting that comes preinstalled is the `FileInfo` class returned by `Get-ChildItem` within the file system provider. This class contains 15 properties. The default format reduces that to 4, groups them, and displays them in a table as shown here:

```
PS C:\Users\Adam> Get-ChildItem
    Directory: C:\Users\Adam
Mode                LastWriteTime     Length Name
----                -------------     ------ ----
d-r--         7/13/2012   7:07 PM            Contacts
d-r--        11/18/2012   8:18 PM            Desktop
d-r--        10/14/2012   9:43 PM            Documents
d-r--        11/21/2012   8:54 PM            Downloads
d-r--         7/13/2012   7:07 PM            Favorites
d-r--         7/13/2012   7:07 PM            Links
d-r--          8/5/2012   8:08 PM            Music
```

Another example is the `RegistryKey` class returned by `Get-ChildItem` within the registry provider. The default formatting for this class organizes the output into a key and property value output that again is much easier to consume. Without formatting, the registry values wouldn't be displayed and the keys wouldn't be grouped:

```
PS HKLM:\Software> Get-ChildItem
    Hive: HKEY_LOCAL_MACHINE\Software
Name                           Property
----                           --------
7-Zip                          Path : C:\Program Files\7-Zip\
Adobe
AGEIA Technologies             PhysX Version   : 9110621
                               PhysX BuildCL   : 1
                               HwSelection     : GPU
                               PhysXCore Path  : C:\Program…
…
```

Several core formatting files are provided with PowerShell that cover many of the .NET types. All formatting files have an extension of *.format.ps1xml. To locate the formatting files installed with PowerShell use the following command:

```
PS C:\> Get-ChildItem $PSHome\*.format.ps1xml

    Directory: C:\Windows\System32\WindowsPowerShell\v1.0

Mode                LastWriteTime     Length Name
----                -------------     ------ ----
-a---         6/10/2009   3:41 PM      27338 Certificate.format.ps1xml
-a---         6/10/2009   3:41 PM      27106 Diagnostics.Format.ps1xml
-a---         7/23/2012   1:12 PM     144442 DotNetTypes.format.ps1xml
-a---          1/3/2012   3:36 PM      14502 Event.Format.ps1xml
-a---         7/23/2012   1:12 PM      21293 FileSystem.format.ps1xml
-a---         7/23/2012   1:12 PM     287938 Help.format.ps1xml
-a---         11/4/2011   8:17 PM      97880 HelpV3.format.ps1xml
-a---         7/23/2012   1:12 PM     101824 PowerShellCore.format.ps1xml
-a---         6/10/2009   3:41 PM      18612 PowerShellTrace.format.ps1xml
```

```
-a---         7/23/2012   1:12 PM       13659 Registry.format.ps1xml
-a---         7/23/2012   1:12 PM       17731 WSMan.Format.ps1xml
```

An easy way to learn the syntax required for one of these files is to look at one of the examples in this directory. Be careful not to edit the formatting files, as it can cause them to fail to load and may prevent formatting from functioning. The XML schema is strictly enforced by the formatting engine, so following another file's example can be helpful. The DotNetTypes.format.ps1xml file contains many commonly used formats for .NET types, whereas formatting files such as the FileSystem.format.ps1xml file contain formatting definitions for file system provider–related types. The PowerShell v3 version of the Integrated Scripting Environment (ISE) provides XML syntax highlighting, basic format validation, and code folding. This makes it a readily available and easy-to-use tool for working with formatting files.

Creating a formatting file

Formatting files define two primary sets of information: views and controls. Views are responsible for selecting properties and laying out data in formats such as list and table view. Controls allow for more advanced control of how data is presented to the user. All formatting files have a root `Configuration` node. To get started open the ISE. Then create a new file and name it PrintSystemJobInfo.format.ps1xml. Although the .format portion of the filename isn't strictly enforced, best practice is to include this in a formatting file's name. The .ps1xml extension is required. Within the format file define the following nodes:

```
<?xml version="1.0" encoding="utf-8" ?>
<Configuration>
  <Controls>
  </Controls>
  <ViewDefinitions>
  </ViewDefinitions>
</Configuration>
```

The `Controls` and `ViewDefinitions` nodes contain the definition for the entire formatting file. Formatting files can define views for multiple .NET types and multiple views for each of those types. The rest of this chapter focuses on defining a single view for the `PrintSystemJobInfo` class.

View definitions

Within the `ViewDefinitions` node you can use the standard `List`, `Wide`, and `Table` views. The different views are triggered when calling the different formatting cmdlets. These include `Format-List`, `Format-Wide`, `Format-Table`, and `Format-Custom`. If only one view is defined in the formatting file it's treated as the default view and is triggered when no formatting cmdlet is specified. Not all object types define a custom view for each standard formatting cmdlet. To list the custom views for a particular .NET type use the `Get-FormatData` cmdlet. Here's an example that returns the custom formatting for the `System.Diagnostics.Process` class:

```
PS C:\> (Get-FormatData System.Diagnostics.Process).FormatViewDefinition

Name                                                  Control
----                                                  -------
process                                               TableControl
Priority                                              TableControl
StartTime                                             TableControl
process                                               WideControl
```

In an effort to make instances of the `PrintSystemInfoJob` class a bit more readable, it may be best to choose the `Format-Table` view. As many print jobs may be running on a machine, formatting as a table allows you to fit many more instances on the screen than with a list view. Within your `ViewDefinitions` node you can define a new view and specify the `TableControl` view like this:

```
<ViewDefinitions>
 <View>
  <Name>System.Printing.PrintSystemJobInfo</Name>
  <ViewSelectedBy>
    <TypeName>System.Printing.PrintSystemJobInfo</TypeName>
  </ViewSelectedBy>
  <TableControl>
  </TableControl>
 </View>
</ViewDefinitions>
```

Note that you can have only one control view per `View` node. If you were to specify a `ListControl` or `WideControl` node you'd get an error when loading the formatting file.

In addition to defining the `TableControl`, the `Name` and `ViewSelectedBy` nodes have been added. The `Name` node needs to be unique among formatting files but doesn't necessarily have to be the .NET type name. The `ViewSelectedBy` node defines at what times this view should be used. In this case you want to use this view when a `System.Printing.PrintSystemJobInfo` is output to the PowerShell host. You can also use `SelectionSet` nodes, which are groups of .NET types, or `ScriptBlock` nodes to define when a particular view should be selected.

Defining table headers

The table output is arranged by column headers followed by the data formatted into rows. Your first job when using the `TableControl` is to define the headers that you want displayed within the view. You can do this by putting a `TableHeaders` node underneath the `TableControl`. Here's the XML structure to accomplish this, which defines six useful properties that will be displayed during output of a `PrintSystem-JobInfo` object:

```
<TableControl>
  <TableHeaders>
    <TableColumnHeader>
      <Label>Identifier</Label>
      <Width>12</Width>
    </TableColumnHeader>
```

```
    <TableColumnHeader>
      <Label>Name</Label>
    </TableColumnHeader>
    <TableColumnHeader>
      <Label>Submitter</Label>
    </TableColumnHeader>
    <TableColumnHeader>
      <Label>Time Submitted</Label>
    </TableColumnHeader>
    <TableColumnHeader>
      <Label>Printer</Label>
    </TableColumnHeader>
    <TableColumnHeader>
      <Label>Size (kB)</Label>
      <Alignment>Right</Alignment>
    </TableColumnHeader>
</TableHeaders>
```

In addition to the header text, the table headers can define the width and alignment of the column. The header text can be arbitrary but should, for good reason, make sense in relation to what's being displayed within the cells beneath it.

Having defined the column structure and header text you can now define the data that will be written to each one of the rows' columns. You can do this with the TableRowEntries node, which falls within the TableControl node, as follows:

```
<TableControl>
  <!—header definition removed for brevity -->
  <TableRowEntries>
    <TableRowEntry>
      <TableColumnItems>
        <TableColumnItem>
          <PropertyName>JobIdentifier</PropertyName>
        </TableColumnItem>
        <TableColumnItem>
          <PropertyName>Name</PropertyName>
        </TableColumnItem>
        <TableColumnItem>
          <PropertyName>Submitter</PropertyName>
        </TableColumnItem>
        <TableColumnItem>
          <PropertyName>TimeJobSubmitted</PropertyName>
        </TableColumnItem>
        <TableColumnItem>
          <ScriptBlock>$_.HostingPrintQueue.FullName</ScriptBlock>
        </TableColumnItem>
        <TableColumnItem>
          <ScriptBlock>$_.JobSize / 1000</ScriptBlock>
          <FormatString>{0:D}</FormatString>
        </TableColumnItem>
      </TableColumnItems>
    </TableRowEntry>
  </TableRowEntries>
</TableControl>
```

Notice that the entry values match the number and order of the header column definitions. This is required, and if there's a mismatch errors will be presented when the formatting file is loaded or data won't appear in the correct column. The most basic type of column data is mapped to a property on the object. For example, the `JobIdentifier`, `Name`, `Submitter`, and `TimeJobSubmitted` are mapped to the column headers defined in the `TableHeaders` node.

The Printer column is mapped to a script block. The `$_` variable refers to the current `PrintSystemJobInfo` instance that the formatting file is processing. The `$this` variable won't work in these script blocks. The script block retrieves the full name of the print queue (printer) within which the job is queued. The second script block divides the `JobSize` property, which is in bytes, by 1000 to return kilobytes. A `FormatString` node is used to format the value into a decimal representation. The `FormatString` node can take any string that a `-Format` operator would accept when formatting string data with PowerShell.

Conditional row entries

You can place conditions on how data is formatted based on the state of the object that's being formatted. The following listing is an example of a conditional and a default table row entry.

Listing 1 Conditional row entries

```
<TableRowEntry>
    <TableColumnItems>
     <TableRowEntry>
      <TableColumnItems>
        <TableColumnItem>
          <PropertyName>JobIdentifier</PropertyName>
        </TableColumnItem>
        <TableColumnItem>
          <PropertyName>Name</PropertyName>
        </TableColumnItem>
        <TableColumnItem>
          <PropertyName>Submitter</PropertyName>
        </TableColumnItem>
        <TableColumnItem>
          <PropertyName>TimeJobSubmitted</PropertyName>
        </TableColumnItem>
        <TableColumnItem>
          <ScriptBlock>
            $_.HostingPrintQueue.FullName
          </ScriptBlock>
        </TableColumnItem>
        <TableColumnItem>
          <ScriptBlock>$_.JobSize / 1000</ScriptBlock>
          <FormatString>{0:D}</FormatString>
        </TableColumnItem>
      </TableColumnItems>
    </TableRowEntry>
```

❶ Default table row entry

Displays only the printer name

```
    </TableColumnItems>
</TableRowEntry>
<TableRowEntry>                                      ❷ Conditional table
   <EntrySelectedBy>                                    row entry
     <SelectionCondition>
        <TypeName>
          System.Printing.PrintSystemJobInfo
        </TypeName>                                    Table row entry
        <ScriptBlock>                                  selection
          $_.HostingPrintServer.BeepEnabled            condition
         </ScriptBlock>
      </SelectionCondition>
   </EntrySelectedBy>
   <TableColumnItems>
        <TableColumnItem>
          <PropertyName>JobIdentifier</PropertyName>
        </TableColumnItem>
        <TableColumnItem>
          <PropertyName>Name</PropertyName>
        </TableColumnItem>
        <TableColumnItem>
          <PropertyName>Submitter</PropertyName>
        </TableColumnItem>
        <TableColumnItem>
          <PropertyName>TimeJobSubmitted</PropertyName>
        </TableColumnItem>
        <TableColumnItem>                                  Displays the printer
          <ScriptBlock>                                    name followed by
             $_.HostingPrintQueue.FullName + " (Beeps)"    "(Beeps)"
          </ScriptBlock>
        </TableColumnItem>
        <TableColumnItem>
          <ScriptBlock>$_.JobSize / 1000</ScriptBlock>
          <FormatString>{0:D}</FormatString>
        </TableColumnItem>
     </TableColumnItems>
   </TableRowEntry>
```

Table row entry ❶ is the default table row entry. It's required to have one and only one default entry that will be selected when no conditional entries match the given object's data. The table row entry ❷ is an example of a conditional table row entry. In this example it's only selected if the print server has beeping enabled. If it's selected the print queue name is followed by the text "(Beeps)." Like table row entries ❶ and ❷, additional table row entries still need to have the same number and order of `TableColumnItem` nodes as the column headers.

When creating formatting files with other views, such as the `List` or `Wide` view, you'll find that they have different nodes and properties from `Table` view. You'll need to study the documentation or find examples to properly develop a formatting file when using those views.

Grouping

As shown earlier, the file system provider groups files based on path. This is a result of the formatting file definition for `FileInfo` objects. You can accomplish this within your custom formatting file as well. You can easily group your print jobs by server and printer using the following `GroupBy` node:

```
<View>
 <GroupBy>
    <ScriptBlock>
    $_.HostingPrintServer.Name+ " : " +
      ➥ $_.HostingPrintQueue.FullName
    </ScriptBlock>
    <CustomControlName>PrintJob-GroupFormatting</CustomControlName>
</GroupBy>
 <!—Other Stuff Removed For Brevity -->
</View>
```

The `GroupBy` node can group objects based on a property value or script block. Grouping can be taken a step further and also define a custom control to use when outputting the header value for each group. In the next section I'll show you how to do this. The `CustomControlName` node is used to define the custom control that will format this header value.

Custom controls

Custom controls allow for advanced control of output in formatting files. You can define custom controls either within the `Controls` node underneath the `Configuration` root node, or within nodes such as the `CustomControl` node within the `GroupBy` node. In the previous `GroupBy` example you saw the `CustomControlName` node referencing the custom control from elsewhere in the document. In that case you'd define the custom control within the global `Controls` node like this:

```
<Configuration>
  <Controls>
    <Control>
      <Name>PrintJob-GroupFormatting</Name>
      <CustomControl>
     <CustomEntries>
       <CustomEntry>
        <CustomItem>
         <Frame>
         <LeftIndent>4</LeftIndent>
          <CustomItem>
          <Text>Printer: </Text>
           <ExpressionBinding>
             <ScriptBlock>$_.HostingPrintServer.Name + " : " +
$_.HostingPrintQueue.FullName </ScriptBlock>
           </ExpressionBinding>
           <NewLine/>
         </CustomItem>
        </Frame>
```

```
          </CustomItem>
        </CustomEntry>
      </CustomEntries>
    </CustomControl>
  </Control>
    </Controls>
    <!—remove ViewDefintions for brevity -->
</Configuration>
```

This custom control is the text that's displayed as a header for the custom grouping operation. Custom controls are customizable and allow for script blocks, numerous types of text formatting, and selection conditions similar to that of views. Custom controls are built around the concept of frames. A frame can control the indentation and hanging of text within the frame. In the example a left indent of four characters is specified. The custom item within the frame formats the object into readable text.

Raw text, like "Printer:", is specified with the `Text` node. Dynamic content, on the other hand, can be generated in several different ways. The example uses a `ScriptBlock` node to run a command to output several properties of the hosting print server to the PowerShell host. Another method of dynamic content is to specify the `PropertyName` node as shown in the following snippet. It outputs the value of the property of the object being formatted:

```
<ExpressionBinding>
   <PropertyName>Name<PropertyName>
</ExpressionBinding>
```

Custom controls also accept conditional statements like table row entries do. For example, you could use the same condition you used for the table row entry to select a particular `CustomEntry` within the custom control. Again, you need to ensure that you define a default `CustomEntry` node along with a conditional custom entry, as in the following listing.

Listing 2 A custom entry

```
<CustomEntry>
    <-- CustomEntry Definition Goes Here -->
</CustomEntry>
<CustomEntry>
     <EntrySelectedBy>
     <SelectionCondition>
        <TypeName>
          System.Printing.PrintSystemJobInfo
        </TypeName>
        <ScriptBlock>
          $_.HostingPrintServer.BeepEnabled
        </ScriptBlock>
      </SelectionCondition>
     </EntrySelectedBy>
</CustomEntry>
```

Default custom entry

Conditional custom entry

Putting it together

The final result of the steps taken throughout this chapter is shown in the following listing. You can place this file anywhere that's readily accessible, as long as you have read access to its location.

Listing 3 A complete extension configuration

```
<?xml version="1.0" encoding="utf-8" ?>
<Configuration>
    <Controls>
        <Control>
              <Name>PrintJob-GroupFormatting</Name>
              <CustomControl>
                 <CustomEntries>
                    <CustomEntry>
                       <CustomItem>
                          <Frame>
                              <LeftIndent>4</LeftIndent>
                              <CustomItem>
                                  <Text>Printer: </Text>
                                  <ExpressionBinding>
                                    <ScriptBlock>
                           $_.HostingPrintServer.Name +
                           ":" +
                           $_.HostingPrintQueue.FullName
                                     </ScriptBlock>
                                  </ExpressionBinding>
                                  <NewLine/>
                              </CustomItem>
                          </Frame>
                    </CustomItem>
                </CustomEntry>
             </CustomEntries>
          </CustomControl>
        </Control>
    </Controls>
    <ViewDefinitions>
        <View>
           <GroupBy>
                <ScriptBlock>
              $_.HostingPrintServer.Name + " : " +
              $_.HostingPrintQueue.FullName
                </ScriptBlock>
                  <CustomControlName>
                   PrintJob-GroupFormatting
                 </CustomControlName>
                </GroupBy>
            <Name>
              System.Printing.PrintSystemJobInfo
            </Name>
            <ViewSelectedBy>
                <TypeName>
                   System.Printing.PrintSystemJobInfo
```

Custom grouping header control

Main view for the `PrintSystemJobInfo` class

Grouping clause

Reference to the custom control

Name of the view

Selection conditions for the view

```
      </TypeName>
    </ViewSelectedBy>
    <TableControl>
      <TableHeaders>
        <TableColumnHeader>
          <Label>Identifier</Label>
          <Width>12</Width>
        </TableColumnHeader>
        <TableColumnHeader>
          <Label>Name</Label>
        </TableColumnHeader>
       <TableColumnHeader>
          <Label>Submitter</Label>
        </TableColumnHeader>
        <TableColumnHeader>
          <Label>Time Submitted</Label>
        </TableColumnHeader>
        <TableColumnHeader>
          <Label>Printer</Label>
        </TableColumnHeader>
        <TableColumnHeader>
          <Label>Size (kB)</Label>
          <Alignment>Right</Alignment>
        </TableColumnHeader>
      </TableHeaders>
      <TableRowEntries>
        <TableRowEntry>
          <TableColumnItems>
            <TableColumnItem>
              <PropertyName>
       JobIdentifier
        </PropertyName>
            </TableColumnItem>
            <TableColumnItem>
              <PropertyName>
                Name
              </PropertyName>
            </TableColumnItem>
            <TableColumnItem>
              <PropertyName>
                Submitter
              </PropertyName>
            </TableColumnItem>
            <TableColumnItem>
              <PropertyName>TimeJobSubmitted</PropertyName>
            </TableColumnItem>
            <TableColumnItem>
              <ScriptBlock>$_.HostingPrintQueue.FullName</
              ScriptBlock>
            </TableColumnItem>
            <TableColumnItem>
              <ScriptBlock>
                 $_.JobSize / 1000
              </ScriptBlock>
              <FormatString>
```

Selection conditions for the view

Specification of the table control

Column header definitions

Default table row entry definitions

```
                                    {0:D}
                                  </FormatString>
                              </TableColumnItem>
                          </TableColumnItems>
                      </TableRowEntry>
                        <TableRowEntry>
                          <EntrySelectedBy>
                              <SelectionCondition>
                                  <TypeName>System.Printing
.PrintSystemJobInfo</TypeName>
                                  <ScriptBlock>-not
$_.HostingPrintServer.BeepEnabled</ScriptBlock>
                              </SelectionCondition>
                          </EntrySelectedBy>
                          <TableColumnItems>
                              <TableColumnItem>
                                  <PropertyName>
                                   JobIdentifier
                                  </PropertyName>
                              </TableColumnItem>
                              <TableColumnItem>
                                  <PropertyName>
                                     Name
                                  </PropertyName>
                              </TableColumnItem>
                              <TableColumnItem>
                                  <PropertyName>
                                    Submitter
                                  </PropertyName>
                              </TableColumnItem>
                              <TableColumnItem>
                                  <PropertyName>TimeJobSubmitted</PropertyName>
                              </TableColumnItem>
                              <TableColumnItem>
                                  <ScriptBlock>
                                   $_.HostingPrintQueue.FullName +
                                   " (Beeps)"
                                  </ScriptBlock>
                              </TableColumnItem>
                              <TableColumnItem>
                                  <ScriptBlock>
                                    $_.JobSize / 1000
                                  </ScriptBlock>
                                  <FormatString>
                                    {0:D}
                                  </FormatString>
                              </TableColumnItem>
                          </TableColumnItems>
                      </TableRowEntry>
                    </TableRowEntries>
                </TableControl>
            </View>
        </ViewDefinitions>
    </Configuration>
```

Default table row entry definitions

Table row entry condition

Conditional table row entry definitions

Loading formatting data

Once you've completed your formatting file you can load it into a PowerShell session using the `Update-FormatData` cmdlet. When used without parameters this cmdlet reloads the format data that has already been loaded into a PowerShell session. When specifying either the `PrependPath` or `AppendPath` parameter it loads the format data from the path specified. This is where you specify the path to your formatting file. The difference between the `AppendPath` and `PrependPath` has to do with the precedence of formatting files. If you use `AppendPath` your formatting file is of a lower precedence than formatting files earlier in the list. The first formatting file to contain a particular type is the formatting file that PowerShell uses to format instances of that type. Using `PrependPath` ensures that your formatting file is the first file found. This is an example of loading the format data:

```
Update-FormatData -PrependPath (Join-Path '$Profile
➥ PrintSystemJobInfo.format.ps1xml')
```

The command loads the formatting file from your PowerShell profile. `Join-Path` combines the path to your profile and the filename before passing it to `Update-FormatData`.

After loading the custom formatting file you can run the same snippet you ran at the beginning of this chapter. The resulting output will look like that shown in figure 1 and, as you can see, it looks quite different from that shown at the beginning of the chapter.

The `Update-FormatData` cmdlet will return any errors found within the formatting file. Errors are generally well defined and point you directly to the node that's causing the problem. After any errors are corrected calling `Update-FormatData` again will attempt to reload the file.

In addition to manually loading a format file, module authors can package and load formatting files by specifying the file in the module's manifest. The `New-ModuleManifest` cmdlet offers a `FormatsToProcess` parameter that accepts an array of strings that can contain the filenames of format files to load during module import. The format files have to reside in the root directory for the module. When the module is

```
PS C:\> foreach($pq in (New-Object -TypeName System.Printing.PrintServer).GetPrintQueues())
>> {
>>     $pq.Refresh()
>>     $pq.GetPrintJobInfoCollection() | Format-Table
>> }
>>

    Printer: \\DRISCOLL-DESK : HP Photosmart C4200 series

Identifier   Name              Submitter      Time Submitted     Printer              Size (kB)
----------   ----              ---------      --------------     -------              ---------
7            Document          Adam           11/19/2012 2:...   HP Photosmart...         1.376


    Printer: \\DRISCOLL-DESK : Epson Stylus C88 Series (M)

Identifier   Name              Submitter      Time Submitted     Printer              Size (kB)
----------   ----              ---------      --------------     -------              ---------
2            Print My Own T... Adam           12/25/2009 5:...   Epson Stylus ...       718.732
6            Document          Adam           11/19/2012 2:...   Epson Stylus ...         1.336
```

Figure 1 Formatted results

either auto-loaded or loaded with `Import-Module` the format files are processed and applied to the session:

```
PS C:\> Get-Help New-ModuleManifest -Parameter FormatsToProcess

-FormatsToProcess <String[]>
    Specifies the formatting files (.ps1xml) that run when the module is
    imported.
    When you import a module, Windows PowerShell runs the Update-FormatData
    cmdlet with the specified files. Because formatting files are not
    scoped, they affect all session states in the session.
```

Summary

Formatting files are an important aspect of PowerShell and are often overlooked by casual users. .NET types can be presented in ways that make it much easier to visually consume output written to the command line. As a module author you can use formatting files to provide a professional edge to your work. As a casual user you can use them to help customize the shell to meet your needs and preferences. Whatever your role, I encourage you to explore and discover this facet of PowerShell's vast ecosystem.

About the author

Adam Driscoll is a software developer and team lead at Dell. He has experience working with Microsoft .NET, Android, SQL, and C++ but focuses primarily on PowerShell API development. As PowerShell is fast becoming the automation tool of choice for both Microsoft and IT administrators, he finds it exciting to contribute to the platform as it evolves and advances. Adam is the author of the Visual Studio 2010 extension PowerGUI VSX. It integrates the PowerGUI PowerShell script editor into Visual Studio. Since its inception it has received over 60,000 downloads. Adam is also an avid blogger and author of *Microsoft Windows PowerShell 3.0 First Look* (Packt Publishing 2012).

15 Scalable scripting for large data sets: pipeline and database techniques

Matthew Reynolds

An online retailer needed to learn which of their Domain Name System (DNS) records were getting the most queries after an advertising campaign. They wrote a script to get this information from their DNS server logs, but as the logs grew, the script slowed to a crawl. Worse, when they tried to run the script on multiple servers remotely the script failed with an `OutOfMemoryException`.

A web search for the terms *PowerShell* and *OutOfMemoryException* returns many thousands of hits. People are clearly struggling to manage large data sets.

The typical problem is the use of a fragile pattern that works in the lab but doesn't scale with real-world production data. In this chapter we'll explore how to write scripts that scale to any size input by processing records in "streams" instead of "water balloons."

The stream and the water balloon

Imagine that you need to measure the amount of water that flows down a mountain stream per hour.

One approach would be to build a huge balloon as a reservoir to stop and hold all the water in one place. Then you would measure the volume of the balloon. This could work, but it could also be slow and expensive. It also scales poorly. What if the requirement changes to measure the amount of water flowing over a year instead of an hour? What if the flow of water is higher than expected? Will the balloon pop?

Instead of using a balloon or any other reservoir you could use a detector to measure the ongoing flow rate of water past a certain point in the stream. This way there's no balloon to build or pop, and by adding up your measurements over time you can determine the amount of water for any time period, from a minute to a decade. This kind of approach, where you deal with small amounts of the stream at a time instead of collecting everything at once, is what I'll refer to as "streaming."

For the IT professional using PowerShell the water in this metaphor is the source data (event logs, database rows, Active Directory objects, log files, and so on) that you want to measure or process in a script. You only have so much memory to work with, which limits the size of any data balloons you could stretch to hold everything at once. Scaling to any size input requires scripting patterns that measure or process items flowing through a stream instead.

Streams and water balloons in PowerShell scripts

Most scripts include lines like the following:

```
$myThings = Get-Thing *
```

The variable `$myThings` is a water balloon in the memory space of the PowerShell session. It will expand with the number and size of objects output by `Get-Thing`, and it could pop if it gets big enough. The imaginary `Get-Thing` command in this example is a stand-in for any cmdlet or method that outputs objects.

The following variation also brings all the "things" into memory at once in a fragile water balloon pattern, though more subtly:

```
Invoke-Thing -InputObject (Get-Thing *)
```

As before, a ballooning array is created to hold "Things" output by `Get-Thing`. In this case, the array is temporary and anonymous, but equally fragile.

The problem: holding everything in memory at once

Using either variation you've brought all of the Things into memory at one time. If there were 100 Things, the script might work well. What if we run it in an environment with 20 million Things?

Pop.

By holding all of the Things in memory at once you consume memory proportional to the number of Things and risk

- Scripts crashing with an `OutOfMemoryException`
- Degrading performance of the machine (and the services it provides) by taxing system memory resources

The following is a realistic example of the fragile water-balloon pattern (holding everything in memory) while processing a modestly large log file (about 500 MB):

```
$logEntries = Import-CSV -Path (Join-Path $env:temp "biglog.txt")
Select-Object -InputObject $logEntries -Property Name
```

NOTE The scripts included with this book include a script (Setup_CreateBigLog.ps1) for generating a similar log file so you can try this snippet for yourself.

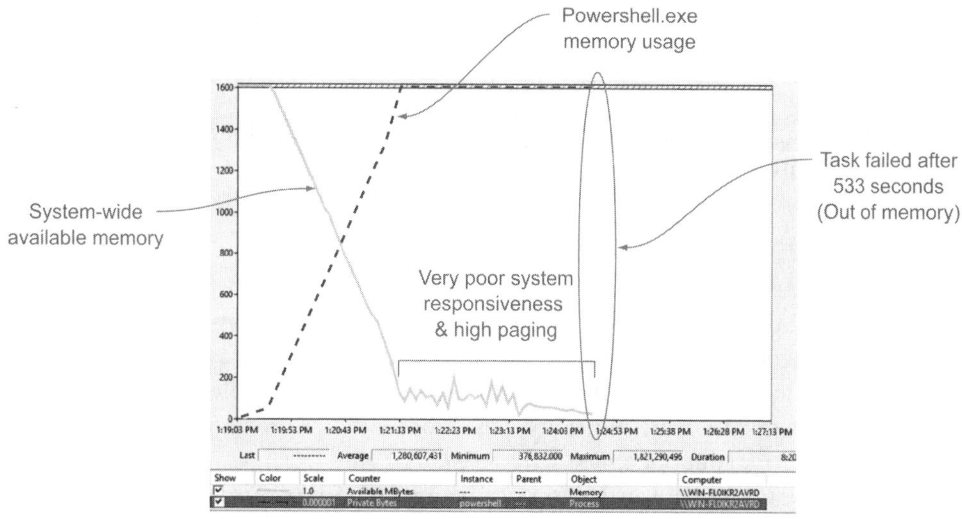

Figure 1 Memory usage of Powershell.exe while processing a 500 MB log file

The first line creates a big, fragile water balloon. It stores all of the objects from `Import-CSV` in `$logEntries`. The battle is already lost.

The second line (`Select-Object`) is included in the example only to imply that you would typically do some task with the log entries once you have them. The real task could be anything. Before you can execute the interesting task, though, you are already at risk because of the potentially large and fragile water balloon created on the first line.

The annotated Performance Monitor graph in figure 1 shows this script causing high memory usage and poor system responsiveness, and eventually failing. The descending line is system-wide available RAM as measured by the performance counter Memory\Available Mbytes. The ascending dashed line is the size of our water balloon as measured by Process\Private Bytes (powershell.exe). This counter reflects how much data is loaded into the powershell.exe process memory address space.

In this example you can see that the available system RAM decreases as the amount of data held in the powershell.exe process grows (the `$logEntries` water balloon). As the machine runs out of available RAM it keeps itself alive through heavy page file usage, resulting in poor system responsiveness. Finally, the script fails with an `OutOfMemoryException` as the powershell.exe instance reaches a maximum allowed size. This example combines two different memory problems (available system RAM and process-level memory limitations) that are subject to different limitations. Available RAM is easy enough to understand, but fewer IT pros are familiar with process-level memory limitations. Even on a server with terabytes of available RAM a 32-bit process can only hold roughly 2 GB of information, and PowerShell remote sessions are further limited to 150 MB of memory by default.

The solution: stream over input items instead of collecting them

How can you write scripts that hold up equally well against 1 Thing or 20 million Things? Wherever possible you should stream over data instead of collecting and looping. You can use command pipelining, as in the following example, to accomplish tasks without creating any water balloons:

```
Import-CSV -Path (Join-Path $env:temp "biglog.txt") |
➥ Select-Object -Property Name
```

In this example you import the log entries and perform a task on each one. As before, the `Select-Object` portion is a stand-in. The task could be anything. By piping the objects from `Import-CSV` into the downstream task cmdlets you avoid creating a water balloon. In this pattern the downstream cmdlets or functions receive and process one item at a time, and you process the entire data set without ever having it all in memory at once.

The graph shown in figure 2, using the same counters as figure 1, shows well-constrained memory usage, good system responsiveness, and a successful script execution.

This script could handle any number of input items without exhausting memory. Not only do you use less memory, but you constrain your memory usage such that it remains flat regardless of the number of input items. The pattern of needing to deal with large data sets a little at a time is well established. Mature data access technologies like LDAP and SQL have "paging" constructs to protect both data providers and consumers from resource exhaustion. In PowerShell you can use the pipeline to similar advantage.

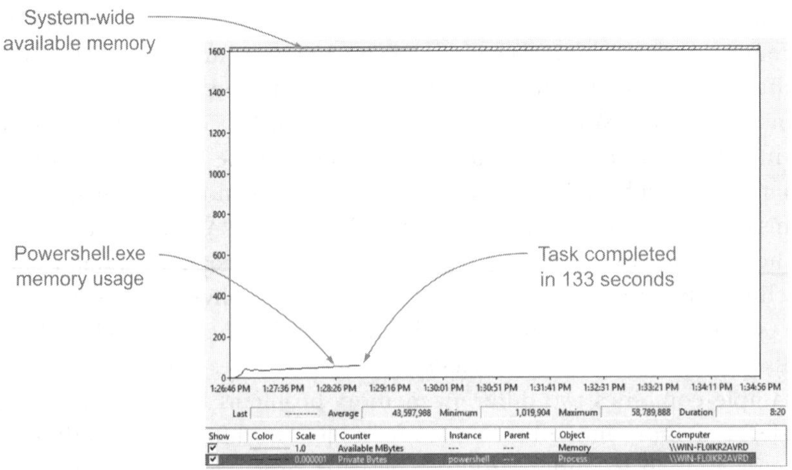

Figure 2 Memory usage stays flat and system responsiveness stays high regardless of input size

Pipelines are not the enemy of efficiency

Many students in scripting classes seem to have heard that pipelines are slow and inefficient compared to water-balloon approaches like collecting objects and then looping over them. This is an area that requires some clarity.

Using a pipeline doesn't magically make scripts efficient. Memory efficiency comes with scripting patterns that avoid cramming lots of data into water balloons. Pipelines together with cmdlets or functions that make good use of their process blocks are a powerful way to accomplish this.

Pipelines (and the related cmdlet binding) do have overhead. They should be used when their benefits outweigh their costs. Pipelines can be an inefficient choice for CPU consumption and execution time when dealing with few objects, when the pipeline will be recreated repeatedly, or when unnecessary cmdlet binding can be avoided. The following example demonstrates inefficient use of pipelines in a simple task (getting the names of files in the Windows directory):

```
Get-ChildItem -Path $env:windir -recurse |
    Foreach-object {
        $_ | Select-Object -expandProperty Fullname
    }
```

Although this example is memory-efficient, it runs slower than it needs to because pipelining is used in a wasteful way. The nested pipeline is created many times and each time only processes one object. This took about 50 seconds per run to complete on a test system. The following is an improved approach:

```
Get-ChildItem -Path $env:windir -recurse |
➥ Select-Object -ExpandProperty Fullname
```

This accomplishes the same task much faster (about 22 seconds per run on a test system). The pipeline is only created once and all the objects are streamed through it.

You could skip the pipeline and use a collect-and-loop (water balloon) pattern instead, as in the following example:

```
foreach($fileOrDir in @(gci -Path $env:windir -recurse) ){
  Select-Object -InputObject $fileOrDir -ExpandProperty FullName
}
```

The preceding took about 55 seconds per run to complete on the same test system. This is similar to the inefficient pipe example and far slower than the efficient pipe example. The following variant gains speed for this specific task by avoiding the overhead of the call to `Select-Object`:

```
foreach($fileOrDir in @(gci -Path $env:windir -recurse) ){
   $fileOrDir.FullName
}
```

This variant completed in about 25 seconds per run on the same test machine.

The lesson is that collect-and-loop (water balloon) can be a fast pattern, but it isn't always faster than using pipes. Also, the "collect" part of collect-and-loop comes with a fragile water balloon. In this example all of the `FileInfo` objects output by `Get-ChildItem` are collected in memory before being looped through.

The goal for the scalable scripter isn't to use pipelines for the sake of it. Collecting the items can be fine where the author is absolutely sure that the number and size of items will always be modest. If the author can't be completely sure that the size of the balloon will always be modest in every context where the script might run, then it's safer to use a streaming pattern instead. Pipelines shine brightest when

- The data set might contain many objects
- The process blocks of cmdlets or functions on the pipeline will process the objects efficiently
- Excessive pipelines (for example, nested single-use pipelines) won't be created unnecessarily

Does embracing pipelines mean you should use `Where-Object` to filter large data sets?

A peculiar notion held by many students in scripting workshops is that the "PowerShell way" to filter data is to pull it all from a source indiscriminately and then use `Where-Object` to filter it. This is wrong. Although `Where-Object` is a capable cmdlet, it's almost always better to filter data natively at its source (for example, using a `-Filter` parameter or similar parameter as part of a `Get-*` cmdlet). Depending on the script or pipeline structure it may not matter to memory efficiency, but there are usually other advantages (CPU, execution time, network I/O, disk I/O) to filtering at the source. Consider the following examples:

```
PS C:\> Measure-Command {
➥ Get-ChildItem -Path $env:windir -recurse |
➥ Where-Object{ $_.Name -eq "netlogon.dll" }
➥ } | Format-List -Property TotalSeconds

TotalSeconds : 36.0082583

PS C:\> Measure-Command{
➥ Get-ChildItem -Path $env:windir -recurse -filter netlogon.dll} |
➥ Format-List -Property TotalSeconds

TotalSeconds : 10.9730405
```

Each of these is safe in terms of memory scalability, as neither collects large numbers of items in memory at once. The latter, however, will run much faster and consume fewer resources by filtering natively at the source data provider.

Making it real: streaming over data in complex realistic tasks

Scripters have two supporting patterns they can use to write streaming scripts that scale:

- Writing effective process blocks in script functions
- Implementing cross-object logic (grouping, averages, sums, trends, and so on) while streaming

We will explore these patterns in the context of a real-world DNS management task.

Imagine your organization wants to get rid of some old static DNS records. Unfortunately, no one feels sure whether some unknown but critical application or device out there might still be querying and relying on these ancient records. Here you enter the "IT paralysis by fear" zone (or alternatively the "discover your dependencies by making cowboy changes" zone).

You don't have to live in fear. To count how many times a given record has been queried you can write a script that parses the debug logs of the DNS Server service.

You might be tempted to write this in a nonscalable way, like in this next snippet. Note that you haven't yet written the `ConvertFrom-DnsLogLine` function, but you will shortly. First, let's sketch out the context of how you would use it. The following is how not to do it:

```
$logLines = Get-Content -Path $dnsLogPath
$parsedLogLines = ConvertFrom-DNSLogLine -InputObject $logLines
$parsedLogLines | Group-Object -Property QueryFQDN
```

This sketch has three scalability bugs:

- It holds all of the raw log lines in memory at once in `$logLines`.
- It holds all of the parsed log lines in memory at once in `$parsedLogLines`.
- It uses `Group-Object` without the `-NoElement` parameter. As a result, `Group-Object` will store yet another copy of each parsed log line and include all the copies in the result.

Let's look at a more scalable way to do this. Note that this is an outline of the proposed flow and you still haven't written the `ConvertFrom-DnsLogLine` function:

```
Get-Content -Path $dnsLogPath | ConvertFrom-DnsLogLine |
➥ Group-Object -Property QueryFQDN -NoElement
```

This example is likely to scale for memory usage much better. Only one log line is in memory at a time as it flows down the pipe, and by using `-NoElement` you're telling `Group-Object` to count the unique instances without collecting them.

`Get-Content` vs. `System.IO.StreamReader.ReadLine()`

Experts in working with large logs might note that `ReadLine()` can be faster per line compared with `Get-Content` (the latter does extra work that takes more time). Either one, however, can output one line at a time and, when used correctly, can be compatible with memory-efficient streaming. Whether you prefer `Get-Content` or `ReadLine()` for reading text, consider using streaming patterns as you process the results.

Also note that `Get-Content -ReadCount 0` writes the entire content of the file to the output pipeline, in a manner similar to `System.IO.StreamReader.ReadAllLines()`. This can be faster for modestly sized files, but it makes streaming harder and will be fragile with large files.

Now that you have a usage sketch you need a `ConvertFrom-DnsLogLine` function. The function should have the following qualities to enable streaming:

- The ability to handle pipeline input elegantly
- The ability to handle any needed cross-object logic (such as trends and sums) without breaking the streaming pattern (that is, it shouldn't secretly collect all the input objects under the mattress)

The following listing demonstrates these attributes. As described in the code annotations, some areas are task specific (parsing this particular log format), whereas other sections illustrate generic streaming patterns.

Listing 1 `ConvertFrom-DnsLogLine`

```
function ConvertFrom-DNSLogLine{
param(
    [Parameter(ValueFromPipeline=$true)]
    [Alias( "DnsLogLine" )]
    [string[]]$InputObject
)
begin{
    $regexForServer2012PacketLines = `
      "(?<Raw_01_Date>^\d{1,2}/\d{1,2}/
     \d{4})\s(?<Raw_02_Time>\d{1,2}\:\d{1,2}\:\
d{1,2}\s\w{2})\s(?<Raw_03_TID>\S{3,4})\s(?<Raw_04_Context>PACKET)\s+(?<Raw_
05_IPI>\S+)\s(?<Raw_06_TCPUDP>[TCUDP]{3})\s(?<Raw_07_SndRcv>[SndRcv]{3})\s(
?<Raw_08_RemoteIP>\S+)\s*(?<Raw_09_XID>\S*)\s(?<Raw_10_QueryResponse>.)\s(?
<Raw_11_OpCode>.)\s+(?<Raw_121314_FlagsCombined>\[.+\])\s+(?<Raw_15_Questio
nType>\w+)\s+(?<Raw_16_QuestionName>.*)"

    $processedLinesCount = 0
    $processedPacketLinesCount = 0
}
process{
foreach( $DnsLogLine in $InputObject ){

    $processedLinesCount++

    if( $_ -match $regexForServer2012PacketLines){
        $processedPacketLinesCount++

        $dateTimeStr = $matches.Raw_01_Date + " " + $matches.Raw_02_Time
        $matches[ "DateTime" ] = [datetime]::Parse( $dateTimeStr )
        $matches[ "RemoteIpAddr" ] = $matches.Raw_08_RemoteIP.trim()
        $matches[ "QuestionType" ]=$matches.Raw_15_QuestionType.trim()
        $qrySplit= [regex]::split($matches.Raw_16_QuestionName,'\(\d+\)')
        $matches[ "QueryFQDN" ] = [string]::Join(".",($qrySplit -ne ""))

        $matches
    }
}
}
end{
    Write-Verbose "Processed total lines: $ProcessedLinesCount"
```

❶ **Input is array and `ValueFromPipeLine`**

❷ **Task work inside `process` and `foreach`**

❸ **Efficient counters for cross-object stats**

```
    Write-Verbose "Processed PACKET lines: $processedPacketLinesCount"
}
}
```

This function processes one item at a time and, therefore, can perform with good memory scalability on the pipeline with any arbitrarily large number of input items. By defining the pipeline input parameter as an array ❶ and including the `foreach` loop inside the process block you can ensure that the function works with piped input or with nonpiped input, such as `-InputObject "a","b","c"`.

The code inside `process` and `foreach` does the task-specific work ❷. In this case a regular expression is used to parse a line from a log file. The resulting `$matches` object is a hash table to which you can add keys. You added a few useful key/value pairs to better describe the logged action and then emitted the object.

This function also avoids secretly building up all the objects in any internal collection along the way. An easy pitfall would have been to add each item processed to some array and then use the `Count` property of that array for the `Write-Verbose` statements at the end. Instead you used integer counters ❸ to keep track of state information that spans across input objects. You can increment these counters millions of times and the memory usage remains flat.

For more complex cross-object state tracking you can often use hash tables. Imagine you want to keep track of query counts by unique source IP address. You could do this in a downstream cmdlet like `Group-Object`, but if you needed something else to be downstream instead you might prefer to track this inside your function. A flexible approach to this task is to create an empty hash table in the begin block. Then for each input item in the process block, update the hash table, where the key is a unique source IP address and the value is an integer counter for how many queries originated at that IP address. As with the standalone counters seen earlier you can increment these integers many times without increasing memory usage. The approach doesn't guarantee perfectly flat memory usage; it will grow slightly with each new unique source IP address (every new key in the hash table). Even so, this approach is far better than collecting all of the input items to accomplish the same.

Using these techniques you can not only process unlimited items, but also calculate metrics across input items (sums, averages, and so on) while still maintaining flat or nearly flat memory usage across potentially huge numbers of input items.

Imagine you've used your script to analyze the logs and found an ancient yet mission-critical device that still relies on those old DNS records. Now the device can be reconfigured, the offending records deleted, and you're a hero in your organization.

As you know, success will only lead to more work, which leads us to our next topic: using databases to store script data.

NOTE These patterns are generic and could be applied to nearly any task. If you want to explore this specific example further, however, you can generate a debug log file like the one expected by this function by enabling debug logging in the DNS Management Console (dnsmgmt.msc) on a Windows Server 2012 machine with the DNS Server role installed. A sample log file is also included in the code download available with this book for immediate use.

If it quacks like a database ...

Sometimes you need random access to a large number of items and all of their properties. Suppose your DNS log-parsing adventure proved so popular in your enterprise that additional use cases started to appear. Rather than summarizing the queries from a single log file on a single server, the organization now wants to analyze trends over time across many logs and many servers. Analysts want to be able to explore the data interactively in Excel and try out new pivots at will. Some analysts want to identify what queries were made by a particular client on a particular day, or analyze query popularity by region, and so on.

You could implement all of this in a script and even do it using streaming-only patterns. Doing it well, however, would require implementing indexing concepts and managing many files and cross-references, and would involve many passes over the data. In order to improve performance and reduce disk IO you would also wind up building out some kind of caching layer that maximizes memory usage for IO efficiency while dynamically limiting memory usage to avoid system exhaustion. That sounds like a lot of work that isn't specific to your business needs.

Fortunately, database engines already know how to do these things and more. Unfortunately, the word *database* can elicit panic from many infrastructure-oriented IT folks. For some reason, the infrastructure folks don't sit at the database administrators' table at lunch. This is a bridge that should be crossed because databases can be a tremendously empowering force. They also couple well with scripting.

Scripts can be a great tool for feeding IT-oriented data (logs, CSVs, WMI, Active Directory) into a database. Once you get the information into a database options abound (such as PowerShell, Excel, Power View, and Reporting Services) for adding to, processing, or deriving meaning from the data.

Imagine a modified version of the earlier DNS log parsing workflow that looks something like this:

```
Get-Content -Path (Join-Path $env:temp "DnsDebugLog01.txt") |
  ➥ ConvertFrom-DnsLogLine | Export-DnsLogLineToDb
```

Note that you haven't created the `Export` function yet. This is an outline of how you would want to use it.

Getting started

If you don't already have a database engine handy an easy way to embark is to use the free LocalDB variant of SQL Server Express. You can install it from http://www.microsoft.com/sqlserver.

For this example you'll create a new database from scratch, including the table and column definitions within the database. You can do this via interactive GUI (SQL Server Management Studio or Visual Studio) or by script. A nice approach is to use SQL Server Management Studio to define the database and tables interactively, and then save out the .SQL script needed to recreate this at will. These clear text .SQL files travel well alongside the related .PS1 scripts so scripters can provision the needed databases anywhere they go.

For brevity the .SQL files aren't printed in these pages, but they're included in the code download that comes with this book. Also included is a script that provisions the database by running the .SQL files against a freshly installed instance of SQL Express on the local machine. To follow along with the rest of this section consider installing SQL Server and running that script, which is shown in listing 2. Note that depending on your machine and database setup specifics you may need to modify parts of the scripts or .SQL files to suit your environment. In particular you may need to change the value for the `-Server` parameter in listing 2 from `(localdb)\v11.0` to `localhost` (if using a non-LocalDB version of SQL Server on the local machine) or some other server/instance name you may be using. Also you may need to adjust the file paths in the DatabaseAsObjectStore__CreateDnsLogDb.sql file (use Notepad to edit) to point to paths that work on your machine (the example uses C:\temp\).

Listing 2 Creating the database and table

```
$serverName = '(localdb)\v11.0'

Import-Module InvokeSqlQuery -ErrorAction Stop        <-- http://powershell4sql.codeplex.com

$Invoc = (Get-Variable MyInvocation -Scope 0).Value
$ScriptPath = Split-Path $Invoc.MyCommand.Path        <-- Get script path to find related files

$relativeNames = @(
    "DatabaseAsObjectStore__CreateDnsLogDb.sql"
    "DatabaseAsObjectStore__CreateDnsPacketsTable.sql"
)

foreach( $scriptName in $relativeNames ){
  $scriptFullPath = Join-Path $scriptPath $scriptName
  Invoke-SqlQuery -Server $serverName -File $scriptFullPath    <-- Run SQL database scripts
}
```

Using Entity Framework or other SQL APIs to map objects to tables

Microsoft Entity Framework (EF) is a technology that maps between the object/property world of .NET (including PowerShell) and the table/column world of a database. With EF, scripters can use normal objects comfortably while still enjoying the advantages of a database behind the scenes for dealing with large volumes of data, sorting, and indexing. EF also allows for complex relationships between objects to be represented naturally. For example, imagine a `Server` object in a script that might have several properties including `Datacenter`. The value of the `Datacenter` property might be an object of another type with various properties (`Country`, `Capabilities`, and others). EF takes care of mapping these relationships in the database and exposing them as properties on the corresponding objects. It also leaves you with the advantages of having domain-specific, strongly typed .NET objects to work with in your script rather than always using `PSCustomObject` or hash-table stand-ins.

As an object-centric database abstraction this would seem an ideal solution for PowerShell scripting. Sadly, it's designed for C# and ASP.NET developers and as such has some sharp edges that make it challenging to get started. Readers who are comfortable with C# and Visual Studio are encouraged to explore EF with PowerShell for working with large data models. The setup is cumbersome but the usage is elegant.

In this chapter I instead use the simple and elegant `Invoke-SqlQuery` function from the `Powershell4SQL` module at http://powershell4sql.codeplex.com/. This is a wrapper around the `System.Data.SqlClient` API.

In this script you created a database on the local SQL Server instance. Within that database you created a table having columns for your data (RemoteIpAddr, QueryFqdn, and so on).

Getting the data to the database

Now that your database is ready you can write and use your `Export-DnsLogLineToDb` function, as follows.

Listing 3 `Export-DnsLogLineToDb`

```
function Export-DnsLogLineToDb {
param(
    [Alias("DnsLogLine")]
    [Parameter(
        ValueFromPipeline=$true
    )]
    [hashtable[]]$InputObject
    , $Server
    , $Database
)
begin{
    Import-Module InvokeSqlQuery
    $sqlConnection = $(
        New-SqlConnection -Server $Server -Database $Database
    )
    $reusableInsertStatement = @"
        INSERT INTO [DnsPackets]
        (QueryFQDN,RemoteIpAddr,DateTime)
        VALUES
        (@QueryFQDN,@RemoteIpAddr,@DateTime)
"@
}
```

Expects piped input from `Convert-DnsLogLine` (annotation on `[hashtable[]]$InputObject`)

Query string with replaceable parameters (annotation on `$reusableInsertStatement`)

```
process{
    foreach( $dnsLogLine in $inputObject ){
        Invoke-SqlQuery `
            -Connection $sqlConnection `
            -Query $reusableInsertStatement `
            -Parameters @{
                QueryFqdn = $dnsLogLine.QueryFqdn
                RemoteIpAddr = $dnsLogLine.RemoteIpAddr
                DateTime = $dnsLogLine.DateTime
            }

    }
}
end{
    $sqlConnection = $null
}
}
```

Now that you have the function you can put it all together per the original outline, as shown in the next listing.

Listing 4 From log to database

```
$server = '(localdb)\v11.0'
$db = "DnsLogDb"

$Invoc = (Get-Variable MyInvocation -Scope 0).Value
$ScriptPath = Split-Path $Invoc.MyCommand.Path

Get-Content (Join-Path $scriptPath "dnsserverlog.txt") |
  ConvertFrom-DnsLogLine |
  Export-DnsLogLineToDb $server $db
```

Get script path to find additional files

Functions defined in previous listings

All of the DNS packets are now represented in that database. They can stay there indefinitely. Tomorrow you could add more entries from other logs and it would all flow together as one cohesive data set. You could add tens of millions more entries over the course of time and the database engine would manage the storage, indexing, and memory usage of that data set, and make it available to whomever you choose. Thank you, SQL Server!

Getting objects and insights back from the database

Now your PowerShell sessions can pull objects back out of the database for further scripted analysis. For example, you can get the queries from a particular client for a particular fully qualified domain name (FQDN), as shown in the next listing.

Listing 5 Querying records from the database

```
$query = @"
    SELECT *
    FROM DnsPackets
    WHERE RemoteIpAddr = @RemoteIpAddr
    AND QueryFqdn = @QueryFqdn
"@
```

```
$parameters = @{
    RemoteIpAddr = "192.168.100.17"
    QueryFqdn = "41397.ds.contoso.com"
}

Import-Module InvokeSqlQuery
Invoke-SqlQuery -Server '(localdb)\v11.0' `
  -Database DnsLogDb -Query $query `
  -Parameters $parameters |
  Out-GridView
```

You can also let the database engine do some of the heavy lifting for analysis. For example, changing the `SELECT *` to `SELECT COUNT(RemoteIpAddr)` causes SQL Server to calculate the count of matching rows without having to bring all the raw data back into your scripting session.

Exploring your PowerShell data outside of PowerShell

Another tremendous advantage of getting the data into a database is that you can easily query it from other tools like Excel, which have their own strengths in exploring and reporting on the data. The brave can draw charts right from PowerShell, or you can go right from PowerShell to Excel without the database (via CSV, for example). In cases when the data set may be very large or may be added to repeatedly over time, when there are relationships between objects, or if you want to expose the data to multiple applications or multiple consumers over the network, the power of the database engine shines. Figure 3 gives an example of using Excel to explore the PowerShell-fed database.

Slicing and dicing the data can bring new insights. It can also be a little addictive (you naturally want to go find out why 192.168.100.17 is issuing so many queries). You

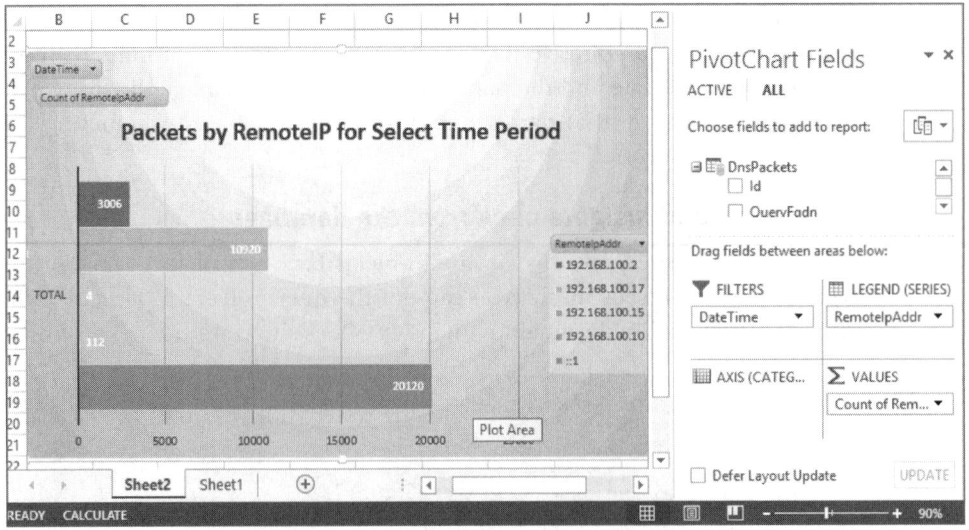

Figure 3 Example of a pivot chart in Excel querying the PowerShell-fed database

may find that you want to add additional properties/columns into your model to allow new pivots. For example, you might find that you want to add a server column to each query, or even a link to a row in a servers table which might have additional properties for each server, such as region or OS. As the set of questions you want to answer from the data evolves you can keep adding to your data model as needed by updating the shape of your PowerShell objects and the corresponding database schema.

Summary

Effective use of pipelines and process blocks can help you to write scalable scripts in the face of any size input. You can be the scripter whose code holds up well in the largest environments and against the longest of data streams—even in memory-constrained remote sessions. These are patterns you can use every day so that your scripts are scalable by default.

Finally, there are some scenarios where you need random access to a huge number of objects, and straightforward streaming isn't enough. Meanwhile, holding everything in memory to access items on demand isn't scalable. In these cases use a database engine that knows how to handle large data sets behind the scenes with appropriate memory usage, durability, and indexing. Use PowerShell to provision and populate the database, and use PowerShell, Excel, Power Pivot, and other tools to explore and analyze the data.

About the author

Matthew Reynolds helps enterprises achieve health and performance with Windows desktop and Active Directory. Through Microsoft's Premier Field Engineering team, Matthew works directly with Fortune 100 customers and also leads development of new diagnostic tools and training to address global customer needs.

Matthew has received multiple awards as a trainer and presenter. He led his team in one of the top-rated sessions at TechEd 2012, developed top-rated training sessions for new Microsoft employees, is a trainer for the Microsoft Certified Masters (aka Rangers) program, is a regular TechReady presenter, and was a tech reviewer for *Windows Powershell in Action,* 2nd edition (Manning 2011).

16 Building your own WMI-based cmdlets

Richard Siddaway

Windows 8 and Windows Server 2012 come with a mass of new PowerShell functionality. Depending on the features installed the server version may have 2,500 or more new cmdlets! Did you know that of that of those 2,500 cmdlets, more than 60 percent are based on Windows Management Instrumentation (WMI)? This chapter explains how you can create your own WMI-based cmdlets.

Discovering WMI-based cmdlets

On a Windows 8 or Windows Server 2012 system try this:

```
PS> Get-ChildItem -Path $pshome\modules\netTCPIP

    Directory: C:\Windows\System32\WindowsPowerShell\v1.0\modules\netTCPIP

Mode                LastWriteTime     Length Name
----                -------------     ------ ----
d----         26/08/2012     14:40            en-US
-a---         02/06/2012     15:32      19097 MSFT_NetIPAddress.cdxml
-a---         02/06/2012     15:32      22334 MSFT_NetIPInterface.cdxml

-a---         17/06/2012     17:08       1979 NetTCPIP.psd1
-a---         02/06/2012     15:32      58379 Tcpip.Format.ps1xml
-a---         02/06/2012     15:32      42813 Tcpip.Types.ps1xml
Display abbreviated for brevity.
```

The last three files are standard module files (manifest, format, and types, respectively)—nothing exciting there. But notice the extension on the first two files: cdxml. That's new!

Now look in the file:

```
PS> Get-Content -Path $pshome\modules\netTCPIP\MSFT_NetIPAddress.cdxml |
  ➥ select -First 5

<?xml version="1.0" encoding="utf-8"?>
<PowerShellMetadata xmlns="http://
```

```
➥ schemas.microsoft.com/cmdlets-over-objects/2009/11">
<Class ClassName="ROOT/StandardCimv2/MSFT_NetIPAddress"
   ClassVersion="1.0.0">
  <Version>1.0.0</Version>
  <DefaultNoun>NetIPAddress</DefaultNoun>
```

Whoa! That's XML. What's it doing in a PowerShell module?

What you've discovered is a CDXML file—*cmdlet definition XML*. In a nutshell, a CDXML file allows you to wrap the use of a WMI class in XML and publish it as a PowerShell module.

In the third line of XML you see this:

```
ClassName="ROOT/StandardCimv2/MSFT_NetIPAddress"
```

Looks like the path to a WMI class. If it is, this should work:

```
PS> Get-CimInstance -Namespace root\standardcimv2
  ➥ -ClassName MSFT_NetIPAddress

IPAddress         : fe80::38ab:4529:2ab6:eb06%13
InterfaceIndex    : 13
InterfaceAlias    : Ethernet
AddressFamily     : IPv6
Type              : Unicast
PrefixLength      : 64
PrefixOrigin      : WellKnown
SuffixOrigin      : Link
AddressState      : Preferred
ValidLifetime     : Infinite ([TimeSpan]::MaxValue)
PreferredLifetime : Infinite ([TimeSpan]::MaxValue)
SkipAsSource      : False
PolicyStore       : ActiveStore
...
```

The root\standardcimv2 namespace is where Microsoft has tucked many new WMI classes. They're only available on Windows 8 and Windows Server 2012. You won't find them if you've upgraded to PowerShell v3 on Windows 7 or any other legacy version of Windows.

Look in the second line of the XML:

```
"http://schemas.microsoft.com/cmdlets-over-objects/2009/11">
```

Cmdlets over objects is Microsoft's technology for making all this happen. This is how WMI is used to deliver so many new cmdlets. A single CDXML file publishes a single WMI class as a module. The module usually consists of the following:

- *A* `Get` *cmdlet*—This is the equivalent of running `Get-CimInstance` using the class. The `Get` cmdlet can have one or more parameters that are based on the WMI class properties and act as filters.
- *Zero or more cmdlets based on the methods of the class*—These cmdlets use parameters to take the method's arguments.
- *Classes that have static methods*—These classes, such as the registry provider (`StdRegProv`), can also be exposed using CDXML files.

The great thing about this is that it's easy to write your own CDXML files and wrap the WMI classes you use as PowerShell modules. Doing so provides a much-improved ease-of-use factor for WMI, especially among junior administrators.

Creating a WMI-based cmdlet

Microsoft is unlikely to wrap any of the root\cimv2 WMI classes as CDXML files any time soon, if at all, so let's see how to create your own CDXML file. We'll use a class everyone accesses—`Win32_NetworkAdapterConfiguration`. The skeleton of the module is shown in the following listing.

Listing 1 Creating `Get-Win33_NetworkAdaptorConfiguration`

```
<?xml version="1.0" encoding="utf-8"?>
<PowerShellMetadata xmlns=
  ➥ "http://schemas.microsoft.com/cmdlets-over-objects/2009/11">      ❶ Header data
  <Class ClassName="root\cimv2\Win32_NetworkAdapterConfiguration">    ❷ WMI class and namespace
    <Version>1.0.0.0</Version>
    <DefaultNoun>Win32NetworkAdapterConfiguration</DefaultNoun>       ❸ Cmdlet noun

    <InstanceCmdlets>
      <GetCmdletParameters DefaultCmdletParameterSet="ByIndex">      ❹ Parameter set
        <QueryableProperties>

          <Property PropertyName="Index">                             ❺ WMI property name
            <Type PSType ="UInt32"/>
            <RegularQuery AllowGlobbing="true">
              <CmdletParameterMetadata PSName="Index"                 ❻ Cmdlet parameter name
                ➥ ValueFromPipelineByPropertyName="true"
                ➥ CmdletParameterSets="ByIndex" />
            </RegularQuery>
          </Property>

        </QueryableProperties>                                        ❼ Closing XML statement
      </GetCmdletParameters>
    </InstanceCmdlets>
  </Class>
</PowerShellMetadata>
```

This file must be saved with a .cdxml extension. The CDXML file starts with two header rows ❶. These are the same for every CDXML file. The working part of the file starts where you define the WMI class name to use ❷. As previously stated, the `Win32_NetworkAdapterConfiguration` class is used. The full path, including namespace, is provided in the definition. A version number is supplied on the next line. This is your version for your module. You can set it to any numbering scheme applicable to your work. The header section closes with a default noun ❸. I usually use the class name without the underscore (_), but you're free to use whatever you want.

TIP Check the nouns of cmdlets already on your system before committing to a final choice.

The middle section of the XML file defines your `Get-Win32NetworkAdapter-Configuration` cmdlet. The cmdlet's verb is set to `Get` by default. The noun is provided by the default noun you supplied earlier. Parameter sets can be defined for the filter parameters ❹. The WMI property name is supplied ❺, and a parameter name is provided ❻. The cmdlet parameter name doesn't have to match the WMI property name, though it often makes sense for it to do so. Additional configuration is supplied for the parameter to allow wildcards (globbing) and for the parameter to accept pipeline input. The file closes with the XML tags ❼ required to complete various sections discussed here.

Using a WMI-based cmdlet

Now you have a CDXML file. How are you going to use it? The answer is simple—just like any other module. Save the CDXML file into a folder on your module path. If you call the module file NetworkAdapterConfiguration.cdxml, save it into a folder called NetworkAdapterConfiguration. You can load the CDXML file during development by using `import-module`:

```
PS> Import-Module .\listing1.cdxml -Force
PS> Get-Module listing1

ModuleType Name                      ExportedCommands
---------- ----                      ----------------
Cim        listing1                  Get-Win32NetworkAdapterConfiguration
```

Use the `-Force` parameter while you're developing. It makes sure the latest version is loaded.

If you have the module on your module path (defined by `$env:PSModulePath`), PowerShell will auto-load it when it starts along with all your other modules. One important point is the module type: it's labeled `Cim`. This indicates a CDXML-based module. If you add a manifest file the module type will change accordingly.

Your new cmdlet is used the same way as any other cmdlet:

```
PS> Get-Win32NetworkAdapterConfiguration | Format-Table -AutoSize

ServiceName DHCPEnabled Index Description
----------- ----------- ----- -----------
Rasl2tp     False       0     WAN Miniport (L2TP)
RasSstp     False       1     WAN Miniport (SSTP)
RasPppoe    False       4     WAN Miniport (PPPOE)
NdisWan     False       5     WAN Miniport (IP)
NdisWan     False       6     WAN Miniport (IPv6)
NdisWan     False       7     WAN Miniport (Network Monitor)
kdnic       True        8     Microsoft Kernel Debug Network Adapter
AsyncMac    False       9     RAS Async Adapter
NVNET       True        11    NVIDIA nForce 10/100/1000 Mbps Ethernet
BthPan      True        17    Bluetooth Device (Personal Area Network)
...
```

This is the equivalent of typing

```
Get-CimInstance -ClassName Win32_NetworkAdapterConfiguration |
Format-Table -AutoSize
```

You're saving a bit of work. But having a cmdlet really scores for you when you want to filter:

```
Get-CimInstance -ClassName Win32_NetworkAdapterConfiguration
  ➥ -Filter "Index=11" | Format-Table -AutoSize
```

This becomes

```
PS> Get-Win32NetworkAdapterConfiguration -Index 11 | Format-Table -AutoSize

ServiceName DHCPEnabled Index Description
----------- ----------- ----- -----------
NVNET       True        11    NVIDIA nForce 10/100/1000 Mbps Ethernet
```

Much simpler. The default display is controlled by PowerShell's Extensible Type System (ETS). You can see the full set of properties by using `Format-List`:

```
Get-Win32NetworkAdapterConfiguration -Index 11 | Format-List *
```

Adding extra filter parameters

Two common filters when you're looking for network adapters are the `DHCPEnabled` and `IPEnabled` properties. You access these, respectively, like this:

```
Get-CimInstance -ClassName Win32_NetworkAdapterConfiguration
  ➥ -Filter "DHCPEnabled = $true"

Get-CimInstance -ClassName Win32_NetworkAdapterConfiguration
  ➥ -Filter "IPEnabled = $true"
```

The next listing shows the extra XML that has to be added to the CDXML file. The full listing is available in the code download available on the book's website.

Listing 2 Adding extra filter parameters

```
<Property PropertyName="DHCPEnabled">
  <Type PSType ="Boolean"/>
  <RegularQuery >
    <CmdletParameterMetadata PSName="DHCPEnabled"
      ➥ ValueFromPipelineByPropertyName="true"
      ➥ CmdletParameterSets="ByEnabled" />
  </RegularQuery>
</Property>

<Property PropertyName="IPEnabled">
  <Type PSType ="Boolean"/>
  <RegularQuery >
    <CmdletParameterMetadata PSName="IPEnabled"
      ➥ ValueFromPipelineByPropertyName="true"
      ➥ CmdletParameterSets="ByEnabled" />
  </RegularQuery>
</Property>
```

Each additional property follows the same format:

1. A property name from the WMI class is required.
2. The type of input—in this case, Boolean—is defined.
3. The cmdlet parameter name is defined.
4. The pipeline capabilities are set.
5. A parameter set is defined.

WMI uses, in some cases, subtly different names for data types. The best way to confirm the data type is to use `Get-CimClass` to investigate the properties:

```
Get-CimClass -ClassName Win32_NetworkAdapterConfiguration |
➥ select -ExpandProperty CimClassProperties |
➥ where Name -like "*Enabled*"
```

The other point to note is that the wildcard (globbing) ability has been removed from these parameters. It makes sense as a Boolean type will only accept `$true`, `$false`, `1`, or `0`.

With two parameter sets your cmdlet's syntax looks like this:

```
PS> Get-Command Get-Win32NetworkAdapterConfiguration -Syntax

Get-Win32NetworkAdapterConfiguration [<CommonParameters>]

Get-Win32NetworkAdapterConfiguration [-Index <uint32[]>]
[-CimSession <CimSession[]>] [-ThrottleLimit <int>] [-AsJob]
[<CommonParameters>]

Get-Win32NetworkAdapterConfiguration [-DHCPEnabled <bool[]>]
[-IPEnabled <bool[]>] [-CimSession <CimSession[]>]
[-ThrottleLimit <int>] [-AsJob] [<CommonParameters>]
```

You can use the new parameters to filter on the enablement of IP, DHCP, or both:

```
Get-Win32NetworkAdapterConfiguration -IPEnabled $true
Get-Win32NetworkAdapterConfiguration -DHCPEnabled $true
Get-Win32NetworkAdapterConfiguration -IPEnabled $true -DHCPEnabled $true
```

The syntax reveals that there isn't a `ComputerName` parameter available on the cmdlet you've created. You do get a `CimSession` parameter, which is how you access remote machines:

```
$sw = New-CimSession -ComputerName $env:COMPUTERNAME
Get-Win32NetworkAdapterConfiguration -DHCPEnabled $true -CimSession $sw
```

You automatically get an additional column called `PSComputerName` that indicates the name of the remote machine. `CimSessions` automatically use Web Services Management (WS-MAN) as the transport protocol, but if you have PowerShell v2 on a remote machine, and therefore WS-MAN v2, it won't work. You have to drop back to using DCOM against machines with PowerShell v2:

```
$o = New-CimSessionOption -Protocol DCOM
$sd = New-CimSession -ComputerName $env:COMPUTERNAME -SessionOption $o
Get-Win32NetworkAdapterConfiguration -DHCPEnabled $true -CimSession $sd
```

You can have multiple computers in a CIM session, and you can mix and match WS-MAN–based sessions with DCOM-based sessions:

```
Get-Win32NetworkAdapterConfiguration -DHCPEnabled $true
  ➥ -CimSession $sw, $sd
```

The other interesting parameter you get for free (PowerShell automatically adds it)—that is, you don't have to do any coding—is -AsJob:

```
PS> Get-Win32NetworkAdapterConfiguration -DHCPEnabled $true -AsJob

Id     Name          PSJobTypeName   State         HasMoreData     Location
--     ----          -------------   -----         -----------     --------
51     CimJob25      CimJob          Running       True            RSLAPTOP01

PS> Get-Job

Id     Name          PSJobTypeName   State         HasMoreData     Location
--     ----          -------------   -----         -----------     --------
51     CimJob25      CimJob          Completed     True            RSLAPTOP01
```

You can use the -AsJob and -CimSession parameters together to access remote machines as a job.

WARNING When you're accessing remote machines the request will fail if the WMI class isn't installed on the remote machine. This isn't a way to bypass having the WMI classes installed.

Creating cmdlets from WMI methods

The Win32_NetworkAdapterConfiguration class has many methods, which you can find like this:

```
Get-CimClass -ClassName Win32_NetworkAdapterConfiguration |
select -ExpandProperty CimClassMethods
```

Two examples of creating cmdlets from these methods are shown in the next listing.

Listing 3 Adding methods as cmdlets

```
<?xml version="1.0" encoding="utf-8"?>
<PowerShellMetadata xmlns=
  ➥ "http://schemas.microsoft.com/cmdlets-over-objects/2009/11">
  <Class ClassName="root\cimv2\Win32_NetworkAdapterConfiguration">
    <Version>1.0.0.0</Version>
    <DefaultNoun>Win32NetworkAdapterConfiguration</DefaultNoun>

    <InstanceCmdlets>
      <GetCmdletParameters DefaultCmdletParameterSet="ByIndex">     ❶ Set Standard parameters
        <QueryableProperties>
          <Property PropertyName="Index">
            <Type PSType ="UInt32"/>
            <RegularQuery AllowGlobbing="true">
              <CmdletParameterMetadata IsMandatory="true" PSName="Index"
                ➥ ValueFromPipelineByPropertyName="true"
                ➥ CmdletParameterSets="ByIndex" />
```

```
      </RegularQuery>
    </Property>
   </QueryableProperties>
</GetCmdletParameters>

<GetCmdlet>                                                      ❷ Get
 <CmdletMetadata Verb="Get"/>                                      cmdlet
 <GetCmdletParameters DefaultCmdletParameterSet="ByIndex">
  <QueryableProperties>
    <Property PropertyName="Index">
      <Type PSType ="UInt32"/>
      <RegularQuery AllowGlobbing="true">
        <CmdletParameterMetadata PSName="Index"
          ➥ ValueFromPipelineByPropertyName="true"
          ➥ CmdletParameterSets="ByIndex" />
      </RegularQuery>
    </Property>
    <Property PropertyName="DHCPEnabled">
      <Type PSType ="Boolean"/>
      <RegularQuery >
        <CmdletParameterMetadata PSName="DHCPEnabled"
          ➥ ValueFromPipelineByPropertyName="true"
          ➥ CmdletParameterSets="ByEnabled" />
      </RegularQuery>
    </Property>
    <Property PropertyName="IPEnabled">
      <Type PSType ="Boolean"/>
      <RegularQuery >
        <CmdletParameterMetadata PSName="IPEnabled"
          ➥ ValueFromPipelineByPropertyName="true"
          ➥ CmdletParameterSets="ByEnabled" />
      </RegularQuery>
    </Property>
   </QueryableProperties>
 </GetCmdletParameters>
</GetCmdlet>

<Cmdlet>                                                         ❸ Renew
  <CmdletMetadata Verb="Invoke" Noun="Win32NACRenewDHCPLease"       IP lease
    ➥ ConfirmImpact="Medium"/>                                     cmdlet
  <Method MethodName="RenewDHCPLease">
    <ReturnValue>
      <Type PSType="System.UInt32"/>
      <CmdletOutputMetadata>
      </CmdletOutputMetadata>
    </ReturnValue>
  </Method>
</Cmdlet>

<Cmdlet>                                                         ❹ Set IP
  <CmdletMetadata Verb="Set" Noun="Win32NACIPAddress"               address
    ➥ ConfirmImpact="Medium"/>                                     cmdlet
  <Method MethodName="EnableStatic">
    <ReturnValue>
      <Type PSType="System.UInt32"/>
      <CmdletOutputMetadata>
```

```
          </CmdletOutputMetadata>
        </ReturnValue>
        <Parameters>
          <Parameter ParameterName="IPAddress" >
            <Type PSType="System.String[]" />
            <CmdletParameterMetadata PSName="IPAddress">
            </CmdletParameterMetadata>
          </Parameter>
          <Parameter ParameterName="SubNetMask" >
            <Type PSType="System.String[]" />
            <CmdletParameterMetadata PSName="SubNet">
            </CmdletParameterMetadata>
          </Parameter>
        </Parameters>
      </Method>
    </Cmdlet>
  </InstanceCmdlets>
</Class>
</PowerShellMetadata>
```

When you load the listing 3 module, you now get three cmdlets:

```
PS> Get-Command -Module listing3

CommandType     Name
-----------     ----
Function        Get-Win32NetworkAdapterConfiguration
Function        Invoke-Win32NACRenewDHCPLease
Function        Set-Win32NACIPAddress
```

The original `Get-Win32NetworkAdapterConfiguration` cmdlet remains, plus `Invoke-Win32NACRenewDHCPLease` and `Set-Win32NACIPAddress`, which you added through the code in listing 3. These cmdlets supply the functionality of the `RenewDHCPLease` and `EnableStatic` methods of the `Win32_NetworkAdapterConfiguration` WMI class, respectively.

Naming conventions

Before we dive into the code, a quick word on naming conventions. You can use anything you want. I stick with the approved verbs (use `Get-Verb` to view them). If I'm changing something I use `Set`—I've used `Set-Win32NACIPAddress` for the `EnableStatic` method because to my mind, it's more natural to think about setting the IP address. I used `Invoke` for the `RenewDHCPLease` method because there wasn't a suitable verb. I created the nouns based on the method name (or item being modified) and the default noun, though I did abbreviate the default noun portion because I'm not competing in the Longest Cmdlet Name in the World competition.

Listing 3 starts off the same way as listing 1 with the same header information. The first change occurs with the definition of standard filter parameters for the cmdlets ❶. A filter parameter is defined based on the `Index` property of the WMI class.

The parameter is made mandatory. This property is only applied to the Invoke-Win32NACRenewDHCPLease and Set-Win32NACIPAddress cmdlets. The original Get-Win32NetworkAdapterConfiguration cmdlet redefines the index parameter as non-mandatory because you don't want mandatory parameters on your Get cmdlet.

An explicit allocation of the verb Get is made to the get cmdlet ❷. The rest of the definition of the Get cmdlet is unchanged using the <GetCmdlet></GetCmdlet> tags.

The new cmdlets are defined within <Cmdlet></Cmdlet> tags. The cmdlet to use the RenewDHCPLease method starts by defining the verb and the noun ❸. The method name is required, and you also define the return value. WMI methods have an integer return value: a return value of 0 means the method worked successfully, and anything else means it went wrong. If you're lucky the class documentation on MSDN will supply a reason to go with the value.

You can test the new cmdlet by first checking the current value of the DHCPLeaseObtained property for the instance you want to reset:

```
Get-CimInstance -ClassName Win32_NetworkAdapterConfiguration
  ➥ -Filter "Index=10" | select DHCP*
```

If you want to renew the lease using the CIM cmdlets you need this code:

```
Get-CimInstance -ClassName Win32_NetworkAdapterConfiguration
  ➥ -Filter "Index=10" | Invoke-CimMethod -MethodName RenewDHCPLease
```

Your new cmdlet is so much easier to use:

```
PS> Invoke-Win32NACRenewDHCPLease -Index 10
0
```

You can put the return code into a variable and use that to return messages based on value. The DHCPLeaseObtained method doesn't take any arguments. Many WMI methods do take arguments; as an example, we'll use the EnableStatic method.

The cmdlet definition starts by defining the verb and noun ❹. The same return code definition is used, and then you define some parameters. The method takes two arguments: an array of IP addresses and an array of subnet masks. The IPAddress parameter keeps the name IPAddress, but the WMI SubNetMask parameter is renamed SubNet for ease of use.

You can discover the parameter requirements using Get-CimClass:

```
PS> $class = Get-CimClass -ClassName Win32_NetworkAdapterConfiguration
PS> $class.CimClassMethods["EnableStatic"].Parameters |
  ➥ Format-Table -AutoSize

Name       CimType     Qualifiers                  ReferenceClassName
----       -------     ----------                  ------------------
IPAddress  StringArray {ID, In, MappingStrings}
SubnetMask StringArray {ID, In, MappingStrings}
```

Now you have a cmdlet definition. How does it work? Like this:

```
$address = @("172.168.5.1")
$subnet = @("255.255.255.0")
```

```
PS> Set-Win32NACIPAddress -Index 11 -IPAddress $address -SubNet $subnet
0
```

This is equivalent to using the much more complicated

```
Get-CimInstance -ClassName Win32_NetworkAdapterConfiguration
  ➥ -Filter "Index=11" | Invoke-CimMethod -MethodName EnableStatic
  ➥ -Arguments @{"IPAddress" = $address; "SubNetMask" = $subnet}
```

Summary

CDXML provides a technology to publish WMI classes as PowerShell modules. This technology is used a lot in Windows 8 and Windows Server 2012 to deliver PowerShell functionality. You can create CDXML files on Windows 7 machines using PowerShell v3, but you must remember that the WMI class your module will use must be installed on that machine. You can't copy or re-create the CDXML files from Windows 8 and expect them to work because the WMI classes won't be present. Expect to see a lot more CDXML-based functionality in the future.

A tool to work with CDXML files called CIM IDE is available at http://archive.msdn.microsoft.com/cimide, but it's still prerelease and requires Visual Studio. I have found it easier to copy the XML from existing CDXML files and modify it.

A white paper describing the XML schema is available from http://mng.bz/xdE9. You can find further information and more examples in *PowerShell and WMI* (Manning 2012) and *PowerShell in Depth* (Manning 2013).

About the author

Richard Siddaway has worked with Microsoft technologies for 25 years and has spent time in most IT roles. He currently works for Kelway (UK) Ltd as an automation consultant. He has a long-standing interest in automation techniques, and PowerShell has been his primary automation tool since the early beta versions. Richard founded the UK PowerShell User Group in 2007 and is a PowerShell MVP. He frequently speaks at PowerShell user groups in the UK, Europe, the US, and elsewhere around the world, and judges the Microsoft Scripting Games. In addition to writing his blog (http://msmvps.com/blogs/RichardSiddaway/), Richard has authored two PowerShell books: *PowerShell in Practice* (Manning 2010) and *PowerShell and WMI* (Manning 2012), and coauthored *PowerShell in Depth* (Manning 2013) with Don Jones and Jeffery Hicks. Currently he is writing an introductory book for Active Directory administrators that features PowerShell.

17 Turning command-line tools into PowerShell tools

Jeffery Hicks

As terrific as PowerShell is as an automation engine and management tool, and despite the new cmdlets that shipped with Windows 8 and Windows Server 2012, there are still times when a command-line (CLI) tool gets the job done. Perhaps there isn't a cmdlet replacement yet, or the CLI tool is easy to run. Or perhaps you have some legacy batch files that you need to use. The downside is that although you can run these tools in PowerShell, you're limited with regard to what you can do with them because CLI tools write text and PowerShell is all about objects.

In this chapter I'll show you how to turn output from CLI tools into something you can work with in a PowerShell pipeline. Ultimately, I think you'll want to create your own PowerShell functions that wrap around a legacy command yet still write objects to the pipeline.

Requirements

Unfortunately, not every command-line tool lends itself to a PowerShell conversion. The tips and techniques I'll show you rely on a few key requirements. If the tool you want to use doesn't fit into the following categories you'll have a hard time transforming the results to a PowerShell-friendly format:

- *The CLI tool must write text using standard out (StdOut).* One easy way to test this is to run your command and redirect it to a file: `netstat > e:\temp\netstat.txt`. If you can't do this, the command isn't a good candidate.
- *The CLI tool should produce formatted or predictable output.* The more structured the output, the easier the transition to PowerShell.
- *The CLI tool should run without any user interaction.* By that I mean you should be able to run the tool with any necessary parameters, press Enter, and get results. If the command requires user interaction such as answering a prompt, it isn't a good candidate.

- *You must be able to run the CLI tool in PowerShell.* It should go without saying, but the whole point is to run the command in PowerShell and then use the results in the pipeline. If the command you want to run has some sort of odd syntax that makes it difficult to execute from a PowerShell prompt, it will be that much harder to transform.

Most Microsoft command-line utilities that I'm aware of should fall into these categories and meet the requirements. But there might be a third-party command-line tool you use that is a little odd. I'm not saying it's impossible to "PowerShell-ize" the output; it just might be a little more difficult.

Table 1 shows a number of common Microsoft command-line tools you may want to turn into PowerShell tools.

Table 1 Potential PowerShell CLI tools

ipconfig	driverquery	schtasks
tasklist	arp	netstat
nbtstat	dnscmd	klist
net [user| localgroup]	qprocess	whoami
quser	getmac	ftype

Conversion techniques

Let me state up front that there is no universal technique for transforming the results of a CLI tool into something PowerShell can use. Depending on the tool you may need to combine these techniques:

- Using PowerShell data formats
- Parsing text output

I also think you'll find it easier to transform a command-line tool into PowerShell using a script or function. Although it's possible to execute many of the examples in this chapter directly in the console, trust me: a script will be much easier because you'll rarely accomplish the conversion with a one-line technique.

Looking for PowerShell data formats

The first technique is an easy one. Look at the command help, and see if the output can be formatted into something that PowerShell already knows how to use, such as CSV or XML. For example, if you look at help for driverquery.exe, as shown in figure 1, there are options to format the results to a CSV format.

This is a useful command-line option because PowerShell already knows how to turn CSV data into objects. In fact, with a single PowerShell expression, you can take the CSV output from `driverquery` and turn it into PowerShell:

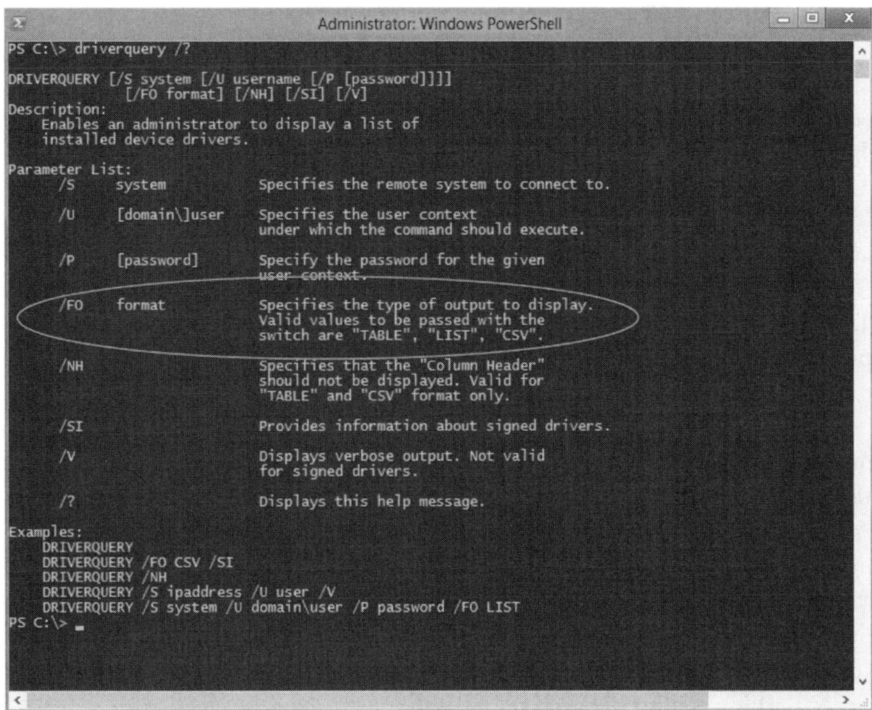
```
PS C:\> driverquery /?

DRIVERQUERY [/S system [/U username [/P [password]]]]
            [/FO format] [/NH] [/SI] [/V]
Description:
    Enables an administrator to display a list of
    installed device drivers.

Parameter List:
     /S     system          Specifies the remote system to connect to.

     /U     [domain\]user   Specifies the user context
                            under which the command should execute.

     /P     [password]      Specify the password for the given
                            user context.

     /FO    format          Specifies the type of output to display.
                            Valid values to be passed with the
                            switch are "TABLE", "LIST", "CSV".

     /NH                    Specifies that the "Column Header"
                            should not be displayed. Valid for
                            "TABLE" and "CSV" format only.

     /SI                    Provides information about signed drivers.

     /V                     Displays verbose output. Not valid
                            for signed drivers.

     /?                     Displays this help message.

Examples:
    DRIVERQUERY
    DRIVERQUERY /FO CSV /SI
    DRIVERQUERY /NH
    DRIVERQUERY /S ipaddress /U user /V
    DRIVERQUERY /S system /U domain\user /P password /FO LIST
PS C:\>
```

Figure 1 DriverQuery.exe help with the format option for CSV

```
PS C:\> driverquery /fo csv | convertfrom-csv

Module Name  Display Name              Driver Type  Link Date
-----------  ------------              -----------  ---------
1394ohci     1394 OHCI Compliant H...  Kernel       11/20/2010 5:44:56 AM
ACPI         Microsoft ACPI Driver     Kernel       11/20/2010 4:19:16 AM
AcpiPmi      ACPI Power Meter Driver   Kernel       11/20/2010 4:30:42 AM
adp94xx      adp94xx                   Kernel       12/5/2008 6:54:42 PM
adpahci      adpahci                   Kernel       5/1/2007 1:30:09 PM
adpu320      adpu320                   Kernel       2/27/2007 7:04:15 PM
AFD          Ancillary Function Dr...  Kernel       12/27/2011 10:59:20 PM
...
```

Once the data has been converted you have objects that you can work with, which means you can do whatever you want with the results. Here are some more examples:

```
PS C:\> driverquery /fo csv | convertfrom-csv |
➥ Group 'Driver Type' -NoElement

Count Name
----- ----
  279 Kernel
   29 File System

PS C:\> driverquery /fo csv | convertfrom-csv |
➥ where {$_."Driver Type" -match "File System"} | sort Displayname
```

```
Module Name    Display Name              Driver Type    Link Date
-----------    ------------              -----------    ---------
Npfs           Npfs                      File System    7/13/2009 7:19:48 PM
Ntfs           Ntfs                      File System    3/10/2011 10:39:3...
rdbss          Redirected Buffering ...  File System    11/20/2010 4:27:5...
NetBIOS        NetBIOS Interface         File System    7/13/2009 8:09:26 PM
...
```

If all you need is basic PowerShell like I've shown here, this should suffice. But there are some potential drawbacks.

First, the property names are taken from the CLI output and might contain spaces. Thus you'll end up with properties like `Module Name` and `Driver Type`. If all you want is pretty output this probably doesn't matter. But when you want to do something with a property you have to remember to enclose it in quotes, as I had to with `"Driver Type"`.

Second, all properties are treated as strings. Again, depending on the CLI tool, that may not matter. But in my example, if you want to filter or sort on `'Link Date'` you won't get the results you expect—at least, not without a little extra work.

Finally, sometimes the property value includes more than meets the eye. Did you notice in the second example, in which I filtered on the driver type for `"File System"`, that I used `-match` and not `-eq`? That's because the actual value has a trailing space that's introduced somewhere in the conversion. It isn't apparent at first glance, until you try to use `-eq` and wonder why nothing is written to the pipeline. So I used `-match`, which is more forgiving.

One way to get around the property-name issue is to specify an alternate header in the CSV file:

```
PS C:\> $h="ModuleName","DisplayName","DriverType","LinkDate"
PS C:\> driverquery /fo csv | select -Skip 1 | convertfrom-csv -Header $h
```

I skipped the first line of the CSV output and told `ConvertFrom-CSV` to use my alternate header. Now my property names are easier to work with.

Handling the property type isn't too difficult, depending on what you need to do. For one-time formatting you might be able to use a cmdlet:

```
PS C:\> driverquery /fo csv | select -Skip 1 | convertfrom-csv -Header $h |
➥ where {$_.Drivertype -match "file"} |
➥ sort @{Expression={$_.LinkDate -as [datetime]}}
```

Here I took my converted data and sorted on a hash table that returned the `LinkDate` property as a `datetime` object. This gets trickier if you want to persist data in this format. Doing so takes a few extra steps, but it can also help with those odd spaces that might crop up in property values. The code in the following listing summarizes everything I just demonstrated.

Listing 1 Converting CLI CSV output to PowerShell

```
#requires -version 3.0

$hash=[ordered]@{
ModuleName=[string]
```

Create an ordered hash table with property names and types

```
DisplayName=[string]
DriverType=[string]
LinkDate=[datetime]
}

$data=driverquery /fo csv | select -Skip 1 |
   convertfrom-csv -Header $($hash.keys)

for ($i=0;$i -lt $data.count;$i++) {
  foreach ($property in $hash.keys) {
    #update each property with a trimmed version
    $data[$i].$property=$data[$i].$property.Trim() -as $hash.$property
  }
}
#write the data to the pipeline
$data
```

Define a header from the hash-table keys

Loop through each object

Get each property, trim any spaces, and cast it to the appropriate type

This technique requires you to know in advance what your output will be and what object types you want to define. You build a hash table with the new property names and assign a type as the corresponding value for each key. Fortunately, PowerShell 3.0 offers ordered hash tables, which make this much easier. You use the hash-table keys for your new header, saving all the results to a variable.

In order to clean up `$data` you have to go through every object and reassign a new value. The new value is the old value trimmed of any trailing or leading spaces and then cast back as the appropriate type.

The end result is that `$data` now has trimmed and properly typed objects. This means you can use `$data` in the pipeline like any other cmdlet output:

```
$data | where DriverType -eq "File System" | sort LinkDate |
  ➥ select -first 5
```

As you can imagine, this technique is much easier to work with in a script.

Parsing text output

If the CLI tool doesn't offer a PowerShell-ready format like CSV you have to parse the output. This is where it's very important that the output is ordered and predictable. There are a number of techniques I think you'll find yourself turning to:

- Use `Select-Object` to skip *X* number of lines. Often a CLI command includes headers you don't really care about.
- Use `Select-String` to select command output lines that you want to transform into PowerShell.
- Use the `Split()` method or operator to break up lines in array. This works well when the command output is structured and predictable.
- Use the `Trim()` method to clean up values. Leading or trailing spaces can lead to unpredictable results.
- Use regular expressions to either identify the data you want to parse or perhaps identify what property type you want to eventually use. You might use regular

expressions on an entire line of output or on individual array elements if you've split up the line.

Let's demonstrate some of these techniques. I'm going to take the output of NBTSTAT /N and turn it into a PowerShell object. I'll work through the process interactively so you can follow along; eventually I could take the steps and turn them into an advanced function.

Here's the original output:

```
PS C:\> nbtstat /n

Local Area Connection:
Node IpAddress: [10.23.36.71] Scope Id: []

                NetBIOS Local Name Table

       Name               Type         Status
    ---------------------------------------------
    QUARK          <20>  UNIQUE      Registered
    QUARK          <00>  UNIQUE      Registered
    JDHITSOLUTIONS <00>  GROUP       Registered

Wireless Network Connection:
Node IpAddress: [0.0.0.0] Scope Id: []
```

What matters in this case is the table of registered names. It looks like a good candidate for a PowerShell object. I already see names I can use for property names, like Name, Type, and Status. So first I'll get the lines of interest:

```
PS C:\> $data=nbtstat /n | Select-String "<"
PS C:\> $data

    QUARK          <20>  UNIQUE      Registered
    QUARK          <00>  UNIQUE      Registered
    JDHITSOLUTIONS <00>  GROUP       Registered
```

I use Select-String to filter and save the results to $data. Next, I'll split each line into an array. The tricky part is that because I used Select-String, each line is a MatchInfo object, not a string, so I need to use the Line property. I'll also trim off spaces while I'm at it:

```
PS C:\> $lines=$data | foreach { $_.Line.Trim()}
PS C:\> $lines
QUARK          <20>  UNIQUE      Registered
QUARK          <00>  UNIQUE      Registered
JDHITSOLUTIONS <00>  GROUP       Registered
```

Next I need to split each line on the spaces between words into another array using the -Split operator and a regular-expression pattern for a whitespace. Because the order is predictable I know what each array element will be, so I can use them to create a new object:

```
PS C:\> $lines | foreach { $temp=$_ -split "\s+"
>> New-Object -TypeName PSObject -Property @{
>> Name=$temp[0]
```

```
>> NbtCode=$temp[1]
>> Type=$temp[2]
>> Status=$temp[3]
>> }
>> }
Name                     NbtCode              Type           Status
----                     -------              ----           ------
QUARK                    <20>                 UNIQUE         Registered
QUARK                    <00>                 UNIQUE         Registered
JDHITSOLUTIONS           <00>                 GROUP          Registered
```

There are potential issues with the techniques I just used. If any property value contained a space I would have had to figure out some other splitting technique. Or if there was a line that had no space between values I would have needed some other splitting technique.

TIP I strongly recommend defining property names without spaces or special characters like commas and apostrophes. You may need to use the `Replace()` method to strip them out. While you're at it, my other best practice recommendation is to trim strings. Also note that if your output has values that you might want to sort on or perhaps measure in some way, it's important that you attempt to cast the text value into the appropriate object type.

Handling CLI errors

Handling errors from your CLI tool and turning them into PowerShell is something you'll have to handle on a case-by-case basis. Assuming you're building a PowerShell script or function to wrap around your CLI tool, you'll need to include some logic to validate data. For example, let's say you're writing a PowerShell function to wrap around the `NET USER` command. When there's no error you can use the techniques I've shown you to parse the output into a PowerShell object. But what if someone tries to get an invalid user?

I would probably do something like this:

```
$data=net user $username 2>$env:temp\err.txt
If ($data) {
   #add your code to process the data
}
Else {
  #add your code to parse the err.txt file to display and handle the error.
}
```

Or you can use a `Try/Catch` block. Because the CLI tool isn't a cmdlet it can't throw a terminating exception. But you can set the error action preference in the `Try` scriptblock to handle that for you:

```
Try {
  $ErrorActionPreference="stop"
  $data=net user $username
}
```

```
Catch {
  Write-Warning "Failed to find $username. $($_.Exception.Message)"
}
if ($data) {
  Write-Verbose "Processing $username"
  #code to parse $data
}
```

A practical example

Let's look at one more practical example. I want to take the output of `ipconfig /displaydns` and turn it into PowerShell output. There's some potentially useful information here that would be easier to work with if I had PowerShell objects.

First, what type of output do I get?

```
PS C:\> ipconfig /displaydns

Windows IP Configuration

    ntp0.cornell.edu
    ----------------------------------------
    Record Name . . . . . : ntp0.cornell.edu
    Record Type . . . . . : 5
    Time To Live  . . . . : 80983
    Data Length . . . . . : 8
    Section . . . . . . . : Answer
    CNAME Record  . . . . : dns3.cit.cornell.edu

    coredc01.jdhlab.local
    ----------------------------------------
    Record Name . . . . . : COREDC01.jdhlab.local
    Record Type . . . . . : 1
    Time To Live  . . . . : 3583
    Data Length . . . . . : 4
    Section . . . . . . . : Answer
    A (Host) Record . . . : 172.16.10.190

    manning.com
    ----------------------------------------
    Record Name . . . . . : manning.com
    Record Type . . . . . : 1
    Time To Live  . . . . : 399
    Data Length . . . . . : 4
    Section . . . . . . . : Answer
    A (Host) Record . . . : 68.180.151.75

    manning.com
    ----------------------------------------
    Record Name . . . . . : manning.com
    Record Type . . . . . : 2
    Time To Live  . . . . : 85593
    Data Length . . . . . : 8
    Section . . . . . . . : Answer
    NS Record   . . . . . : yns2.yahoo.com

    Record Name . . . . . : manning.com
    Record Type . . . . . : 2
```

```
    Time To Live  . . . . : 85593
    Data Length . . . . . : 8
    Section . . . . . . . : Answer
    NS Record   . . . . . : yns1.yahoo.com
...
```

I could create objects that would include all these properties, but I've decided all I really need is the record name and the PTR or A record—essentially, anything that has *record* in the name. After some initial testing I realize I need to select lines that have the word *Record* followed by a space:

```
PS C:\> $data=ipconfig /displaydns | select-string "Record "
```

This should give me three lines of data for each record:

```
PS C:\> $data[0..2]

    Record Name . . . . . : JDHIT-DC01.jdhitsolutions.local
    Record Type . . . . . : 1
    A (Host) Record . . . : 172.16.10.1
```

The challenge is to go through `$data` and group by threes. A `For` loop will work as long as I increase my counter by three every time instead of the usual one. Assuming I don't get any odd entries, this command should verify that the every third record is a record name:

```
PS C:\> for ($i=0;$i -lt $data.count;$i+=3) {$data[$i]}

    Record Name . . . . . : JDHIT-DC01.jdhitsolutions.local
    Record Name . . . . . : ntp0.cornell.edu
    Record Name . . . . . : JDH-NVNAS.jdhitsolutions.local
    Record Name . . . . . : COREDC01.jdhlab.local
    Record Name . . . . . : manning.com
    Record Name . . . . . : manning.com
    Record Name . . . . . : manning.com
    Record Name . . . . . : yns2.yahoo.com
    Record Name . . . . . : yns1.yahoo.com
    Record Name . . . . . : incsrc.manningpublications.com
    Record Name . . . . . : powershell.com
```

Good. Because I know what the order will be I can build an ordered hash table (which is a new PowerShell v3 feature) for each group of record data and then use those hash tables as properties for `New-Object`. In v3 I could also use `[pscustomobject]` instead of `New-Object`:

```
for ($i=0;$i -lt $data.count;$i+=3) {

    $hash= [ordered]@{
      Name=$data[$i].toString().Split(":")[1].Trim()
      Type=($data[$i+1].toString().Split(":")[1].Trim()) -as [int]
      Value=$data[$i+2].toString().Split(":")[1].Trim()
    }

    New-Object -TypeName PSobject -Property $hash

}
```

```
Administrator: Windows PowerShell
    Record Name . . . . . : yns1.yahoo.com
    Record Type . . . . . : 1
    A (Host) Record . . . : 98.136.43.32
    Record Name . . . . . : incsrc.manningpublications.com
    Record Type . . . . . : 1
    A (Host) Record . . . : 66.98.170.92
    Record Name . . . . . : powershell.com
    Record Type . . . . . : 1
    A (Host) Record . . . : 65.38.114.170

PS C:\> for ($i=0;$i -lt $data.count;$i+=3) {
>>
>>     $hash= [ordered]@{
>>       Name=$data[$i].toString().Split(":")[1].Trim()
>>       Type=($data[$i+1].toString().Split(":")[1].Trim()) -as [int]
>>       Value=$data[$i+2].toString().Split(":")[1].Trim()
>>     }
>>
>>     New-Object -TypeName PSobject -Property $hash
>>
>> }
>>

Name                                                        Type Value
----                                                        ---- -----
JDHIT-DC01.jdhitsolutions.local                                1 172.16.10.1
ntp0.cornell.edu                                               5 dns3.cit.cornell.edu
JDH-NVNAS.jdhitsolutions.local                                 1 172.16.10.100
COREDC01.jdhlab.local                                          1 172.16.10.190
manning.com                                                    1 68.180.151.75
manning.com                                                    2 yns2.yahoo.com
manning.com                                                    2 yns1.yahoo.com
yns2.yahoo.com                                                 1 98.139.247.192
yns1.yahoo.com                                                 1 98.136.43.32
incsrc.manningpublications.com                                 1 66.98.170.92
powershell.com                                                 1 65.38.114.170

PS C:\> _
```

Figure 2 Converting a group of lines into PowerShell objects

Each item is a `MatchInfo` object that I need to convert to a string. Each string is then split into an array on the colon. The property value will be the second item in the array, so I trim it up. I know I want the type to be an `[int]` so I cast it accordingly. Figure 2 depicts the results.

Now that I have rough PowerShell code that works, I can go ahead and build an advanced function to turn this into a PowerShell tool, as shown in the next listing. My function requires PowerShell v3 because I'm using an ordered hash table. If you remove the `[ordered]` attribute it should work in PowerShell v2.

Listing 2 Get-IPConfigDNS

```
#requires -version 3.0

Function Get-IPConfigDNS {

[cmdletbinding()]
Param()

Write-Verbose "Getting DNS cache information"
$data=ipconfig /displaydns | select-string "Record "

Write-Verbose ("Retrieved {0} entries" -f $data.count)
Write-Verbose ("There should be {0} dns records" -f ($data.count/3))

for ($i=0;$i -lt $data.count;$i+=3) {
    Write-Verbose $data[$i]
```

```
    $hash=[ordered]@{
      Name=$data[$i].toString().Split(":")[1].Trim()
      Type=($data[$i+1].toString().Split(":")[1].Trim()) -as [int]
      Value=$data[$i+2].toString().Split(":")[1].Trim()
    }

    New-Object -TypeName PSobject -Property $hash
}
Write-Verbose "Finished parsing DNS cache data"
}
```

I didn't worry about error handling because the `ipconfig` command should always return data. The end result is that I have a tool I can reuse in a PowerShell expression. Figure 3 shows my function in action. There isn't a PowerShell command to handle the local DNS cache, so I wrote my own!

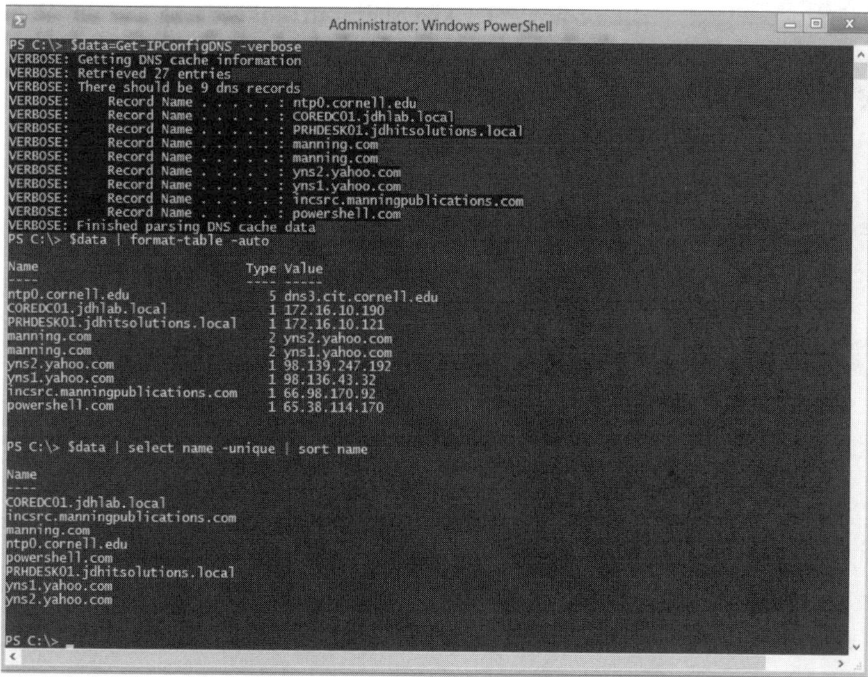

Figure 3 A CL- to-PowerShell tool in action

Summary

As I hope you've seen, it isn't necessarily difficult to transform a CLI tool into a PowerShell-based tool. The easiest approach is to use a CLI tool that writes results in a PowerShell-friendly format like CSV. Barring that, look for a tool that writes a predictable and structured format so that you can parse the results into objects. In any event, always look at help for the command you want to convert.

Once you've mastered the techniques I've demonstrated here you might want to take your PowerShell tools further by incorporating custom formatting or type extensions. Or you could incorporate similar command-line tools into a module. But most important, I hope you'll share your work with the PowerShell community.

About the author

Jeffery Hicks is a Microsoft MVP in Windows PowerShell, a Microsoft Certified Trainer, and an IT veteran with over 20 years of experience, much of it spent as an IT consultant specializing in Microsoft server technologies. He works today as an independent author, trainer, and consultant. Jeff writes the popular Prof. PowerShell column for MPCMag.com and is a regular contributor to the Petri IT Knowledgebase and 4SysOps.

PART 3

PowerShell for developers

Edited by Oisín Grehan

PowerShell is a scripting language. Scripting is for IT pros. Are these two statements true? Yes, of course, they are—I don't think anyone would disagree with that. But, I believe that these two truisms are often misinterpreted. This stems from the artificial line drawn between the two major disciplines. That is to say, people assume there is a tangible demarcation between what IT pros and developers do. But, scripting is programming, and programming is scripting. UNIX administrators have always known this. Lord knows, working with SED, AWK, and their ilk is often more like programming than…uh…programming.

If you think PowerShell is not for coders then maybe it's time you sat back and thought about that. When's the last time you needed to do a quick calculation? Debug a regular expression? Figure out the correct incantation to format that pesky date string the way the dumb specification says? Opened up your favorite decompiler to try to figure out how that poorly documented third-party library works? Had to toggle a flag in the registry? Needed to generate or modify a fiddly XML document? Had to decode something quickly in Base64 or unravel some triple URL-encoded parameter that is screwing up your web application? Had to test a remote web service? Or address any one of many other one-off or repeating tedious tasks? In all my years coding, I've had to do all those things any number of times.

If you've been in one of the positions above, you've probably fired up Visual Studio and coughed up yet another throwaway WinForms or Console project to figure out how to do what your frazzled brain is refusing to process, despite knowing how to do it. We've all been there. I think the first inkling that there had to be a better way was when I discovered the fun that is the Immediate Window in Visual Studio. It's typically available during a debugging session, which devalues it a little, but the ability to have your .NET code immediately evaluated in an interactive console seemed a blindingly obvious and useful thing to have as a developer. Well, you have it already: it's called PowerShell—and it is amazeballs!

PowerShell makes all things possible in IT, and the chapters in Part 3 illustrate ways to use PowerShell that you may have never thought about before.

Source control for PowerShell-related projects should be on everybody's radar. Starting in this section, Trevor Sullivan shows how to set up a free and open source product with PowerShell in chapter 18.

PowerShell has embraced XML from the very beginning. In chapter 20 Josh Gavant demonstrates how easy it is to work with XML from a PowerShell prompt. PowerShell 3.0 also uses XML, in the form of CDXML, to create new CIM-based tools. PowerShell MVP Richard Siddaway walks you through this arcane structure and explains how easy it is to build your own CIM-based commands in chapter 19.

If you aren't building CIM-based commands, then you are likely creating advanced PowerShell functions. PowerShell MVP and developer Karl Prosser shows in chapter 21 how to integrate remoting into your scripting projects.

Finally, PowerShell MVP and software engineer Jim Christopher offers chapter 22 on managing software builds with PowerShell and psake—a use for PowerShell that goes beyond what anyone may have originally thought.

About the editor

Oisín Grehan cut his teeth programming with an Amstrad CPC 464 way back in 1984. He was born in Dublin, Ireland, and lives in Montreal, Canada, with his wife Carly, his daughter Mena, and his two cats: Betsy (thin) and Peanut (fat). He currently works as a software developer and technical architect and builds all sorts of stuff for all sorts of people. Oisín has been a PowerShell MVP since 2008.

18 Using Source Control Software with PowerShell

Trevor Sullivan

Windows PowerShell is a phenomenal tool for automation, but with great power comes great responsibility. Over time you'll find that your script repository will grow larger and larger, and you'll frequently need to modify scripts to provide additional functionality, fix bugs, or make your code more readable. As your repository grows and morphs it's important to maintain a history of changes to your script files. The benefits of keeping track of history are many, most importantly including the ability to revert to an old version of a script if you make a breaking modification.

In this chapter I'll describe the benefits of using source control and how to perform basic source control functions. It's my hope that you'll begin to appreciate the benefits that using source control software can provide to you, and will seek a deeper understanding of its capabilities.

Requirements

For this chapter of PowerShell Deep Dive you'll need several pieces of software:

- Microsoft Windows 7/8 system running Windows Management Framework 3.0
- Microsoft .NET Framework 4.0 (required for PowerShell v3)
- TortoiseHg, available from http://tortoisehg.bitbucket.org
- Mercurial (included with TortoiseHg)

As of this writing the Release to Manufacturing (RTM) version of Windows PowerShell 3.0 is available for Windows 7. It's extremely stable, and offers an array (no pun intended) of new functionality over version 2.0. PowerShell version 2.0 is the version built into Windows 7 out of the box. To determine which version of PowerShell you are running, simply type the following command at the console:

```
$PSVersionTable.PSVersion
```

You can download the Windows Management Framework Core 3.0 release at http://goo.gl/ixOkQ.

When to use source control

As discussed in the introduction, source control should be used in any circumstance where having the ability to roll back or review and audit changes is crucial. In production environments the smallest change can have a massive impact, and having the ability to rapidly revert to known-working code is vital.

Source control systems are also great for keeping track of small, individual projects. Rather than having a single, large code repository full of random script code it's advisable to subdivide your code into logical groupings. PowerShell modules are good candidates for self-contained Mercurial repositories, as they generally are designed to represent a cohesive block of functionality.

Another great use of source control is to integrate with a continuous integration system, which can build different versions of your software project, no matter where you're at in the development cycle. Having this integration means that you can rapidly deploy any software version into a production environment and avoid interrupting your development cycle to manually roll back code to a known working version.

Introduction to Mercurial

There are many version control software (VCS) packages available; however in this chapter we'll focus on Mercurial. Mercurial is a very popular VCS package. Due to its decentralized nature it's highly portable, meaning that a code repository can be synchronized with any other team member's repository. With this in mind, it isn't necessary to have a centralized server, although in a team environment having a central server would still be desirable.

Like most other VCS packages, Mercurial has a basic concept called a repository. A repository keeps track of changes to files that have been added to it. Thanks to the TortoiseHg graphical user interface (GUI) tools you can easily create a new repository. In Mercurial parlance this is known as repository initialization (figure 1).

Once you've created a repository you'll want to add files to that repository, which instructs Mercurial to keep track of change to those files. When files are added, changed, or removed, those changes are detected during the next commit operation, and can be reviewed for errors prior to finalizing the commit. When you commit changes to a source code repository you have the opportunity to add a commit message which helps you and other developers to identify what changes have occurred since the last commit operation.

As you develop your code you'll continue the process of adding or removing files from change tracking, and when you make significant changes you'll regularly commit them back to the repository. Once you've reached a certain point you may be ready to share your code with others. In this case you can push or pull your code to or from a remote repository. Thanks to Mercurial's decentralized nature you aren't

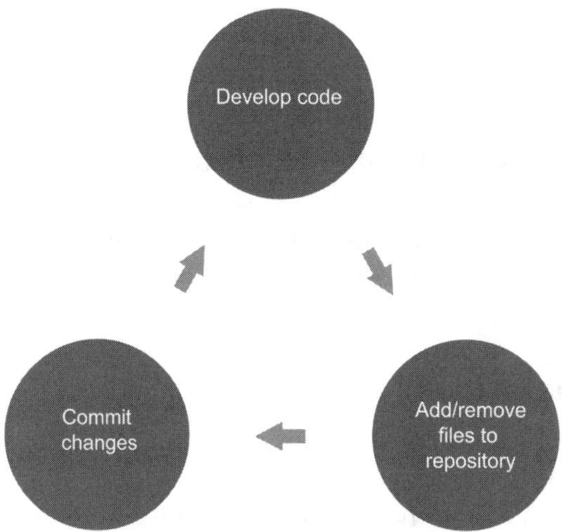

Figure 1 The high-level process of using Mercurial once a repository has been initialized

forced to synchronize with any central repository unless all of the developers on a project agree to it at the beginning of the project. This means you can push/pull code changes with any replica of your repository. If you're working on an open source project you might synchronize your local repository with a hosted service, such as Microsoft's CodePlex open source website Bitbucket.org, or any other source code hosting provider who supports Mercurial repositories.

Command line versus GUI

The TortoiseHg package includes both GUI tools and the Mercurial command line executable, hg.exe. For most operations either tool can be used, and it's up to you to determine which one you're most comfortable with. It has been my experience that using the GUI tools can make it more convenient to view changes, insert commit messages, and add and remove files, but there are many people who prefer to stay true to the command line tools.

One benefit of using the TortoiseHg GUI instead of the command line utility is that it will save your settings and credentials for a remote repository. This helps to avoid the necessity of typing out the remote repository URL and your credentials each time you want to synchronize (push / pull) your local repository with the remote one.

Using the command line over the GUI has its benefits as well. For example, you can use the command line to automate common tasks in Mercurial and save yourself precious typing time. We'll explore more about how to use Mercurial from PowerShell later in this chapter. Most of the tasks you perform using the command line interface consist of a structure similar to

```
hg.exe <Action> <ParametersForAction>
```

If you're just getting started with Mercurial for the first time you can always type either of these commands to help you learn the command line utility:

```
hg.exe help
```

or

```
hg.exe help <action>
```

The actions you can perform are very user-friendly and easy to remember. Additionally, many of the actions have aliases, making them even easier to type when you're deep in the middle of a coding session.

I think you'll find both the command line and GUI interfaces to be beneficial tools as you get started with Mercurial. In the next section we'll discuss some common functions you'll use when working with Mercurial.

Common source control operations

During your development workflow you'll interact with a number of core functions in any version control software. In this section we'll go over some of the most common source control operations that you should become familiar with in Mercurial. You'll use these functions on a daily basis as you develop your code. Using these operations is critical to ensuring that you get the most usefulness out of your source control repository. If you neglect to use these you'll still have your code, but you won't gain the benefits of having revision history and rollback capabilities.

Initializing a repository

As discussed in the previous section, the first step to using Mercurial is to initialize a code repository. Let's assume that we'll be creating a PowerShell module at the path c:\code\Modules\ConfigMgr2012. You can perform the repository initialization using the following command line tool:

```
Set-Location -Path c:\code\Modules\ConfigMgr2012
hg.exe init
```

Figure 2 demonstrates the TortoiseHg UI control used to initialize a repository.

Once the code repository has been created you'll notice that an .hg folder is created in the root, along with an .hgignore file. These files are used by Mercurial to keep track of the repository and shouldn't be modified by the end user under normal circumstances.

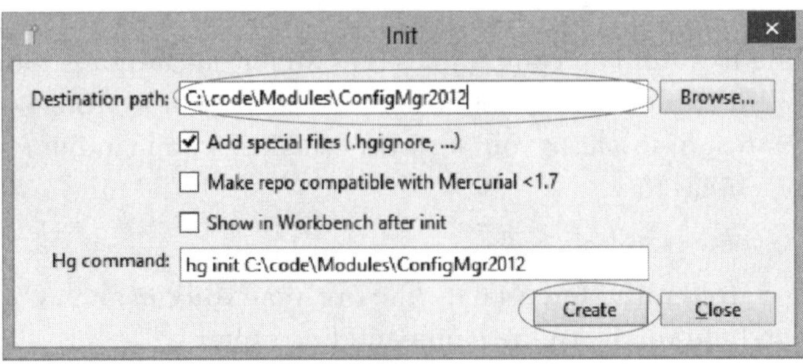

Figure 2 The TortoiseHg repository initialization screen

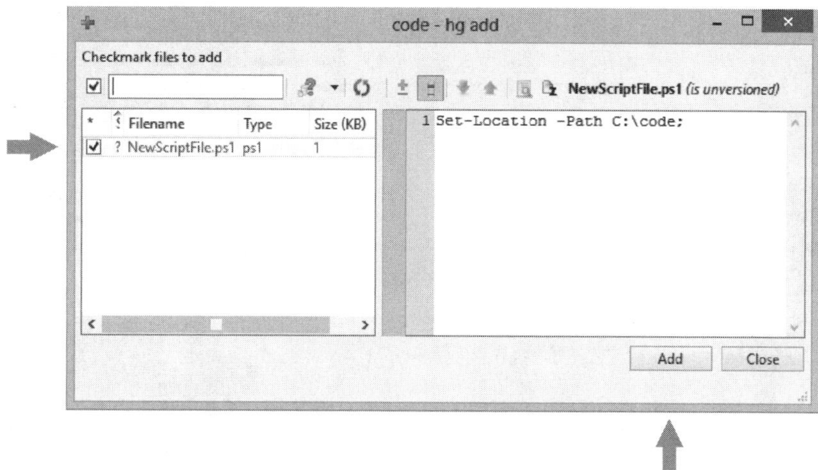

Figure 3 The TortoiseHg add files screen

Adding files

Once you've initialized a code repository you'll want to add some files to it. You can use the command line or GUI for this purpose. Using hg.exe run the command below:

```
Set-Location -Path c:\code\Modules\ConfigMgr2012;
New-Item -ItemType File -Name NewScriptFile.ps1;
hg.exe add NewScriptFile.ps1;
```

Figure 3 shows what the TortoiseHg GUI tool looks when adding files to a repository. You can simply uncheck the files that you don't want to add to the source control repository, and leave checked the ones that you want added.

NOTE Keep in mind that adding files doesn't create any changes to the repository. In order to actually make the newly added files become part of the repository you must commit them, which will be demonstrated in the next section.

Committing a new changeset

Once you have added files to your repository you'll want to commit changes to the repository. Performing this action creates what is known as a Mercurial *changeset*. A changeset represents a series of changes that have been performed since the last changeset was committed.

In order to commit a new changeset using the command line simply run the following command:

```
Set-Location -Path c:\code\Modules\ConfigMgr2012;
hg.exe commit -m "Commit message" -u "Trevor Sullivan (pcgeek86@gmail.com)"
```

The Commit dialog box in TortoiseHg looks similar to figure 4.

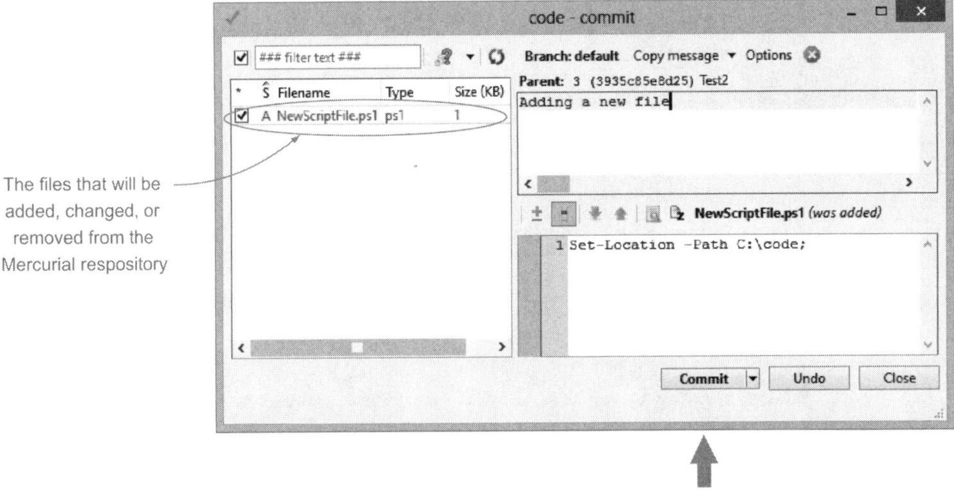

Figure 4 The TortoiseHg commit dialog box

Removing files

The remove action is similar to the add action. The remove action removes a file from change tracking in the Mercurial repository that you're currently operating on (the current working directory). To remove files from change tracking use this command:

```
Set-Location -Path c:\code\Modules\ConfigMgr2012
hg.exe remove NewScriptFile.ps1
```

Figure 5 shows the TortoiseHg remove dialog box. The left-hand pane shows the files that will be removed, while the right-hand pane shows a preview of the currently selected file.

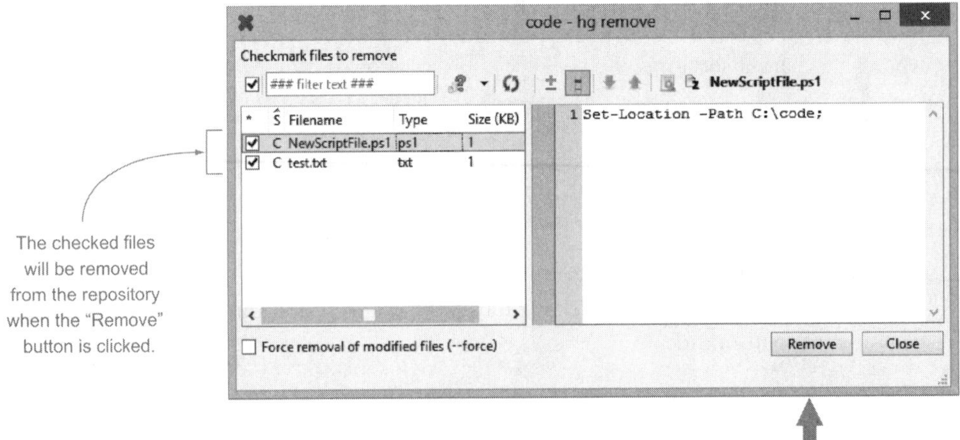

Figure 5 The TortoiseHg remove file dialog box

Using Mercurial from PowerShell

As an end user of Mercurial you can automate many of its functions from PowerShell. This is easy to do since the product was built around the command line. Unfortunately there's no .NET library for Mercurial. You can, however, easily call the command line utility, which we've already discussed.Automating Mercurial tasks can help to streamline your workflow as a software developer, and can also be incorporated into build scripts that run on a continuous integration service such as Cruise Control .NET or JetBrains TeamCity.

Script to initialize a repository

The following listing shows how to wrap a Mercurial repository initialization command in a PowerShell function.

Listing 1 The `New-MercurialRepository` PowerShell Function

```
function New-MercurialRepository {
    [CmdletBinding()]
    param (
        [Parameter(Mandatory = $true)] [string] $Path
    )

    if (Test-Path -Path $Path -PathType Container) {
     Start-Process -FilePath hg.exe -ArgumentList ('init "{0}"' -f $Path)
    }
}

New-MercurialRepository -Path c:\code\Modules\ConfigMgr2012
```

Script to commit a changeset

Listing 2 demonstrates how to perform a commit operation using a PowerShell script cmdlet. There are parameters to pass in a commit message, the path to the Mercurial repository, and an optional username. By default the function uses the username with which you're logged into a Windows session.

Listing 2 The `Commit-MercurialChangeset` PowerShell Function

```
function Commit-MercurialChangeset {
    [CmdletBinding()]
    param (
      [Parameter(Mandatory = $true,
HelpMessage = 'Please enter a commit message.')]
      [string] $Message
      , [Parameter(Mandatory = $true,
HelpMessage = 'Please enter the path to the repository.')]
          [string] $Path
        , [Parameter(Mandatory = $false)]
[string] $Username = $env:USERNAME
    )

    $Path = '{0}\.hg' -f $Path
```

```
    if (Test-Path -Path $Path -PathType Container) {
        $Arguments = 'commit -u "{1}" -m "{0}"' -f $Message, $Username;
        Write-Host -Object $Arguments
        $Process = Start-Process -FilePath hg.exe -ArgumentList $Arguments
          ➥ -NoNewWindow -PassThru -Wait -WorkingDirectory $Path
        $Process.ExitCode
    }
    else {
        throw ('Path ({0}) does not exist!' -f $Path)
    }
}
Commit-MercurialChangeset -Message 'Test commit message.' -Path
  ➥ c:\code\Modules\ConfigMgr2012 -Username 'Trevor Sullivan'
```

NOTE The Commit verb is not an officially recognized PowerShell verb; however you can use any verb you like to name your function. If this function is imported as part of a PowerShell module you'll receive this warning: *WARNING: Some imported command names include unapproved verbs which might make them less discoverable.*

Working with Mercurial in teams

In team environments Mercurial provides the ability for team members to commit to a single, centralized repository. By working off of a centralized repository multiple people can make changes to the same code repository and see what each other are working on. Although it's quite rudimentary Mercurial includes a built-in command line webserver, which can be launched using this command:

```
Set-Location -Path c:\code\Modules\ConfigMgr2012
hg serve
```

NOTE In order to run the "hg serve" command the current directory must be set to a folder containing a Mercurial repository. If you attempt to run the command without navigating to a folder containing a Mercurial repository you will receive this error message: abort: there is no Mercurial repository here (.hg not found)!

Once the webserver has been launched on a remote system you can use the push and pull commands in Mercurial to synchronize your local repository with the remote repository. When you push changes from your local repository to the remote repository any changesets that you've created will be sent up to the remote repository. If you pull changes from the remote repository to your local repository any changesets that other team members have pushed to the remote repository will be pulled down to your local repository. When pulling or pushing you can also specify a changeset ID that you'd like to be pushed or pulled, rather than pushing or pulling *all* changes.

If you need to work on a project that exists on a remote server but you don't have a local copy of the repository you'll need to use the clone command before you can push or pull changesets. In this scenario the clone command replaces the init command that was discussed earlier in this chapter.

Alternative Mercurial web services

To reiterate, the built-in Mercurial webserver is quite simplistic in its nature and doesn't provide a very wide set of features such as user authentication, authorization, bug tracker integration, or a web interface to manage code repositories. If you require these features there are software packages available that can accommodate this need.

For example, there's a free solution – albeit in its alpha stages – called HgLab available at http://hglabhq.com. This package is written in C# using the Microsoft .NET Framework; it's built on top of the HgSharp .NET library. According to its website it offers Active Directory integration for user authentication and authorization, repository management, and a source code browser.

Kiln, developed by Fog Creek Software, is another centralized Mercurial solution that is proprietary. A unique feature of this package is that it integrates with Fog Creek's own FogBugz bug tracking software and allows Mercurial changesets to be tied back to software support tickets.

I'll leave further research into these tools up to you, dear reader. Be aware that there are solutions out there beyond the basic, built-in Mercurial webserver.

Summary

In this chapter we discussed when to use a version control system (VCS) with PowerShell projects, as well as some basics of how to get started with Mercurial as a VCS. We also examined how to call Mercurial commands from PowerShell using wrapper functions and looked at the two main methods of interfacing with Mercurial repositories from the GUI and command line. I trust that this chapter has given you some new ideas and can help take your coding workflow to the next level.

About the Author

Trevor Sullivan is a pursuer of all types of knowledge and is particularly passionate about information technology and technical communities. He has been working primarily with Microsoft solutions since 2004 and is entirely self-taught. Trevor has received public recognition from Microsoft for his contributions to the Windows PowerShell community, and has also written several guest posts for the Microsoft *Hey, Scripting Guy!* blog and *PowerShell Magazine*. One of his more notable achievements is the release of the PowerEvents module for PowerShell, which is available on Microsoft's CodePlex open source website. Trevor also enjoys giving presentations and has presented on the topic of PowerShell & WMI, in addition to two guest appearances on the weekly PowerScripting podcast.

19 Inline .NET code

Richard Siddaway

PowerShell is .NET-based. This enables you to use the .NET framework in your PowerShell scripts by loading the relevant assemblies into PowerShell (if they aren't part of the default assembly set) and then using them via `New-Object`. You can create intricate GUI applications as a front end to your scripts, for instance. Whether you should or not is a discussion for another time.

You can also use .NET code directly in your scripts, which is the topic of this chapter. You'll see two ways of using .NET directly in your scripts. The first way involves creating a .NET class that you can then use for output or future processing. The second way enables you to create a class with methods you can use in your script to perform an action. You could access the method without creating a class, but ultimately, creating the class gives you more flexibility. Let's start by looking at how to create a class for output.

.NET class for output

The PowerShell mantra is *output objects*. Executing a simple piece of PowerShell such as the following produces output onscreen:

```
PS> Get-CimInstance -ClassName Win32_OperatingSystem |
  ➥ select CSName, Caption, OSArchitecture, LastBootUpTime, CountryCode

CSName         : RSLAPTOP01
Caption        : Microsoft Windows 8 Enterprise
OSArchitecture : 32-bit
LastBootUpTime : 17/08/2012 10:02:11
CountryCode    : 44
```

Output types

If you look at the output type by piping this code into `Get-Member` you'll see it's a `Selected.Microsoft.Management.Infrastructure.CimInstance` object. It's a modified version of the object produced by the `Get-CimInstance` cmdlet but still an object that can be put onto the PowerShell pipeline for further processing.

Such output is common when investigating computer configuration. Another common requirement is to retrieve information about the computer hardware. Here's an example:

```
PS> Get-CimInstance -ClassName Win32_ComputerSystem |
➥ select DNSHostName, TotalPhysicalMemory, Manufacturer, Model, Domain

DNSHostName         : RSLAPTOP01
TotalPhysicalMemory : 2951135232
Manufacturer        : Hewlett-Packard
Model               : HP G60 Notebook PC
Domain              : WORKGROUP
```

Outputting single objects is straightforward. When working interactively, outputting multiple objects in a sequential manner is easy. What happens when you run these two sets of code in a script? The two WMI classes work together, but you can get a formatting error because the default formats for the two classes clash. Also, outputting two objects from a single script or advanced function makes further processing of the output problematic if not impossible.

Creating a .NET class for output

At this point you may be thinking that you can combine the two outputs into a single object. There are a number of ways of performing this task. Using `New-Object` to create a custom object is the most commonly used, but there's an alternative: create and compile a .NET class as part of your script. This class becomes part of the .NET framework loaded into PowerShell and can be accessed and used like any other class. It may seem that this is an additional complication you don't need—and in many cases, you would be correct. But using this technique offers some benefits:

- Class properties are strongly typed.
- The class has a unique name, which means it works easily with PowerShell's format and type files.

Strongly typed is a way of saying that the value you pass to a property must be of the correct data type or be automatically convertible to the correct data type. If you define a property as an integer and try to pass it a string value, PowerShell attempts to convert the string to an integer. If the conversion works, everything is fine and processing continues. If the conversion fails, PowerShell throws an error.

So how do you get this to work? An example is shown in the next listing. The source code is supplied at the start of the script. `Add-Type` compiles the code, after which it can be accessed like any other .NET class.

Listing 1 Creating a class for output

```
$source = @"
public class MySystemData                            ❶ Class definition
{
  public string ComputerName {get; set;}
  public string DNSHostName  {get; set;}
```

```
  public string OSName       {get; set;}
  public string OSArchitecture {get; set;}
  public string Manufacturer   {get; set;}
  public string Model          {get; set;}
  public int    CountryCode  {get; set;}
  public double Ram    {get; set;}
  public System.DateTime   BootUpTime {get; set;}
}
"@
Add-Type -TypeDefinition $source -Language CSharpVersion3

function get-computersystem {
[CmdletBinding()]
param (
 [Parameter(ValueFromPipeline=$True,
              ValueFromPipelineByPropertyName=$True)]
 [ValidateScript({Test-Connection -Computername $_ -Count 1 -Quiet})]
 [string]$computername = $env:COMPUTERNAME
)
$os = Get-CimInstance -ClassName Win32_OperatingSystem `
-ComputerName $computername |
select CSName, Caption, OSArchitecture, LastBootUpTime, CountryCode

$cs = Get-CimInstance -ClassName Win32_ComputerSystem `
-ComputerName $computername|
select DNSHostName, TotalPhysicalMemory, Manufacturer, Model, Domain

$props = @{
  ComputerName = $os.CSName
  DNSHostName = $cs.DNSHostName
  OSName = $os.Caption
  OSArchitecture = $os.OSArchitecture
  Manufacturer = $cs.Manufacturer
  Model =  $cs.Model
  CountryCode = $os.CountryCode
  Ram = [math]::round($($cs.TotalPhysicalMemory / 1GB), 2)
  BootUpTime = $os.LastBootUpTime
}

New-Object -TypeName MySystemData -Property $props
}
```

❶ Class definition
❷ Compile class
❸ Function definition
❹ Get operating system
❺ Get computer system
❻ Set property values
❼ Create object

The .NET code is defined ❶ using a here string. The class definition is supplied first. It looks like this:

```
public class MySystemData
{
}
```

The `class` keyword says you're creating a class. It's given a name: `MySystemData`. The `public` keyword indicates that the class is visible to PowerShell. Within the class definition are a number of property definitions of this form:

```
public string ComputerName {get; set;}
```

`Public` is again used to make the property visible. The data type is defined as a `string`. The property is named `ComputerName`. The final part of the definition makes the property readable (`get`) and writable (`set`). The common data types you'll need are shown in the listing; other types can be found in the .NET documentation.

`Add-Type` ❷ is used to compile the code. The language is expected to be C# version 3, but you can use a different version of C#, Visual Basic, J#, F#, or another language if you have the appropriate compiler installed on your system.

NOTE You can't unload a type or change it once you've successfully compiled the code. You have to change the type (class) name or start a new instance of PowerShell.

The code now reverts to the PowerShell you know and love. A function is defined ❸ with one parameter: a computer name that can be supplied by parameter or through the pipeline. `Test-Connection` is used as part of the validation process to ensure that the computer is reachable.

Calls to `Get-CimInstance` retrieve the operating system data ❹ and the computer hardware information ❺. You could substitute `Get-WmiObject` for `Get-CimInstance`, although I recommend moving to the CIM cmdlets for new work.

A hash table is used to create the property set ❻. Together with `New-Object` ❼ it creates an object using the class name used in the source code.

The function can be loaded as part of a module or script and is used exactly the same way as any other advanced function. Running it on my test machine produces these results:

```
PS> get-computersystem

ComputerName   : RSLAPTOP01
DNSHostName    : RSLAPTOP01
OSName         : Microsoft Windows 8 Enterprise
OSArchitecture : 32-bit
Manufacturer   : Hewlett-Packard
Model          : HP G60 Notebook PC
CountryCode    : 44
Ram            : 2.75
BootUpTime     : 02/09/2012 19:27:41
```

One objection that many people have raised to using `New-Object` to create a custom object is that the order of the properties isn't maintained. This is because of the way hash tables work. Compare the order of creation in the code and what is produced when you display the hash table:

```
PS> $props

Name                           Value
----                           -----
OSName                         Microsoft Windows 8 Enterprise
Ram                            2.75
Manufacturer                   Hewlett-Packard
ComputerName                   RSLAPTOP01
CountryCode                    44
BootUpTime                     02/09/2012 19:27:41
```

```
OSArchitecture                    32-bit
DNSHostName                       RSLAPTOP01
Model                             HP G60 Notebook PC
```

Creating an object this way using .NET preserves the order of properties; compare the output with the source code.

The other advantage of creating objects like this is that you define the type:

```
PS> (get-computersystem ).getType()

IsPublic IsSerial Name                   BaseType
-------- -------- ----                   --------
True     False    MySystemData           System.Object
```

You can then create new type and format definitions if required.

That concludes our look at using inline .NET code to create an object for output. The second major way to use .NET code is to create a class with methods you can call.

.NET class with methods

Adding methods to your .NET code is a bit more complicated than adding properties. For example, the code in the next listing provides a way to use the .NET `MessageBox` class in your scripts.

Listing 2 Creating a class with methods

```
$source = @'                                          <-- ❶ Source code definition
using System.Drawing;
using System.Windows.Forms;

public class Messages
{
  public static System.Windows.Forms.DialogResult OK(      <-- ❷ Method definition
    ➥ string message, string caption)
  {
    return MessageBox.Show(message, caption,
      ➥ System.Windows.Forms.MessageBoxButtons.OK);
  }
  public static System.Windows.Forms.DialogResult YesNo(
    ➥ string message, string caption)
  {
    return MessageBox.Show(message, caption,
      ➥ System.Windows.Forms.MessageBoxButtons.YesNo);
  }
}
'@

Add-Type -TypeDefinition $source -Language CSharpVersion3     <-- ❸ Compile code
  ➥ -ReferencedAssemblies System.Drawing, System.Windows.Forms

[Messages]::OK('Hello, this is to inform you that you have    <-- ❹ Use methods
  ➥ a decision to make', 'Information')
$yn = [Messages]::YesNo('Do you want to take this further',
  ➥ 'Decision Time')
switch ($yn){
```

```
  'Yes' {[Messages]::OK('Well done - this technique may
    ➥ help you in the future','Decision Made')}
  'No'  {[Messages]::OK('OK - the technique is here
    ➥ if you need it','Decision Made')}
}
```

The source code is defined in a here string ❶. The first two lines define other assemblies that you need to reference:

```
using System.Drawing;
using System.Windows.Forms;
```

The language is C# again, because that's what I'm most comfortable with. Other languages are available. The class name is supplied—in this case, `Messages`. Each method ❷ has its own definition block:

```
  public static System.Windows.Forms.DialogResult OK(
    ➥ string message, string caption)
  {
    return MessageBox.Show(message, caption,
      ➥ System.Windows.Forms.MessageBoxButtons.OK);
  }
```

The `public` keyword means you can find and use the method. The methods are `static`, meaning you don't need to create an object to use them. The return object type is defined; in this case, it's a `System.Windows.Forms.DialogResult` object. The method name is `OK`. Two parameters are defined for the method named `message` and `caption`. Each parameter is defined to accept a string.

The working part of the method is as follows:

```
return MessageBox.Show(message, caption,
   ➥ System.Windows.Forms.MessageBoxButtons.OK);
```

This line defines the `return` information. A call to the `MessageBox` class invokes the `Show()` method. The message and caption parameters provide the `message` to be displayed and the Window `caption`, respectively. A final parameter defines the style of buttons to be used, in this case a simple OK button. A second method supplies the option of having two buttons: one labeled Yes and one labeled No.

`Add-Type` is used to compile the code ❸. Notice that the assemblies you want to reference are repeated in the call to `Add-Type`. If you don't do this you'll get a confusing error with a message regarding `Drawing` not being found.

The class is now ready to use ❹:

```
[Messages]::OK('Hello, this is to inform you that you have
   ➥ a decison to make', 'Information')
```

The message is `'Hello, this is to inform you that you have a decision to make'`. The second parameter, `'Decision Time'`, provides the caption for the pop-up window. Click the OK button, and the window disappears. The second method asks for a yes/no choice; the result is returned in the `$yn` variable. A `Switch` statement processes the result.

You might ask how to discover the values for the System.Windows.Forms.DialogResult enumeration. You can look them up on MSDN or use the following function:

```
function Get-Enum {
param (
[string]$class
)
[enum]::GetNames("$class") |
foreach {

$exp = "([$class]::$($_)).value__"

 New-Object -TypeName PSObject -Property @{
   Name = $_
   Number = Invoke-Expression -Command $exp
 }
}
}
```

The function accepts a .NET class as a parameter and uses the GetNames() method of the System.Enum class to provide the list of named values. Each name has a numeric value associated with it, which can be discovered by using the value__ property. Unfortunately you can't put the class into a type definition via a variable, so I created a string with the required code. I used string substitution to populate it and then called Invoke-Expression to execute the code.

Summary

This chapter has shown you how to create .NET objects that you can use to combine data from multiple objects. It has also shown how to create your own .NET class that you can call from PowerShell.

The techniques presented in this chapter are advanced and won't be required by every PowerShell user. When you need to extend PowerShell just that little bit further, they may supply you with the answer.

About the author

Richard Siddaway has worked with Microsoft technologies for 25 years and has spent time in most IT roles. He currently works for Kelway (UK) Ltd as an automation consultant. He has a long-standing interest in automation techniques, and PowerShell has been his primary automation tool since the early beta versions. Richard founded the UK PowerShell User Group in 2007 and is a PowerShell MVP. He frequently speaks at PowerShell user groups in the UK, Europe, the US, and elsewhere around the world, and judges the Microsoft Scripting Games. In addition to writing his blog (http://msmvps.com/blogs/RichardSiddaway/), Richard has authored two PowerShell books:

PowerShell in Practice (Manning 2010) and *PowerShell and WMI* (Manning 2012), and coauthored *PowerShell in Depth* (Manning 2013) with Don Jones and Jeffery Hicks. Currently he is writing an introductory book for Active Directory administrators that features PowerShell.

With thanks to Tobias Weltner for the discussion on using the `-ReferencedAssemblies` *parameter.*

20 PowerShell and XML: better together

Josh Gavant

In the words of PowerShell creator Jeffrey Snover in his 2002 "Monad Manifesto" (www.jsnover.com/Docs/MonadManifesto.pdf), "[t]he traditional model for administrative automation ... requires clumsy, lossy, imprecise text manipulation utilities." Command-line input and answer files are unstructured text; output is a hodgepodge of details that the command's authors deem helpful. To use the text output from one command as input for another, that text has to be parsed, and the script author has to pray that the chosen parsing works consistently. In fact, Snover coined the term *prayer-based parsing*, and defines it as follows:

DEFINITION *Prayer-based parsing* is when you parse the text and pray that you got it right. Examples include, cutting off the first three lines and praying that it wasn't four, cutting out columns 30–40 and praying that those spaces aren't tabs, or casting as an integer and praying that it's 32 bits. ("Monad Manifesto," p. 4, note 7)

Figure 1 provides a simple example of prayer-based parsing gone wrong. In the first series, the word "quick" is replaced with "slow" and all is well. In the second series, because the input file now uses the four-letter "fast" instead of the five-letter "quick," the parser unintentionally removes a space between words. A small difference, but it could easily crash a script or a program.

Spoken languages and text are imprecise. We may each use different adjectives to indicate the same characteristic, we may choose to separate words with spaces, line breaks, or tabs, and we may include an attribute when describing something that someone else would not. But the reality is that we humans ultimately need to describe things in spoken languages and text. Perhaps the ideal way to identify the Windows Update service would be a 16-byte GUID; it's guaranteed to be unique and have a 100-percent predictable structure. But a report that indicates

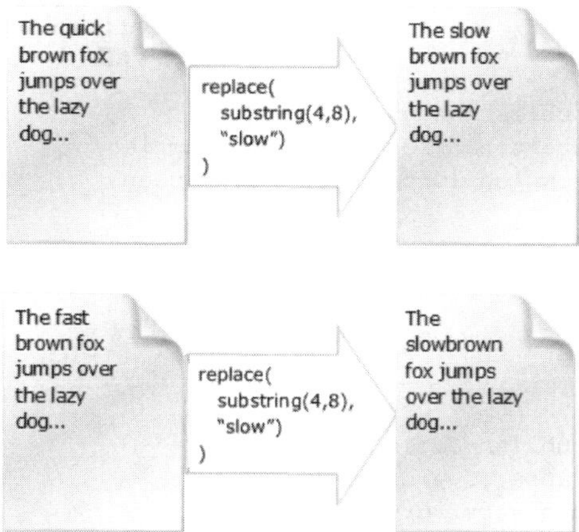

Figure 1 Prayer-based parsing of the input at the left produces the output at the right. The prayer is unanswered in the second series, leading to incorrect output.

"`service {17AE3EB7-F6B1-4C22-B55E-746767EC7346} is in state 1`" is useless; humans need to be told that "`WUAUSERV is Running.`"

Structure and definition make our solutions more efficient, more resilient, and less error-prone. But too much structure can make these solutions unwieldy and difficult to use. What allows us to attain PowerShell's goal of structure as we preserve the benefits and friendliness of human-readable text? Enter XML.

What is XML?

No doubt we've all worked with XML before, but let's go back and begin at the foundation to set a common understanding from which to build.

XML may be defined as data and markup stored in a text file in a structured format. But what purpose is this structured collection of data and metadata meant to serve, and what benefits does it provide over other data storage formats? In answering this question, I'll use the following listing as an example XML document (books.xml), which presents metadata about a small collection of books. (The example is available here: http://msdn.microsoft.com/en-us/library/windows/desktop/ms762271.aspx.)

Listing 1 Books.xml example

```
<?xml version="1.0"?>
<catalog>
   <book id="bk101">
      <author>Gambardella, Matthew</author>
      <title>XML Developer's Guide</title>
      <genre>Computer</genre>
      <price>44.95</price>
      <publish_date>2000-10-01</publish_date>
      <description>An in-depth look at creating applications
      with XML.</description>
   </book>
   <book id="bk102">
      <author>Ralls, Kim</author>
```

Structured data about book

Attribute specifying book's ID

```
        <title>Midnight Rain</title>               <-- Element containing
        <genre>Fantasy</genre>                         book's title
        <price>5.95</price>
        <publish_date>2000-12-16</publish_date>
        <description>A former architect battles corporate zombies,
        an evil sorceress, and her own childhood to become queen
        of the world.</description>
    </book>
    <book id="bk103">
        <author>Corets, Eva</author>
        <title>Maeve Ascendant</title>
        <genre>Fantasy</genre>
        <price>5.95</price>
        <publish_date>2000-11-17</publish_date>
        <description>After the collapse of a nanotechnology
        society in England, the young survivors lay the
        foundation for a new society.</description>
    </book>
</catalog>
```

XML provides a defined, structured, predictable way to organize textual information. The document in listing 1 is like the bookshelf shown in figure 2: each book is exactly the same size; each takes an exact space on the shelf; the title of each book is in an exact place on the cover; the author's name is at a specific, predictable location; and an ID number is at a specific position. A robot could be told to follow an exact sequence over and over to discover all details about each book on this bookshelf. In the same way, an automated parser could discover all details about all books in this XML document by repeatedly processing the text in the same way.

The sample XML document contains a relatively *readable* set of data about several books, including each book's ID, title, and author. An automated parser can identify and return specific pieces of information and their relationships to other information in the document. The structure in XML allows you to create collections of in-memory objects from XML and vice versa.

Whereas listing 1 looks like a simple text file, XML is more than structured text. The first sentence in the W3C XML specification states "XML describes a class of *data*

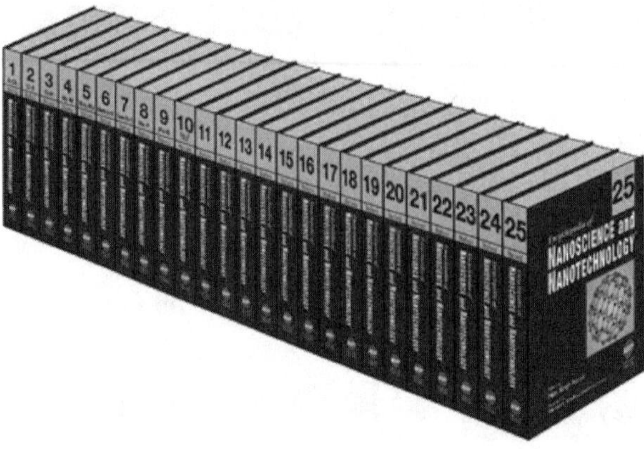

Figure 2 A well-organized bookshelf (from www.aspbs.com/)

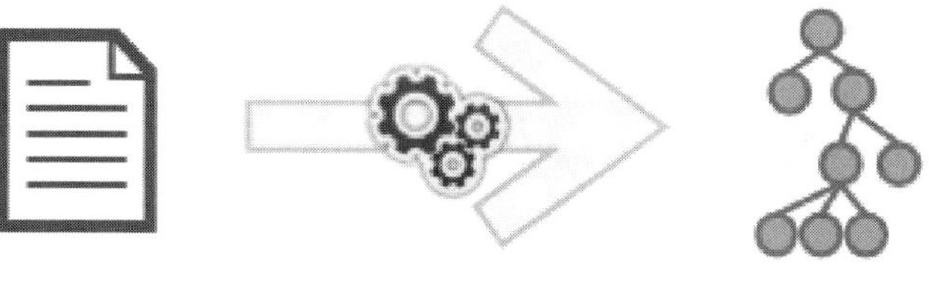

Figure 3 Processing an XML document into an XML Document Object Model (DOM) tree

objects called XML documents" (World Wide Web Consortium, www.w3.org/TR/xml/; emphasis added). XML documents are *stored* as readable text, but they're *defined* from the start as data *objects*. The perspective that these objects are stored as formatted text instead of `1`'s and `0`'s is incidental; XML is an object framework with its own members and semantics for access and storage.

When data is retrieved into memory it isn't typically stored as text, so before applications and scripts can work with an XML document a processor converts it into an appropriate in-memory model, as illustrated in figure 3. The in-memory version of an XML document is a hierarchical tree of items defined by the XML Document Object Model (DOM). Once the document has been converted into a DOM object applications and scripts can access its data and manipulate it.

In Microsoft .NET, instances of `System.Xml.XmlReader` and derived classes analyze and process XML documents, returning DOM-compatible representations of their nodes and contents. Instances of `System.Xml.XmlDocument` store these representations in memory and provide continuing read/write access to them. Utilities and APIs such as LINQ to XML, XPath navigation, and PowerShell's XML facilities are built on top of these core elements.

XML as text

All of this emphasis on complex XML processors and XML being more than text may be leaving you scratching your head. After all, on many occasions it's convenient to skip the formalities and treat XML documents as simple text. I'm sure that, like me, you sometimes do that by opening XML documents in Notepad and making quick edits. I'm not telling you not to.

But when you're writing reusable scripts for automation relying on ad hoc reading and editing is a practice that will lead to problems. Only conforming XML processors, such as those provided by .NET and PowerShell or other libraries, should be relied upon for the consistency and dependability needed for production-level, reusable scripts and code. The XML standard has many subtleties that simple text-oriented parsing will likely not be aware of, such as XML Schemas, entities, and enumerable attribute values, to name a few. Although text editing is sometimes convenient for quick fixes, stick to standards-based processors for long-term consistency and reliability.

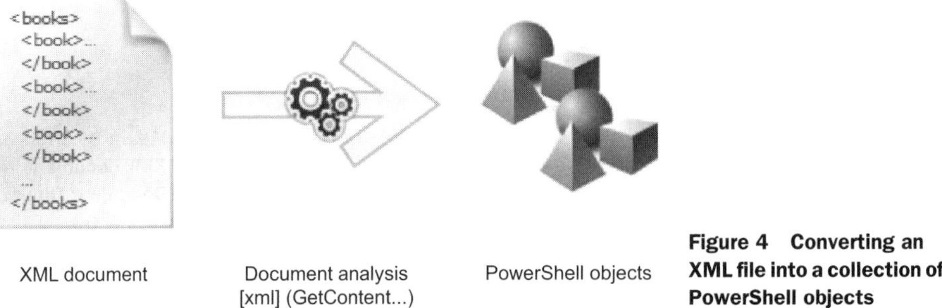

Figure 4 Converting an XML file into a collection of PowerShell objects

If you didn't follow all the nitty-gritty details of the past few paragraphs, don't fret. Your key takeaway should be that XML documents are, in fact, objects, and that this makes them a perfect fit for PowerShell and the structure it emphasizes. Now let's see how PowerShell capitalizes on this.

XML in .NET and PowerShell

Having described what XML files and objects are and the structure and predictability they provide, I'll show you these pieces at work and use PowerShell to parse and return information from an XML document. As illustrated in figure 4, you'll read the sample XML document (books.xml) and turn it into a collection of PowerShell objects. As I demonstrate each command I'll explain in depth what it's doing.

Your first step is to load the text file and convert it to an `XmlDocument` object. Store this object in a variable titled `XMLDoc`:

```
PS C:\> $XMLDoc = [xml] (Get-Content C:\books.xml)
```

The `Get-Content` cmdlet retrieves text from a file and creates an array of strings (as opposed to one long string with line breaks). Each string is one line from the original file.

Get-Content

When `(Get-Content C:\books.xml)` runs an array of strings is generated. Try it:

```
PS C:\ > Get-Content C:\books.xml
<?xml version="1.0"?>
<catalog>
   <book id="bk101">
      <author>Gambardella, Matthew</author>
      <title>XML Developer's Guide</title>
      <genre>Computer</genre>
      <price>44.95</price>
      <publish_date>2000-10-01</publish_date>
      <description>An in-depth look at creating applications
      with XML.</description>
   </book>
   <!-- ...other <book> items omitted... -->
</catalog>
```

To prove that the content is retrieved as an array of strings run this command:

```
PS C:\ > (Get-Content .\books.xml).Length
32
```

It returns 32, the number of elements in the array, which corresponds to the number of lines in the original file. If a single long string were returned the value of Length would be 1.

[xml]

Next let's consider the [xml] symbol. This is a *type literal*, a reference to a type. In this case it's a type *accelerator*, which is a shorthand reference to a full type name. [xml] represents the [System.Xml.XmlDocument] type, the .NET type encapsulating an XML DOM data tree.

When a type literal like [xml] is placed before an expression, it represents a conversion of the expression to the type represented by the literal. In this case, your array of strings is converted into a System.Xml.XmlDocument object. PowerShell accomplishes this by concatenating all the strings together into one long string, then calling the XmlDocument.Load method to process the text and load the data into an XmlDocument object. Remember, the XmlDocument object represents the in-memory model (DOM) for the XML file. The process described here is PowerShell's implementation of the analysis illustrated in figure 3.

NOTE Those accustomed to C# and other .NET languages may be surprised by this conversion; casting a string directly to an XmlDocument in C# isn't supported. This is an example of PowerShell extending the basic .NET casting logic with its own conversion algorithms.

The output following this conversion is demonstrated by the following command:

```
PS C:\> [xml] (Get-Content C:\books.xml)

xml                                     catalog
---                                     -------
version="1.0"                           catalog
```

Most XML documents converted into PowerShell XML objects look like this by default, with a property representing the XML declaration, and a property representing the root element of the document.

The following code is a more complete demonstration of all of the properties of a PowerShell XML object. The XML DOM for a document node specifies most of the capitalized properties. Some of the raw XML content has been removed for the sake of brevity:

```
PS C:\> [xml] (Get-Content C:\books.xml) | Format-List -Property *

xml                  : version="1.0"
catalog              : catalog
NodeType             : Document
ParentNode           :
```

Properties added to XmlDocument by PowerShell

```
DocumentType        :
Implementation      : System.Xml.XmlImplementation
Name                : #document
LocalName           : #document
DocumentElement     : catalog
OwnerDocument       :
Schemas             : System.Xml.Schema.XmlSchemaSet
XmlResolver         :
NameTable           : System.Xml.NameTable
PreserveWhitespace  : False
IsReadOnly          : False
InnerText           :
InnerXml            : <?xml version="1.0"?><catalog><book
                      id="bk101"><author>Gambardella,
                      Matthew</author><title>XML Developer's Guide
                      </title><genre>Computer</genre><price>44.95
                      </price><publish_date>2000-1001</publish_date>
                      <description>An in-depth look at creating
                      applications with XML.</description></book>
                      ...
                      </catalog>
SchemaInfo          : System.Xml.Schema.XmlSchemaInfo
BaseURI             :
Value               :
ChildNodes          : {xml, catalog}
PreviousSibling     :
NextSibling         :
Attributes          :
FirstChild          : xml
LastChild           : catalog
HasChildNodes       : True
NamespaceURI        :
Prefix              :
OuterXml            : <?xml version="1.0"?><catalog><book
                      id="bk101"><author>Gambardella,
                      Matthew</author><title>XML Developer's Guide
                      </title><genre>Computer</genre><price>44.95
                      </price><publish_date>2000-1001</publish_date>
                      <description>An in-depth look at creating
                      applications with XML.</description></book>
                      ...
                      </catalog>
```

Most of these properties will be familiar if you've encountered the DOM before, but you'll be surprised by the xml and catalog properties, which PowerShell has added. In the next section I'll explain where these properties come from and how you can take advantage of them.

Adapted objects and XMLNodeAdapter

PowerShell treats objects from many different frameworks as first-class citizens. Members of a first-class object are available as direct children (via dot notation) of the containing object. Integration of multiple object frameworks in PowerShell is achieved via the Adapted Type System (ATS). In this system, pluggable type adapters provide a translation layer between the underlying objects in their original framework and the objects as represented in PowerShell. Figure 5 shows how this system works for Common Information Model (CIM)/Windows Management Instrumentation (WMI) classes and objects.

NOTE Windows Management Instrumentation (WMI) is Microsoft's implementation of a Common Information Model (CIM) service. In this section I use the terms CIM and WMI interchangeably.

Familiar examples of adapted first-class object frameworks in PowerShell include CIM/WMI, ADSI, XML, and ADO.NET. Even .NET objects are adapted by a .NET type adapter. To ease you into this concept I'll demonstrate type adaptation with CIM/WMI first. Afterward we'll walk through the same process with XML.

CIM (WMI) adapted objects

CIM/WMI in C# and .NET isn't truly a first-class citizen. You can't directly access members (for example, properties and methods) of a CIM instance as members of the parent object (via dot notation). Instead you must index into an intermediary collection. C# code to retrieve the `TotalPhysicalMemory` property of a Win32_ComputerSystem WMI object looks like this:

```
String ComputerName = System.Environment.MachineName;
ManagementObject comp = new ManagementObject(
String.Format(@"\\.\ROOT\cimv2:Win32_ComputerSystem.Name=""{0}""",
ComputerName));
var mem = comp.Properties["TotalPhysicalMemory"].Value.ToString();
Console.WriteLine("Memory: " + mem);
Console.ReadKey();
```

WMI properties retrieved via intermediary collection

After creating the `ManagementObject` object (a classic WMI API in .NET), it's still necessary to reference the intermediary `Properties` property of the object and index into this collection to retrieve individual WMI properties. When members must be accessed indirectly in this way the object framework is considered a second-class citizen of the language.

One of several consequences of second-class citizenship is lack of IntelliSense for the framework, as shown in figure 6.

In PowerShell the CIM framework is a first-class citizen. The PowerShell equivalent of the previous C# would be:

```
PS C:\> $Instance = Get-CimInstance Win32_ComputerSystem
PS C:\> $Instance.TotalPhysicalMemory
17057411072
```

Much simpler. In PowerShell CIM/WMI properties are directly accessible as children of the object, via dot notation, without indirection or an intermediary collection. As a result, the Integrated Scripting Environment (ISE) displays detailed properties in its IntelliSense for CIM, as shown in figure 7.

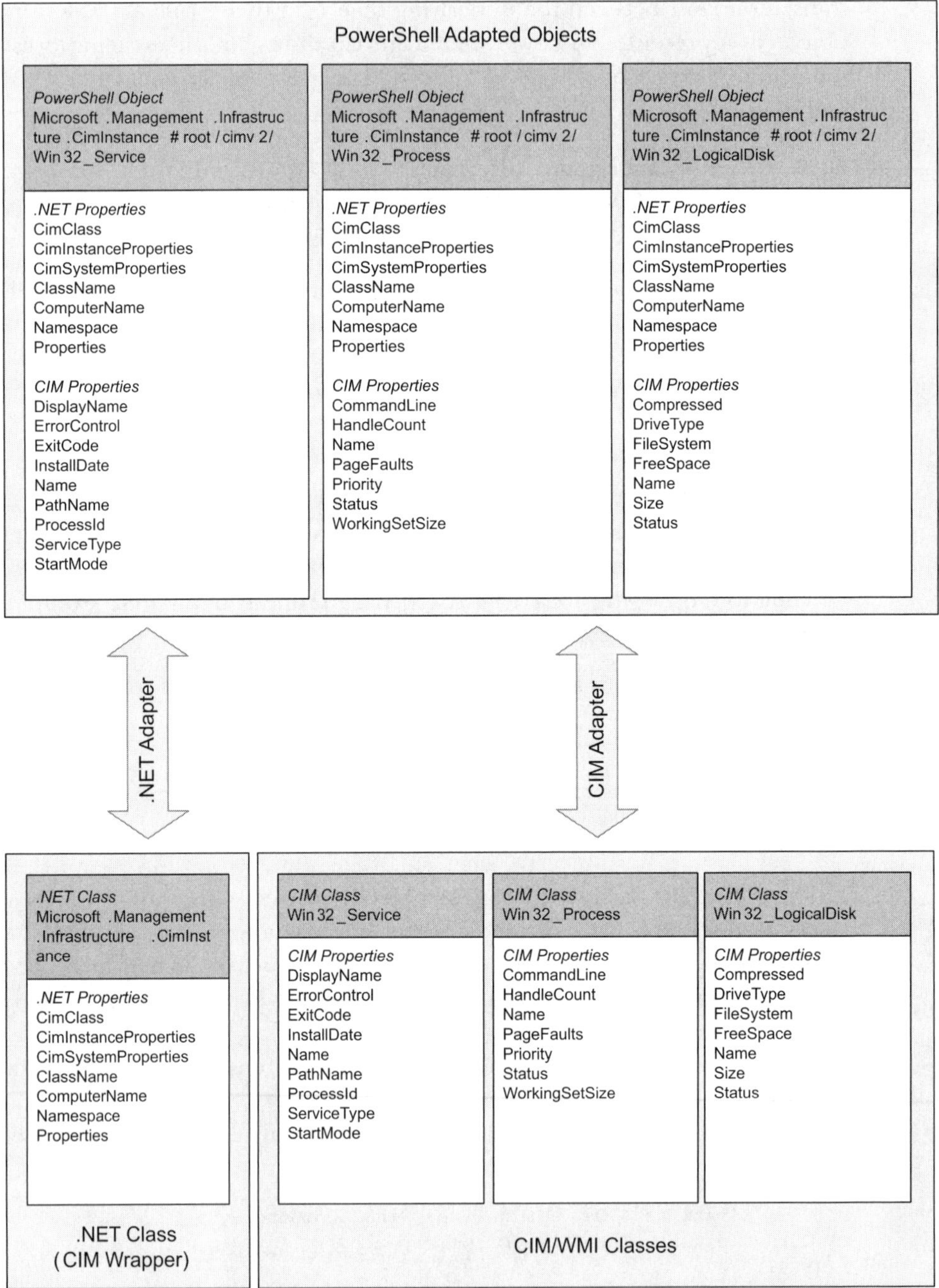

Figure 5 PowerShell objects expose members from different object frameworks as first-class citizens. In this example, the .NET `CimInstance` class and the specific CIM (WMI) class of an instance both contribute properties to the PowerShell object.

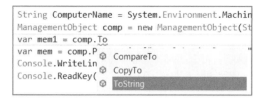

```
String ComputerName = System.Environment.Machin
ManagementObject comp = new ManagementObject(St
var mem1 = comp.To
var mem = comp.P   CompareTo
Console.WriteLin   CopyTo
Console.ReadKey(   ToString
```

Figure 6 WMI objects aren't first-class objects in C# and .NET, so Visual Studio IntelliSense can't display specific properties.

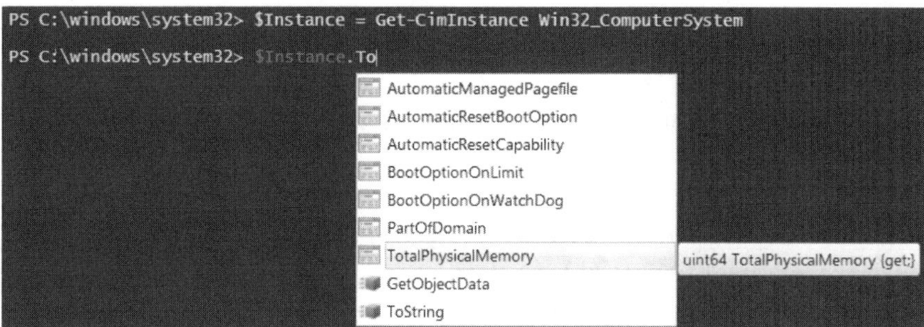

Figure 7 Because CIM/WMI is a first-class citizen in PowerShell, ISE IntelliSense can display detailed information about CIM properties (unlike Visual Studio IntelliSense for C#).

PowerShell elevates the CIM/WMI framework to a first-class citizen via an adapter for the Adapted Type System (ATS). I started with this adapter as a familiar example. Next, let's see how the XML adapter elevates XML to first-class citizenship as well.

XML adapted objects

I described previously how XML processors convert XML documents into in-memory objects implementing the XML Document Object Model (DOM). To understand how PowerShell adapts XML I'll discuss the parts that make up this in-memory DOM object.

In the DOM each and every part of the document is a base Node as well as a more specific, derived kind of node. Common derived node kinds and corresponding .NET classes are listed in table 1.

Table 1 Each XML DOM Node kind corresponds to a specific .NET class. All .NET classes are in the `System.Xml` namespace.

Node kind	.NET class
`Node`	`XmlNode`
`Document`	`XmlDocument`
`Element`	`XmlElement`
`Attribute`	`XmlAttribute`
`CDataSection`	`XmlCDataSection`
`Text`	`XmlText`

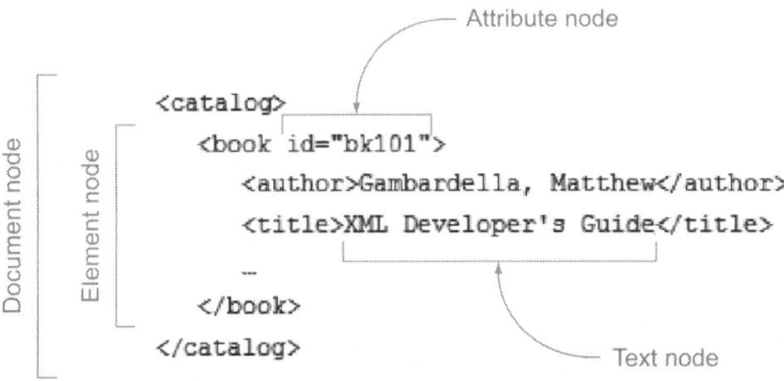

Figure 8 Everything in an XML document is a node of some kind. Typical nodes are shown here.

Examples of where and how different node kinds (types) appear in an XML file are shown in figure 8.

PowerShell's XML type adapter adapts .NET `XMLNode` objects. Because all other node classes derive from `XMLNode` the type adapter targets all of the kinds of XML nodes by targeting this shared base class.

To demonstrate and explain the XML type adapter let's build on your manipulation of the books.xml file by adding a second command:

```
PS C:\> $XMLDoc = [xml] (Get-Content C:\books.xml)
PS C:\> $XMLDoc.catalog.book | Format-Table title,author,price

title                  author                price
-----                  ------                -----
XML Developer's Guide  Gambardella, Matthew  44.95
Midnight Rain          Ralls, Kim            5.95
Maeve Ascendant        Corets, Eva           5.95
```

The root node of the books.xml document (listing 1) is titled `catalog`, and it contains a number of children titled books. The book elements have their own children, including those named `title`, `author`, and `price`. In C# and other .NET languages you access the `catalog` element in the XML document as follows:

```
String nodeName = "catalog";
XmlNode node = null;
var XmlDoc = new XmlDocument();
XmlDoc.Load("C:\books.xml");
foreach (XmlNode childNode in XmlDoc.ChildNodes) {
    if (childNode.LocalName == nodeName) {
        node = childNode;
        Console.WriteLine("Found node: " + node.LocalName);
        break;
    }
}
// do something with node
Console.ReadKey();
```

Child node retrieved via `ChildNodes` intermediary property

This code helps you retrieve the root `catalog` node of your document. Similar routines let you retrieve its child book nodes. The child nodes of the current node are not accessible via dot notation (that is, as first-class members). Instead, you must use the intermediary `ChildNodes` collection. Even there, you can't index into the collection by the name of the element (catalog); instead, you loop until you find a child element with the correct name.

> **XML DOM methods and APIs**
> The XML DOM interface includes methods, such as `GetElementsByTagName` and `GetElementById`, which simplify retrieval of individual attributes and child elements. Other APIs also are available, such as XPath and LINQ to XML, which simplify querying and parsing of XML documents. These methods and APIs, like PowerShell, wrap and hide the generality of the underlying XML DOM and Node model.

PowerShell makes working with XML nodes and their children simpler via the `XmlNodeAdapter`. In the same way that the CIM adapter adapts CIM properties for PowerShell objects, the `XmlNodeAdapter` translates XML nodes into properties of PowerShell XML objects, as shown in figure 9.

XMLNODEADAPTER

As its name implies, PowerShell's `XmlNodeAdapter` operates on `XmlNode` and `XmlNode`-derived objects, such as `XmlDocument`, `XmlElement`, and `XmlAttribute`. It finds child elements (`XmlElement`) and attributes (`XmlAttribute`) of the current node and adapts these to be direct children of that parent node, named by their original tag name and accessible via dot notation. In PowerShell it isn't necessary to find a node in the `ChildNodes` collection, as it is in C#; if it exists in the document it's a property of its parent node.

The following example shows how you can use PowerShell to easily achieve what was previously so complex with C# and work directly with the child elements and attributes of an XML node. Start by loading the books.xml file into an `XmlDocument` object, storing it in a variable, and verifying that the variable contains what you expect, an `XmlDocument` node:

```
PS C:\> $XMLDoc = [xml] (Get-Content .\books.xml)
PS C:\> $XMLDoc

xml                                         catalog
---                                         -------
version="1.0"                               catalog
```

`$XmlDoc` contains an `XmlDocument` object, which represents the entire original document.

XMLDOCUMENT OBJECT

The adapted child nodes of the `XmlDocument` include the XML Declaration (`<?xml version="1.0" ?>`) and the root element of the document—in this case, the element named catalog. To review all of the properties available on `XmlDocument` objects execute the following:

```
PS C:\> $XMLDoc | Format-List *
```

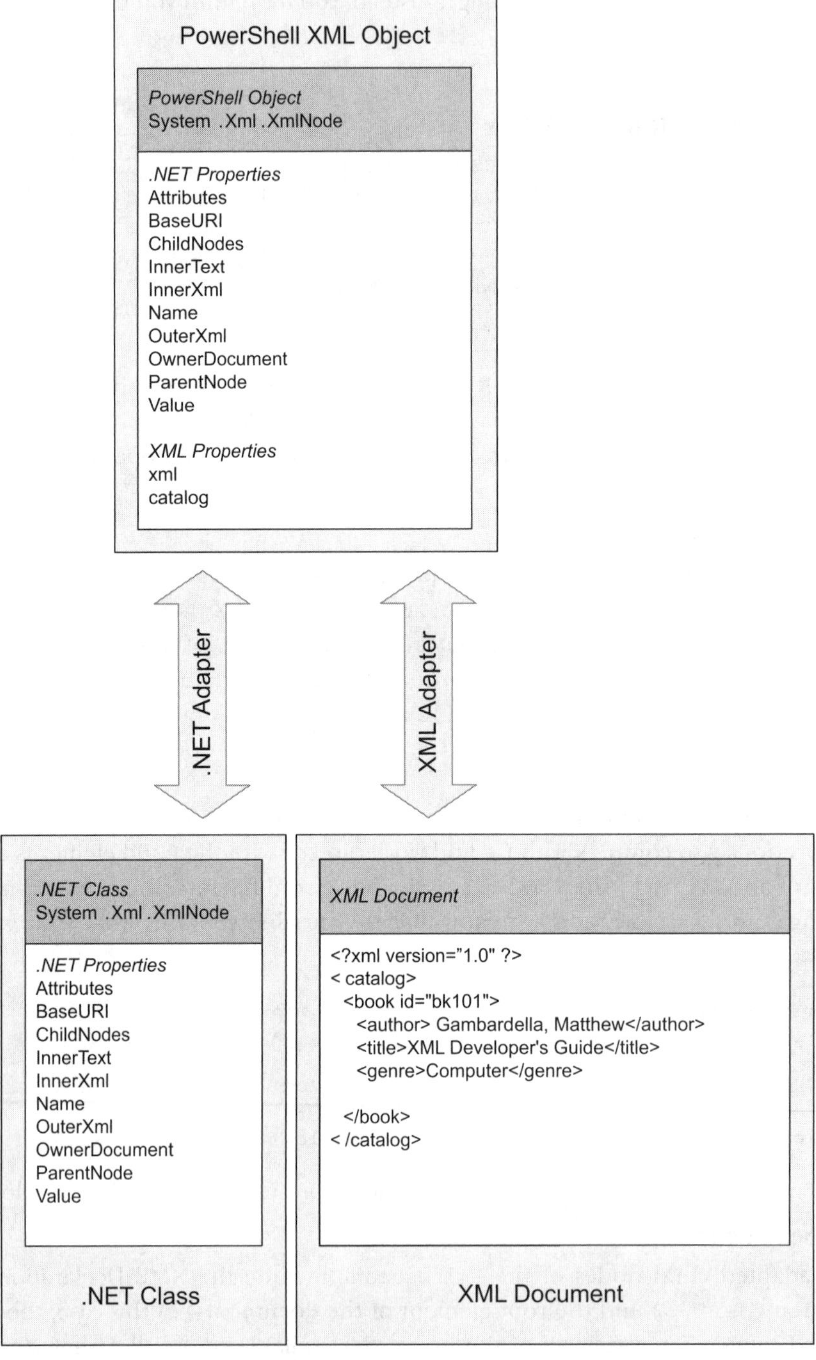

Figure 9 PowerShell uses the .NET and XML adapters to surface members of PowerShell XML objects.

Remember that the document node and all other node kinds are all derived from the more generic node kind. To prove that the .NET DOM APIs implement this as well, execute the following:

```
PS C:\ > $XMLDoc.GetType().BaseType

IsPublic IsSerial Name         BaseType
-------- -------- ----         --------
True     False    XmlNode      System.Object
```

GetType() returns the type of the object stored in $XMLDoc, which is XmlDocument. The BaseType property of this type returns the base type of XmlDocument, which is XmlNode.

Next retrieve the root element of the document:

```
PS C:\> $XMLDoc.catalog

book
----
{book, book, book}

PS C:\> $XMLDoc.catalog | Format-List -Property *

book             : {book, book, book}
Name             : catalog
LocalName        : catalog
NamespaceURI     :
Prefix           :
NodeType         : Element
ParentNode       : #document
OwnerDocument    : #document
IsEmpty          : False
Attributes       : {}
...output truncated
```

XMLELEMENT OBJECTS

The root Element Node of the XML Document is a first-class member of its parent and can be accessed via $XMLDoc.catalog. catalog is a node of the kind Element, .NET type XmlElement, as shown here:

```
PS C:\> $XMLDoc.catalog.GetType()

IsPublic IsSerial Name
-------- -------- ----
True     False    XmlElement
```

PowerShell's XmlNodeAdapter has created this property (catalog) of the parent XML document object based on the original XML document hierarchy.

The child elements of the catalog element are each titled book. Multiple child elements sharing the same name are grouped into an array of nodes at the shared property name. In this example, three XmlNode objects titled book are aggregated at the property book of the parent XmlElement object titled catalog.

As with any array in PowerShell, when you access the array all individual elements are listed (that is, the array is "unwrapped"). In this case, each XmlElement node titled book is returned. Child elements and attributes of these nodes are recursively adapted and displayed. Id is an attribute of a book element; author, title, and genre are child elements. Despite this difference (attribute versus element), all are adapted and displayed uniformly by PowerShell. Output of retrieving the book property is as follows:

```
PS C:\> $XMLDoc.catalog.book

id           : bk101
author       : Gambardella, Matthew
title        : XML Developer's Guide
genre        : Computer
price        : 44.95
publish_date : 2000-10-01
description  : An in-depth look at creating applications
               with XML.

id           : bk102
author       : Ralls, Kim
title        : Midnight Rain
genre        : Fantasy
price        : 5.95
publish_date : 2000-12-16
description  : A former architect battles corporate zombies,
               an evil sorceress, and her own childhood
               to become queen of the world.

id           : bk103
author       : Corets, Eva
title        : Maeve Ascendant
genre        : Fantasy
price        : 5.95
publish_date : 2000-11-17
description  : After the collapse of a nanotechnology
               society in England, the young survivors
               lay the foundation for a new society.
```

Running the following proves that the book property of catalog is an array:

```
PS C:\> $XMLDoc.catalog.book.GetType()

IsPublic IsSerial Name
-------- -------- ----
True     True     Object[]
```

XMLATTRIBUTE AND SIMPLE XMLELEMENT OBJECTS

You may be surprised to find that `$XMLDoc.catalog.book[0].id.GetType()` yields the .NET `String` type and not the `XmlAttribute` type. You may likewise be surprised that `$XMLDoc.catalog.book[0].author.GetType()` also yields the `String` type and not `XmlElement`. Conveniently (or perhaps not), PowerShell's XML type adapter converts attributes and simple elements with only inner text and no attributes into `String` objects representing the attribute value or element inner text. This allows you to use these leaf nodes as input variables in scripts and other scenarios, as you'll see in the next section.

If you need to make complex changes to the original `XmlElement` or `XmlAttribute` objects, such as adding nested elements to an element or changing parent, child, and sibling relationships of an attribute, you'll need to bypass the adapter and index into the intermediary collection, as in the following:

```
PS C:\> $XMLDoc.catalog.book[0].Attributes['id']

#text
-----
bk101
```

This completes my coverage of the internals of how PowerShell captures and presents XML documents as flexible and fluent DOM objects. Let's now use this understanding to provide some practical solutions.

Read and write XML documents

Reading and modifying XML documents will probably be your most important XML task in PowerShell. As examples of this, I'll first present how to read and use a simple XML answer file and then discuss how to modify .NET application configuration files.

Read an XML answer file

Using an XML answer file in coordination with a script is a good way to separate configuration details from the script itself, while still providing a persistent store of those details. The logic to be executed is stored generically in the script, whereas specific names and values are stored in one or more answer files specific to various configurations. In this arrangement the script retrieves and parses the XML file, using its data to fill in parameter and settings values, as shown in figure 10.

Robust, reusable answer files require some forethought and planning to ensure that the XML structure is logical and that script editors can easily target the information they need. For our purposes, let's assume that the work of planning the XML structure has already been done and focus on the semantics of reading the prepared XML file.

Listing 2 provides a truncated SharePoint farm creation answer file as an example. The file contains a name for the farm, database names and servers, Active

Figure 10 Separating configuration-specific details from a script's implementation and execution is more complicated up front, but makes both easier to maintain.

Directory accounts to use, URLs and names for associated web applications, and details about a SharePoint site. Although you won't use many of these details here, I present this more intricate answer file to demonstrate how one might be written for a complex application.

Listing 2 A custom XML answer file for SharePoint farm configuration

```
<?xml version="1.0" ?>
<SharePointElements>
  <Farm Name="SP2013"
        DatabaseServer="SQL01"
        FarmAccountName="CONTOSO\svcSPFarm"
        FarmAccountPassword="Pass@word1"
        FarmPassphrase="Pass@word1" />
  <ManagedAccounts>
    <ManagedAccount AccountName="CONTOSO\svcSPWebAppPool"
                    AccountPassword="Pass@word1" />
    <ManagedAccount AccountName="CONTOSO\svcSPServiceAppPool"
                    AccountPassword="Pass@word1" />
  </ManagedAccounts>
  <ServiceApplicationPools>
    <ServiceApplicationPool Name="SharePoint Web Applications"
                            AccountName="CONTOSO\svcSPWebAppPool" />
    <ServiceApplicationPool Name="SharePoint Service Applications"
                            AccountName="CONTOSO\svcSPServiceAppPool" />
  </ServiceApplicationPools>
  <WebApplications>
    <WebApplication Name="Intranet"
                    AppPoolName="SharePoint Web Applications"
                    AppPoolAccount="CONTOSO\svcSPWebAppPool"
                    HostHeader="intranet.contoso.com"
                    Port="80"
                    SSL="false"
                    DatabaseName="Intranet"
                    DatabaseServer=""
                    >
      <Sites>
        <Site Name="Intranet"
              RelativeUrl=""
              OwnerAlias="CONTOSO\Josh"
              Template="STS#0" >
                <Users>
                  <User Alias="User01"
                        PermissionLevel="FullControl" />
                </Users>
        </Site>
      </Sites>
    </WebApplication>
  </WebApplications>
</SharePointElements>
```

This answer file is used as input for a script that builds a SharePoint farm. I'll demonstrate the first few commands from that script.

LOAD THE FILE

To use the details in this file in a script it must first be loaded into the script's PowerShell session. You can accomplish this in one of two ways, the first being the simple syntax introduced previously:

```
PS C:\> $XMLDoc = [xml] (Get-Content -Path "C:\sharepoint.xml")
```

You may encounter scenarios in which greater control of document processing is required. For example, you may want to validate XML schemas or require a higher level of security by ignoring certain text that could represent an attack vector. For more control of these settings, load an XML file by first creating and configuring an `XmlReaderSettings` object, and then creating a `XmlReader` based on those settings, as in the following:

```
PS C:\> $XmlSettings = New-Object System.Xml.XmlReaderSettings `
    -Property @{
        IgnoreComments = $true
        IgnoreProcessingInstructions = $true
        IgnoreWhitespace = $true
        ValidationType = "None"
    }
PS C:\> $Reader = [System.Xml.XmlReader]::Create("C:\sharepoint.xml",
  ➥ $XmlSettings)
```

With your custom `XmlReader` in hand, use the reader as the foundation of an `XmlDocument` like this:

```
PS C:\> $XMLDoc = New-Object xml
PS C:\> $XMLDoc.Load($Reader)
```

Both the simple and full-control approach demonstrated result in a `System.Xml.XmlDocument` object stored in the `$XMLDoc` variable and ready for further work.

USE VALUES FROM THE FILE

Next, use the answer file to create a new SharePoint farm and configuration database. For ease of access, begin by storing the root element from the XML object in its own variable. Remember, the `$XMLDoc` variable contains an `XmlDocument` object, which itself contains the root element of the document:

```
$SP = $XMLDoc.SharePointElements
```

The SharePoint farm creation cmdlet has a parameter that takes a `PSCredential` object specifying the farm service account. The value for this parameter is taken from the account name and password stored in the XML file, and you need to complete the following steps to prepare the value:

1. Convert the password into a `SecureString` object.
2. Create a `PSCredential` object using the secure password together with the plain-text account name.
3. Set the names of the farm's configuration and administration databases.

Steps 1 and 2 are accomplished via the following two commands (values taken from the XML file are shown in bold):

```
$Password = ConvertTo-SecureString `
                -String $SP.Farm.FarmAccountPassword `
                -AsPlainText `
                -Force

$FarmAccount = New-Object `
    -TypeName System.Management.Automation.PSCredential `
    -ArgumentList $SP.Farm.FarmAccountName, $Password
```

This code steps through the Farm element in the XML file to the FarmAccountName and FarmAccountPassword attributes and uses those values to parameterize the script. The script remains generic; all specific values are contained in the XML answer file.

Your final preparatory step is to build strings for the names of the farm's configuration and administration databases. The following code uses the same information from the XML configuration file in two different commands. Because the information is retrieved from the same source your script guarantees a consistent naming convention for the databases, which database administrators are likely to appreciate:

```
$ConfigDBName = '{0}_Config' -f $SP.Farm.Name
$AdminDBName  = '{0}_AdminContentDB' -f $SP.Farm.Name
```

With your parameter values prepared, you're ready to call the farm creation cmdlet, adding in the last necessary values (shown in bold):

```
New-SPConfigurationDatabase `
      -DatabaseServer $SP.Farm.DatabaseServer `
      -DatabaseName $ConfigDBName `
      -AdministrationContentDatabaseName $AdminDBName
      -FarmCredentials $FarmAccount `
      -Passphrase $SP.Farm.FarmPassphrase
```

BENEFITS OF ANSWER FILES

In this example you read values from an XML configuration file to govern the actions of your script. In practice, these commands would be part of a greater script or series of scripts, which could carry out complete deployment of a SharePoint environment.

Although my purpose here has been to show you how to read and use data in XML files, let's not pass up an opportunity to acknowledge several of the advantages of using an answer file to set up complex environments:

- The script itself doesn't have to be modified for various configuration implementations. For example, if a different destination database server is to be used for a SharePoint farm in a quality assurance environment, only the XML file must be modified; the script stays the same.
- Implementation- and environment-specific details are documented separately from the script in the answer file. Multiple answer files can represent multiple scenarios, such as one for production and one for QA. Store these files for documentation and disaster recovery and use them to replicate environments for

testing. For example, the farm name and service account password may be different in XML files representing different farms.

- Names and strings can be standardized by reusing values from XML elements and attributes in multiple places in the script.

Now that you've learned to read XML data, let's discuss how to make changes to data and save them back to a file.

Modify and save XML data

.NET application configuration files typically end with a .config extension and are stored in the same directory as the application they reference. These files provide declarative settings in XML that govern runtime behavior of the associated .NET application. For example, application-specific web proxy settings and trace settings can be set here. Settings are applied via a cascading hierarchy of files, with a file named machine.config shared by all applications at the root of the hierarchy.

TIP For more details on configuration files see http://msdn.microsoft.com/en-us/library/vstudio/1xtk877y(v=vs.110).aspx.

In this example you'll set the web `processModel autoConfig` value to `true` on the local machine.config file. This causes all local ASP.NET web applications to use an optimized number of worker and I/O threads (for more details, see http://msdn.microsoft.com/en-us/library/7w2sway1(v=vs.100).aspx).

Begin by finding the correct machine.config file path. This file is stored in the main Microsoft.NET folder, the path to which differs based on the .NET version number and the bitness (32 or 64) of the .NET version. The following command fills in the appropriate pieces of this path and saves it to the appropriately named `$MachineConfigFilePath` variable:

```
PS C:\> $MachineConfigFilePath =
➥ '{0}\Microsoft.NET\Framework{1}\v{2}\Config\machine.config'
➥ -f $env:SystemRoot,
➥ (& {if ([System.Environment]::Is64BitOperatingSystem)
➥ {"64"} else {""}}),
➥ ([System.Environment]::Version.ToString(3))
```

Next, load the XML document from this path using the simple load process described previously:

```
PS C:\> $MachineConfigDoc = [xml] (Get-Content -Path
➥ $MachineConfigFilePath)
```

MODIFY THE XML DOCUMENT

You can now modify elements and attributes of this document in the same way you can modify properties of other objects in PowerShell. All access and modification of these elements effect the same in-memory representation. Set the `autoConfig` attribute of the `processModel` element to `true`. The relevant part of the original XML is shown here, with the `autoConfig` property value shown in bold:

```
<configuration>
     <system.web>
        <processModel autoConfig="false"/>
     </system.web>
</configuration>
```

In the PowerShell command to change the value you refer to the nodes (elements and attributes) by their names, treating them like properties of parent objects:

```
PS C:\>$MachineConfigDoc.configuration.'system.web'.processModel.
➥ autoConfig = 'true'
```

NOTE The `'system.web'` property has a dot in it. To avoid confusion with the dot operator, the property name is enclosed in single quotation marks. This is a convenient, though possibly unintentional, artifact of the manner in which PowerShell processes member names (it's unlikely to work in other languages).

SAVE THE XML DOCUMENT TO DISK

Finally, save the changed `XmlDocument` back to disk as an XML file, overwriting the current file:

```
PS C:\> $MachineConfigDoc.Save($MachineConfigFilePath)
```

The `autoConfig` property is now set to `true`.

The `Save` method is the simplest way to write an XML document object back to disk. But just as the `XmlReaderSettings` object together with `XmlReader` provided additional settings for reading and validating XML input, an `XmlWriterSettings` object together with `XmlWriter` can provide additional control over writing XML back to disk. For example, you may prefer to improve readability of the saved file by having new lines between nodes and indenting child elements, an option you can specify. To demonstrate, we'll change a value in the SharePoint farm configuration file used previously and save the file with specific indentation parameters.

First, retrieve the SharePoint XML configuration file as shown previously:

```
PS C:\> $XMLFilePath = 'C:\sharepoint.xml'
PS C:\> $XMLDoc = [xml] (Get-Content -Path $XMLFilePath)
```

Next, change the value of the `Name` attribute of the `Farm` element:

```
PS C:\> $XMLDoc.SharePointElements.Farm.Name = "SP2010"
```

Finally, specify a custom `XmlWriterSettings` object together with an `XmlWriter`:

```
PS C:\> $WriterSettings = New-Object `
    -TypeName System.Xml.XmlWriterSettings `
    -Property @{
        Encoding = [System.Text.Encoding]::UTF8
        Indent = $true
        IndentChars = "`t"
    }
PS C:\> $Writer = [System.Xml.XmlWriter]::Create(
➥ $XMLFilePath,$WriterSettings)
```

Use the custom `XmlWriter` to write your in-memory XML document to a file. You must also call `Flush` to ensure all data is written to disk, and then call `Close` to release the open handle to the file, as follows:

```
PS C:\> $XMLDoc.WriteTo($Writer)
PS C:\> $Writer.Flush()
PS C:\> $Writer.Close()
```

In this section I demonstrated reading and writing data from and to XML files. To work with collections of XML files you can scale the paradigms I presented here with loop constructs. With these typical scenarios covered, let's conclude by discussing some advanced uses of XML in PowerShell.

Special XML cases

I've discussed how PowerShell handles generic XML documents and how you can use PowerShell to read and write your own application XML files, but XML's rigorous structure also makes it ideal for persistent storage or transfer of structured data between applications and systems. In this last section we'll take a look at how this capability is exploited for .NET and PowerShell serialization and for web service (SOAP and REST) operations.

Object serialization

As long as you remain within the confines of a single .NET AppDomain you can largely ignore how your objects are stored. The common language runtime (CLR) manages the objects in memory and access and modifications to them. But as your domain of operation expands you need to transfer objects across process and system boundaries, and you also need to persist information and objects to long-term storage. To achieve this the objects must first be converted into transferable, interoperational, and persistable formats and encodings.

The process of converting objects from their in-memory representation to transferable and storable forms is called *serialization*. Conversely, conversion of serialized objects back into forms appropriate for use in a .NET application is known as *deserialization*. Generally, the result of serialization is a text or binary file that can be stored to disk or transferred across networks. Common serialization formats include base64-encoded byte arrays and XML and JSON documents, as illustrated in figure 11.

XML SERIALIZATION IN POWERSHELL (CLIXML)

XML plays a prominent role in serialization within the .NET framework, and PowerShell is no exception. Two cmdlets in PowerShell help serialize objects into XML for storage on disk and transfer across networks: `Export-CliXml` and `ConvertTo-Xml`. The difference in the output produced by these two commands isn't only cosmetic; the CliXml produced by `Export-CliXml` is designed to provide high-fidelity deserialization of the original object in other PowerShell sessions. Objects produced by deserializing CliXml (using the `Import-CliXml` cmdlet) can often be plugged into a command in place of the original object, depending on what members of the original

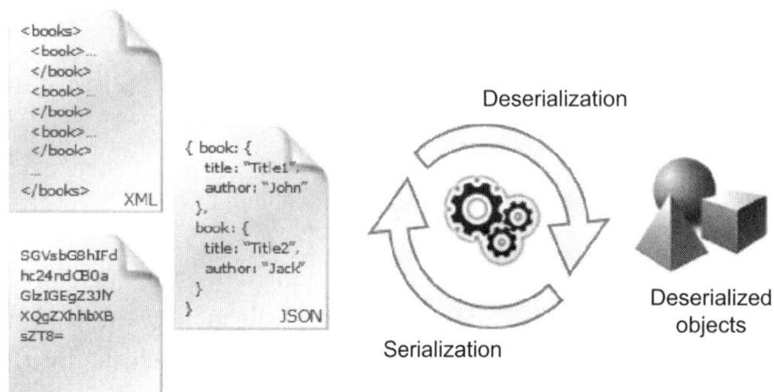

Figure 11 Objects are serialized for persistent storage and deserialized to bring them back into memory. Base64, XML, and JSON are common serialization formats.

object are needed. The standard XML produced by `ConvertTo-Xml` is only intended to produce information about the original object; it isn't a true serialization of the original object, and it can't be deserialized back into the original.

TIP Use `Export-CliXml` when you expect to deserialize and reuse exported objects within another PowerShell session. Use `ConvertTo-Xml` to save object data for reporting and logging purposes outside of PowerShell, such as in a web report using XSLT.

To demonstrate each form of XML export we'll export a service object (the Windows Update service, known internally as `wuauserv`) as CliXml, import it back into the session, and review it using `Get-Member`:

```
PS C:\> Get-Service wuauserv | Export-Clixml C:\serviceCLI.xml

PS C:\> Import-Clixml C:\serviceCLI.xml | Get-Member

   TypeName: Deserialized.System.ServiceProcess.ServiceController

Name                    MemberType
----                    ----------
ToString                    Method
Name                  NoteProperty
RequiredServices      NoteProperty
CanPauseAndContinue       Property
CanShutdown               Property
CanStop                   Property
Container                 Property
DependentServices         Property
DisplayName               Property
MachineName               Property
ServiceHandle             Property
ServiceName               Property
ServicesDependedOn        Property
ServiceType               Property
Site                      Property
Status                    Property
```

Deserialized object retains relationship with original ❶

When CliXml is imported into a PowerShell session, as we discussed previously, a deserialized version of the original object is created. Note that the `TypeName` of the deserialized version is prefixed with the `Deserialized` tag ❶. The deserialized versions of most .NET objects are simple objects (like property bags or dictionaries) representing the properties and saved values of the original object. Even in this diluted form they more closely represent the original object than would a standard XML document, as you'll see next.

Now we'll export the service object as standard XML and import it back in as well. We'll then check its properties and `TypeName` via `Get-Member`.

```
PS C:\> Get-Service wuauserv | ConvertTo-Xml -As String |
  ➥ Set-Content -Path C:\service.xml

PS C:\> [xml] (Get-Content C:\service.xml) | Get-Member

   TypeName: System.Xml.XmlDocument

Name                        MemberType
----                        ----------
ToString                    CodeMethod
AppendChild                 Method
Clone                       Method
CloneNode                   Method
CreateAttribute             Method
CreateCDataSection          Method
...
```

Objects exported as standard XML and then imported back into PowerShell, as in this example, are represented as standard XML document objects. The original object is lost, and you'll have to do some fancy footwork to find its original properties and saved values. Although neither CliXml nor standard XML necessarily provide full fidelity to the original object, objects created by importing CliXml can be more easily used in place of the originals.

Notably, the CIM objects and classes introduced in Microsoft Management Infrastructure and the PowerShell v3 `CimCmdlets` module were designed to be able to be serialized and deserialized for network transfer and storage persistence with complete fidelity to the original object. Properties are dynamically retrieved and even CIM methods can be called on the deserialized object. This is demonstrated in the following:

```
PS C:\> Get-CimInstance -ClassName Win32_Process -Filter 'Name =
  ➥ "explorer.exe"' | Export-CliXml -Path C:\processCLI.xml

PS C:\> Import-Clixml -Path C:\processCLI.xml | Get-Member

   TypeName:                                              Imported object
     ➥ Microsoft.Management.Infrastructure.CimInstance     is the same as
     ➥ #ROOT/cimv2/Win32_Process                           exported object

Name                       MemberType      Definition
----                       ----------      ----------
Handles                    AliasProperty   Handles = Handlecount
ProcessName                AliasProperty   ProcessName = Name
```

```
VM                          AliasProperty  VM = VirtualSize
WS                          AliasProperty  WS = WorkingSetSize
Clone                       Method         System.Object IClone...
Dispose                     Method         void Dispose(), ...
Equals                      Method         bool Equals(System.Object obj)
GetCimSessionComputerName   Method         string GetCimSess...
GetCimSessionInstanceId     Method         guid GetCimSession...
GetHashCode                 Method         int GetHashCode()
GetObjectData               Method         void GetObjectData(...
GetType                     Method         type GetType()
ToString                    Method         string ToString()
Caption                     Property       string Caption {get;}
```

Unlike the deserialized .NET service object we previously discussed, the `TypeName` of the deserialized CIM object isn't prefixed with `Deserialized`. It's the same type of object as the one created directly in the current process with `Get-CimInstance`.

The same qualities that make XML a good serialization format for the .NET framework make it an ideal medium for web communications, which must cross network and system boundaries. Most web services accept input and produce responses as XML documents. Let's examine the facilities provided by PowerShell to easily parse these XML responses.

Web service communication

The `Invoke-RestMethod` cmdlet (first introduced in PowerShell v3) retrieves a response from a web resource identified by a Uniform Resource Identifier (URI). If the response is XML it's converted into an `XmlDocument` object for output. This effectively means that web service responses, like XML documents, are first-class citizens in PowerShell. In addition, Atom feeds such as those produced by OData services are automatically further processed to retrieve the internal XML of individual items in the collection as a collection of PowerShell objects.

The following examples demonstrate both standard XML responses and the special treatment of Atom/OData feeds. The public Northwind OData web service is used. Northwind, available at http://services.odata.org/Northwind/Northwind.svc, is a collection of sample data made publicly and anonymously available by the OData organization for testing.

What is OData?

OData is an extension of the Atom and RSS standards that defines and standardizes REST patterns for publication and modification of data entities and collections on the internet. OData defines specific URL and HTTP structures for querying and modifying this data.

With only the URI parameter specified, `Invoke-RestMethod` sends an `HTTP GET` request to the URI and receives an XML document with a response:

```
PS C:\> $Uri = 'http://services.odata.org/Northwind/Northwind.svc'

PS C:\> Invoke-RestMethod -Uri $Uri

xml                                     service
---                                     -------
version="1.0" encoding="utf-8" stand... service
```

The XML is automatically converted into an `XmlDocument` object and adapted by PowerShell. You can interact with the response as you can with any XML document, as shown in the following:

```
PS C:\> $Response = Invoke-RestMethod -Uri $Uri
PS C:\> $Response.service.workspace.collection

href                                title
----                                -----
Categories                          Categories
CustomerDemographics                CustomerDemographics
Customers                           Customers
Employees                           Employees
Order_Details                       Order_Details
Orders                              Orders
Products                            Products
Regions                             Regions
...
```

❶ **Data collection**

A request to the base URL of an OData service returns a metadata document, which lists all data collections that the service publishes. Having discovered from the initial request that you have a collection of data named `Customers`, call the standard URI to retrieve that collection from the Northwind service. Because the data collection is returned as an Atom feed, the individual entries in the feed are converted individually into `XmlDocuments` and each returned separately (only the first two results are shown here):

```
PS C:\> $Uri =
  ➥ 'http://services.odata.org/Northwind/Northwind.svc/Customers'

PS C:\> Invoke-RestMethod -Uri $Uri

id       : http://services.odata.org/Northwind/Northwind.svc/Customers(
           'ALFKI')
title    : title
updated  : 2012-09-11T23:50:25Z
author   : author
link     : {link, link, link}
category : category
content  : content

id       : http://services.odata.org/Northwind/Northwind.svc/Customers(
           'ANATR')
title    : title
updated  : 2012-09-11T23:50:25Z
author   : author
link     : {link, link, link}
category : category
content  : content
```

As a bonus example, you can use the standard query parameters provided by OData to retrieve only a subset of the collection:

```
PS C:\> Invoke-RestMethod -Uri $Uri -Method Get -Body @{
    '$filter' = "Country eq 'Germany'"
    '$top' = "3"
}

id       : http://services.odata.org/Northwind/Northwind.svc/Customers(
           'ALFKI')
title    : title
updated  : 2012-09-11T23:49:54Z
author   : author
link     : {link, link, link}
category : category
content  : content

id       : http://services.odata.org/Northwind/Northwind.svc/Customers(
           'BLAUS')
title    : title
updated  : 2012-09-11T23:49:54Z
author   : author
link     : {link, link, link}
category : category
content  : content

id       : http://services.odata.org/Northwind/Northwind.svc/Customers(
           'DRACD')
title    : title
updated  : 2012-09-11T23:49:54Z
author   : author
link     : {link, link, link}
category : category
content  : content
```

The XML facilities provided by PowerShell become the foundation for serialization, web communications, and other important tasks and utilities.

Summary

I began this chapter by positing that XML documents are not, in fact, standard text files but instead a special kind of object saved as text. This explains XML's special place in PowerShell, a language built from the ground up on the principle of rejecting unstructured text as input or output. As PowerShell is to legacy scripting languages, so is XML to unstructured text files.

Respecting this special place, XML documents are adapted in PowerShell into first-class citizens, their nodes and attributes immediately accessible like the members of any other object. This easy accessibility makes XML the perfect format for input answer files and output data files in PowerShell; it also makes PowerShell an ideal language for manipulating other XML data and configuration files.

Not coincidentally, the foundations laid for XML in PowerShell lead to further practical uses in domains where XML is a primary means of message transport and encoding, such as in object serialization and web service communications protocols like SOAP and REST.

Whenever and wherever you face input and output needs in PowerShell, consider the structure provided by XML and the facilities provided by PowerShell to control and manipulate it. It's likely that XML is part of the solution you're seeking.

About the author

Josh Gavant is a senior program manager with Microsoft Open Technologies (http://msopentech.com), where he helps define and support industry standards, such as XML, and ensures that Microsoft software adheres to them. Following his belief that knowledge is best when shared, Josh publishes technical insights via his blog at http://blogs.msdn.com/besidethepoint and via occasional tweets @joshugav.

21 Adding automatic remoting to advanced functions and cmdlets

Karl Prosser

This chapter's goal is to present a design pattern to help you produce PowerShell modules that contain professional-grade cmdlets that are easy and intuitive for users to run both locally and remotely with a commercial-grade user experience. This chapter focuses on the intricacies of using a PowerShell script to create cmdlets that are robust and have built-in remoting functionality. I'll talk briefly at the end about nuances and strategies for turning your functions into enterprise-grade modules. This chapter presumes familiarity with PowerShell remoting. If you're not familiar with the ins and outs of fan-in and fan-out in PowerShell remoting, then `get-help About_Remote` is a good place to start.

Delivering economic value

For the most part, solutions have their value in solving a quantifiable problem. Compared to other languages and platforms, distributed computing with PowerShell remoting is easier and can save you time. Something that may take weeks to engineer on another stack may be completed in half an hour by a seasoned PowerShell scripter. The problem is that most users of your cmdlets are not seasoned PowerShell scripters, and even if they were, half an hour is longer than the 5 or 10 seconds that it would take to call your cmdlet locally. Let's produce a user experience in which running your cmdlet against a set of computers is as easy for the user as running `Get-Process` locally.

Jeffrey Snover, the architect of PowerShell, mentions a number of differentiating value propositions of PowerShell. One of them is the consistency of verb/noun and parameters, which allows you to learn something once and apply what you've learned even when you begin using PowerShell against a completely different technology and different set of commands. Consistency gives you the ability to guess what the command, parameter, or usage pattern will be, regardless of the environment. Even if you can't guess, you should be able to discover it relatively easily.

Many built-in cmdlets, whether using PowerShell Remoting or another mechanism, expose a `-ComputerName` property. You can use `-ComputerName` with `Invoke-Command` or with cmdlets, such as `Get-Process`, `Get-Service`, `Get-EventLog`, `Invoke-WmiMethod`, and `Get-WmiObject`. A nuance of our goal is to make our cmdlets as easy to use, guessable, and discoverable as these. The example in this chapter shows you how a scripter takes something made locally and runs it remotely, and you'll also see the overhead that this process involves. You'll see how this functionality should be set up and how it can be simple and discoverable and can even provide tab-completion support.

At a minimum, you'll want to surface a `-ComputerName` parameter, but we'll go further and provide full `Invoke-Command` parity. In the real world, people may have to run the code in existing sessions, with specific credentials or authentication protocols, or on specific remoting endpoints.

An automatic remoting example

I'll use a function that you can run locally, one without too much real-world value, and show you how to transform it, step by step, into a robust automatic remoting–enabled cmdlet. PowerShell v2 is the lowest common denominator: v1 doesn't support remoting, and although v3 gives you some new, shiny features, it's not needed for this example. I'll refer to a few v3 features, however, particularly the way Windows PowerShell Workflow (PSWF) is implemented in v3, which sets some precedents you can follow.

Start by wrapping `Get-Module` in your own function, and pass a wildcard for your `Name` parameter. The function returns a list of available modules for a single machine:

```
function Get-AvailableModule([string]$Name = "*") {
  Get-Module -ListAvailable -Name $Name
}
```

Running the function, like this

```
PS C:\> Get-AvailableModule -Name *power*
```

produces the following result:

```
ModuleType Name                                ExportedCommands
---------- ----                                ----------------
Manifest   Microsoft.PowerShell.Diagnostics    {Get-WinEvent, Get-Counte...
Manifest   Microsoft.PowerShell.Host           {Start-Transcript, Stop-T...
Manifest   Microsoft.PowerShell.Management     {Add-Content, Clear-Conte...
```

I prefer this example because it's pithy, but let's modify it. You're going to add a property to indicate where the command was run so that you can easily determine this when you run the command against multiple computers.

You may ask, "What about `PSComputerName`?" Well, that's a good question. `PSComputerName` is important, and I'll cover it, but the PowerShell formatting engine has a "nice" habit of often hiding PSComputerName, and you want to see your results. Also, PSComputerName contains the name that you requested. For example, if you did self-remoting to 127.0.0.1, then that would be the value.

For your initial local function, do the following:

- Add a property called WhereRan and give it the computer name from the environment variables.
- Grab the Name and Version properties of the PSModuleInfo object. (The formatting view of the previous result shows only a few columns, but the PSModuleInfo object contains many more properties.)

Here's the resulting function:

```
function Get-AvailableModule([string]$Name = "*")
{
   Get-Module -ListAvailable -Name $Name |
   Select Name,Version |
   Add-Member -Name WhereRan `
              -Value $ENV:ComputerName `
              -MemberType NoteProperty -PassThru
}
```

Running the function like this

```
PS C:\> Get-AvailableModule -Name *power*
```

produces the following result:

```
Name                        Version              WhereRan
----                        -------              --------
Microsoft.PowerShell.D...  3.0.0.0              BOOKBOX
Microsoft.PowerShell.Host  3.0.0.0              BOOKBOX
Microsoft.PowerShell.M...  3.0.0.0              BOOKBOX
```

Before you transform this into an automatic remoting-enabled function, let's look at some of the pain points of running the function as an end user with Invoke-Command.

The pain of manual Invoke-Command

To run this function remotely, put the body of the function inside the script block, which you're passing to Invoke-Command, and hardcode the parameters inside the script block.

You don't want to lose the function, so embed the function and a line that runs the function. The parameters are still hardcoded inside the Invoke-Command script block, but on the line that calls the function, as shown in the following listing.

Listing 1 Manual remoting with hardcoded parameters

```
Invoke-Command -ComputerName localhost -ScriptBlock {
  function Get-AvailableModule([string]$Name = "*")
  {
     Get-Module -ListAvailable -Name $Name |
     Select Name,Version |
```

```
    Add-Member -Name WhereRan `
               -Value $ENV:ComputerName `
               -MemberType NoteProperty -PassThru
  }
  Get-AvailableModule -Name "*power*"
}
```

You may think, "Well, that isn't too hard." But it's the users who have to do this themselves every time they run the function remotely, and they have to get it right themselves every time rather than having the function do it for them. Also, they have to hardcode the parameter. In most cases, users want to pass in the parameters themselves—mix that in with other complexities that we'll cover later, and the complexity keeps growing.

The function invocation in listing 1 produces the following result:

```
Name           : Microsoft.PowerShell.Diagnostics
Version        : 3.0.0.0
WhereRan       : BOOKBOX
PSComputerName : localhost
RunspaceId     : eb9bedcb-45b5-4050-90ad-803ae4198908

Name           : Microsoft.PowerShell.Host
Version        : 3.0.0.0
WhereRan       : BOOKBOX
PSComputerName : localhost
RunspaceId     : eb9bedcb-45b5-4050-90ad-803ae4198908
```

Note that remoting added a `PSComputerName` and `RunspaceId` to each object. Also, the `PSComputerName` is based on what you passed to `Invoke-Computer`, which in this case was `localhost`, and it differs from the name of the computer, which you populate with the `WhereRan` property.

The next step is adding the ability to pass your single parameter from your PowerShell environment to the remote environment.

The pain of increasing complexity

To add this functionality with `Invoke-Command`, you have the receiving script block accept parameters, and then pass all of your parameters as an array using the `-ArgumentList` parameter, as shown in the following listing.

Listing 2 Manual remoting with `-ArgumentList` parameter passing

```
Invoke-Command -ComputerName localhost -ScriptBlock {
  param(
    [string]$PassedName
  )
  function Get-AvailableModule([string]$Name = "*")
  {
   ...                                                    <- Removed for brevity
  }
  Get-AvailableModule -Name $PassedName
} -ArgumentList @("*power*")
```

NOTE You'll see lengthier listings throughout this chapter, so I may omit parts, such as in listing 2, if they've been shown in a previous listing or aren't germane.

In this listing you must accept a parameter in your script block and pass in the value through `-ArgumentList`. You may argue that this solution isn't too complex, but now you have three levels of script blocks in the mix and many things that can go wrong for an admin who wants to use your function. Additional complexities that you should be aware of include the following:

- Passing optional parameters
- Passing switches
- Passing script blocks
- Passing dependent functions
- Passing entire modules and saving to a temporary file on the target machine
- Passing dependent DLLs
- Checking for dependencies that should exist on the target machine

If users are dealing with issues related to this list of facets, they could spend many hours, or even a week, getting things in order to be able to call your function remotely. These are difficult challenges and some of them will require a lot of work to implement, but we can implement them once and the user can consume them often. It's a good economy of scale, and we can develop patterns and procedures that allow us to more quickly implement each additional function we wrap. We'll have to deal with these pains ourselves (covered later in the chapter) but in dealing with these pains, and abstracting these complexities ourselves, we simplify tasks for our users and solve the problem with our cost of development once, versus the user's cost of development every single time.

Defining the user experience

So far I've mentioned the user several times. What should their experience be like? Is the pattern I'm designing a good pattern or an antipattern? Does it leave a good code smell? Am I going with the grain of PowerShell or against it? These are important questions, and in this section, we'll look at PowerShell itself to help answer them.

It all starts with ComputerName

Previously I mentioned a partial list of cmdlets that have their own `-ComputerName` property. Many of these cmdlets existed before PowerShell remoting and use a remoting technology built into the underlying technology they expose, whether Windows processes, event logs, or WMI.

Run the following to get a list of these cmdlets:

```
Get-Command | where  {
  $_.Parameters | foreach { $_.keys -contains "ComputerName" }
  }
```

On my v3 machine, this command returns 38 cmdlets from the PowerShell built-in cmdlets. I'm not sure how well `ComputerName` is used in third-party cmdlets, whether Exchange, Hyper-V, SQL, or VMware. I know that some cmdlets have alternative ways to pass in a computer name: some use a fully qualified domain name (FQDN) as a different parameter, some cache the computer name, and some run only on the target machine. Also, topological complexities complicate the matter, such as with SharePoint, in which you aren't dealing with a flat list of computer names, but rather a structured topology of machines and roles. Based on the built-in cmdlets, however, you can infer that this is probably a good pattern.

Inspiration from Workflow

When determining whether we're designing a good pattern or an antipattern, another validation of our pattern comes from PowerShell Workflow (PSWF) in v3.

When you define a workflow in v3, PowerShell automatically generates a wrapper function and adds remoting-specific parameters. Let's create a simple workflow in v3:

```
workflow add( [int]$a, [int]$b){$a+$b}
```

When you call it, note that pressing the Tab key provides tab completion for a plethora of parameters, including `PSComputerName`. You can even run the following function:

```
PS C:\> add -PSComputerName BOOKBOX -a 5 -b 3
8
```

Holy guacamole, Batman! What manner of stealth is enabling such trickery? The workflows in PSWF, are, in fact, XAML-based Windows Workflow Foundation (WF) workflows. PowerShell creates a big wrapper around each, giving a consistent and predictable user experience. Sound familiar? Yes, that's the same goal we have. But what's this wrapper? And what parameters does it add?

`$function:add.ToString()` reveals the secret behind PSWF, and it's neither pithy nor pretty. In fact, for this simple one-line workflow, `$function:add.ToString().split('`n') | Measure-Object` reveals that the wrapped function is 480 lines long. As for the parameters, our two parameters get transformed into 32 lines of code per `(Get-Command Add).Parameters.Count`.

Parameters added to the PSWF remoting function are the following:

Parameter Names		
a	b	PSParameterCollection
PSComputerName	PSCredential	PSConnectionRetryCount
PSConnectionRetry-IntervalSec	PSRunningTimeoutSec	PSElapsedTimeoutSec
PSPersist	PSAuthentication	PSAuthenticationLevel
PSApplicationName	PSPort	PSUseSSL

Parameter Names (continued)		
PSConfigurationName	PSConnectionURI	PSAllowRedirection
PSSessionOption	PSCertificateThumbprint	PSPrivateMetadata
AsJob	JobName	InputObject
Verbose	Debug	ErrorAction
WarningAction	ErrorVariable	WarningVariable
OutVariable	OutBuffer	

Some, such as `ErrorAction`, are the ubiquitous parameters added to any advanced function. Others are specific to PSWF, such as `PSPersist`, but many of them are related to remoting. An interesting thing to note is that while `Invoke-Command` has parameters such as `ComputerName` and `Authentication`, the remoting wrapper function has `PSComputerName` and `PSAuthentication`. Which convention should we use? The burden of quantity in the built-in cmdlets lends itself to `ComputerName`. Also, understanding the reason why PSWF uses `PS*` helps cement the decision. PSWF prepends `PS` because it's wrapping *your* functions, and it doesn't want to risk a conflict between the user's own parameters and those it autogenerates. In this case, however, you're sculpting your own function from beginning to end, so using the same remoting parameters that `Invoke-Command` uses is the most predictable and consistent approach.

Another interesting parameter that PSWF adds is the `AsJob` switch. Though not covered in this chapter, I think it would be perfect for this pattern: a function that can run locally, on remote machines, and as a background job!

The PSWF takeaway is even more amazing than what we're doing. You not only can consume but also author the workflow in a user-friendly experience. The tips and tricks in this chapter will teach you to be effective and efficient in producing automatic remoting-enabled cmdlets; you may even decide to build your own functions that can automatically wrap any function.

Is ComputerName alone sufficient?

Is supporting `ComputerName` alone sufficient? I once thought so until I inherited a function that supported it, but I needed to specify a nonstandard PowerShell remoting endpoint and then call it with Credential Security Support Provider (CredSSP) authentication with an alternative credential. This function had automatic remoting but only supported `ComputerName`, so for my needs it was a hindrance and not a help. To make automatic remoting useful we need to support the full surface area of remoting as `Invoke-Command` does.

Of parameters and parameter sets

Since we agree that `Invoke-Command` is our model, we want functional and parameter parity with it. What are the parameters and parameter sets of `Invoke-Command`? In v2 there are 28 parameters and 32 in v3. While we want to target v2 here, you could write clever code that also supports v3 parameters and throws errors if running under v2.

The remaining parameters, barring the ubiquitous parameters, are listed below.

Parameter Names		
`Session`	`ComputerName`	`Credential`
`Port`	`UseSSL`	`ConfiguationName`
`ApplicationName`	`ThrottleLimit`	`ConnectionUri`
`AsJob`	`HideComputerName`	`JobName`
`ScriptBlock`	`FilePath`	`AllowRedirection`
`SessionOption`	`Authentication`	`InputObject`
`ArgumentList`	`CertificateThumbprint`	

That's 20 parameters, but you won't need several of them:

- `FilePath` isn't relevant.
- `ScriptBlock` isn't necessary because you're effectively supplying that.
- `InputObject` is up to you and depends on whether you're building the function to support pipeline input, which, in this case, we aren't doing at first, so that can be scrapped.
- `ArgumentList` is redundant because you'll have explicit parameters and take care of passing them to the script that does the remote work for you.
- `AsJob` is twofold; although you want to support it for remoting, which is the only context for `Invoke-Command`, the design pattern you're implementing also uses it locally. You therefore need to call `Start-Job` internally instead of `Invoke-Command` when running locally.

That leaves us with 15 core parameters that seem essential to support full-spectrum remoting with the v2 feature set plus `-AsJob`.

To double-check, let's compare this list with the parameters in the PSWF wrapper. The Workflow wrapper adds many `PS*` parameters for its own reasons, with the exception of ThrottleLimit, Session, and HideComputerName. Keep this in mind as we proceed.

Next, we'll look at parameter sets. `Invoke-Command` has seven. Suppose you're wrapping something that already has three parameter sets; the combinatorial complexity would demand 21 parameter sets. If that were the case, you'd want to follow the example of the wrapper function that PSWF sets, where it has all of these parameters and more and uses only one parameter set. However, the PSWF wrapper code has more than 200 lines of code that work out the correct combinations of parameters. Since your function has only one parameter set to start with, use the seven parameter sets of `Invoke-Command`, and strip out what doesn't make sense for you.

Implementing your solution

Now that you understand how PSWF operates, let's get to work. To help build the scaffolding for your function we'll use another nifty PowerShell feature: proxy functions. The code in the next listing saves a proxy function, which wraps `Invoke-Command`, to your hard drive. The great thing about this is it also utilizes steppable pipelines, which allows you to implement pipeline-streamable functions if you so desire.

Listing 3 Generate proxy function from `Invoke-Command`

```
$MetaData = New-Object System.Management.Automation.CommandMetaData (
  Get-Command  Invoke-Command)
$proxy = [System.Management.Automation.ProxyCommand]::Create($MetaData)
$proxy | out-file -width 500 c:\temp\invoke-commandproxy.ps1
```

This proxy function produces an advanced-function styled script block that is approximately 200 lines long and uses steppable pipelines. It has a number of parameters and seven parameter sets. What do you do with this code? First, make it look like your function, which involves removing the parameters that you don't want or need and adding your own parameters, which in this case is only one: `-Name`. This poor script block is also "orphaned," so we'll give it a home by wrapping it in a function declaration.

Let's start with some pruning. To customize the proxy function, first determine which parameters you can omit:

- To run your function remotely, you'll pass it to `Invoke-Command` as a script block, so you can get rid of all the parameter sets that are related to running a file: `FilePathUri`, `FilePathComputerName`, and `FilePathRunspace`.

You've almost halved the parameter sets already. Now let's get to the parameters.

- Remove `FilePath` for the same previous file-related reason.
- Remove the four v3-only parameters.

  You could support these if you want to support v3 only, or you could implement some clever techniques to gracefully degrade or error out, but for this chapter, remove them.
- Also remove `InDisconnectedSession`, `SessionName`, `NoNewScope`, and `EnableNetworkAccess`.
- Although `ScriptBlock` and `ArgumentList` are important, you'll provide these internally to `Invoke-Command`, so they can be demoted from a parameter to an implementation detail.
- Finally, remove some autogenerated PowerShell help-related info and links.

All of this pruning makes room to add your own parameter, the core parameter of your own function: `-Name`. The start of your function now looks like the following listing.

Listing 4 Start of outer function

```
function Get-AvailableModule {
[CmdletBinding(DefaultParameterSetName='InProcess')]
param(

    [Parameter(ParameterSetName='InProcess',Position=0)]
    [Parameter(ParameterSetName='Uri',Position=1)]
    [Parameter(ParameterSetName='ComputerName',Position=1)]
    [Parameter(ParameterSetName='Session',Position=1)]
    [string]$Name = "*",

    [Parameter(ParameterSetName='Session', Position=0)]
    [ValidateNotNullOrEmpty()]
    [System.Management.Automation.Runspaces.PSSession[]]
    ${Session}
    ...                                                      <- Truncated
```

If you run the function as is, it's going to break because you don't yet have any of your own logic in it, and the inner call to `Invoke-Command` doesn't yet provide any script block to run.

Inner and outer functions and script blocks

I used to confuse myself and colleagues by talking about local functions and remote functions. Is the remote function the code that's running on the target machine? Or is it the function that's doing the remoting? Is the local function running locally where you're running it from (which is local to you), or local where it's affecting the system?

Now, for lack of a better set of words, I call them the *inner* and *outer* functions. The inner function is what does the work, running on the specific machine. It knows nothing of `Invoke-Command` or remoting. The outer function wraps the inner function and enables the remoting or job invoking.

The outer function is the user experience, and it abstracts the complexity of PowerShell remoting, whereas the inner function is simple, knows only the machine it runs on, and contains the "business logic" for what you're doing.

In this case, the start of the outer function is shown in listing 4; the inner function was introduced previously. We'll leave the outer function with the name `Get-AvailableModule` because it's the user experience. We'll rename the inner function to `Get-InnerAvailableModule` because the user never sees or experiences this function.

Inserting the inner function and making it work

The generated proxy wrapper of `Invoke-Command` has code inside the `begin`, `process`, and `end` blocks. The `begin` is where the proxy function sets up the steppable pipeline, and this is where you insert your function and pass your own argument (`Name`) to `Invoke-Command`.

Let's look at the `begin` block before and after round one of our makeover; the following listing shows the block before we insert the inner function.

Listing 5 Process block: before

```
begin
{
  try {
      $outBuffer = $null
      if ($PSBoundParameters.TryGetValue(
            'OutBuffer', [ref]$outBuffer))
      {
          $PSBoundParameters['OutBuffer'] = 1
      }
      $wrappedCmd = $ExecutionContext.InvokeCommand.GetCommand(
        'Invoke-Command',
        [System.Management.Automation.CommandTypes]::Cmdlet)
      $scriptCmd = {& $wrappedCmd @PSBoundParameters }        ❶ Invokes wrapped command
      $steppablePipeline = $scriptCmd.GetSteppablePipeline(
        $myInvocation.CommandOrigin)
      $steppablePipeline.Begin($PSCmdlet)
  } catch {
      throw
  }
}
```

The trick here is where `ScriptCmd` is invoking the wrapped command and *splatting* `PSBoundParameters` ❶.

DEFINITION *Splatting* is a PowerShell feature added in v2 that allows you to pass a hash table in as a parameter to a function or script block.

To insert the inner function, you modify the hash table of bound parameters that gets splatted. Pass the function as a script block and the name parameter as an argument, as shown in the following listing.

Listing 6 Process block: after

```
begin
{
  function Get-InnerAvailableModule([string]$Name = "*")      ❶ Inner function
  {
     Get-Module -ListAvailable -Name $Name |
     Select Name,Version |
     Add-Member -Name WhereRan `
                -Value $ENV:ComputerName `
                -MemberType NoteProperty -PassThru
  }

  try {
      $outBuffer = $null
      if ($PSBoundParameters.TryGetValue(
            'OutBuffer', [ref]$outBuffer))
      {
```

```
            $PSBoundParameters['OutBuffer'] = 1
        }
        $wrappedCmd = $ExecutionContext.InvokeCommand.GetCommand(
          'Invoke-Command',
          [System.Management.Automation.CommandTypes]::Cmdlet)

        $NameToPass= $Name
        $null = $PSBoundParameters.Remove("Name")
        $PSBoundParameters.Add("Scriptblock",
              ${function:Get-InnerAvailableModule})
        $PSBoundParameters.Add("ArgumentList",@($nametopass))

        $scriptCmd = {& $wrappedCmd @PSBoundParameters }
        $steppablePipeline = $scriptCmd.GetSteppablePipeline(
          $myInvocation.CommandOrigin)
        $steppablePipeline.Begin($PSCmdlet)
    } catch {
        throw
    }
}
```

❷ Backs up and removes parameters

❸ Passes inner function to Invoke-Command

❹ Passes arguments to Invoke-Command

The first thing you'll notice is that inside the `begin` block I've embedded a fully named function inside the code ❶, which I reference as `${function:Get-InnerAvailableModule}` when I pass it to `Invoke-Command` ❸. Many people declare the embedded function as a script block variable with `$sb = { param(x,y,z) ...}`. When writing distributed code, however, I find that giving the function a name based on a naming convention makes it easier to work out what code is running locally and what code is running remote.

Because the proxy code splats `Invoke-Command` with `$PSBoundParameters`, and our own `Name` parameter isn't a valid parameter for `Invoke-Command`, I have to remove it from `$PSBoundParameters` ❷, but I back it up to another variable so that I can pass it in the `ArgumentList` parameter ❹.

Does it work?

Testing your solution

Grab the full source for listing 6 from www.manning.com/hicks/ to run a few examples. First, run it without parameters:

```
PS C:\>Get-AvailableModule

Name                      Version                   WhereRan
----                      -------                   --------
BitLocker                 1.0.0.0                   BOOKBOX
BitsTransfer              1.0.0.0                   BOOKBOX
...
```

It ran locally here. How is that when we didn't add any code to check for local and run it locally? Well, `Invoke-Command` itself has that ability, and the `InProcess` parameter set of both `Invoke-Command` and the proxy-derived function is called. If you want to add local machine `AsJob` support, then have your own parameter set and conditionally have your own code run it locally.

We didn't add all of this infrastructure to run it locally, so let's run it remotely and target more than one machine at the same time.

Pass in the name parameter positional to make sure the parameter sets are working, and pass in a list of two computers as the computer name:

```
PS C:\>Get-AvailableModule branch* -ComputerName localhost,BOOKBOX

Name           : BranchCache
Version        : 1.0.0.0
WhereRan       : BOOKBOX
PSComputerName : localhost
RunspaceId     : ba92ad8f-c11f-4832-b35d-97ecd708a520

Name           : BranchCache
Version        : 1.0.0.0
WhereRan       : BOOKBOX
PSComputerName : BOOKBOX
RunspaceId     : 8da7bc35-5338-48d5-85d0-f5bb429588ab
```

You use loopback remoting on the same computer for this example, but you can see that it ran on those machines, with the true computer name specified in the WhereRan property and what you passed specified in the PSComputerName.

Feel free to play with all of the parameters and parameter sets, using credentials, different authentications, and sessions. In fact, if you were building production code, you'd want to build unit tests around all of those different parameters and parameter sets.

Making it more standard

To get that first function out the door, I added a few bad code smells. Your eventual goal is to have a pattern that's so consistent, using a technique similar to proxy functions, that you can generate a wrapper around any function. (We won't deliver an autogenerated wrapper solution in this book.) The main problem is that the code is specific to the script block, with the arguments list containing the one specific parameter relevant to your code.

Let's pass a different "generic" script block that takes the script block as a parameter and then a hash table of arguments to splat. This helps get around the limitations of the ArgumentList parameter, which flattens the dynamic PowerShell mix of named and positional parameters and forces all parameters to be positional.

This process may get confusing because your main function already wraps a proxy, to which you then pass your "inner" function. Now you'll pass a different script block to be run remotely, and then pass your inner function to that as a parameter. It's like the matrix inside the matrix, so let's let the code in the following listing do the talking.

Listing 7 Process block: revised

```
begin
{
  function Get-InnerAvailableModule([string]$Name = "*")
```

```
{
 #in previous listings
}
try {
    $outBuffer = $null
    if ($PSBoundParameters.TryGetValue('OutBuffer',
        [ref]$outBuffer))
    {
        $PSBoundParameters['OutBuffer'] = 1
    }
    $wrappedCmd = $ExecutionContext.InvokeCommand.GetCommand(
        'Invoke-Command',
        [System.Management.Automation.CommandTypes]::Cmdlet)
    $null = $PSBoundParameters.Remove("Name")
    $RemoteScriptBlock = {
      param($scriptblockToRun, [hashtable]$arguments)
        $scriptblockToRun = [scriptblock]::Create($scriptblockToRun)
        &$scriptblockToRun @arguments
    }
    $Arguments = @{name = $Name}
    $PSBoundParameters.Add("Scriptblock",$RemoteScriptBlock )
    $PSBoundParameters.Add("ArgumentList",
      @(${function:Get-InnerAvailableModule},$Arguments ))
    $scriptCmd = {& $wrappedCmd @PSBoundParameters }
...
```

Annotations: Removed for brevity (previous listings); 1 New remote workhorse ($RemoteScriptBlock); Passes arguments as hash table to splat ($Arguments); Passes new workhorse (Scriptblock); Script block is an argument (ArgumentList); Removed for brevity (...).

You now have a generic `$RemoteScriptBlock` to which you pass your own payload. The remote script block can take any script block and any hash table of parameters ❶. One thing to note is the use of `[scriptblock]::Create()`. Although PowerShell serializes and deserializes many types over the remoting wire successfully, it sends script blocks as strings, so you have to turn it back into a script block on the target machine to execute it.

Before we move on to the pipeline, grab the full source for this listing (www.manning.com/hicks/), and run some examples against it to make sure everything is working.

Enabling pipeline support

The pipeline is key to PowerShell, and, shame on us, this current example doesn't support it. Not to worry, though, let's jump through some hoops and get it working. You'll wire the `Name` parameter so that it can be accepted in the pipeline. The first step, shown here, is to give the `$Name` parameter the ability to accept the value from the pipeline in all parameter sets:

```
[Parameter(ParameterSetName='InProcess',Position=0,
           ValueFromPipeline=$true)]
[Parameter(ParameterSetName='Uri',Position=1,
           ValueFromPipeline=$true)]
[Parameter(ParameterSetName='ComputerName',Position=1,
           ValueFromPipeline=$true)]
[Parameter(ParameterSetName='Session',Position=1,
           ValueFromPipeline=$true)]
[string]$Name = "*"
```

That only allows the data to be piped in. Now you need to process it and make sure it works remotely. The inner function isn't pipeline-friendly, either; no matter what plumbing you do, you won't get pipelining. The following listing shows how to get the inner function working with the pipeline.

Listing 8 Pipeline-enabled inner function

```
function Get-InnerAvailableModule(
  [Parameter(ValueFromPipeline = $true)]      <- Adds ability to accept pipeline input
  [string]$Name = "*"
  )
 { process                                    <- Moves logic into process block
   {
     Get-Module -ListAvailable -Name $Name |
     Select Name,Version |
     Add-Member -Name WhereRan `
                -Value $ENV:ComputerName `
                -MemberType NoteProperty -PassThru
   }
 }
```

To test the listed function that now supports pipelined input, run the following command:

```
PS C:\>"br*","v*" | Get-InnerAvailableModule
Name                      Version                   WhereRan
----                      -------                   --------
BranchCache               1.0.0.0                   BOOKBOX
VpnClient                 1.0.0.0                   BOOKBOX
```

Now you can put the inner function back in the main function; however, you first need to modify the remote script block. To stream the data into your function, update the remote script block, as shown in the following listing.

Listing 9 Updated remote script block

```
$RemoteScriptBlock = {
  param($scriptblockToRun, [hashtable]$arguments)
    $scriptblockToRun = [scriptblock]::Create($scriptblockToRun)
    if($input) {                                  <- 1 Processes differently if piped data
        $arguments.remove("Name")
        $input | &$scriptblockToRun @arguments    <- 2 Pipes in $input
      }
    else {
       &$scriptblockToRun @arguments              <- 3 Processes without pipeline data
    }
}
```

Here we've broken our "generic" remote script block goal by specifying to remove the `Name` parameter. With a bit more work, you could make this updated block generic again.

In this case, the code behaves differently if data is piped in. In ❶, you're testing whether the built-in PowerShell variable `$Input` has a value or not. If it does, there is pipeline input, and you want to pipe data in and remove the `Name` parameter ❷ or binding will fail. Otherwise, you invoke the script block as you did previously ❸.

Go ahead and grab the full source for listing 9 and run the following test:

```
PS C:\>"br*","v*" | Get-AvailableModule -ComputerName localhost
```

And we have results:

```
Name           : BranchCache
Version        : 1.0.0.0
WhereRan       : BOOKBOX
PSComputerName : localhost
RunspaceId     : 06a4479b-ca67-42a3-8798-349c960f628c

Name           : VpnClient
Version        : 1.0.0.0
WhereRan       : BOOKBOX
PSComputerName : localhost
RunspaceId     : 06a4479b-ca67-42a3-8798-349c960f628c
```

Take a look at the following example, for which I won't show the results, and observe the pattern in action. With this pattern, combined with some awesome engineering in PowerShell remoting and `Invoke-Command`, you can achieve the epitome of distributed asynchronous coolness:

```
"secureboot","NetSecurity","wdac","WindowsDeveloperLicense" |
foreach {sleep 10  ;$_} |
Get-AvailableModule -ComputerName localhost,bookbox |
foreach { write-host -fore red "amazing" ; $_ }
```

What's going on here? Well, it's pipeline and fan-out remoting on steroids. You pass in data to remoting, use the sleep loop to delay the input, fan-out to two computers, and then process the results asynchronously as they come in.

Read that again.

First, `secureboot` is sent to both computers, which process it in their own time. As soon as they get the data, it's streamed back to you and travels along the pipeline, where you output it to the screen with the word "amazing." All the while, more data is going every 10 seconds to each computer, and it carries on until it's all done. Typically, this sort of fan-out—asynchronously processed and received—is rare and difficult to pull off in most languages and frameworks. Here, it flows naturally like a normal pipeline, and there are no complex callbacks.

Dealing with the real world and gotchas

In the real world, you often have dependencies that don't fit so nicely inside your inner script block, and this is when the pattern seems to break down.

Accommodating PowerShell versions

With remoting, you'll be dealing with PowerShell v2 and v3. Your code may require v3 on the target machine, or it may be required to run as 32-bit or 64-bit. If so, you'll have the privilege, or rather pain, of finding out whether the target machine is running a compatible version or bitness. You may choose to throw an error, if appropriate, or start a job in another PowerShell version or bitness.

Dealing with modules

If your code depends on a third-party module to preexist on a destination machine, then you can check for it. You'll have to load the module or Snap-In inside your inner function. You can fail gracefully with an error if it doesn't exist, but the command may still succeed on other machines.

If the module is one of your own or you're responsible for it being on the target machine, then you have a more difficult challenge. For example, in a corporate LAN environment, I've often coded my inner function to test whether the module exists and whether it's the latest version. If not, the function copies it from a network share to the destination machine. But this approach doesn't work over URLs, and you must have a share that can be read by the user the script is running under. If possible, you can convert a script module into a dynamic module and include it in the inner function.

Another approach I've taken is to pass in all text-based module files as strings through arguments. Then I write them to a temporary folder on the destination machine and load the module from there, cleaning up afterward. This allows you to skip copying, but your script payload and network traffic can get large, depending on the module size. In the context of remoting, this is often a negligible overhead. If it's a binary module, or you depend on a binary DLL, then you have an extra challenge, which is explained next.

Streaming binary DLLs to the target server

This common scenario often causes a lot of pain, and developers end up requiring that modules and DLLs be installed on all destination computers, negating the benefits of central administration using this pattern.

I approach this issue with a three-step process:

1. Encode the DLL in a Base64 string.
2. Pass the resulting string as part of my script to the target computer.
3. Load the DLL from a byte stream.

If, however, you're dealing with multiple DLLs that depend on each other, you'll have to stream it over, save the DLLs to a temporary folder, and load them from there.

To demo this, we'll invent an unlikely scenario: suppose that for some manufactured reason, you won't trust PowerShell to do your math, so you take an already-compiled C# Assembly project and run a script on it to preprocess it into Base64 so it can be included in the text of the PowerShell function. It's then passed via remoting to the target computer, where it's unencoded and loaded directly into the memory, as shown in the following code:

```
using System;
namespace AddDLL
{
    public class AddClass
    {
        public static int Add(int a, int b)
        {
            return (a + b);
        }
    }
}
```

After you compile the C# DLL in Visual Studio you can process the resultant DLL into a Base64-encoded string (step 1):

```
[byte[]]$Data = Get-Content "C:\temp\add.dll" -Encoding Byte
[system.convert]::ToBase64String($Data) | `
Set-Content c:\temp\encoded.txt
```

Now you have a 4KB DLL encoded into a 6KB string that is on one single line. You could add extra logic to insert carriage returns into the string and remove them during decoding if you wish.

Let's take this string and inline it into the function (step 2):

```
function Add-InnerNumber($a,$b)
{
 $code = 'TVqQAAMAAAAEAAAA//8AALgAAAAAAAAA...'          <-- Truncated for space
 $ByteArray = [System.Convert]::FromBase64String($code);
[System.Reflection.Assembly]::Load($bytearray) | out-null
[AddDLL.AddClass]::Add($a,$b)
}
Add-InnerNumber 4 5
```

The `$code` line in the real listing is more than 5,000 characters wide, but it's a complete example of embedding a DLL in a function, and this function can be sent remotely in the same manner as the previous examples. For the sake of space I'm not going to wrap this in a complete automatic remoting-enabled function. In this example, you take the Base64-encoded DLL, decode it, then load it into memory and test it (step 3).

Making your cmdlets production-ready

You now have a strategy for wrapping a function so that it has automatic fan-out remoting abilities without having to install anything custom on your target machines. The wrapped function also supports pipeline streaming and some DLL dependencies. Still, you need to address the following issues before selling the result of your labor and retiring in the Caribbean:

- Although it's unlikely you have one function that lives in isolation, I suggest that you wrap it all up in a module. This module doesn't get installed on the target machines; it's where the module runs from.
- Implementing comprehensive help that includes examples and full details for each parameter is essential to producing a useable and marketable module.

- If you plan on selling your module or using it in a well-controlled corporate environment, I strongly recommend signing your script, too.
- Parameter validation is another area to master. `-Confirm` and `-WhatIf` support is common in well-written PowerShell functions, and how you deal with those over the remoting boundary is a challenge with some interesting facets.
- As always, error handling is a big deal. Be aware that PowerShell transforms terminating errors into nonterminating errors when they cross the remoting boundary.

"Protecting" intellectual property and positioning your module as a product

With scripts, and even .NET in general, it's hard, or even impossible, to fully "protect" your intellectual property from a technical perspective. Reverse engineering is almost always possible; it's just a matter of how much effort is required. Our goal is to make it difficult enough that 90 percent of people won't bother. Scripts often yell "don't buy me, copy and paste me" to one set of audiences, and "tweak me, but still blame the author when I don't work anymore" to others. To get around this, I use a few obfuscation techniques:

- I encode the begin, end, and process blocks of my function as Base64. (Sometimes I may add some true encryption and a few other things to discourage somebody by having them jump through one-too-many steps to get the code.)
- I then decode the string, create a script block, and dot source it.
- After that, I sign the script, which discourages tampering even further.

Here is a small but complete example with one function:

```
function say-hello($name)
{
 "hello $name"
}
```

I take the body and encode it as Base64:

```
$sb = { "hello $name" }
$bytes  = [System.Text.Encoding]::UTF8.GetBytes([string]$sb);
[System.Convert]::ToBase64String($bytes);
```

This results in a nice small string `"ICJoZWxsbyAkbmFtZSIg"`, though in the real world, this would be large, and you'd likely need to update the algorithm to add carriage returns every so many characters.

To execute the encoded body of script, I update my function to decode the string, create a script block, and execute it:

```
function say-hello($name)
{
  $sb ='ICJoZWxsbyAkbmFtZSIg'
  . ([scriptblock]::Create(
        [System.Text.Encoding]::UTF8.GetString(
            [System.Convert]::FromBase64String($sb)
```

```
            )
        )
    )
}
say-hello "it works"
```

Use these obfuscation techniques to protect your code when it goes out into the world.

Summary

There you have it, now go and build some great functions, add automatic remoting, document them, wrap them in a module, add `-whatif` support, make sure error handling is excellent, obfuscate your logic, sign your scripts, and start selling them.

You may be thinking that Mr. X and Company Y won't buy a script module no matter what. And it's true, some organizations won't pay for scripts and won't trust scripts, but they'll happily trust a binary, despite both entities running under the same user credentials with the same permissions. Also, some entities won't trust DLLs or executables but will happily trust a script module. Maybe you'll have to cater to both audiences. You can take the script assets you've developed here and go a step further and wrap them in C# binary cmdlets inside a binary module, but that's an adventure for another day.

About the author

Karl Prosser, a PowerShell MVP since 2007, founded Shell Tools LLC, which developed the first PowerShell IDE—PowerShell Analyzer, and then later PowerShell Plus. He also developed Portable PowerShell, and in recent years he's used PowerShell as part of his toolkit in helping to automate the Office 365 infrastructure for Microsoft.

22 Taming software builds (and other complicated processes) with psake

Jim Christopher

Managing the build for a software project has a lot in common with a child trying to tell a lie. The build and the lie both start as deceptively simple things, but over time missing details are added that demand more scrutiny. As the build (or the lie) expands to sustain itself, the likelihood of a catastrophic failure increases significantly. For both the build master and the child, the consequences of such a failure can be severe.

I learned long ago the fundamental nature of any lie, but only recently have I drawn the same conclusion about build systems: there's no such thing as a perfect one. The build needs to grow along with the project, swallowing up manual processes and digesting them into an ever-expanding battery of reports and artifacts. Adequate build systems encourage this type of growth; the better ones do it without getting in the way. This chapter introduces you to one of these better build systems: the psake PowerShell module.

NOTE *psake* is pronounced like *sake* (the Japanese rice wine). It doesn't rhyme with *make* as you might expect.

Complexity abounds in our field, and as simple as it is, psake will likely have you reconsidering your approach to many forms of automation. I find that the task-oriented nature of psake and its simple integration with PowerShell lend it to many situations: provisioning virtual machines, scripting upgrades of versioned databases, even generating boilerplate Visual Studio projects for a new client.

Building software

The point of any build system is to automate software production as much as possible. This may start with a compiler slurping up some source files and spitting out some form of binary output, but it doesn't end there.

One of the more complicated builds I've been charged with was able to accomplish the following steps without user intervention:

1. Compile a moderately large code base into several hundred assemblies
2. Execute a battery of unit tests against the assemblies
3. Email a report of the unit test results to the development team
4. Package the assemblies into a Microsoft Windows Installer (MSI) file
5. Package the assemblies and the MSI into a zip archive
6. Copy the archive to a release point on the network
7. Spool a virtual machine inside the quality assurance (QA) environment
8. Deploy and install the MSI onto the virtual machine
9. Execute a battery of integration tests on the QA virtual machine
10. Email a report of the integration test results to the development and QA teams
11. Create a manifest of assembly digital signatures and store them in a database
12. Produce a deployment image to be delivered to industry regulators for approval

The workflow continues from there, but you get the idea. The point is that the build has almost nothing to do with the creation of *binaries*, but rather the production of *software*—creating, verifying, and tracking a deliverable release candidate. Consider the list of technologies touched in this build workflow: the compiler, the file system, the network, the virtualization server, the database, email, and multiple proprietary file formats. Clicking either Rebuild All or Publish in Visual Studio doesn't get you far down this path. It's only a first step—albeit a necessary one—in the software production process.

In this light, driving a software build doesn't demand new tooling as much as it demands glue for tools that already work well. MSBuild does fine at wrapping the compiler to make binaries. Hyper-V does a great job of managing virtual machines. SQL is great at storing stuff. The build needs a way to make these things work together with as little friction as possible.

psake helps PowerShell become the glue for these tools so you can do wonderful things more easily. Driving a build with psake makes it easy to automate functionality anywhere in the software development cycle.

Introducing psake

The psake module uses PowerShell semantics to create a domain-specific language for build scripts. The syntax of a psake script is inspired largely by other scripted build systems like Ruby's Rake (see http://rake.rubyforge.org).

psake is an open source project hosted on GitHub at https://github.com/psake/psake. In addition, a psake-contrib sister project (https://github.com/psake/psake-contrib) exists to capture useful applications of psake, such as source control or continuous integration interfaces.

NOTE At the time of this writing psake is at version 4.2.0. If you find yourself using a newer version, consult the official project wiki at https://github.com/psake/psake/wiki and the included module help for the latest project information.

Installing psake

To install psake

1. Download the zip file of the project from https://github.com/psake/psake-contrib/zipball/master.
2. Unblock the downloaded zip file. You can do this manually by right-clicking the zip file in Windows Explorer, selecting Properties, and then clicking the Unblock button. You can do this at the console using the `unblock-file` command available in PowerShell v3; or, if you're using v2, this command is also available in the PowerShell Community Extensions module (available at http://pscx.codeplex.com).
3. Extract the zip archive into a folder named psake on your PowerShell Module path. Most commonly this will be My Documents\Windows PowerShell\Modules\psake. If you're unsure about your module path you can find it in the value of the `PSModulePath` environment variable: `$env:psmodulepath`.
4. Verify the module install by running the following command in a fresh PowerShell console: `import-module psake`. If you receive an error indicating that the psake module couldn't be located, double-check that the psake folder is located on your module path.

psake commands

Once you have psake installed, open a new shell and import the psake module. Use the `get-command` PowerShell cmdlet to check out the commands available in the module:

```
PS C:\> import-module psake
PS C:\> get-command -module psake

CommandType     Name                              Definition
-----------     ----                              ----------
Function        Assert                            ...
Function        Exec                              ...
Function        FormatTaskName                    ...
Function        Framework                         ...
Function        Include                           ...
Function        Invoke-psake                      ...
Function        Invoke-Task                       ...
Function        Properties                        ...
```

```
Function        Task                          ...
Function        TaskSetup                     ...
Function        TaskTearDown                  ...
```

Only two of the eleven commands exposed by psake conform to the PowerShell `verb-noun` convention: `invoke-psake` and `invoke-task`. These two commands provide the means to *execute* a build script; the other nine commands comprise the domain language you use to *define* a build script.

psake build scripts

A psake build script is nothing more than a PowerShell script that uses commands exposed by the psake module; these scripts capture build workflows as a set of named *tasks*. Each task isolates one small part of the build as a piece of PowerShell code. For example, the following listing contains a simple psake build script that defines four build tasks.

Listing 1 A minimal psake build script

```
task -name Build -action { write-host 'running task build' }

task -name Clean -action { write-host 'running task clean' }

task -name Rebuild -depends Clean,Build -action {
    write-host 'running task rebuild'
};

task -name default -depends Build;
```

Each task is given a name using the `-name` parameter: `Build`, `Clean`, `Rebuild`, and `default`. The `Build`, `Clean`, and `Rebuild` tasks contain instructions in the form of script blocks passed in the `-action` parameter. You can almost read the task declaration as plain English: "For task `Build`, do the action `{ write-host 'running task build' }`."

NOTE Use the psake `task` statement to define a new build task.

In addition to an `-action` script block, the `Rebuild` task declares that it's dependent on the `Clean` and `Build` tasks by listing their names in the `-depends` parameter. This means that `Rebuild` won't run until the `Clean` and `Build` tasks have run first. The `default` task is special. First, it's required—every psake script must contain a task named `default` to avoid an error when the build is run. In addition, the `default` task isn't allowed to have an action; it may only declare dependencies on other tasks.

NOTE Always include a task named `default` in your psake build script.

TIP The parameter names for the `-name` and `-action` parameters of the task command are optional. You may find the more concise task declaration an easier read: `task Build { write-host 'running task build' }`.

Running the build script

You use the psake module command `invoke-psake` to run a psake build script. Let's say the build script in listing 1 is saved to the file listing_1.ps1. To run the script, import the psake module and call the `invoke-psake` command, passing the path of the script in the `-buildfile` parameter, like this:

```
PS C:\> import-module psake
PS C:\> invoke-psake -buildfile .\listing_1.ps1
psake version 4.2.0
Copyright (c) 2010 James Kovacs

Executing Build
running task build

Build Succeeded!
```

NOTE To run a build script, use the psake module command `invoke-psake`.

TIP The `-buildfile` parameter is optional. If unspecified, psake looks for a build script named default.ps1 in the current directory.

Did you notice that only the `Build` task is executed? Because you didn't specify which task(s) to run when you called `invoke-psake`, the `default` task is executed. In this build script the `default` task depends on the `Build` task, so that's the only task run.

You can list specific task names to execute in the `-task` parameter of `invoke-psake`. For example, to run the `Rebuild` task defined in our build script try the following:

```
PS C:\> invoke-psake -buildfile .\listing_1.ps1 -task rebuild
psake version 4.2.0
Copyright (c) 2010 James Kovacs

Executing Clean
clean
Executing Build
build
Executing rebuild
rebuild

Build Succeeded!
```

You invoked the `Rebuild` task, but the `Clean` and `Build` tasks ran first, as `Rebuild` depends on these other tasks. `Invoke-psake` ensures that those dependent tasks have been run before the target task is executed. These dependent tasks are executed in the order they are listed in the task `-depends` parameter.

This doesn't mean that running `Rebuild` will always run `Clean` and `Build`. Only dependent tasks that haven't already executed are run. If you run the `Build` task manually before trying to run `Rebuild`, `invoke-psake` won't run the `Build` task more than once:

```
PS C:\> invoke-psake -buildfile .\listing_1.ps1 -task build,rebuild
psake version 4.2.0
Copyright (c) 2010 James Kovacs
```

```
Executing build
build
Executing Clean
clean
Executing rebuild
rebuild

Build Succeeded!
```

Build task executed once, explicitly

Clean task executed once, as a dependency

This implies two important things about psake tasks:

- Each task will execute *at most* one time per build, regardless of how often it's depended upon by other tasks.
- The ordering of task execution is contingent on the task dependency tree and the task names passed to `invoke-psake`.

Keep these things in mind when breaking apart your build process into tasks.

Building Visual Studio projects

It's time to build some code. Listing 2 defines the build for a Visual Studio project named MyProject. For your purposes, the type of project isn't relevant—MyProject could be a class library, web application, Windows Presentation Foundation (WPF) client, or whatever.

Listing 2 MyProject build script

```
task -name Build -action {
    exec {
        msbuild ./MyProject/MyProject.csproj /t:Build
    }
}

task -name Clean -action {
    exec {
        msbuild ./MyProject/MyProject.csproj /t:Clean
    }
}

task -name Rebuild -depends Clean,Build;
task -name Default -depends Build;
```

Wrap console commands in `exec` to handle exit codes

The `Build` and `Clean` tasks delegate to the MSBuild command-line tool to perform their respective actions. The psake `exec` command transforms unsuccessful exit codes from old-school console applications like MSBuild into first-class PowerShell errors. If the MSBuild commands fail, `exec` will raise an error. Without the `exec` wrapper the MSBuild command could fail without stopping the build, resulting in the `Rebuild` task trying to `Build` after a failed `Clean`, which is certainly not what you want to happen.

NOTE Use the psake `exec` statement to wrap any calls to native applications that use exit codes, so they can correctly interact with the psake build process.

Isn't that cheating?

You may call foul on the fact that I had you delegate build logic from your psake script to Microsoft's build tool, MSBuild. As I stated in the beginning of this chapter, psake isn't a replacement for your existing tools. It's a way to glue them together and extend their reach.

You're also free to point out that MSBuild is an extensible build system, but it's hardly a simple process. Consider the workflow for creating a custom task for an MSBuild script:

1. Stop what you're working on and open another Visual Studio project.
2. Define the new MSBuild task in managed code.
3. Build the task assembly and copy it into your original project tree.
4. Edit the XML for your project file to import the assembly containing your build task.
5. Add your custom MSBuild task XML element(s) to the project file.
6. Reload your updated project file in Visual Studio, addressing the security dialogs warning you about your "suspicious build task."

Now compare that to the workflow for adding the same task to your psake script:

1. Modify the psake script.
2. There's no step two. You're done.

The output of running your `Build` task shows the MSBuild activity in line with the psake script output, as in the following:

```
PS C:\>invoke-psake .\listing_2.ps1
psake version 4.2.0
Copyright (c) 2010 James Kovacs

Executing Build
Microsoft (R) Build Engine Version 4.0.30319.1
[Microsoft .NET Framework, Version 4.0.30319.296]
Copyright (C) Microsoft Corporation 2007. All rights reserved.

Build started 1/21/2013 3:52:04 PM.
Done Building Project "C:\MyProject\MyProject.csproj" (Build target(s)).

    Build succeeded.
    0 Warning(s)    0 Error(s)
Time Elapsed 00:00:00.21

Build Succeeded!

----------------------------------------------------------------------
Build Time Report
----------------------------------------------------------------------
Name   Duration
----   --------
Build  00:00:00.2593068
Total: 00:00:00.2713013
```

Using MSBuild to create binaries from source code is neither cheating nor bad form. It's an example of why PowerShell is a great choice for these kinds of problems. As you're about to see, this build script provides a way to extend the Visual Studio build workflow with things Visual Studio was never designed to do.

Using PowerShell in psake tasks

psake is PowerShell, so build scripts can use any PowerShell modules, scripts, or commands at their disposal. Use psake, and your build can suddenly do anything PowerShell can do.

Archiving binaries into a zip file is a common build activity. Listing 3 expands your build with a task named `PackageZip` that stuffs the MyProject binaries into a zip archive. I regularly use the `write-zip` command from the PowerShell Community Extensions module (available at http://pscx.codeplex.com/) to archive files in PowerShell, and now you can use it in your build too.

Listing 3 Adding the `PackageZip` task

```
task -name PackageZip -depends Build -action {
    import-module pscx;
    dir ./MyProject/bin/debug |
    write-zip -output ./MyProject.zip;
}

task -name Build -action {
    exec {
        msbuild ./MyProject/MyProject.csproj /t:Build
    }
}

task -name Clean -action {
    exec {
        msbuild ./MyProject/MyProject.csproj /t:Clean
    }
}

task -name Rebuild -depends Clean,Build;
task -name Default -depends Build;
```

`PackageZip` uses the PSCX `write-zip` cmdlet

The `PackageZip` task imports the PowerShell Community Extensions (PSCX) module and uses the `write-zip` command to archive the MyProject build output. Because packaging doesn't make a lot of sense without a completed build, `PackageZip` depends on the `Build` task. You can see the `Build` task is run implicitly when invoking the `PackageZip` task:

```
PS C:\>invoke-psake .\listing_3.ps1 -task PackageZip
psake version 4.2.0
Copyright (c) 2010 James Kovacs

Executing Build …

Executing PackageZip
```

```
Mode           LastWriteTime       Length Name
----           -------------       ------ ----
-a---     1/21/2013  4:01 PM         9859 MyProject.zip

Build Succeeded!

----------------------------------------------------------------------
Build Time Report
----------------------------------------------------------------------
Name       Duration
----       --------
Build      00:00:00.1787477
PackageZip 00:00:00.0826554
Total:     00:00:00.2900772
```

At this point the build is being automated past the initial "create some binaries" phase. Extending the reach of this build is a simple matter of adding more tasks, but what do you do if you need your build tasks to adapt their behavior? How can you configure these tasks?

Configuring the build with properties

The sample build scripts so far have assumed many things. The `Build` and `Clean` tasks assume a debug build, as they don't specify any value for the `Configuration` MSBuild property. You need to add the ability to build a release version of your project.

On a related matter, `PackageZip` assumes that the build output will be in the \bin\debug directory:

```
dir ./MyProject/bin/debug | …
```

This location will change in a release build, and the `PackageZip` task will need to adjust its behavior accordingly. How do you configure these things when you run the build?

psake exposes a set of configurable properties to each task. These properties are just PowerShell variables, but they're called properties because you define them using the `properties` psake command. The following listing declares a single property you can use to toggle the build configuration of MyProject between debug and release.

Listing 4 Configuring the build script

```
properties {                                              ❶ Declaration of psake properties
    $config = 'Debug';                                    ❷ A $config property defaulting to "debug"
};

task -name PackageZip -depends Build -action {
    import-module pscx;
    dir ./MyProject/bin/$config |                         ❸ Use $config to determine the output directory
    write-zip -output ./MyProject.zip;
}

task -name Build -action {
    exec {
        msbuild ./MyProject/MyProject.csproj              ❹ Use $config to toggle the build configuration
          ➥ /p:Configuration=$config /t:Build
```

```
    }
}

task -name Clean -action {
    exec {
        msbuild ./MyProject/MyProject.csproj
          ➥ /p:Configuration=$config /t:Clean
    }
}
...
```

❺ **Use `$config` to toggle the clean configuration**

The `properties` statement ❶ requires a script block. This script block initializes each task, so any changes made to these variables inside of one task won't affect other tasks.

NOTE Use the psake `properties` statement to declare a set of configurable properties used by your build tasks.

A single property named `$config` ❷ is defined and assigned a default value of "debug". The property is referenced in the `Build` ❹ and `Clean` ❺ tasks to set the value of the `Configuration` build property in MSBuild. In addition, the property is used in the MyProject output path in `PackageZip` ❸.

The default value of `$config` results in a debug build, so running the psake build script in listing 4 produces the same output as listing 3. To see the property in action you need to set the `config` property when you call `invoke-psake`. You do this by passing a hash table to the `-properties` parameter of `invoke-psake`, where each item name specifies a property to set (`config`) and its value ("release"):

```
PS C:\> invoke-psake .\listing_4.ps1 -task build
  ➥ -properties @{'config'='release'}
psake version 4.2.0
Copyright (c) 2010 James Kovacs

Executing Build
Microsoft (R) Build Engine Version 4.0.30319.1
[Microsoft .NET Framework, Version 4.0.30319.269]
Copyright (C) Microsoft Corporation 2007. All rights reserved.

Build started 9/28/2012 3:18:02 PM.
Project "C:\MyProject\MyProject.csproj" on node 1 (Build target(s)).
...
CopyFilesToOutputDirectory:
  Copying file from "obj\x86\release\MyProject.exe" to
    ➥ "bin\release\MyProject.exe".
  MyProject -> C:\MyProject\bin\Release\MyProject.exe
  Copying file from "obj\x86\release\MyProject.pdb" to
    ➥ "bin\Release\MyProject.pdb".
Done Building Project "C:\MyProject\MyProject.csproj" (Build target(s
)).
...
```

Setting the value of `$config` to "release"

MyProject output is placed in the "release" directory

NOTE To set build properties at runtime pass a hash table to the `-properties` parameter of `invoke-psake`.

Why can't I declare variables and use them in my tasks?

The reason you can't declare variables and use them in your tasks has to do with the way invoke-psake executes tasks. Any variable you declare in the build script will exist in the scope of that script file. Tasks aren't executed in this scope; instead, they're executed in the scope of the psake module, where your variables aren't defined. The script block defined by the properties statement is executed as a part of each task, in effect defining a unique set of variables inside the scope of each individual task.

Validating property values

Property values passed to `invoke-psake` override the values of the corresponding properties defined in the build script. This enables your build to toggle between build and release configurations. But what prevents someone from setting the `config` property to something other than "debug" or "release"?

```
PS C:\> invoke-psake .\listing_4.ps1 -task build
➥ -properties @{'config'='kipplefish'}

psake version 4.2.0
Copyright (c) 2010 James Kovacs

Executing Build
Microsoft (R) Build Engine Version 4.0.30319.1
[Microsoft .NET Framework, Version 4.0.30319.296]
Copyright (C) Microsoft Corporation 2007. All rights reserved.

Build started 1/21/2013 4:03:54 PM.
Project "C:\ MyProject.csproj" on node 1 (Build target(s)).
c:\Windows\Microsoft.NET\Framework64\v4.0.30319\Microsoft.Common.targets:
     error : The OutputPath property is not set for project
     'MyProject.csproj'. Please check to make sure that you have specified a
     valid combination of Configuration and Platform for this project.
     Configuration='kipplefish'  Platform='x86'.
Done Building Project "C:\MyProject.csproj" (Build target(s)) -- FAILED.

Build FAILED.
```

The previous output shows a failed build resulting from the user specifying an invalid build configuration, and as verbose as the error output is, it doesn't inform the user how to avoid the failure. It would be nice to prevent this error from happening and perhaps offer a more informative error in its place. To do this, modify the build so it validates the value of the `config` property, raising an error when it doesn't match an expected value.

TIP Validate the values of all build properties at the beginning of the build, before any potentially dangerous operations are executed against user-supplied data.

Validating `config` needs to be done by the `Build`, `Clean`, and `PackageZip` tasks, but it only needs to happen once during each build. It makes sense to have a single validation task on which these other tasks depend, as shown in this listing.

Listing 5 Validating property values as a Build task

```
properties {
    $config = 'Debug';
};

task -name ValidateConfig -action {
    assert -condition (
     ➥ 'debug','release' -contains $config )
     ➥ -failureMessage "Unrecognized config
     ➥ property value: $config; valid values
     ➥ include 'debug' and 'release'"
}

task -name PackageZip -depends Build -action {…}

task -name Build -depends ValidateConfig -action {…}
task -name Clean -depends ValidateConfig -action {…}

task -name Rebuild -depends Clean,Build;
task -name Default -depends Build;
```

ValidateConfig validates the $config property

Build and Clean tasks depend on ValidateConfig task

The ValidateConfig task uses the psake assert statement to ensure a valid value has been supplied for config. When the -condition parameter is false, the error message specified in the -failureMessage parameter is raised as an error and the build is stopped. In your case, the -condition statement checks that config matches one of the expected values, and the -failureMessage indicates the values allowed for the property.

NOTE Use the psake assert command to validate conditions during the build and issue informative error messages.

The new error message is far more helpful than the previous one and no dangerous build tasks were executed using the invalid config property value:

```
PS C:\>invoke-psake .\listing_5.ps1 -properties @{ 'config'='kipplefish' }
psake version 4.2.0
Copyright (c) 2010 James Kovacs

Executing ValidateConfig
1/21/2013 4:11:13 PM: An Error Occurred:
Assert: Unrecognized config property value: kipplefish; valid values include
     'debug' and 'release'
```

With tasks and configuration in your toolbox you're ready to automate your software development process. Before you find yourself lost in a sea of build scripts, let's look at ways to keep that automation organized.

Managing psake script growth

As a build matures the number of tasks in your psake scripts will flourish. Keeping tasks structured and discoverable is important to both your sanity and the manageability of the build. The information in the next few sections will help you keep your build scripts wieldy.

Identifying public tasks

Generally only a handful of tasks are meant to start a build workflow: tasks like `Build`, `Clean`, `Rebuild`, `Package`, and `Install`. I consider these tasks *public*. The rest of the tasks are there to support these operations but aren't meant to be directly invoked by a user. I regard these tasks as *private*.

I differentiate the two using a naming convention. I designate names of private tasks with a leading underscore (_), and name public tasks normally:

```
task -name _ValidateConfig -action {…}                          <-- Private task
task -name Build -depends _ValidateConfig -action {…}           <-- Public task
```

This naming convention neither hides the private tasks from view nor prevents anyone from running them directly. But it does identify which tasks are the starting points in the build workflows. When tasks start to number in the dozens this information becomes imperative.

TIP Differentiate public and private tasks.

Describing your tasks

Adding a description to each build task will help make them discoverable. The `task` command accepts a `-description` string parameter you can use to describe the task to the user. This feature can also enforce the notion of private and public tasks, as shown in the following listing.

Listing 6 Using the `Description` task parameter

```
properties {
    $config = 'Debug';
};
$private = '(do not run this task directly)'
task -name _ValidateConfig
  ➥ -description $private -action {…}

task -name PackageZip -depends Build
  ➥ -description "Creates a ZIP the project" -action {…}

task -name Build -depends _ValidateConfig
  ➥ -description "Builds out-of-date binaries" -action {…}

task -name Clean -depends _ValidateConfig
-description "Removes all build artifacts" -action {…}

task -name Rebuild -depends Clean,Build
  ➥ -description "Rebuilds the entire project";

task -name Default -depends Build;
```

Private tasks get a shared generic description

Public tasks each get a unique description

TIP Provide a description for every task in your build.

Users see these task descriptions when they request the psake script documentation using the -docs parameter of invoke-psake:

```
PS C:\> invoke-psake .\listing_6.ps1 -docs
psake version 4.2.0
Copyright (c) 2010 James Kovacs

Name            Description                        Depends On      Default
----            -----------                        ----------      -------
_ValidateConfig (do not run this task directly)
Build           Builds out-of-date binaries        _ValidateConfig True
Clean           Removes all build artifacts        _ValidateConfig
PackageZip      Creates a ZIP of the project       Build
Rebuild         Rebuilds the entire project        Clean, Build
```

Using generic descriptions for private tasks helps focus the user on those public tasks they are meant to run.

NOTE Use the `-docs` parameter of `invoke-psake` to view a list of available tasks in a build script.

Grouping tasks into files

Isolate related tasks into files to keep your build scripts small. My preference is grouping tasks by purpose, where each file holds tasks related to one build activity, such as generating code, building source files, packaging the build output, and managing data bases.

For larger projects I tend to have one main build script containing public build tasks like `Build`, `Clean`, `Rebuild`, `Test`, `Package`, `Install`, `Uninstall`, and `Deploy`. These public tasks depend on private tasks that are isolated in other psake script files.

TIP Isolate related tasks into their own file. Reference the file from a main build script.

For example, suppose you have a set of tasks related to packaging the build output. Group those tasks in a file named packaging.ps1:

```
task -name _PackageZip -action {…}
task -name _PackageInstaller -action {…}
task -name _PackageNuget -action {…}
task -name _PackageChocolatey -action {…}
```

In the main psake build script, reference these tasks by dot-sourcing the packaging.ps1 file:

```
. ./packaging.ps1
task -name Package -depends _PackageZip, _PackageInstaller,
  ➥ _PackageNuget, _PackageChocolatey
  ➥ -description "Package all the things!"
```

Builds tend to grow rather than shrink. Doing these simple things goes a long way in keeping your build scripts working and manageable.

Summary

The expectations around modern software development mandate the use of automation to ensure a consistent and reliable build, and rightfully so—it improves quality, speeds up release cycles, and provides a consistent feedback loop for everyone involved. Meeting these expectations is hard enough without your tools getting in the way. Build automation hinges on these tools working together easily, and given the state of the art, PowerShell is the best choice to make this happen on Windows.

Where PowerShell provides the technological reach and flexibility to get your tools working together, psake provides the structure necessary to map out the crooked paths the build tends to wander. Combining these creates a powerhouse of automation, allowing you to take the build process well beyond the starting point of producing a binary.

Many consider managing the build an evil, but a necessary one (this may or may not correlate with your moral stance on lying). My hope is that this chapter pushes you to give psake a whirl. If you do, you'll be surprised at what you accomplish and how little effort it takes.

And that's no lie.

About the author

Jim Christopher has been developing software since the age of nine. With 18 years of professional experience across industries such as gaming, education, and defense, his drive is designing software, systems, and user experiences for automation. This theme earned him Microsoft MVP awards for PowerShell from 2011 to 2013. Jim has published several open source projects targeting PowerShell, including the StudioShell automation environment for Visual Studio (http://studioshell.codeplex.com). Jim currently runs Code Owls LLC (www.codeowls.com), a small software development company in Charlotte, North Carolina, which focuses on helping people do awesome things and publishes the SeeShell data visualization module for PowerShell (www.codeowls.com/seeshell).

PART 4

PowerShell platforms

Edited by Aleksandar Nikolić

If you've made it this far in the book chances are you're a PowerShell fan, but by itself, PowerShell is irrelevant. Richard Siddaway once told Jeffrey Snover that PowerShell didn't matter. After Jeffrey's initial shock, Richard clarified that it's what you can *do* with it that matters. This section is all about putting PowerShell to work.

PowerShell solutions for products and servers continue to arrive from Microsoft product teams and third-party vendors. PowerShell is a management engine and more of the stuff we deal with on a daily basis is being plugged into this engine.

There's so much that could be written about using PowerShell to manage this platform or that application. In some cases entire books could be devoted to topics such as managing Exchange Server or SQL Server with PowerShell. Some of those books have been written and others are in the works.

The chapters in this section touch on a few areas that many IT pros are likely to have to deal with such as IIS, WSUS (Windows Server Update Services), and Active Directory. But even if you don't need to manage these things, you should still take the time to look through the chapters. Often a technique or concept can be applied to other platforms.

The material in these chapters tends to rely on scripts and functions, which you can download from Manning. We encourage you to look at the code and test in a non-production environment, following along with each chapter.

When the time comes to develop your own PowerShell platform-specific solution and you need some help, we recommend using the forum at PowerShell.org.

About the editor

Aleksandar Nikolić is a Microsoft MVP for Windows PowerShell, a cofounder of PowerShellMagazine.com, and the community manager of PowerShell.com. He is an experienced presenter and speaker about Microsoft automation solutions, and has more than 17 years of experience as a system administrator. He is also available for one-on-one online PowerShell trainings. You can find him on Twitter: @alexandair.

23 PowerShell and the SQL Server provider

Ben Miller

This chapter is written for the DBA who needs an efficient way to get information from or manage SQL Servers in their environment with just a few commands by using native PowerShell methods. When you're looking at the options for managing or getting information from a SQL Server by using PowerShell your choice is driven by a few scenarios. One use case might be to find out how many databases are in the instances you maintain while using the simplest way to reference these instances. Another might be to find out whether a certain object exists in a Software as a Service (SaaS) environment with thousands of databases and multiple servers while upgrading in a phased upgrade methodology. You may want to know which database has the object so you don't attempt to upgrade that database in the second wave and find that the object exists. When faced with these or other scenarios you can quickly accomplish your goal with part PowerShell methods and part SQL Server provider.

You have a few options for managing SQL Server using PowerShell. You can use straight Shared Management Objects (SMOs) by loading the SMOs individually or by using the SQL Server provider. This chapter discusses the SQL Server provider that was released with SQL Server 2008/2008 R2. The provider for SQL 2008/R2 is implemented as a Windows PowerShell snap-in (PSSnapin) and is implemented as a module in SQL Server 2012. The provider for SQL Server 2012 has a few more cmdlets and more properties and methods on the SMOs, but the functionality is the same. I'll start by introducing you to the SQL Server provider and then I'll show you practical ways to use the provider to get at SQL Server information using PowerShell cmdlets.

Requirements

Many modules and providers come with PowerShell in Windows, but the SQL Server provider is a separate element that you install like any other Windows application. It's installed when you install SQL Server 2008, 2008 R2, or 2012 Management Tools, or you can download and install a copy of the Feature Pack for 2008 R2 at http://mng.bz/ccVK or for 2012 at http://mng.bz/m8po. You'll need to download and install the following components for 2008/R2:

- 1033\x64\PowerShellTools.msi
- 1033\x64\SharedManagementObjects.msi
- 1033\x64\SQLSysClrTypes.msi

For 2012 you install the following components:

- Microsoft Windows PowerShell Extensions for Microsoft SQL Server 2012
- Microsoft SQL Server 2012 Shared Management Objects

These components for 2008/R2 are listed for the x64 platform, and the corresponding items are available for IA64 and x86. With the components installed and with access to a SQL Server you can start exploring the capabilities of the SQL Server provider.

Introduction to the SQL Server provider

Two snap-ins are registered with PowerShell when you install the SQL Server provider components for 2008/R2: `SqlServerCmdletSnapin100` and `SqlServerProviderSnapin100`. You can verify that the snap-ins are available by using the first command in the following code. You can add them a couple of different ways, as shown:

```
Get-PSSnapin -Registered

Add-PSSnapin SqlServerCmdletSnapin100
Add-PSSnapin SqlServerProviderSnapin100
```

Alternatively you can use Wildcards, but be sure that you only get what you want:

```
Add-PSSnapin *SQL*
```

The first snap-in contains two cmdlets that you can use to execute commands against a SQL Server. The first cmdlet, `Invoke-PolicyEvaluation`, is used in SQL Server policy-based management in SQL Server 2008 and above. The second is `Invoke-SqlCmd`, which is a query executer. These two cmdlets are useful, and in future versions of the provider there are more cmdlets available.

The second snap-in is the SQL Server provider. It's used for navigating SQL Server objects in a manner similar to navigating a directory structure, folders, and items in folders. Think of a directory like C:\WINDOWS and how you can use the `dir` command to access the items in that folder. The objects that are returned from the SQL Server provider are SMO-based. You can do a search on "SQL SMO objects" and see the richness these objects can bring. We're familiar with objects in SQL Server because we deal with tables, columns, and indexes. SMOs represent SQL Server objects and have properties and methods to interact with objects in SQL Server, such as dropping an object, getting properties of an object, and altering an object. This provider becomes powerful when automating certain processes or information-gathering procedures by simplifying the syntax to get these objects. Let's dive in and learn how to use this provider's power.

Using the SQL Server provider

The SQL Server provider is exposed as a PSDrive (PowerShell Drive) by using paths into the hierarchy of SQL Server objects. A PSDrive is a way to access items in a way that's similar to a directory structure. After you load the provider you can use the PowerShell command `Get-PSDrive` to show all the drives available for PowerShell to reference in a fashion similar to a file system.

The list of drives includes a SQLSERVER: drive when the provider is loaded. This drive begins the process of accessing SQL Server objects through a series of paths. Table 1 shows the drive structure and what each level represents.

Table 1 SQL Server provider paths

Path	Description
SQLSERVER:	The drive you use to access SQL, just as you would use C:. The root of this drive contains the following paths to explore: SQL SQLPolicy SQLRegistration DataCollection Utility DAC
SQLSERVER:\SQL	The root of the SQL services on the local machine, and the beginning of the path in SQL Server via the provider.
SQLSERVER:\SQL\Computer-Name	The beginning of SQL Server's journey in the provider. The computer name is the next part of the path and it can be local or remote. This doesn't include the instance name (default or named). Executing `Get-ChildItem` gets information about *all* instances on this machine, including the default, and shows you their properties.
SQLSERVER:\SQL\Computer-Name\Instance	The path that connects you to the instance of SQL Server and tries to log you in via your Windows credentials. The following folders are available: Audits BackupDevices Credentials CryptographicProviders Databases Endpoints JobServer Languages LinkedServers Logins Mail ResourceGovernor Roles ServerAuditSpecifications SystemDataTypes SystemMessages Triggers UserDefinedMessages

With an understanding of this information you can begin to use the SQL Server provider in a powerful way. The information in table 1 will be a valuable reference for you regarding where you can go in SQL Server because most of the objects are represented in the provider and SMO.

As I've said, the real power of the provider syntax is that it's like a directory structure. Think of what the path to a table would look like. Listing 1 demonstrates the basic use of the provider from a console or the Integrated Scripting Environment (ISE); this can eventually be wrapped in a function, where you can pass parameters for the server, instance, and other parameters. It also shows using path-like structures in PowerShell with the SQL Server provider. You can extend this to your advantage in other pieces of automation.

Listing 1 Path-like access to SQL objects

```
$server = "localhost"
$instance = "default"
$dbname = "AdventureWorks"
$tblname = "HumanResources.Employee"

$path="SQLSERVER:\SQL\$server\$instance\Databases\$dbname\Tables\$tblname"
If(Test-Path $path)
{
  Get-Item $path
}
```

The more you use the SQL provider the more you'll want to become familiar with the paths that exist in the provider if you're planning to do any work in SQL Server with PowerShell.

Examples of using the SQL Server provider

Let's get some objects and see what you can do with this tool. Listing 2 shows a function that prepares the provider for use in the various versions of SQL Server; this function is reused throughout this chapter. It includes an example of using the provider to get information from SQL Server. The listing uses code from http://mng.bz/4sXz to load the assemblies so the function is reusable.

Listing 2 Function to load the SQL Server provider

```
function Load-SQLSnapins
{
   [CmdletBinding()]
   Param()

    $ErrorActionPreference = "Stop"

    $sqlpsreg="HKLM:\SOFTWARE\Microsoft\PowerShell\1\ShellIds\
      ➥ Microsoft.SqlServer.Management.PowerShell.sqlps"

    if (Get-ChildItem $sqlpsreg -ErrorAction "SilentlyContinue")
    {
        throw "SQL Server Provider for Windows PowerShell is not installed."
```

```
    }
    else
    {
        $item = Get-ItemProperty $sqlpsreg
        $sqlpsPath = [System.IO.Path]::GetDirectoryName($item.Path)
    }

    Set-Variable -scope Global -name SqlServerMaximumChildItems -Value 0
    Set-Variable -scope Global -name SqlServerConnectionTimeout -Value 30
    Set-Variable -scope Global -name SqlServerIncludeSystemObjects -Value
     $false
    Set-Variable -scope Global -name SqlServerMaximumTabCompletion -Value
     1000

    Push-Location
    cd $sqlpsPath

   if (!(Get-PSSnapin -Name SQLServerCmdletSnapin100 `
-ErrorAction SilentlyContinue))
   {
      Add-PSSnapin SQLServerCmdletSnapin100
      Write-Verbose "Loading SQLServerCmdletSnapin100..."
   }
   else
   {
      Write-Verbose "SQLServerCmdletSnapin100 already loaded"
   }

   if (!(Get-PSSnapin -Name SqlServerProviderSnapin100 `
-ErrorAction SilentlyContinue))
   {
      Add-PSSnapin SqlServerProviderSnapin100
      Write-Verbose "Loading SqlServerProviderSnapin100..."
   }
   else
   {
      Write-Verbose "SqlServerProviderSnapin100 already loaded"
   }

    Update-TypeData -PrependPath SQLProvider.Types.ps1xml
    update-FormatData -prependpath SQLProvider.Format.ps1xml
    Pop-Location
}

<#
namespaces based on
http://msdn.microsoft.com/en-ca/library/ms182491(v=sql.105).aspx

SQL2005
root\Microsoft\SqlServer\ComputerManagement"

SQL2008
root\Microsoft\SqlServer\ComputerManagement10"

SQL2012
\\.\root\Microsoft\SqlServer\ComputerManagement11\instance_name
```

```
#>
function Prepare-SQLProvider
{
   [CmdletBinding()]
   Param()
   $namespace = "root\Microsoft\SqlServer\ComputerManagement"
   if ((Get-WmiObject -Namespace $namespace -Class SqlService `
-ErrorAction SilentlyContinue)
   )
   {
      Write-Verbose "Running SQL Server 2005"
      #load Snapins
      Load-SQLSnapins
   }
   elseif ((Get-WmiObject -Namespace "$($namespace)10" -Class SqlService `
-ErrorAction SilentlyContinue))
   {
      Write-Verbose "Running SQL Server 2008/R2"
      #load Snapins
      Load-SQLSnapins
   }
   elseif ((Get-WmiObject -Namespace "$($namespace)11" -Class SqlService `
-ErrorAction SilentlyContinue))
   {
      Write-Verbose "Running SQL Server 2012"
      Write-Verbose "Loading SQLPS Module ... "
      Import-Module SQLPS
   }
}
```

Listing 3 shows how to get a list of the database names on your server. It's simple if you think of your SQL Server like a file system. For each file in a file system, properties give information about that file. Similarly, in the SQL Server provider you can access your databases like you do files in a directory.

Listing 3 Displaying a list of database names from SQL Server

```
Prepare-SQLProvider
cd SQLSERVER:\SQL\localhost\default
cd Databases
Get-Childitem | Select Name
```

The example in listing 4 takes you a little further into the hierarchy to get a list of tables. This isn't much harder than the previous example, because the Tables folder is another level in the hierarchy. The path is similar to SQLSERVER:\SQL\localhost\default\Databases\AdventureWorks\Tables. You can either use `Get-ChildItem` to get the tables or you can use `Where-Object` to filter them by property. In this case, you need to use the `Where-Object` because the SQL Server provider doesn't have support for filters. Figures 1 and 2 show the output from listing 4.

Listing 4 Getting a list of tables

```
Prepare-SQLProvider
CD SQLSERVER:\SQL\localhost\default\Databases\AdventureWorks\Tables
Get-ChildItem | Select DisplayName
Get-ChildItem | Where-Object { $_.DisplayName -match "HumanResources[.]" |
 Select DisplayName
```

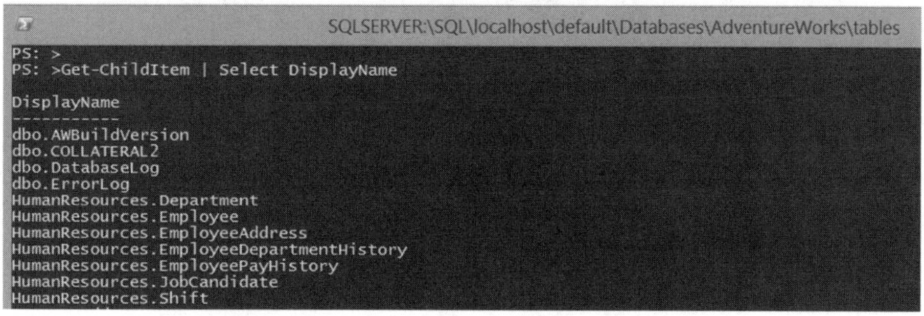

Figure 1 Output of getting a list of tables

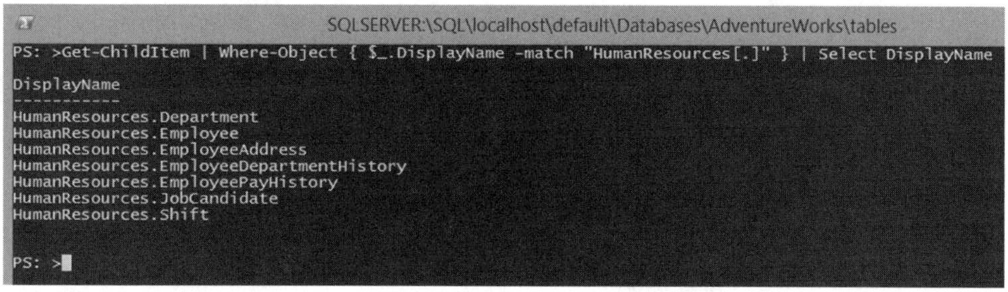

Figure 2 Output of the second command with the `Where-Object` clause

Last but not least, when you aren't in the mood or can't use the provider to get information but you need to use some of the objects it provides you can take advantage of the fact that the return objects are SMO-based. You use a server object to get some properties, or when you need access to the server object later in your code you can use `Get-Item` and the provider path to the server to get a server object. This is illustrated in the following listing. Figure 3 shows the output.

Listing 5 Getting a server object using the SQL Server provider

```
Prepare-SQLProvider
$server = Get-Item SQLSERVER:\SQL\localhost\default
$server.GetType() | Format-Table -Auto
$server | Get-Member
```

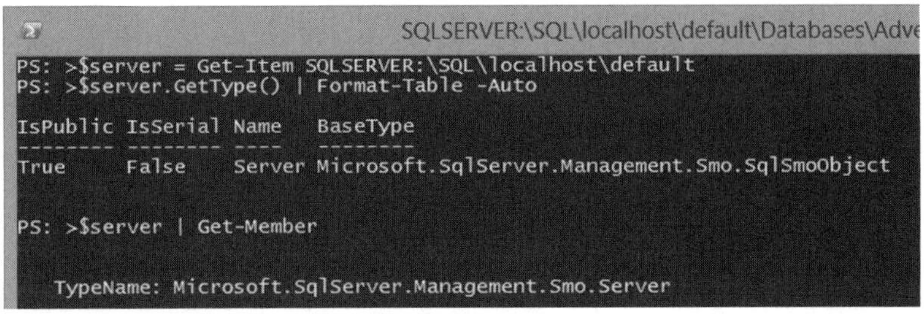

```
SQLSERVER:\SQL\localhost\default\Databases\Adve
PS: >$server = Get-Item SQLSERVER:\SQL\localhost\default
PS: >$server.GetType() | Format-Table -Auto

IsPublic IsSerial Name   BaseType
-------- -------- ----   --------
True     False    Server Microsoft.SqlServer.Management.Smo.SqlSmoObject


PS: >$server | Get-Member


   TypeName: Microsoft.SqlServer.Management.Smo.Server
```

Figure 3 Using `Get-Item` to get an SMO server object

Notice in figure 3 that you see the type: the server object is a `Microsoft.SqlServer.Management.Smo.SqlSmoObject`. More specifically, in the second statement it's a `Microsoft.SqlServer.Management.Smo.Server` object. You can use this approach with databases, tables, and stored procedures to get and manipulate objects, all in a path to the object.

Getting a count of databases in an instance

The next listing uses the SQL Server provider to get a count of databases using functions to load the provider for whichever version of SQL Server is installed.

Listing 6 Get-DatabaseCounts function

```
function Get-DatabaseCounts
{
    [CmdletBinding()]
    Param(
        [Parameter(Position=0,Mandatory=$true)]
        [alias("server")]
        [string]$serverName,

        [Parameter(Position=1,Mandatory=$true)]
        [alias("instance")]
        [string]$instanceName
    )

   $results = @()
   (Get-Item SQLSERVER:\SQL\$serverName\$instanceName).Databases |
   Foreach-Object {
       $db = $_

       $db.Tables |
       Foreach-Object {
          $table = $_

          $hash = @{
             "Database"        = $db.Name
             "Schema"          = $table.Schema
             "Table"           = $table.Name
             "RowCount"        = $table.RowCount
             "Replicated"      = $table.Replicated
          }
```

```
            $item = New-Object PSObject -Property  $hash
            $results += $item

        }
    }
    $results

}

Prepare-SQLProvider -Verbose
Get-DatabaseCounts -server "localhost" -instance "DEFAULT" | Out-GridView
```

This listing shows the count of databases in the localhost\DEFAULT instance of SQL Server using the `Get-DatabaseCounts` function.

Finding a table in many databases

This use case is a common one when you're dealing with upgrades to a database or when you're deploying new code that relies on a new table that was created during development. There are different ways to find a table in the midst of many databases. Listing 7 shows a function that uses the provider to find the table, and listing 8 still uses the provider but with a script.

Listing 7 Finding the existence of a table in many databases

```
Function Get-SQLTableInDB {
    [CmdletBinding()]
    Param(
       [Parameter(Position=0,Mandatory=$true)]
       [alias("server")]
       [string]$serverName,

       [Parameter(Position=1,Mandatory=$true)]
       [alias("instance")]
       [string]$instanceName,

       [Parameter(Position=2,Mandatory=$true)]
       [alias("table")]
       [string]$tableName
    )

    (Get-Item SQLSERVER:\SQL\$serverName\$instanceName).Databases |
     Foreach-Object {
       $db = $_

       $db.Tables |
       Foreach-Object {

          $sqltable = $_
          If($tableName -eq $($sqltable.Name)) {
             Return $db.Name
          }
       }
     }
}
```

```
Prepare-SQLProvider
Get-SQLTableInDatabases -server "localhost" -instance "DEFAULT" `
-table "Table1"
```

Listing 8 Finding the existence of a table in many databases using the provider

```
Prepare-SQLProvider

$servername = "localhost"
$instance = "default"
$tableName = "backupset"
$schema = "dbo"

$instpath = "SQL\$servername\$instance\Databases"
foreach($db in (Get-ChildItem SQLSERVER:\SQL\$instpath)) {
 $dbname = $db.Name
 if(!(Test-Path SQLSERVER:\$instpath\$dbname\Tables\$schema`.$tableName))
 {
   Write-Output $db.Name
 }
}
```

Summary

In this chapter you've seen how to get the SQL Server PowerShell provider for 2008/R2 and how to add it to your PowerShell session. The SQL Server provider for PowerShell is provided as a snap-in and is loaded with the `Add-PSSnapin` command; you access the structure of SQL Server using a path structure. You can add the provider to any Windows machine by downloading the PowerShell objects in the SQL Server Feature Packs.

Whether you're retrieving objects individually or detecting their existence a path structure provides a powerful way to use PowerShell and SQL Server together. This is just the tip of the iceberg when it comes to what you can do with the provider and how it all works, but I hope you caught the vision of where you can take it.

Chapter 25 discusses SMO and how to use objects in SQL Server with SMO; that chapter is a great companion to what you learned here. SQL Server 2012 wasn't covered in this chapter, but the concepts apply to the SQL Server 2012 provider; it's just loaded as a module (SQLPS) instead of a snap-in. Now, go execute some PowerShell!

About the author

Ben Miller is a database architect for HealthEquity, Inc. in Draper, Utah, the largest US Health Savings Account (HSA) trust organization. He is a SQL Server MVP and an MCM: SQL Server 2008. He has been in the industry for over 20 years and has focused on SQL Server and automation for the past 12 years. He has held various positions at companies like Microsoft and the LDS Church. He regularly speaks on SQL Server and PowerShell topics, and he is president of the Utah County, Utah SQL Server User Group. Ben lives in Lehi, Utah, with his beautiful wife and two children.

24 Creating flexible subscriptions in SSRS

Donabel Santos

If you create reports using SQL Server Reporting Services you may get requests—for example, for specific reports with varying formats and criteria to be emailed out to clients on the fifteenth of every month, or created and stored in a shared folder every Monday. SQL Server Reporting Services (SSRS) supports subscriptions but can be inflexible and rigid. PowerShell can help IT and SQL Server professionals with flexible report scheduling and delivery that support dynamic parameters and ever-changing user requirements.

In this chapter we'll look at implementing something similar to a data-driven subscription using a list in a CSV file and PowerShell. What I'll show you is just an example of how you can implement data-driven subscription in PowerShell from start to finish. Not everyone who is reading this chapter is familiar with SSRS or the SSRS environment, so the first few sections are devoted to explaining what the environment looks like. The formats and names I've chosen in this chapter may or may not work for you, but the good thing about this approach is that it's very flexible. You should be able to easily change any of the names (file, parameter, variable) or formats and adjust your PowerShell script.

Understanding SSRS subscriptions

Before we dive in to how you can create SSRS subscriptions using PowerShell, it's important to understand what's already available with SSRS, what the limitations are, and why PowerShell can be the vehicle that overcomes this gap. SSRS subscriptions are discussed in detail in the MSDN entry "Subscriptions and Delivery (Reporting Services)" (http://mng.bz/gVRN). To summarize:

- SSRS supports standard and data-driven subscriptions.
- Standard subscriptions only support static values, which can't be changed during report processing. To quote from the MSDN entry: "For each standard

subscription, there is exactly one set of report presentation options, delivery options, and report parameters."

- Data-driven subscription, which is a feature available only in SQL Server Enterprise or Business Intelligence Edition, can dynamically retrieve parameters, format, and scheduling information from a data source other than the subscription window for report processing. As mentioned in the MSDN entry, "You might use data-driven subscriptions if you have a very large recipient list or if you want to vary report output for each recipient. To use data-driven subscriptions, you must have expertise in building queries and an understanding of how parameters are used."

More often than not, different departments or groups in a company require customized reports. They have different (or multiple) report formats and scheduling preferences. For example, they may want both a PDF and an Excel report, each manager receives only their territory's reports, and they may want to supply a list of clients every month in addition to their territory clients.

If the company only has the Standard Edition of SQL Server—which is the situation for many small to medium-sized businesses—then this feat isn't doable using the subscription feature that comes with SSRS. Remember that standard subscription only supports static values. The best solution is to create the subscription using a combination of .NET programming, SQL stored procedures, and perhaps some batch files.

If a company has the Enterprise or Business Intelligence Edition, then most of this is doable but still requires a fair bit of management from the report administrator or DBA. Each format requires its own subscription. Each territory needs to be its own subscription. Having numerous subscriptions to manage will eventually become cumbersome to deal with.

Toward this end, PowerShell can both simplify and automate subscriptions without having to wrestle with SSRS editions or set up and manage multiple subscriptions from the SSRS administration interface.

Environment settings

To follow along with this chapter, you must have already installed and configured the SQL Server 2012 database engine and SSRS 2012 in native mode. This chapter doesn't cover step-by-step installation, but you can use this MSDN article as a reference: http://mng.bz/VPws.

To provide context to the example, table 1 lists the settings of the environment I used.

The example uses a very simple report that accepts multiple parameters of different data types. For simplicity I named the parameters based on their data types. This helps differentiate the formats you're passing to your PowerShell script later.

When this report is accessed from the SSRS Report Manager the parameter bar displays the individual parameters differently depending on the data type, as shown in figure 1. For example, strings, integers, and floats are presented as text boxes.

Table 1 Demo environment settings

SQL Server instance name	KERRIGAN
Report server URL	http://KERRIGAN/ReportServer
Report name	Sample Report
Absolute path to report	/PowerShell Deep Dives/Sample Report
Report parameters	`StringParam`—Accepts any string `IntParam`—Accepts any integer `BoolParam`—Accepts true or false `DateParam`—Accepts any valid date format `FloatParam`—Accepts any float

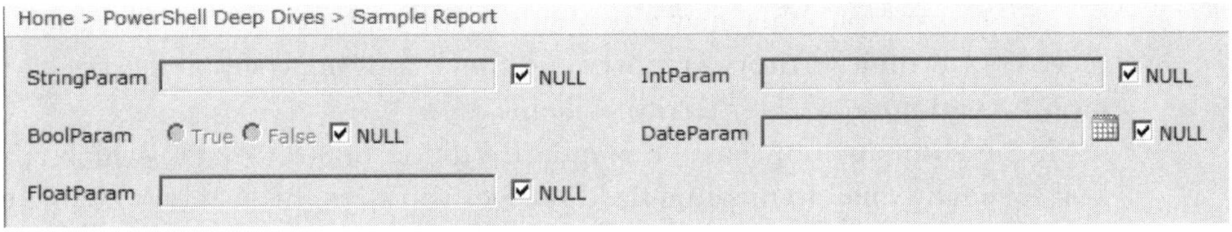

Home > PowerShell Deep Dives > Sample Report

StringParam [ ] NULL IntParam [ ] NULL

BoolParam True False NULL DateParam [ ] NULL

FloatParam [ ] NULL

Figure 1 Sample report parameter bar

Boolean parameters are shown, by default, as True/False radio buttons. Date parameters are shown with a date picker.

Requirements

This section identifies what you need to create report subscriptions using PowerShell.

SQL Server and PowerShell requirements

The example uses SSRS 2012 and PowerShell v3, but you aren't tied to these versions. With minor script changes you should be able to use the scripts in this chapter on older versions of SSRS and PowerShell.

You can also use the Microsoft Report Viewer 2010 Redistributable to render your reports. The Microsoft Report Viewer 2010 Redistributable Package, which can be used for SSRS 2008 or higher, can be downloaded from http://mng.bz/eA9a.

Subscription requirements

To create your own data-driven subscriptions using PowerShell a few pieces need to be in place:

- A location to store your subscriptions. This can be a file of any format, as long as you can easily parse different pieces of information. If you prefer, this could also be a database table.
- A way to determine active subscriptions and subscription preferences in terms of report format and report delivery.

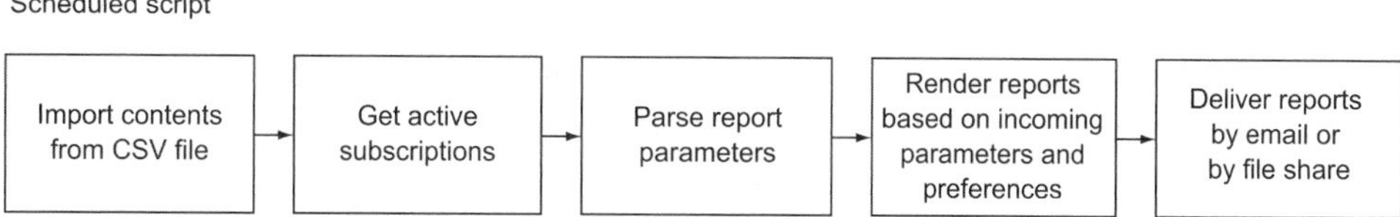

Figure 2 PowerShell SSRS subscription process flow

- A method to render and deliver reports to the appropriate subscribers.
- A means to pass in, and parse, different report parameters.
- An approach to schedule the script to run.

Your process flow can be mapped as shown in figure 2.

You also need to collect some typical pieces of information before you can service report subscriptions. Table 2 enumerates typical information you need to collect, which you'll consume later in your scripts.

Table 2 Subscription parameters

CSV header or table column name	Description
FirstName	Subscriber first name.
LastName	Subscriber last name.
Delivery	Delivery preference, either email or shared folder.
EmailAddress	Email address.
SharedFolder	Shared folder in UNC notation.
ReportPath	Report path: the path to the report from the root of the report manager. For example: /Reports/Financial Report
ExportFormat	Subscriber's preferred report format. SSRS supports the following rendering extensions: XML, NULL, CSV, ATOM, PDF, RGDI, HTML4.0, MHTML, EXCEL, EXCELOPENXML, RPL, IMAGE, WORD, and WORDOPENXML. In your subscription you allow only PDF, IMAGE, MHTML, WORD, WORDOPENXML, EXCEL, and EXCELOPENXML. Note that WORD and EXCEL refer to the 2003 version (.doc and .xls), and WORDOPENXML and EXCELOPENXML refer to the 2007/2010 versions (.docx and .xlsx).
ReportParameters	Parameters accepted by that report, in the following format: `parameters={param1=value|param2=value|param3=value}`
SubscriptionYear	Subscription year. * if subscribed for all years, or comma delimited if subscribed for multiple years.
SubscriptionMonth	Subscription month. * if subscribed for all months, or comma delimited if subscribed for multiple months.
SubscriptionDay	Subscription day. * if subscribed for all days, or comma delimited if subscribed for multiple days.

Subscription in action

Let's look at the scripts you can use to implement subscriptions. We'll start with the main script and subsequently dissect the different functions you use to complete the process flow. Note that to run the script the functions on which the main script is dependent must be loaded first:

```
PS C:\Path\to\scripts>. .\Load-SSRSAssembly.ps1
PS C:\Path\to\scripts>. .\Get-SSRSParameterArray.ps1
PS C:\Path\to\scripts>. .\Get-SSRSSubscription.ps1
PS C:\Path\to\scripts>. .\Send-SSRSSubscription.ps1
```

Main script

The main script that retrieves all active subscriptions and sends out the reports is presented in listing 1. For this example active subscriptions are saved in a CSV file. Two sets of parameters are included in this CSV file: subscription parameters, itemized in table 2, which are delimited by semicolons; and `ReportParameters`, which are enclosed in curly braces and delimited by pipes or vertical bars. This example uses semicolons and pipes as delimiters because there's a slimmer chance that these are part of a valid subscription or `ReportParameter` value.

Listing 1 Main subscription script

```
[CmdletBinding()]
param(
  [ValidateScript({Test-Path $_})]
  [string]$SubscriptionList="c:\temp\ssrs-subscription.csv",
  [string]$ReportServer="http://localhost/ReportServer"
)

Load-SSRSAssembly

Import-CSV -Delimiter ";" -Path $SubscriptionList |
Get-SSRSSubscription |
Send-SSRSSubscription -ReportServer  $ReportServer
```

Annotations: **Loads the ReportViewer assembly** (Load-SSRSAssembly); **Gets subscription list from CSV file** (Import-CSV); **Filters and returns current active subscriptions** (Get-SSRSSubscription); **Renders and delivers reports to subscribers** (Send-SSRSSubscription)

The first function you use is `Load-SSRSAssembly`, shown in the next listing, which loads the assembly required to use the `ReportViewer WinForms`.

Listing 2 `Load-SSRSAssembly` function

```
function Load-SSRSAssembly {
  Add-Type -AssemblyName "Microsoft.ReportViewer.WinForms, Version=11.0.0.0,
    Culture=neutral, PublicKeyToken=89845dcd8080cc91"
}
```

Later, should you need additional SSRS assemblies, such as the `ReportViewer WebForm`, you can update this function to load those assemblies as well.

The code lines following `Load-SSRSAssembly` are discussed in detail in the succeeding sections. After you load the required assemblies you read a CSV file that contains all of your subscriptions. You then pass the results of this `Import-CSV` to another function, `Get-SSRSSubscription`, which filters only for active subscriptions. Active subscriptions are then passed to another function, `Send-SSRSSubscription`, which takes care of the actual report rendering and delivery.

Storing subscriptions

For this example you store subscription information in a semicolon-delimited file. You capture in this file the information outlined in table 2. To help you visualize what it looks like, here's an example of one line in this file:

```
john;doe;email;john.doe@queryworks.local;\\KERRIGAN\Reports\;
➥ /PowerShell Deep Dives/Sample Report;PDF;parameters=
➥ {IntParam=2013|BoolParam=true|FloatParam=9.4|DateParam=6/30/2012
➥ 12:00:00 AM|StringParam=Data Warehousing};*;*;*
```

Of course, information here can be stored in different formats depending on your needs. You can adjust the PowerShell script to read from an XML file, a JSON file, or even a SQL Server table similar to the following.

Listing 3 Subscription table creation T-SQL script

```
CREATE TABLE [dbo].[Subscription]
    (
      [FirstName] [varchar](100) NULL ,
      [LastName] [varchar](100) NULL ,
      [Delivery] [varchar](100) NULL ,
      [EmailAddress] [varchar](100) NULL ,
      [SharedFolder] [varchar](100) NULL ,
      [ReportPath] [varchar](100) NULL ,
      [ExportFormat] [varchar](100) NULL ,
      [ReportParameters] [varchar](1000) NULL ,
      [SubscriptionYear] [varchar](20) NULL ,
      [SubscriptionMonth] [varchar](20) NULL ,
      [SubscriptionDay] [varchar](20) NULL
    )
ON  [PRIMARY]
```

Note that this is a pretty simplistic table—you're just trying to create a table that will store information equivalent to what's in your text file. In reality, there are many structural and design considerations when creating this subscription table, such as the primary key, indexes, and timestamp columns.

If you decide to capture subscription information in a table you need to update the script that reads your subscriptions.

Retrieving subscriptions

Your subscription list, which is stored in a semicolon-delimited text file format, contains a list of all subscribers, including those whose subscriptions may have already lapsed. Table 3 lists some possible subscription frequency values.

Table 3 Sample subscription frequency values

Subscription year, month, and day	Description
`*;*;*`	Always active
`2011;*;1`	Subscribed for every first of the month for the year 2011
`*;*;15`	Subscribed every fifteenth of the month
`*;3,6,9;15,20`	Subscribed every fifteenth and twentieth of March, June, and September

The function `Get-SSRSSubscription` retrieves only the current subscribers and returns the list to the pipeline, as shown in the next listing.

Listing 4 `Get-SSRSSubscription` function

```
function Get-SSRSSubscription  {
[CmdletBinding()]
param(
        [Parameter(Mandatory=$true,
        ValueFromPipeline=$true)]
        [string]$subscriptions
)
BEGIN {
        $currYear = (Get-Date).Year
        $currDay = (Get-Date).Day
        $currMonth = (Get-Date).Month
}

PROCESS {
        $item = $_
        $yearArray = $item.SubscriptionYear -split ","
        $monthArray = $item.SubscriptionMonth -split ","
        $dayArray = $item.SubscriptionDay -split ","

        if ( -not $item.ReportPath) { return }
        if($item.SubscriptionYear -contains $currYear -or `
$item.SubscriptionYear -eq "*")
        {
                if($monthArray -contains $currMonth -or `
$item.SubscriptionMonth -contains "*")
                {
                        if($dayArray -contains $currDay -or `
$item.SubscriptionDay -contains "*")
                        {
                           $item
                        }
                }
        }
        }
END {}
}
```

Gets the current year, month, and day

Parses the subscription year, month, and day values into their own respective arrays

Returns the subscription item if and only if the subscription is currently valid

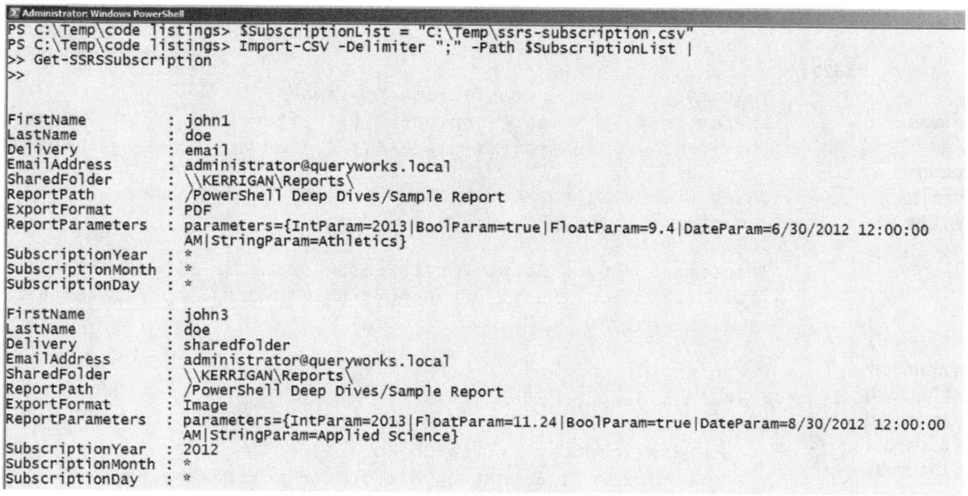

```
Administrator: Windows PowerShell
PS C:\Temp\code listings> $SubscriptionList = "C:\Temp\ssrs-subscription.csv"
PS C:\Temp\code listings> Import-CSV -Delimiter ";" -Path $SubscriptionList |
>> Get-SSRSSubscription
>>

FirstName          : john1
LastName           : doe
Delivery           : email
EmailAddress       : administrator@queryworks.local
SharedFolder       : \\KERRIGAN\Reports\
ReportPath         : /PowerShell Deep Dives/Sample Report
ExportFormat       : PDF
ReportParameters   : parameters={IntParam=2013|BoolParam=true|FloatParam=9.4|DateParam=6/30/2012 12:00:00
                     AM|StringParam=Athletics}
SubscriptionYear   : *
SubscriptionMonth  : *
SubscriptionDay    : *

FirstName          : john3
LastName           : doe
Delivery           : sharedfolder
EmailAddress       : administrator@queryworks.local
SharedFolder       : \\KERRIGAN\Reports\
ReportPath         : /PowerShell Deep Dives/Sample Report
ExportFormat       : Image
ReportParameters   : parameters={IntParam=2013|FloatParam=11.24|BoolParam=true|DateParam=8/30/2012 12:00:00
                     AM|StringParam=Applied Science}
SubscriptionYear   : 2012
SubscriptionMonth  : *
SubscriptionDay    : *
```

Figure 3 Sample invocation of `Get-SSRSSubscription`

This function checks whether a subscription is active. How do you check it? You take the incoming parameter and store it in an array. For example, `SubscriptionYear` can come in as either a single year (`2012`), an asterisk (`*`), or a series of years (`2010,2011,2012`). You compare the incoming value with the current year and an asterisk. If there's a match then you know this is an active subscription for that year. You do the same for `SubscriptionMonth` and `SubscriptionDay`. If the subscription is active you output that object so it can be consumed by the next function or cmdlet in the pipeline. An example invocation of this function is provided in figure 3.

Parsing parameters

Let's talk about parsing parameters before we discuss the function that renders and sends subscriptions. To parse the parameters that are passed with each subscription you use the function `Get-SSRSParameterArray`. This function takes the report parameters from the CSV file in this format:

```
params={IntParam=2013|FloatParam=8.89|BoolParam=false|DateParam=1/30/2012
  ➥ 12:00:00 AM|StringParam=Sample}
```

`Get-SSRSParameterArray` then converts them into a `ReportParameter` array that can be used to render the report, as shown in the following listing.

Listing 5 `Get-SSRSParameterArray` function

```
function Get-SSRSParameterArray {
[CmdletBinding()]
param(
        [Parameter(Mandatory=$True,
        ValueFromPipeline=$True)]
```

```
        [string]$paramstr
)
BEGIN{
        $paramstr = $paramstr -replace "params=",""
        $paramstr = $paramstr -replace "[{}]",""
        $paramstr = $paramstr -replace "[|]","`n"

        $hash = ConvertFrom-StringData -StringData $paramstr
        $numparams = $hash.Count

        [Microsoft.Reporting.WinForms.ReportParameter[]]$params =
        ➥ New-Object 'Microsoft.Reporting.WinForms.ReportParameter[]'
        ➥ $numparams

        $counter = 0;
        foreach ( $key in $hash.keys )
        {
           $params[$counter] = New-Object
           ➥ Microsoft.Reporting.WinForms.ReportParameter($key,
           ➥ "$($hash.$key)", $false)
           $counter++
        }

        return $params
}
PROCESS{}
END {}
}
```

Removes parameters= from the parameter string

Removes {} from the parameter

Places each set of parameters into its own line

Converts the parameter string into a hash

Creates a ReportParameter array based on the number of parsed parameters

Creates a ReportParameter object for each parameter passed in, and assigns it back to the array

In your CSV you pass the report parameters as a single string in the following format:

```
parameters={label=value|label=value}
```

This format allows you to be flexible with the parameters. This demonstrates that you can pass different number of parameters to reports, and different types, as long as you can properly parse the string that contains the parameter list.

In the `Get-SSRSParameterArray` function you convert the incoming parameter string to a hash and eventually into a `ReportParameter` array that you can use to render the report. To convert the parameter string into a hash you remove `parameters={}` and place each `label=value` into its own line:

```
label=value
label=value
:
```

In the code, this looks like

```
IntParam=2013
FloatParam=8.89
BoolParam=false
DateParam=1/30/2012 12:00:00 AM
StringParam=Sample
```

You can create a hash from this string format by passing this string to the cmdlet `ConvertFrom-StringData`. When you have the hash you iterate through it and create a

Microsoft.Reporting.WinForms.ReportParameter object for each item in the hash. You store this in a Microsoft.Reporting.WinForms.ReportParameter[] array and later pass it as a parameter to the SetParameter method of the ReportViewer object.

Delivering subscriptions

Once you retrieve active subscriptions and parse their corresponding parameters you can pass this information to another function called Send-SSRSSubscription, shown in the next listing. This function does the bulk of the report rendering and delivery work.

Listing 6 Send-SSRSSubscription function

```
function Send-SSRSSubscription {
[CmdletBinding()]
param(
        [Parameter(Mandatory=$True,
        ValueFromPipeline=$True)]
        [string[]]$Subscriptions,
        [Parameter(Mandatory=$True,
        ValueFromPipeline=$True)]
        [string]$ReportServer = $null,
        [string]$SmtpServer = "queryworks.local",
        [string]$ReportSender = "ssrs-powershell@queryworks.local",
          $TempFolder = $ENV:TEMP,
        $LogFile = "C:\Temp\SSRS PowerShell Subscription.log"
)
BEGIN {}
PROCESS {
        $item = $_
        if ( $item.ReportPath -eq $null ) { return }

        $ts = Get-Date -Format "yyyyMMdd_hhmmt"
        $fileName = "$($item.LastName)_$($item.FirstName)_$($ts)"     <-- Composes the timestamped filename

        #message for display, or logging
        $msg = "$ts Report for $($item.FirstName) $($item.LastName) "

        $mimeType = $null                        <-- Declares variables needed for rendering the report
        $encoding = $null
        $extension = $null
        $streamids = $null
        $warnings = $null
        $params = $null

        $rv = New-Object Microsoft.Reporting.WinForms.ReportViewer     <-- Creates a ReportViewer object
        $rv.ProcessingMode =
     [Microsoft.Reporting.WinForms.ProcessingMode]::Remote
        $rv.ServerReport.ReportServerUrl = $ReportServer
        $rv.ServerReport.ReportPath = $item.ReportPath
        [Microsoft.Reporting.WinForms.ReportParameter[]]$params =
          ➥ Get-SSRSParameterArray $item.ReportParameters       <-- Creates the ReportParameter array based on the incoming string
        $rv.ServerReport.SetParameters($params)

        #render the report
        $bytes = $rv.ServerReport.Render($item.ExportFormat,
                                          $null,
```

```
                                         [ref] $mimeType,
                                         [ref] $encoding,
                                         [ref] $extension,
                                         [ref] $streamids,
                                         [ref] $warnings)        <-- Renders the report
        $FileName = "$($FileName).$($extension)"     <-- Assigns the proper extension to the report that is being rendered

        $msg += " $FileName "
        $file = Join-Path $TempFolder $FileName
        $fileStream = New-Object System.IO.FileStream($file,
          ➥ [System.IO.FileMode]::OpenOrCreate)           <-- Creates the actual file
        $fileStream.Write($bytes, 0, $bytes.Length)
        $fileStream.Close()

        #deliver according to preference
        switch($item.Delivery)                 <-- Determines delivery method
        {
            "email"
            {
                $msg += " - emailed to $($item.EmailAddress)"
                Send-MailMessage `
                    -SmtpServer "$SmtpServer" `
                    -To "$($item.EmailAddress)" `
                    -From "$ReportSender" `
                    -Subject "Report for $($item.FirstName)
                      ➥ $($item.LastName) - $file - $ts" `
                    -Body "Report Generated" `
                    -Attachments $file

            }
            "sharedfolder"
            {
                $msg += "- saved to folder $($item.SharedFolder)"
                 Copy-Item  -Path $file -Destination $item.SharedFolder
            }
        }

        Write-Verbose $msg
        Add-Content $LogFile -value $msg

        #remove temp file
        Remove-Item -Path $file
        }
    END {}
}
```

This is a longer script. Instead of discussing each line I'll focus on some of the key items.

The bulk of the rendering work is done by the `ReportViewer` object:

```
$rv = New-Object Microsoft.Reporting.WinForms.ReportViewer
```

Some of the settings for this object are outlined in table 4. `ReportViewer` has many other properties and methods documented in MSDN (http://mng.bz/9YxQ) that give you more granular control over how you render and process the report.

Table 4 **`ReportViewer` settings**

Property/Method	Description
`ProcessingMode`	Specifies where the report will be processed. Accepts two values: `Local` and `Remote`. `Local` specifies that the report will be processed on the client, and `Remote` indicates that the report will be processed on the report server.
`ServerReport.ReportServerUrl`	Report server URL.
`ServerReport.ReportPath`	Report path, starting from the root. In this case: /PowerShell Deep Dives/Sample Report.
`ServerReport.Render()`	Method that renders the report. Two of the parameters that need to be passed to this method are `format` and `parameters`. This method also returns the extension you can use with the rendered report. You can learn more about this method from MSDN (http://mng.bz/k3re).

The report is rendered after the `ServerReport.Render()` method has finished executing. You need to capture what's returned by this method and pass it to `System.IO.FileStream`, which lets you turn the contents into an actual file in your file system. You use `System.IO.FileStream` instead of the `Out-File` cmdlet because you allow different file formats in the subscription, such as PDF, TIFF, XLSX, and DOCX, which aren't supported natively by `Out-File`. For this example's purposes you only temporarily store this file in C:\Temp, which is stored in the variable `$TempFolder`. Once the file is created you then determine how to deliver the report. You get this preference from the subscription data.

If the delivery preference is `email` you get the email address of the subscriber and send an email using the `Send-MailMessage` cmdlet. You attach the report to this email.

If the delivery preference is `shared folder` you copy the report to the shared folder using the `Copy-Item` cmdlet. You may need to adjust this section in the script, depending on where this folder is in your environment. For example, if you have any cross-domain folders you need to provide additional authentication before this section will be successfully executed.

For the example you display the message *and* add this message to your log file:

```
Write-Verbose $msg
Add-Content $logfile -value $msg
```

The last bit removes the temporary report that was stored in the location specified in `$TempFolder`. Of course, you don't have to delete this; you can choose to keep the file in a permanent location.

Scheduling the script

With the script in place you need to determine how you can schedule it and how frequently you should run it. The frequency should be defined by your business

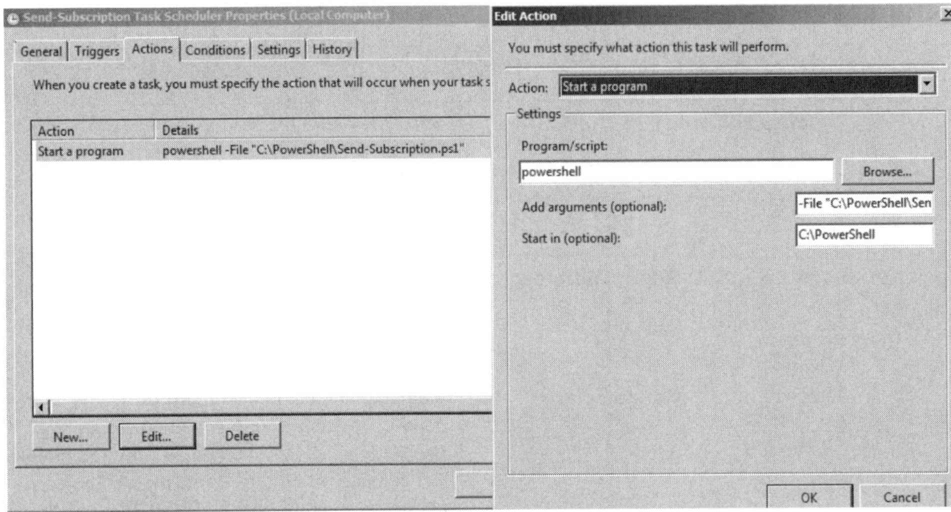

Figure 4 Example settings for creating a new Windows task schedule

requirements, but a nightly run is typically sufficient. After the script is scheduled the reports are rendered and delivered based on the subscription preferences stored in the CSV file. The subscribers of the reports can now expect a report, whether through email or via a shared folder.

There are different ways to schedule the script. You can use Windows Task Scheduler to schedule it: enter `powershell` in the Program/Script field and the complete path to your PowerShell script in the Add Arguments section, as shown in figure 4.

You can also use SQL Server Agent to schedule the script. To do so, create a new job and use `CmdExec` for the job step type. Depending on what the script does you may also need to create a proxy in SQL Server and use that proxy in the Run As section. A sample set of values is provided in figure 5.

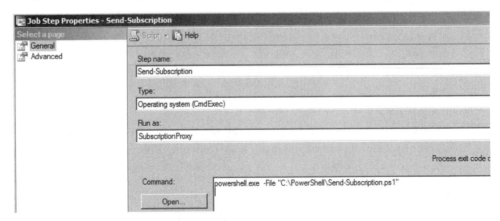

Figure 5 Example settings for SQL Server Agent job step

Taking it further

The scripts in this chapter are basic enough to illustrate how to use PowerShell to create and send subscriptions. To create more flexible scripts you can look at doing the following:

- Using and parsing an XML or JSON file to store subscription information, or storing this information in a table
- Adding more exception handling to the scripts
- Expanding the PowerShell code to use script blocks for conditions, or packaging the code into modules
- Using additional ways of delivering the report(s), such as SFTP
- Logging results to a table instead of a text file

Summary

The scripts presented in this chapter should provide a starting point for creating subscriptions in SSRS using PowerShell even without having a SQL Server Enterprise version. Often, meeting vastly differing requirements for subscriptions can be a huge challenge. Even the data-driven subscription that comes with SQL Server Enterprise doesn't provide flexibility when it comes to dynamic parameters, dynamic schedules, and dynamic rendering formats. PowerShell can help you address those challenges, as presented in this chapter. Using a CSV file and a few custom functions you can create a subscription framework that works in your environment.

About the author

Donabel Santos (SQL Server MVP, MCT, MCITP) is the senior SQL Server developer/DBA/trainer at QueryWorks Solutions, a consulting and training company in Vancouver, BC. She has worked with SQL Server in numerous development, tuning, reporting, and integration projects with ERPs, CRMs, SharePoint, and other custom applications. She is also the lead instructor for a number of SQL Server courses at British Columbia Institute of Technology (BCIT). Donabel is a proud member of the Professional Association of SQL Server (PASS). She blogs (sqlmusings.com), tweets (@sqlbelle), speaks (SQLSaturday, VANPASS, Vancouver TechFest), and writes (Packt, Idera, Manning). You can reach her at donabel.santos@queryworks.ca.

25 Inventory database table statistics using PowerShell and SQL Server Management Objects

Robert C. Cain

SQL Server Management Objects, or SMO, were the only way to interact with SQL Server in the PowerShell v1 days. Although the release of the SQL Provider simplified interacting with SQL Server from PowerShell, there are still many reasons to understand and use SMO with PowerShell. Performance increases, finely tuned control, and access to a large base of existing code samples are but a few of the benefits to understanding and using SMO.

In this chapter you'll create a script to inventory all of the databases on an instance of a SQL Server. The script will query the databases to get statistics for each table in each database—things such as row counts, data space used, and index space used. It will take this data and insert it into a new database named PSMVP, which the script will create if it's not present. In order to achieve the desired results you need to start with a brief overview of SMO.

Understanding SMO

SMO is a set of .NET Framework libraries—dynamic-link libraries (DLLs) you can use from PowerShell. These libraries expose a set of classes from which you can create various objects. If you were to look at the Object Explorer in SQL Server Management Studio you'd soon notice parallels in the SMO libraries. Almost every object in the tree has a corresponding class in SMO.

Using these libraries can be preferable to using the SQL Provider for a few reasons. First, the SQL Provider is heavily reliant on SQL, which is great for database administrators, but a .NET developer will likely find the object model of SMO more natural to work with. Second is the performance issue. When iterating over a large database, using the object model is measurably faster than using the SQL Provider. Finally, a large base of PowerShell code that uses SMO is available on the web. Knowing how to use SMO allows a PowerShell developer to use these code samples confidently.

At the heart of SMO is the `Server` class. Everything in SMO derives from the `Server` class. This class is slightly misnamed, however, as what it represents is the name of the server plus the instance name, as you'll see shortly.

Once you instantiate a `Server` object, as you'll do in this chapter, you can begin to explore your SQL Server, primarily by iterating over the various collections the `Server` object exposes, such as the `Databases` collection.

You can also create SQL Server objects at levels other than the server. For example, you could create a variable that represents a database. This database would come from a specific database in the `Server` objects `Databases` collection. I'll show you an example of that, but first let's see how to set up SMO so you can use it in your PowerShell session.

NOTE The examples in this chapter assume you're executing the code on a computer with SQL Server 2008 or later installed and that you have administrator rights on the SQL Server.

Loading SMO

Before you can begin using the SMO libraries you have to tell PowerShell how to find them. You do this the same way you would for any other set of .NET libraries. First, assign the names of the SMO assemblies into an array, then use `LoadWithPartialName` to load each one, as shown in the following listing.

Listing 1 Loading the SMO libraries

```
$assemblylist =
  "Microsoft.SqlServer.ConnectionInfo",
  "Microsoft.SqlServer.SmoExtended",
  "Microsoft.SqlServer.Smo",
  "Microsoft.SqlServer.Dmf",
  "Microsoft.SqlServer.SqlWmiManagement",
  "Microsoft.SqlServer.Management.RegisteredServers",
  "Microsoft.SqlServer.Management.Sdk.Sfc",
  "Microsoft.SqlServer.SqlEnum",
  "Microsoft.SqlServer.RegSvrEnum",
  "Microsoft.SqlServer.WmiEnum",
  "Microsoft.SqlServer.ServiceBrokerEnum",
  "Microsoft.SqlServer.ConnectionInfoExtended",
  "Microsoft.SqlServer.Management.Collector",
  "Microsoft.SqlServer.Management.CollectorEnum"

foreach ($asm in $assemblylist)
{
  [void][Reflection.Assembly]::LoadWithPartialName($asm)
}
```

You can load these assemblies into memory in several different ways. You can

- Put the code shown in listing 1 directly in the current script you're running
- Place the code in its own PS1 file in a central folder, and then execute it from your current script
- Place the code in your profile, if you'll be interacting with SQL Server on a daily basis, so the SMO libraries will always be available and ready for use

The Server object

Once you've loaded the libraries you can start using SMO. To do so you'll need to know the name of the server you wish to work with. You could hard-code the name into your script. Or many people place the names of their servers into a text file, from which they can load them and loop through all the servers repeating the same set of commands.

Another way, one that's portable (especially if you're working with one server at a time), is to use the computer name environment variable, or `$env:COMPUTERNAME`. This will return the name of the computer on which the current script is running. This makes script reuse much easier, as you won't have to change your scripts for each server you want to run on.

If you recall from the "Understanding SMO" section, the `Server` object represents a server plus an instance. If the instance you want to work with is the default instance on the server you may omit the instance name. If you're working with a named instance you could include the instance name with your list of stored server names, or any other method from which you could result in the final server/instance name combination. For the purpose of this chapter, assume you're using the default instance, also known as localhost, which you can omit.

For the rest of the chapter the following code line will indicate the current server and instance:

```
$instance = "$env:COMPUTERNAME"
```

After all that, creating a `Server` object is pretty simple, as you can see here:

```
$instance = $env:COMPUTERNAME
$Server = New-Object Microsoft.SqlServer.Management.Smo.Server("$instance")
```

`New-Object` is PowerShell's cmdlet for creating a new object from a class in a .NET library. `Microsoft.SqlServer.Managment.Smo` is the specific path in your library where your class can be found. `Server` is the class you're going to create a new object from. Finally, you pass the server and instance, in the form of the `$instance` variable, to the `Server` class's constructor.

These two lines of code will be the launching point for the rest of your project. It's through the `Server` object that you can use the rest of the SMO library.

Creating the inventory database using SMO

The first thing you need is a database to hold the results of your inventory. The following listing creates the database.

Listing 2 Creating the database

```
$instance = $env:COMPUTERNAME
$server = New-Object Microsoft.SqlServer.Management.Smo.Server("$instance")

if ($Server.Databases.Contains("PSMVP") -eq $false)
{
  $db = New-Object
    ➥ Microsoft.SqlServer.Management.Smo.Database($server, "PSMVP")

  $fg = New-Object
    ➥ Microsoft.SqlServer.Management.Smo.FileGroup ($db, 'PRIMARY')
  $db.Filegroups.Add($fg)

  $mdf = New-Object
    ➥ Microsoft.SqlServer.Management.Smo.DataFile($fg, "PSMVP_Data")
  $fg.Files.Add($mdf)
  $mdf.FileName = "C:\SQLdata\PSMVP_Data.mdf"
  $mdf.Size = 30.0 * 1KB
  $mdf.GrowthType = "Percent"
  $mdf.Growth = 10.0
  $mdf.IsPrimaryFile = "True"

  $ldf = New-Object
    ➥ Microsoft.SqlServer.Management.Smo.LogFile($db, "PSMVP_Log")
  $db.LogFiles.Add($ldf)
  $ldf.FileName = "C:\SQLlog\PSMVP_Log.ldf"
  $ldf.Size = 20.0 * 1KB
  $ldf.GrowthType = "Percent"
  $ldf.Growth = 10.0

  $db.Create()
}
```

In this listing you first check to see if the database already exists on your server. The `.Databases` after the `Server` variable represents a list, or a collection, of all the databases on the server. You can check to see if PSMVP is already in the collection by using the `Contains()` method. If `false` is returned, the `if` statement is triggered to create the database.

You then create a new database *object*. Note the stress on the word *object*. At this point the database only exists as a construct in memory—that is, as an object. You haven't written it to the server yet.

Next you start assembling the various pieces that make up a SQL Server database. You create a file group object, then define the location and sizes for the database and log files. As each piece is created it's added to the database object.

The last line ties it all together. You call the `Create()` method of the database object. With this command you write the database to the SQL Server.

Creating the TableStats table using SMO

Once a database exists to hold your inventory you need to ensure there's a table to hold the table statistics you want in your inventory. Just as the server has a collection of databases, each database object has a collection of table objects. The `Contains()` method works here as well, and you'll use it to see if your TableStats table already exists. If not you'll need to create it. The following listing creates the table.

Listing 3 Creating the table

```
$instance = $env:COMPUTERNAME
$Server = New-Object
  ➥ Microsoft.SqlServer.Management.Smo.Server("$instance")
$db = $Server.Databases["PSMVP"]
if ($db.Tables.Contains("TableStats") -eq $false)
{
  $table = New-Object                                                    ❶ Create table object
    ➥ Microsoft.SqlServer.Management.Smo.Table($db, "TableStats")
  $col1 = New-Object                                                     ❷ Create columns
    ➥ Microsoft.SqlServer.Management.Smo.Column ($table, "TableStatsID")
  $col1.DataType = [Microsoft.SqlServer.Management.Smo.Datatype]::Int
  $col1.Nullable = $false
  $col1.Identity = $true
  $col1.IdentitySeed = 1
  $col1.IdentityIncrement = 1
  $table.Columns.Add($col1)
  $col2 = New-Object
    ➥ Microsoft.SqlServer.Management.Smo.Column ($table, "DatabaseName")
  $col2.DataType =
    ➥ [Microsoft.SqlServer.Management.Smo.Datatype]::NVarChar(250)
  $col2.Nullable = $false
  $table.Columns.Add($col2)
  $col3 = New-Object
    ➥ Microsoft.SqlServer.Management.Smo.Column ($table, "TableName")
  $col3.DataType =
    ➥ [Microsoft.SqlServer.Management.Smo.Datatype]::NVarChar(250)
  $col3.Nullable = $false
  $table.Columns.Add($col3)
  $col4 = New-Object
    ➥ Microsoft.SqlServer.Management.Smo.Column ($table, "FileGroup")
  $col4.DataType =
    ➥ [Microsoft.SqlServer.Management.Smo.Datatype]::NVarChar(250)
  $col4.Nullable = $false
  $table.Columns.Add($col4)
  $col5 = New-Object
    ➥ Microsoft.SqlServer.Management.Smo.Column ($table, "TableOwner")
  $col5.DataType =
    ➥ [Microsoft.SqlServer.Management.Smo.Datatype]::NVarChar(250)
```

```
    $col5.Nullable = $false
    $table.Columns.Add($col5)

    $col6 = New-Object
      ➥ Microsoft.SqlServer.Management.Smo.Column ($table, "RowCount")
    $col6.DataType = [Microsoft.SqlServer.Management.Smo.Datatype]::Int
    $col6.Nullable = $false
    $table.Columns.Add($col6)

    $col7 = New-Object
      ➥ Microsoft.SqlServer.Management.Smo.Column ($table, "DataSpaceUsed")
    $col7.DataType = [Microsoft.SqlServer.Management.Smo.Datatype]::Int
    $col7.Nullable = $false
    $table.Columns.Add($col7)

    $col8 = New-Object
      ➥ Microsoft.SqlServer.Management.Smo.Column ($table, "IndexSpaceUsed")
    $col8.DataType = [Microsoft.SqlServer.Management.Smo.Datatype]::Int
    $col8.Nullable = $false
    $table.Columns.Add($col8)

    $col9 = New-Object
      ➥ Microsoft.SqlServer.Management.Smo.Column ($table, "Replicated")
    $col9.DataType =
      ➥ [Microsoft.SqlServer.Management.Smo.Datatype]::NVarChar(20)
    $col9.Nullable = $false

    $table.Columns.Add($col9)                               <-- 3 Add columns to table

    $table.Create()                                         <-- 4 Create the table

    $pk = New-Object Microsoft.SqlServer.Management.Smo.Index(   <-- 5 Create primary key
      ➥ $table,"PK_TableStatsId")
    $pk.IndexKeyType =
      ➥ [Microsoft.SqlServer.Management.Smo.IndexKeyType]::DriPrimaryKey

    $ic = New-Object                                        <-- 6 Add the index to the column
      ➥ Microsoft.SqlServer.Management.Smo.IndexedColumn($pk, "TableStatsID")
    $pk.IndexedColumns.Add($ic)

    $table.Indexes.Add($pk)

    $table.Alter()                                          <-- 7 Add index to table
}
```

In this listing you begin by creating a table object ❶. At this point the table only exists as an item in memory; you haven't written it to the database yet.

Next you define each column you want in the table ❷, providing a name, along with the data type and size, and whether it's nullable. For the column that will become the primary-key column you add the attributes to indicate it's an identity column.

Once you create each column as an object in memory you add that column object to the columns collection of the table object ❸.

After adding the columns you can write the table to the database using the `Create()` method ❹ of the table object. But you're not done yet!

As a final task you should create a primary key. You'll use the first column you defined, `TableStatusId`, as your key ❺.

The flow is similar to other tasks in SMO. Begin by creating a new object of type `SMO.Index`. Next define what type of index it is, in this case a primary-key index.

Next create an object that will contain the first (and in this case only) column of your index. Map that index column to the `TableStatusId` column in the table. Then add this index column to the index columns collection of your index object.

As the next-to-last step, add the new index to the indexes collection of your table object, using the `Add()` method ❻. Finally, modify the existing table by using the `Alter()` method ❼. At this point the new index is written to the database.

Resetting from previous runs

It's likely that you'll run this script many times. When you do you should remove any data from previous runs. The following listing accomplishes this.

Listing 4 Removing rows from previous runs

```
$instance = $env:COMPUTERNAME
$Server = New-Object
  ➥ Microsoft.SqlServer.Management.Smo.Server("$instance")
$db = $Server.Databases["PSMVP"]
$tb = $db.Tables["TableStats"]
if ($tb.RowCount -gt 0)
{
  $dbcmd = "TRUNCATE TABLE dbo.TableStats"
  $db.ExecuteNonQuery($dbcmd)
}
```

In this script you first get a reference to the TableStats table. Then you check to see if there are any rows by querying the `RowCount` property.

If there are rows put a SQL statement in a variable, in this case a command to truncate the table. Then run the command by using the `ExecuteNonQuery()` method of the database object. `ExecuteNonQuery()` will run a command on the SQL Server but not expect any result to be returned.

Gathering inventory data

Now we come to the heart of the script—gathering your inventory data. The following listing accomplishes this.

Listing 5 Gathering the inventory data

```
$instance = $env:COMPUTERNAME
$Server = New-Object
  ➥ Microsoft.SqlServer.Management.Smo.Server("$instance")
$db = $Server.Databases["PSMVP"]

foreach($database in $Server.Databases)
{
  $dbName = $database.Name.Replace("[", "").Replace("]","")
```

```
  foreach($table in $database.Tables)
  {
    $tableName = "$dbName\$($table.schema).$($table.Name)"
    $tableName

    $dbcmd = @"
      INSERT INTO dbo.TableStats
        ( [DatabaseName]
        , [TableName]
        , [FileGroup]
        , [TableOwner]
        , [RowCount]
        , [DataSpaceUsed]
        , [IndexSpaceUsed]
        , [Replicated]
        )
      VALUES
        ( '$dbName'
        , '$($table.schema).$($table.Name)'
        , '$($table.FileGroup)'
        , '$($table.Owner)'
        , $($table.RowCount)
        , $($table.DataSpaceUsed)
        , $($table.IndexSpaceUsed)
        , '$($table.Replicated)'
        )
"@

    $db.ExecuteNonQuery($dbcmd)
  }
}
```

You start by getting a reference to the server you want to gather stats on. You also get a reference to the PSMVP database, as you'll need it to issue SQL commands against.

The script has two `foreach` loops. The outer loop iterates over each database in the server's database collection. The inner loop iterates over each table in the current database from the outer loop.

Next, for each table, you assemble an `INSERT` SQL command within a PowerShell here-string and use the various properties of the current table object to supply data for your SQL statement.

Note that for this example I've chosen a few of the most common properties of a table to include in the inventory table. Many more properties are available to choose from.

The complete list of all objects of the SMO, along with their properties, is available on MSDN at http://msdn.microsoft.com/en-us/library/ms162209.aspx.

As the final step you use `ExecuteNonQuery()` to insert your row into the inventory table.

Querying the data

Now that your inventory database is populated with table data, it would be nice to recover that data within PowerShell. There's a parallel to the `ExecuteNonQuery()`

method named `ExecuteWithResults()`. This method allows you to pass in a SQL `SELECT` statement and return the results to a variable, as shown in the following listing.

Listing 6 Returning data from the inventory

```
$instance = $env:COMPUTERNAME
$Server = New-Object
  ➥ Microsoft.SqlServer.Management.Smo.Server("$instance")
$db = $Server.Databases["PSMVP"]

$dbcmd = @"
  SELECT [TableStatsID]
       , [DatabaseName]
       , [TableName]
       , [FileGroup]
       , [TableOwner]
       , [RowCount]
       , [DataSpaceUsed]
       , [IndexSpaceUsed]
       , [Replicated]
    FROM [dbo].[TableStats]
"@

$ds = $db.ExecuteWithResults($dbcmd)

$dt = $ds.Tables[0]

$dt | Format-Table -Property DatabaseName, TableName, RowCount -Autosize
```

The variable that's created is called a `DataSet` and is analogous to a database. It contains a collection of one or more tables, only here they're of a variable type `DataTable`. Each `DataTable` has a collection of `DataRow` objects, similar to rows in a table.

In listing 6, because you only have one `DataTable` being returned, you can use array-style notation to grab it and assign it to a variable. Otherwise you could have used a `foreach` to iterate over each `DataTable` in the `DataSet`.

Here are the first few lines of results from the last line in listing 6:

```
DatabaseName         TableName                     RowCount
------------         ---------                     --------
AdventureWorks2012 dbo.AWBuildVersion                     1
AdventureWorks2012 dbo.DatabaseLog                     1597
AdventureWorks2012 dbo.ErrorLog                           0
AdventureWorks2012 HumanResources.Department             16
AdventureWorks2012 HumanResources.Employee              290
```

One of the nice things PowerShell does for you is to take the column names from the database and convert them to property names in the data table. In this example the selection is limited to three columns so they fit on the printed page.

Other ways to use the data

You can use the data you retrieve in several ways. For example, you can save it to a CSV file for use as documentation in the future:

```
$dt | Export-Csv -Path C:\Temp\PSMVP.csv
```

You can also iterate over each row of the returned data table in a `foreach` loop, as is shown in the following listing. This example lists tables with more than 100,000 rows, but you can do anything you want within the `foreach` loop. (Be sure to run listing 6 first in order to put data in the `$dt` variable.)

Listing 7 Iterating over each row

```
Write-Output "Tables with a row count in excess of 100,000 rows`r`n"
foreach($row in $dt)
{
  if ($row.RowCount -gt 100000)
  {
    "$($row.DatabaseName).$($row.TableName) has $($row.RowCount) rows."
  }
}
```

Here's the output from listing 6 on my system:

```
Tables with a row count in excess of 100,000 rows

AdventureWorks2012.Production.TransactionHistory has 113443 rows.
AdventureWorks2012.Sales.SalesOrderDetail has 121317 rows.
AdventureWorks2012_CS.Production.TransactionHistory has 113443 rows.
AdventureWorks2012_CS.Sales.SalesOrderDetail has 121317 rows.
AdventureWorksDW2012.dbo.FactProductInventory has 776286 rows.
BigNumbers.dbo.BigNumbers has 1000000 rows.
BIxPress.dbo.SSISDataFlowExecutionLog has 1036118 rows.
BIxPress Stress Test.Destination.BigNumbersTarget has 116297048 rows.
BIxPress Stress Test.Source.BigNumbers has 10000000 rows.
Global Change 1.dbo.BigNumbers has 1000000 rows.
Global Change 1.dbo.BigNumbersTarget has 1000000 rows.
SSISDB.internal.event_message_context has 252334 rows.
SSISDB.internal.event_messages has 1237112 rows.
SSISDB.internal.executable_statistics has 157719 rows.
SSISDB.internal.operation_messages has 1237112 rows.
```

You can also produce a nice-looking report by taking the output of listing 6 and piping it through several common cmdlets, as shown in the following listing.

Listing 8 Formatting the data table

```
$dt |
  Select-Object DatabaseName, TableName, RowCount |
  Where-Object {$_.RowCount -gt 100000 } |
  Sort-Object RowCount -Descending |
  Format-Table @{ Label='Database Name'
                  Expression={$_.DatabaseName}
                },
               @{ Label='Table Name'
                  Expression={$_.TableName}
                },
               @{ Label='Number of Rows'
                  Expression={$_.RowCount}
                  FormatString='#,0'
                  Width=15
                } -AutoSize
```

Here's the output from listing 8:

```
Database Name          Table Name                         Number of Rows
-------------          ----------                         --------------
BIxPress Stress Test   Destination.BigNumbersTarget          116,297,048
BIxPress Stress Test   Source.BigNumbers                      10,000,000
SSISDB                 internal.event_messages                 1,237,112
SSISDB                 internal.operation_messages             1,237,112
BIxPress               dbo.SSISDataFlowExecutionLog            1,036,118
BigNumbers             dbo.BigNumbers                          1,000,000
Global Change 1        dbo.BigNumbers                          1,000,000
Global Change 1        dbo.BigNumbersTarget                    1,000,000
AdventureWorksDW2012   dbo.FactProductInventory                  776,286
SSISDB                 internal.event_message_context            252,334
SSISDB                 internal.executable_statistics            157,719
AdventureWorks2012     Sales.SalesOrderDetail                    121,317
AdventureWorks2012_CS  Sales.SalesOrderDetail                    121,317
AdventureWorks2012     Production.TransactionHistory             113,443
AdventureWorks2012_CS  Production.TransactionHistory             113,443
```

In listing 8 `Select-Object` limits your results to only three columns. Next, `Where-Object` removes all tables with 100,000 rows or fewer. Note that the PowerShell v2 syntax of `Where-Object` is used for backward compatibility.

Next, `Sort-Object` sorts the tables so that the one with the most rows will be presented first, followed by the rest of the tables in descending order. Finally, you use `Format-Table`, using expressions to print and nicely format each column.

Summary

The techniques shown in this chapter are only the tip of the iceberg when it comes to SMO. You can expand this script to hold inventory data for indexes, stored procedures, and so on; just about any object in SQL Server can be inventoried and stored.

The SMO model is deep; with it, you can accomplish any task within SQL Server. Because you're going right to the objects you'll often get much better performance than with the SQL Provider. Finally, having a good understanding of SMO allows you to take advantage of all those wonderful code samples available on the internet.

About the author

Robert C. Cain (http://arcanecode.com) is a Microsoft MVP in SQL Server and a Microsoft Certified Technology Specialist in Business Intelligence. He works as a senior consultant for Pragmatic Works, is a technical contributor to Plurasight Training, and has coauthored three books. A popular speaker, Robert has presented at events such as TechEd, SQL Rally, SQL PASS, SQL Saturdays, and PowerShell Saturdays. Robert has over 25 years' experience in the IT industry, working in a variety of fields ranging from manufacturing to telecommunications to nuclear power.

26 WSUS and PowerShell

Boe Prox

Windows Software Update Services (WSUS) ensures that all of your system's patching remains up-to-date and provides a way to report the status of patches and clients. The UI can be clunky and slow, but you can automate some processes with a WSUS API, a Windows Server 2012 module, or an open source WSUS module called `PoshWSUS` that I wrote for PowerShell (http://poshwsus.codeplex.com) to quickly manage and generate reports.

Instead of looking at the existing cmdlets available in the Windows Server 2012 `UpdateServices` module, I'll show you some API tricks for using PowerShell to manage WSUS configuration and events, provide reporting on various client and patch statuses, start and view synchronization progress and history, and view and create automatic installation rules to simplify patch management by approving common updates.

WSUS server configuration and events

In WSUS two of the most basic administration tasks are client management and patch management. Before Windows Server 2012 the only ways to manage these tasks were to work with the UI or dig into the API via scripts or the open source module, `PoshWSUS`. With Windows Server 2012 the WSUS module called `UpdateServices` makes it easier to manage clients. The `UpdateServices` module is available only on the WSUS server, allowing you to manage the server remotely using PowerShell. If you're not using Windows Server 2012 you'll need to use the API to manage a remote WSUS server.

Initial connection

To make a connection to the WSUS server both locally or remotely with the API you must install the WSUS Administration console on the system from which you'll make the connection. Once the console is installed you'll have access to the assemblies required for the WSUS connection. Let's load the assembly and make the initial connection to the WSUS server:

```
[reflection.assembly]::LoadWithPartialName(
  ➥ "Microsoft.UpdateServices.Administration") |
  ➥ out-null
```

For the connection attempt, I'm using the `Microsoft.UpdateServices.Administration.AdminProxy` class along with the `GetUpdateServer()` method. This method accepts one of three parameter sets based on your WSUS configuration and whether it's a remote or local connection. For the remote connection I need to supply the remote system name, a Boolean value that designates whether the connection is secure or not, and the remote port that I need to connect to on the WSUS server. Acceptable ports for WSUS are 8080 and 8530 (for nonsecure ports) and 443 and 8531 (for SSL):

```
$Wsus =
  ➥ [Microsoft.UpdateServices.Administration.AdminProxy]::GetUpdateServer(
                                                         "Boe-PC",
                                                         $False,
                                                         "8530"
                                                      )
$Wsus

WebServiceUrl                      : http://BOE-PC:8530/ApiRemoting30/WebSe..
BypassApiRemoting                  : False
IsServerLocal                      : True
Name                               : BOE-PC
Version                            : 6.2.9200.16384
IsConnectionSecureForApiRemoting   : True
PortNumber                         : 8530
PreferredCulture                   : en
ServerName                         : BOE-PC
UseSecureConnection                : False
ServerProtocolVersion              : 1.8
```

From here you can see information such as the version number of the WSUS software. The most important thing here is that we successfully connected to the WSUS server.

Viewing WSUS configuration

Once the initial connection is made you can look at the internal configuration settings of the WSUS server using the `GetConfiguration()` method of the `Microsoft.UpdateServices.Internal.BaseApi.UpdateServer` object:

```
$wsus.GetConfiguration()

UpdateServer                                :
Microsoft.UpdateServices.Internal.BaseApi.UpdateServer
LastConfigChange                            : 9/17/2012 2:22:43 AM
ServerId                                    : 64ad0f03-e81d-4539-…
SupportedUpdateLanguages                    : {he, cs, fr, es...}
TargetingMode                               : Server
SyncFromMicrosoftUpdate                     : True
```

```
IsReplicaServer                                  : False
HostBinariesOnMicrosoftUpdate                    : False
UpstreamWsusServerName                           :
UpstreamWsusServerPortNumber                     : 8530
UpstreamWsusServerUseSsl                         : False
UseProxy                                         : False
ProxyName                                        :
ProxyServerPort                                  : 80
UseSeparateProxyForSsl                           : False
SslProxyName                                     :
SslProxyServerPort                               : 443
AnonymousProxyAccess                             : True
ProxyUserName                                    :
ProxyUserDomain                                  :
HasProxyPassword                                 : False
AllowProxyCredentialsOverNonSsl                  : False
...
```

This method returns a marginal number of 121 properties. You can set and easily update the majority of these properties from PowerShell, but use caution when making any changes to the properties here as it could leave you troubleshooting the server to find out what changed. For example, accidentally updating `IsReplicaServer` to `True` forces your WSUS server to be a replica of the upstream server, which inherits the computer groups and approvals of the upstream server.

Viewing the WSUS database connection

You can look at the database connection and database properties from your WSUS server using the `GetDatabaseConfiguration()` method or the `CreateConnection()` method from the created `Microsoft.UpdateServices.Internal.DatabaseConfiguration` object:

```
$wsus.GetDatabaseConfiguration()

UpdateServer                    :
Microsoft.UpdateServices.Internal.BaseApi.UpdateServer
ServerName                      : MICROSOFT##WID
DatabaseName                    : SUSDB
IsUsingWindowsInternalDatabase  : True
AuthenticationMode              : WindowsAuthentication
UserName                        :
Password                        :

$wsus.GetDatabaseConfiguration().CreateConnection()

QueryTimeOut       : 150
LoginTimeOut       : 60
ConnectionPooling  : True
ApplicationName    : WSUS:powershell:1824
UserLoginName      :
UseIntegrated      : True
ConnectionString   :
MaxPoolSize        : 100
DoRetry            : False
DefaultRetryTimes  : 3
```

```
ServerName          : MICROSOFT##WID
DatabaseName        : SUSDB
Password            :
IsConnected         : False
InTransaction       : False
```

The level of detail that you can get about the database is helpful, such as the database name and database instance name. In fact, you could delve deeper into the database if you want to perform queries using the `ExecuteReader()` method, but that's beyond the scope of this chapter.

Viewing WSUS event history

If you're interested in viewing the event history of the WSUS server, call the `GetUpdateEventHistory(StartDate,EndDate)` method and supply a `StartDate` and an `EndDate`. In this case I want to look at the events that have occurred during the past hour:

```
$wsus.GetUpdateEventHistory("$((Get-Date).AddHours(-1))","$(Get-Date)")

UpdateServer            : Microsoft.UpdateServices.Internal....
HasAssociatedUpdate     : False
UpdateId                : Microsoft.UpdateServices....
HasAssociatedComputer   : False
ComputerId              :
Status                  : Unknown
WsusEventId             : ContentSynchronizationSucceeded
WsusEventSource         : Server
Id                      : f01cb84f-9a0b-4da8-a12a-39a6866c5787
CreationDate            : 9/23/2012 7:08:20 PM
Message                 : Content synchronization succeeded.
IsError                 : False
ErrorCode               : 0
Row                     : Microsoft.UpdateServices.Internal....
UpdateServer            : Microsoft.UpdateServices.Internal.BaseApi...
HasAssociatedUpdate     : True
UpdateId                : Microsoft.UpdateServices.Administrati...
HasAssociatedComputer   : False
ComputerId              :
Status                  : Unknown
WsusEventId             : ContentSynchronizationFileDownloadSucceeded
WsusEventSource         : Server
Id                      : 0c7ade08-87d6-4019-b676-0f50ce486591
CreationDate            : 9/23/2012 7:08:20 PM
Message                 : Content file download succeeded. Di...x86_830994754
                          ba721add8a13bd0266d2e092f21cab0.exe
Destination File:
                          F:\WsusContent\B0\....
IsError                 : False
ErrorCode               : 0
Row                     : Microsoft.UpdateServices.Internal....
```

With this information you can audit for any possible failures that have occurred due to a recent synchronization or another problem that might have caused a WSUS issue.

Automatic approval rules

With WSUS you can automate patch approvals by creating and configuring automatic approval rules. You can specify categories and target groups, among other things, to use for the rules.

Locating approval rules

To locate the rules currently on the WSUS server, use the `GetApprovalRules()` method from the `Microsoft.UpdateServices.Internal.BaseApi.UpdateServer` object created from the initial connection:

```
$wsus.GetInstallApprovalRules()

UpdateServer   : Microsoft.UpdateServices.Internal.BaseApi.UpdateServer
Id             : 2
Name           : Default Automatic Approval Rule
Enabled        : False
Action         : Install
Deadline       :
CanSetDeadline : True
```

The result does not show all of the information for the approval rules. To learn what target groups, classifications, and categories are in the `Microsoft.UpdateServices.Internal.BaseApi.AutomaticUpdateApprovalRule` object, use the `GetUpdateClassifications()`, `GetComputerTargetGroups()`, and `GetUpdateCategories()` methods, respectively:

```
$approvalRules = $wsus.GetInstallApprovalRules()

$wsus.GetInstallApprovalRules()[0].GetUpdateClassifications()    <-- Gets classifications
UpdateServer                : Microsoft.UpdateS...
Id                          : e6cf1350-c01b-414d-a61f-263d14d133b4
Title                       : Critical Updates
Description                 : A broadly released fix for a specific problem
                              addressing a critical, non-security related
                              bug.
ReleaseNotes                :
DefaultPropertiesLanguage   :
DisplayOrder                : 2147483647
ArrivalDate                 : 9/23/2012 6:51:37 PM

UpdateServer                : Microsoft.UpdateService...
Id                          : 0fa1201d-4330-4fa8-8ae9-b877473b6441
Title                       : Security Updates
Description                 : A broadly released fix for a product-specific
                              security-related vulnerability. Security
                              vulnerabilities are rated based on their
                              severity which is indicated in the Microsoft®
                              security bulletin as critical, important,
                              moderate, or low.
ReleaseNotes                :
DefaultPropertiesLanguage   :
DisplayOrder                : 2147483647
ArrivalDate                 : 9/23/2012 6:40:34 PM
```

```
$wsus.GetInstallApprovalRules()[0].
GetComputerTargetGroups()                                         <-- Gets target groups
UpdateServer             Id                       Name
------------             --                       ----
Microsoft.UpdateService... a0a08746-4dbe-4a37-9adf... All Computers

$wsus.GetInstallApprovalRules()[0].GetCategories()                <-- Gets categories
Type                       : Product
ProhibitsSubcategories     : True
ProhibitsUpdates           : False
UpdateSource               : MicrosoftUpdate
UpdateServer               : Microsoft.UpdateServices....
Id                         : a105a108-7c9b-4518-bbbe-73f0fe30012b
Title                      : Windows Server 2012
Description                : Windows Server 2012
ReleaseNotes               :
DefaultPropertiesLanguage  :
DisplayOrder               : 2147483647
ArrivalDate                : 9/23/2012 6:47:20 PM
```

Now that you know what rules already exist on the WSUS server you can create new rules to automate server tasks.

Creating approval rules

Creating an approval involves the following steps:

1. Create the approval object with a name.
2. Fill in the blanks for the configuration details (target groups, categories, classifications, and so on) of the object.
3. Deploy the object on the server.

Before you create the object get a list of the current rules to verify that the new rule (2012Servers) doesn't already exist:

```
$wsus.GetInstallApprovalRules()

UpdateServer   : Microsoft.UpdateServices.Internal.BaseApi.UpdateServer
Id             : 2
Name           : Default Automatic Approval Rule
Enabled        : False
Action         : Install
Deadline       :
CanSetDeadline : True
```

No rule exists with the name "2012Servers", so you can create the new approval rule, as shown in the following listing.

Listing 1 Creating the 2012Servers approval rule

```
[cmdletbinding()]
Param (
  [parameter(ValueFromPipeline=$True,Mandatory=$True,
  HelpMessage="Name of WSUS server to connect to.")]
  [Alias('WSUSServer')]
```

```
    [string]$Computername,
    [parameter()]
    [Switch]$UseSSL
)
[reflection.assembly]::LoadWithPartialName(
  "Microsoft.UpdateServices.Administration"
) | out-null
$Wsus = `
[Microsoft.UpdateServices.Administration.AdminProxy]::GetUpdateServer(
  $Computername,$UseSSL,$Port
)

$newRule = $wsus.CreateInstallApprovalRule("2012Servers")

$updateCategories = $wsus.GetUpdateCategories() | Where {
  $_.Title -LIKE "Windows Server 2012*"
}

$categoryCollection = New-Object `
Microsoft.UpdateServices.Administration.UpdateCategoryCollection
$categoryCollection.AddRange($updateCategories)

$newRule.SetCategories($categoryCollection)

$updateClassifications = $wsus.GetUpdateClassifications() | Where {
  $_.Title -Match "Critical Updates|Service Packs|Updates|Security Updates"
}

$classificationCollection = New-Object `
Microsoft.UpdateServices.Administration.UpdateClassificationCollection
$classificationCollection.AddRange($updateClassifications )

$newRule.SetUpdateClassifications($classificationCollection)

$targetGroups = $wsus.GetComputerTargetGroups() | Where {
  $_.Name -Match "All Computers"
}

$targetgroupCollection = New-Object `
Microsoft.UpdateServices.Administration.ComputerTargetGroupCollection
$targetgroupCollection.AddRange($targetGroups)

$newRule.SetComputerTargetGroups($targetgroupCollection)

$newRule.Enabled = $True
$newRule.Save()

$newRule.ApplyRule()
```

Creates new rule object

Gets, creates, and adds categories collection

Gets, creates, and adds classification collection

Gets, creates, and adds target groups collection

Runs rule against target group

Again, get a list of the current rules, this time to verify that the new rule exists:

```
$wsus.GetInstallApprovalRules()

UpdateServer   : Microsoft.UpdateServices.Internal.BaseApi.UpdateServer
Id             : 2
Name           : Default Automatic Approval Rule
Enabled        : False
Action         : Install
Deadline       :
CanSetDeadline : True
```

```
UpdateServer    : Microsoft.UpdateServices.Internal.BaseApi.UpdateServer
Id              : 6
Name            : 2012Servers
Enabled         : True
Action          : Install
Deadline        :
CanSetDeadline  : True
```

Now we have a new approval rule that approves only the updates specified for Windows Server 2012 systems. Keep in mind that the automatic approval rules run after the WSUS synchronizes, and only the synched updates are eligible for the rule unless you run the rule manually.

Reporting in WSUS

With WSUS you have options available for reporting on updates, clients, and synchronizations. With PowerShell you can create various reports not only on all of these items but also on conditions to narrow the scope of the reports. For example, you could report on only the updates that failed to install on the clients. The following sections show scripts for reporting with PowerShell. Each of the following reporting scripts outputs objects that can be exported to a CSV file or used for an HTML file, if needed.

Failed update installations

When updates fail to install from a WSUS server, you need to identify those failed patches on each system.

The following report runs the function `Get-FailedUpdateInstallation`, which queries for all updates that reported back to the WSUS server as `Failed`. The report returns additional information, including the client that couldn't install the update:

```
Get-FailedUpdateInstallation

InstallationState : Failed
TargetGroup       : Windows 2003
Computer          : DC1
ApprovalAction    : Install
Update            : Security Update for Windows Server 2003 (KB2731847)
```

The code for the `Get-FailedUpdateInstallation` function is shown in the following listing.

Listing 2 `Get-FailedUpdateInstallation`

```
Function Get-FailedUpdateInstallation {
  [cmdletbinding()]
  Param (
    [parameter(ValueFromPipeline=$True,
    HelpMessage="Name of WSUS server to connect to.")]
    [Alias('WSUSServer')]
    [string]$Computername,
```

```
    [parameter()]
    [ValidateSet(80,443,8530,8531)]
    [Int]$Port = 80,
    [parameter()]
    [Switch]$UseSSL
  )
  Begin {
    [reflection.assembly]::LoadWithPartialName(                 <-- Loads required assemblies
 "Microsoft.UpdateServices.Administration") | out-null
    $Wsus = `
[Microsoft.UpdateServices.Administration.AdminProxy]::GetUpdateServer(
      $Computername,$False,$Port
    )
    $updateScope = New-Object
     Microsoft.UpdateServices.Administration.UpdateScope         | Creates and
    $updateScope.IncludedInstallationStates = `                 | configures
[Microsoft.UpdateServices.Administration.UpdateInstallationStates] | update scope
  ➥ ::Failed
  }
  Process {
    $wsus.GetComputerTargets() | ForEach {
      $_.GetUpdateInstallationInfoPerUpdate($UpdateScope) | ForEach {
        $object = New-Object PSObject -Property @{
          Computer = $_.GetComputerTarget().FullDomainName
          Update = $_.GetUpdate().Title
          TargetGroup = `
$wsus.GetComputerTargetGroup($_.UpdateApprovalTargetGroupId).Name
          InstallationState = $_.UpdateInstallationState
          ApprovalAction = $_.UpdateApprovalAction
        }
        $object.pstypenames.insert(0,"wsus.updateinstallation")
        $object
      }
    }
  }
}
```

Iterates through computers and pulls installation information

The `Get-FailedUpdateInstallation` rule automates the process of determining which updates failed to install so you can monitor and resolve failures more efficiently.

Auditing approvals

Sometimes you want to know who approved an update during a patching cycle or what has been approved since the last Patch Tuesday[1].

The following report runs the function `Get-ApprovalAudit`, which pulls the update approvals for all patches synchronized since a specified date. The `StartDate` and `EndDate` parameters designate the synchronization date, but not the approval date, for the patches. In this report example I'm looking for everything approved since the last Patch Tuesday:

---

1 Patch Tuesday is the second Tuesday of every month when Microsoft regularly releases security updates.

```
Get-ApprovalAudit -Computername Boe-PC -Port 8530 -StartDate "09/10/2012"

Action            : Install
Deadline          : 12/31/9999 11:59:59 PM
CreationDate      : 9/29/2012 3:38:20 AM
TargetGroup       : All Computers
AdministratorName : WUS Server
GoLiveTime        : 9/29/2012 3:38:20 AM
Title             : Update for Windows 7 (KB2735855)

Action            : Install
Deadline          : 12/31/9999 11:59:59 PM
CreationDate      : 9/29/2012 3:41:32 AM
TargetGroup       : All Computers
AdministratorName : WUS Server
GoLiveTime        : 9/29/2012 3:41:32 AM
Title             : Update for Windows Server 2008 R2 for Itanium-based
     Systems (KB2735855)

Action            : Install
Deadline          : 12/31/9999 11:59:59 PM
CreationDate      : 9/29/2012 3:43:47 AM
TargetGroup       : All Computers
AdministratorName : WUS Server
GoLiveTime        : 9/29/2012 3:43:47 AM
Title             : Update for Windows Server 2008 R2 x64 Edition (KB2735855)
```

The account that approved the patches, WUS Server, gave approval using an automatic approval rule. The `CreationDate` lists when the WSUS server approved this update for installation.

The code for the `Get-ApprovalAudit` function is shown in the following listing.

Listing 3 Get-ApprovalAudit

```
Function Get-ApprovalAudit {
  [cmdletbinding()]
  Param (
    [parameter(Mandatory=$True,ValueFromPipeline=$True,
    HelpMessage="Name of WSUS server to connect to.")]
    [Alias('WSUSServer')]
    [string]$Computername,
    [parameter()]
    [ValidateSet(80,443,8530,8531)]
    [Int]$Port = 80,
    [parameter()]
    [Switch]$UseSSL,
    [parameter()]
    [DateTime]$StartDate,
    [parameter()]
    [DateTime]$EndDate
  )
  Begin {
    [reflection.assembly]::LoadWithPartialName(
"Microsoft.UpdateServices.Administration") | out-null
    $Wsus = `
```

```
[Microsoft.UpdateServices.Administration.AdminProxy]::[GetUpdateServer(
      $Computername,
      $UseSSL,
      $Port
    )
    $updateScope = New-Object `
Microsoft.UpdateServices.Administration.UpdateScope
    If ($PSBoundParameters['StartDate']) {
      $updateScope.FromCreationDate  = $StartDate
    }
    If ($PSBoundParameters['EndDate']) {
      $updateScope.ToCreationDate = $EndDate
    }
  }
  Process {
    $wsus.GetUpdateApprovals($updatescope) | ForEach {
      $object = New-Object PSobject -Property @{
        TargetGroup = $_.GetComputerTargetGroup().Name
        Title = `
($wsus.GetUpdate([guid]$_.UpdateId.UpdateId.Guid)).Title
        GoLiveTime = $_.GoLiveTime
        AdministratorName = $_.AdministratorName
        Deadline = $_.Deadline
        CreationDate = $_.CreationDate
        Action = $_.Action
      }
      $object.pstypenames.insert(0,"wsus.approvalaudit")
      $object
    }
  }
}
```

Creates and configures update scope

Retrieves approval information

You can see how the `Get-UpdateApprovals` function allows you to track information such as which administrator approved updates, the date and time the updates ran, which computers received the update(s), and which server sent them.

Client update status

The final report runs the function `Get-ClientUpdateStatistics`, which shows a summary of all clients and their current patch status: installed, downloaded, waiting to install, or pending reboot:

```
Get-ClientUpdateStatistics -Computername Boe-PC -Port 8530

Installed     : 122
Failed        : 0
NotInstalled  : 56
PendingReboot : 0
Computername  : dc1.rivendell.com
Downloaded    : 8
Unknown       : 0

Installed     : 0
Failed        : 1
NotInstalled  : 52
PendingReboot : 0
```

```
Computername  : boe-pc
Downloaded    : 1
Unknown       : 0
```

As you can see, some patches were downloaded for installation, as well as a patch that failed at some point during its installation.

The code for the Get-ClientUpdateStatistics function is shown in the following listing.

Listing 4 Get-ClientUpdateStatistics

```
Function Get-ClientUpdateStatistics {
  [cmdletbinding()]
  Param (
    [parameter(ValueFromPipeline=$True,
    HelpMessage="Name of WSUS server to connect to.")]
    [Alias('WSUSServer')]
    [string]$Computername,
    [parameter()]
    [ValidateSet(80,443,8530,8531)]
    [Int]$Port = 80,
    [parameter()]
    [Switch]$UseSSL
  )
  Begin {
    [reflection.assembly]::LoadWithPartialName(
"Microsoft.UpdateServices.Administration") | out-null
    $Wsus = `
[Microsoft.UpdateServices.Administration.AdminProxy]::GetUpdateServer(
$Computername,$False,$Port)
    $updateScope = New-Object`
Microsoft.UpdateServices.Administration.UpdateScope
    $computerScope = New-Object `
Microsoft.UpdateServices.Administration.ComputerTargetScope
  }
  Process {
    $wsus.GetSummariesPerComputerTarget
      ($updateScope,$computerScope) |
ForEach {
      $object = New-Object PSObject -Property @{
        Computername = $wsus.GetComputerTarget(
       $_.ComputerTargetID).FullDomainName
        Installed = $_.Installedcount
        Failed = $_.Failedcount
        Downloaded = $_.DownloadedCount
        NotInstalled = $_.NotInstalledCount
        Unknown = $_.UnknownCount
        PendingReboot = $_.InstalledPendingRebootCount
      }
      $object.pstypenames.insert(0,"wsus.clientupdate.statistics")
      $object
    }
  }
}
```

Creates update scope

Creates computer scope

Displays update statistics

The `Get-ClientUpdateStatistics` function creates a summary of each client and its update status, making it easier to determine which computers have successfully installed updates and which have not.

Summary

In this chapter I showed how you can use PowerShell and the available APIs to manage your WSUS server, view the server's configuration settings, and audit events. You can also use APIs to audit and build automatic approval rules to provide detailed reporting.

With Windows Server 2012 you can use the `UpdateServices` module to perform basic WSUS administration tasks, such as patch approvals. For more advanced configurations and reporting, the APIs are definitely the way to go as they provide additional flexibility into the WSUS infrastructure that is not currently available through the `UpdateServices` module. In addition, the module I wrote called `PoshWSUS` provides cmdlets that allow for more advanced administration (http://poshwsus.codeplex.com). With multiple options for automating your WSUS server, you can't go wrong. If you write scripts for your own WSUS server I hope that you'll share them with the rest of the community.

About the author

Boe Prox is a Senior Windows Systems Administrator. He has been in the IT industry since 2003 and has been working with Windows PowerShell since 2009. He is also the recipient of the Microsoft Community Contributor award for 2011 and 2012. Boe holds several IT certifications, including MCITP Enterprise Administrator, VCP4, and Microsoft Certified Solutions Associate (MCSA). You can find him on Twitter (@proxb) and at his blog (http://learn-powershell.net). He is also a moderator on the "Official Scripting Guys Forum!" His current projects are published on CodePlex: PoshWSUS (http://poshwsus.codeplex.com), PoshPAIG (http://poshpaig.codeplex.com), and PoshChat (http://poshchat.codeplex.com).

27 Provisioning IIS web servers and sites with PowerShell

Jason Helmick

The following scenario is common if you're an administrative web master, and here's how it was delivered to me: "Deploy a highly available web farm (four servers) with a couple of websites, including certificates, for a new secure shopping site. Make sure to enable graphical remote management for IIS Manager so that other admins and developers can make changes; and, by the way, did we mention we're moving to Windows Server 2012 Core?" (See figure 1.)

This isn't a complicated project, thanks to the support of PowerShell and the Internet Information Services (IIS) cmdlets, but you may encounter tricky spots and gotchas along the way.

Initially I solved this problem by using PowerShell interactively to complete the required tasks. As a smart and lazy admin, I saved the commands to a script so that in the future I could automate similar deployments without all the typing. I even turned some of the tasks into advanced functions so that other admins could accomplish some of the trickier stuff.

In this chapter you'll see how I interactively solved this deployment scenario, and I'll also show you how to automate it. The entire process from beginning to end involves these tasks:

- Deploy IIS to the Windows Server 2012 Core remote servers.
- Prepare the remote servers with website files and certificates.
- Enable remote-management support for the graphical IIS Manager.
- Create a load-balanced web farm.
- Create a secure load-balanced website using Secure Sockets Layer (SSL).
- Automate the process.

Let's get started and deploy the web servers and websites.

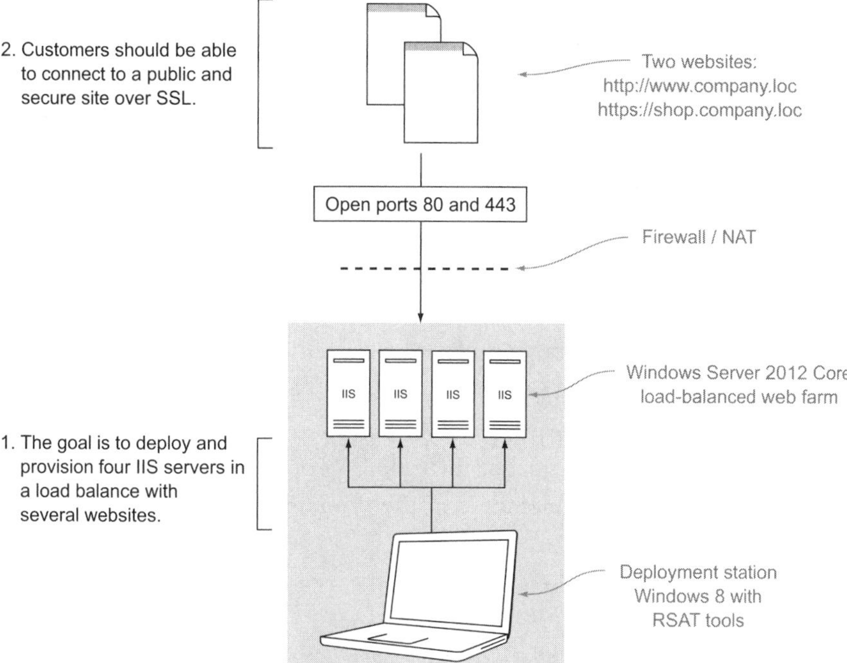

Figure 1 The deployment goal of a web farm with multiple websites

Setting up the lab environment

I created a lab environment to write this chapter. If you want to follow along you can create a similar environment.

Although I'm using Windows Server 2012 Core, this deployment solution also works on Windows Server 2008 R2, with or without a graphical desktop. I use some of the newer networking commands from Server 2012 for the Domain Name System (DNS) settings, but if you're using Windows Server 2008 R2 you can work around that with the GUI. I also use the dynamic module-loading feature in PowerShell v3; if you're using PowerShell v2 I'll warn you when you need to import a module.

These are the items that I set up in advance:

Deployment station—Windows 8 Pro running Remote Server Administration Tools (RSAT). I'll use local RSAT cmdlets in this chapter.

Four Windows Server 2012 Core servers—Each server is assigned an IP address and is a member of the domain, although this is not required for middle-tier web servers. You can set up the IP address through SConfig.cmd or the networking cmdlets.

Remoting—This feature is enabled for all Windows Server 2012 products; you'll need to enable it if you're using Windows Server 2008 R2. (This is a requirement.)

Script execution—This should be enabled on the servers.

SSL certificate—For a lab environment you can use a self-signed certificate, but for production use a good web server certificate or even an Extended Validation (EV) certificate. I created a certificate in Active Directory Certificate Services (AD CS) and exported it to a Personal Information Exchange (.pfx) file.

Rapid IIS deployment

To begin the deployment we'll use PowerShell Remoting to connect to the remote servers. Some tasks won't be completed over remoting, so store a list of computer names in a variable that you can pipe to commands.

1 Gather the computer names of the future web servers and store them to a variable, `$Servers`, using one of the following options.

   If the servers are members of the domain, use the Active Directory cmdlet `Get-ADComputer`:

```
PS> $Servers = Get-ADComputer -Filter "name -like 's*'" |
  ➥ Select-Object -ExpandProperty name
```

NOTE If you're using PowerShell v2, be sure to import the `Active Directory` module first.

   You can also get the list from a CSV or TXT file:

```
PS> $Servers = Import-Csv c:\servers.csv |
  ➥ Select-Object -ExpandProperty ComputerName

PS> $Servers = Get-Content c:\servers.txt
```

2 Create a PowerShell remote session to the servers. Store the sessions in a variable `$Sessions` for easy access later:

```
PS> $Sessions = New-PSSession -ComputerName $Servers
```

3 Determine what software is needed to support all of the tasks for this project.

   The remote servers require the following roles and features for this deployment solution, but you can add to the list if you need additional components to support your websites:

   – *Web Server (IIS) (`web-server`)*—The primary role for a web server. This installs the components of IIS and creates the default website.
   – *ASP.NET (`web-asp-net`)*—Provides support for ASP.NET websites.
   – *Network Load Balancing (`NLB`)*—I'm using Microsoft's built-in layer-3 NLB software. You can substitute your own hardware load balancer or Microsoft's layer-7 Application Request Routing (ARR) balancer. ARR has cmdlets for easy management and is one of my favorite products. ARR also includes additional features beyond load balancing but requires greater in-depth

knowledge, so I'm sticking with the straightforward, built-in, and useful Microsoft NLB.

- *Management Service* (`Web-Mgmt-Service`)—Required component for remote management of IIS with IIS Manager.

4 Install the required components on the remote servers with `Invoke-Command`:

```
PS> Invoke-Command -Session $Sessions {Install-WindowsFeature
  ➥ web-server,web-asp-net,NLB,Web-Mgmt-Service}
```

> **PowerShell v2 notes**
>
> If you're using PowerShell v2 on Server 2008 R2 you'll need to import the `Server Manager` module first:
>
> ```
> Invoke-Command -Session $Sessions {Import-Module ServerManager}
> ```
>
> Also I'm using the new `Install-WindowsFeature` cmdlet. In PowerShell v2 use the `Add-WindowsFeature` cmdlet.

Installing the software components to all four servers, as shown in figure 2, takes only a few minutes (5 minutes to be exact).

The IIS installation process creates the default website automatically. Let's test this default website on each server before continuing with the next task.

Testing ensures that the web server is functioning properly and reduces future troubleshooting if something goes wrong:

5 Use the `$Servers` variable to pipe the server names to Internet Explorer:

```
PS> $Servers | ForEach-Object {Start-Process iexplore http://$_}
```

Four separate browsers automatically launch and test the default website on each individual server.

With the initial software deployment completed the next task is to deploy (copy) the website files and certificate out to the servers. PowerShell makes this a snap.

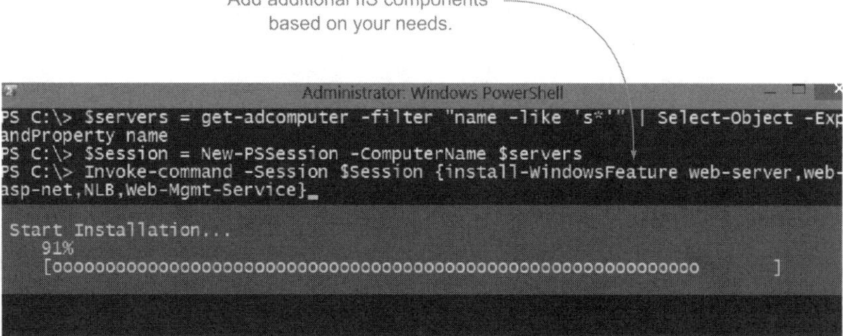

Figure 2 Performing a rapid install of the required software on multiple servers

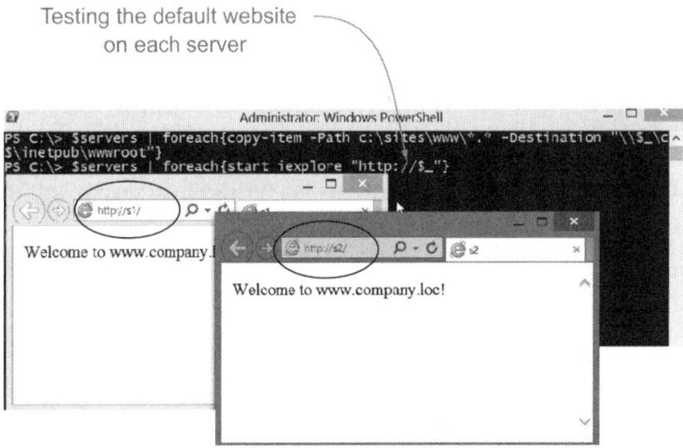

Figure 3 Successful deployment of the default website to multiple web servers

Transferring website files and certificates

IIS supports storing your website files and applications on a central share from a clustered file server. Some organizations, such as small companies, don't have this capability, so we'll copy the websites from a central location (my computer) out to the individual web servers. Because these web servers will be load-balanced, each server needs to have the same files.

DEPLOYING THE DEFAULT WEBSITE

1 Copy the new default website to each web server's c:\inetpub\wwwroot path:

```
PS> $Servers | ForEach-Object {Copy-Item -Path c:\sites\www\*.*
  ➥ -Destination "\\$_\c$\inetpub\wwwroot"}
```

2 Test the default website after the file transfer (see figure 3):

```
PS> $Servers | ForEach-Object {Start-Process iexplore http://$_}
```

With the default website successfully deployed we can focus on the new secure shopping site.

DEPLOYING THE SHOPPING WEBSITE

Most of the websites that you'll copy out to the web servers won't be in the default path (InetPub). I prefer to use a directory called sites, with each website in its own folder:

1 Create the folder structure on the remote servers (C:\sites\shopping), and then copy the new website:

```
PS> Invoke-Command -Session $Sessions {New-Item -Path c:\sites\shopping
  ➥ -ItemType directory -Force}
PS> $Servers | ForEach-Object {Copy-Item -Path c:\sites\shopping\*.*
  ➥ -Destination "\\$_\c$\sites\shopping"}
```

2 Generate a certificate for SSL for the secure shopping site.

(I previously generated and stored a trusted certificate on my local Windows 8 computer in c:\sites\certpfx.)

3 Copy the certificate to the remote servers, and then use CertUtil.exe to import the certificate:

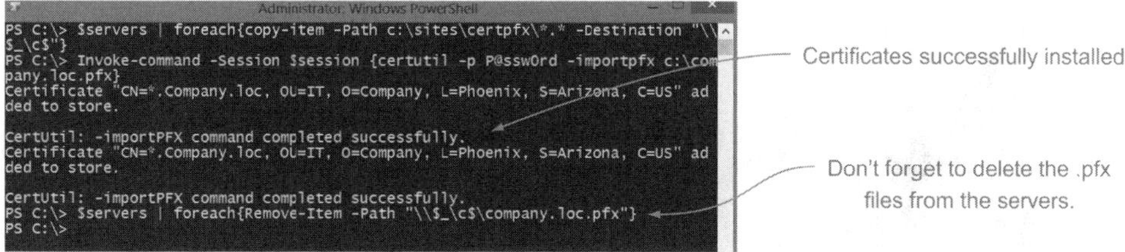

Figure 4 Deploying and installing a certificate for SSL

```
PS> $Servers | ForEach-Object {Copy-Item -Path c:\sites\certpfx\*.*
  ➥ -Destination "\\$_\c$"}
PS> Invoke-Command -Session $Sessions {certutil -p P@ssw0rd
  ➥ -importpfx c:\company.loc.pfx}
```

I sent the password in clear text because PowerShell Remoting is secure and encrypted. I wouldn't do this in a script. The certificate imports successfully, as shown in figure 4.

4 Remove (delete) the .pfx file from the remote servers:

```
PS> $Servers | ForEach-Object {Remove-Item -Path
  "\\$_\c$\company.loc.pfx"}
```

The website files are copied to the remote servers and each server has the certificate for the secure site. Before you finish creating and configuring the secure site you need to enable IIS remote management so that the websites can be managed using IIS Manager.

Enabling remote management for IIS Manager

IIS remote management adds the capability of managing websites on remote servers from IIS Manager. It's best to enable and configure this feature using IIS Manager run locally on each server; it's not a friendly feature to enable through the command line or on Windows Server 2012 Core. In addition, we need to replace the temporary, self-signed certificate, which is assigned to remote management.

Let's break this into two steps: enabling the service and replacing the certificate.

ENABLING THE SERVICE

1 Enable the remote management service in the registry, and then start the Web Management Service (WMSVC).

WMSVC has a startup type of `Manual`, so change the startup to `Automatic` before starting the service:

```
PS> Invoke-Command -Session $Sessions {Set-ItemProperty
  ➥ -Path HKLM:\SOFTWARE\Microsoft\WebManagement\Server
  ➥ -Name EnableRemoteManagement -Value 1}
PS> Invoke-Command -Session $Sessions {Set-Service wmsvc
  ➥ -StartupType Automatic}
PS> Invoke-Command -Session $Sessions {Start-Service wmsvc}
```

Figure 5 illustrates the successful start of WMSVC on the remote computers.

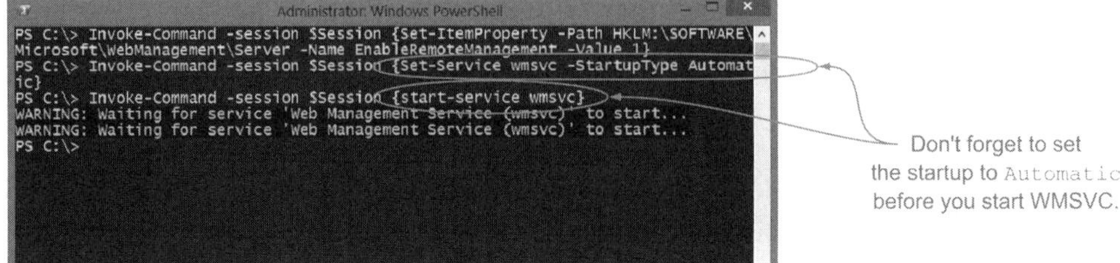

Figure 5 Enabling IIS remote management and starting WMSVC

At this point you can connect IIS Manager to the remote computers, but you can't use IIS Manager to manage and change the certificates for the remote service.

REPLACING THE CERTIFICATE

The IIS remote management service uses port 8172 and binds a temporary certificate to "all unassigned" IP addresses. You need to change this binding, and this is where things get a little strange. To remove the old SSL binding for port 8172 and add a new one you need to access the `IIS:` provider. Because PowerShell cmdlets and this provider don't work together as well as they could, extra steps are required to complete the process:

1 Get the thumbprint of the trusted certificate that you imported previously and store it to a variable (`$cert`).

Perform this step over PowerShell Remoting so that the variable can be used for later commands:

```
PS> Invoke-Command -Session $Sessions {$cert = Get-ChildItem
➥ -Path Cert:\LocalMachine\My | where {$_.subject -like "*company*"} |
➥ Select-Object -ExpandProperty Thumbprint}
```

2 Access the IIS: drive.

When IIS is installed, a module called `WebAdministration` is added, which includes cmdlets and an IIS: provider. To ensure that the provider is loaded, import the `WebAdministration` module:

```
PS> Invoke-Command -Session $Sessions {Import-Module WebAdministration}
PS> Invoke-command -Session $Sessions {cd IIS:\SslBindings}
```

Bindings are stored in IIS:\SslBindings as path items.

3 Remove the binding that contains the temporary certificate:

```
PS> Invoke-command -Session $Sessions {Remove-Item -Path
➥ IIS:\SslBindings \0.0.0.0!8172}
```

NOTE Usually IIS binding information is entered and displayed as `IPaddress:port:hostname`, as in `*:80:*`, but PowerShell interprets the colon (`:`) as a path indicator. When using the cmdlets to work with bindings for IIS, replace the colon with an exclamation mark (`!`), as in `*!80!*`.

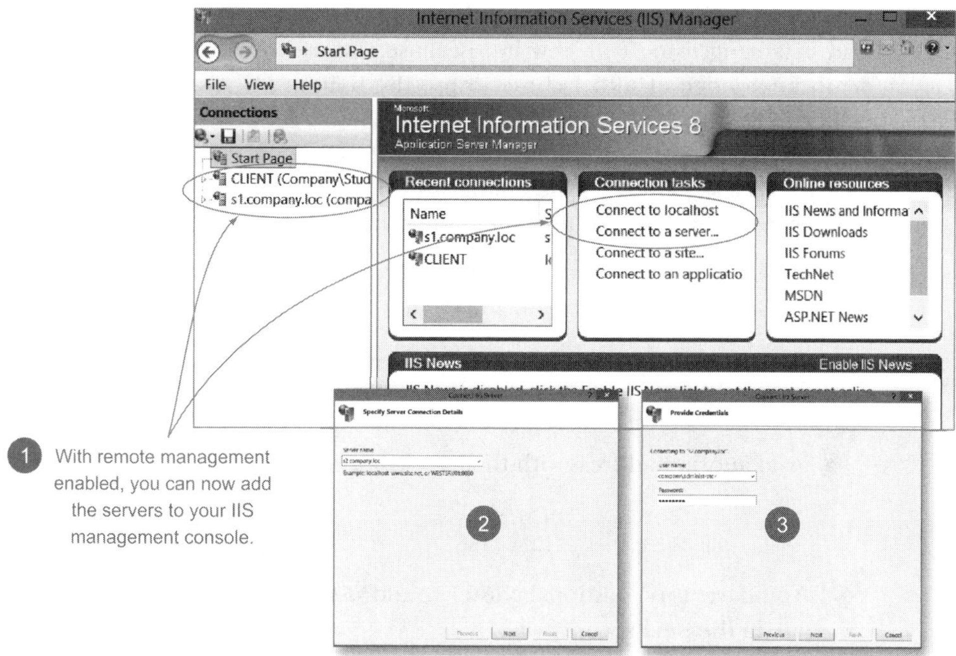

Figure 6 Adding the remote servers to IIS Manager

4 Create a new binding that uses the new trusted certificate.

Use the `Get-Item` command to retrieve the correct certificate based on the thumbprint stored in `$cert`. The certificate is piped to `New-Item`, which creates the new binding for all IP addresses on port 8172:

```
PS> Invoke-Command -Session $Sessions {Get-Item
➥ -Path "cert:\localmachine\my\$cert" |
➥ New-Item -Path IIS:\SslBindings\0.0.0.0!8172}
```

5 Start IIS Manager (`PS> Start inetmgr`), and create connections to the remote servers as shown in figure 6.

With the remote management capabilities of IIS enabled we can finish off our deployment and provisioning web server project with two final tasks: building the web farm and creating a new secure website. Let's start with the web farm.

Creating a load-balanced web farm

For many companies a hardware load balancer that provides high availability is the only choice for their web farms; it's fast, efficient, and provides certificate management. Not everyone can afford (or even needs) this level of performance, so other options are available. My favorite is the layer-7 load balancer for IIS from Microsoft called Application Request Routing (ARR). It's free, an excellent product, can be downloaded from www.iis.net, has cmdlets for management, includes many more features in addition to load balancing, and, did I mention, it's free. ARR performs load balancing using URL rewrite. Because URL rewrite is complex and requires in-depth knowledge of ARR I chose to use the built-in Microsoft NLB for this example deployment situation. NLB works well and doesn't require the additional installation and knowledge overhead to make a great solution.

For this task I'm using the cmdlets from the `NLB` module on my Windows 8 computer. Alternatively you could issue these commands over PowerShell Remoting:

1 Create the load balance on server `S1` with the `New-NlbCluster` cmdlet, and create a cluster IP address for the default website:

```
PS> New-NlbCluster -HostName s1 -InterfaceName Ethernet -ClusterName web
➥ -ClusterPrimaryIP 192.168.3.200 -SubnetMask 255.255.255.0
➥ -OperationMode Multicast
```

2 Add another address with the `Add-NlbClusterVip` cmdlet:

```
PS> Get-NlbCluster -HostName s1 | Add-NlbClusterVip -IP 192.168.3.201
➥ -SubnetMask 255.255.255.0
```

You'll use this additional cluster IP address for the secure website that you'll create in the next section.

3 Add the second server (`S2`) as a node in the load balance with the `Get-NlbCluster` cmdlet:

```
PS> Get-NlbCluster -HostName s1 | Add-NlbClusterNode -NewNodeName s2
➥ -NewNodeInterface Ethernet
```

4 Repeat step 3 for the other two servers in this scenario.

The return information from the `Get-NlbCluster` cmdlet informs you if you have any problems converging the load balance.

5 Launch the graphical Network Load Balancing Manager (on a Windows 8 computer) from the Administrative Tools to verify the status (see figure 7).

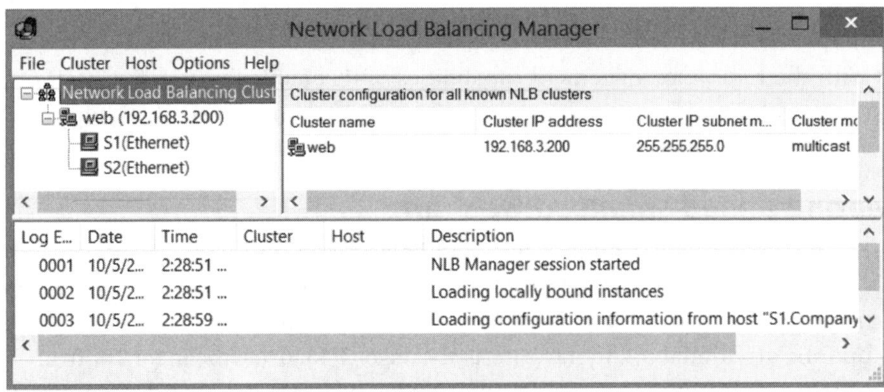

Figure 7 Verifying the load balance in the Network Load Balancing Manager

6 Test the load balance with full name resolution.

Create a www record in DNS that points to the cluster IP address, and then launch a browser using the new address:

```
PS> Add-DnsServerResourceRecordA -Name www -ZoneName company.loc
  ➥ -IPv4Address 192.168.3.200 -ComputerName DC.company.loc
PS> Start-Process iexplore http://www.company.loc
```

Finally, after all this work, it's time for the final task: creating a new and secure website for the web farm. Let's make a website!

Creating an SSL website

To make a new website on the remote servers use the IIS (web) cmdlets from the `WebAdministration` module. Remember that we already copied the files for this new website to the location c:\sites\shopping:

1 Create an application pool for the new website with the `New-WebAppPool` cmdlet:

```
PS> Invoke-Command -Session $Sessions
{New-WebAppPool -Name Shopping-Pool}
```

Figure 8 shows the graphical version of creating a pool in IIS Manager.

The new application pool is created with default settings for items such as the recycle times and identity. This is a good time to add your own application pool commands to alter those defaults, if desired. (See the sidebar for an example.)

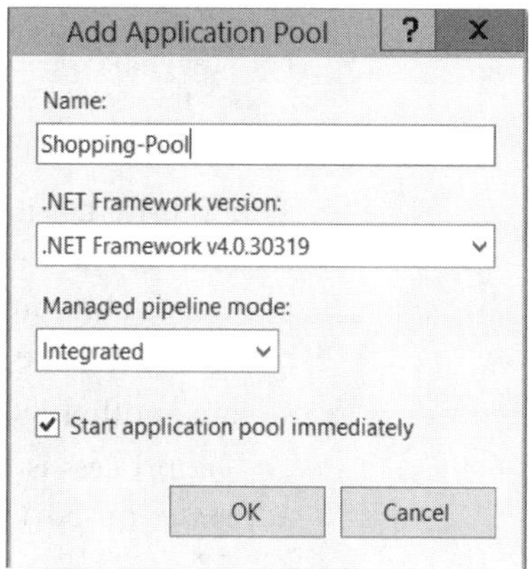

Figure 8 Creating a pool in IIS Manager

Changing the application pool identity

Usually, for application pools of `ApplicationPoolIdentity`, the default identity is sufficient as a restricted identity. In cases where multiple customers have websites located on the same server (multitenant), isolating each pool with its own identity provides unique security for every customer. To set the pool identity IIS uses a number representing the identity. The default value is `4`, but if you want to have isolation you can create individual accounts and assign those accounts to each pool as in the following example:

```
LocalSystem = 0
LocalService = 1
NetworkService = 2
SpecificUser = 3
ApplicationPoolIdentity = 4
```

```
PS> Invoke-Command -Session $Sessions {Set-ItemProperty
  ➥ -Path IIS:\AppPools\MyTest -Name processmodel.identityType -Value 3}
```

```
PS> Invoke-Command -Session $Sessions {Set-ItemProperty
  ➥ -Path IIS:\AppPools\MyTest -Name processmodel.username
  ➥ -Value Administrator}

PS> Invoke-Command -Session $Sessions {Set-ItemProperty
  ➥ -Path IIS:\AppPools\MyTest -Name processmodel.password -Value
         P@ssw0rd}
```

2 Create a new website named `Shopping`.

After you create the application pool the `New-Website` cmdlet does the rest of the work:

```
PS> Invoke-Command -Session $Sessions {New-Website -Name Shopping
  ➥ -HostHeader shop.company.loc -PhysicalPath C:\sites\shopping
  ➥ -ApplicationPool Shopping-Pool -Port 443 -ssl -SslFlags 0}
```

The website has a host header of `shop.company.loc` and points to the physical location of the website files. The new site is assigned to the correct application pool and a binding on port 443 is set. The `-SslFlags` tells the website to use a normal certificate.

3 Create another SSL binding for the new site.

The process is the same as discussed previously, but the binding is for all IP addresses on port 443:

```
PS> Invoke-Command -Session $Sessions {$cert=Get-ChildItem
  ➥ -Path Cert:\LocalMachine\My | where {$_.subject -like "*company*"} |
  ➥ Select-Object -ExpandProperty Thumbprint}
PS> Invoke-Command -Session $Sessions {Import-Module WebAdministration}
PS> Invoke-Command -Session $Sessions {Get-Item
  ➥ -Path "cert:\localmachine\my\$cert" | New-Item -Path
  ➥ IIS:\SslBindings\0.0.0.0!443!Shop.company.loc}
```

As shown in figure 9, the new binding is successfully created on all remote servers.

4 Test the new website.

Add a DNS record that points to the cluster IP address previously defined for the website and then launch a browser using the address:

```
PS> Add-DnsServerResourceRecordA -Name shop -ZoneName company.loc
  ➥ -IPv4Address 192.168.3.201 -ComputerName DC.company.loc
PS> Start-Process iexplore https://shop.company.loc
```

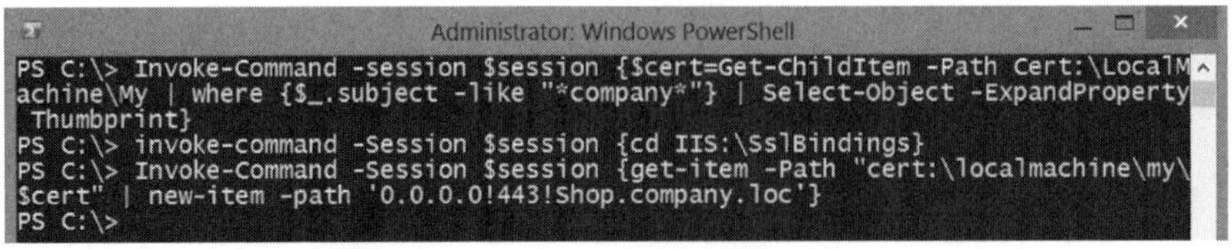

Figure 9 Successful creation of the new SSL binding

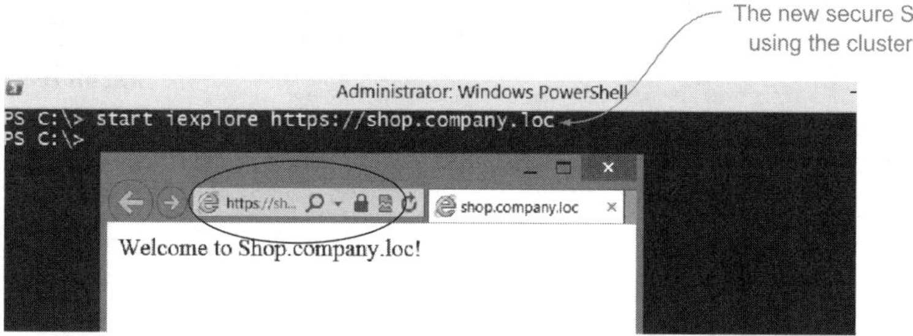

Figure 10 Successful test of the new website using SSL

As shown in figure 10, the new website successfully passes the test using the trusted certificate over SSL.

Total time for this project, using PowerShell interactively, is approximately 30 minutes. Storing these commands in a .ps1 file helps me script future deployment projects. Why do all that typing again? I wrote the tricky tasks, such as enabling remote management, as advanced functions so that other admins have the tools they need without all the hassle. I increased my value to the company and managed to get a little more time on the beach.

Automating the process

Automating the deployment process is as simple as sticking the commands in a script file, but I went further and built in more flexibility. PowerShell Remoting and the `Invoke-Command` cmdlet make life easy. For example, have you ever tried the switch option for `Invoke-Command -FilePath`? This switch option eliminates the need to copy scripts to remote computers before executing them. You write a script that performs the tasks as if it were running on the local computer. To send that script to your remote computers use `Invoke-Command`.

In this section I'll first show you the script that does the hard work, and then I'll show you how I call and use the script. The only changes from the commands you've already seen are the following:

- I removed all of the `Invoke-Command` cmdlets.
- I changed how the certificate password is passed to the script. I don't want the password hardcoded in the script, so I used a PowerShell v3 feature to pass a variable to the script with `$Using:CertPassword`.
- I left out the NLB commands, in case you already have a load-balance solution, but you can always add them.

Here's the script, which I named `Deploy-WebServer.ps1`.

Listing 1 Deploy-WebServer.ps1

```
Install-WindowsFeature web-server,Web-Mgmt-Service          <-- Installs required components

Set-ItemProperty -Path HKLM:\SOFTWARE\Microsoft\WebManagement\Server `
-Name EnableRemoteManagement -Value 1                        <-- Enables remote management

Set-Service wmsvc -StartupType Automatic
Start-Service wmsvc

certutil -p $Using:certPassword -importpfx c:\Wildcard.company.loc.pfx
Remove-Item -Path c:\Wildcard.company.loc.pfx                <-- Removes the certificate file

Import-module -Name WebAdministration
$cert = Get-ChildItem -Path Cert:\LocalMachine\My |
where {$_.subject -like "*company*"} |
Select-Object -ExpandProperty Thumbprint

Remove-Item -Path IIS:\SslBindings\0.0.0.0!8172

Get-Item -Path "cert:\localmachine\my\$cert" |
New-Item -Path IIS:\SslBindings\0.0.0.0!8172

New-WebBinding -Name "Default Website" -Protocol https

Get-Item -Path "cert:\localmachine\my\$cert" |               Creates new SSL binding
New-Item -Path IIS:\SslBindings\0.0.0.0!443
```

To use the Deploy-WebServer.ps1 script I run interactive commands to set up the remoting connections and set a few variables. Then I call the deployment script with a single `Invoke-Command` cmdlet:

1 Build a remote session to the computers that will become web servers.

   Put the server names in a variable—you'll need that later, so don't cheat and make this a one-liner:

```
PS> $Servers='server1','server2', 'server3'
PS> $Sessions=New-PSSession -ComputerName $Servers
```

2 Set a variable to contain the password to install the certificate.

   This information is passed over the remoting session encrypted:

```
PS> $CertPassword="P@ssw0rd"
```

3 Interactively copy the website files and certificates to the remote servers:

```
PS> $servers | ForEach-Object{New-Item -Path \\$_\C$\inetpub\wwwroot
  ➥ -ItemType Directory -Force}
PS> $servers | ForEach-Object{Copy-Item -Path c:\sites\www\*.*
  ➥ -Destination \\$_\C$\inetpub\wwwroot -Force}
PS> $servers | ForEach-Object{Copy-Item -Path c:\sites\CertPFX\*.*
  ➥ -Destination \\$_\C$\ -Force}
```

   If you put these commands in the Deploy-WebServer.ps1 file you'll run into a double-hop issue—the remote computers connecting to another remote server to get the files.

NOTE If you copy files to Windows Server 2012 Core you'll first need to install the `FS-FileServer` role to access the `C$` share.

4 Run the deployment script using the `-FilePath` parameter:

```
PS> Invoke-Command -Session $Sessions -FilePath C:\scripts\deploy-
➥ WebServer.ps1
```

All the target servers now have a web server, website, and certificates installed and are ready for action!

Summary

This chapter covered the deployment of multiple web servers with multiple websites, which included building a web farm and installing certificates for SSL. The concepts and tactics demonstrated here could easily be applied to other roles, features, and products, such as SharePoint web servers and Client Access Server (CAS) arrays for Microsoft Exchange. I gleaned the following takeaways during this real-life project:

- I can use PowerShell interactively to solve each task, even for a more complicated deployment.
- There may not be specific cmdlets for every situation, such as enabling the remote management of IIS, but there are ways around those issues.
- PowerShell Remoting must be enabled to permit these larger-scale management solutions. While it's the default for Windows Server 2012, you need to enable it now even if you're not at that version yet.

Thanks to PowerShell I get an amazing amount of work done quickly and without traveling to a cold data center. If you have any questions about the script or commands I discussed in this chapter visit the forums at http://www.powershell.org, and I'll be happy to help!

About the author

Jason Helmick is a teacher, author, consultant, and 25-year IT veteran focusing on Microsoft enterprise technologies. Jason is a strong proponent of automation with PowerShell and is a board member of PowerShell.Org. He is the author of *Learn Windows IIS in a Month of Lunches* (Manning, 2013). You can follow and contact Jason on Twitter: @theJasonHelmick.

28 Active Directory Group Management application

Chris Bellée

Windows PowerShell offers a wide range of management features, from its immediate and intuitive command shell in which "one-liners" rule, to interacting with the Win32 API environment. With such breadth and interoperability to offer, PowerShell is well-positioned for lightweight application development duties.

In this chapter I demonstrate how to use PowerShell in collaboration with other Microsoft technologies to produce a graphical tool for managing Active Directory group memberships. A common customer request is for a tool that can manage temporary group membership. For example, a customer may request an application for managing group membership around a project timeline. By automating additions and removals from a group, such an application removes reliance on human intervention as well as the inherent security risk of users retaining unneeded groups.

Before diving in and writing any PowerShell code let's evaluate the scope of the project.

Requirements

Before writing any PowerShell code we must first define the specifications of the group management application:

- *User interface (UI)*—Help desk staff require an easy-to-use UI to view and manage users, ideally in a single window.
- *Data Storage*—User and group membership data must be persisted in a store that can be backed up and restored in event of an outage.
- *Automated updates*—Group membership changes should be handled automatically, regardless of whether the Group Management UI is running.
- *Auditing*—Active Directory group changes must be logged to a file.

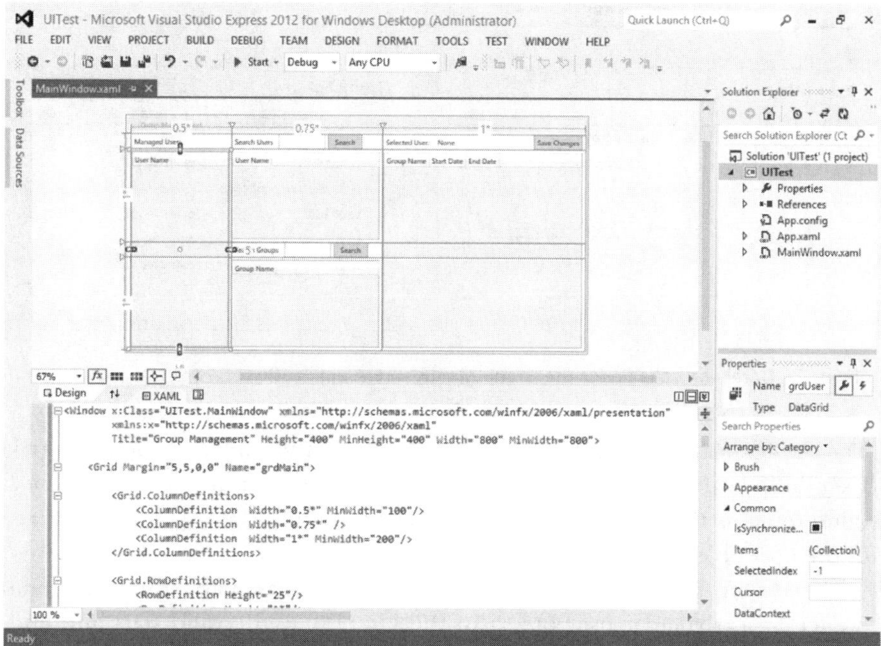

Figure 1 Visual Studio 2012 Express for Windows Desktop provides a free and fully featured development environment.

User Interface development tools

We'll build the UI with Windows Presentation Foundation (WPF) technology. To design the interface we'll use the freely downloadable Microsoft Visual Studio Express 2012 for Windows Desktop (http://www.microsoft.com/en-us/download/details.aspx?id=34673), shown in figure 1.

Visual Studio automatically generates XAML code (an XML-based markup language) when you use its visual UI designer.

Data storage tools and design

Active Directory is unsuited for easily storing relationships between users, groups, and dates. Many relational database products are available to store this information, and for this project I'll use the freely downloadable Microsoft SQL Server 2012 Express (http://www.microsoft.com/en-us/download/details.aspx?id=29062).

To store the one-to-many relationship between a user, a user's group memberships, and the membership start and end dates, we'll need to create two database tables (see figure 2):

- *UserTable*—Stores user accounts.
- *GroupTable*—Stores the user's group membership information, such as the group `ObjectGUID`, `SamAccountname`, a reference to the user account `ObjectGUID`, and the group membership start and end dates.

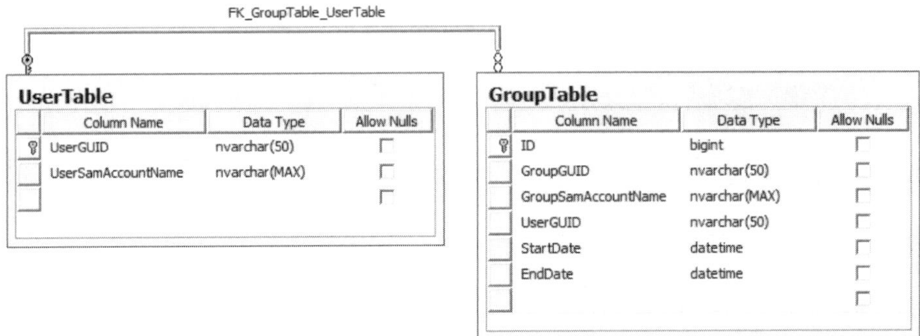

Figure 2 Database schema for the Group Management application

The `ObjectGUID` attribute of the Active Directory user object is the primary key in the UserTable both because this value must be unique within a forest, and because this value remains the same over a user account's lifetime. The `SamAccountName` attribute of the user object is also stored for UI display purposes.

The GroupTable stores an entry for each group of which a user is a member, a reference to a particular user object in the UserTable, the valid start and end dates of group membership, and the group's `SamAccountName` value. The primary key column (ID) is an automatically incremented integer, as many duplicate `ObjectGUID`'s could exist in the table. The UserGUID column has a foreign key constraint relationship with the UserTable's UserGUID column.

Automation and auditing

The final point to consider is the way in which group membership changes, which are persisted in the SQL database, are applied to the Active Directory database. The solution, for this example application, is to execute a PowerShell script via a scheduled SQL Server Agent job. The script modifies the group membership of users if the membership start or end dates have elapsed.

Active Directory group modifications are not taken lightly in the majority of organizations, so the inclusion of some form of auditing feature in the tool is mandatory. For auditing we'll log the changes to a text file. Alternatively, for a more secure solution, you could write them to a custom Windows event log file.

NOTE The script and database files for the Group Management application are available for download at http://manning.com/hicks. You'll need to modify the T-SQL script file that creates the database (Create_SQL_DB.sql) so that the `FILENAME` parameters match the correct paths for the database and the log files on the reader's machine. You'll also need to modify the SQL job script (Create_SQL_Job.sql) to match the path to the SQLJob.ps1 script.

Organizing the project files

Now that we've made the supporting technology decisions we'll divide the code and markup into the three files listed in table 1.

Table 1 The Group Management application functionality divided into three files

File Name	Purpose
UI.xaml	XAML markup text file that defines the UI
Main.ps1	Central script that performs the following functions: renders the UI defined in UI.xaml, wires up the WPF control event handlers to PowerShell code, and defines helper functions to perform operations against the database and search Active Directory
SQLJob.ps1	Script run as a job by the SQL Server Agent to make changes in Active Directory

Let's start by creating the XAML file and laying out the interface.

Designing the UI

WPF, the successor to the Windows forms library, is a vector-based presentation system that uses an XML-based markup language to implement the UI's appearance. All form elements are positioned relatively, which allows the form to be resized automatically without having to write any code, making it an ideal UI layer for a PowerShell script.

To create a new WPF project open Visual Studio 2012 Express and select New Project. The project type should be WPF Application (the .Net language choice is irrelevant).

The form layout is defined by a Grid control (`grdMain`), which consists of three columns and four rows (see figure 1). Each user control is assigned to one or more grid cells. Controls can be dragged onto the empty WPF form from the Toolbox panel at the left to occupy one of the cells.

As shown in figure 3, each control instance has a unique name so that it can be referenced from the PowerShell script.

The form uses three WPF control types: `DataGrid`, `TextBox`, and `Button`. See table 2.

Table 2 The Group Management application's three types of form controls

Control Type	Control Name	Description
`DataGrid`	`grdUser`	Displays users managed by the application
`DataGrid`	`grdSearchUser`	Displays users returned by an Active Directory search
`DataGrid`	`grdSearchGroup`	Displays groups returned by an Active Directory search
`DataGrid`	`grdSelectedGroup`	Displays group memberships for an existing user
`TextBox`	`txtSearchUser`	Searches string input for Active Directory user search
`TextBox`	`txtSearchGroup`	Searches string input for Active Directory group search

Table 2 The Group Management application's three types of form controls *(continued)*

Control Type	Control Name	Description
`Button`	`btnSearchUser`	Executes an Active Directory search for user objects
`Button`	`btnSearchGroup`	Executes an Active Directory search for group objects
`Button`	`btnSaveChanges`	Saves group membership changes to the database

A collapsed view of the WPF XAML markup is shown in figure 4.

Using WPF as a presentation layer neatly separates concerns, decoupling the UI design from the underlying PowerShell script that drives it.

TIP The PowerShell 3.0 ISE now automatically color-codes XML markup.

Rendering the UI

Once you've designed the UI in Visual Studio, copy the resulting XAML markup to a new text file saved with the .xaml file extension. The UI rendered using a couple of lines of PowerShell.

NOTE To render a Visual Studio-created .xaml file using the technique described in this section, the following attribute, shown in bold, must be removed from the enclosing `<Window>` node in the xml markup. This attribute is used only by Visual Studio to associate the UI and the program code class.

```
<Window x:Class="GroupManagementWPF.MainWindow" xmlns="http://
schemas...
```

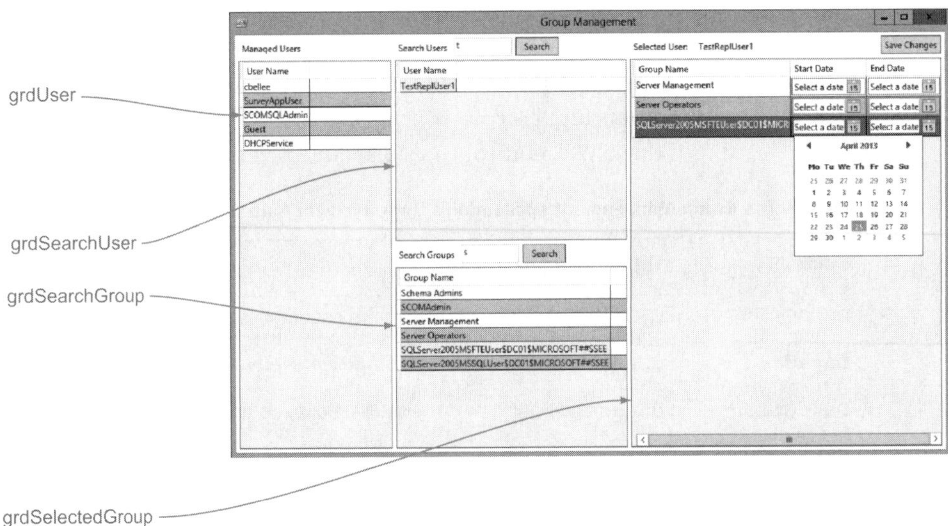

Figure 3 The WPF UI for the Group Management application

```
UI.xaml X
<Window xmlns="http://schemas.microsoft.com/winfx/2006/xaml/presentation"
        xmlns:x="http://schemas.microsoft.com/winfx/2006/xaml"
        Title="Group Management" Height="400" MinHeight="400" Width="800" MinWidth="800">

 <Grid Margin="5,5,0,0" Name="grdMain">

   <Grid.ColumnDefinitions>...</Grid.ColumnDefinitions>

    <Grid.RowDefinitions>...</Grid.RowDefinitions>

        <Label Name="lblManagedUsers" Grid.Column="0" Grid.Row="0" Content="Managed Users" />

        <StackPanel Grid.Column="1" Grid.Row="0" Orientation="Horizontal">
            <Label Name="lblSearchUser" Content="Search Users" />
            <TextBox Name="txtSearchUser" AcceptsTab="True" TabIndex="1" Margin="5,0,0,0"  Width="80" />
            <Button Name="btnSearchUser" Content="Search" Width="60" Margin="5,0,0,0" Padding="5,0,5,0"/>
        </StackPanel>

        <StackPanel Grid.Column="1" Grid.Row="2" Orientation="Horizontal">
            <Label Name="lblSearchGroup" Content="Search Groups"/>
            <TextBox Name="txtSearchGroup" AcceptsTab="True" TabIndex="2" Margin="5,0,0,0"  Width="80" />
            <Button Name="btnSearchGroup" Content="Search" Width="60" Margin="5,0,0,0" Padding="5,0,5,0"/>
        </StackPanel>

        <StackPanel Grid.Column="2" Grid.Row="0" Orientation="Horizontal">
            <Label Name="lblSelectedUser" Content="Selected User:"/>
            <Label Name="lblSelectedUserName" Margin="5,0,0,0" Content="None"/>
        </StackPanel>

        <Button Name="btnSaveChanges" Grid.Column="2" Grid.Row="0" Content="Save Changes" Margin="5,0,5,0"

        <DataGrid Name="grdUser" IsReadOnly="True" ItemsSource="{Binding Path=Table}" Grid.Column="0" Grid

        <DataGrid Name="grdSearchUser" IsReadOnly="True" ItemsSource="{Binding Path=Table}" Grid.Column="1

        <DataGrid Name="grdSearchGroup" IsReadOnly="True" ItemsSource="{Binding Path=Table}" Grid.Column="

        <DataGrid Name="grdSelectedGroup" IsReadOnly="True" ItemsSource="{Binding Path=Table}"  Grid.Colum

</Grid>
</Window>
```

Figure 4 XAML markup syntax in PowerShell 3.0 ISE

As shown in the following snippet from the Main.ps1 file, code execution starts with importing the WPF assemblies needed to instantiate the UI objects, followed by reading the `UI.xaml` file and casting it to an XML data type. The helper function, `Get-PSScriptRoot`, resolves the path of a file name to the folder where the script was executed:

```
Add-Type -Assembly PresentationCore, PresentationFrameWork, WindowsBase    <-- Imports assemblies

[xml]$xmlUI = Get-Content (Get-PSScriptRoot -File UI.xaml)    <-- Reads .xaml file
```

Next, an `XmlNodeReader` object is created to read the `XmlDocument`:

```
$xmlNodes = New-Object System.Xml.XmlNodeReader($xmlUI)
```

Finally, the `XamlReader` class's `Load() static` method is used to render the XAML markup on the screen. The `$window` variable holds a reference to the entire WPF form object and is how PowerShell configures the form's behavior:

```
$window = [Windows.Markup.XamlReader]::Load($xmlNodes)    <-- Loads XAML and renders form

# UI event handling code goes here...

$window.ShowDialog()    <-- Displays form
```

Next we'll write the event-handling code in the Main.ps1 file.

Adding UI event-handling logic

Before the form can be shown using the Window's `ShowDialog()` method we must define the PowerShell code to run when a UI control event is fired, such as clicking a button or changing the selected item in a data grid.

To reference each control defined in the XAML markup use the `FindName()` method of the WPF `Window` object (`$window` variable):

```
$grdUser = $window.FindName("grdUser")
$grdGroup = $window.FindName("grdGroup")

$grdSearchUser = $window.FindName("grdSearchUser")
$grdSearchGroup = $window.FindName("grdSearchGroup")

$grdSelectedUser = $window.FindName("grdSelectedUser")
$grdSelectedGroup = $window.FindName("grdSelectedGroup")
```

Table 3 outlines which UI control event handlers are "wired-up" to PowerShell code.

Table 3 Form event handlers

Control Name	Event	Description
`btnSearchUser`	`Click()`	Searches for users
`btnSearchGroup`	`Click()`	Searches for groups
`grdSearchUser`	`SelectionChanged()`	Selects a user object from the search result
`grdSearchGroup`	`SelectionChanged()`	Adds groups to the `grdSelectedGroup` `DataGrid`
`grdUser`	`Loaded()`	Populates the user list when the form loads
`grdUser`	`SelectionChanged()`	Adds selected user's groups to the `grdSelectedGroup DataGrid`
`btnSaveChanges`	`Click()`	Saves the changes in `grdSelectedGroup` to the database

The PowerShell code to run when the event is fired is defined between the event's left and right parentheses, in a regular PowerShell script block.

The following example demonstrates how to bind a `datasource` to a control, such as a `DataGrid`. In this example a call to the SQL Server database—to return all groups of which the currently selected user is a member—is assigned to the `DataGrid`'s `DataContext` property like this:

```
$grdUser.Add_SelectionChanged({

if ($grdUser.Items.count -gt 0)
{
   $grdSelectedGroup.DataContext = @(Get-GroupData -UserGUID `
$grdUser.SelectedItem.UserGUID)
$lblSelectedUserName.Content = $grdUser.SelectedItem.UserSamAccountName
}

})
```

The database read operation is encapsulated in the `Get-GroupData` helper function, which uses the `System.Data.SqlClient` namespace classes to query the database for all groups of which the current user is a member. This function has a single input parameter, the Active Directory `objectGUID` attribute of the user for whom we want to return the group memberships from the SQL database. (See listing 3.)

To display the data returned from the `Get-GroupData` function in the `grdSelected-Group DataGrid` you can take advantage of its default setting (`AutoGenerateColumns="True"`) and set the `ItemsSource` binding path to `Table`. You can do this in the Visual Studio GUI editor environment.

For more control over how data is bound to the `DataGrid` you can optionally define a collection of column objects manually in the `UI.xaml` file. Each column has a nested `DataGridTemplateColumn` object on which you can set a column header and many other optional parameters.

The following listing shows the XAML code of the finished UI with several of these types of parameters set. Remember that you need to make these changes manually in the `UI.xaml` file rather than using the Visual Studio editor.

Listing 1 Complete UI.xaml code

```
<Window xmlns=http://schemas.microsoft.com/winfx/2006/xaml/presentation
        xmlns:x="http://schemas.microsoft.com/winfx/2006/xaml"
        Title="Group Management"
        Height="600" MinHeight="600"
        Width="1000" MinWidth="1000">

        <Grid Margin="5,5,0,0" Name="grdMain">

            <Grid.ColumnDefinitions>
            <ColumnDefinition
               Width="0.5*" MinWidth="100"/>
            <ColumnDefinition
               Width="0.75*" />
            <ColumnDefinition
               Width="1*" MinWidth="200"/>
            </Grid.ColumnDefinitions>

            <Grid.RowDefinitions>
                <RowDefinition Height="25"/>
                <RowDefinition Height="1*"/>
                <RowDefinition Height="25"/>
                <RowDefinition Height="1*"/>
            </Grid.RowDefinitions>

             <Label Name="lblManagedUsers" Grid.Column="0"

Grid.Row="0" Content="Managed Users" />

     <StackPanel
             Grid.Column="1"
             Grid.Row="0"
             Orientation="Horizontal">
        <Label Name="lblSearchUser" Content="Search Users" />
```

Annotations: Defines WPF form start (Window element); Contains all UI elements (Grid); Specifies relative sizes (ColumnDefinitions); Specifies both absolute and relative sizes (RowDefinitions); Contains other objects horizontally (StackPanel).

```
        <TextBox
             Name="txtSearchUser"
             AcceptsTab="True"
             TabIndex="1"
             Margin="5,0,0,0"  Width="80" />
        <Button
             Name="btnSearchUser"
             Content="Search"
             Width="60"
             Margin="5,0,0,0" Padding="5,0,5,0"/>
     </StackPanel>

     <StackPanel Grid.Column="1" Grid.Row="2" Orientation="Horizontal">
        <Label Name="lblSearchGroup" Content="Search Groups"/>
        <TextBox Name="txtSearchGroup" AcceptsTab="True" TabIndex="2"
Margin="5,0,0,0"  Width="80" />
        <Button Name="btnSearchGroup" Content="Search" Width="60"
Margin="5,0,0,0" Padding="5,0,5,0"/>
     </StackPanel>

     <StackPanel Grid.Column="2" Grid.Row="0" Orientation="Horizontal">
         <Label Name="lblSelectedUser" Content="Selected User:"/>
    <Label Name="lblSelectedUserName" Margin="5,0,0,0"
Content="None"/>
     </StackPanel>

    <Button Grid.Column="2" Grid.Row="0" Name="btnSaveChanges"
Content="Save Changes" Margin="5,0,5,0" Padding="5,0,5,0"
HorizontalAlignment="Right"/>

    <DataGrid IsReadOnly="True" ItemsSource="{Binding Path=Table}"
 Grid.Column="0"
 Grid.Row="1"
 Grid.RowSpan="4"
 Margin="0,5,5,5"
 Name="grdUser"
 AlternatingRowBackground="LightBlue"
 AutoGenerateColumns="False">

                <DataGrid.Columns>

                    <DataGridTemplateColumn Header="User Name">
                        <DataGridTemplateColumn.CellTemplate>
                            <DataTemplate>
                                <TextBlock Text="{Binding
Path=UserSamAccountname}" />
                            </DataTemplate>
                        </DataGridTemplateColumn.CellTemplate>
                    </DataGridTemplateColumn>

                    <DataGridTemplateColumn Header="UserGuid"
Visibility="Collapsed">
<DataGridTemplateColumn.CellTemplate>
                            <DataTemplate>
                            <TextBlock Text="{Binding Path=UserGUID}" />

                             </DataTemplate>
                        </DataGridTemplateColumn.CellTemplate>
                     </DataGridTemplateColumn >
```

Contains other objects horizontally

Binds to DataTable from SQL query at runtime

Binds to column in DataTable by name

```
                </DataGrid.Columns>

            </DataGrid>

            <DataGrid IsReadOnly="True" ItemsSource="{Binding Path=Table}"
Grid.Column="1" Grid.Row="1" Margin="0,5,5,5" Name="grdSearchUser"
AlternatingRowBackground="LightBlue" AutoGenerateColumns="False">

              <DataGrid.Columns>

                <DataGridTemplateColumn Header="User Name">
                    <DataGridTemplateColumn.CellTemplate>
                        <DataTemplate>
                            <TextBlock Text="{Binding
Path=UserSamAccountName}" />
                        </DataTemplate>
                    </DataGridTemplateColumn.CellTemplate>
                </DataGridTemplateColumn>

                <DataGridTemplateColumn Header="UserGuid"
Visibility="Collapsed">
                    <DataGridTemplateColumn.CellTemplate>
                        <DataTemplate>
                            <TextBlock Text="{Binding Path=UserGUID}" />
                        </DataTemplate>
                    </DataGridTemplateColumn.CellTemplate>
                 </DataGridTemplateColumn >

                 </DataGrid.Columns>

            </DataGrid>

            <DataGrid IsReadOnly="True" ItemsSource="{Binding Path=Table}"
Grid.Column="1" Grid.Row="3" Margin="0,5,5,5" Name="grdSearchGroup"
AlternatingRowBackground="LightBlue" AutoGenerateColumns="False">

              <DataGrid.Columns>

                <DataGridTemplateColumn Header="Group Name">
                    <DataGridTemplateColumn.CellTemplate>
                        <DataTemplate>
                            <TextBlock Text="{Binding
Path=GroupSamAccountName}" />
                        </DataTemplate>
                    </DataGridTemplateColumn.CellTemplate>
                </DataGridTemplateColumn>

                <DataGridTemplateColumn Header="UserGuid"
Visibility="Collapsed">
                    <DataGridTemplateColumn.CellTemplate>
                        <DataTemplate>
                            <TextBlock Text="{Binding Path=GroupGUID}" />
                        </DataTemplate>
                    </DataGridTemplateColumn.CellTemplate>
                 </DataGridTemplateColumn >

                </DataGrid.Columns>

            </DataGrid>
```

```
        <DataGrid IsReadOnly="True" ItemsSource="{Binding Path=Table}"
Grid.Column="2" Grid.Row="1" Grid.RowSpan="3" Margin="0,5,5,5"
Name="grdSelectedGroup" AlternatingRowBackground="LightBlue"
AutoGenerateColumns="False">
            <DataGrid.Columns>

                <DataGridTemplateColumn Header="Group Name">
                    <DataGridTemplateColumn.CellTemplate>
                        <DataTemplate>
                            <TextBlock Text="{Binding
Path=GroupSamAccountname}" />
                        </DataTemplate>
                    </DataGridTemplateColumn.CellTemplate>
                </DataGridTemplateColumn>

                <DataGridTemplateColumn Header="Start Date">
                    <DataGridTemplateColumn.CellTemplate>
                        <DataTemplate>
                            <DatePicker SelectedDate="{Binding
Path=StartDate, Mode=TwoWay,UpdateSourceTrigger=
PropertyChanged}" />
                        </DataTemplate>
                    </DataGridTemplateColumn.CellTemplate>
                </DataGridTemplateColumn>

                <DataGridTemplateColumn Header="End Date">
                    <DataGridTemplateColumn.CellTemplate>
                        <DataTemplate>
                            <DatePicker SelectedDate="{Binding
 Path=EndDate, Mode=TwoWay,UpdateSourceTrigger=PropertyChanged}" />
                        </DataTemplate>
                    </DataGridTemplateColumn.CellTemplate>
                </DataGridTemplateColumn>

                <DataGridTemplateColumn Header="GroupGuid"
Visibility="Collapsed">
                    <DataGridTemplateColumn.CellTemplate>
                        <DataTemplate>
                            <TextBlock Text="{Binding Path=GroupGUID}" />
                        </DataTemplate>
                    </DataGridTemplateColumn.CellTemplate>
                </DataGridTemplateColumn>

                <DataGridTemplateColumn Header="UserGuid"
Visibility="Collapsed">
                    <DataGridTemplateColumn.CellTemplate>
                        <DataTemplate>
                            <TextBlock Text="{Binding Path=UserGUID}" />
                        </DataTemplate>
                    </DataGridTemplateColumn.CellTemplate>
                </DataGridTemplateColumn >

                <DataGridTemplateColumnHeader="UserSamaccountName"
Visibility="Collapsed">
                    <DataGridTemplateColumn.CellTemplate>
                        <DataTemplate>
```

1 Updates DatePicker on DataTable change

```
                                <TextBlock Text="{Binding
Path=UserSamAccountName}" />
                            </DataTemplate>
                        </DataGridTemplateColumn.CellTemplate>
                    </DataGridTemplateColumn >
                </DataGrid.Columns>
            </DataGrid>
        </Grid>
</Window>
```

Defines WPF form end

In this example the `UserGUID` column's visibility is set to `Collapsed`, hiding it in the UI, but preserving its data. The `Header` property specifies a custom column header. The Start Date column contains a `DatePicker` object whose `SelectedDate` property is populated with the datasource's StartDate column data. Because the `DatePicker` can be updated by the user you must set the binding mode to `TwoWay` and the `UpdateSourceTrigger` property to a UI event ❶. This allows the changes to be written to the underlying `DataTable`.

To complete the application we'll need to add two database operations.

Handling database interactions

We need one database operation to read user and group information from the database into the application and another to modify user and group relationships and commit the changes back to the database.

Three PowerShell functions handle these interactions: `Get-UserData`, `Get-GroupData`, and `Set-GroupData`. Each function uses classes from the `System.Data` .NET namespace to execute SQL statements against the database. Each function uses the same .NET classes to open the database connection and execute the SQL statement.

Executing SQL statements

The steps required to execute SQL statements against the database are as follows:

1. Define the database connection string.
2. Create a new `SqlConnection` object, passing in the connection string to the object constructor method.
3. Create a new `SqlCommand` object, and set its connection property with the connection string.
4. Set the `CommandText` property of the `SqlCommand` object, entering the SQL statement to execute.
5. Create a local `DataSet` object to store the results of the database query.
6. Create a `DataAdapter` object, and set its `selectCommand` property to the `SqlCommand` object.
7. Use the `Open()` method of the `SqlConnection` object to open the database connection.
8. Use the `Fill()` method of the `SqlDataAdapter` object to assign the results to the local `DataSet`.

The three functions are the result of translating these steps to PowerShell code. Listings 2 and 3 show code excerpts from the `Get-UserData` and `Get-GroupData` functions.

Listing 2 `Get-UserData` function

```
function Get-UserData {

$strConnection = "Data Source=$script:SQLServer;
Initial Catalog=$script:DBName;Integrated Security=SSPI"

$sqlConnection = New-Object `
System.Data.SqlClient.SqlConnection($strConnection)

$strSQL = @"
SELECT dbo.UserTable.UserSamAccountname, dbo.UserTable.UserGUID
FROM UserTable
"@

$sqlCommand = New-Object System.Data.SqlClient.sqlCommand
$sqlCommand.CommandText = $strSQL
$sqlCommand.Connection = $sqlConnection

$sqlDataSet = new-object System.Data.DataSet
$sqlDataAdapter = new-object System.Data.SqlClient.SqlDataAdapter
$sqlDataAdapter.selectCommand = $sqlCommand

try
{
$sqlConnection.open()

    [void]$sqlDataAdapter.Fill($sqlDataSet,"LocalData")

    $sqlConnection.Close()
    $sqlCommand.Dispose()
    return $sqlDataSet.Tables[0]
    }

    catch
    {
    write-host $_.exception
    $sqlConnection.Close()
    $sqlCommand.Dispose()
    }
}
```

Annotations: Defines connection string; Creates SQLConnection object; Stores SQL Select statement; Creates SQLCommand object; assigns SQLConnection object; Creates local DataSet object; Creates SqlDataAdapter object; assigns SQLCommand object; Catches database connectivity issues

Notice the use of `try{} catch{}` blocks around the `Open()` and `Fill()` methods to catch database connectivity issues.

Listing 3 `Get-GroupData` function

```
function Get-GroupData {

param
(
$UserGUID
)

$strConnection = "Data Source=$script:SQLServer;
Initial Catalog=$script:DBName; Integrated Security=SSPI"
```

Annotation: Defines connection string

```
$sqlConnection = New-Object `
System.Data.SqlClient.SqlConnection($strConnection)
$sqlConnection.open()

$sqlCommand = New-Object System.Data.SqlClient.sqlCommand
$sqlCommand.Connection = $sqlConnection

$strSQL = @"
SELECT dbo.GroupTable.GroupSamAccountname,
dbo.GroupTable.StartDate,
dbo.GroupTable.EndDate,
dbo.GroupTable.GroupGUID, dbo.UserTable.UserGUID,
dbo.UserTable.UserSamAccountname
FROM UserTable
INNER JOIN GroupTable
ON
dbo.UserTable.UserGUID = dbo.GroupTable.UserGUID
WHERE
dbo.UserTable.UserGUID = @UserGUID
"@

$sqlCommand.CommandText = $strSQL

[void]$sqlCommand.Parameters.AddWithValue("@UserGUID", $UserGUID)

$sqlDataSet = new-object System.Data.DataSet
$sqlDataAdapter = new-object System.Data.SqlClient.SqlDataAdapter
$sqlDataAdapter.selectCommand = $sqlCommand

    try
    {
    [void]$sqlDataAdapter.Fill($sqlDataSet,"LocalData")
    $sqlConnection.Close()
    $sqlCommand.Dispose()

    $sqlDataSet.tables[0].DefaultView.AllowNew = $true
    $sqlDataSet.tables[0].PrimaryKey =
    ➥ $sqlDataSet.tables[0].Columns.Item("GroupGUID")

    return $sqlDataSet.tables[0]
    }

    catch
    {
    write-host $_.exception
    $sqlConnection.Close()
    $sqlCommand.Dispose()
    }
}
```

Creates SQLConnection object

Opens DB connection

Creates SQLCommand object; assigns SQLConnection object

Stores SQL Select statement

Creates local DataSet object

Creates SqlDataAdapter object; assigns SQLCommand object

Catches connectivity errors

Admittedly you could achieve the same result using a SQL stored procedure, but that requires moving the SQL statement to the server, making the function more difficult to understand.

Implementing UI error handling

When the user clicks the "Save Changes" button, the database updates the changes in the `grdSelectedUser DataGrid`. Before the rows of data are piped to the `Set-GroupData` function (to write the changes to the SQL database) you must ensure that 1) the start and end dates aren't empty and 2) the end date occurs after the start date.

To achieve this create a Boolean variable `$dateError` and set it to `$false`. Next evaluate the current row's start and end date fields to verify that they aren't empty. If that check passes ensure that the end date occurs after the start date. If either of these evaluation fails the `$dateError` variable is set to `$true`.

After you complete the checks evaluate the `$dateError` variable:

- If the variable holds `$true` the user is presented with a popup box and the save operation is abandoned.
- If it's `$false` any modified rows are written back to the database.

Notice that you can access the `DataGrid`'s bound `DataTable` object using its `ItemsSource` property. Also you can return a collection of only the modified rows using the `GetChanges()` method as shown:

```
if ($dateError)
{
$wsh = New-Object -ComObject wscript.shell
$wsh.popup("Date is null or EndDate before StartDate",$null,"Error",0)
}
else
{
$changedRows =
  ➥ ($grdSelectedGroup.ItemsSource.Table.DefaultView.Table.GetChanges())

    if ($changedRows)
    {
    $changedrows.Rows | Set-GroupData
    }
 }
```

Because the `Set-GroupData` function has the `begin{}`, `process{}`, and `end{}` blocks defined, you can use the pipeline to pass the collection of modified rows to the `Set-GroupData` function.

The final task is to create a script that reads the SQL database information and makes the relevant changes in Active Directory.

Writing the Active Directory modification script

The script must run automatically on a regular schedule to eliminate the need for human intervention. To satisfy this requirement the SQL database Job Agent will run the script once an hour. The `SQLJob.ps1` script contains the logic to complete the tasks shown in table 4.

Listing 4 shows the logic used to add a user/group membership defined in the SQL database to Active Directory. The `Get-SQLData` function returns the result of the SQL statement and an array of custom PowerShell objects, rather than a `DataSet` object, which makes the data far easier to work with.

Table 4 SQLJob.ps1 functionality

Task	Description
Run SQL query	Returns all user and group information where group membership start date is less than the current date and end date is greater than the current date
Run SQL query	Returns all user and group information where group membership start and end dates are both less than the current date
Process results of first query	Binds to user and group objects in Active Directory Determines whether the user is already a member of the group If not a group member, adds the user to the group
Process results of second query	Binds to user and group objects in Active Directory Checks that the user is a member of the group Removes the user from the group

Listing 4 Read SQL database and add user group membership

```
$sqlAddGroups = @"
SELECT dbo.GroupTable.GroupGUID,
dbo.GroupTable.GroupSamAccountname,
dbo.GroupTable.UserGUID,
dbo.GroupTable.StartDate, dbo.GroupTable.EndDate,
dbo.UserTable.UserSamAccountName
FROM GroupTable
INNER JOIN UserTable
ON
dbo.UserTable.UserGUID = dbo.GroupTable.UserGUID
WHERE dbo.GroupTable.StartDate <= GETDATE()
AND dbo.GroupTable.EndDate >= GETDATE()
"@

Get-SQLData -strSQL $sqlAddGroups |
ForEach-Object {

$strUser = [String]::Format("LDAP://<GUID={0}>",$_.UserGUID)
$User = [ADSI]$strUser

$strGroup = [String]::Format("LDAP://<GUID={0}>",$_.GroupGUID)
$Group = [ADSI]$strGroup

    if (-not $Group.member.Contains($User.DistinguishedName.ToString()))
    {
        try
        {
        $Group.psbase.Invoke("Add",$User.Path)
        Add-Content -Value "$(get-date -f 'yyyy-MM-dd HH:mm:ss'); `
Added $($User.DistinguishedName) To $($Group.DistinguishedName)" `
-Path $logFilePath
        }
        Catch
        {
        return $_.exception
        }
    }
}
```

Stores SQL Inner Join statement

Executes SQL query and processes group membership additions

Binds to user object

Binds to group object

If user is not already a member of the group, adds user

When the user and group objects are accessed in Active Directory the `objectGUID` attribute value is used in the `LDAP://` binding moniker. Using the `objectGUID` attribute ensures that the correct objects are found because this attribute can't be modified on any directory object.

Summary

Developing a full-fledged GUI application using PowerShell can be rather daunting because it forces you to interact with technologies, such as WPF and SQL Server, that lie outside of the regular PowerShell environment most administrators are familiar with.

The example in this chapter could be improved with several features, such as adding a mechanism in the UI to remove users from groups, and the ability to automatically send emails to the users affected by group membership changes, to name a few. I hope this chapter has demonstrated how PowerShell can be the glue that joins different technologies together to solve a real-world problem.

About the author

Chris Bellée is a Senior Premier Field Engineer (PFE) who works for Microsoft Services in Sydney, Australia. His background is in IT Administration, and he specializes in Directory Services and PowerShell automation, delivering proactive and reactive services for Microsoft's Premier customers. Originally from the island of Jersey in the Channel Islands (UK), Chris traveled to Australia eight years ago and liked it so much that he stayed—and met his future wife. He and his wife now have a daughter who keeps them constantly on their toes!

index

A

D

E

F

G

H

I

J

K

L

M

N

O

P

Q

R

S

T

X

RELATED MANNING TITLES

Windows PowerShell in Action, Second Edition
by Bruce Payette

ISBN: 978-1-935182-13-9
1016 pages, $59.99
May 2011

SharePoint 2010 Workflows in Action
by Phil Wicklund

ISBN: 978-1-935182-71-9
360 pages, $44.99
February 2011

SQL Server MVP Deep Dives
Edited by Paul Nielsen, Kalen Delaney, Greg Low, Adam Machanic, Paul S. Randal, and Kimberly L. Tripp

ISBN: 978-1-935182-04-7
848 pages, $59.99
November 2009

SQL Server MVP Deep Dives, Volume 2
Edited by Kalen Delaney, Louis Davidson, Greg Low, Brad McGehee, Paul Nielsen, Paul Randal, and Kimberly Tripp

ISBN: 978-1-617290-47-3
688 pages, $59.99
October 2011

For ordering information go to www.manning.com